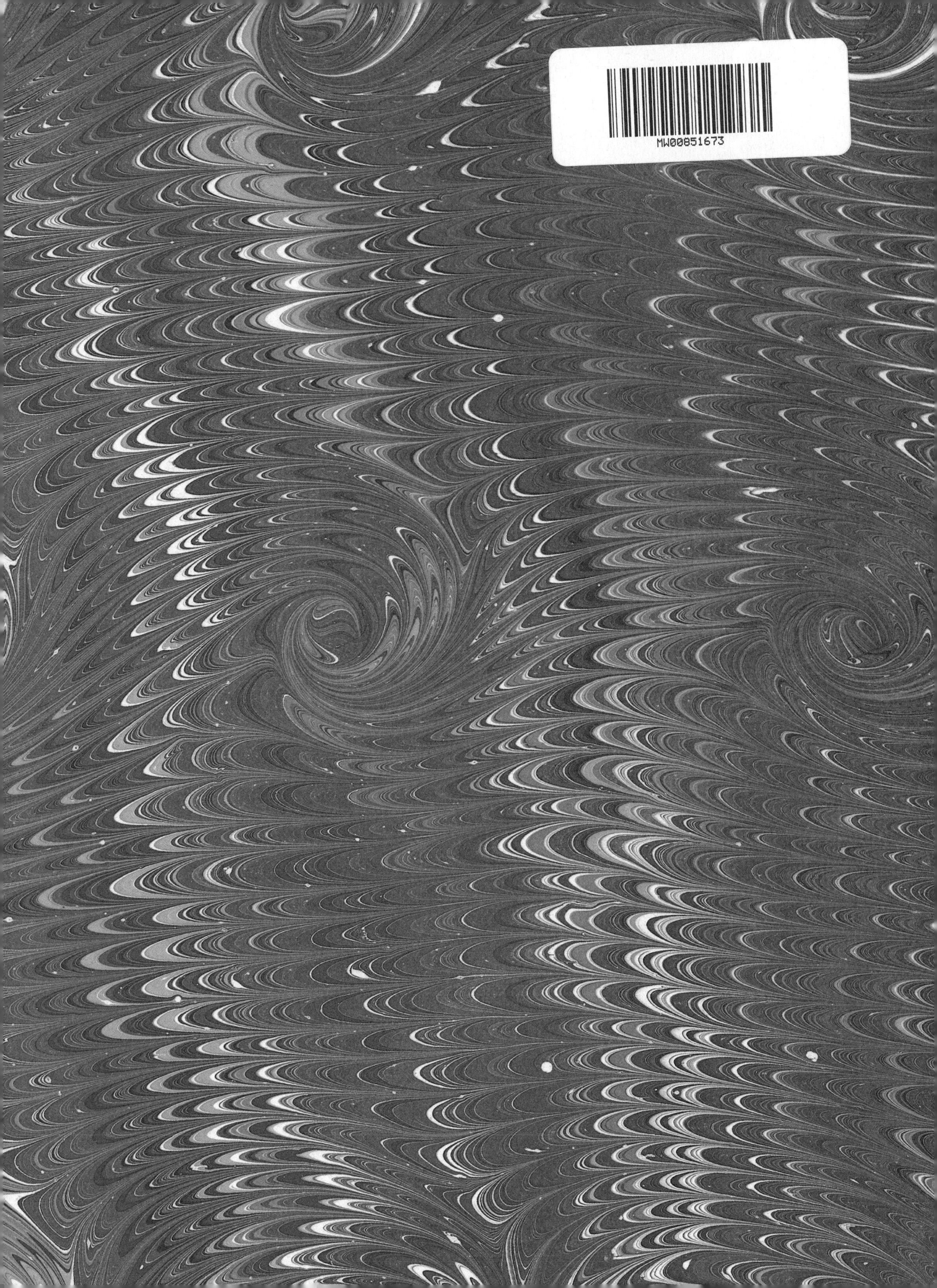
MW00851673

# THE ZEPPELIN IN COMBAT

Douglas H. Robinson

# The Zeppelin in Combat

# A HISTORY OF THE GERMAN NAVAL AIRSHIP DIVISION 1912-1918

**Schiffer Military/Aviation History**
Atglen, PA

*Dedicated*
*to the memory of the 748 men of four nations*
*who lost their lives in Rigid Airships*
*1913-1937*

Book Design by Robert Biondi


Library of Congress Catalog Number: 93-84500



Printed in the United States of America.
ISBN: 0-88740-510-X

We are interested in hearing from authors with book ideas on related topics.

Published by Schiffer Publishing Ltd.
77 Lower Valley Road
Atglen, PA 19310
Please write for a free catalog.
This book may be purchased from the publisher.
Please include $2.95 postage.
Try your bookstore first.

# Contents

# *PREFACE TO THE ORIGINAL EDITION*

At a time when there is increasing interest in the English-speaking countries in aerial operations in World War I, the second reprinting of *The Zeppelin in Combat* ten years after its first appearance emphasizes the status it has achieved as the standard work on the German rigid airships in World War I. Most gratifying to me personally has been its enthusiastic acceptance by the old time airship men of the German Navy who survived while so many of their comrades died, and who today are banded together in the *Marine-Luftschiffer-Kameradschaft,* of which I have the honor to be a full member. I am proud that a copy of *The Zeppelin in Combat* is today enshrined at Nordholz in the *Traditionsraum* of the *Marinenfiegergeschwader 3* "Graf Zeppelin" of the German Navy, charged with carrying on the traditions of the Imperial Navy's Zeppelins in World War I.

Of those who so greatly assisted me in preparing the original work, Rear Admiral E. M. Eller USN (Ret.) has retired as Director of Naval History, as have his subordinates who proved so helpful in going through the microfilmed archives of the German Navy, Miss Lauretta MacCrindle and Mrs. Mildred Mayeux. Of the officers of the former Imperial German Navy who gave so generously of their time in answering my countless questions about their service in airships, Joachim Breithaupt, Walter Dose, Guido Wolff-Vorbeck, and Erich Blew have passed on. So have Heinrich Hoyer, Ernst Lehmann, Max Pruss, Erich Rutzen, August Siem, Ernst Weiss, and Hermann Wolff among the ratings. Dr. Walter Bleston, formerly of the *Luftschiffbau Schütte-Lanz,* has also died. Heinrich Ellerkamm, and Wilhelm Tinchon and Peter Vossen in the East Zone, have not been heard from in years. Still living in Hamburg is the doyen of surviving airship officers, Martin Dietrich, and also Richard Frey in Hannover.

Friedrich Moch, the archivist of the *Kameradschaft,* who helped me so generously with information, did not live to see the first printing

*OPPOSITE:*
*A bow view of L 30 entering the construction shed at Friederichshafen. Note the head resistance offered by the gondolas slung under the body, and particularly by the side propeller brackets. The large ropes coming from beneath the nose are attached to runners (so-called Laufkatzen) rolling on rails extended from the hangar out onto the field. (Luftschiffbau Zeppelin)*

of the book. His incomparable collection of 6,000 airship photographs is held intact by the *Kameradschaft* in Hamburg. Frau Hertha Mathy, widow of the late *Kapitänleutnant* Heinrich Mathy, who has taken a constant interest in this work, still writes frequently from a retirement home in Schleswig. Dr. Karl Arnstein, formerly of the *Luftschiffbau Zeppelin* and Goodyear Zeppelin Corporation, and Captain Garland Fulton USN (Ret.), who so greatly helped me to understand the design and technology of the rigid airships they helped to design and build, are happily still with us today.

To the late Sir Egbert Cadbury I owe almost the whole of the story of the secret salvage operation on the wreck of the *L 70,* which he, together with Air Marshal Robert Leckie, shot down in flames in the last raid on England. The details of the salvage operations are related for the first time in book form in this printing, with assistance from Air Marshal Leckie and Mr. Byron Midgley, Clerk of the Immingham Parish Council.

To the other members of the quadrumvirate who have specialized in rigid airship history, Dr. Robin Higham, Mr. Charles Keller, and Dr. Richard K. Smith, go my thanks for their constant interest through the years.

I wish to thank the following publishers for permission to quote from works published by them: Cassell & Co, Constable & Co, Faber and Faber, Eyre and Spottiswood, Andrew Melrose, Oxford University Press and *Blackwood's Magazine.*

The reader's attention is called to the fact that all times in the text have been converted to Central European Standard Time, an hour later than Greenwich Time. For those consulting original records, it is further necessary to remember that both belligerents began using Summer Time in 1916.

Distances at sea are given in nautical miles, and on land in statute miles.

References are made to the German Navy's squared position chart of the North Sea: a portion of this will be found reproduced on page 10.

# INTRODUCTION

Korvettenkapitän Peter Strasser, Commander of the Naval Airship Division, to Vizeadmiral Reinhard Scheer, Commander-in-Chief of the High Seas Fleet:

**SECRET !**

Nordholz, August 10, 1916

Naval Airship Division No.2804

The performance of the big airships has reinforced my conviction that England can be overcome by means of airships, inasmuch as the country will be deprived of the means of existence through increasingly extensive destruction of cities, factory complexes, dockyards, harbor works with war and merchant ships lying therein, railroads, etc.

The determining consideration for the establishment of 18 airships assigned to the Imperial Command was that the number was necessary and sufficient for the scouting needs of the High Seas Fleet. This is still generally true.

On the other hand, the number of airships cannot be estimated high enough for a quick and effective conquest of England. In the interest of a prompt and victorious ending of the war, attacks must be made with all the airships the building works can produce.

I therefore respectfully request the Imperial Command to effect an increase of the establishment of airships assigned to the Imperial Command from 18 to 22 . . .

The above proposal naturally requires an early increment of 4 airship crews with 4 commanders and 4 executive officers.

I am well aware of the generally prevailing personnel problems, but believe that the personnel must be made available, if necessary through reduction in other areas, since the airships offer a certain means of victoriously ending the war.

Strasser

To: Imperial Command, High Seas Fleet

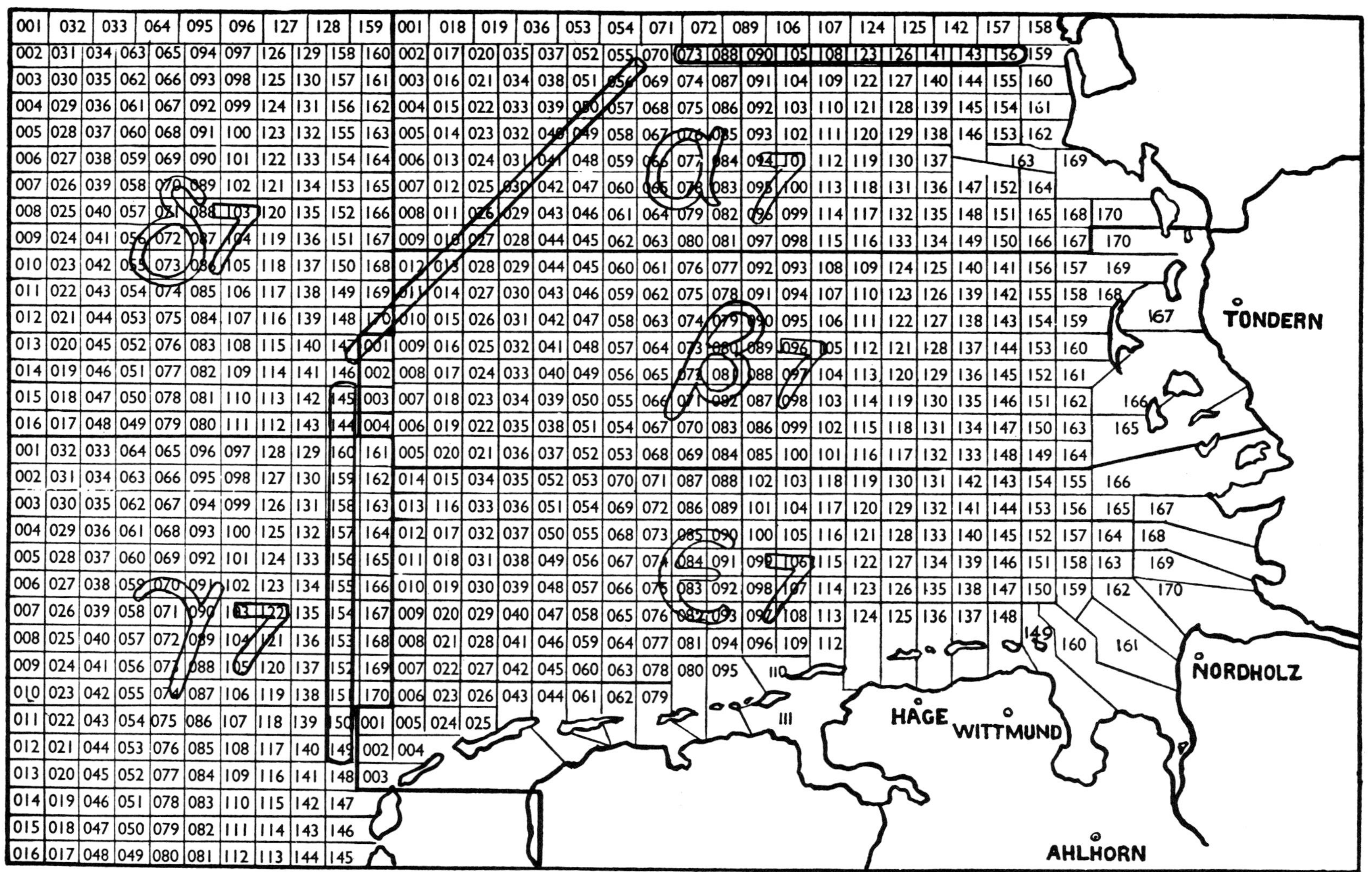
TONDERN
NORDHOLZ
HAGE
WITTMUND
AHLHORN

# CHAPTER I

# HYDROGEN & FLAMING BULLETS

London on the evening of Saturday, September 23, 1916. London at the beginning of the third year of the First World War, the political and mercantile heart of the British Empire, and the symbol of the pomp, the might and the wealth of the Victorian era, now going down in a twilight of blood. A hundred miraculous years of peace, progress and security have accustomed the beneficiaries of this Golden Age to believe that it will last for ever. The cataclysmic events of the past two years have been a rude shock. The tale has been long – Mons and Ypres, Gallipoli and Kut-el-Amara, Dogger Bank and Jutland. "Rule Britannia!" will never sound the same again.

Some Londoners tonight will be in hectic pursuit of pleasure. At the Strand Theatre they can see *The Rotters; a Tale of a Disreputable Family*. The more durable *Peg O' My Heart* is continuing a long run at the Globe. But the war intrudes even in entertainment. The Special Sunday Concert to be held next afternoon at the Royal Albert Hall "Under the Patronage of Their Majesties the King and Queen," will be in aid of Canadian Base Hospitals, with the Canadian Massed Bands of 250 performers being conducted by Sir Thomas Beecham. Madame Tussaud's Wax-Works Exhibition, "The Most Inexpensive, Interesting and Instructive House of Entertainment in London," is featuring "Life-like Portrait Models" of the late Captain Fryatt, a merchant marine officer whose recent execution by the Germans as a *franc-tireur* has created a wave of anger throughout England; and of John Travers Cornwell, a boy of 16 who, in dying at his gun aboard the cruiser *Chester* at the recent Battle of Jutland, has won the Victoria Cross. The personal columns of the London Times reflect the war: "REVINGTON, John Hulett, 2nd Lieutenant, Devons. Wounded Sept. 4. Any news please COMMUNICATE to John Revington, Clonalour, Tralee, Ireland." "Naval Officer's Widow, income greatly reduced by war, requires POST abroad or at home." The "National Rumanian Relief Fund" is soliciting money "to present Her Majesty the Queen of Ru-

*OPPOSITE:*
*Airship patrol lines "North", "Middle" and "West" established July 18, 1917, by order of C.-in-C., High Seas Fleet, with a portion of the German Navy squared position chart of the North Sea.*

mania" – that luckless country – with "Field Hospitals, Motor Ambulances, &c, so urgently required by the Rumanian Red Cross." And an incongruous note on an inner page: "Though the Thames is low and bright, anglers are making good mixed baskets of roach, dace and gudgeon; perch, pike and chub have also been landed." The principal feature of the October number of the *London Magazine* will be "the first of a series of articles by Mr. Churchill on 'The War by Land and Sea', in which he proposes to deal with the course of the naval and military operations." And another Mr. Churchill, a Broker to the Marshal of the Admiralty, announces the Prize Court sale at auction on September 26 of "the ex-S.S. *Bolmen* at Leith, ex-S.S. *Sommelsdyk* (per *Maasstroom*) at London," and many other ships seized by Britain's blockade of the Central Powers.

The war news, heavily censored, is always good. In three months the British Army has suffered a third of a million casualties on the Somme, the French are being bled white on the altar of Verdun, but the Military Correspondent of *The Times* writes: "The fighting on the Somme and at Verdun continues to show an uninterrupted series of military successes for the Franco-British Allies . . . In front of both General Foch and Sir Douglas Haig the Allies are steadily eating into the German lines and blasting their way forward to the Meuse . . . The last two attacks of the Armies have been the sharpest and most successful of any." The whole of the opposite page is filled with the "Roll of Honour," the names of the dead, wounded and missing of the British Army reported in the last 24 hours – 304 names of officers, 4,200 other ranks, overflowing on to a later page. "VAUGHAN. Killed in action on the 15th September 1916 Major George Edmund Vaughan (Military Cross), Coldstream Guards, younger son of the late Edmund Mallet Vaughan of Lapley, Staffordshire, age 35. R.I.P." And many, many others.

London itself stands in the front line. The Germans, with diabolical cleverness, have built airships – the fabulous Zeppelins – to raid England, flying through the skies in defiance of the all-powerful Royal Navy. So far, in the whole of England, their bombs have killed 413 people, including 113 in London. Almost all of these are civilians. The British, with no comparable weapon, are unable to retaliate. The German air crews are stigmatized as "Huns," "barbarians," and "baby-killers," their activities are dastardly and murderous outrages. Many in London anxiously look up to the clear

*L 32 landing at Nordholz. The dark fabric on the top of the ship is a loose weave whereby the hydrogen escapes from the interior of the hull. Only with the L 34 ship were gas valves at the bottom of the cells which exhausted the hydrogen through a fabric chute. (Moch)*

*L 32 brought into Nordholz. L 32 was shot down in flames over England on September 24, 1916. (Kameradschaft)*

evening sky tonight, wondering if the Zeppelins are coming. The new moon is only three days away – and the Germans send out their vulnerable gas bags only in the dark of the moon.

At the Admiralty building in Whitehall a handful of men in Room 40 – the Naval Intelligence Division under the legendary Admiral Sir Reginald Hall – know there will be a raid before the night is over. Two years before, by an extraordinary stroke of fortune, the secret code book, signal book and cipher keys of the German Navy fell into their hands, and with untiring patience and skill, aided by the talkativeness of the enemy, they have again and again divined his secret purposes through reading and decoding his radio messages. At the moment Hall's men are handicapped. The Germans, suspicious, have changed the signal book. But the British have taken in the usual radio messages which tell them that the Zeppelins have taken off to raid England. A secret alert goes out via G.H.Q. Home Forces to searchlight and gun positions around the coast, and to grass-covered flying fields where a handful of youngsters stand ready to fly into the night in flimsy biplanes.

Actually twelve Zeppelins are in the air. From bases on the North German coast – each with an array of giant hangars an eighth of a mile long – the monsters have "weighed off" shortly after noon. Most of them are steering via the North Sea for cities in the north of England. But three of them, the biggest and newest, commanded by officers who are the cream of the Imperial Navy, have headed south, to reach London by a protected route that will take them over friendly territory. *L 31*, *L 32* and *L 33* are flying in loose formation, at fifty miles an hour and 5,000 feet up.

Each of these primitive strategic bombers is a marvel of mechanical ingenuity. The giant bubble of hydrogen gas – or rather, nineteen bubbles in separate cells, totaling two million cubic feet – can lift 70 tons into the air. But over half of this is eaten up by the weight of the ship herself. A delicate trellis-work of duralumin girders and taut steel wires, weighing 12 tons, holds the bubbles of hydrogen in a streamline shape, 650 feet long and 78 feet in diameter. Underneath are hung four tiny nutshells containing the six roaring, deafening Maybach engines. The foremost is the control car, where the officers and the steersmen guide and fly the giant. Navigation is crude – a small liquid compass, liable to freeze at high altitudes; an altimeter, a thermometer, an airspeed meter, are the only instruments. The commander who knows where he is over England at night is lucky. For most of them, one bay, headland or river looks like any other. Each ship has a powerful radio set, and radio bearings of doubtful accuracy can be obtained. How inaccurate, the Germans never find out while the war is in progress.

All these components – the "fixed weight" of the ship herself – amount to nearly 40 tons. Depending on the temperature, barometric pressure, "superheat," and many other factors, the Zeppelins can carry a "useful load" of 25 to 30 tons. *L 31* today has a useful load of just under 27 tons. Twenty men, figured at 176 pounds each in leather fur-lined flight clothes. One thousand, seven hundred and fifty gallons of petrol, enough to last for 21 hours, in thirty aluminum tanks hung along the keel that runs from end to end at the bottom of the giant hull. A hundred and fifty-nine gallons of lubricating oil for the engines. Also carried through the length of the keel are more than 10 tons of water ballast in rubberized cloth sacks. Machine guns and ammunition amount to just under 1,000 pounds, for the Zeppelin must be defended against attacking planes. Some of the guns are in the gondolas, but three on the top platform on the ship's back are served by lookout men who stand in the icy blast of the slipstream, and risk frost-bitten noses, ears and fingers. Amidships, in the bomb rooms, is carried the "pay load" – four fat, pear-shaped 660 pounders, forty more explosive bombs weighing 128 pounds, and sixty incendiaries – "fire-buckets" – 25 pounds each of thermite wrapped in tarred rope. But the leviathan herself is merely a giant bomb. The hydrogen burns on the slightest provocation, and when mixed with air, has the blasting force of dynamite. The petrol, liquid or vapor, is dangerously inflammable. Even though the men wear special shoes to avoid striking sparks, and give up matches before going on board, accidents are always happening. Forty per cent of the picked flight crews – 379 officers and men – will die violently during the war in their flaming ships. Yet there is never a lack of volunteers. "I'm appalled when I think how dangerous it was," says one former crewman, looking back with astonishment on his life as a sailmaker in Zeppelins, "but we were all young, we loved the excitement and adventure. And we always thought nothing would ever happen to us – it would be the other fellow." But for many of them, life is short. Aboard *L 32*, commissioned only seven weeks ago, are twenty-two men who will never see another dawn. And *L 33*, only three weeks in service, is on her first raid, which will also be her last.

There is no trouble, no mishap, as the Zeppelins soar majestically over the soil of the Fatherland – 175 miles south to Cologne. From their vantage point among the clouds the crews look down proudly on the green fields, the dark forests and the smoky cities of the Reich – Osnabrück, Dortmund, Wupperthal, the teeming industries of the Ruhr. At Cologne the ships turn west-southwest; beyond Aachen they leave Germany astern, and skirting neutral Dutch territory, enter occupied Belgium. In the early evening hours they cross its big cities – Liege, Louvain, Brussels, Mechelen and Antwerp – retracing the victorious advance of the German Army in 1914. In twilight, towards 8 p.m., the airships stand out to sea from the Belgian coast between Ostend and Blankenberghe. Waiting for darkness, they steer west over the Channel. As the stars come out, they separate, each commander to follow his own plan of attack.

*Kapitänleutnant der Reserve* Alois Böcker of *L 33*, old merchant marine skipper, chooses – unwisely – to head for London directly, and therefore is the first over land. Coming up the broad reaches of the lower Thames, he is fired on by alert destroyers, comes inland over Foulness Point, and keeps on going over the heavy anti-aircraft defenses east of the capital. But the guns are aimed by sight, and

Böcker has a stratagem for dealing with them. Twice he drops parachute flares, and the dazzling radiance of the blazing magnesium, suspended for five minutes below his ship, blinds the gunners. Dropping all ballast he can spare in anticipation of the coming ordeal, Böcker gets his ship up to 13,000 feet. It is not enough. "The gunfire from all sides," Böcker writes later, "was extraordinarily heavy, more so than I had ever experienced." Down go his bombs over eastern London – two 660-pounders, eight 220s, twenty-two 110-pound explosives and twenty incendiaries. Flames spring up, fire storms through a lumber yard and oil depot. But the Zeppelin is held in the glare of a myriad searchlights – "one can read a newspaper in the control car" – and her every move is followed. Chief Machinist's Mate Adolf Schultz, in the gangway amidships, looks out through a ventilation hatch, counts thirty searchlights, and knows the ship must be a perfect target. A storm of shells is exploding outside. Suddenly there is a terrific crash overhead. A shell has burst inside one of the forward gas bags. Splinters rip through the adjacent cells, and the hydrogen – the ship's life-blood – pours out in gusts. Amazingly, she does not catch fire. Other near-misses pepper the after-cells with fragments.

The air defense of London has by now sent five airplanes aloft – fragile, stick-and-wire, cloth-covered biplanes with go h.p. engines, which, with the pilot, a .303 caliber machine gun, and a few drums of ammunition, take nearly an hour to climb to the Zeppelins' attack altitude. One of the pilots, a New Zealander, Second Lieutenant Alfred de Bathe Brandon, sees *L 33* enmeshed in the searchlights and heads for her. Brandon is having trouble with his unreliable crate – the fuel pump has failed, and he is pumping petrol by hand. Coming up behind the wounded giant, he pulls his machine gun down to load it – and gun, mount, and ammunition tumble into his lap. He has two more chances, and fires over a drum of incendiary and explosive bullets, seeing them burst all along the hull – but she still does not catch fire. The Zeppelin's crew know he is out to kill them – his bullets zip through fuel tanks, petrol spurts out into the keel and pours along the gangway. But the volatile fumes do not burn. Gunners on top of the whale-like hull see the little biplane with the red, white and blue roundels flitting like a moth in the searchlights' beams, but they do not dare shoot for fear of igniting the hydrogen pouring up from the torn gas cells.

The attack is over. As *L 33* heads for the coast, ominous reports of damage pour into the control car. In four minutes she falls over 3,000 feet. Trying to keep her in the air, Böcker flies the cripple with her nose pointing so high that the crew have to hold on to keep from sliding aft. Overboard goes every item that can be torn or pried loose. The British trace her course by the jetsam scattered through Essex – jackets, boots, an ammunition box here, a machine gun there, a case of tools further on. Böcker dumps petrol and oil – only an hour's supply remains on board. The sailmaker and his mates, with flashlight and dope-can, scramble high in the hull, crawling from girder to girder, trying to find and patch the holes in the gas-bags. Still she goes down and down. Brandon and the guns have been left far behind. At 1:30 a.m. the radio-man sends, in the clear, "need help mouth of the Thames, *L 33*," then throws his set out of the window piece by piece. But Böcker cannot reach even the coast. Her tail dragging, her nose pointing to the stars, her altitude only 500 feet, *L 33* is out of control. A downdraft seizes her, she crashes into a field, is picked up and carried a hundred yards further, and comes to rest close to a farmer's cottage. Still, as if she were made of asbestos, there is no explosion, no flame. The twenty-two men on board, miraculously uninjured, leap out of the cramped gondolas – and one of them falls heavily and breaks some ribs. Böcker piles the crew's papers and the ship's secret documents in the control car, fires a signal ball into the pools of petrol in the gangway, and at last the inflammable monster blazes up. Flames tower high in the air, some machine-gun ammunition pops off with a clatter, and a blast of exploding oxyhydrogen in one of the leaky cells knocks the survivors off their feet. At last there is nothing but a glowing tangle of red-hot girders. Twenty-two German seamen – the only armed invaders to set foot in England in four years of war, are free to go where they will in the silent countryside.

Böcker hopes to get to the coast, seize a boat and flee across the North Sea. But as the crew march

*Wreck of L 33 being examined at Little Wigborough, England.*

along the country lanes, they are aware of a gathering crowd following them. The ship's fall has been seen, the alarm has been spread, soldiers are hurrying from the nearest town, the Germans are surrounded and must surrender. Ahead of them lie endless interrogations, accusations, years of imprisonment. For them the war is over.

The other two Zeppelins, with *L 31* in the lead, have turned west-south-west, and are steering down-Channel. *L 31*'s commander is Heinrich Mathy, thirty-three years old, a former destroyer skipper, three years in naval airships, with a reputation for boldness, determination and navigational genius that has caused friend and foe alike to place him in the first rank. A year ago, with a lucky ship ironically numbered "*L 13*," he started fires in the heart of London that did half a million pounds' worth of damage. His men worship him. His faith in the airship is boundless, and, clumsy and dangerous though it is, he almost makes it look like a decisive weapon of war. Mathy has noted in his previous London raid, a month before, that the defenses on the south side of the capital are much weaker than those on the north and east. He is going to come up from the south, and *L 32*'s commander, *Oberleutnant zur See* Werner Peterson, a gay youngster with the reputation of being the best ship-handler in the service, will follow the same route.

At 10:45 p.m. the two Zeppelins are off Dungeness Point, whence they will steer a course of 320 degrees for the attack on London. Mathy has dropped nine-tenths of his water ballast and two tanks of precious fuel, but cannot get his craft higher than 11,000 feet. The temperature here is 40 degrees F., which makes it a warm night. Were it seasonably cold, Mathy could reach 13,000 feet with his full bomb load. Some of it has to be sacrificed, and ten of the 128-pound bombs are aimed, unsuccessfully, at the Dungeness Lighthouse. *L 32*, possibly suffering engine trouble, slows down and circles near her landfall, but *L 31* presses straight on – huge, menacing, droning across the darkened countryside. Dropping parachute flares to see what lies below, Mathy soon discovers one of the main railway lines entering London from the south. With no hesitation, he follows the "iron compass" straight into the suburbs on the southern fringe of the capital. With satisfaction, Mathy sees that another Zeppelin – Böcker's – is already at work over eastern London, with two big fires in her wake. Twenty minutes after midnight *L 31* is at 12,500 feet over Croydon, and the first bombs whistle down. Mathy's dramatic entrance makes an unforgettable impression on the London *Times'* ace reporter, Michael MacDonagh:

> I was sitting in my room reading about twelve o'clock last night when, through the slightly parted curtains of the glazed door (leading to a balcony which overlooked the grounds of the Notre Dame Convent, Clapham Common), there penetrated a ray of intense white light. Wondering what it could be I stepped out on to the balcony, and saw the convent and its grounds made more vivid to the eye by the dazzling light streaming from the sky than I have ever seen them in sunlight. My conjecture that the light was associated with an air raid was confirmed by an explosion which had in it something of the roaring crackling of forked lightning. Then suddenly the strange light went out and the sheltering darkness of night enveloped the familiar scene.
>
> I went to the front door of my house, facing south-east, and again the light appeared, revealing a wide area, and I heard explosions of bombs in quick succession apparently near at hand. It then occurred to me that the mysterious light implied that the Germans with their devilish ingenuity had invented a bomb of a terribly destructive kind, which was being used by the raiders.[1]

But the world has to wait nearly thirty years for the atomic bomb. MacDonagh has actually seen Mathy's last parachute flares drifting down as he drops his explosives in a long line from south to north across the enemy metropolis. Though he is sure he has plastered the City – the financial heart of London – the bulk of Mathy's cargo falls in residential areas south of the River Thames, and he does not live to learn of his mistake. Lightened by the 9,000 pounds of bombs sent down over London, *L 31* climbs to 13,000 feet, and with wide-open engines driving her at 65 m.p.h., she races on north. Mathy's proverbial luck is holding – a low ground fog is spreading over the valley of the River Lea, and choosing his course above it, he is concealed from the powerful gun defenses north of the capital. At 2:15 in the morning Mathy, pursued by a heavy cannonade, goes out to sea at Great Yarmouth. His escape produces some heart-burning among the British defenders, and ungrudging tributes to his skill in the secret files of G.H.Q. Home Forces.

Werner Peterson is not so fortunate. Heading inland at last, and following an hour behind Mathy, he deviates to the east and at 1 a.m., when he reaches the River Thames, he is twelve miles east of London. If he realizes the error in his navigation, he has no chance to correct it. South of the river the airship has been hidden by mist, but now she comes out into clear air. Searchlights flash up – *L 32* at 13,000 feet is dazzled and lit up like a deer transfixed by the poacher's lantern-beam. The guns bark, bombs tumble from the Zeppelin's racks, and Second Lieutenant Frederick Sowrey kicks the rudder-bar of his little biplane to head for the uproar. Coming up beneath the giant fish, whose crew must be blinded by the light which sparkles from the tautly doped hull, the vibrating struts and wires, and the spinning discs of the six propellers, he gets off three drums of ammunition. At last, tiny flames spurt out of the fabric underside of the doomed raider and, as Sowrey turns away, they coalesce, lick up the sides, and tower high above the airship's back in a giant pillar of flame. Still she soars on, a ghastly pyramid of fire blotting out the stars and shedding a bloody radiance over miles of country. Gouts of flame – gas tanks, gondolas, structure – break off and hiss tumbling down through the black night. Hoarse cries of triumph and execration swell from a million throats as all eyes on the ground

1 Michael MacDonagh, *In London During the Great War* (London: Eyre & Spottiswoode, 1935), p. 127.

turn to the apocalyptic vision in the heavens. The glowing skeleton tips towards the vertical and, trailing a red banner of burning gas, 40 tons of ruined airship slide gently down through two and a half miles of sky.

The roar of the flames rouses the people of the sleepy village of Little Burstead, but the derelict crashes a mile beyond in a hilltop beet field on Snail's Hall Farm. A laborer and his wife awaken at the noise to see the tangled wreckage flaming across the fields. Almost at their feet sprawls the body of an officer, lying on his back half-imbedded in the ground. It is *Leutnant zur See* Karl Brodrück, *L 32*'s executive officer, who has leaped from the blazing hell in the sky rather than burn to death. Rivers of petrol from burst fuel tanks feed the fire for nearly an hour and only with dawn can Flying Corps personnel cut their way into the tangled mass. In shattered gondolas, crushed under heaps of corroded girders, they find the charred bodies of the twenty-one remaining members of the crew. Many human reminders are strewn through the wreckage – a blood-stained red leather cushion in an engine gondola; a half-burned chair in the smashed debris of the control-car, and the remains of the crew's breakfast – greasy black war bread, bacon, and potatoes delicately sliced – which have not cooked in spite of the blow-torch heat of the burning hydrogen. In the woods half a mile away are found the huge elevating planes and rudders, one with its fabric covering still intact. A propeller complete with hub and gear case is picked up three miles from the scene. Thousands of fragments of the gas-bags and cotton outer cover are strewn over the surrounding fields, where they are eagerly sought by souvenir-hunters. In the ruins of the control car a flying squad of Captain (later Admiral) Hall's Naval Intelligence men make a priceless discovery – the new secret signal book of the German Navy, burned but usable – but they leave without saying anything, not even when Brodrück is misidentified as the commander.

Three days later the crew of *L 32* is buried in the little churchyard of Great Burstead. Despite outcries by the yellow press, which wants to see the "baby-killers" consigned to Potters' Field, the Royal Flying Corps renders military honors to fellow airmen. Six months later they will cause to be inscribed over the graves of another dead airship crew, "Who Art Thou That Judgest Another Man's Servant? To His Own Master He Standeth Or Falleth."[2]

Thus *L 31* returns alone next morning to her base at Ahlhorn, and a silent and anxious crew climb down from her swaying gondolas as soon as she is berthed in the "Albrecht" shed. The ground crew waits in vain for her mate, *L 32*. Mathy and his men have seen the blazing portent a bare fifteen miles away in the eastern sky as they dash north from London for the coast. The attacking plane cannot be seen at this distance, and Mathy reports that the guns set *L 32* on fire. The memory of their shipmates burning to death haunts Mathy's crew for their few remaining days of life. Mathy writes to his young wife, in East Frisia with their baby:

> Peterson is dead, Böcker a prisoner. Hertha, the war is becoming a serious matter. We have both of us always remembered this, and in our own good fortune have given heartfelt thanks for the blessed Providence that has preserved Gisela's father to her. It is my most earnest wish that you may both be spared this most heavy sacrifice for the Fatherland and that I may remain with you to surround you with love as with a garment. During these days, when you lay our little daughter down to sleep, a good angel will see you and will read what is in your heart, and he will hasten to guard my ship against the dangers which throng the air everywhere about her.

It is not to be. Seven days after writing these lines, Mathy, once again daring to attack the British capital, perishes with all his crew when *L 31* is shot down in flames at Potters Bar.

---

2 Romans, 14:4.

# CHAPTER II

# THE EARLY HISTORY OF THE RIGID AIRSHIP

The rigid airship was first conceived and developed by Count Ferdinand von Zeppelin, and will always be associated with his name. An intensely patriotic aristocrat of the South German state of Württemberg, and a career army officer who had fought with distinction in the Franco-Prussian War, the Count might never have become famous through his contributions to aeronautics if politics had not forced his retirement in 1890, when he was only 52. A too-frank memorandum protesting against the domination of the Württemberg Army by the Prussian War Ministry had aroused the wrath of the Kaiser, and a few months later, told that he was unfit for high command, Zeppelin's career was at an end.

Immediately the Count set himself to develop his dream of the giant rigid airship. Though he had made his first flight in a balloon at St. Paul, Minnesota, during a visit to the American Civil War, it was in 1874 that the Count had conceived his unique idea after reading a lecture by the German Postmaster-General on "World Mail and Airship Travel." Military considerations came to the fore in 1884 with the qualified success of the small non-rigid dirigible "La France," in the hands of Germany's arch-rival. Count Zeppelin began to feel concern lest the Fatherland be outstripped in the air. As the years passed, it might be said that his intense and persistent efforts to build a huge "air cruiser" stemmed from patriotic convictions that Germany needed such an airship for military purposes, and that it was his duty to provide it.

In 1894 a commission of scientists and aeronautical experts, headed by Professor Hermann von Helmholtz, was appointed by the Kaiser to examine Zeppelin's proposals. The Count's "Deutschland" design, prepared with the assistance of a young engineer, Theodore Kober – for the inventor had no technical training – was a flat-ended monstrosity, 384 feet long, 36 feet in diameter, powered by two 11 h.p. Daimler motors each weighing 1,100 pounds, and intended to tow

*LZ 1, Count Zeppelin's first rigid airship. A giant for its time, 420 ft. long, it made three flights with 8 h.p. engines, and was then dismantled. (Luftschiffbau Zeppelin)*

separate rigid-framework cylindrical sections, coupled together like railway coaches, carrying passengers and cargo. The Commission found the Count's speed calculations overly optimistic, offered valid criticisms of the utterly impractical rigid framework composed of seamless tubing and flat discs, and advised against spending government money on the design.

Subsequently, with the assistance and encouragement of Professor Müller-Breslau, a member of the commission, Zeppelin made many necessary improvements. Not only was the "aerial express train" abandoned in favor of the conventional cigar-shaped hull, but the adoption of the "Schwedler cupola" with braced transverse rings produced a rigid structure both light and adequately strong. Thus was developed the characteristic "Zeppelin" design, for which Müller-Breslau never received credit.[1]

Aided by the distinguished Union of German Engineers, Count Zeppelin formed in May, 1898, the "Joint Stock Company for Promotion of Airship Flight," and within a year began the construction of his first rigid airship in a floating shed near Friedrichshafen on his native Lake Constance. The hull, built of aluminum girders, was 420 feet long, 38 feet 6 inches in diameter, and contained 400,000 cubic feet of hydrogen in seventeen separate gas cells. Truly the ship was a giant for her day. But she was ridiculously underpowered. In each of the two gondolas was a Daimler engine producing only 15 h.p. for a weight of 850 pounds, the two motors together producing a speed of only 16 m.p.h. instead of the 28 m.p.h. that the Count had hopefully predicted. The first take-off of *LZ 1* (*Luftschiff Zeppelin I*) on July 2, 1900 revealed insufficient speed, lack of control, and weakness in the hull. Two more ascents were made in the autumn. These three flights, totaling 2 hours 1 minute, had exhausted the Joint Stock Company's resources and the ship was broken up early in 1901.

Not until 1905 was Zeppelin able to begin construction of his second ship. *LZ 2* resembled the first craft but was more strongly built and carried two greatly improved engines developing 85 h.p. each. On her second flight, in January, 1906, she was carried off in a high wind when both motors

1 Professor Dr.Ing. Müller-Breslau, "Zur Geschichte des Zeppelin-Luftschiffes," *Verhandlungen zur Beförderung des Gewerbfleisses*, January, 1914, p. 35.

failed. She landed successfully twenty miles away, but during the night a storm destroyed her at her moorings.

Though the public felt that Zeppelin would now give up his mad experiments, the inventor scraped together the last sources of his private fortune and commenced a third ship. In October, 1906, *LZ 3* was completed and made her first ascent. With her the Count at last achieved a measure of success. In September, 1907, he astonished the world with a flight of eight hours' duration. The Army showed interest, and agreed to purchase a ship if she could make a continuous journey of twenty-four hours, cover a distance of 435 miles, reach a predetermined goal and return to her base.[2] Since *LZ 3* lacked the endurance for such a flight, the Count proposed to build a larger ship.

*LZ 4* was completed in June, 1908. The gas capacity was increased to 530,000 cubic feet, amidships there was a small passenger cabin, and the two engines delivered 105 h.p. each. Following a successful twelve-hour flight over Switzerland on July 1, Zeppelin set out on August 4 to carry out the test. His goal was Mainz, but after 11 hours in the air he was forced to land on the Rhine river when a motor failed. After repairing the engine and landing five of the twelve people on board, the Count went on in the night to Mainz and there turned south for Friedrichshafen. Next morning, however, there was another engine failure and the ship landed at Echterdingen near Stuttgart. While mechanics were rushing repairs, a sudden thunderstorm blew up, the airship was torn from her moorings, and took fire in the air. A half mile away she fell, a total wreck.

This disaster, the last and worst in a long series, was actually the turning-point in Zeppelin's career. His stubborn determination to build an airship for the Fatherland had made him a national symbol. From all parts of the nation voluntary contributions poured into Zeppelin's offices in Friedrichshafen, the sum in time amounting to more than £300,000. Successfully resisting the attempt of the Prussians in Berlin to impose on him a "Board of Trustees," the Swabian hero set up the "Zeppelin Foundation for the Promotion of Aerial Navigation," which became the parent company for all his enterprises.

With a fifth ship the Count early in 1909 carried out the 24-hour requirement, and the War Ministry purchased *LZ 3* and *LZ 5*. But the latter showed up badly in a competition which favored the short-range non-rigid craft, and *LZ 6*, built in anticipation of further Army orders, remained unsold. In an effort to demonstrate the rigid airship's superior range and carrying capacity, Count Zeppelin,

2 *Luftschiffbau Zeppelin, Das Werk Zeppelins, Eine Festgabe zu seinem 75.* Geburtstag (Stuttgart: Kommissionsverlag Julius Hoffman, 1913), p. 30.

*LZ 4, with more powerful engines, flew to Zürich in twelve hour flights.*

in November, 1909, founded the world's first commercial airline, the German Airship Transportation Company, popularly known as the DELAG. Large German cities subscribed most of the capital, each agreeing to build a shed. But a succession of accidents destroyed the first three passenger ships, and once again the Zeppelin enterprise faced ruin.

The old aristocrat played his last card with the completion of *LZ 10*, named *Schwaben*, on July 15, 1911. And with her, "the lucky ship of the DELAG," at last came success. Commanded by Dr. Hugo Eckener, later famous as commander of the *Graf Zeppelin, Schwaben* carried 1,553 passengers in 218 flights, and when she burned at Düsseldorf on June 28, 1912 – happily without loss of life – the German people had come to take for granted the safe and dependable operation of Count Zeppelin's airline.

At the time of *Schwaben*'s loss, the DELAG was already operating *Viktoria Luise*, and two more ships were later added, *Hansa* and *Sachsen*. Though some German authorities have suggested that these craft maintained a regular scheduled service between cities, this was not the case. Pleasure cruises, averaging two hours at a time, were made in the vicinity of the sheds during the spring, summer and autumn. Twenty passengers were carried in comfort in a cabin amidships equipped with wicker chairs and tables, and a cold menu and generous wine list added to the *Gemütlichkeit* of these excursions. During these cruises, and sometimes between passenger flights, Army and Navy airship crews were trained by Dr. Eckener and DELAG personnel. By July 31, 1914, 10,197 passengers had been carried on 1,588 voyages, covering 107,231 miles.

In the last years before the war a rival to the Zeppelin firm had appeared – the Luftschiffbau Schütte-Lanz of Mannheim-Rheinau. Founded in 1909 by Dr. Johann Schütte, Professor of Naval Architecture at the University of Danzig, and a group of powerful Mannheim industrialists, it proposed to build rigid airships of laminated plywood girders, which the professor believed would be lighter and more elastic than the aluminum girders of the Zeppelins. The firm enjoyed from the beginning the special favor of the War Ministry, which encouraged the Schütte-Lanz firm in order to foster technical competition with the Zeppelin Company.

*OPPOSITE: "Victoria Louise" (named for the Kaiser's only daughter) flew for DELAG, carrying up to twenty passengers for two hour joy rides. With the start of the war, the ship was taken over by the Navy, and after 1000 flights was retired in 1915. (Luftschiffbau Zeppelin)*

*OVERLEAF: DELAG passenger carrier "Schwaben" landing at Johannisthal, 1912. (Moch)*

Their first ship, *SL 1*, flew on October 17, 1911. Her streamlined hull was built of helically arranged longitudinals which crossed each other in a diamond-shaped pattern. She was bought by the Army, but the design was not repeated. *SL 2* which was completed on February 28, 1914, had a plywood girder framework with longitudinals and transverse frames. The new craft embodied a whole series of revolutionary advances, and deserves to be called the first modern rigid airship. The hull was carefully streamlined, simple cruciform fins, rudders and elevators were fitted at the stern, the commander and helmsmen were accommodated in a comfortable, fully enclosed control car forward, and the four Maybach engines were directly coupled to propellers at the rear of the streamlined gondolas. The triangular keel was inside the ship, and cloth shafts led hydrogen exhausted from the gasbags to the top of the hull. Many of these features were patented by the Schütte-Lanz Company – patents which in August, 1914 were taken over by the German Government.

During the war years, as the Zeppelin design was refined and developed, many of these features appeared in their ships. The accusation has been made that the Zeppelin designers were mere copyists imitating the Schütte-Lanz model with the blessing of the German Government. A fair statement of the merits of this controversy might be as follows:

Up until about 1912 the Zeppelin Company was a small organization with a small design staff, dominated by the Count's ideas, and he built his ships along conservative lines. In a public lecture in the year 1908, he indicated that he was aware of the studies on streamlining by Professor Helmholtz (the chairman of the 1894 commission which criticized his designs), but chose to disregard them:

Bosch-Magnetos

SCHWABEN

*SL 2 was the second ship built by Schütte-Lanz in Mannheim. It was remarkable for its modern features: streamlined hull, enclosed control car, and four engines in suspended gondolas. However, its glued wooden girders tended to fail because of humid conditions during operations over the North Sea. (Luftschiffbau Schütte-Lanz)*

> The consideration that the speed of a ship varies only slightly from the speed of wave propagation, while the fastest airship is more than 20 times slower than the air waves caused by its progress, led me, in opposition to Helmholtz, to the conviction that the laws of motion relating to ships could not be directly applied to airships, and, for example, a fining-away of the hull aft from a midships frame would not have the same effect on the speed of an airship as it would have with a surface vessel. This led me to the shape of a cylinder of small cross-section with ogival ends, to present the least possible head resistance.[3]

As early as 1910, wind-tunnel experiments on models by Ludwig Prandtl, the first Professor of Aeronautical Engineering at the University of Göttingen, had shown that this characteristic "pencil-form" Zeppelin hull shape "was not the optimum for low air resistance, [and] a more favorable bow shape could be found."[4] Yet the Count ignored these studies, arguing that this inefficient hull form, with its many identical transverse frames, was easy to build. The deep external keel, which increased the height of the ship and also its lateral area, was considered necessary to separate the engines from the gas cells filled with inflammable hydrogen. The clumsy propellers on brackets high on the hull, with their vulnerable bevel gears and long shafting, were placed near the center of resistance of the airship hull – a feature the Count considered important – and in addition they could be run ahead or in reverse with the ship on the ground, an important asset in maneuvering. The uncomfortable, completely open gondolas expressed the Count's conviction that the ships could be landed safely only if

3 Dr.Ing. Graf Zeppelin, *Erfahrungen beim Bau von Luftschiffen* (Berlin: Verlag von Julius Springer, 1908), p. 5.

4 *Luftschiffbau Zeppelin*, p. 83

*SL 2 in the Rheinau shed before the war. Schütte-Lanz took a major step by building a control car, as was usual with later airships. (Bleston)*

*Detail of the structure of a Schütte-Lanz airship at Rheinau. Note gun pit, and at least five sockets around the gun pit. Early in World War I, airships and even airplanes were so armed, however the socket arrangement was later dropped. (Schütte-Lanz)*

*SL 17 building in Rheinau. Note the elevators and rudders, and the delicate structure abaft the rudders. (Bleston)*

*SL 7 under construction at Rheinau. (Bleston)*

the commander felt the wind in his face. Extreme turbulence around the blunt stern, which made the control surfaces ineffective, necessitated the multiple array of box rudders and elevators with their excessive drag.

Beginning in 1912 the Zeppelin organization came under fire from outside engineering experts. As shall be seen, the German Navy, with its first order for a Zeppelin airship, put pressure on the company to change and enlarge its designs. Experienced naval constructors and naval architects concerned themselves with developing the ships for long scouting flights at sea. With this, Count Zeppelin began to lose interest in his creation. On the outbreak of war the Zeppelin Company became a national asset and expanded rapidly. There was a great influx of engineers and designers, among whom should be mentioned Dr. Paul Jaray and Dr. Karl Arnstein, who undertook extensive basic research in aerodynamics and structures, improving greatly the empirically evolved basic Zeppelin design. These men were far too highly trained and talented to be mere copyists, and if their work presently resembled the Schütte-Lanz creations, it was because they themselves recognized the value of the features which the Schütte-Lanz firm had pioneered between 1909 and 1914.

*OPPOSITE: SL 5 under construction at Darmstadt. (Bleston)*

# CHAPTER III

# THE EARLY HISTORY OF THE GERMAN NAVAL AIRSHIP DIVISION

It is surprising to find that the rigid airship, developed successfully in Germany, was almost entirely neglected by the German Navy in the years before World War I. Great Britain, on the contrary, had an exaggerated impression of the value which her potential enemies placed on the Zeppelin. In July, 1912, two members of the Technical Sub-Committee of the British Committee of Imperial Defence reported, after a flight in *Viktoria Luise*:

> In favorable weather the German airships can already be employed for reconnaissance over vast areas of the North Sea, and one airship, owing to the extensive view from high altitudes under favorable weather conditions, is able to accomplish the work of a large number of scouting cruisers. It is difficult to exaggerate the value of this advantage to Germany. By a systematic and regular patrol of the approaches to the coast, it will be possible in fair weather for German airships to discover the approach of an enemy and to give timely warning of the attack.[1]

Yet the German Navy at this time did not possess a single airship, and appeared indifferent to the advantages so obvious to its future enemies.

Even the advocacy of the Kaiser's brother, Admiral Prince Henry of Prussia, and of the Emperor himself counted for naught against the implacable opposition of the Navy Minister, *Großadmiral* Alfred von Tirpitz. Since 1897 he had dedicated himself to building the German Fleet into a mighty instrument of national policy. In this he was aided by the young Kaiser Wilhelm II, who took a special interest in the Navy and in advancing his country towards a predominant position in the markets of the world. It was Tirpitz' conviction that Great Britain, which throughout the nineteenth century had dominated

*OPPOSITE:*
*Fregettenkapitän Peter Strasser, Chief of the Naval Airship Service, October 1913 to December 1916; Leader of Airships from December 1916 to his death in action over England on August 5, 1918. He is shown here at Ahlhorn on September 4, 1917 when he was awarded the Pour le Mérite. (Moch)*

---

1 Sir Walter Raleigh, *The War in the Air* (Oxford: at The Clarendon Press, 1922-35), I, p. 181.

*Fuhlsbuttel, Hamburg airport. DELAG flew civilians in the summer, while the Navy flew out of the double shed for maneuvers. L 1 made her last flight from this shed on September 9, 1913. (Moch)*

world commerce, would oppose – by force if necessary – the competition of German trade and industry. He wished to believe that his battle fleet would deter England from the risk of a war against Germany. The "risk Navy," in a sense, was not built to fight, but to impress its possible enemies. Still a poor relation of the Army, the Navy had to fight for funds, and Tirpitz spent them on offensive weapons – battleships and destroyers.

Neither would Tirpitz waste money developing novel weapons of unproven worth. In his biography he states:

> I refrained from the premature adoption of new devices, but acted energetically as soon as I saw that the matter contained some real possibility of development. I have always found this method to be the only right one. It was very often a difficult part of my duties to prevent myself, as Secretary of State, from getting agitated by the impatient throng of inventions which came rushing in from all sides during this epoch, but it was also a very important one, if we were to set up a first class navy with the limited means in the short time instead of a museum of experiments.[2]

Official records of this period indicate that as early as 1906, Tirpitz showed an interest in the airship as a scouting weapon, but this project was but one of many concerns of the ruthless and energetic creator of the modern German Navy. No visionary, aviation was to him a side issue, and rather than spend money on it, he preferred to be an observer

[2] Alfred von Tirpitz, *My Memoirs* (New York: Dodd, Mead & Co., 1919), I, p. 47.

*Friedrichshafen, Zeppelin works. The largest shed is number III, then number II shed then the Ring Shed where airships were assembled flat. The airship shadow is that of the Los Angeles. (Moch)*

of the Army's experiments with the early Zeppelins. Above all, Tirpitz insisted throughout the prewar years that the airship – to be an efficient naval weapon – must be a large craft of long range. And Count Zeppelin, equally stubborn, refused to build craft big enough to meet the Navy's specifications. The Navy's requirements in fact were not fulfilled until after the war broke out.

In September, 1907, when *LZ 3* made her 8-hour flight over Lake Constance, the official commission on board included the Navy's *Fregattenkapitän* Mischke. Admitting in his report to Tirpitz that numerous difficulties remained to be overcome, Mischke claimed that "Count Zeppelin had enjoyed a decisive success, which showed that the path he was following would lead to his goal."[3] In a memorandum of April 23, 1908, Tirpitz' own Dockyard Department chief saw the airship as especially suited for strategic scouting at sea, particularly in the event of a blockade of the German coast, while "also they will eventually be able to be used with great success for independent operations against the enemy coast (attack on vital objectives thereon by dropping shells, etc.)."[4] The same memorandum called for a craft with a range of 1,000 sea miles and a speed superior to a wind velocity of 33.5-47 miles per hour. Yet Dr. Eckener, Count Zeppelin's collaborator, had to admit of the craft lost that same year at Echterdingen:

> What the ship still needed was greater speed, which would have given greater dy-

3 *Kriegrswissenschaftliche Abteilung der Luftwaffe, Die deutschen Luftstreitkräfte von ihrer Entstehung bis zum Ende des Weltkrieges 1918. Die Militärluftfahrt bis zum Beginn des Weltkrieges 1914* (Berlin: E.S. Mittler u. Sohn. 1941), p. 235.

4 *Die Militärluftfahrt*, p. 238.

> namic lift for overcoming temperature fluctuations, and a greater possibility of making progress against strong winds. In the shape and performance of *LZ 4* the airship was still incapable of practical employment.[5]

The Echterdingen catastrophe did nothing to increase the Navy's confidence in Zeppelin's craft, and Tirpitz minuted: "the thing itself is not very safe; whether the concept is safe is very much in dispute."[6]

In 1910, Tirpitz went so far as to assign a talented naval architect, *Marine-Schiffbaumeister* Felix Pietzker, to observe more closely developments on the Bodensee. Yet despite the Zeppelin craze then sweeping the country, Pietzker advised that the contemporary craft were too slow to fight winds in the North Sea, very susceptible to wind and weather, and lacking in range. By increasing the size and improving the lines, Pietzker believed that an efficient ship could be produced with a speed of 45 miles per hour. He submitted sketches for a craft of 1,223,100-cubic-foot capacity with six engines of 140 h.p. But Tirpitz felt the £150,000 needed to procure the ship, together with base, shed and equipment, could not possibly be obtained from the *Reichstag*, while Count Zeppelin insisted that he would need several years more to develop designs for large airships.

When, in the summer of 1911, Tirpitz finally changed his mind, it was in response to pressure from the Emperor and public opinion, and to increasingly disquieting reports from his attaches of airship progress in foreign navies. According to Alfred Colsman, the business manager of the Zeppelin Company, Tirpitz was persuaded to order an airship only by the threat that the firm, then in dire financial straits, would otherwise sell a ship to the English.[7] Discussions with the Zeppelin Company led to a contract being placed for *L 1* (*Luftschiff I*) on April 24, 1912. The firm wished to build a ship of the current production model of 706,200 cubic feet; Tirpitz favored a larger 4-engine design of 882,750 cubic feet, although this craft still would not have met Navy requirements; and the airship finally ordered was a compromise between these figures. The fourteenth craft in the company's series, the new Navy Zeppelin was practically a replica of the low-performance DELAG passenger carriers and the Army airships of the day.

*A "Laufkatze" – "trolley" in English. With big ships being drawn out of their sheds, crosswinds might swing the ships into the wind. These rolling trolleys were drawn out by members of the ground crew until the ship was out and could be swung into the wind. The double shed in the background is the "Norman" shed at Nordholz. (Moch)*

Navy officers and civilian experts began looking over possible sites for an airship base on the North Sea coast, and finally recommended the purchase of an open spot near the village of Nordholz, south of Cuxhaven. £83,400 was set aside to purchase and develop the site, exclusive of the cost of building a shed, and the transaction was handled so quietly that only in December, 1912, did the Brit-

5 Hugo Eckener, *Graf Zeppelin* (Stuttgart: J.G. Cott'sche Buchhandlung Nachfolger, 1938), p. 166.

6 *Die Militärluftfahrt*, p. 239.

7 Alfred Colsman, *Luftschiff Voraus!* (Stuttgart & Berlin: Deutsche Verlags-Anstalt, 1933), p. 154.

*Bow view of the first German naval airship, L 1 (LZ 14), taking off for a trial flight at Friedrichshafen on October 7, 1912. Note the triangular keel under the hull, the open gondolas fore and aft, the cabin amidships, side propellers on brackets, and multiple control surfaces at the stern. (Luftshiffbau Zeppelin)*

ish learn that the area was not intended for a "rifle range." Construction of a double revolving shed commenced there in April, 1913, and meanwhile the Navy rented for four years the DELAG hangar at Fuhlsbüttel, near Hamburg.

Tirpitz' next concern was the personnel for the new Naval Airship Division. By May 21, 1912, he had *Kapitänleutnant* Carl-Ernst Hanne as commander of the first crew, and was looking for further volunteers. They should preferably be unmarried, and able to pass a medical examination that gave special attention to heart, eyes, ears, and possible nervous conditions. On July 1, the first crew was detailed for training aboard the DELAG ship

*Viktoria Luise*. During the summer they handled her, and later her sister-ship *Hansa*, on passenger flights from the shed at Fuhlsbüttel. By July 1, 1912, Tirpitz had also found a senior officer, *Korvettenkapitän* Friedrich Metzing, to be chief of the organization.

On September 25, 1912, their ship was completed. She was the largest Zeppelin built up to that time, with 793,600 cubic feet of hydrogen. The thin, "pencil-form" hull, with its long parallel portion amidships and abruptly rounded bow and stern, was 518 feet 2 inches long and 48 feet 6 inches in diameter. On October 7, 1912, *L 1* made her first flight. On October 13, with Count Zeppelin in command and twenty people on board, the new naval airship left Friedrichshafen for an endurance cruise over North Germany. On her return next day she had voyaged 900 miles and had flown for six hours at an altitude of 5,000 feet.

This splendid flight, of more than thirty hours' duration, was hailed throughout Germany as proof of the capabilities of airships for long-range reconnaissance. But in England it lent credence to alarmist rumors of night flights by darkened aircraft over the British coast. Several people in Sheerness were certain that *L 1* had flown over the town during the evening of October 13. The tale finally came to Count Zeppelin's ears and he vigorously denied that *L 1* had flown to England during her endurance cruise. Nevertheless, the reports of "phantom airships" over England persisted in the manner of the "flying saucer" craze of our own day, and levelheaded people, who did not believe that the German naval airship had flown over England, feared for the future when they realized that she could easily have done so.

*Forward gondola of L 1, which was commisioned on October 17, 1912. Paul Puzicha, with visor cap, is fourth from the left in the gondola. It was soon recognized that the open gondolas were unsuited to North Sea weather. L 1 was forced into the sea by extreme vertical squalls on September 9, 1913. Of the twenty on board, only six survived. (Kameradschaft)*

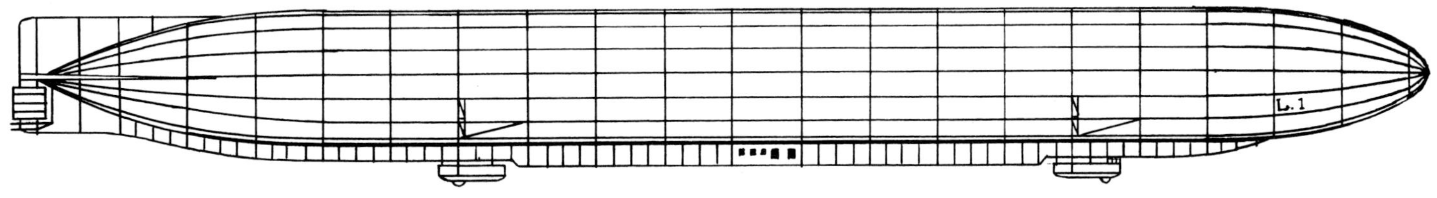


**L 1**

| | | | |
|---|---|---|---|
| Gas capacity | 793,000 ft.[3] | Engines | 3 Maybach C-X, of 180 h.p. |
| Length | 518.2 ft. | Propellers | 4 L.Z. aluminum sheet |
| Diameter | 48.9 ft. | Weight empty | 36,800 lbs. |
| Useful lift | 20,700 lbs. | Maximum speed | 47.5 mph |
| Gas cells | 18 | Ceiling | 9000 ft. |
| Crew | 14 | Full speed endurance | 1750 miles |

On October 17, 1912, the airship flew from Friedrichshafen to Johannisthal, near Berlin, where the Navy had hired a shed for her use during the training period. Through the rest of the autumn and winter, *L 1* made short flights almost daily. Tirpitz recognized the need for thorough training in airship handling before going on to the military portion of the experiment. Several more officers were assigned for instruction, hut not all of them proved suitable. One, intended to be the commander of a second airship, was "washed out" with the comment:

> He lacks the "feel of the air" and particularly a feel for the weight of the ship at various altitudes. More experience will not help this

*LZ 14 over the Friedrichshafen shed. Note multiple elevators and rudders. (Illustrated London News)*

matter, and using him as commanding officer could cause the loss of the ship.

Influenced by "advances in airship construction," together with "the intervention of the public in all phases of aviation,"[8] Tirpitz on January 18, 1913, requested and obtained the Emperor's consent to a 5-year program which would put Germany ahead of all other powers in the airship field. He called for:

(1) Purchase of 10 Zeppelins for two squadrons, each to comprise four operating craft with one in material reserve.

(2) Construction at Nordholz of a central airship base with four double revolving sheds and two fixed sheds.

(3) Subsidizing the construction of private airship hangars for use in wartime.

On January 30 the Admiralty contracted for the first ship of the new program, which was laid down in May, 1913, under the factory designation of *LZ 18*. Pietzker had prepared a design for a larger craft which, in case of war, could reach the English coast with a load of bombs, and the Zeppelin Company agreed to build it, despite some misgivings. Though surpassing her predecessor in volume, *L 2* still would have to fit inside the Fuhlsbüttel hangar. Her length therefore was 518 feet 2 inches, the same as *L 1*. *L 1*'s overall height of 62 feet likewise could not be exceeded, for the doors of the Friedrichshafen construction shed were only 65 feet 6 inches high. It would not be the last time that the size of a rigid airship would be dictated by the dimensions of the sheds available.

Yet Pietzker had some ingenious ideas for increasing the gas volume of the new ship. Firstly, he proposed to have the deep external keel inverted and placed inside the hull. Then, he insisted on placing the open engine gondolas close up against the hull. Both steps saved height, so that the hull diameter could be increased by six feet while the overall height remained at 62 feet. The Zeppelin Company staff strongly opposed these changes, which placed the engines only a few feet from the hydrogen-filled gas-bags. Yet Pietzker not only imposed his wishes with respect to these alterations, but even had windscreens fitted at the bow of each engine car, completely filling the narrow space between the gondolas and the hull. With this last victory Pietzker sealed his own death warrant and those of twenty-seven other men. But the terrible penalty was still in the unforeseeable future, and when the new ship was completed, Count Zeppelin so far forgot his misgivings as to congratulate Pietzker on the radical design features.

*L 2*, with a gas volume of 953,000 cubic feet, was thus the largest airship built before the war. Because of her increased size, she had four 165 h.p. Maybach engines in two gondolas, while the commander and the controls were housed in a separate fully enclosed car attached directly to the hull some 25 feet ahead of the forward engine car.

During the summer *L 1* was very active, making numerous short flights from Johannisthal to train new crews under *Kapitänleutnants* Freyer and Homeyer. One other person, though not a member of the Naval Airship Division, was also taking the commanders' course – *Kapitänleutnant* Heinrich Mathy. A determined and far-sighted officer, Mathy as early as 1907 had been inspired by a vision of the airship playing a dominant role in naval warfare. In his skillful hands the clumsy and vulnerable Zeppelin would become a spectacular offensive weapon.

Even though she was experimental, Tirpitz felt that *L 1* should participate in the autumn maneuvers of the High Seas Fleet, and on August 15, 1913, she was transferred to Fuhlsbüttel. The chief of the division, *Korvettenkapitän* Metzing, also moved his headquarters to Hamburg. Fog and high winds prevented *L 1* from participating in the combat exercises on September 1 and 2. On the first day of the strategic maneuvers, on September 8, the airship reported the position of the "enemy's" main blockading force, as well as the activities of his cruisers and destroyers, while the surface scouting craft were still under way to the scene of action. The Commander-in-Chief of the High Seas Fleet observed that:

> These reports may be regarded as a complete success for the scouting activities of the airship,

[8] Die Militärluftfahrt, p. 254.

> and indicate how scouting by airships without employment of surface vessels may be extended to great distances by utilizing their high speed, as is possible with favorable weather conditions.[9]

On the morning of September 9, *L 1* was prepared for another scouting mission. Twenty officers and men were assigned to the flight, including *Kapitänleutnant* Hanne and his crew of sixteen officers and men; *Korvettenkapitän* Metzing, *Oberleutnant zur See* Peter Wendt, an officer in training, and *Oberleutnant zur See* Grimm, assigned as observer from a battleship squadron with which *L 1* was to cooperate. It was Grimm's first flight in an airship. At his post in the after gondola was the warrant machinist, Ernst Lehmann, who, as the last survivor of this first naval airship crew, has contributed his recollections of this flight nearly half a century later.[10]

During the morning, Metzing and Hanne examined weather maps and received reports from Heligoland and the Fleet offshore, and had a pilot balloon sent up from the field. At 1.25 p.m. when *L 1* took off on her 68th flight, the weather was calm and sunny. It remained pleasant as the ship climbed to her "pressure height" of 1,650 feet over the Elbe estuary, and continued so as far as Heligoland, which she crossed at 3 p.m. Here the airship received a radio forecast of bad weather developing in the evening. Metzing had to abandon the idea of continuing on to the north-north-west, as he had

9 *Die Militärluftfahrt*, p. 260.

10 Ernst Lehmann, former warrant officer in the Imperial German Navy, is not to be confused with Ernst A. Lehmann, Dr. Eckener's collaborator in the period between the wars, who died of injuries in the Hindenburg disaster in 1937.

*The end of the German Navy's first Zeppelin, L 1, blown into the sea off Heligoland on September 9, 1913. Of the crew of twenty, fourteen drowned, and six were rescued by the trawler "Orion" of Geestemünde. "Orion" is to the right of the photo, and what remains of L 1 shows above water to the left. (Moch)*

*Stern view of the naval airship L 2 (LZ 18) at Friedrichshafen, showing how the engine gondolas were placed close up against the hull. Note the profuse array of rudders and elevators, characteristic of the Zeppelins of the time. (Luftschiffbau Zeppelin)*

been ordered, and *L 1* was in fact directed to stay close to the destroyers of the fleet. A falling barometer heralded the approaching storm, which struck at 6.30 p.m. when she was only 16 miles east-southeast of Heligoland.

A torrent of rain beat down on the ship, a violent down-draft seized her, and Lehmann saw the lead weight at the end of the 260-foot radio antenna plunge into the sea, while water streamed from the ballast sacks along the keel. The following up-draft whirled the Zeppelin uncontrollably upward to 5,200 feet, far above her pressure height. Then she began rapidly to fall. In a desperate attempt to keep his ship under control, Hanne ordered "flank

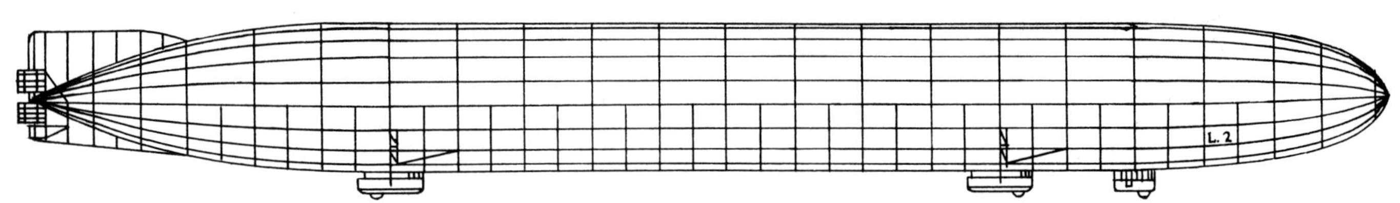


**L 2**

| | | | |
|---|---|---|---|
| Gas capacity | 953,600 ft.$^3$ | Engines | 4 Maybach C-X, of 180 h.p. |
| Length | 518.2 ft. | Propellers | 4 L.Z. aluminum sheet |
| Diameter | 54.4 ft. | Weight empty | 44,500 lbs. |
| Useful lift | 24,500 lbs. | Maximum speed | 47.5 mph |
| Gas cells | 18 | Ceiling | 9200 ft. |
| Crew | 17 | Full speed endurance | 1300 miles |

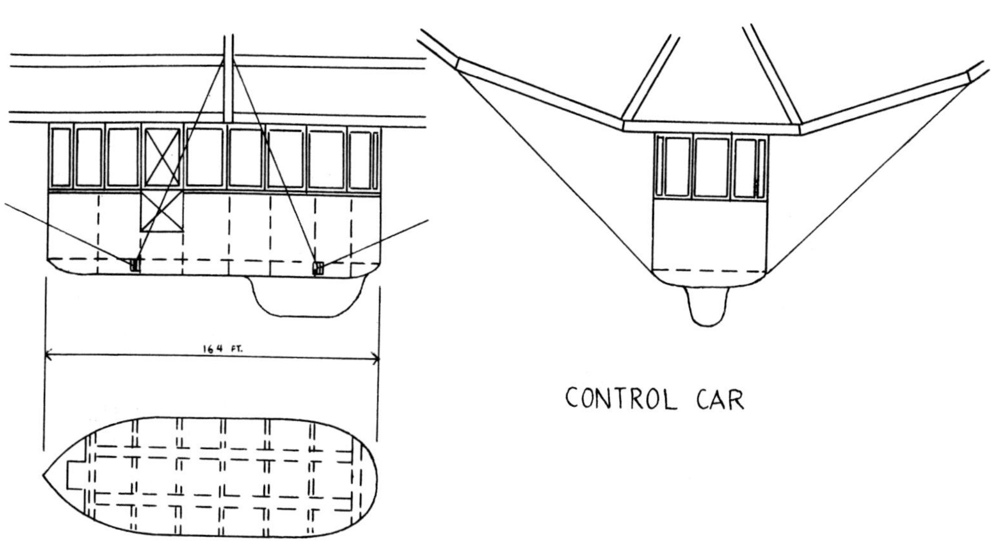


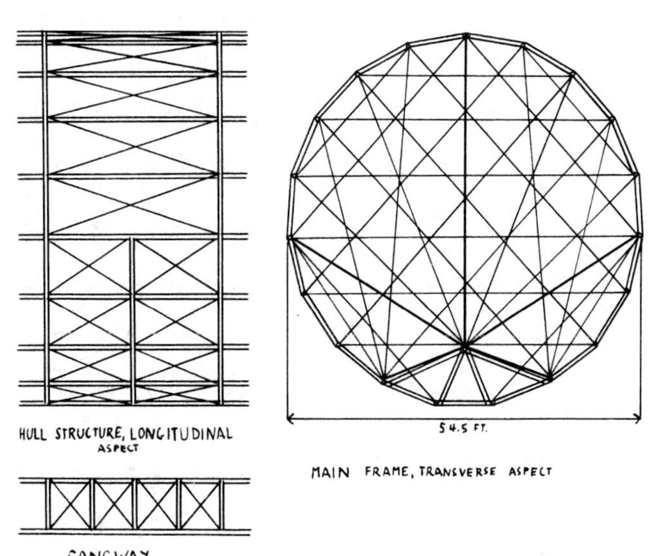


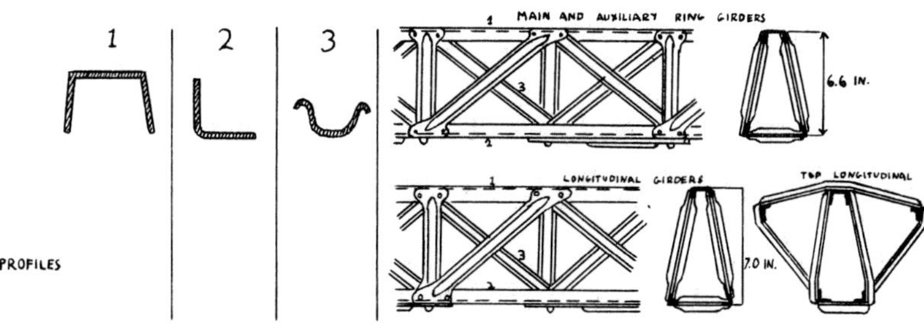


**L 2 Class Detail**

(after Dürr)

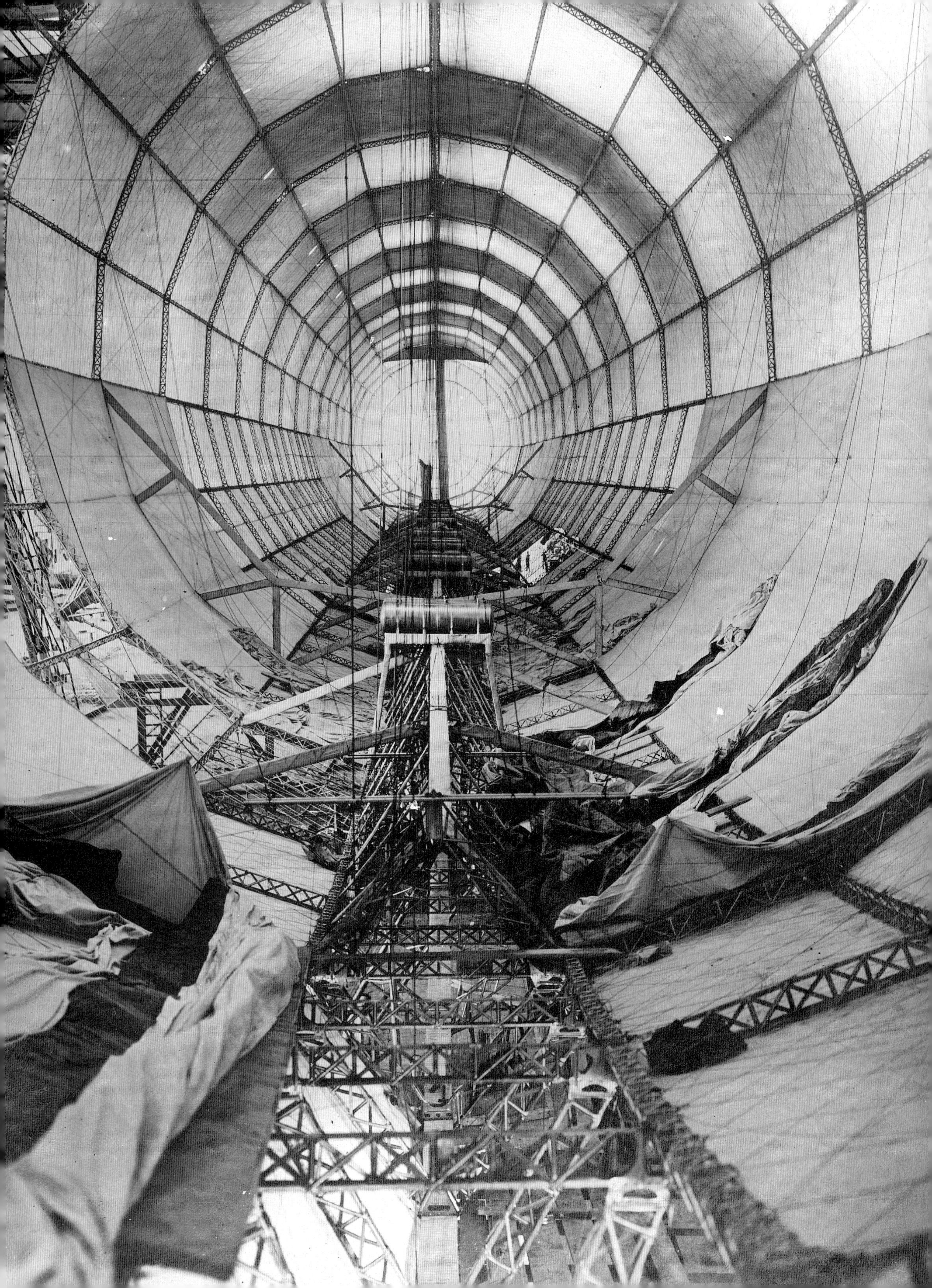

speed" on all engines, dropped all ballast, and sent his executive officer through the ship to order fuel tanks to be slipped. Lehmann raced from the after gondola to drop fuel amidships, but a few moments later *L 1*, with engines running wide open and at a marked angle down by the bow, plunged into the foaming sea. Lehmann heard a rending crash and the shriek of tearing metal as the hull broke in two amidships over his head, the bow, breaking free abaft the forward gondola, reared up vertically a hundred feet in the air, and the stern sank almost out of sight. The ship's hull, crushing down on the open gondolas, apparently trapped their occupants, for none of them was ever seen alive again. Only the midships section with the cabin still floated, with Lehmann, the two radio-men, and another machinist clinging desperately to the wreckage. Lehmann saw two officers, *Leutnants* Wendt and Grimm, who apparently had been thrown out of the gangway when the ship broke up, swimming after the bow section. Within ten minutes the trawler *Orion*, which had watched the Zeppelin fall, was alongside and rescued the two swimmers. Following her came the battleship *Hannover*, which sent out a boat and picked up the four amidships. Not another living soul did they find, and while they searched the broken wreck of the first naval airship sank beneath the waves.

All Germany was shaken by the disaster. Incredible as it may seem, in view of the catastrophe at Echterdingen, the burning of *Schwaben*, and the dangerous combination of hydrogen and petrol in his airships, this was the first time that the loss of one of Count Zeppelin's craft had taken human life. The disaster was much like that to the United States Navy's *Shenandoah* twelve years later, even to a similarity in causes, and it produced a similar reaction. Although Tirpitz exonerated the lost crew of *L 1* from any blame, charges of naval incompetence soon began to appear in the press. Dr. Eckener, the experienced operations chief of the DELAG, charged that the airship was not lost by "the action of a Higher Power," but because she was overloaded. This the Admiralty denied. However, with the unusual weather prevailing that day, she was in fact overloaded for the conditions. The violent line squall which tossed her up and down like a toy balloon was undoubtedly the accompaniment of a "cold front" – a mass of cold air advancing from the polar regions and pushing up on top of itself the warm air in its path. Meteorological science of that day was hardly acquainted with such phenomena of the upper air, and certainly in no position to forecast them. *L 1* had ridden up on the ascending air ahead of the front, and had then been dragged down by violent down-drafts in the cold air behind. She lost so much gas during her involuntary rise that she could no longer sustain herself in the air. Try as they might, *L 1*'s crew simply could not keep the heavy ship aloft in the vicious turbulence in the wake of the cold front.

*OPPOSITE: Looking forward inside the hull of the L 2. The uninflated gas-bags lie on the lower inner covering to right and to the left. At the bottom of the hull is the triangular internal gangway, with fuel tanks rigged horizontally overhead. (Luftschiffbau Zeppelin)*

*L 2 gondola. In flight, vacuum behind the windshields of the engine cars sucked hydrogen down from the gangway which caught fire. The ship fell from 1000 feet, killing all 28 on board. (Moch)*

Down in Friedrichshafen, *Kapitänleutnant* Freyer and the crew of *L 2* were ready to carry on for their dead chief and lost shipmates. Their new Zeppelin had made her first ascent on September 9, 1913, and several more factory test flights were made between then and September 20, when she flew to Johannisthal for her naval acceptance trials. Three new crews reported there for training on October 1, and had some opportunity to participate in the height, speed and endurance tests being carried out by a mixed factory and naval crew.

*Children got a thrill out of aviation as far back as 1913. The younger generation at Friedrichshafen watching the L 2 take off from the Zeppelin Company's field. (Luftschiffbau Zeppelin)*

*L 2*'s tenth flight, an altitude trial, was scheduled for October 17. During the morning the ship was brought out of her shed, and twenty-eight people took their places on board – *Kapitänleutnant* Freyer and fourteen of the regular Navy crew; Captain Gluud and four engineers from the Zeppelin Company; and a party from the Admiralty Aviation Department, including its chief, *Korvettenkapitän* Behnisch, and his key assistant, *Marine-Schiffbaumeister* Pietzker. Because of the number of passengers, the radio set was removed and the two radio-men, two steersmen, and the executive officer, *Oberleutnant zur See* Klaus Hirsch, remained on the ground.

There was a delay. The port engine in the rear gondola refused to start, and for two hours the ship lay on the field while mechanics took down and reassembled the ignition system. Meanwhile a hot sun broke through the morning mist and expanded the hydrogen in the airship's gas cells. At ten o'clock the engines were started, and *L 2*, already light from the "superheat" picked up in the warm sun, leaped off the ground, circled the field, and headed west in a steep climb. All eyes followed her on her way, the morning sun glistening on her taut sides, the war flag fluttering proudly at her stern.

Some of those on the ground were puzzled that the hatch was open from the forward engine car to the keel, yet nobody was coming down. Then they saw a sight that petrified them with horror: a long tongue of fire shot from the forward engine gondola, followed by an explosion that blasted flame throughout the airship's length. Blazing like a giant torch, she fell faster and faster. For an instant, as the fire licked off the outer cover, the spectators saw the bulging after gas cells revealed, then they too were consumed by the flames. Half-way to the ground the bare framework crumpled up in a second explosion that shattered windows half a mile away. As the wreckage struck the ground, several fuel tanks blew up with loud reports.

A company of Army engineers was working nearby. They tried to throw earth on flaming petrol and oil, but were driven back by the searing heat and had to wait for the fire to die down before they could cut their way into the glowing wreckage. Three men, horribly burned and injured, were found alive, but two of them expired on the spot, and the third died that night in a Berlin hospital.

*OPPOSITE: The burning wreck of the L 2 photographed at the instant it hit the ground, leaving a long trail of smoke in the air. (Illustrated London News)*

*Firemen searching the wreckage of the L2 at Johannisthal – remains of a gondola in the foreground, tail planes in the distance. (Luftschiffbau Zeppelin)*

The rest, Behnisch, Freyer, Gluud, the Navy crew, the Zeppelin Company's men – and Pietzker, who had received so much praise for the ship's design – all had perished in the inferno of blazing hydrogen.

Dr. Eckener broke into print again, charging the Admiralty with short-sightedness in overruling the Zeppelin Company's designers on the structural innovations in the ship. Eckener contended that the large windscreens at the front of the engine gondolas had formed a partial vacuum in flight, and had sucked down an explosive mixture of hydrogen and air from the internal gangway close overhead.

The official findings agreed generally with Dr. Eckener's conclusions. Since the gas had been expanded by the heat of the sun while she was still on the ground, *L* 2 had taken off with the gas cells completely filled. As she rose rapidly to 2,000 feet, quantities of hydrogen had spilled out through the automatic valves on the underside of the cells. Not until 1916 were gas exhaust trunks fitted in Zeppelin airships, so the hydrogen had mixed with the air in the gangway, forming an explosive mixture. Some of this was sucked down into the forward engine car and ignited, whereupon the gas in the gangway had exploded and set fire to the whole length of the ship.

Count Zeppelin and *Großadmiral* Tirpitz exchanged bitter words at the funeral of the airship victims. The Count publicly blamed the dead Pietzker and the Admiralty for the disaster, until Colsman, Zeppelin's business manager, fearful that he would open a permanent breach between the Company and the Navy, reminded the old aristocrat that he had congratulated Pietzker on the changes in the ship. From this time forth, Count Zeppelin, increasingly lonely and embittered, became more and more a figurehead. He turned to the construction of giant airplanes, and shortly before his death in 1917 was heard to say, "whatever was done with the airships was all the same to him."[11]

Practically all the experienced naval airship personnel were lost in the *L 1* and *L 2* disasters. There remained only the three new and untrained crews under *Kapitänleutnants* Beelitz, Fritz and von Platen. Without a ship and apparently without a future, they were in a demoralizing position. The ambitious 10-ship program was forgotten, and Tirpitz, though he did not want to abandon the experiment, was reluctant to order more airships unless they could be built larger. Probably considerations of prestige and national pride motivated the Admiralty's decision to continue the Naval Airship Division. But the small organization which survived into the World War was barely sufficient for "window-dressing," and completely inconsistent with the scouting requirements of the High Seas Fleet.

The Naval Airship Division was, however, taken very seriously by its new chief, a man of remarkable organizing ability, indomitable energy and great personal charm, who during the succeeding years made his mark as one of the outstanding naval leaders on either side in the First World War. Two weeks after the loss of *L 1*, *Korvettenkapitän* Peter Strasser, a gunnery specialist serving in the shipboard ordnance department of the Admiralty, had been asked to take the position of Chief of the Naval Airship Division in Metzing's place. Strasser, though he had volunteered for aviation duty as early as 1911, could hardly have been enthusiastic. But as his superiors well knew, he became completely absorbed in every new duty assignment. From the beginning, the possibilities of the rigid

---

11 Colsman, p. 181.

*"Sachsen" passenger airship in 1913. It was 140 meters in length, and could carry up to 24 passengers. It was later turned over to the Army in August 1914, and bombed Antwerp later in the war. (Luftschiffbau Zeppelin)*

„Luftschiff SACHSEN."

airship seized on him and made him the driving force behind all the remarkable achievements of the Navy's Zeppelins in the World War.

At the time of *L 2*'s loss, Strasser was in Leipzig, learning airship handling from Captain Ernst A. Lehmann of the commercial airship *Sachsen*. Hurrying to Johannisthal on the day of the crash, Strasser took energetic measures to restore the morale of his subordinates. He insisted that the Admiralty hire *Sachsen* as a temporary training ship, and since neither he nor anyone else in the Naval Airship Division was qualified to command an airship, he persuaded the DELAG to part with Dr. Eckener and Captain Lehmann to supervise flight operations. A few days after the disaster at Johannisthal, the three naval crews were once more in the air.

On December 7, 1913, *Sachsen*, under Dr. Eckener's command, transferred to Fuhlsbüttel, and thereafter made almost daily flights, training the naval crews in navigation over the sea as well as in airship handling. During this period Strasser quickly rose to the true leadership of the reconstituted Naval Airship Division. Without Eckener's experience he would have been helpless, yet there was never any friction between the two men. "It was Eckener's operating knowledge and Strasser's military spirit that cemented the new organization into one of efficiency."[12] In a service that emphasized strict discipline, Strasser on duty could be a veritable martinet. Any act of carelessness was soon rewarded with a "black cigar" – the German Navy term for a first-class dressing down. But Strasser in off hours showed a rarely attractive personality. He soon came to know all the officers and most of the enlisted men of the small pre-war airship division, and took a personal interest in them and their problems. In later years, Strasser showed a special affection and friendship towards the officers of his "Old Guard," and those who joined the greatly expanded service during the war noticed the difference and were accustomed to call themselves the "Parvenus."

Recognizing that the Division must have a ship of its own, Tirpitz was persuaded to order another craft. But the Zeppelin Company, after the *L 2* disaster, flatly refused to depart from its proven design for small Army airships. Reluctantly, because the ship did not meet the Navy's specifications, Tirpitz on March 21, 1914, contracted with the Zeppelin Company for *L 3*.

His acceptance of this inferior design is remarkable inasmuch as Professor Schütte had written to Tirpitz in October, 1913, offering to build an airship with a gas capacity of 1,112,265 cubic feet, and a useful lift of 32,000 pounds. This craft would have had the internal gangway, simple tail surfaces, bomb rooms, and four engines with direct-drive propellers as in *SL 2*, and was expected to have a speed of 47 miles per hour. Though much larger and with better performance than the contemporary Zeppelins, she would still have fitted inside the Fuhlsbüttel shed. Admiral Dick, the head of the Dockyard Department which included the Aviation Department at the Admiralty, was very favorably impressed by this design, which corresponded to the Navy's requirement for an airship of 1,060,000 cubic feet. But Schütte's difficult personality almost certainly antagonized Tirpitz, as it did so many others with whom he had to deal.

The third naval airship, *L 3*, was completed on May 11, 1914. Her engines were more powerful, but otherwise she was almost a replica of *L 1*. After an endurance flight of 35 hours, she was accepted by the Navy and on May 28 stationed at Fuhlsbüttel.

The Naval Airship Division followed its usual practice of short flights and longer training cruises during the early summer months of 1914. *L 3* put in an appearance during Kiel Week, a splendid round of balls, banquets and regattas in which a powerful British battle squadron was the guest of the German Navy. The gaiety came to an abrupt conclusion with the assassination on June 28 of the Austrian heir, the Archduke Franz Ferdinand. Yet the High Seas Fleet proceeded on its annual Norwegian cruise, and the Kaiser left for his usual vacation aboard the yacht *Hohenzollern*, while the chancelleries of the Great Powers drifted steadily towards war.

During the last days of peace, *L 3* made a 22-hour flight which was a model for the long scouting patrols with which Strasser planned to cover

12 Ernst A. Lehmann and Howard Mingos, *The Zeppelins* (New York: J.H. Sears & Co., Inc., 1927), p. 265.

the interior of the German Bight in time of war. Taking off from Fuhlsbüttel at 5 a.m. on July 18, the Zeppelin proceeded via Heligoland and Norderney westward along the Frisian Islands, and turned back during the evening off the Dutch coast. At 2 a.m. next morning she crossed the big naval base at Wilhelmshaven, and landed an hour later in front of her shed. During the entire cruise the airship was in constant touch with her base, and, it is said, made radio direction-finding experiments. Though the British were impressed, such a journey could be made only in exceptionally favorable circumstances, due to the low performance of the *L 3* type of Zeppelin.

On July 25 the High Seas Fleet hurriedly left Norway for Kiel and Wilhelmshaven, and on July 29 its reserve ships mobilized. Five days later, on August 3, Germany declared war against France, and at midnight on August 4, England entered the war against Germany.

# CHAPTER IV

# THE AIRSHIP COMES INTO ITS OWN

To all appearances, the German Navy was ready for war with the world's greatest sea power. Officers and men were splendidly trained and filled with martial ardor, and they manned a firstline High Seas Fleet of 13 dreadnoughts, 3 battle cruisers, 6 light cruisers and 77 destroyers. Yet in another sense the Imperial Navy was fatally unprepared. Due to the incredible division of authority, indecision and personal intrigue in the High Command, there was no effective leadership and no real plan for war with England.

The responsibility for this state of affairs rested with the Kaiser, the constitutional head of the Navy, who autocratically refused to delegate his powers on the one hand, yet was too frivolous and impractical to give serious attention to the needs of a great service. On his accession to the throne in the year 1888, he had deliberately fragmented the command organization of the German Navy in order to exercise closer control over it than had his predecessors. The various departments functioned independently of each other and were united only by their subservience to the Supreme War Lord. The Navy Minister was reduced to directing the bureau of the Admiralty – an assignment which after 1897 occupied all the energies of *Großadmiral* von Tirpitz, who gave only passing thought to the employment of the powerful fleet he was creating. The Chief of the Naval Staff, in theory the Emperor's chief naval adviser, was a pale shadow of his prestigious counterpart, the Chief of the Great General Staff of the Army. His war plans reflected the amateur strategic ideas of his Imperial master, rather than the genius of a Moltke or a Schlieffen. More courtier than sea dog, *Admiral* Georg von Müller, the Chief of the Naval Cabinet – nominally in charge of all officer personnel – had over many years made himself indispensable to the weak monarch and wielded a sinister influence over him. Though the Commander-in-Chief of the High Seas Fleet might have been expected to concern himself with problems of wartime strategy, he immersed himself in routine administration and training.

*OPPOSITE:*
*A bow view of the German naval airship L 7. (Luftschiffbau Zeppelin)*

L3

*PREVIOUS: The naval airship L 3 on a trial flight at Friedrichshafen. Compare with the earlier photo of the L 1 on page 35. The L 3 was the German Navy's only Zeppelin in service at the start of World War I, and was a participant in the first Zeppelin raid on England January 19, 1915. (Luftschiffbau Zeppelin)*

Before 1914 the German Navy never really faced the problems of fighting a war against England. Tirpitz advocated offensive action, but played no part in planning and after 1908 the war plans were kept secret even from him. Though he was the creator of the superb fighting machines which gave and took so much punishment at Jutland, he thought of the Fleet as a political instrument which by its menace alone would cause England to yield to Germany her "place in the sun." (Too late, the purblind old admiral realized that the Zeppelin itself was a potent instrument of international blackmail.) The Naval Staff had convinced itself that the British Fleet, as in the Napoleonic Wars, would impose a close blockade on the North German coast. Thus it would conveniently offer itself to attack by the powerful German torpedo flotillas, and the "decisive battle" that would follow would end in German victory. As late as May, 1914, when Tirpitz, during maneuvers, asked the Commander-in-Chief of the High Seas Fleet what he would do in a war with England if the enemy failed to appear in the Heligoland Bight, he received no answer.[1]

On the outbreak of war the Kaiser, though preoccupied with the campaign on land, insisted on directing naval operations and issued orders which were intolerable to Tirpitz and to many officers of the Fleet. The Emperor's treasured battleships must be conserved, and only the smaller units could be risked. Tirpitz' memoirs reveal a passive strategy which yielded the initiative to the enemy:

> The plan of operations which, in accordance with the Cabinet Order of July 30, 1914 . . . was now laid before me by von Pohl, the (Chief of the Naval Staff, in the event of an English declaration of war, consisted, as I found to my surprise, of short instructions to the Commander of the North Sea Fleet to wage for the present only guerrilla warfare against the English, until we had achieved such a weakening of their fleet that we could safely send out our own.[2]

The preconceived idea of the close blockade died hard. It was many months before the Fleet Command ceased to expect a British descent on the German coast heralding the "decisive battle." The North Sea remained empty – but the High Seas Fleet must be on guard. Yet the requisite patrols put an intolerable strain on its all-too-few cruisers and destroyers. A solution seemed to lie at hand – the airship, it was hoped, could fulfill the role of the scouting cruiser, could cover an even wider area more rapidly and do it cheaper. An airship could be built in six weeks, a cruiser took over two years. For the officers and men of the neglected Naval Airship Division, this meant recognition beyond their wildest dreams. Yet it is doubtful if even Strasser foresaw the host of aerial leviathans, the far-flung bases, the crucial roles in Fleet operations, which were to be his in the coming years. After all, the Kaiser had said, "when the leaves fall, we will be back home again," and nobody expected the war to last more than a few months.

Through no fault of its chief, this abrupt change in official attitude towards the airship found Strasser's organization totally unprepared. It was not even up to its authorized strength of 414, including five flight crews, and on the outbreak of war numbered only 12 officers and 340 men, including three flight crews, headquarters personnel and ground troops.[3] Its only ship, *L 3*, was entirely incapable of patrolling the North Sea and Baltic together. The Navy's own "airship harbor" at Nordholz, with its double revolving shed, was still not completed, and the rented hangar at Fuhlsbüttel was the only one on the North Sea. No bombs had been developed,[4] and the armament of the big "air cruiser" was limited to two machine guns on the top platform near the nose.

The senior officers who met at the Admiralty early in August, 1914, were looking ahead not more

1 Admiral Hopman, *Das Logbuch eines deutschen Seeoffiziers* (Berlin: August Scherl G.m.b.H., 1924), p. 393.

2 Tirpitz, I, p. 87.

3 *Kriegswissenschaftliche Abteilung der Luftwaffe, Mobilmachung, Aufmarsch und ersten Einsatz der deutschen Luftstreitkräfte in August, 1914* (Berlin: E.S. Mittler u. Sohn, 1939), p. 96.

*The naval Schütte-Lanz airship SL 3. Note the "modern" appearance of this craft, which as early as 1914 embodied most of the features of all post-war rigid airships. (Luftschiffbau Zeppelin)*

than a year in their plans for expanding the German Naval Airship Division. Indeed, the greater part of their "crash" program was to have been completed by the spring of 1915. Airships and airship sheds were ordered wholesale, several thousand men were assigned to the Airship Division, and it is hard to believe that the war was not used as an excuse for a certain amount of "empire-building." War certainly enabled the Admiralty to force the Zeppelin firm to produce larger craft with improved performance.

The Zeppelin Company initially was in no position to comply with the Navy's demands, having neither a design for big airships nor a shed large enough to build them. Geared to the production of five or six small craft every year, it had in August, 1914, only two building berths in the cramped 1909 construction shed in Friedrichshafen.[5] As a stopgap measure, the Zeppelin Company was permitted to build 800,000 cubic foot airships of the *L 3* type, and ten of these units of pre-war vintage were completed up to February, 1915, when new and more efficient designs were ready.[6]

4 Though attacks on English military facilities were part of the intended mission of the airships in war, experiments were still going on to develop aerial bombs – a pointed illustration of the official lack of interest in the airship. It was intended that *L 3* should carry 8.2 inch naval shells on her six bomb releases. Not until October, 1914, were fifty 110-pound explosive bombs delivered, and the first experimental 660-pound bomb (the "Grand Slam" of its day) was dropped by the semi-rigid airship *M IV* at Biesdorf on December 18, 1914.

5 For statistics concerning the wartime increases in the numbers of employees of the airship building firms, see Appendix D.

6 Bitter disputes raged for months over the division of these craft between the Navy and the Army, which within four weeks of the start of the war had lost four of its six Zeppelins. There was an uneasy agreement that the services would divide these hips equally, but the Army could not resist demanding the Navy Zeppelins also when their need was desperate. Thus, as the Navy's *L 5*, *L 6* and *L 7* approached completion, the General Staff demanded each in turn, repeating its demand for *L 5* a week after she had been commissioned as a naval vessel!

On the outbreak of war a prototype airship of improved performance was already on the drawing board. In the summer of 1914 the Zeppelin Company had started the construction of a passenger carrier for the DELAG, the *LZ 26*. With 880,000 cubic feet of gas, she was roughly the same size as her predecessors, but introduced many improvements. The framework was of duralumin – a new aluminum alloy containing small percentages of copper, manganese and silicon – which permitted the hull to be built lighter without sacrificing strength. For the first time since the disastrous experiment with *L 2*, the gangway was placed partially inside the body. The gondolas were slung well below the hull, and were completely enclosed, which not only decreased the risk of fire, but added greatly to the crew's comfort and efficiency. The hull was better streamlined, with simple, effective fins and control surfaces.

On August 5, 1914, Zeppelin Company representatives proposed to design an enlarged version of *LZ 26*, with all her improved features, a gas volume of 1,126,000 cubic feet, a fully enclosed keel, and a fourth engine. At the same time, to provide building facilities for these bigger ships, a new, larger construction shed was started at Friedrichshafen with Navy funds, and a large Army shed approaching completion at nearby Löwenthal, and the DELAG hangar at Potsdam, were taken over for construction. With a minimum of red tape and delay, the first Zeppelin of this new type, *LZ 38*, was completed in the new hangar at Friedrichshafen on April 3, 1915, and was so successful that she became the standard for both services and was duplicated in quantity.

Unlike the Friedrichshafen firm, the Schütte-Lanz Company already had a design for a big ship of 1,147,500 cubic feet – with slight modifications, the same as had been submitted to Tirpitz in October, 1913. But the firm was unable immediately to exploit this advantage. No further contracts had been forthcoming after the sale of *SL 2* to the Army in May, 1914, and in August the plant at Mannheim-Rheinau was operating with a skeleton staff,[7] while their construction shed was being enlarged. Three ships were in the Navy's first contract, and the first of them, *SL 3*, was ready in February, 1915. At that time she was the largest airship in the world, and two months ahead of the first big Zeppelin.

Although they continued to find favor with the War Ministry, the Schütte-Lanz ships never became popular with the Navy. Strasser was undoubtedly prejudiced against the wooden-framed craft, and was known to refer contemptuously to their supporters as "glue-potters." After two and a half years of war, he wrote:

> The Schütte-Lanz airships are not really combat-worthy . . . I consider it would be a mistake to build more Schütte-Lanz ships, for experience has thoroughly demonstrated that wood is an unsuitable material for airship construction, because it weakens and breaks with even a moderate degree of humidity . . . Building more wooden ships would only increase the number of ships useless for combat and would create personnel problems for the crews of combat-worthy aluminum ships.

[7] For statistics concerning the wartime increases in the numbers of employees of the airship building firms, see Appendix D.

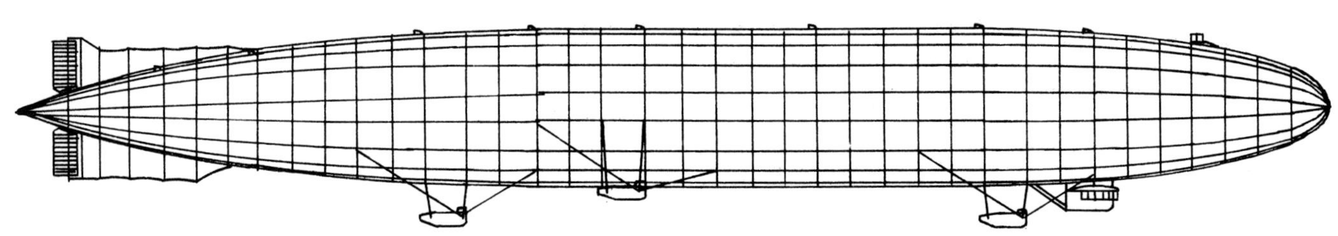

**SL 2**

| | | | |
|---|---|---|---|
| Gas capacity | 882,750 ft.$^3$ | Crew | 14 |
| Length | 472 ft. | Engines | 4 Maybach C-X, of 180 h.p. |
| Diameter | 60 ft. | Maximum speed | 55 mph |
| Useful lift | 17,900 lbs. | Ceiling | 9200 ft. |
| Gas cells | 15 | Full speed endurance | 6200 miles |

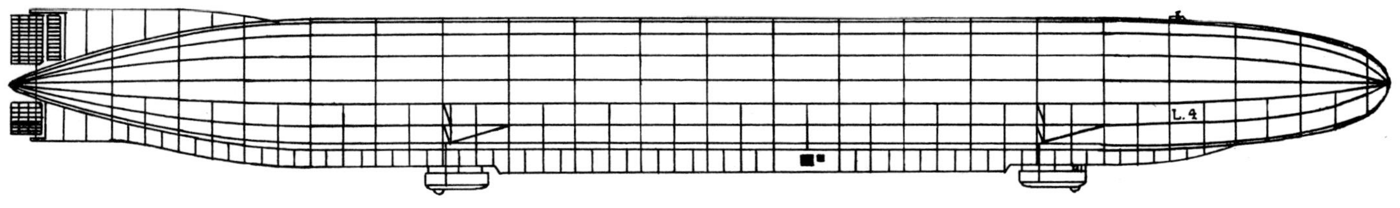


**L 4**

| | | | |
|---|---|---|---|
| Gas capacity | 793,600 ft.³ | Engines | 3 Maybach C-X, of 210 h.p. |
| Length | 518.2 ft. | Propellers | 4 L.Z. aluminum sheet |
| Diameter | 48.9 ft. | Weight empty | 37,500 |
| Useful lift | 19,600 lbs. | Maximum speed | 52 mph |
| Gas cells | 18 | Ceiling | 9300 ft. |
| Crew | 14 | Full speed endurance | 1375 miles |

The Mannheim firm later claimed to have solved the moisture problem with a special casein glue, and impregnation of the plywood girders with a waterproofing substance, but Strasser then refused to use the ships on front-line duty because their performance was inferior to that of contemporary Zeppelins. After years of experiments with duralumin tube girders, the Schütte-Lanz firm finally switched to metal structure – too late to finish any of these ships before the Armistice.

The need for airships was so urgent that the Admiralty even flirted briefly with the small, short-range "pressure airship." The Navy on August 9 requisitioned the Parseval non-rigid *PL 6*, familiar to pre-war Berliners as a sky sign carrier for the Stollwerck Chocolate Company, and flew her from her builder's shed at Bitterfeld to a private hangar at Kiel. Prince Henry, the admiral commanding in the Baltic, found her "militarily useless" and used her for training and a few local patrols in calm weather. On September 17 a second Parseval, *PL 19*, also came to Kiel. One of four ships building under a contract with the British Admiralty, she was seized at the outbreak of war for the German Army, and then ceded to the Navy with an Army crew. During the next few months she made a number of scouting and antisubmarine flights over the Baltic of up to 11 hours' duration, carrying up to 1,260 pounds of bombs.

Strasser had as violent a dislike for the Parseval ships as for the Schütte-Lanz craft. As early as September 22, 1914, he had written, "the Division is of the opinion that pressure airships are unsuited for naval purposes, and also for operations over land, because of low ceiling and ease with which they are damaged by gunfire." A few days later, when *PL 19* force-landed short of her base through loss of gas from a leaky valve – a minor defect – he

*The Army airship Z IX in front of the Maybach engine works at Friedrichshafen. This ship was the first Zeppelin to have simple cruciform control surfaces instead of box rudders, and set the type for the L 4 and the other ships in the Army and Navy's first wartime expansion programs. (Luftschiffbau Zeppelin)*

*The German naval airship L 5 on the Fuhlsbüttel landing ground. (Kriegsmarinesammlung)*

wrote: "this shows again the uselessness of pressure airships at sea." In fact, only one more Parseval airship was accepted by the Navy – *PL 25*, building at the start of the war on an Army order.

The Parseval airships actually were small, cheap and handy, and though they were indeed vulnerable to gunfire, they would have been well suited for local patrolling and anti-submarine warfare. The United States Navy in World War II found similar airships exceedingly useful for these purposes. It must be admitted that rubber for their fabric envelopes eventually became unobtainable in Germany; but Strasser erred in failing to comprehend the merits of the Parseval design, while his superiors likewise erred in an absurd attempt to procure Parseval airships rivaling the Zeppelins in size.

Less glamorous than the airships, but equally necessary, were the giant hangars needed to house them. On the outbreak of war the Admiralty placed contracts for eight, and on September 16, 1914, wrote to the Chief of the Naval Staff to suggest locations for them. Nordholz and Fuhlsbüttel could cover the interior of the Heligoland Bight, but additional bases should be set up at the outer limits of this strategic body of water. Thus the Admiralty proposed that two hangars should be erected "at Emden" in the west; one "opposite Sylt" in the north; two sheds should expand the existing Nordholz base, which had only the double revolving hangar; and three should go to Belgium, which had been overrun by the field-grey juggernaut in the first month of the war. Since the sheds in Belgium could contribute in no way to the security of the High Seas Fleet, this proposal reveals a passionate determination on the part of high naval officers to win from the Army the glittering triumph of making the first air attack on England. Ultimately, new bases were laid out at Hage near Norden in East Frisia, at Tondern in Schleswig-Holstein, and at Namur, far forward in Belgium.

With extreme optimism, the Admiralty had promised completion of the first sheds by the end of October or early November, and the last ones by the end of November. Actually none was finished at the end of 1914. This deplorable situation reveals a great clashing of gears in the supposedly well-oiled German war machine. No night work could be done at Nordholz because the commandant of the fortress of Cuxhaven enforced a total blackout within his domain. Strange as it may sound in our era of total warfare, there was no direction of labor, and half the ironworkers brought from the Rhineland to set up the Hage sheds drifted away within two weeks.

The crisis developed at the end of the year, when the new *L 7* and *L 8*, badly needed for Fleet operations in the North Sea, had to be housed wherever space could be found in the interior. Not until January 23, 1915, was the first of the new sheds put in service at Nordholz. The first airship was berthed in Tondern on March 23, and the first at Hage on April 10. The base at Namur was not completed until June, by which time the British Royal Naval Air Service at Dunkirk had become so aggressive that no airships could be risked there. The shed scandal could have been even more serious if airship deliveries had not been similarly delayed. While the stop-gap ships of the *L 3* type were, in some cases, rushed to completion in less than 5 weeks, *L 9*, the Navy's only example of the *LZ 26* class, was delayed by extensive modifications from January 10 until March 8, 1915. In November, 1914, the Admiralty had predicted that the Navy's first big million-cubic-foot Zeppelins, *L 10* and *L 11*, would be completed in January, 1915. Actually they were not commissioned until May 13 and June 7, 1915. Schütte-Lanz deliveries were likewise delayed – *SL 3*, *SL 4* and *SL 6*, expected to enter service in December, 1914, January and February, 1915, were actually completed in February, June and October, 1915.

The overriding importance of the Naval Airship Division in the German Navy's scheme of defense is further underlined by the generosity with which its personnel requirements were met. Trained officers and petty officers were at a premium, yet the first five new airship crews reported to the Naval Airship Division on September 20, 1914. By November 26, 1914, Strasser had a total of 25 flight crews – 412 officers and men – in service or in training. On October 8, Strasser set up the Airship Detachment Leipzig-Mockau, with the old passenger-carrier *Viktoria Luise* operating from this inland base as a training ship.[8] Each crew spent at least six months in elementary and advanced school ships, and then, on proceeding to the "Front," took over older airships in which their duties were not too demanding.

The need for more men in the ground troop – the "ground floor acrobats," as the flight crews were prone to call them – was more easily met by calling up older or less physically fit reservists. Thus, four months after the start of the war, Strasser's original 352 officers and men had expanded to a total of 3,740 at nine separate bases.[9]

Rarely has a mere three-striper wielded such power, or directed the destiny of so large an organization. Strasser had his own ideas on the use of airships in support of Fleet operations, and as bomb carriers which might directly determine the war's outcome by attacking enemy Cities. The time would soon come when he could translate his concepts of aerial warfare into action.

---

8 Dr. Eckener, enrolled in the Navy as a "volunteer airship pilot," directed the training of the naval crews. On March 15, 1915, when the Leipzig shed was turned over to the Schütte-Lanz firm for construction purposes, the school was transferred to Dresden. *L 6*, the advanced training ship, operated from Fuhlsbüttel after September 21, 1915, and from September 19, 1916, until the end of the war, all airship training was centralized in Nordholz.

9 For statistics concerning the wartime increases in personnel of the Naval Airship Division, see Appendix D.

*The German naval airship L 6 in the hands of the ground crew at Nordholz. Note the machine-gun on the top platform near the bow. The revolving shed appears on the left. (Luftschiffbau Zeppelin)*

L 21

# CHAPTER V

# EARLY OPERATIONS: THE CHRISTMAS DAY RAID

At the outbreak of war the Naval Airship Division was subordinated to *Konteradmiral* Franz Hipper, the commander of the High Seas Fleet's scouting forces. During the first hectic weeks, Hipper gave orders to Strasser directly. But Hipper could not supervise personally the large air organization now being planned. On August 29, 1914, the Navy's nine operational seaplanes and the naval airships were combined under *Konteradmiral* Philipp, who received the title of Chief of the Naval Air Forces.

Even before the outbreak of war, the German Navy, on July 30, had taken measures to protect the German Bight. Cruisers by day, and destroyers by night, patrolled stations in the "wet triangle" from Langeoog on the Frisian coast to Heligoland, and east to the Eider River in Schleswig-Holstein. On August 3, when war was declared against France, all sorts of rumors were rife, and French aircraft were falsely reported over Wilhelmshaven. On August 4 followed the British declaration of war.

At this time *L 3* was assigned to patrol the inner destroyer line. She was supposed to reconnoiter early in the morning and just before dark. But, though she was in the air every day making training flights, *L 3* made only two cruises along the coast in the first week of the war. "When giving orders to any of the air units," wrote the German official historian, "one had to consider that this weapon was still in its earliest stages of trial and development.[1]

On the night of August 11 the German light cruiser *Rostock* and a flotilla of destroyers ran down the Dutch coast, and reported seeing two mine-layers. While the High Seas Fleet prepared for the expected British attack, Hipper sent *L 3* to the area next morning. Off the island of Terschelling the Zeppelin found the Dutch battleship *de Zeven Provincien* and four destroyers. This flight of 170 miles from Fuhlsbüttel was the first under war conditions in which an airship carried out a

*OPPOSITE:*
*L 21 was one of the first ships to raid the English midlands. (Kameradschaft)*

---

1 Otto Groos, *Der Krieg in der Nordsee* (Berlin: E.S. Mittler u. Sohn, 1920-27), I, p. 36.

*L 6 at Nordholz (shed "Normann"). (Moch)*

*L 11 landing at Nordholz. Radio masts to the right, and revolving shed at center. (Kameradschaft)*

*This photo is said to be of L 4, of which no other known photo exists. Note multiple rudders and elevators. (Kameradschaft)*

*L 21 at Nordholz revolving shed. Note the machine guns on the top platform. On November 28, 1916, L 21 was shot down by British aircraft. (Kameradschaft)*

specific mission, and the accurate identification of the Dutch warships reflected credit on her commander, *Kapitänleutnant* Hans Fritz. Unfortunately, some later instances of faulty ship recognition demonstrated that the airship as a scouting weapon was no better than the training of her personnel.

August 17 marked the first long war flight, when Hipper, on learning that the British Fleet was operating off the Skagerrak, sent out *L 3* to reconnoiter. During the day she flew 300 miles north from her base, reaching a line between Hanstholm in Denmark and Ryvingen in Norway, and saw nothing of the enemy – a report which must have been reassuring to the fleet command. During the coming months, as the number of airships increased, the Fleet came to rely increasingly on them to check the numerous reports and rumors of British operations in the eastern North Sea.

Though the Germans saw nothing of British surface vessels, from the first days of the war the "D" and "E" class submarines of the Harwich Flotilla kept up a constant patrol near Heligoland. The British commanders saw the destroyers putting to sea in the evening, and the cruisers standing out to relieve them each morning. They saw nothing of the German big ships, which, according to British intelligence, were swinging to their anchors in Schillig Roads off Wilhelmshaven. Taking advantage of this situation, the light cruisers and destroyers of the Harwich Force, supported by battle cruisers, descended on the German patrols on the early morning of August 28. Though the German light cruisers tried to fight back, Admiral Beatty's heavy ships had the last word, and *Mainz*, *Köln* and *Ariadne* were sunk, with no British losses.

The Naval Airship Division failed the surface forces badly in this first sea battle of the war. Ordered out by Hipper when the first news of the action arrived, *L 3* at 8:40 a.m. met her own destroyers fleeing eastward towards the shelter of Heligoland and their own cruisers, and in the mist farther to the west glimpsed the pursuing British vessels. Unexpectedly *L 3* found herself under fire from the "friendly" destroyers, which drove her off to the east and away from the scene of action. A few minutes later *L 3* radioed to Hipper, "8:50 a.m.

*OPPOSITE BELOW: The standard German bombing aircraft was the "p" type. There were 22 of these type which flew many German Army missions. Later they were withdrawn because of the inability to keep up with the "q" ships. LZ 38 initiated the reach for greater altitude because of British and French aircraft. (Author)*

*L 11 taking off from the Löwenthal field. (Luftschiffbau Zeppelin)*

Turned back before enemy cruiser in 142 ε (about ten miles north-west of Heligoland). Returning to Fuhlsbüttel for technical reasons." Had the Zeppelin continued north and west as intended, she might well have discovered Beatty's big ships and thereby have saved the three light cruisers. But she was on her way home long before *Lion*, *Queen Mary* and *Princess Royal* burst into the Bight.

The decisive Battle of the Heligoland Bight had as great an influence on the conduct of the naval war as did the Battle of Jutland. Even the "activists" in the German Navy never recovered from the fear of another British advance right into their own waters, while those who believed that British naval power could be whittled down by guerrilla warfare now had a tangible excuse for keeping the battle fleet in harbor. The "lesson of August 28," as interpreted by the Naval Staff, led directly four years later to the mutiny in the High Seas Fleet and the downfall of the German Empire itself. Yet British capital ships never again appeared off the German bases. Obsessed with the fear of mines, submarines, and torpedoes, Admiral Jellicoe, the British Commander-in-Chief, resolved in an historic letter of October 30, 1914, to hold his fleet on the defensive in the northern part of the North Sea.

On the 17th of October the High Seas Fleet sacrificed a half-flotilla of old destroyers to the timorous policy of the Kaiser and his advisers. Sent out unsupported to lay mines before the Thames Estuary, they were overhauled and sunk by ships of the Harwich Force. This "slaughter of the innocents" gave Admiral von Ingenohl, the Commander-in-Chief of the High Seas Fleet, an argument with which to gain the Imperial consent to using the big ships. He planned to bombard the port of Great Yarmouth with the battle cruisers, taking the battle fleet to sea in support. Dissatisfied with the reports

*Navy airship base at Hage. The four hangars were identical, but were eventually too small when the 55,000 cubic meter ships were developed. (Kriegsmarinesammlung)*

of destroyer flotillas sent out at night to reconnoiter the proposed route, he turned to the airships. On October 19, *Oberleutnant zur See* Hirsch in *L 5* made a fine flight of 16 hours to within 60 miles of Great Yarmouth, without seeing British vessels. This encouraged von Ingenohl to go ahead with his plans for the raid on the 28th. But in the meantime, on October 25, the British appeared in the Bight. Only later did the Germans learn that the Harwich Force, with several primitive seaplane carriers, had attempted an air attack on the naval airship sheds believed to be at Cuxhaven. A "deluge of rain" prevented the seaplanes from getting off the water. *L 4*, scouting westward that day past the German offshore islands of Norderney and Borkum, must have passed close to the British force, but saw nothing in fog and rain.

Early on the morning of November 3, Hipper's battle cruisers appeared off Great Yarmouth and fired a few shells harmlessly in the direction of the town. On their way home the Germans were shadowed by light cruisers and destroyers of the Harwich Force, but did not fight an action. The Kaiser had especially ordered air reconnaissance to the north of the returning High Seas Fleet, but bad weather prevented the airships from going out.

On November 21, *L 7*, approaching completion in Friedrichshafen, barely escaped destruction when the British Royal Naval Air Service made a daring attack on the Zeppelin works. Three Avro 80 h.p. biplanes, carrying four 20-pound bombs each, made the 120-mile flight from Belfort in France to Friedrichshafen. One plane was lost, but the British claimed that *L 7* was badly damaged and the gas works destroyed. This assertion is refuted by the detailed report which *L 7*'s commander, *Oberleutnant zur See* Werner Peterson, sent next day to Admiral Philipp. Peterson believed that

*The revolving shed at Nordholz. Originally each shed was 597.1 feet long. As the Zeppelins grew larger, extensions ("Busen") made them 656 feet long. The entire 4000 ton double shed could be rotated in one hour. (Moch)*

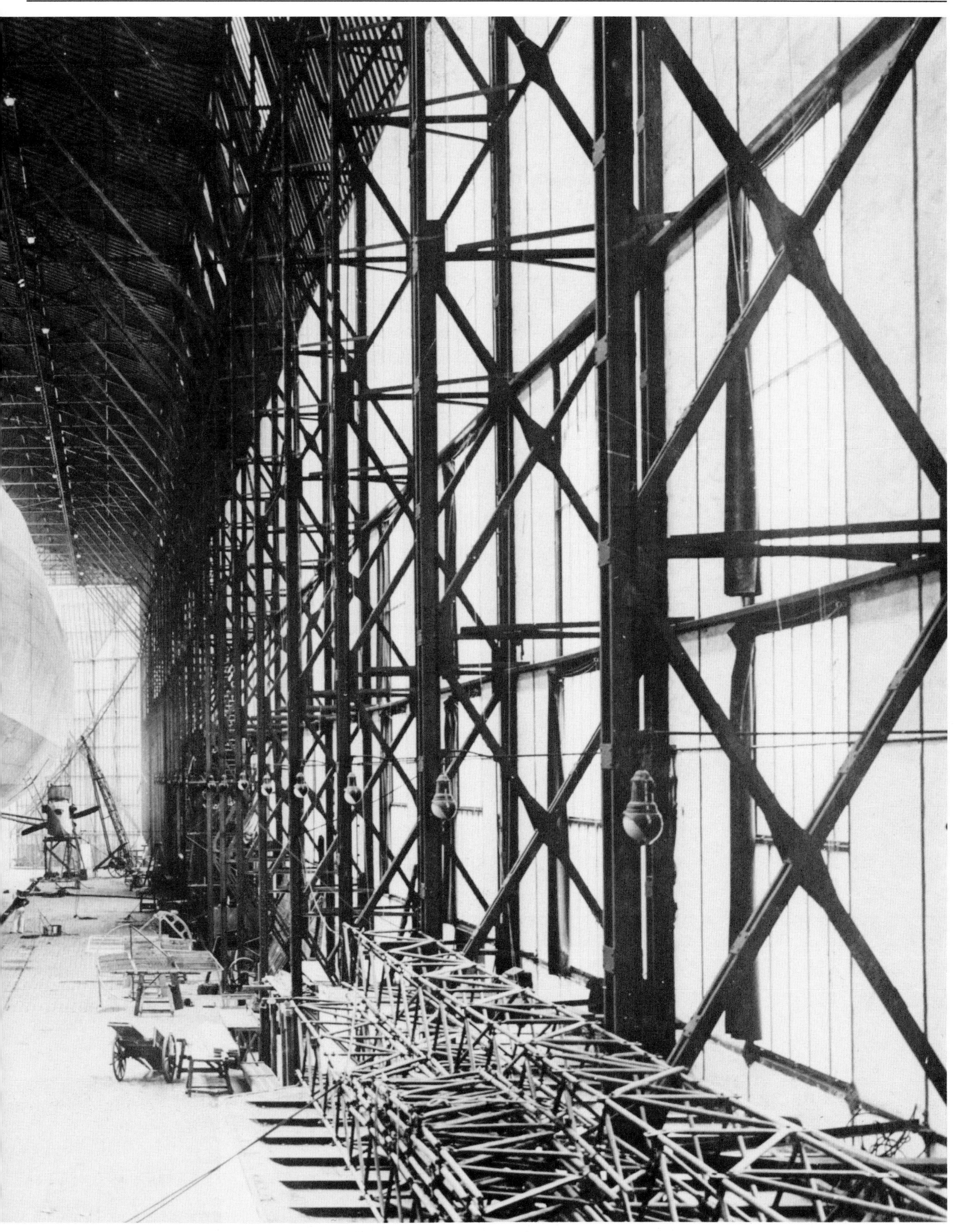

*PREVIOUS: SL 14 at Schütte-Lanz, Mannheim-Rheinau. A trench in the floor of the hangar was to accomodate larger ships. SL 14 was badly damaged on field at Wainoden and was dismantled November 19-22, 1917. (Moch)*

spies had reported the inflation of *L 7* on November 20, but the Avros had arrived in Belfort only on November 13, and the 21st was the first day of good flying weather.[2] Peterson was impressed by the courage and determination of the flight leader, Squadron Commander E.F. Briggs, who came down to 500 feet in the face of heavy rifle and machine-gun fire to aim two bombs at the Zeppelin hangars. One burst between the sheds, but Briggs, with a head wound, a shattered gas tank, and ten bullet holes in his plane, was forced to land on the field. A bomb from the second plane blew out a window of the smaller shed with *L 7* inside; if it had traveled sixty feet farther it would have destroyed the ship, but actually she was unscratched. Though the results must have seemed encouraging, the British never repeated the attempt, even when the Zeppelin menace was causing them great concern. Neutral Switzerland had complained that the Avros had crossed her territory, and though this was denied, presumably the British wished to avoid further trouble with the Swiss Government.

On December 16 the German battle cruisers bombarded Hartlepool, Whitby and Scarborough. The British official air history states that a Zeppelin reconnoitered the Humber on the preceding day,[3] but the airship war diaries show that on December 15 none of them was able to make even local practice flights. Again on the 16th the weather prevented the airships from covering the operation.

2 J.M. Bruce, *British Airplanes 1914-18* (London: Putnam & Co., Ltd., 1957), p. 42.

3 H.A. Jones, *The War in the Air* (Oxford: at The Clarendon Press, 1922-35), III, p. 86.

*The dogs of war. Most German airships had pets as mascots. Most were dogs, however, a few had cats. This photo shows the crew of the Army ship SL 2 with their mascot at Liegnitz, August 1914. This crew later disappeared in SL 10 over the Black Sea. (Bleston)*

*SL 4, built at Sandhofen. On December 11, 1915, the doors of the "Selim" shed opened during a gale and SL 4 was blown out on to the field and was a total loss. (Bleston)*

In fact the first reconnaissance flights of the month were on December 23, when *L 4* and *L 5* were out, the former, in spite of losing a propeller, pushing on to 50 miles west of the Dutch island of Texel. On December 24, *L 5* and *L 6* were forced by heavy clouds to turn back over the inner waters of the Bight. Thus the airships were unable to give warning of the Christmas Day raid on Cuxhaven.

Like the previous attempt, this attack was intended for the airship sheds which in fact were at Nordholz, about eight miles south of Cuxhaven. The British squadron consisted of two light cruisers and eight destroyers of the Harwich Force escorting the seaplane carriers *Engadine*, *Riviera* and *Empress*. These small, fast cross-Channel steamers, had been taken over at the start of the war and had

*Count Zeppelin aboard L 6 on a training flight. In the foreground from left to right: Hauptmann Manger, Hugo Eckener, Count Zeppelin, Hermann Kraushaar, and Leutnant zur See Westphal.*

*Bombs carried by naval Zeppelins. In order of size: 660 lb., 220 lb., 110 lb., and 22 lb. explosives, and a pair of incendiaries in the cart to the left and right. The men are holding bomb-fuses, and a parachute flare stands in front of the 660 lb. bomb. (Moch)*

*SL 3 lifting off at Rheinau. (Bleston)*

had a hangar built aft to house three Short seaplanes which carried two men and a few 20-pound bombs. Ten British submarines were to work close in to the German coast, and the Grand Fleet took station far out in the North Sea, hopeful that the Germans could be provoked into a major battle.

During the night of December 24 a U-boat encountered the British force. At dawn the enemy was sighted from Heligoland, and the watchers on the island alarmed the whole North Sea coast. At 7 a.m. the carriers hove-to and swung out their planes, and by 8 a.m. seven were in the air. Two more had failed to get off the water.

*SL 5 was taken out for a flight on July 5, 1915, when its wooden structure broke up within sight of a British POW camp, whose inmates wrote home about the destruction of a German airship. It was later dismantled (opposite below). (Pochhammer)*

The German Naval Airship Division could bring only half its strength to bear. Only the day before, *L 3* had been taken out of service in Fuhlsbüttel to have her control surfaces modified. But this probably made no difference, for the war diary of her shedmate, *L 4*, records for this date, "could not fly, thick fog." Nordholz, however, was clear, and at 7:31 a.m. *L 6* took off, followed at 8:49 by *L 5*.

From 8:30 on, alarm messages poured in all along the German coast. *L 5* sighted three of the seaplanes over the River Weser at 9:12 a.m., steering a course for Nordholz. Hirsch sent a warning message to his base, and continued westward.

The weather, which at first had been crisp and clear, now turned against the attackers. A low, thick fog drifted in from the sea. At 9:20 a.m. one of the British planes was heard in the fog over Nordholz, and a few minutes later an anti-aircraft machine-gun battery sighted the Englishman and opened fire. The plane glided down to a thousand feet and steered for the revolving hangar, but turned away and crossed the battery. Neither the machine guns nor rifles in the hands of the ground troop seemed to damage it, and it headed straight for the gasometer, holding a million cubic feet of hydrogen. Two bombs intended for this target missed and fell in the pine woods. As far as the Nordholz base was concerned, this ended the attack.

Out at sea, German airships and seaplanes were just beginning to make matters interesting for the British. *L 6*, passing Heligoland at 8:30, received the searchlight message, "enemy bears north by east." A few minutes later, and fifteen miles north of the island, *Oberleutnant zur See* Horst Baron von

*SL 3 under construction at Rheinau. Note different sized girders. (Bleston)*

Buttlar sighted the British force. He correctly identified the two light cruisers and eight destroyers, and distinguished three "steamers with funnels painted black," but failed to recognize them as seaplane carriers. Quickly von Buttlar coded a message, but at the first attempt to send it, the radio generator failed. *L 6* then steered north-west after two vessels separated from the main body, but soon after 10 a.m. returned to the larger group. One seaplane carrier, *Empress*, was having condenser trouble and had fallen behind. Dropping three tanks of fuel and all water ballast except three "breeches," von Buttlar got his ship up from 1,600 to 5,800 feet, and using for cover some scattered clouds, steered the huge gas-bag to attack the straggler. British versions describe the desperate plight of Empress at the center of a forest of bomb bursts, and claim she was rescued only when a 6-inch shell from the cruiser *Undaunted* badly damaged the Zeppelin. Von Buttlar states that the one 110-pound bomb he aimed at *Empress* missed by at least a hundred feet, and the other three bombs were later dropped as ballast. He noticed the carrier's crew firing at him with rifles, and replied with the machine guns in the airship's gondolas. He states he was unable to repeat the attack due to heavy gunfire from the ships below, and on taking his Zeppelin into the clouds for safety, he lost sight of the enemy. Von Buttlar then steered for Schillig Roads, where he descended to 400 feet to drop a written report on the quarter-deck of the armored cruiser *Roon*. An hour later, at 1:30 p.m., he landed at Nordholz. Though the gas cells showed nine holes from rifle bullets when the ship was checked next day, she was 1,300 pounds light at the landing and

*OPPOSITE: SL 2 at Rheinau. Note tapered fuel tanks, and the light and heavy girders. Gas cells are hung up awaiting gas. (Bleston)*

*PL 26 Parseval pressure ship with four engines is shown at Bitterfeld. This ship burned November 19, 1915 the same day this photo was taken.*

von Buttlar had to valve gas to get her down. Hirsch, on his way to the scene of action in *L 5*, had further adventures with the British seaplanes. Of the seven that started, only two returned to the carriers. Another was picked up by the destroyer *Lurcher*, and towards 11:30 a fourth dropped down by the British submarine E. 11, lying half-submerged off Norderney. The submarine had just taken off the crew of this plane when two more landed nearby. At the same time *L 5* came in sight. E. 11 took off the remaining airmen and just managed to submerge as two bombs burst on the surface overhead. Hirsch then went off to the west, sighted the British cruisers and destroyers, and followed them through their maneuvers. Whenever he came back to the three seaplanes, he descended close to the water and shot them up with his machine guns. At 12:25 the British squadron put on speed and disappeared in the haze to the west, and due to the deteriorating visibility, Hirsch turned back for Nordholz. On the way he found the three seaplanes drifting forlornly near the Norderney Lightship. He reported their position by radio and went down close enough to observe their identification markings – a red circle on top of the wings, and a Union Jack underneath – and to read their numbers, 120, 814 and 815.

The last of the seven British aviators landed near a Dutch trawler and was taken into Ymuiden. Here he was classified as a "shipwrecked mariner" and was shortly returned to England.

This attack forced the Germans to look to the security of the airship bases. 88mm and 37mm anti-aircraft cannon were mounted, and the giant hangars and broad shed doors, which could be seen shining from 12 miles away in the early morning light, were daubed with camouflage paint. Each base received a flight of defending airplanes. The Navy fighter aircraft were identical with those used by the German Army on the Western Front.

Foul weather set in again, and no further scouting flights were made for the rest of the month. On December 29, during a south-east gale, part of the roof of the Nordholz revolving shed blew off and a large beam fell through a gas cell of *L 5*. Only a miracle prevented the hangar and the two airships it housed from going up in flames. The crew and

*OPPOSITE: SL 13 at Wildeshausen. SL 13 is identical with SL 11, the first German airship shot down in flames over London on September 3, 1916. (Pochhammer)*

XVI
16
16

*LZ 26 built by LZ at Frankfurt to carry passengers (see cabin amidship). This photo is probably of the first flight on December 14, 1914. The engine cars are open as in earlier DELAG ships, but were fitted with light fabric and bows to cover engine cars. (Provan)*

maintenance party turned to at once, repaired and refilled the cell, and stood by all night, while the shed had to be turned four times during the night due to shifting winds. On the 19th of January the Harwich Force appeared in the outer German patrol line, with the battle cruisers in support. A seaplane was the first to sight the British ships. At 8:17 a.m., Hirsch took off from Nordholz in *L 5* to scout on a west-northwest course. At 11:15 he spotted many British warships, including the battle cruisers, 60 miles north-west of Heligoland. The men in Beatty's big ships, glimpsing the Zeppelin at a great distance mid snow-laden clouds, remembered her as the only German craft they sighted on this cruise. At 2 p.m. Hirsch radioed that the British had gone home, and turned back to Nordholz where he landed at 4:26 p.m.

*L 5*'s reconnaissance was not the only flight made on this day. On the following morning, the war-fevered country was electrified by this announcement:

Berlin, January 20 Official:

> On the night of January 19-20 naval airships undertook an attack on several fortified places on the English east coast. Numerous bombs were dropped successfully in misty weather and rain. The ships were fired on, but returned undamaged.

The Deputy Chief of the Naval Staff
(signed) Behncke.[4]

---

4 *Kölnische Zeitung*, January 21, 1915.

# CHAPTER VI

# LUFTPOLITIK AT IMPERIAL HEADQUARTERS

The emotions which swept over the German people in August, 1914 as their armies stormed through Belgium and France, included a wave of rage against England. Through the years, while the *Reichstag* had voted millions to expand the Army and Navy, and while the Kaiser had rattled the sabre in crisis after crisis, the Germans had persisted in the belief that England would be friendly, or at least neutral, while they settled accounts with France and Russia. The intervention against them of the most powerful empire in the world must have seemed an omen of the disaster which ensued four years later. Starting spontaneously, their wrath burst out in such mad imprecations as Lissauer's "Hymn of Hate." The "nation of shopkeepers" should be punished like France and Belgium, whom the Germans professed to believe had been duped by their arch-enemy. But how? The sea stood between the German Army and "perfidious Albion," and the sea was held by the overpowering might of the Royal Navy. Only through the air could England be attacked. Remembering the impressive spectacle of the giant airships soaring overhead, the German people turned to old Count Zeppelin. In the autumn of 1914 even the children were singing:

*Zeppelin, flieg,*
*Hilf uns im Krieg,*
*Fliege nach England,*
*England wird abgebrannt,*
*Zeppelin, flieg!*[1]

"Fly, Zeppelin! Fly to England! England shall be destroyed with fire!"

This must have seemed simple enough to the German public, accustomed to the propaganda-inflated exploits of the DELAG craft, and ignorant of the frailties of the 1914 Zeppelins. But the vaunted

[1] Dr. Adolf Saager, *Zeppelin* (Stuttgart: Verlag Robert Lutz, 1915), p. 214.

fleet of "giant air cruisers" had been sadly decimated in the first month of the war, when the Army had lost four of its six Zeppelins – three as a result of sending them out on daylight reconnaissance's low over the enemy's troops. A fifth, *Z IX*,[2] was destroyed in her shed at Düsseldorf on October 8 by a daring British naval pilot who made the 100-mile flight from Antwerp the day before the city fell to the German Army. For nearly three months thereafter the Army airship force in the west consisted of the aged *Sachsen* and Schütte-Lanz *SL* 2, and the new *Z X* of the *L* 3 type – hardly equal to the destruction of England.

And it was even longer before they were permitted to make the attempt. The Kaiser, so often represented as the blood-thirsty advocate of *Schrecklichkeit*, was in fact the chief obstacle to the air war on England. The records show his generals and admirals, forced to bend to the vacillating will of the All Highest, living in an agony of apprehension and uncertainty as to the day-to-day future of their plans. In particular, the Supreme War Lord felt a tender solicitude for historic monuments in London and for the personal safety of his royal cousins, the King and Queen of England.

Fantastic though it may seem, hard-headed admirals in control of the German Navy shared the exaggerated expectations of the uninformed populace. The wish that England, particularly London, should be destroyed from the air inspired the conviction that this was possible. A deep sense of inferiority to the British Navy may have led the Kaiser's admirals to hope they could leap over the wall of ships to strike at the enemy's heart. This emotionally motivated campaign started in the earliest days of the war. Its consistent advocate was *Konteradmiral* Paul Behncke, the Deputy Chief of the Naval Staff, who had been left in charge in Berlin when his superior, Admiral Hugo von Pohl, went off with the Kaiser to Imperial Headquarters in Luxemburg. But von Pohl, the man to whom everybody looked for a decision, was weak and hesitant, driven hither and thither by the fear of displeasing his Imperial master and by the demands of his subordinates. Unwilling to urge that the Navy be allowed to attack England, he waited on the Army to develop a joint plan of operations.

As early as August 20, 1914, Behncke, excited by the news of the fall of Liege and Brussels, wrote to von Pohl on the possibilities opening up for aerial warfare. The Army might be expected, he wrote, to seize the Belgian and French coasts as far west as Cape Gris Nez (his prophecy nearly came true, the trenches eventually reaching the sea west of Nieuport in Belgium), in which case airship bases could be set up at Nieuport, Ostend and Zeebrügge in Belgium or Dunkirk and Calais in France. From these he predicted that Navy Zeppelins, carrying twenty 110-pound bombs, could travel 460 miles – as far north as a line drawn through Scotland from Glasgow to Dundee. (Later experience would show that the *L* 3 type of Zeppelin, under favorable cold-weather conditions, could lift enough fuel to fly barely 400 miles, together with not more than 1,000 pounds of bombs.) Behncke pointed out the importance of bombing London, its docks, and the nerve-center of the British Navy, the Admiralty building in Whitehall. Such attacks "may be expected, whether they involve London or the neighborhood of London, to cause panic in the population which may possibly render it doubtful that the war can be continued." Next to London, the naval bases at Dover and Portsmouth would be the most important targets, while the Humber and the Tyne, the Firth of Forth, Plymouth and Glasgow were also mentioned. Behncke concluded:

> In general, air attacks with planes and airships from the Belgian and French coasts, particularly with airships, promise considerable material and moral results. They must therefore be considered an effective means of damaging England.

---

2 The German Army system of numbering their rigid airships requires special explanation. Up until December, 1914, their Zeppelins were designated by the letter Z and a Roman numeral (*Z I*), but they were not numbered consecutively, lost or decommissioned ships were replaced with a new one bearing a similar "ersatz" number (Ersatz *Z I* or *EZ I*), and when this last ship was lost, she was succeeded by an "Ersatz *EZ I*." Fearing to have a "*Z XIII*," the Army in January, 1915, began using the builder's numbers of the Zeppelin works (*LZ 34*) Shortly afterwards, they began the practice of adding "30" to the Zeppelin Company's works number (thus *LZ 42* became *LZ* 72). This system was followed until the end of the Army airship service in 1917. Army Schütte-Lanz airships were designated with the builder's number in Roman numerals (*SL VII*).

In practice, the number was rarely painted on the ship, Army Zeppelins having merely the letters "*LZ*" and Schütte-Lanz ships the letters "*SL*" painted under the bows.

Only two Zeppelins, *L 3* and *L 4*, were on hand when von Pohl replied on September 4 to Behncke's letter. The High Seas Fleet was short of cruisers, and von Pohl's insistence that the small number of airships on hand should be reserved for scouting and not risked on raids was entirely realistic. Yet such was the determination to destroy England that there were occasions when the Commander-in-Chief of the Fleet was ordered to hold back a bare minimum of airships for scouting, and to send the rest out against the enemy's homeland.

Admiral Philipp, in a letter to Tirpitz and von Pohl on October 2, presented a detailed plan for using *L 3* in an attack on England. He agreed that the primary mission of the Naval Airship Division must be scouting in the North Sea, but if enough airships were on hand, an "expedition" to England could be considered. Leaving Hamburg-Fuhlsbüttel at 7 a.m., one could reach the British coast at 7 p.m., operate with the onset of darkness over London or Chatham, and next morning could be back over the Elbe. October would be a month of suitably calm and cool weather, while November could be expected to be stormy. Though the Navy had started work on the base at Namur, in Belgium, Philipp was opposed to using a Belgian base to attack England. There was still considerable civil disturbance, and he feared that as the ships hovered low on take-off or landing, an incendiary bullet from a house or a bush could destroy them. Also, "if a ship is sent to Belgium the Army High Command will try to commandeer it for their own purposes." After delivery of *L 6*, anticipated for October 17, the Naval Airship Division would have four Zeppelins, and one could be spared for raiding. When it was certain that the Navy would get *L 6* (and the Army was then demanding her), Philipp proposed that Strasser be given authority to send out one airship to raid whenever the weather seemed favorable.

A few days later, Behncke wrote to von Pohl supporting Philipp's request, agreeing that there would be enough ships after *L 6* was delivered, and that the fine October weather should not be wasted. The Zeppelins of the *L 3* class, Behncke submitted, could reach the Thames from Nordholz, and possibly even the west coast of England if lightened of equipment and personnel. The first raid should be on London and the banks of the Thames down to Woolwich. Damage in the center of the capital would have the greatest moral effect. Behncke further indicated his ideas by a draft of a proposed order (which was never issued) to the Commander-in-Chief of the High Seas Fleet:

> (1) As soon as possible, an airship is to carry out an attack on England. The time of the attack and choice of airship will be decided by the Commander-in-Chief of the High Seas Fleet.
>
> (2) Target area will be London and the Thames region from London to Woolwich-Becton [sic] inclusive. Chief target within this area is the Admiralty with its radio station. Further targets are: main telegraph office, gas works in London-Becton, harbor works west and south of Woolwich, oil tanks at Greenwich and Woolwich and the Woolwich Arsenal.
>
> Buildings of historic value, monuments, etc., are to be spared as far as possible.
>
> (3) After completing the operation against London or if the operation against London cannot be carried out, other places in England may be attacked. These primarily include: Immingham,[3] Dover, Portsmouth, Southampton, Liverpool and Manchester.

Behncke added that a particular moral effect would result from bombing Liverpool and Manchester because of their great distance from the German bases. His letter is given in some detail because, for what it is worth, this "master bombing plan" is what guided the naval airships through four years of war. He concluded, "we dare not leave untried any means of forcing England to her knees, and successful air attacks on London, considering the well-known nervousness of the public, will be a valuable measure."

On October 10, 1914, *General* Erich von Falkenhayn, the Chief of the Army General Staff, telegraphed his intention of starting raids on England in three weeks, and requested the Navy's cooperation. The Army proposed to stage its Zeppelins for-

3 A seaport in Lincolnshire on the south bank of the Humber.

ward from the Rhineland bases to hangars in occupied Belgium and France. The Navy would then be permitted to use the Rhineland sheds which would be closer to England than the North Sea bases. Next day a conference at the Admiralty suggested that at least two Zeppelins should be assigned to make raids in cooperation with the Army, though the final decision should be left to the Naval Staff.[4] Yet nothing came of these plans. On this date, the Army in fact had only the old ex-passenger carrier Sachsen in the west, and the sheds in France and Belgium were not ready until March, 1915.

Belatedly, Behncke thought of international law in relation to this novel way of making war. In a memorandum of October 22, 1914, he saw no legal obstacle to his plans. The first Hague Declaration of 1899 had forbidden dropping shells or explosives from the air, but it had not been renewed when it expired in 1904. Article 25 of the Land Warfare Convention of 1907 (which Germany had not ratified) forbade bombardment of undefended places "by any means whatever," but Article 2 of the Naval Convention stated that all military installations in undefended places might be bombarded. Behncke argued that London possessed "military installations" in its docks and factories, also in its known anti-aircraft batteries. Furthermore, claimed Behncke, three land forts and ten redoubts on the south side of the capital, and a fort to the north, made London a "defended place."

A small incident at the end of October illustrates the intense jealousy and rivalry between the Army and Navy in their efforts to be the first in bombing England. A War Ministry memorandum dated October 25 came into the hands of Behncke and von Capelle, the Deputy Chiefs of the Naval Staff and of the Admiralty in Berlin. The memorandum quoted von Pohl as saying that the Navy would soon have ten airships (actually, due to losses, it reached this number only in June, 1915), and since only three would be needed for scouting over the North Sea, the remaining seven could be put at the disposal of the General Staff for operations against England. The Army wished to know if the Navy was prepared to supply and maintain the seven Navy ships to be *turned over* to the Army with their crews. In horrified unison, both admirals protested in the strongest possible terms to their erring superior at Imperial Headquarters. When it came to assisting the Army, it would seem that there were no airships to spare. Behncke pointed out that the Navy would not have ten ships until the following year at the earliest. Three at least would be needed for scouting in the North Sea, two more were required to reconnoiter over the Channel in advance of some hypothetical naval operations from the Belgian coast, and one should be held in reserve in each area. Von Pohl should take a stiffer attitude towards the War Ministry – "I respectfully beg Your Excellency to put forward these points of view in further negotiations with the Army."

On November 9, von Falkenhayn sent to von Pohl another plan for joint aerial operations against England beginning on December 1. He proposed a joint conference at Imperial Headquarters on November 18 of the aviation personnel who would be involved in the first joint Army and Navy air attack. Admiral Philipp, attending with Strasser on behalf of the Navy, was not impressed: "Airship matters in the Army," he reported, "are not handled and directed as is necessary in the interest of the war effort, considering the importance of the arm." Philipp met *Major* Köppen, of the General Staff, who "seemed to be" in charge, but "did not appear to be well oriented concerning the weapon he was representing at the conference." "No particular senior officer could be found directing the Army airships and their employment," Philipp alleged. "If any decision is required, the Army officers get together either spontaneously or by order of the Army Command and reach a decision after a conference."

But French planes were beginning to bomb German towns, and the Army instead began planning retaliatory raids on French cities. On Christmas Day the Army Command advised von Pohl that it was sending its ships against Nancy, Dunkirk and Verdun, and suggested the Navy's airships be sent out in simultaneous operations. Strasser, growing impatient, had telegraphed from Nordholz, "generally favorable weather conditions for distant un-

4 The conference noted that bombs were finally on hand – fifty 110-pound explosive bombs had already been delivered, and one hundred 220- and one hundred 660-pound bombs would be ordered at once.

dertaking against England." Impulsively von Pohl, without consulting anyone, wired to the Commander-in-Chief of the Fleet, "Army General Staff ordering their airships to attack French fortresses. Suggest taking advantage of favorable weather conditions for operations of naval airships against English east coast with exception of London. Attack on London will take place later in cooperation with Army airships." Too busy to think of "Peace on Earth, Good Will towards Men," von Pohl spent Christmas dinner at Imperial Headquarters discussing this decision with Tirpitz. Next day the fork-bearded old *Großadmiral* sent von Pohl his views in writing: he advised no piecemeal efforts; considering:

> The great fragility and vulnerability of our airships, all available ships should be concentrated on London . . . The measure of the success will lie not only in the injury which will be caused to the enemy, but also in the significant effect it will have in diminishing the enemy's determination to prosecute the war, which will be greater than if the bombs are scattered singly.

On December 4, and again on December 19, primitive French long-range bombers had caused heavy civilian casualties in Freiburg – acts which, to Tirpitz and to other Germans, seemed to cry out for retaliation. Yet, Tirpitz admitted sadly, a decision by His Majesty would seem unavoidable.

Von Falkenhayn, the Chief of the General Staff, expressed his, serious concern about the effect on both services' plans for aerial warfare if bombs fell in the wrong places in England and the Kaiser took umbrage. Von Pohl belatedly agreed, and at noon on December 26, "because speed was urgent," he telegraphed directly to Strasser, by-passing the chain of command, to order the raids postponed. To the Commander-in-Chief of the High Seas Fleet he explained on December 27, "with respect to an air attack on London, there prevail at this time in other circles [i.e., the Kaiser] very serious scruples which will first have to be resolved."

"Order, counter-order, disorder!" It was too much for Philipp, who exploded in a letter to von Pohl: "Recently London, then the whole of England, was forbidden to the naval airships for special operations because the Army is now using their airships in the ground fighting in France and apparently does not want the Navy to go ahead by itself." Though plenty of airships were available, the Navy had been forced to let good weather opportunities slip by. Unfavorable hot summer days might arrive while the Army and Navy were still trying to coordinate their operations from different bases with different weather conditions.

> If the Army uses ships in France indefinitely, and the Navy is forced to wait for a plan of common operations, the great fighting capacity of the Navy ships will remain completely unused for a long time. They will be destroyed without results by enemy plane attacks. For these reasons, and because the Army lacks a determined and expertly trained leadership, I ask that an effort be made to give the Navy a free hand in its efforts against London and the rest of England, and if the Army has ships participating, the Navy should be directing the overall operation.

Although his post as chief naval adviser to the Kaiser carried with it the right of the *Immediatvortrag* – access to the Emperor whenever a decision on high naval policy was required – von Pohl had still made no direct attempt to get the Supreme War Lord's consent to opening raids on England – nor to many other measures being demanded by officers of the Fleet. Now, goaded on by his subordinates, von Pohl on January 7, 1915, demanded an audience with the Kaiser. The written agenda covered the entire naval war. Heading "f–Air Warfare" read:

> The primary mission of the airships and planes remains scouting in cooperation with the High Seas Fleet.
>
> Further, it is anticipated that offensive employment of the airships against England in the months of January and February will be particularly worth while, as calm and cool weather can be anticipated. Primary attack targets would be the militarily important areas of London and

*The canvas covered shed at Liegnitz. The ship is SL 2. (Bleston)*

the military installations of the lower Thames, because of the moral impression as well as the high significance which would not be involved in attacks on objectives of lesser importance. Historic buildings and private property will be spared as much as possible.

Cooperation with the Army is not practical, since this would mean a further postponement of the offensive, which the Commander-in-Chief of the Fleet is pressing for, and weather conditions on the coast are not always the same as in the interior of Germany.

Von Pohl came away with a partial victory: "Air attacks on England approved by the Supreme War Lord," he telegraphed to the Commander-in-Chief of the High Seas Fleet on January 10. "Targets not to be attacked in London but rather docks and military establishments in the lower Thames and on the English coast."

# CHAPTER VII

# "ENGLAND SHALL BE DESTROYED BY FIRE"

Strasser must have prepared his attack plan well in advance, for on that same January 10 he forwarded it to the Commander-in-Chief of the Fleet. Raids would be made on the Tyne, the mouth of the Humber, Great Yarmouth and Lowestoft, Harwich and the Thames mouth "with exception of objectives in London itself." Three ships would be held for raids and one for scouting in accordance with a recent Fleet order. The airships would approach England by day, attack in the evening, and return at night. The day approach would permit scouting the sea areas along their course while at night there would be better prospects for a surprise attack, and darkness would conceal the Zeppelins from defensive gunfire and pursuing planes. (Strasser could have added that the airships would be sent out only during the dark of the moon – the so-called "attack period", lasting usually from eight days before the new moon until eight days afterwards.) The airship commanders would be given discretion to continue or turn back over the North Sea depending on their estimate of the weather, and would choose their targets according to the wind direction – working to windward to attack, so as to have a following wind for the return. The attack order would be: "Distant scouting to west, take only *Handelsschiffsverkehrsbuch*."[1]

The initial raid attempt was made with the first break in the weather on January 13, and in Strasser's absence on an inspection trip, was a somewhat impromptu affair. The Fleet Command order to hold one ship for scouting was disregarded, and all four North Sea

---

1 The *Handelsschiffsverkehrsbuch* (abbreviated H.V.B.) was the Navy's signal book for communicating with German merchant ships. It was known to be compromised, therefore no harm would be done if the airship was lost and the book fell into British hands. On March 15, 1915, Admiral Philipp ordered that the German Navy signal book, the War Signal Book Cipher Key, Wireless Calls of the German Navy, and Cipher Key III, which the naval airships ordinarily carried, were to be left behind when raiding England. Yet this order was sometimes disregarded, occasionally with disastrous results for the German cause. The airships were required to radio to the Commander-in-Chief of the Fleet as soon as they departed on a raid, "Naval Airship L – taking off for distant scouting, course –, only H.V.B. on board." The British soon learned that "H.V.B." invariably meant an attack on England.

*LZ 39, built for the Army, was a sister ship of L 9. Seen here at Friedrichshafen, it flew over the eastern front. (LZ)*

Zeppelins went out – *L 5* and *L 6* from Nordholz, and *L 3* and *L 4* from Fuhlsbüttel. The leader of the raid was none other than *Kapitänleutnant* Heinrich Mathy. Transferred from a destroyer to the Naval Airship Division on January 10, 1915, he was determined to have a ship of his own and had been assigned to command the next new craft, *L 9*. Meanwhile he had been acting as Strasser's administrative *alter ego* in Nordholz. On this first raid attempt Mathy was aboard *L 5*. The weather steadily deteriorated as the Zeppelins steered west along the offshore islands, heavy rain weighted them down, and Mathy ordered them back at 2:54 p.m.

Improved weather five days later encouraged Strasser to order *L 6*, *L 3* and *L 4* to stand by for a "distant mission to the west, only H.V.B. on board." Strasser himself intended to lead the three ships against England. No arm-chair superior, Strasser tried to participate in one raid each month to judge for himself the state of the enemy defenses and the performance of his ships and men in combat.

*L 3* and *L 4* took off from Fuhlsbüttel just before 11 a.m. on January 19 with orders to attack the River Humber. *L 6*, ordered to raid the Thames, left Nordholz at 9:38 a.m. with Strasser on board. Cold winter weather – the temperature at Fuhlsbüttel was 27 degrees F. – permitted the primitive Zeppelins to lift a maximum load. *L 3* and *L 4* were carrying fuel for 30 hours, sixteen men, and eight 110-pound explosive bombs and ten or eleven 25-pound incendiaries. *L 6*, which was going further, carried 33 hours' fuel, only eleven men besides her passenger, and ten 110-pound explosive and twelve incendiary bombs.

Strasser was destined to be disappointed, for at 2:45 p.m., when she was north-east of the Dutch island of Terschelling, the crankshaft in *L 6*'s port engine broke. There were still go miles to go to the English coast, and if the ship should encounter freezing rain during the night, the weight of ice on the envelope might be more than she could carry with only two engines. "I therefore decided," wrote Strasser, "in agreement with the commander of *L 6*, but with a heavy heart, to turn back."

The other two Zeppelins found clear, frosty weather at first, mist over the sea, and variable snow and rain. At 4:15 they were off Terschelling, whence they steered by compass across the open sea.

Fritz in *L 3* had to drop a third of his ballast to reach 3,300 feet, the altitude he had been ordered to maintain over the sea. Towards 6:30 p.m. it appeared that the wind, which had been south-west, had veered to the north and freshened to 15 miles per hour, and he decided to steer for Norfolk, which was nearer than the Humber. At 8:50 p.m. *L 3* reached the coast – the first German Zeppelin over England – and from the trend of the shoreline Fritz recognized that he was over northern Norfolk. Somewhere to the south was the port of Great Yarmouth, a minor naval base which had been on Strasser's January 10 target list. Dropping parachute flares as he circled low, Fritz recognized the village of Haisbrough and the lighthouse at Winterton, and set his course for Yarmouth. At 9:20 p.m. Fritz sighted the town and dropped another parachute flare. He had been ordered to attack from 7,500 feet, but found it impossible to get his ship higher than 5,000 feet, due to a heavy load of rain. Fritz reported that a battery fired shells at the flare, whose dazzling illumination hid him from the ground. *L 3* dropped six of the 110-pound explosive bombs and seven incendiaries, more or less at random, as she crossed the town from north to south.

> The first bomb fell on the recreation ground, and did no harm. The second fell into a garden in Norfolk-square, adjoining the beach station, and according to the statement of a corporal, sent up a column of flame. The corporal went to the spot when the flame disappeared, and on striking a match, discovered a hole in the ground two feet wide and rather less in depth, from which came the fumes of sulfur and petrol.
>
> The aircraft dropped several bombs in rapid succession as it passed over the center of the town, and it is evident that in most cases they failed to hit the spots aimed at. Near St. Peter's Church the enemy evidently had a definite objective. In the Drill Hall a hundred yards from the church was stationed a company of the Na-

*L 3, the only airship in naval service in August, 1914, being walked into the DELAG shed at Fühlsbüttel bei Hamburg. Note the open gondola, and clumsy propellers on brackets attached to the hull. (Moch)*

> tional Reserve. The hall has a glass roof which, although reduced in transparency by a coating of paint, is still far from opaque, and must have afforded a good target for the raiders. Their bomb, however, landed about so yards south of the hall, at a point where St. Peter's Plain, the cross street between the hall and the church, widens into a small square. It was here that two lives were lost and the gravest damage done to property. Continuing its southerly course, the airship dropped a bomb on the South Quay near Trinity wharf, but without doing much harm. Presently it reached the gasworks, and launched a bomb at them. Again, however, the mark was missed, and the bomb fell about fifty yards south of its objective. Finally, the Zeppelin crossed the race-course, and dropped a bomb in front of the grandstand, where it made a large hole in the ground and destroyed some yards of the railings around the course. Then, having bombarded the town for about ten minutes in all, the enemy made off to sea.[2]

Fritz deserves credit for having found and accurately identified Great Yarmouth with no navigational aids except parachute flares, on an unusually foul and dark night. On his way home, freezing rain built up a coating of ice on the fabric outer cover, the drive shafts and bracing wires which Fritz estimated to weigh 4,400 pounds. Delayed by fog, *L 3* landed at Fuhslbüttel at 9:40 a.m.

*Kapitänleutnant* Magnus Count von Platen-Hallermund in *L 4* held on for the Humber. At 9:30 p.m. he crossed a coastline running from north-west to south-east, and assumed he was south-east of Grimsby at the mouth of the River Humber. Claiming he had been fired at from the ground, he dropped two incendiaries, and a third over another unidentified place. Actually, as von Platen himself realized a few days later when he read the English papers, he had made his landfall at Bacton in Norfolk, very near the spot where Fritz had come in earlier, and nearly eighty miles south-east of the Humber. From Bacton he turned north-west, passed over Cromer without seeing it, and his first two bombs fell in the tiny village of Sheringham. From here, says von Platen, "I turned off north, in order to get behind the sea front and to reach and attack the Humber industrial area from the land side. Against expectations, I did not find the north bank of the Humber on a north-west course." To orient himself, von Platen steered west, descended to 800 feet, saw some lights and dropped two incendiaries. Then, because he believed he had been fired on, he released an explosive bomb. This place, he was later forced to conclude, must have been Sandringham, the site of a royal palace. In fact, this attack was made on the small village of Snettisham. From here *L 4* wound her way south, actually crossing Sandringham (where the royal family was not in residence) and other villages, until the lights of King's Lynn appeared on the dark curve of the southern horizon. Von Platen by now was sure he was not over the Humber; from the small hamlets below he believed he was north of it! Though he could not identify the "big city", von Platen, claiming to have received "heavy artillery and infantry fire," attacked it with seven explosive and six incendiary bombs. These smashed several small houses and killed a woman and a boy.

> In almost every part of the town there was a litter of glass interspersed with occasional fragments of masonry. Except in the places where the bombs fell, there was little excitement in the town. Most of the people were already in bed, and various warnings which have been issued lately deterred them from going into the streets. Those who were abroad say that the airship circled twice around the town, at times seeming to hang almost motionless. As the bombs fell and explosions occurred, great flashes of light leaped up and the reports were terrific.[3]

After this last bombardment, von Platen headed due east, passing close to the large town of Norwich. At 12:45 a.m. he radioed his attack report: "Successfully bombed fortified places between the Tyne and Humber." *L 4* was also heavily loaded with ice on the way home. She landed at Fuhlsbüttel seven minutes after *L 3*.

2 *The Times*, January 21, 1915.

3 *The Times*, January 21, 1915.

## AIRSHIP RAID, JANUARY 19–20, 1915

| *Ship* | *Flt. No.* | *Take-off* | | *Landing* | | *Time in air* | *Distance (miles)* | *Av. speed (m.p.h.)* | *Max. alt. (feet)* | *Temp. (°F.)* | *Crew* | *Fuel (lb.) loaded/used* | *Oil (lb.) loaded/used* | *Ballast loaded (lb.)* | *Bombs (lb.)* | *Gas used (cubic feet)* |
|---|---|---|---|---|---|---|---|---|---|---|---|---|---|---|---|---|
| *L 3* | 134 | F'sbüttel | 10.45 a.m. | F'sbüttel | 9.40 a.m. | 22h. 51m. | 1,052 | 46·0 | 5,090 | 32 | 16 | 7,610/5,340 | 591/269 | 6,530 | 1,100 | 136,700 |
| *L 4* | 45 | F'sbüttel | 10.57 a.m. | F'sbüttel | 9.45 a.m. | 22h. 50m. | 935 | 40·9 | 4,580 | 28·4 | 16 | 7,840/6,020 | 574/331 | 5,740 | 1,100 | 198,000 |
| *L 6* | 31 | Nordholz | 9.38 a.m. | Nordholz | 6.30 p.m. | 8h. 52m. | | | | | 11 | 8,710/1,985 | 448/46 | 6,840 | 1,430 | 76,400 |

*Weather:* Moderate S.W. winds on Norfolk coast. Sky overcast with mist and drizzling rain.
*Bombs:* 24 (2,155 lb.).
*Casualties:* 4 killed, 16 injured.
*Monetary damage:* £7,740.

## *L 3* DECK LOG IN RAID OF JANUARY 19–20, 1915

| *Central Europ. time* | *Altitude (feet)* | *Temperature (°F) Air* | *Gas* | *Pressure height (feet)* | *Release of ballast* | *Wind Direction* | *Strength* | *Course* | *Distance (miles)* | *Speed (m.p.h.)* | *Position* | *Weather* | *Engines* |
|---|---|---|---|---|---|---|---|---|---|---|---|---|---|
| 10.49 a.m. | 50/ 1000 | 28·4 | 28·4 | 100 | | Calm | | 282° | | | Takeoff | Clear at take off, towards 12 noon gradually clouding up; from 12 noon on, misty. Between 3 and 4 p.m. variable clouds. From 4 p.m. on, clouds developing over water at 1,300 ft., upper limit of cloud layer about 6,500 ft. | All Full |
| 10.53 a.m. | 50/ 1000 | 24·8 | 29·3 | 1,000 | 6,000 water and 2 fuel tanks | N.E. by N. | 1·5 | 282° | | | | | 10.57–11.20 all half speed. |
| 2.03 p.m. | 1000/ 1300 | 32·0 | 37·4 | 1,300 | | S.W. | 3·0 | 282° | 157 | 48·5 | Borkum | | 3 p.m.–8.55 p.m. stbd. engine 850 r.p.m. |
| 3.15 p.m. | 1300/ 2600 | 32·0 | 35·6 | 2,600 | 6 bombs @ 110 = 660 | W.S.W. | 2·5 | 276° | | | 026 ϵ | | 12.20 a.m. port engine stopped for short time. |
| 4.15 p.m. | 2600/ 1650 | 32·0 | 34·7 | 2,600 | 9 incendiaries @ 22 = 198 | W. | 4·0 | | 59·6 | 27·1 | Terschelling | | |
| 9.22 p.m. | 5,100 | 32·0 | 34·0 | 5,100 | | N.W. | 6·0 | 275° As directed | 202 | 39·1 | Yarmouth | | |
| 12.45 a.m. | 3,300 | 30·2 | 32·0 | 5,100 | | S.W. | 6·0 | 12.45–2.00 N.N.W. | | | Dutch Coast in sight | | 2.45 a.m., forward engine stopped for short time, fuel line broken. |
| 8.00 a.m. | 1300/ 1000 | 26·6 | 31·1 | 5,100 | about 51,200 cu. ft. gas valved | S.W. | 8·0 | 2–3 N., 3–4 E.S.E., 4–5 E.S.E. | 594 | 56·3 | Lübeck | | |
| 9.40 a.m. | 650/ 50 | 32·0 | 32·0 | 5,100 | | S.W. by S. | 7·0 | 5–6 S.E., 6–8 S.S.W. | 39 | 23·5 | Landing | | 4.40 a.m. stbd. engine stopped, 2 cyls. cracked |

Admiral Behncke's announcement of the raid produced the wildest enthusiasm throughout Germany. The *Kölnische Zeitung* echoed general sentiments in its editorial of January 21, 1915:

> German warships have already bombarded English seaports, German airmen have dropped bombs on Dover and other places, and now the first Zeppelin has appeared in England and has extended its fiery greetings to our enemy. It has come to pass, that which the English have long feared and repeatedly have contemplated with terror. The most modern air weapon, a triumph of German inventiveness and the sole possession of the German Army, has shown itself capable of crossing the sea and carrying the war to the soil of old England! . . .
>
> An eye for an eye, a tooth for a tooth, only in this way can we treat with England. This is the best way to shorten the war, and thereby in the end the most humane. Today we congratulate Count Zeppelin, that he has lived to see this day, and offer him the thanks of the nation, for having placed it in possession of so wonderful a weapon.[4]

Such enthusiasm could hardly be dampened by the relatively truthful reports that presently began to come through Holland. At Yarmouth, suggested the *Berliner Lokalanzeiger*, "after the first bomb fell the inhabitants fled shrieking into their houses and hid in the cellars. This explains the fact that although

4 *Kölnische Zeitung*, January 21, 1915.

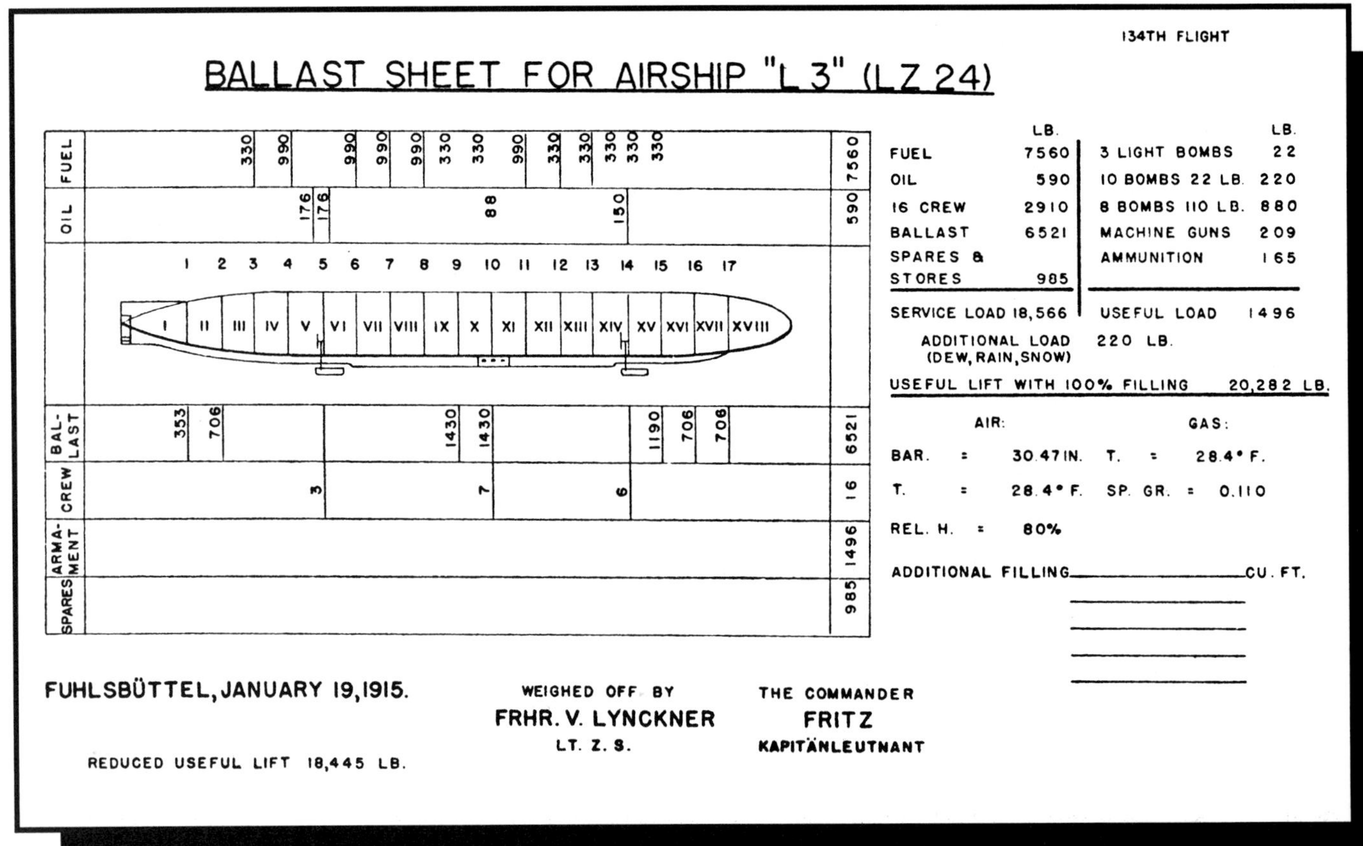

134TH FLIGHT

BALLAST SHEET FOR AIRSHIP "L 3" (LZ 24)

FUEL: 330 990 990 990 990 330 330 990 330 330 330 330 330 — 7560
OIL: 176 176 88 150 — 590
1 2 3 4 5 6 7 8 9 10 11 12 13 14 15 16 17
I II III IV V VI VII VIII IX X XI XII XIII XIV XV XVI XVII XVIII
BALLAST: 353 706 1430 1430 1190 706 706 — 6521
CREW: 3 7 6 — 16
ARMAMENT: 1496
SPARES: 985

| | LB. | | LB. |
|---|---|---|---|
| FUEL | 7560 | 3 LIGHT BOMBS | 22 |
| OIL | 590 | 10 BOMBS 22 LB. | 220 |
| 16 CREW | 2910 | 8 BOMBS 110 LB. | 880 |
| BALLAST | 6521 | MACHINE GUNS | 209 |
| SPARES & STORES | 985 | AMMUNITION | 165 |
| SERVICE LOAD 18,566 | | USEFUL LOAD | 1496 |

ADDITIONAL LOAD (DEW, RAIN, SNOW) 220 LB.

USEFUL LIFT WITH 100% FILLING 20,282 LB.

| AIR: | | GAS: | |
|---|---|---|---|
| BAR. = | 30.47 IN. | T. = | 28.4° F. |
| T. = | 28.4° F. | SP. GR. = | 0.110 |
| REL. H. = | 80% | | |

ADDITIONAL FILLING ________ CU. FT.

FUHLSBÜTTEL, JANUARY 19, 1915.

WEIGHED OFF BY FRHR. V. LYNCKNER LT. Z. S.

THE COMMANDER FRITZ KAPITÄNLEUTNANT

REDUCED USEFUL LIFT 18,445 LB.

great material damage was done, only a slight human casualty list is indicated." The German public continued to hug to itself the delusion of England's fear of the Zeppelins. But at higher levels there was doubt and discord. The day after the raid, Chancellor Theobald von Bethmann-Hollweg addressed a tart letter to von Pohl:

> According to information received, for Zeppelins to drop bombs on apparently undefended places makes a very unfavorable impression on foreign neutrals, particularly in America. Also doubt exists in responsible circles there, as military importance and success is not readily apparent. Prompt explanation to this effect seems urgently necessary.

Von Pohl was also disturbed by the report of the commander of *L 4*, which, with a covering report from Strasser, was forwarded to Imperial Headquarters. The Kaiser, after reading the documents, praised the conduct of the raid, but "once more emphasized that only the docks of London and military establishments of the lower Thames and the British coast could be taken as bombing targets." What about von Platen's admission that he had dropped two incendiaries at Sandringham before he was fired on? If it was proved that he had not strictly followed the Emperor's orders, there was a danger that raids would be forbidden even on the British coast. Von Pohl agreed with von Ingenohl, the Commander-in-Chief of the High Seas Fleet, that the Zeppelins should be permitted in self-defense to retaliate with bombs when attacked by rifle fire over "undefended places." But royal palaces – including Sandringham – were not to be bombed.

The British authorities, while not particularly alarmed by this first raid, were concerned that the Germans had avoided the few defenses already installed around London and important military targets. Though it had been realized before the war that the German airship services might try to bomb England, the British hoped that the Germans would respect the provisions of the Hague Convention, and made no attempt to defend unfortified towns. While both the War Office and the Admiralty claimed the responsibility, most of the anti-aircraft guns and crews protecting naval harbors and maga-

*Z IV was typical of the German Army's airships in service in August 1914, and is shown here at her base in Königsberg, East Prussia. Z IV made scouting flights and some bombing raids against invading Russian armies in August 1914, then was relegated to training, and later broken up in the autumn of 1916. (Author)*

zines were provided by the Navy. On September 3, 1914, since all the Army's resources were required in France, formal responsibility for the defense of England against air attacks passed to the Admiralty.

To the energetic young First Lord, who took a personal interest in combating the Zeppelin menace, attack seemed the best defense. As early as July 29, 1914, Winston Churchill had minuted, "In the present state of aeronautics, the primary duty of British aircraft is to fight enemy aircraft, and thus afford protection against aerial attack."[5] On August 27 an odd collection of ten British naval airplanes flew to Ostend, and five days later the squadron was ordered to remain in Dunkirk "to deny the use of territory within a hundred miles of Dunkirk to German Zeppelins, and to attack with airplanes all airships found replenishing there."[6] One of its planes destroyed the Army Zeppelin *Z IX* at Düsseldorf on October 8, 1914, and the Royal Na-

5 Winston S. Churchill, *The World Crisis* (New York: Scribner's, 1923-31), I, p. 220

6 Raleigh, I, p. 375.

*Z XII was a transitional ship built for DELAG and had its cabin amidship, as well as duralumin metal for girders. It initially had open gondolas, but later received a light covering as shown.*

val Air Service in Dunkirk continued to be a thorn in the side of the German air services in Belgium. Churchill was also behind the air raid on Friedrichshafen, and the seaplane attacks on the naval airship bases in the North Sea. Also, before the first Zeppelin raid had occurred, the Admiralty mounted more guns at the naval bases, and placed others so as to cover the government buildings in London.

But in this first airship raid, the attackers had avoided the fixed defenses. To cover East Anglia, the Admiralty formed the Eastern Mobile Section, equipped with old acetylene searchlights and Boer War pompoms and Maxims mounted on trucks – scarcely a menace to attacking Zeppelins, but reassuring to the civilian population. The trucks were not intended to chase Zeppelins, but were sent out to lie in wait along the routes which it seemed the airships might follow.

Meanwhile there were renewed demands in Germany that raids on London be authorized. Behncke, on January 11, had drawn up a list of dozens of targets "of direct service to the war effort," which were excluded by the Kaiser's order that only the docks could be attacked. These not only included the Admiralty, the War Office, military barracks, and Woolwich Arsenal, but also the Bank of England, the Stock Exchange, the Central Telegraph Office, the Foreign Office, the Mint, the main railroad stations, the London Water Works at Hampton, and the water, gas and electric plants at Waltham Abbey and Chelmsford. Behncke urged particular attention to the "dangerous zone" in the heart of the City of London between Aldersgate Street and Moorgate Street – the "soft goods quarter" crowded with inflammable textile warehouses. This had been the site of a disastrous conflagration in 1897 which had not failed to impress the German military authorities.

An Imperial Order of February 12 stimulated the rivalry between the Army and Navy to carry the air war to England:

> 1. His Majesty the Kaiser has expressed great hopes that the air war against England will be carried out with the greatest energy.
>
> 2. His Majesty has designated as attack targets: war material of every kind, military establishments, barracks, and also oil and petroleum tanks and the London docks. No attack is to be made on the residential areas of London, or above all on royal palaces.

Though the Kaiser's directive did not specifically permit attacks on London, the Army General Staff construed it to mean that their airships could bomb targets east of a line drawn through Charing Cross Station in the center of the capital. Admiral Bachmann, who had replaced von Pohl as Chief of the Naval Staff, learned of the General Staff's interpretation on February 18, and wrote to the Fleet Command that a similar order should be promulgated for the naval airships: "Through this limitation the avoidance of artistic monuments, particularly the royal palaces, which was ordered by H.M. the Kaiser, will be assured." Thus the way to London seemed open at last, though Admiral Behncke's favorite target, the Admiralty, was still on the wrong side of the line. The Army drew up a grandiose plan, code-named FILM FETWA, for attacking London. All possible targets in the capital east of the bombing line were listed, together with the location of known anti-aircraft guns. The Army Zeppelins were to be held ready for raids on London after February 23, and on receipt of the code word JAUSE ("afternoon tea"), their *SL 2*, *Z X*, *LZ 35*, and new *Z XII* would proceed from their permanent stations in the Rhineland to advanced bases in occupied territory.

Before the Army could act, the Navy had made its attempt on London, and had failed. Due to the shed shortage in the North Sea, *L 8*, completed on December 22, 1914, had been flown to Düsseldorf and had lain there ever since. In consequence of the Kaiser's order of February 12, her commander, *Kapitänleutnant* Helmut Beelitz, had been instructed to raid London at the first opportunity. On his first attempt, on February 26, he had to turn back because of head winds and landed at the Army base at Gontrode, near Ghent, in Belgium. On March 1, as the Army needed the Gontrode shed, Beelitz was ordered to return to Düsseldorf. He thought this authorized him to throw in a raid on his way back, and when he finally left Gontrode on the evening

*Above: First flight of navy L 9 at Friedrichshafen on March 8, 1915. Note better streamlining compared to open cars, and also multiple rudders on the stern. Below: L 9 probably at Hage. Note machine gun on top platform. (Moch)*

of March 4, he had 70 incendiary bombs on board. Beelitz set his course for Mersea Island on the coast of Essex, but at intervals came down through the overcast to check his position by sight of the ground. The first time he descended was near Bruges; the second time, about 9 p.m., was west of Ostend. Unfortunately, nobody had told Beelitz that five and a half miles west of Ostend the Belgian trenches came down to the sea. As *L 8* appeared over Nieuport and fired recognition signals from a height of less than a thousand feet, the Belgians riddled her with rifle and machine gun fire. Dumping fuel, all his bombs, and the last drop of water ballast, Beelitz forced his ship up out of range and turned back, with his gas cells pouring hydrogen. By-passing the nearby Army bases in Belgium, he tried to make it back to Düsseldorf. But at 1 a.m. near Tirlemont, 85 miles short of his goal, his luck ran out. First the forward engine had to be stopped for lack of water, then the port motor failed. De-

*Two views of the wreck of L 8 on March 5, 1915 at Tirlemont after gunfire damage. C.O. Helmut Beelitz was so ashamed of his performance, that he removed and destroyed the L 8 log book from archives at the Admiralty where he later worked. (both - Moch)*

prived of the thrust needed to sustain her in the air dynamically, *L 8* began to slide stern-first towards the ground. First the tail, then the after gondola, caught in some trees. The bow slammed against a row of poplars, tossing out the occupants of the forward car, and within a few minutes the wind had battered the hull into a formless tangle of metal and fabric. Thus, four months before completion of its costly base at Namur, ended the Navy's first and last attempt to raid England from Belgium.

Early in March the Army's ships were transferred from the Rhineland to the advance bases in Belgium and France. On March 11 they received the code signal FETWA EINS, which meant, "until further orders, bombing flights are to be made, if possible on military targets in England, particularly in London.[7] In their first attempt, on March 17, the Army airships encountered heavy fog and could not find England. *Z XII*, using her sub-cloud car,[8] dropped bombs on Calais, but damaged herself in a bad landing and was out of service for 14 days. A few days later, FETWA ZWEI was transmitted, meaning that London no longer could be attacked. The Kaiser had vetoed the General Staff's interpretation of his order as going beyond his wishes and desires. On March 20 the three remaining ships set out to raid Paris, but *Z X* was lost en route home, and on April 13, *LZ 35* was damaged by anti-aircraft guns and "written off" in a forced landing near Ypres. The old *SL 2* was then withdrawn to be rebuilt and enlarged.

The Kaiser's irresolution was a trial to both services, particularly to Admiral Bachmann. It was not enough for him that the London Docks could still be bombed. Admiral von Müller, speaking for the Kaiser, advised him that "if the Naval Staff proposes that naval air attacks should be extended to the City, a further expression of the Imperial Will must be obtained with the cooperation of the Chancellor." At the end of April, the Kaiser was pressed to give consent to raids on London, and on May 5 his decision was promulgated in writing: "London east of the longitude of the Tower permitted for air attacks; within this area military installations, barracks, oil tanks may be attacked, particularly the docks." Yet this order was held up until the end of the month.

It was now the turn of the naval airships in the North Sea. In preparation for a mine-laying expe-

7 Ernst A. Lehmann and Leonhard Adelt, *Auf Luftpatrouille und Weltfahrt* (Leipzig: Schmidt u. Günther, 1936), p. 68.

8 The sub-cloud car (Spahkorb), invented by Captain Lehmann of *Z XII* and his executive officer, Freiherr von Gemmingen, was extensively used in the Army airship service. A small streamlined nacelle hanging in clear air half a mile below the Zeppelin and connected by telephone with the control car, it enabled an observer to direct the airship hidden in the clouds above. With its steel cable and winch driven off one of the airship's engines, it weighed over half a ton. Strasser had some tests made with the sub-cloud car in *L 17* in November, 1915, but rejected it for naval service. "The car can be useful only with a solid cloud ceiling," he wrote. "This occurs rarely and cannot be predicted accurately over the target area. In all other circumstances – clear weather, variable clouds, rain and snow – it is just a useless weight. With electrical atmospheric disturbances it will pose a great danger for the airship. Therefore I do not believe that the sub-cloud car will ever play more of a role than that of a very occasional weapon of opportunity." A story that Strasser insisted himself on being lowered in the car, and that he was almost thrown out when its tail became entangled in the airship's radio antenna, cannot be confirmed from official documents. (See photo on page 190).

dition to the Swarte Bank, *L 9* on the morning of April 14 took off from the new Hage base to scout to the west beyond Terschelling. She had ten 110-pound explosive and 40 incendiary bombs on board, and was to return before dark. But after flying within 100 sea miles of Flamborough Head without sighting enemy vessels, Mathy, her commander, obtained "liberty of action" to carry out a raid at his discretion since the weather seemed unusually favorable. Mathy's choice of objective fell on the shipyards of the Tyne area, because the older Zeppelins could not reach them, and because "effective use of incendiaries in this industrial area would cause more disturbance in the already restless mass of British workers."

Mathy confidently states that, "since sunshine had accompanied the ship almost the whole day, the course could be set precisely, so that Tynemouth was hit 'on the nose' at 8:45 p.m." Actually, his fatal mistake was in making his landfall at Blyth, a coastal mining town on the River Wansbeck which Mathy mistook for the Tyne nine miles to the south. An open-air recruiting meeting was in progress, and one of the speakers, "had just been describing the barbarities which would follow a German invasion when the drone of the airship engines was heard. 'Here they come,' he exclaimed."[9] There is no record of whether the Teuton *Deus ex machina* had the desired effect on recruiting.

Mathy wrote that, "bombs were dropped on a winding course over Jarrow, Hebburn, Carville, Walker and Newcastle" – all large shipbuilding and industrial centers. Mining villages north of the Tyne were the actual targets, but damage was limited to a barn roof scorched by an incendiary bomb. Mathy did not fail to note the few signs of life below, but attributed this to the general darkening of the industrial area over which he thought he was flying. Towards 9:45 Mathy actually reached the Tyne at Wallsend, but the remaining few bombs merely injured two people and slightly damaged a house. At 10 p.m. *L 9* left the coast south of the Tyne.

Before criticizing the conduct of this raid, it should be pointed out that Mathy was "discovering a new country,"[10] as he himself stated. Yet its ineffectiveness strikingly illustrates the difficulties of bombing by dead reckoning, particularly when the original point of reference is in error.

Mathy's report encouraged Strasser to lead three airships against the Humber on the following day, April 15. Until news arrived later from England via Holland, none of the commanders could report where they had been. *Kapitänleutnant der Reserve* Alois Böcker, who had taken command of *L 5* only the day before, found a large town where he dropped most of his six 110-pound explosive and forty incendiary bombs. These set fire to a lumber yard which could still be seen burning an hour after the airship left the coast. Only 5,200 feet in the air, the men in *L 5*'s open gondolas could hear fire sirens shrieking as they crossed the town. Böcker apparently believed he was somewhere near the Humber, and only later learned that he had attacked the seaport of Lowestoft.

Von Buttlar in *L 6* reported that a lighted city came in sight, he was lit up by searchlights and fired on with machine guns and cannon, and accordingly dropped all his bombs. He had no idea where they had fallen, and turned back to the coast and headed for Fuhlsbüttel. He had bombed from 5,200 feet, but must have been a good target for rifle and gun fire from the ground, for Cell 11 amidships ran completely empty en route home and was found to have eight tears and seventeen bullet holes, while Cells 7 and 13 aft and forward were also damaged and had run half empty. *L 6*'s bombs landed in fact in the town of Maldon in Essex and in the adjacent parish of Heybridge.

Peterson in *L 7*, with Strasser as a passenger, was unable to report success. The ratings, particularly, came to regard Strasser as something of a "Jonah," for his presence on board during a raid seemed to be an almost certain guarantee of engine trouble, head winds, or zero-zero visibility. A head wind estimated at 34 m.p.h. held *L 7* in almost the same spot, and at 2:30 a.m., with only ten hours' fuel remaining, Peterson turned about for the Dutch coast. Curiously, British records show that *L 7* touched land at the eastern edge of the Wash at 2:40 a.m. and followed the coastline east until 3:35 a.m., when she passed out to sea over Great

9 *The Times*, April 16, 1915.

10 *New York World*, September 22, 1915.

Yarmouth. Because of the lighting restrictions her commander never realized he was over England.

This first series of raids taught Strasser that conventional navigational methods – dead reckoning at sea, and pilotage through identifying rivers, harbors, or cities over land – had failed completely. Only Fritz had been able to find his position in any raid, and even Mathy, who later was to show an uncanny accuracy in orienting himself by the lay of the land, had been out in his reckoning. Wind directions and velocities could not be measured precisely from an airship over the sea, particularly when she was flying above clouds, hence large drift errors often made dead reckoning positions worthless. Over England at night, particularly with impaired visibility, little detail could be distinguished in the blacked-out countryside, headlands, rivers and cities looked alike, and wishful thinking played a large part in a commander's guess as to where he was. At twilight one might occasionally take star sights from the top platform of the airship, using an ordinary marine sextant, but the celestial bodies had to be visible as well as a sharp cloud or sea horizon.

The need for radio navigational aids had been foreseen, and at this time the first German direction-finding stations were being completed at Nordholz and Borkum to serve the Naval Airship Division. At first the airship called up the shore station, which measured the direction of her signals and radioed the bearings to the Zeppelin, where they were plotted on a chart. The Germans ignored the fact that British direction-finding stations could likewise locate the airships by their radio calls, and when the system was replaced early in 1918 by a method in which the airship was silent, it was not for the sake of security but because the special airship wavelength had become too overloaded with all the traffic required by the old procedure. The whole science of radio communication was in its infancy, and such phenomena as "night effect" and "airplane effect," which later were proved to introduce gross errors in the apparent direction of the signals, were entirely unknown in 1914-18. *L 9* on April 19, 1915, was apparently the first airship to use the direction-finding stations. At this date the bearings were given, not in degrees but in compass directions, thus "north-west by north." A commander might have to be satisfied with only one bearing instead of two, and bearings which failed to intersect, or which otherwise when plotted proved obviously false, were common.

Attempting to raid England in the obsolete *L 5*, Böcker on May 12 experienced a remarkable combination of troubles, and came near to losing his ship. At 12:30 p.m. he left Nordholz with Strasser on board, carrying six 110-pound explosive and thirty incendiary bombs. During the afternoon the Zeppelin passed through rain and snow which coated the envelope with ice. Within sight of the Norfolk coast *L 5* was put on a north-east course, lest she arrive over the defenses before darkness fell. At 9 p.m. Böcker set a course for the Humber, flying at 4,800 feet. The temperature at this altitude was 23 degrees F. At 9:20 the oil line to the forward engine choked up with congealed lubricant and the motor had to be stopped. An hour later, with the Humber in sight, the port engine failed. With only one motor running and a heavy load of ice, the ship stalled and fell, and only by dropping all the bombs as ballast could *L 5* be prevented from crashing into the sea. Böcker turned back, fighting a stiff head wind. At 10:40 the port engine was set running at two-thirds speed, and at 3:10 a.m. the fore engine was running at half-speed. Progress against the head wind was slow, and at 4 a.m., after consulting with Strasser, Böcker decided to steer for Belgium as he could not reach Germany with the fuel remaining. Because of the danger to the ship, Böcker did not hesitate to cross neutral Holland above the clouds, and at 9:20 a.m., when he descended for a look at the ground, he was relieved to see soldiers in German uniforms. He then steered for Namur, where he landed at 12:25 p.m. Not until May 20 was *L 5* able to return to Nordholz.

This experience convinced Strasser that the ships of the *L 3* class, with their low speed, ceiling and endurance, were unequal to raiding England. In cold weather, with a useful lift of about 20,000 pounds, they could barely reach the English coast with half a ton of bombs. In warmer weather – the ground temperature at Nordholz when Böcker took off was 55 degrees F. – the useful load would be less. *L 5* on this day lifted only 17,165 pounds, and

Böcker had tried to skimp on water ballast, with near-fatal results.

It was only logical to withdraw the older types from raiding, for more efficient ships were now being delivered. On May 17 there arrived in Nordholz *L 10*, the first naval Zeppelin of the 1,126,000 cubic foot type, of which the Admiralty purchased ten during the course of the year. She was 536 feet 5 inches long, 61 feet 4 inches in diameter, and stood 79 feet 4 inches high, and was powered by four 210 h.p. Maybach C-X engines. *L 10*'s useful lift of 35,000 pounds was higher than that of her later sisters, which had the range to reach the west coast of England with more than two tons of bombs. These ships were found extremely satisfactory and handy until the need was felt for a higher ceiling in raids on England than the 11,000 feet of which they were capable.[11]

Meanwhile the Army airship service had replaced its losses, and was proceeding with the campaign against England with no competition from the Navy. For Admiral Philipp had written on April 28:

> The activities of the airships in the most recent operations have shown how very valuable airship scouting will be for Fleet operations with the arrival of more favorable weather. I therefore feel it is the chief requirement to station a large number of the newest ships in the bases on the German Bight . . . A steady use of the [Belgian] sheds can be considered only when the bases in the German Bight are completed with airships.

During May the Army *Z XII* was joined in Belgium by three new ships, *LZ 37*, *LZ 38*, the first of the million-cubic-foot, four-engine Zeppelins, and *LZ 39*. Beginning on April 29, *LZ 38*, under *Hauptmann* Erich Linnarz, made a series of attacks on Bury St. Edmunds, Southend and Ramsgate. In the last days of May the Kaiser authorized release of the order permitting London to be bombed east of the Tower, and on the night of May 31, *LZ 38* made the first air attack on the capital of the British Empire. She dropped 3,000 pounds of bombs on northeast London, and though only seven people were killed and £18,596 damage was done, the British Admiralty considered the consequences serious enough to impose a strict censorship of newspaper accounts of the raid. Before Linnarz had left the country they issued the following announcement:

*Major Erich Linnarz who commanded LZ 38 in the early attacks on England.*

> The press are specially reminded that no statement whatever must be published dealing with the places in the neighborhood of London reached by aircraft, or the course proposed to be taken by them, or any statement or diagram

11 Later in the year it was found necessary to improve the performance of the *L 10* type by adding two gas cells amidships. This brought the length up to 585 feet 5 inches, permitting these Zeppelins to fit into the shortest of the old standard hangars with less than five feet to spare. The volume rose to 1,264,100 cubic feet, the useful lift was increased by about 5,500 pounds, and the ceiling on raids went up by 1,500 feet or so. The first of the lengthened ships, *L 20*, was commissioned on December 22, 1915, and four more were delivered before a new and larger type was ready at the end of May, 1916.

which might indicate the ground covered by them.

The Admiralty *communiqué* is all the news which can properly be published.

These instructions are given in order to secure the public safety, and the present intimation may itself be published as explaining the absence of more detailed reports.[12]

Henceforth the Admiralty restricted the reporting of raids to the enumeration of casualties, with very meager descriptions of the effects. The region attacked was never more closely designated than "the East Coast," "home counties," etc., the purpose being to keep the Zeppelin commanders in the dark as to where they had been. Thus, the German commanders were denied information that might have served to correct their gross errors in navigation over England, and in particular, they were kept in ignorance of the unreliability of the radio bearings on which the Zeppelins increasingly depended as the war progressed. Yet the long and circumstantial accounts of the insignificant damage to small towns that had appeared in the English press up to the time of Linnarz's raid had tended to discredit the bombing campaign among neutrals, and even in Germany. Now the German claims – frequently exaggerated – were answered by almost complete silence, which appeared to confirm their success.

The Army's victory in the race for London was a blow to the Navy, which promptly found that it was possible after all to give priority to attacks on England instead of scouting for the Fleet. On June 2 the Naval Staff ordered Philipp to use the newest ships for raiding England, saving the older craft for reconnaissance and mine search in the German Bight.

The Navy entered the contest on June 4. At 1:20 p.m. Hirsch in *L 10* left Nordholz with orders "to attack the English south-east coast, target London," carrying two 220-pound, twenty 110-pound explosive and ninety incendiary bombs. At 1:44 p.m. *Kapitänleutnant* Fritz Boemack followed in *SL 3*, to scout to the west and raid the mouth of the Humber if the weather seemed favorable.

During the afternoon Hirsch flew west out of sight of the Dutch Islands, lest agents stationed there should telegraph warning of his approach. At 10:15 p.m. he thought he saw Lowestoft Lighthouse, but actually the wind had carried him south to the mouth of the Thames. In his war diary Hirsch stated that as he proceeded south from Lowestoft, rockets shot up from the Cork Lightship to alarm the coast. Finding that a rising head wind would prevent him from reaching London before dawn, he decided to attack the Harwich naval base instead. Though it was well darkened, he believed he could recognize Harwich from the course of its rivers and scattered lights. With the "air chart" of Harwich in his hand, Hirsch sent down his bombs on the arms of water where destroyer and submarine buoys were supposedly located, and on the town itself. "The City of Ipswich, off to the west, was brightly lit and offered an excellent aid to navigation."

These were in fact the lights of London. After reaching the mouth of the Thames, *L 10* had made a big circle over the Isle of Sheppey and had then flown up the darkened course of the river to Gravesend. Here the nine explosive and eleven incendiary bombs that were traced injured six people and burned out the Yacht Club, which was being used as a military hospital. If Hirsch had known how near he was to London he certainly would not have wasted his bombs on Gravesend.

Boemack in *SL 3* came inland at 12:30 a.m. just south of the prominent landmark of Flamborough Head, planning to attack Hull from the north. But he made slow progress over the ground, and as he watched the lights of a south-bound train pull away from him he recognized that a fresh head wind had sprung up. The moon was rising, and already the early midsummer dawn was beginning to grey the east as he decided to turn back. Three bombs, aimed at a "railway junction," fell in open country, and since the airship had not been fired on, Boemack carried his remaining bombs back to Nordholz.

This was one of the few appearances of a Schütte-Lanz airship over England. With a performance inferior to the Zeppelins, they could not safely be sent on raids. *SL 3*'s useful lift, 31,380 pounds when new, had diminished as her wooden framework, cover and gas cells soaked up mois-

12 *The Times*, June 1, 1915.

ture in the damp North Sea air. On this flight she could carry only 27,985 pounds, and she had been unable to ascend higher than 6,200 feet.

By coincidence rather than prearrangement, both the military and the naval airships attempted to raid England on June 6. *L 9*, the only naval craft participating, had orders to "attack London if possible, otherwise a coastal town according to choice." The shortness of the June night, and high temperatures persisting after sundown, made an attack on London hazardous, so Mathy decided to bomb Hull. Mist blanketed land and sea, and only after a painstaking two-hour search with parachute flares did Mathy recognize Bridlington and from this point of reference set a course for Hull. At 12:50 a.m. *L 9* was over the large East Coast port, illuminated the docks with a flare, and for several minutes hovered over the same area while she released ten explosive and fifty incendiary bombs. A "light battery without searchlights" was avoided by rising to 6,500 feet. Mathy reported that "eight big fires in the docks and an explosion, apparently in the gas works to the north-east, were observed."

The "light battery without searchlights" was the 4-inch gun armament of the small scout cruiser *Adventure* in drydock – Hull's sole defense. Considering the lack of protection, it is not surprising that Mathy was able to cause the greatest destruction of any raid undertaken up to that time. The official announcement of the Secretary of the Admiralty admitted fires in "a drapery establishment, a timber yard and a terrace of small houses," but this alone would hardly account for direct damage of £44,795. The incidental damage amounted to considerably more, for rioting broke out in Hull and mobs sacked many German or supposedly German shops in the city.

The Army airships were not so fortunate. Linnarz' *LZ 38* had to return with engine trouble soon after taking off, and early next morning two naval pilots from Dunkirk bombed her shed at Evere, near Brussels. The first London raider took fire and was destroyed. The other Zeppelins did not reach England. Near Ghent *LZ 37* was bombed in the air by another Dunkirk pilot, Flight Sub-Lieutenant Warneford. The Zeppelin burst into flames and fell on a convent, killing all but one of her crew.[13] *LZ 39* was likewise attacked by a plane near Ghent, but shook it off by diving into a cloud bank.

This double success by the Dunkirk squadron greatly heartened the small force that was trying to defend England against the Zeppelin menace, and had a depressing effect on the Germans. The Army later used the base at Namur briefly during attack periods, but most of their raids were made from the Rhineland sheds. In fact, the Army's airship activities against England will appear only twice more in this history. The military airship service had important commitments on the Russian Front and in the Balkans, and after the first months of the war, when prestige was all-important, England was for them a secondary theater.

The Navy was affected likewise. Envious of the Army's success against London, Philipp had reconsidered his earlier decision, and on June 6 had written to von Pohl to suggest that only six ships be retained in the North Sea, and the remainder – possibly three or four Zeppelins – should be sent to Belgium, "to take advantage of the shorter distances from the western bases to make raids, an advantage demonstrated by *LZ 38* recently." After the disasters to *LZ 37* and *LZ 38*, nothing more was heard of this proposal, and naval airships used the Belgian sheds only in emergencies.

Two Zeppelins left Nordholz on June 15 to attack the mouth of the Tyne, but the new *L 11* had to return with a broken crankshaft in the forward engine. Hirsch in *L 10* steered directly to the Northumberland coast. At 9:45 p.m. he was in sight of England, but it was still full daylight and he steered north and south offshore, waiting for darkness. At 10:25 the lookout on the upper platform reported an enemy airplane coming up from astern. Hirsch had been hovering at 1,300 feet, but he now dropped two fuel tanks and climbed to 5,900 feet. The lookout must have been deceived, for the only British aircraft up that night were two that ascended from Whitley Bay almost at the end of the raid. At 11 p.m. *L 10* was put back on a westerly course, and at 12:25 a.m. she came inland. To port appeared a large number of blast furnaces, and on approach-

---

13 For an account by the sole survivor see Alfred Mühler, "Mit *LZ 37* aus 2000 m. Brennend Abgestürzt," *Kyffhäuser*, Nr. 19, 8. Mai 1938.

**AIRSHIP RAID, JUNE 15–16, 1915**

| *Ship* | *Flt. No.* | *Take-off* | *Landing* | *Time in air* | *Dis-tance (miles)* | *Av. speed (m.p.h.)* | *Max. alt. (feet)* | *Temp. (°F.)* | *Crew* | *Fuel (lb.) loaded/used* | *Oil (lb.) loaded/used* | *Ballast loaded (lb.)* | *Bombs (lb.)* | *Gas used (cubic feet)* |
|---|---|---|---|---|---|---|---|---|---|---|---|---|---|---|
| *L 10* | 12 | Nordholz 1.30 p.m. | Nordholz 9.27 a.m. | 19h. 53m. | 969 | 48·7 | 8,850 | 37·5 | 15 | 9,770/6,840 | 871/293 | 8,050 | 5,840 | 353,000 |
| *L 11* | 6 | Nordholz 2.04 p.m. | Nordholz 12.20 a.m. | 10h. 16m. | | | | | | | | | | |

*Weather:* Moderate wind on N.E. coast. Fine, clear sky.
*Bombs:* 53 (3,536 lb.).
*Casualties:* 18 killed, 72 injured.
*Monetary damage:* £41,760.

ing, Hirsch made out a winding river and many industrial plants. Suddenly, he says, *L 10* was heavily fired on by shore batteries. Because the blast furnaces and factories offered a good target, and because he was being fired on, Hirsch decided to unload all his bombs. He reported seeing whole factories collapse, giant explosions in the blast furnaces, and many fires. Yet Hirsch did not know where he was. "The place involved in the bombing attack I would assume to be Sunderland or Blyth. I would not consider Shields likely, because from there the city of Newcastle would be visible." Hirsch started his return at 1 a.m., and observed the glow of fire until he was 80 miles out at sea.

Only after the war did the Germans learn that *L 10*'s bombs had fallen in the South Shields district. Hirsch had made his landfall at Blyth, and had come south so fast that most of the industrial plants along the Tyne were caught unawares with all their lights burning. His first bombs, on Wallsend, damaged machinery at the Marine Engineering Works to the value of £30,000. He then crossed the river to Palmer's shipyard at Jarrow, which was building the super-dreadnought *Resolution* and two monitors for the Royal Navy. Here seven explosive bombs and five incendiaries did great damage to the engine construction department. Seventeen workmen were killed, and seventy-two injured. Returning to the north bank, Hirsch damaged a chemical plant at Willington and killed a policeman, and dropped the rest of his bombs on collieries at South Shields on his way out to sea. From the point of view of military damage, this was one of the most successful raids of the war. But such ideal conditions would not recur. No searchlights were in action, and Hirsch actually was fired on only by the guardship in the Tyne, the ancient cruiser *Brilliant*.

Hirsch, in his report, commented on the first attempt to use radio bearings over England. The procedure seemed promising, but the results were inconclusive as the two direction-finding stations at Borkum and Nordholz were nearly in line with *L 10's* position over the Northumberland coast. Additional stations were later erected at List, on the island of Sylt near the Danish border, and at Bruges in Belgium, to give more accurate "fixes." Hirsch further urged very strongly that the June and July nights were too short and light to be suitable for raids. Since it never became fully dark on the night of June 15, he considered that a well-trained airplane pilot could have stayed in the air all night. Strasser heeded his advice, and henceforth attempted no raids in June and early July – with one exception, two years later, which ended in catastrophe.

This, therefore, was the last raid for nearly two months, and when the Zeppelins came again, it was in a systematic assault on London.

# CHAPTER VIII

# THE DOGGER BANK BATTLE & OTHER NAVAL ACTIONS

Less than a week after the first triumphant strafing of England, there occurred the Battle of the Dogger Bank, second only in importance to the Battle of Jutland. For the first and only time in history, an airship was present above a naval battle, providing information for its admiral from direct observation of the enemy.

On the afternoon of January 23, 1915, Admiral Hipper departed from Schillig Roads with four battle cruisers, four light cruisers and nineteen destroyers to reconnoiter the Dogger Bank. Incredibly, von Ingenohl, the Commander-in-Chief of the High Seas Fleet, had no intention of proceeding to sea in support. The British Navy's radio intelligence had learned from wireless messages passing to and fro in Wilhelmshaven, not only that Hipper was sailing, but also where he was going. Thus they were able to place Admiral Beatty with five battle cruisers at the very spot where Hipper arrived at 8:15 a.m. on the morning of the 24th. The German commander at once turned for home, with his weakest ship, the *Blücher*, at the rear of the line. The faster British vessels soon came within range and succeeded in crippling *Blücher*. At the same time German shells disabled Beatty's flagship, the *Lion*. In the resulting confusion the remnant of the German squadron ran off to Wilhelmshaven, while the other British battle cruisers halted and sank *Blücher*.

It was 3:30 in the afternoon before von Ingenohl, hastily putting to sea, joined up with the surviving three battle cruisers. Nearly two hours previously the British had disappeared to the northwest. Von Ingenohl conceivably could have chased and sunk the crippled Lion, which by this time was proceeding in tow to Rosyth, had the Naval Airship Division observed Beatty's predicament.

Hirsch, flying a routine patrol in *L 5*, first learned of the battle at 10:03 a.m. when he received Hipper's message, "am in action with a battle cruiser squadron, 109 δ 7 [145 miles west-northwest of Heligoland]. Am steering S.E. 1/4 S." Approaching from the north-east, Hirsch soon had the whole magnificent panorama at his feet – the fleeing German battle cruisers sending up great clouds of smoke in the foreground, and the low, black silhouettes of the five British "cats" slinking along on the distant horizon. Steering on the disengaged side of the German heavy ships, Hirsch soon came under fire from British light cruisers trying to work around to the north side of the retreating Germans. At 12:07 they forced *L 5* up into the low clouds and out of range. From then on, Hirsch saw little of the enemy's maneuvers, for he considered it his duty to guard Hipper's rear. Consequently, he did not observe that *Lion* was damaged. From a distance he watched *Blücher* go down in a circle of enemy small craft. The British blamed *L 5* for dropping bombs amid the destroyers rescuing survivors, but these actually came from an interloping seaplane from Borkum. At 2:29 came a query from Hipper, "How many enemy battle cruisers?" Hirsch's answer, "Four enemy battle cruisers," encouraged the Germans to claim that they had sunk H.M.S. *Tiger*.

It is clear that Hirsch lost track of *Lion* when she dropped astern of her four consorts, and did not notice her difficulties. It is clear also that no doctrine had as yet been evolved or promulgated for employing airships in fleet actions. Obviously, Hirsch would have served his superiors better if he had clung to the enemy ships, observing their movements, rather than following along in the wake of his own retreating forces.

Von Ingenohl paid for the faulty dispositions which had led to the loss of *Blücher* by being removed from his command, and was succeeded by none other than von Pohl, the erstwhile Chief of the Naval Staff. Von Pohl's policy continued to be to preserve the German capital ships from damage or loss, and while a number of operations were undertaken during his administration, he never took the High Seas Fleet far from its own waters. Due in part to the Kaiser's wishes, these fleet operations were preceded and accompanied by elaborate airship scouting, and it was actually von Pohl, who could not feel safe at sea without a ring of airships in the sky, who expanded the Naval Airship Division beyond the wildest dreams of its pre-war supporters.

On the night of February 16, Strasser received orders from the Naval Staff to send two airships to look for British patrols off the Norwegian coast, as the steamer *Rubens* was sailing by that route with supplies for German East Africa. *L 3* and *L 4* had flown to within sight of the Norwegian coast more than once in the preceding autumn, but such a flight in winter was a much riskier undertaking. Strasser assigned his most experienced commanders – Fritz of *L 3* and von Platen of *L 4*. At 4 a.m. on the morning of the 17th the two ships left Fuhlsbüttel, with orders to look for enemy ships as far north as the Skagerrak.

A clear dawn brought a light north wind, but within a few hours it veered into the east and finally settled down to blow hard from the south. For *L 3* the situation was particularly critical, as one of her three engines had failed completely shortly after the take-off. Accordingly, at 8:40 a.m. Fritz radioed that he was turning back. He was then 35 miles to the west of Lyngvig on the Danish coast, and about 225 miles from his base. He had seen nothing on the grey, wind-streaked waters below. Von Platen held on until within sight of Christiansand in Norway, on the north side of the Skagerrak. He went on west to the Lister Fjord, without seeing any British warships. Here, at 9:45, he turned back for Fuhlsbüttel – 360 miles to the south, and every mile of the way against a head wind which by now was blowing half a gale.

At 12:59 p.m. the crippled *L 3* radioed, "In trouble in 160 α 7, will attempt to stand by Danish coast. Request send destroyers to help." Yet Fritz must have known that the surface vessels could not possibly arrive before the early winter darkness. Late in the afternoon *L 3* had made good only thirty miles to the south when another engine failed. Swinging his ship inshore, Fritz at 5:45 p.m. brought her down on the Danish island of Fanö. Without shelter and without a landing crew, *L 3* hit the ground hard and buckled amidships, but none of the sixteen men on board was injured. Fritz destroyed his confidential documents, and regretfully set fire to his late command.

Nor was *L 4* spared. At 5:25 p.m. her Telefunken signals were heard: "One engine and radio sender out of order. Position 161 α 7. Request wind mea-

*Danish fishermen examining the twisted and fire-blackened wreckage of the L 3 on the beach at Fanö. A gondola lies bottom-up at the right; at the left, the nose cap and tail planes of the jack-knifed hull. (Illustrated London News)*

surements." Soon afterwards a second engine failed. At 6:30 p.m., unable to make headway with only the engine in the forward car, von Platen came in at a low altitude towards the Danish coast at Blaavands Huk. A sudden downdraft forced the nose of the ship into the foaming surf. Woodwork splintered, girders buckled. In the forward gondola it was every man for himself, as the officers and crew leaped overside and struggled shoreward through the icy water. No one had time to pull the cords of the maneuvering valves on the gas-bags – and the Zeppelin, lightened by the weight of eleven men, whirled upward and disappeared in the gathering darkness. With her went four machinists in the after gondola. Somewhere in the freezing waters of the North Sea, the stricken *L 4* went down with the luckless remnants of her crew –the Naval Airship Division's first dead in World War I. Their commander and the remaining survivors (one with a broken leg) surrendered to Danish gendarmes.

The southerly gale had been entirely unexpected. In a later tribute to Strasser, Admiral Scheer wrote:

> He was particularly gifted in estimating meteorological conditions. He had an almost prophetic instinct for the weather. How often we have had to apologize mentally to him, when in apparently favorable weather the airships did not go out; for he was always right, and shortly afterwards there was invariably a change in the weather which would have endangered the ships and made their return impossible.[1]

[1] Reinhard Scheer, *Germany's High Seas Fleet in the World War* (London: Cassell & Co., Ltd., 1920), p. 209.

*Army Zeppelin Z VI was the first to drop bombs in World War I. Setting out from its shed in Cologne, Z VI flew to Liege to bombard enemy forts. However, returning to Cologne, and going against a strong head wind, Z VI ran out of fuel and was badly damaged as it fell into the forest surrounding the city. (Grosz)*

*OPPOSITE: L 9 covering the High Seas Fleet. (Moch)*

The double catastrophe to *L 3* and *L 4* represented dearly bought experience in the development of Strasser's weather knowledge. Henceforth, until larger and more powerful airships were available, flights to the Skagerrak were rarely attempted.

Ever since von Pohl had taken command of the Fleet at the beginning of February, the German Navy had been on the defensive. Towards the middle of March the Fleet staff began making plans for a cautious excursion into the North Sea. In the words of *Kapitän zur See* von Trotha, one of the Navy's "activists," this excursion (and those that followed) were "only undertaken because it was certain that the Fleet could not find anything to attack,"[2] and only exposed its units to useless loss through mines and submarine attacks. The Naval Airship Division, however, came out of this operation with its credit higher than ever. "The undertaking was finally remarkable for the fact that . . . the airships were able for the first time to cooperate tactically with the Fleet, although they several times flew into heavy snow squalls."[3] It is clear that neither von Pohl nor anyone else understood the possibility of using airships for long-distance strategic scouting – covering the remote areas of the North Sea to find where the British Grand Fleet in fact was located. Instead, von Pohl held them in a close defensive girdle around the Fleet, almost within sight of each other and of the flagship.

On March 29, the day of the operation, it at first seemed unlikely that the airships would be able to fly at all. Three of them should have sortied early,

2 Groos, IV, p. 71 (footnote).

3 Ibid, p. 71.

*Army Zeppelin Z XIII, completed December 14, 1914. This ship introduced the duraluminum framework, closed cars, and direct-drive propellers in the Zeppelin airships. Note that the gangway was only partially enclosed. (Luftschiffbau Zeppelin)*

but *L 5*, the only Zeppelin that had taken off at 3:50 a.m., had to turn back due to a freshening east wind, and because girders had broken in a midships ring while trying to valve gas. Later in the morning the weather improved, and between 10 and 11 a.m. three airships left their bases in a light east-south-east wind. While *L 6* stayed close to the Fleet, *L 7* patrolled to the north-west, and *L 9* flew ahead of the Fleet to the region around Terschelling, where von Pohl expected that the enemy might assemble for a counterstroke. "Unfortunately," comments Otto Groos, the German official historian, "the airships limited themselves to a purely tactical reconnaissance around the Fleet."[4] Otherwise, he believes, they might have discovered that the Grand Fleet was also at sea. But the doctrinal error was von Pohl's, and besides, the British dreadnoughts had broken off their sweep prematurely while still in the far northern part of the North Sea.

May was marked by a succession of attempted air strikes by the Harwich Force, with a new feature – the Sopwith Schneider seaplane fighter, carried to attack the Zeppelins which the British now knew would be hovering about whenever they appeared in clear weather. In addition to the lumbering Short seaplane bombers, *Engadine*, *Riviera* and the newly-converted *Ben-my-Chree* each carried one or two of the little single-seaters whose prototype, in April, 1914, had captured the Schneider Trophy for Britain at a speed of 87 m.p.h. With a 100 h.p. rotary engine and a single upward-firing Lewis gun, the Schneiders took 35 minutes to climb to 10,000 feet. But if they could only fly off the water, they would be a real threat to Zeppelins whose ceiling by day in summer was considerably lower.

The Harwich Force, with the three carriers, was off the German coast on May 3 to attempt to bomb the German naval radio station at Norddeich, not far from Hage, but a choppy sea made it impossible to fly the planes off the water. Nor did the force see any Zeppelins. Only one was out that day – *L 9*, which missed the surface vessels, but had a dramatic encounter with the Harwich submarines. At 12:50 that afternoon Mathy was flying at 900 feet, twenty miles north-west of Terschelling, when he sighted four submarines on the surface, steering for stations in the Heligoland Bight, although the main operation had been called off. Though only one boat, E. 5 had a gun, Mathy thought that all four opened fire on *L 9*, which rose, as Mathy decided to attack, to 3,300 feet. Three of the submarines dived as the Zeppelin headed in their direction, but the fourth stayed on the surface until the airship was overhead. Four 110-pound bombs with delayed-action fuses burst close to the diving submarine, and Mathy, observing air bubbles and an oil slick, believed the enemy vessel had been destroyed; but she was undamaged. E. 5, on the other hand, erroneously thought she had hit the Zeppelin. Mathy went off to the south-west, hoping to deceive the submarines into believing he had departed permanently. On returning at 1:25 p.m., flying at 3,300 feet, Mathy saw a submarine ahead on the surface and ran up astern of her to attack. Suddenly he observed a second submarine rising half a mile to starboard:

> *L 9* thereupon turned with rudder hard over and attacked the boat, caught as she was rising to the surface, with five bombs with instantaneous fuses. The boat was undoubtedly hit and vanished immediately without leaving a trace. The clearly visible wake was as if cut off.

Though Mathy reported the certain destruction of this submarine, which was D. 4, she was lucky to escape with a severe shaking-up which loosened rivets in the conning-tower casing and scattered a layer of paint and chips throughout the boat. She was saved because her commander had seen *L 9* close aboard through the canted prism of his periscope and was diving to 60 feet when the bombs exploded. At 2:30 p.m. *L 9* sighted one of the submarines on the surface; she turned towards the Zeppelin, firing, but dived before *L 9* got close enough to aim her last bombs. Mathy remained cruising over the area till 3:10 without seeing any more of the Britishers.

On May 11 the Harwich Force put to sea in a last attempt to bomb Norddeich. At 5 p.m., while still in the western North Sea, the warships sighted a Zeppelin about 70 miles away low on the eastern horizon. Commodore Tyrwhitt ordered the carri-

[4] Groos, IV, p. 72.

*Kapitänleutnant Heinrich Mathy, "the greatest airship commander of the war." His death in a raid on London was a turning point in the history of the German Naval Airship Division. (Luftshiffbau Zeppelin)*

ers to launch fighters, and *Ben-my-Chree* attempted to fly a Schneider seaplane off an improvised launching track forward; but a bad engine backfire wrecked the staging. At 9 p.m. the Admiralty ordered the force to return because of an approaching north-east storm.

Yet the Harwich Force on this occasion was not reported by the Zeppelin, which, due to the great distance and visibility conditions, had been seen without herself seeing. Almost certainly it was *L 9*, which had taken off from Hage shortly before noon to raid England. At 2:30 p.m. she had again encountered four submarines 15 miles west-north-west of Texel, proceeding eastward in connection with the air attack planned for the next day. The boats opened fire, and *L 9* rose to 4,900 feet and dropped five 110-pound bombs thirty feet astern of one of them. Three of the submarines dived, but a fourth, staying on the surface, was attacked seven minutes later with five bombs which fell sixty feet astern. The four submarines were seen proceeding east-north-east submerged; at 3:15 Mathy aimed five more bombs at one as she was attempting to surface, but they fell short. His last bombs, two 220-pounders, missed in an attack on a surfaced submarine at 4:03 p.m. Mathy made no claims, and the British boats were not damaged. With no bombs left, Mathy had to give up his raid on England.

On June 2 the airships showed their value in protecting the minesweeping flotillas. At 12:35 p.m. that day *L 5*, patrolling to the west, radioed that she had sighted three light cruisers proceeding south-east. Thanks to the timely warning, the minesweepers and their attendant destroyers were able to flee to safety ahead of the British warships.

For a while *L 5* was in great danger. Böcker had suddenly come on the cruisers in low visibility, and their first shells had burst very close. Climbing to 4,000 feet, he put clouds between himself and the enemy. It was in fact the Harwich Force. The sea was smooth, the light cruiser *Arethusa* quickly swung out her Sopwith Schneider, and the little seaplane roared off the water. But the first and only occasion when one of the float plane fighters succeeded in getting into the air in German waters ended in a fiasco: at 1,800 feet the pilot turned back when he mistook the smoke made by destroyers for a recall signal, and the Zeppelin escaped.

On the evening of July 3 the Harwich Force appeared in the German Bight. The primary objective was to send up fighter seaplanes next morning to attack patrolling Zeppelins, but reconnaissance flights were to be made over the Ems River and Borkum to check reports that the Germans were collecting transports there. Three light cruisers and sixteen destroyers covered the seaplane carriers *Engadine* and *Riviera*.

Tyrwhitt's ships were promptly reported by a U-boat, but instead of sending to sea a strong force of surface vessels, von Pohl merely ordered an extensive air reconnaissance on the following morning. Between 1:30 and 2:28 a.m. six airships took off with orders to seek out the enemy seaplane car-

*Schütte-Lanz SL III at Nordholz. The wooden framework was prone to breakage under load. It was distinguishable from Zeppelins by the separate control car, and the forward engine gondola. SL III was lost May 1, 1916 when it dove into the Baltic Sea after the elevators jammed down while flying at high speed. (Moch)*

riers and attack with bombs. Since the airships might have to ascend quickly in case of meeting the British unexpectedly, they carried a relatively large amount of ballast and only a light load of fuel and bombs. A gentle north-west wind was bringing in mist from the sea as they took off, and over the Bight, low, solid clouds extended down to within 300 feet of the water, at first preventing any view of the surface. As the sun rose, the clouds shredded and dissolved, but the atmosphere was still so hazy that the observers in the sky could hardly see more than eight miles.

With the early dawn the British force hove-to near the Dutch island of Ameland, and put over the Short seaplanes to make the 60-mile flight to Borkum and the Ems. The *Engadine*'s single plane split her propeller in the wake of a destroyer, and had to be hoisted in. The *Riviera*'s four Shorts were all in the air by 3:10 a.m., but two of them presently returned with engine trouble.

The two Zeppelins from Hage were the first to sight the Harwich Force. At 3:36 a.m., *Kapitänleutnant* Odo Loewe in *L 9* saw smoke and soon afterwards the British warships, only nine miles

*Naval Zeppelin L 9 on the field at Friedrichshafen. In this ship the gangway was totally enclosed within the hull. Note covered after car in foreground, with side propellers and gun pit in the tail of the gondola. (Luftschiffbau Zeppelin)*

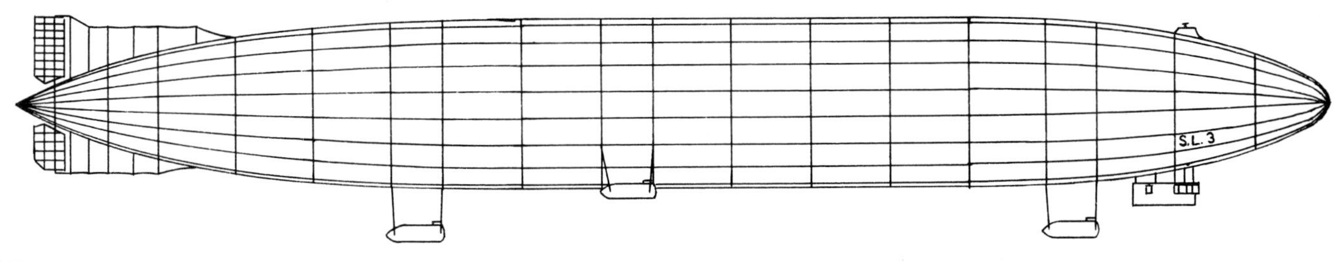


**SL 3**

| | | | |
|---|---|---|---|
| Gas capacity | 1,147,575 ft.$^3$ | Crew | 14 |
| Length | 513 ft. | Engines | 4 Maybach C-X, of 210 h.p. |
| Diameter | 64 ft. | Maximum speed | 53.7 mph |
| Useful lift | 29,500 lbs. | Ceiling | 7900 ft. |
| Gas cells | 17 | | |

north of Ameland. At 4:18 he reported, "the enemy force includes a light cruiser, twelve destroyers, and two seaplane carriers, course east. Under fire; keeping contact." Loewe could not see whether the carriers had sent off their planes or not. Repeatedly one of the light cruisers and four destroyers fired at *L 9* and tried to drive her off. The Zeppelin could not attack, as it was by now broad daylight, there was no cloud cover, and Loewe could not force her higher than 5,000 feet, which he considered within easy gun range. At 6:51 a.m. Loewe saw a seaplane land alongside one of the carriers and be hoisted aboard. This was the only one to reconnoiter Borkum and the Ems, and return; the pilot had seen no transports. The last seaplane, after crossing Juist and Borkum, became lost in the clouds, missed the British squadron, and landed near a Dutch trawler which took the pilot and observer to Holland.

Close behind *L 9* came *Kapitänleutnant* Joachim Breithaupt in *L 6*, which at 4 a.m. sighted smoke to starboard, then found numerous enemy destroyers, one cruiser and "two steamers." By dropping all ballast except two "breeches" fore and aft, two slip-tanks of fuel and one bomb, Breithaupt drove his ship up to 5,200 feet and moved to attack, but changed his mind when he came under heavy antiaircraft fire. As the ships moved off to the west, *L 6* followed, flying nose up at an angle of 15 degrees. Later, when three other airships were in company, Breithaupt felt he could head back east to re-examine a Norwegian steamer he had considered suspicious. While searching for her at an altitude of 150 feet, he encountered a light cruiser and two destroyers running west-north-west at high speed. Breithaupt's recognition signals were answered with 6-inch gunfire, and only then did he realize they were British. Shells burst close above and below the Zeppelin, but she was undamaged.

The three Nordholz ships, put on the alert by *L 9*'s contact message, were flying west in company. At 7:20 a.m. *L 10* sighted a cruiser and five destroyers which chased her to the east. At 7:23 *SL 3* saw

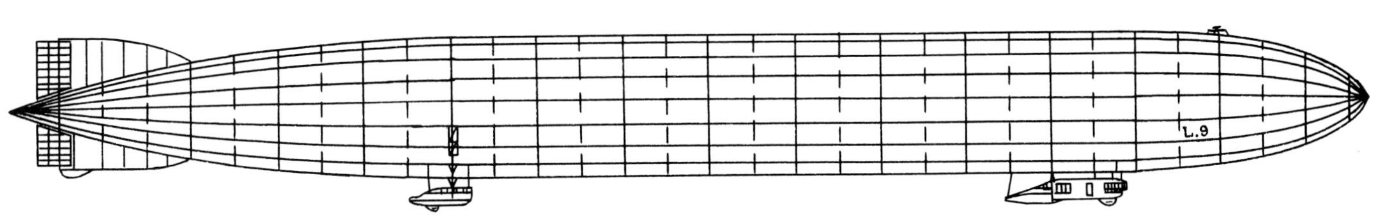


**L 9**

| | | | |
|---|---|---|---|
| Gas capacity | 879,500 ft.$^3$ | Bombs | 5300 lbs. |
| Length | 529.4 ft. | Gas cells | 15 |
| Diameter | 52.5 ft. | Crew | 14 |
| Useful lift | 24,450 lbs. | Engines | 3 Maybach C-X, of 210 h.p. |
| Fixed weights | 39,200 | Propellers | 3 Lorenzen |
| Fuel | 1110 Gal. | Maximum speed | 53 mph |
| Oil | 119 Gal. | Ceiling | 9000 ft. |
| Ballast | 1110 Gal. | Full speed endurance | 1750 miles |

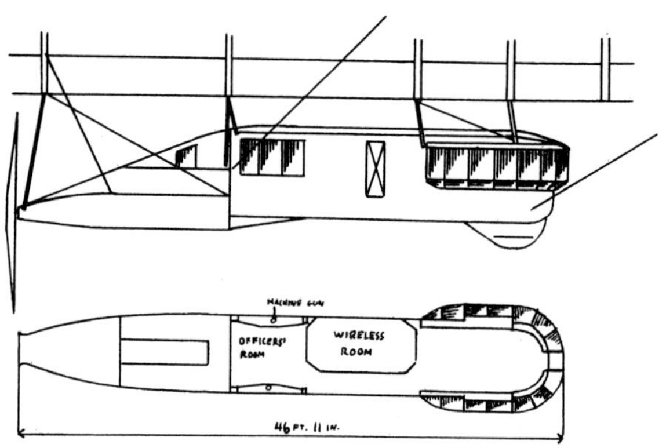


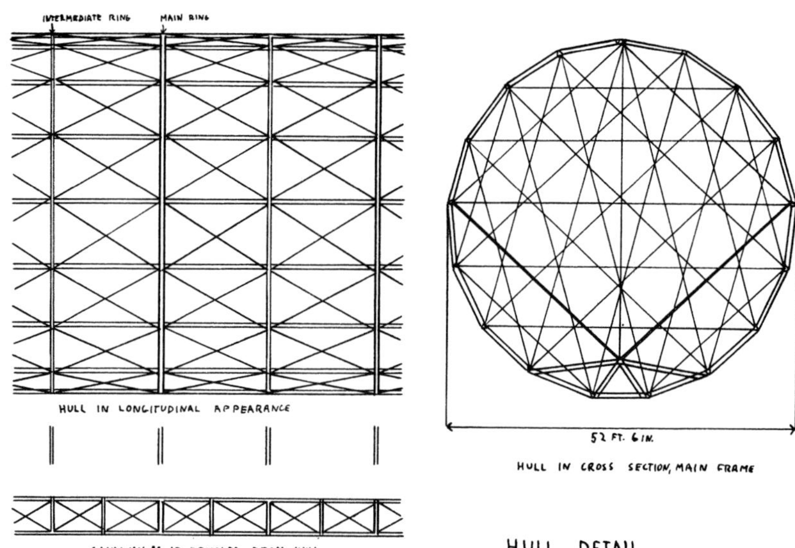


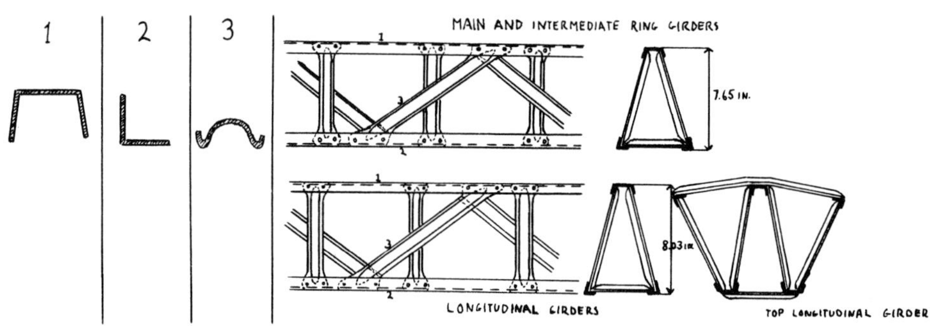


**L 9 Class Detail**

(after Dürr)

*L 9 landing at Hage. One of two ships (the other Army LZ 39) as an intermediate design between early types with open gondolas, and multiple control surfaces, and later models. (Moch)*

one seaplane carrier, one light cruiser and twelve destroyers. Two other airships were on either side, and Boemack fell in at the rear. *L 11* likewise found the force off Ameland. Proceeding further west, von Buttlar claimed to have found a covering force, including a battle cruiser of the *Indomitable* class, off Vlieland. He alleged that the battle cruiser drove him back to the east with the fire of her 12-inch guns; but no British capital ships were present.

The Zeppelins had risen to the bait, but the trap failed to go off. With four airships in sight, *Engadine* swung out her three brand-new Sopwith Schneider seaplane fighters, but the moderate sea was too rough for them, their plywood floats broke up, and two of them sank, though the pilots were rescued.

The last Zeppelin was back on the ground by 4:20 p.m. Only *L 7*, coming from Tondern in the north, had failed to sight the Harwich Force. The airship crews were jubilant, unaware that they themselves had been the prime targets of the attackers, and had narrowly escaped disaster. "Their intentions were frustrated," wrote Breithaupt, who had commanded *L 6* in the operation. "A large-scale air attack had been planned on the German Frisian coast; but no aviator had reached a German target."[5]

Throughout the day the High Seas Fleet made no move, and the airships reaped all the glory. They were criticized for errors in position, and for sending more messages than the shore stations could handle, but:

> All in all they had succeeded in causing the enemy undertaking to be broken off by their early appearance at the edge of the German Bight. All the more was it to be regretted that the great tactical advantage which the airship reconnaissance gave to the German Fleet Command was not utilized at the very latest by sending surface vessels out simultaneously with the airships.[6]

5 Joachim Breithaupt, "Hochsee-Aufklärung", *In der Luft Unbesiegt*, ed. Georg Paul Neumann (München: J.F. Lehmanns Verlag, 1923), p. 279.

6 Croos, IV, p. 206.

*L 9 at Hage. The ground troop handles line from the nose, as well as the after gondola. Ammunition dump at distant right of the photos. (both - Kameradschaft)*

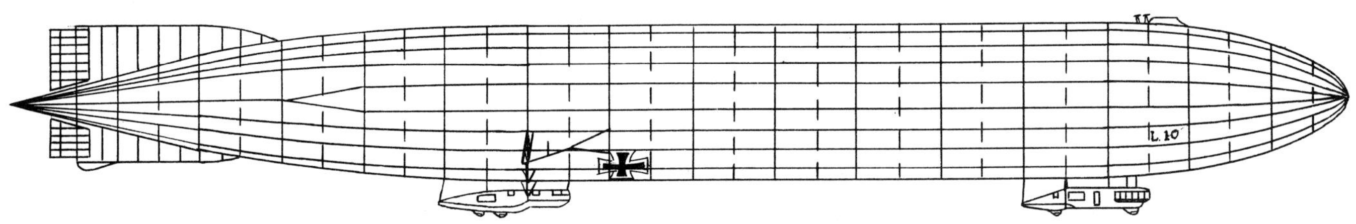


**L 10**

| | | | |
|---|---|---|---|
| Gas capacity | 1,126,700 ft.$^3$ | Engines | 4 Maybach C-X, of 210 h.p. |
| Length | 536.4 ft. | Propellers | 4 Lorenzen |
| Diameter | 61.35 ft. | Maximum speed | 57.7 mph |
| Useful lift | 35,050 lbs. | Ceiling | 10,500 ft. |
| Gas cells | 16 | Full speed endurance | 2700 miles |
| Crew | 18 | | |

On the British side, the fiasco with the seaplane fighters caused profound disillusionment, and had far-reaching consequences:

> An exceptional opportunity had been lost. Much had been risked to give the seaplanes their chance. Their repeated failures created a distrust of the Naval Air Service among many responsible naval commanders. Not until January of 1916 were any further combined operations against the German coast attempted.[7]

[7] Jones, II, p. 361.

On August 6 the German auxiliary cruiser *Meteor* sailed to lay mines off the British Grand Fleet base at Cromarty. Von Pohl did not dare to risk major surface vessels to escort her out of the German Bight, and trusted to the airships, destroyers and submarines to get her safely to sea. At 7 a.m. on August 6, *SL 3* left Nordholz to scout ahead of the minelayer. During the morning, shore weather stations reported south to south-west winds, heralding a storm. At 1:40 p.m. the Schütte-Lanz ship turned back from a position off Blaavands Huk. On the way home, *SL 3* flew through steady rain, and soaked up such a load of water that her commander

*Naval Airship L 10 at Friederichshafen. Note new rear gondola with propeller at stern of car, and gun platform over forward car. The L 10 was the first naval airship to bear the Maltese Cross aircraft recognition mark, painted here just ahead of the side propeller brackets. (Luftschiffbau Zeppelin)*

had to drop almost all ballast. The landing at Nordholz was delayed till 9 p.m. by a thunder-squall, and with the gas cooled and little ballast remaining, *SL 3* fell hard and sustained damage that kept her out of service until August 24.

*Meteor* laid her mines, and at daylight of August 8 sank the British armed boarding steamer *Ramsey*. Her commander then steered for Wilhelmshaven, and by the morning of August 9 was on the outer edge of the German Bight. Although he could not know it, Commodore Tyrwhitt with five light cruisers of the Harwich Force, and two light cruiser squadrons of the Grand Fleet, were already coming up from the south and west to cut him off from the Jade. Von Pohl might have expected that the British would pursue the minelayer, but instead of taking the Fleet to sea, he merely ordered "strong air reconnaissance." At 4:30 a.m. on the 9th, *L 7* took off from Tondern, followed at 5 a.m. by *PL 25*, to look for *Meteor* off Horns Reef. At 9 a.m. a German seaplane reported Tyrwhitt's cruisers off Terschelling. Von Pohl now ordered Strasser and his Leader of Submarines to send "all available units" against this squadron – a futile gesture which he backed up only by ordering "heightened preparedness" in the High Seas Fleet.

Meanwhile, at 10 a.m. *Kapitänleutnant der Reserve* Max Dietrich of *L 7* had found a "black painted merchant ship, one funnel, two masts, no name visible, no flag or distinguishing marks, does not answer recognition signals." It was *Meteor*, but Dietrich failed to recognize her and searched on towards the south. At 10:35, *L 7* received the seaplane's message, and at 11 a.m. found Tyrwhitt's vessels (which she identified as "four armored cruisers and one destroyer") 75 miles north-west of Heligoland. Dietrich did what he could to save the cornered minelayer by radioing the position, course and speed of the British vessels, and even tried to decoy them away to the north-east, but they ignored the Zeppelin and held to their course.

At 11:30 a.m., when Dietrich's first message was decoded aboard *PL 25*, her commander, the Army officer *Hauptmann* Kuno Manger, steered for the indicated position. At 1 p.m. he sighted *L 7* following the enemy to the north. At the same time the airship commanders saw Tyrwhitt's five cruisers scatter into line abreast at ten-mile intervals, and in this formation they swept up the Jutland coast. They were making 29 knots, and *PL 25* could not make enough speed against a 22-mile-per-hour headwind to keep them in sight. At 2:20 p.m. *L 7* saw the British 1st Light Cruiser Squadron approaching to close the trap from the west. *L 7* likewise could not keep pace with the British warships, but Dietrich knew that nothing more could be done to save the slow minelayer. At 2 p.m. *Meteor*'s commander saw the cruisers racing up from the south and west, set explosive charges and took to the boats. The Royal Navy had scored another victory on the High Seas Fleet's doorstep, and even though the German loss was small, the moral effect still further paralyzed their Fleet Command. As the British official naval history comments:

*The "Rubber Cow", the Parseval non-rigid airship PL 25 shown here at Nordholz, though it was usually stationed at Tondern. Note the cumbersome single gondola hung on wires, and the top machine-gun platform above. It was built for the German army but was later turned over to the Navy. PL 25 was dismantled in August 1917. (Luftschiffbau Zeppelin)*

*The giant Nordholz base in 1918. In the foreground are the 853 foot hangars "Nordstern" and "Nogat." To the right are the small single hangars "Nora" and "Norbert." At left rear is the double revolving shed "Nobel." In the distance is the "Normann" shed, which was able to house eight large and two small Zeppelins. (Moch)*

> Thanks to the completeness of the enveloping plan, all that the aircraft had been able to do in their first effort to intervene in a regular naval operation was no more than to spare us the trouble of sending to the bottom the ship they had come out to save. The weakness of operating with minor naval types unsupported by surface ships of force could scarcely require more cogent illustration.[8]

But Admiral von Pohl, it must be remembered, felt bound by the order of his Emperor to withhold from combat the battleships and battle cruisers which could have intervened decisively to save Meteor. The "minor naval types" thus had achieved an artificial prominence. Not only was von Pohl tempted to believe that the Zeppelin could replace surface combat ships in the North Sea; with his ever-present fear of being brought to battle, he turned to the airships to protect the High Seas Fleet against surprise. On June 4, 1915, he had written to the Navy Minister a letter which resulted in elevating the Naval Airship Division to a permanent arm of the Fleet, and which largely determined the Navy's policy on lighter-than-air craft for the rest of the war. He wrote:

> The experiences of the last few months have confirmed the great value of airships for naval warfare . . . The most important types of employment for them are as follows:
>
> (1) With the shortage of suitable fast cruisers, extensive airship reconnaissance with operations of the High Seas Fleet is a prerequisite.
>
> (2) Combating enemy submarines by means of airships promises great success, judging by recent experiences.
>
> (3) The Minesweeping Division will require far-ranging air reconnaissance for their work in

8 Sir Tulian S. Corbett, *History of the Great War – Naval Operations* (London: Longmans, Green & Co., 1920-31), III, p. 124.

the mine-infested waters of the German Bight, in order to protect the sweepers against enemy surprise attacks.

(4) It has been demonstrated that with favorable light conditions, airships are able to locate certain minefields.

(5) Operation of the airships against enemy territory from the North Sea airship bases will have greatly improved prospects of success and significance if the airships can be kept continuously informed of their exact position with the aid of the directional radio equipment now under construction.

(6) Cooperation between airships and submarines seems promising but requires practical testing, which is planned for the future . . . Considering the extraordinarily great significance of the airships for naval warfare, I consider it urgently necessary to give priority to building more airship sheds by every possible means.

To protect the High Seas Fleet in its advances at least six sectors must be patrolled by airships, in order to cover the surrounding sea area completely. For lengthy operations a second group of airships must be available, for experience has shown that after lengthy cruises (20 hours or more) the airships are not able to fly for at least 24 hours. This results in an overall requirement for 12 operational airships. Considering possible losses and the frequently necessary lengthy repair periods, an estimated total of 18 airships must be available in order to be able to count on 12 operational airships at any one time.

*The Staaken airship construction facility, operated by Luftschiffbau Zeppelin. Altogether eleven large Zeppelins were built here. However, Staaken builders were unable to build lighter ships, as senior airship captains demanded a Friederichshafen product, with its better altitude performance. (Moch)*

Up to this time, with airships being built as fast as possible by the Zeppelin and Schütte-Lanz firms, no establishment had been defined. Now the Admiralty and Naval Staff approved the 18-ship figure as well as plans for increasing the number of sheds.

Though in June, 1915, there were eighteen berths in the North Sea and Baltic sheds built or building, they would not suffice for eighteen airships, as it was Strasser's well justified policy to hold one or two berths empty at larger bases to receive ships that could not land at their home fields.[9] Accordingly, on June 17 representatives of the German Admiralty, the Naval Staff and the Fleet Command met and decided to erect six giant double hangars, all of the same inner dimensions – 790 feet long, 197 feet wide and 110 feet high. One would be added at Nordholz, and one in the Baltic.[10] The remaining four would form an entirely new base to serve the High Seas Fleet, surpassing Nordholz in size. They would be sited inland because of the danger of air attack from the sea, because of the prevalence of fog along the coast, and because the longer-range ships now in service could easily reach the sea or England from such a location. Dr. Eckener and Admiralty officials spent eight days looking over sites in the vicinity of Bremen, and finally settled on an open heath near the rustic village of Ahlhorn, nearly sixty miles from the sea. The German Admiralty approved their recommendation on July 21, 1915, and the four Ahlhorn sheds were officially completed on September 11, 1916.

In ordering such large hangars, the Admiralty was looking ahead to the delivery of Zeppelins of a new and greatly enlarged type. Even before completion of the first million-cubic-foot Zeppelin on April 3, 1915, the Admiralty had requested the airship firms to prepare designs for even larger craft. Shortly afterwards the Admiralty contracted with the Zeppelin Company for a "big 6-engine ship" with the unprecedented volume of nearly two million cubic feet.

Von Pohl was not alone in his advocacy of the rigid airship. The airplane was still a frail toy, not to be taken seriously by tradition-minded military men, and the Zeppelin reigned supreme in the minds of Army and Navy officers and civilians alike. Not only in Berlin and Wilhelmshaven, but also at Imperial Headquarters in France, and in Poland, where Hindenburg directed the war on the Eastern Front, there was a clamor for more and more airships. The Army's Chief of Field Aviation, Colonel Thomsen, was determined that new building works should be erected in the heart of the country, lest the existing Friedrichshafen and Mannheim-Rheinau plants, on Germany's borders, should be destroyed by air attack. In the summer of 1915 the Zeppelin Company began constructing a whole new factory at Staaken, near Berlin, with two large single sheds. The Schütte-Lanz firm likewise erected a new building plant with a single hangar at Zeesen, near Berlin. Thomsen's foresight eventually benefited the Navy even more than the Army.

Thus, on the first anniversary of the outbreak of war, the airship arms of both services looked forward confidently to the future. Encouraged by their exaggerated estimate of the damage done in the early raids, and foreseeing no obstacles to their victorious progress in the skies, they were ready for the first serious attempt to destroy the city of London.

---

9 As far as possible, the revolving hangar at Nordholz, which could always be turned parallel to the wind, was kept free for such emergencies.

10 On August 28, 1915, the Admiralty decided to build it at Seerappen Rear Königsberg.

# CHAPTER IX

# SQUADRON RAIDS ON LONDON

The City, the financial heart of the British Empire, the site of the Stock Exchange and the Bank of England, the ancient square mile packed with the counting houses and warehouses of great mercantile firms, was still forbidden territory. The Kaiser's order of May 5, 1915, still restricted air attacks to London east of the Tower. Admiral Bachmann, the Chief of the Naval Staff, could not accept this limitation. The destruction of the City would deal a crippling blow to the British economic offensive against Germany. And farther to the west was the Admiralty in Whitehall. A French air raid on Karlsruhe on June 15 gave Bachmann the excuse to ask that the Navy be freed to wage unrestricted air war against the heart of the Allied coalition. Von Falkenhayn, the Chief of the General Staff, agreed in principle, but recommended waiting until the two services could muster a large squadron of airships, accompanied by bombing and fighter planes – all under Army direction. But the Navy, with four ships of the new *L 10* class, was ready to start squadron raids against the City. The Army, by contrast, had transferred the only ships in the west – the low-performance *Z XII* and *LZ 39* – to the Russian Front, and would have no replacements for them until mid-July.

His hand strengthened by von Falkenhayn's endorsement, Bachmann on July 9 approached the Chancellor and obtained his support on condition that the City be attacked only on weekends, and that historical monuments, such as St. Paul's and the Tower, be spared. Bachmann knew that the former restriction was impractical. Invoking the right of the *Immediatvortrag,* on July 20 he petitioned the Emperor:

> But really effective attacks are possible only if the City, the heart of London commercial life, is bombed. The Chancellor has agreed to raids on the City, but requests on humanitarian grounds that

*Naval airship L 12 dropping her trail-ropes for a landing at Friedrichshafen. (Luftschiffbau Zeppelin)*

these be made only on week-ends, from Saturday to Monday morning, so that buildings in the City would be unoccupied. This limitation is unacceptable because of the dependence of the airships on the weather. Every night the City empties of people regardless of the weather, also the enemy shows no regard for humanitarian behavior in attacks on Karlsruhe and elsewhere. Therefore I request Your Majesty to withdraw this prohibition and to authorize the Commander-in-Chief of the Fleet and the Chief of the Flanders Naval Forces to designate the City of London as a target; monuments like St. Paul's Cathedral and the Tower will be spared as far as possible.

The Kaiser gave in completely, and henceforth permitted the air services to attack London without

restriction, except that royal palaces and historic edifices were not to be bombed.

The moon was new on August 10, and the first squadron raid on London was set for the 9th. Instead, the airships on that day were ordered out against the British cruisers hunting *Meteor*. In the afternoon Strasser, embarked in *L 10*, was permitted to proceed with the raid. At 2:19 p.m. he radioed, "*L 9* to *L 13* assemble in 107 ε 7," ten miles north of Borkum, and by 2:50 the five Zeppelins were proceeding west in company. *L 9*, detached at 3:50 p.m. to attack the mouth of the Humber, was the only airship to get anywhere near her objective. After delaying off the coast to wait for darkness, her commander, Loewe, came inland at 11:15 p.m. and headed more or less for Hull. Though the night was clear, a ground mist made it impossible for Loewe to tell whether he was over land or water; while the blackout made it difficult to orient himself by the lights of towns. Also a broken rud-

AIRSHIP RAID, AUGUST 9–10, 1915

| *Ship* | *Flt. No.* | *Take-off* | *Landing* | *Time in air* | *Distance (miles)* | *Av. speed (m.p.h.)* | *Max. alt. (feet)* | *Temp. (°F.)* | *Crew* | *Fuel(lb.) loaded/used* | *Oil (lb.) loaded/used* | *Ballast loaded (lb.)* | *Bombs (lb.)* | *Gas used (cubic feet)* |
|---|---|---|---|---|---|---|---|---|---|---|---|---|---|---|
| *L 9* | 48 | Hage 11.50 a.m. | Hage 7.35 a.m. | 19h. 45m. | 910 | 47·0 | 7,200 | 41·0 | 17 | 7,100/5,500 | 716/342 | 3,750 | 2,515 | 176,000 |
| *L 10* | 22 | Nordholz 12.52 p.m. | Nordholz 8.38 a.m. | 19h. 46m. | 877 | 44·4 | 9,200 | 35·6 | 17 | 10,550/5,030 | 951/335 | 6,220 | 4,070 | 300,000 |
| *L 11* | 18 | Nordholz 12.28 p.m. | Nordholz 5.14 a.m. | 16h. 46m. | 761 | 45·3 | 8,200 | 39·2 | 17 | 9,830/4,890 | 989/282 | 8,380 | 4,790 | 353,000 |
| *L 12* | 14 | Hage 12.05 p.m. | | | | | 10,500 | | | 9,480/ | | 8,830 | 4,520 | |
| *L 13* | 5 | Hage 12.30 p.m. | Hage 4.45 a.m. | 16h. 15m. | | | | | | | | | | |

*Weather:* Wind light and variable, mainly from south. Cloudy and dull with some rain and mist.
*Bombs:* 79 (5,580 lb.).
*Casualties:* 17 killed, 21 injured.
*Monetary damage:* £11,992.

der cable caused the Zeppelin to make two complete circles before the defect was remedied. Thus it is not surprising that Loewe thought he was over Hull when he actually found Goole, twenty miles to the west, by the reflection of its shaded lights on the wet pavement beneath. Here *L 9*'s bombs killed sixteen people, destroyed ten dwellings and damaged some warehouses. Loewe believed he had caused very severe damage in the Hull docks, and further reported he had been heavily fired at while making for the coast after the attack. "The ship escaped heavy damage only by luck," Loewe wrote, and suggested that a greater altitude would be needed to attack defended places.

The newer ships to the south ran into deep, low-hanging thunder squalls and had to drop much of their ballast, and even some fuel, to compensate for heavy loads of rain. Towards 8:30 p.m. the confidential signal books were weighted and dropped in deep water. At the same time Strasser issued his general orders to all ships by searchlight:

> Remain together until 9:45, then each ship shall independently attack the London Docks, then the City. Attack course west, then turn north and run off to the north-east.

None of the Zeppelins came within sight of London that night. Mathy in *L 13* turned back near the coast with engine trouble; on the way home he had to dump 120 incendiary bombs in the sea to lighten the ship. *L 10*, groping through thick rain-clouds, glimpsed the Thames by the light of a parachute flare, and, convinced that he was over eastern London, her acting commander, *Oberleutnant zur See der Reserve* Friedrich Wenke, sent down his bombs and thought he saw several burst among shipping. Actually he was far down near the mouth of the river. Twelve of his bombs fell in a line across the landing-ground of the Eastchurch naval air station on the island of Sheppey. Von Buttlar in *L 11*, wishfully concluding he was over Harwich, dumped all his bombs when he came under fire from some naval 12-pounders at Lowestoft. Most of them fell in the sea, where the British mistook them for water flares.

*L 12* made her landfall at Westgate, south of the Thames, but Peterson, her commander, thought he was far to the north on the Norfolk coast. "On a southerly course," he reported, "passed Yarmouth and Lowestoft, and finally Orfordness Lighthouse." These places he confused with Margate, Ramsgate, Deal and other towns along the Kentish coast. Finally he identified as Harwich the cluster of lights marking Dover Harbor. Deciding that he was too late to reach London, Peterson determined to attack here, and forced his ship up from 6,500 to 9,500 feet. He thought that he saw his bombs burst in Harwich itself, and in "the fortifications of Felixstowe." Of his cargo of two 220-pound and twenty 110-pound explosive bombs, and seventy incendiaries, only three incendiaries fell on land, injuring three men and doing negligible damage. The local 3-inch gun fired ten rounds, the second or third of which seemed to hit the Zeppelin aft, for she was seen to falter as she disappeared from view behind a "smoke screen," actually the spray of falling water ballast.

*Army LZ 38 was the first London raider on May 31/June 1, 1915, and was larger than any Zeppelin in service at that time.*

*All three photos show German army LZ 37 at Cologne. On June 7, 1915 in Brussels LZ 37 was bombed while on the ground and destroyed. (three - Elias-Müher)*

The Dover gunners had aimed well. As *L 12* made off to the east, ominous reports of damage aft came to Peterson in the control car:

> An examination showed several large holes in Cells 3 and 4, so that Cell 4 was completely empty thirty minutes later, while Cell 3, in spite of efforts to patch it, slowly ran out three-fourths empty. The ship began to sink slowly but steadily, in spite of being driven at an increasingly steep angle. Towards 2:40 all available spare parts, machine guns, provisions, etc., were thrown overboard. It was clear that the ship could stay in the air only a short time.

Peterson saw it was hopeless to try to gain his North Sea base, and steered south-east for occupied Belgium. Even this refuge was beyond his reach. Shortly after three o'clock, at an altitude of 2,000 feet, he dropped his last ballast, including the radio cabinet and its contents, but still the ship fell. At 3:40 a.m. she settled stern-first on the foggy waters of the Channel. One of the engineers in the after car, Machinist's Mate Richard Fankhänel, was thrown from the gondola roof into the water, and for half an hour, as the wreck drifted before a light north wind, he swam after her before scrambling aboard.

At first, *L 12* had floated lightly on the bottom of the after gondola, but gradually this had sunk until it was entirely submerged. Several men tried to get aft to cut away the car, for Peterson thought he might be able to proceed with the forward engine alone. But leaking hydrogen and petrol and oil fumes overpowered them, and in a short time the waves broke up the hull structure enclosing the empty gas cells. Peterson could only hope for rescue with daylight, and when this happened, his executive officer was to empty a can of petrol in the keel and set the ship on fire.

The first vessel sighted was a German torpedoboat, whose commander informed Peterson that he was not far from Zeebrügge. At Peterson's request he passed a hawser that was made fast to the mooring-point under the nose, and slowly the Zeppelin was towed in the direction of Ostend. Towards noon she was brought alongside the quay. As there was no means of repairing the hull, Peterson decided to have *L 12* dismantled.

The Allied forces in Belgium were not long in learning that one of the raiders was down at sea, and even before the airship reached Ostend, three British naval air pilots from Dunkirk attempted to destroy her. Their bombs missed, and one of them was shot down and killed. Later six planes attacked *L 12* at Ostend, but they met heavy fire over the target and scored no hits. With the help of Army airship personnel from Gontrode, Peterson detached the two gondolas and lifted them out of the water. But as the intact forepart of the hull was being swung on to the pier by a crane, it suddenly exploded and burned. The after section, which was still in the water, received no harm and its cover, framework and gas cells were salvaged.

Although the Zeppelins had not reached London, and one of them had come to grief, Strasser was not discouraged. On the afternoon of August 12, four airships took off, but only two reached England. Finding a head wind of 40 to 45 m.p.h. at his altitude of two miles in the air, Wenke in *L 10* steered for Harwich. With uncanny accuracy, he identified the towns below – Woodbridge, Ipswich, and ultimately the east coast naval base. At 12:15 a.m. the Zeppelin appeared over Harwich, and dropped the rest of her cargo. Wenke claimed that the electric power plant and railroad station, marked on the air map of Harwich, loomed up conspicuously and were directly hit, but British records state that his bombs only wrecked two houses.

Von Buttlar in *L 11* appeared briefly over the North Foreland, but went home without dropping any bombs. Forty minutes before midnight, when *L 11* was forty miles west of The Helder, he had to alter course to northeast by north to avoid a series of heavy thunderstorms. One was over the Rotterdam and Amsterdam area, the other covered the Dutch islands from Texel to Terschelling; and there were continuous flashes of vivid lightning. Presently von Buttlar realized that the storms were moving rapidly out to sea. An attempt to race around them to the north failed, and shortly before 2 a.m., *L 11* was overtaken on the Dogger Bank. Though he intended to fly through them at 4,600 feet – 1,300 feet below "pressure height" – the Zep-

*L 10 was the first of the "p" ships which carried the war to the British and Russian homelands until the "r" 2,000,00 cubic feet ships were developed. L 10 was struck by lightning as she approached Nordholz on September 3, 1915 and was destroyed with all nineteen crewmen killed. Revolving shed in background. (Moch)*

pelin was tossed violently up and down in the black, boiling clouds, sometimes to within a thousand feet of the water. Rain lashed down in torrents, blinding flashes of lightning surrounded the ship, leaping from cloud to cloud and from cloud to sea, and everything was heavily charged with electricity. The executive officer, who had climbed to the top platform to conn the ship between the squalls, reported that bluish-violet tongues of St. Elmo's Fire a foot long burned on the machine-gun sights, and the lookouts' heads were haloed in flame attracted by the wire grommets in their caps. Down in the control car, von Buttlar observed the same cold bluish flame spraying from his fingers when he held them out of the window. Acutely aware that he was nearly a mile up in the air in a vessel supported by a million cubic feet of inflammable hydrogen, the young commander was worried. But he was safe as long as he did not rise over "pressure height" – the altitude at which diminishing atmospheric pressure allowed the gas to expand to the point where it completely filled the cells. Had *L 11* done so, the hydrogen pouring from the automatic valves would have instantly taken fire from the electrical discharges, and the ship would have burned in the air.

*Above: Naval airship L 11 landing at Löwenthal. (Luftschiffbau Zeppelin)*

*OPPOSITE: L 11 taken from another airship, circa 1915. Note the drag-producing propeller bracket, and three radiators for the three engines on the gondola at left. (Moch)*

Four more Zeppelins took off on August 17, ordered "according to possibilities and weather situation [to] attack City of London with bombs." Two of them had mechanical trouble and did not reach England. For the first time, but not the last, von Buttlar turned in a dramatic report of having bombed London, when he had not been within 40 miles of the capital. Twenty-one of *L 11*'s bombs descended on the village of Ashford in Kent, and she then went north to Faversham. Nearby was a gun-powder factory to which the Admiralty had allotted an anti-aircraft gun and a searchlight. But the gunners were unable to fire, as the manager had cut off the electricity for the searchlight for fear it would betray the factory's position! Consequently von Buttlar met no opposition as he dropped forty-one bombs in nearby fields.

Wenke in *L 10* turned in a much more competent performance, and was the first naval officer to bomb London. Once again, with confident accuracy, he made his landfall where he expected to, at Orfordness. Despite a ground mist, he was able to check his course and position by the lights of towns and villages below. At 10:35 p.m. a glow like an aurora loomed on the south-west horizon – the lights of London. An hour later *L 10* began her attack on the capital:

> Since it had turned into a clear, starry night, I steered for the west end of the city, in order to have the wind abaft the beam. At 11:30 p.m. turned on to an easterly course and crossed the center of the city at 3,100 meters (10,200 feet), a little north of the Thames. Bomb dropping was ordered to begin between Blackfriars and London Bridges. Collapse of buildings and big fires could be observed.

In his "Remarks," Wenke added that "the London searchlights cannot hold a ship at 3,100 meters in clear weather even if they have found her" – encouraging news for Strasser, who had not yet been able to reconnoiter London in person.

Although Wenke did indeed reach London, he did not drop his bombs in the heart of the capital. The northeast suburbs of Leyton and Wanstead Flats suffered, with ten dead, forty-eight injured, the Leyton railroad station partly wrecked, a trolley car garage damaged and many houses destroyed. Why Wenke believed he was over the center of London when he was only on its outskirts is a minor mystery that has puzzled several chroniclers of the raids.[1]

Once again commanded by Hirsch, *L 10* was one of the four airships out on reconnaissance on September 3. In the afternoon she radioed that she would land at Nordholz at 3:30, and the ground crew was ordered to stand by. "In the direction of Cuxhaven," Strasser later reported, "was a circumscribed local thunderstorm, and considerable thunder and lightning were apparent. Suddenly, at about 3:20 p.m., personnel on the airship base at Nordholz saw, in the direction of Cuxhaven whence the ship was expected, a large flash of flame like that of an explosion, which left a large cloud of smoke." At once the telephone began ringing with the dread tidings that a Zeppelin had fallen afire near Neuwerk Island. Observers in the coastal batteries near Cuxhaven had a much closer view of the tragedy. A sentry who had been watching *L 10* fighting her way shoreward with the upper portion of the hull hidden in cloud saw a flash of lightning, then a red flame burst out of the hull between the nose and the forward gondola. An officer saw the fire climbing up the envelope, then the bows of the airship canted downward to an angle of 80 degrees and she slowly fell, smothered in flame, to the tide flats where she continued to burn with heavy clouds of smoke. The commander of a picket boat offshore saw two men leap from the blazing airship. He could not reach the wreckage, which lay in six feet of water, until 4:15. Forcing his boat through a tangle of girders, he opened the door of the control car and pulled out a leather jacket with the badges of a warrant quartermaster. Its owner and the rest of the 19 aboard had perished – the first naval airship crew to die in the war. Next day some wreckage and 11 bodies were recovered, also *L 10*'s recording barograph which showed that just

---

1 On p. 51 of *The German Air Raids on Great Britain, 1914-1918*, Captain Joseph Morris claims that Wenke confused a model yacht pond at Wanstead Flats with the River Thames. On pp. 53-56 of *War on Great Cities*, Albert H. Ross suggests that Wenke mistook a chain of large reservoirs along the River Lea for the Thames, and the solid ground between them for the bridges mentioned in his report.

*Kapitänleutnant Klaus Hirsch (left) and Oberleutnant zur See Freiherr Treusch von Buttlar Brandenfels in the Kasino at Nordholz. (Luftschiffbau Zeppelin)*

before the final plunge the airship had risen to 2,400 feet. Strasser in his report noted:

> Shortly before the crash the ship – whether on purpose or not cannot be ascertained – went over pressure height . . . The ship was thus valving gas at the time. This could have led to her being set on fire by lightning. Airships should in all circumstances try to go around thunderstorms. If this is not possible, they should go through as far as possible under pressure height as the squalls will allow. The airships of the Division now have such orders; also in thunderstorms they are ordered to reel in antennas.

On the night of September 7 the Army airships *LZ 74* and *SL 2* raided London. The rebuilt Schütte-Lanz struck a spectacular blow at the Millwall, Deptford, Greenwich and Woolwich docks.[2] After dumping most of her 4,400 pound bomb load on greenhouses at Cheshunt, *LZ 74* had only one incendiary bomb left when she later found herself over the City of London – the first to reach this fabulous goal, and the last Army airship but one to appear in the London area for the rest of the war.

Not to be outdone by the rival service, Strasser sent four ships out next day to raid England. Loewe's *L 9* was as usual restricted to the north of England by her orders to attack the benzol works at Skinningrove on the north Yorkshire coast. On reaching the coast at 10:15, Loewe searched carefully for the benzol works, but could not discover it. Though he believed he identified Hartlepool, Whitby and Stockton, Loewe complained he could not recognize the River Tees, and "a false street was laid out and lit on Seal Sand." In desperation, Loewe began dropping his bombs in a line where he believed the benzol plant to be. He was luckier than he knew:

> One incendiary bomb made a direct hit on the benzol house, but it failed to penetrate the concrete. Another, a high-explosive, fell within ten feet of it, and although the bomb broke the water-main and the electric light cables, and did other minor damage, it failed to damage the benzol house. Had the bomb hit this or the tanks, which held 45,000 gallons of benzol, not much of the works could have survived. The works had one other extraordinary escape, as a bomb which made a direct hit on a T.N.T. store failed to explode. Many other attacks were to be made on the Skinningrove Iron Works, but none was to come so near to destroying them as this one, although the damage actually done was slight and there were no casualties.[3]

Of the southern airships, *L 11* and *L 14* experienced engine trouble, and only *L 13* reached London. Mathy made his landfall near Wells-next-the-Sea on the Norfolk coast at 8:35 p.m., but for an hour stood offshore waiting for darkness. At 9:45 he came inland over King's Lynn. For the first few miles, Mathy followed the River Ouse and the Bedford Level Canal, while the villages below, lit up as fully as in peace-time, assisted his navigation. But from north of Cambridge, while still more than sixty miles from the capital, Mathy was able to dispense with maps and compass, as the reflection of the lights of the world's largest city glowed on the southern horizon.

---

2 On her return from this raid, *SL 2* had a fantastic escape from destruction. With only one of her four engines working she landed outside the Berchem Ste. Agathe base near Brussels, and fell on a small house which penetrated inside the rigid hull. A fire was burning on the hearth, but by extraordinary luck the chimney was forced up between two gas cells and a gas shaft carried away the heat and smoke.

3 Jones, 111, p. 119.

AIRSHIP RAID, SEPTEMBER 8–9, 1915

| *Ship* | *Flt. No.* | *Take-off* | | *Landing* | | *Time in air* | *Dis-tance (miles)* | *Av. speed (m.p.h.)* | *Max. alt. (feet)* | *Temp. (°F.)* | *Crew* | *Fuel (lb.) loaded/used* | *Oil (lb.) loaded/used* | *Ballast loaded (lb.)* | *Bombs (lb.)* | *Gas used (cubic feet)* |
|---|---|---|---|---|---|---|---|---|---|---|---|---|---|---|---|---|
| *L 9* | 59 | Hage | 2.20 p.m. | Hage | 7.30 a.m. | 17h. 0m. | 795 | 46·7 | 7,550 | 41·0 | 14 | 7,160/4,490 | 660/330 | 4,740 | 2,255 | 159,000 |
| *L 11* | 28 | Nordholz | 1.20 p.m. | Nordholz | 2.25 p.m. | 1h. 5m. | | | | | | | | | | |
| *L 13* | 15 | Hage | 2.10 p.m. | Hage | 9.10 a.m. | 19h. 2m. | 811 | 42·4 | 11,150 | 30·2 | 16 | 8,650/7,050 | 880/660 | 10,070 | 3,965 | 373,000 |
| *L 14* | 9 | Nordholz | 1.00 p.m. | Nordholz | 8.20 a.m. | 19h. 20m. | 706 | 36·6 | 9,200 | 32·9 | 16 | 9,250/4,400 | 795/320 | 9,350 | 3,560 | 216,000 |

*Weather:* Light variable winds. Fine with local mist.
*Bombs:* 152 (8,895 lb.), includes 70 (3,730 lb.) on London.
*Casualties:* 26 killed (22 in London), 94 injured (87 in London).
*Monetary damage:* £534,287 (£530,787 in London).

At 11:40 p.m., as he was approaching from the north-west, Mathy sent down five bombs to check the setting of his bomb sight. Over the capital he had little difficulty fixing his position from the lights below: "For example, Regent's Park could be clearly recognized from the 'Inner Circle' which was lit as in peacetime." Members of the crew eagerly pointed out targets, but Mathy, who had spent a week in London in 1909, only smiled and shook his head. Finally he had to say, "There are still better objectives. Only have patience!"

His first bombs, two incendiaries which fell in Upper Bedford Place, did little damage. The third, an explosive, landed a hundred yards away in Queen's Square and shattered all the glass in the surrounding buildings. Farther east, an explosive bomb in Theobald's Road badly damaged the offices of the National Penny Bank. Nearby a falling explosive bomb was detonated in the air by striking the lamp at the entrance to Lamb's Conduit Passage. Spraying fragments of metal killed a man standing outside the Dolphin public house, and demolished the front of the pub. Four more casualties – all children – resulted from a direct hit on a block of apartments further to the east.

Among Mathy's cargo was a 660-pound explosive bomb, the first of its size to be carried over England. Shortly after midnight this descended in the middle of Bartholomew Close. The blast wave and flying fragments blew out glass and shattered

*L 13* DECK LOG IN RAID OF SEPTEMBER 8–9, 1915

| *Central Europ. time* | *Altitude (feet)* | *Temperature (°F) Air* | *Gas* | *Pressure height (feet)* | *Release of ballast* | *Wind Direction* | *Strength* | *Course* | *Distance (miles)* | *Speed (m.p.h.)* | *Position* | *Weather* | *Engines* | *Remarks* |
|---|---|---|---|---|---|---|---|---|---|---|---|---|---|---|
| 2.08 | — | 63·4 | 69·8 | | 220 lb. | N.E. by N. | 2–3 | | | | Take-off | Clear | 2·25–7·20 | |
| 2.18 | 1,970 | 55·4 | 70·8 | | 1980 lb. | N.E. | 2 | | 7·5 | 44·7 | Norderney Light | | 2 Engines stopped | |
| 8.25 | 2,630 | 57·2 | 67·1 | | 4.20, 1540 lb. | | | 270° | 276·0 | 45·2 | 032 ε 5 | | | |
| 8.30 | 3,600 | 53·6 | 61·7 | | 5.40, 880 fuel<br>7.10, 3,090 lb. | | | N.W. | 4·6 | 61·4 | 014 ε 5 | | | |
| 8.50 | 4,900 | 48·2 | 53·6 | | 7.40, 440 lb.<br>9.00, 1,100 lb. | N.E. | 3 | N. | 18·4 | 53·8 | 012 ε 5 | | | 11.35–11.50, 3,970 lb. bombs dropped |
| 9.20 | 6,600 | 45·5 | 45·5 | | 11.35 –11.50 | | | S. | 25·4 | 50·7 | 014 ε 5 | | | |
| 11.50 | 10,500 | 39·2 | 42·8 | | 3,970 lb. bombs | | 4 | 210° | 93·2 | 37·3 | London | | | |
| 12.15 | 11,150 | 29·3 | 34·7 | | | E.S.E. | 8 | N.N.W. | 24·2 | 58·1 | St. Albans | | | |
| 2.00 | 10,500 | 30·2 | 32·0 | | | E.S.E. | 6 | 60° | 91·1 | 52·1 | Norwich | | | |
| 8.00 | 9,850 | 35·6 | 56·3 | | Ship used | N.E. | 4 | 85° | 230·1 | 37·3 | 095 ε 7 | | | |
| 9.10 | — | 60·8 | 68·0 | | 373,000 cu. ft. | E. | 2 | | 40·4 | 40·4 | Landing Hage | | | |

the walls of the buildings on the four sides of the enclosure. Mathy, watching from above, was impressed: "The explosive effect of the 300 kg. bomb must be very great, since a whole cluster of lights vanished in its crater."

It was among the textile warehouses lining the crooked lanes north of St. Paul's that the real damage of the raid was done. This was the "soft goods quarter," and for the first and last time, Admiral Behncke's dream of starting a conflagration in the "dangerous zone" was coming true. Wood Street, Silver Street, Addle Street and Aldermanbury were all ablaze, and despite the efforts of twenty-two fire engines, many valuable buildings were destroyed with their contents.

By this time all twenty-six guns of the London defenses were in action, even those at Woolwich, which were far out of range. At least six of them were small pom-poms, whose shells exploded only on impact, and considerable damage to property was caused by these and by fragments of anti-aircraft shells. "Ideas both as to the height and size of the airship appear to have been somewhat wild,"[4] is the restrained comment of the official record, and not until Mathy had set the City ablaze did the gun at Parliament Hill put a shell close to the airship. But Mathy was sufficiently impressed to report on his return:

> Within the range of the anti-balloon guns of London an airship can remain only a short time with a clear sky, in my opinion. Therefore in clear weather it will hardly be possible to aim at individual targets.

Mathy at this point forced his ship up from 8,500 to 11,200 feet, finding cover behind a light layer of cloud from the 20 searchlights he had counted. But in the excitement he failed to take aim at the Bank of England and Tower Bridge. Still ahead of *L 13* lay Liverpool Street Station, and Mathy's last four bombs were directed at this target. One of them burst on the roadbed north of the station, but merely tore up a few feet of track. The other three, though falling very close to the terminal, did not damage it. But two of them scored direct hits on motor-buses, raising the night's death toll from seven to twenty-two.

[4] Great Britain, Air Ministry. *Air Raids, 1915*. Airship Raids, Aug.-Sept. 1915. Compiled by the Intelligence Section, G.H.Q. Home Forces, February, 1918.

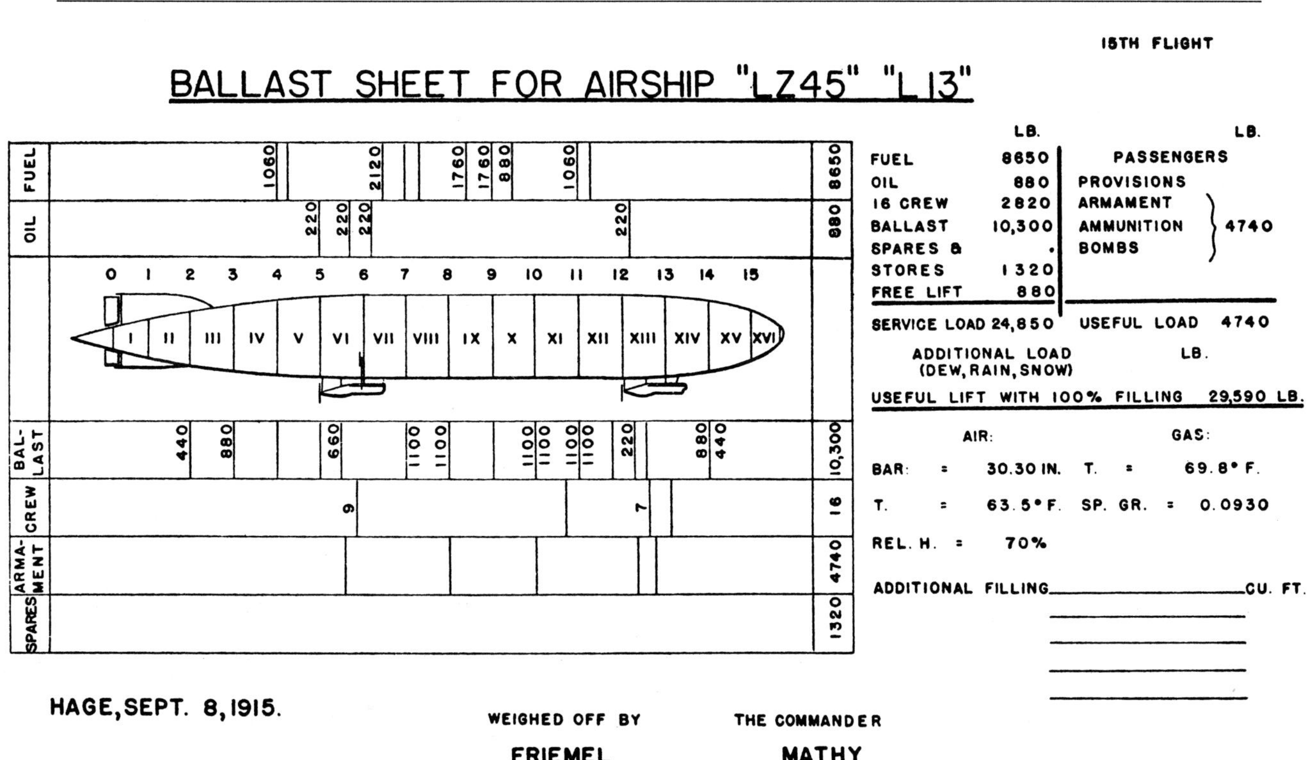

15TH FLIGHT

BALLAST SHEET FOR AIRSHIP "LZ45" "L 13"

FUEL: 1060, 2120, 1760, 1760, 880, 1060 — 8650
OIL: 220, 220, 220, 220 — 880
0 1 2 3 4 5 6 7 8 9 10 11 12 13 14 15
I II III IV V VI VII VIII IX X XI XII XIII XIV XV XVI
BALLAST: 440, 880, 660, 1100, 1100, 1100, 1100, 1100, 1100, 220, 880, 440 — 10,300
CREW: 9, 7 — 16
ARMAMENT: 4740
SPARES: 1320

| | LB. | | LB. |
|---|---|---|---|
| FUEL | 8650 | PASSENGERS | |
| OIL | 880 | PROVISIONS | |
| 16 CREW | 2820 | ARMAMENT | 4740 |
| BALLAST | 10,300 | AMMUNITION | |
| SPARES & | • | BOMBS | |
| STORES | 1320 | | |
| FREE LIFT | 880 | | |
| SERVICE LOAD | 24,850 | USEFUL LOAD | 4740 |

ADDITIONAL LOAD (DEW, RAIN, SNOW) LB.

USEFUL LIFT WITH 100% FILLING 29,590 LB.

AIR: BAR: = 30.30 IN. T. = 63.5° F. REL. H. = 70%

GAS: T. = 69.8° F. SP. GR. = 0.0930

ADDITIONAL FILLING ______ CU. FT.

HAGE, SEPT. 8, 1915.

REDUCED USEFUL LIFT 32,859 LB.

WEIGHED OFF BY FRIEMEL OBLT. Z. S.

THE COMMANDER MATHY KAPITÄNLEUTNANT

*Kapitänleutnant Heinrich Mathy in L 13. (Frau Mathy)*

"As seen from below, the airship gave an impression of absolute calm and absence of hurry,"[5] records one witness, and there was general exasperation at the inability of the defenses to prevent the enemy from bombing London at leisure. As a result of press agitation the Admiralty placed Admiral Sir Percy Scott, a fiery enemy of "red-tapism," in charge of the London defenses. Though Scott had made his reputation as a gunnery expert, he soon foresaw that the airplane would become "the Zeppelins' worst enemy."

The monetary loss in this raid totaled £534,287, of which £530,787 resulted from the fires Mathy started in the City – the most injury inflicted in any airplane or Zeppelin raid throughout the war, and over a sixth of the total air-raid damage in the United Kingdom in World War I.

On September 18, Mathy was summoned to Berlin, and described this raid in an interview with Karl von Wiegand of the *New York World*.[6] He was also commanded to an audience with Admiral von Müller, the Chief of the Emperor's Naval Cabinet. The Kaiser and Kaiserin, alarmed by reports of bomb damage in the heart of London, wished to be certain that no harm had been done to Buckingham Palace, churches or historical buildings. The young airship commander solemnly assured the old courtier that "all the bombs were accurately aimed," and was told that Their Majesties would be greatly relieved![7]

The first chance to follow up Mathy's success came on September 13, with three naval airships taking off to raid London. Thunderstorms and head winds were encountered, and only *L 13* kept going. At 12:10 a.m. Mathy reached the coast, and from a glimpse through a hole in the clouds he correctly determined that he was over Orfordness on the Suffolk coast. Mathy still hoped to reach and bomb London about 4 a.m., and to get away from the country before daylight. At 1 a.m. six searchlights opened up on *L 13* from Harwich, with a heavy bombardment by shrapnel and incendiary shells. Five minutes later "a shell struck in the gangway almost vertically from below, pierced Cells 11 and 12, the fuel line and the radio power cable." Mathy turned back at once, dumping his bombs to

5 Ibid.

6 *New York World*, September 23, 1915.

7 Interview with Mathy's brother-in-law, Hermann Haakh, July 25, 1957, at Bad Soden im Taunus.

*Naval commanders in Hage, fall 1915. Left to right: Peterson, L 16; Breithaupt, L 15, Dietrich L 9, Mathy, L 13. (Photo was a gift to the author from Martin Dietrich)*

*L 13 taking off at Friedrichshafen. (Luftschiffbau Zeppelin)*

lighten the ship. The port engine failed with a broken wrist-pin. As the two damaged midships gas cells rapidly became 80 to 85 per cent empty, despite attempts to patch them, the Zeppelin became very heavy and was in a critical situation. Mathy headed for home by the shortest route, deliberately flying across Holland to save his ship. Before reaching the Dutch coast he dumped 1,750 pounds of fuel. At 3:10 a.m. Mathy was over Ymuiden, and fifty-five minutes later he left Dutch territory at Delfzijl. At 5:20 a.m. *L 13* was over Hage. Mathy would have preferred to wait for sunrise to warm and expand the remaining hydrogen, but thunderstorms threatened to load the ship with soaking rain and he decided to land immediately. Though he dropped 1,100 pounds more of oil, spare parts and radiator water in the Ems, the ship fell heavily in landing. Girders were broken over the control car, gondola struts and side propeller shafts were bent, but the damage was made good in four days.

*L 13* had been hit by one of twelve rounds fired by the sixpounder gun at Felixstowe, across the harbor from Harwich. The British never discovered why Mathy had turned back so precipitately, for the Zeppelin had been hidden in clouds and the gun had been aimed by sound alone.

The first series of raids on London was received with jubilation by the Navy, which had outstripped the Army in the air war against England, and by the country as a whole. But the Army General Staff professed to be concerned that the Allies might retaliate. On September 12, *General* von Falkenhayn wrote that the Army airships had been ordered not to bomb London except for the docks and harbor works, and would not attack the City of London itself as long as the enemy refrained from attacking open German towns. The reply of Admiral von Holtzendorff, Bachmann's recent successor as Chief of the Naval Staff, showed an obvious wish to press the Navy's advantage. In view of existing Navy policy and the military importance of the raids, he could not agree with von Falkenhayn, but on September 14 he ordered that "in the future the air raids should be restricted once more as far as possible to those parts of London on the banks of the Thames, as to which no restrictions had been made by the German authorities, and that the northern quarter of the City inhabited chiefly by the poorer classes should as far as possible be avoided." Displeased by this restriction, the Commander-in-Chief of the High Seas Fleet decided to call off the raids until the next new-moon period, and to use all his airships to assist the mine sweepers in clearing the German Bight.

On October 5, with the return of the darker nights, Admiral von Pohl ordered Strasser to make

AIRSHIP RAID, OCTOBER 13–14, 1915

| *Ship* | *Flt. No.* | *Take-off* | *Landing* | *Time in air* | *Distance (miles)* | *Av. speed (m.p.h.)* | *Max. alt. (feet)* | *Temp. (°F.)* | *Crew* | *Fuel(lb.) loaded/used* | *Oil (lb.) loaded/used* | *Ballast loaded (lb.)* | *Bombs (lb.)* | *Gas used (cubic feet)* |
|---|---|---|---|---|---|---|---|---|---|---|---|---|---|---|
| *L 11* | 37 | Nordholz 12.22 p.m. | Nordholz 8.02 a.m. | 19h. 40m. | 895 | 44·9 | 8,550 | 39·2 | 17 | 9,840/5,510 | 727/209 | 11,630 | 3,345 | 424,000 |
| *L 13* | 22 | Hage 1.40 p.m. | Hage 10.30 a.m. | 20h. 50m. | 881 | 40·4 | 11,150 | 35·6 | 16 | 8,480/7,820 | 880/660 | 10,130 | 4,370 | 339,000 |
| *L 14* | 18 | Nordholz 12.40 p.m. | Nordholz 3.20 p.m. | 26h. 40m. | 949 | 39·9 | 10,200 | 36·5 | 16 | 8,820/8,640 | 1,058/760 | 9,800 | 3,900 | 307,500 |
| *L 15* | 7 | Nordholz 12.50 p.m. | Nordholz 12.20 p.m. | 23h. 40m. | 1,089 | 45·4 | 10,200 | 35·6 | 16 | 10,120/9,880 | 660/485 | 10,680 | 3,250 | 371,000 |
| *L 16* | 5 | Hage 1.30 p.m. | Hage 7.25 a.m. | 18h. 0m. | 854 | 47·4 | 9,530 | 41·0 | 17 | 8,700/7,600 | 655/353 | 10,120 | 3,715 | 441,000 |

*Weather:* Light winds, mainly from the south. Mist on East Coast and in Kent.
*Bombs:* 189 (13,672 lb.), includes 81 (5,635 lb.) on London.
*Casualties:* 71 killed (47 in London), 128 injured (102 in London).
*Monetary damage:* £80,020 (£50,250 in London).

every effort to raid Liverpool. American supplies and munitions were beginning to pour in through this West Coast port, and any interruption of this traffic would be of prime military importance. On October 6 the newer airships were ordered to "clear for a raid." But bad weather held them in their sheds for a week, and when they were finally sent out on October 13, conditions were only good enough to permit an attack on London.

Five Zeppelins started – *L 11*, *L 14* and *L 15* from Nordholz shortly after noon, and *L 13* and *L 16* an hour later from Hage. During the afternoon the ships kept together, flying over a solid overcast that reached up to 2,600 feet. At Ameland they took their departure for the Winterton-Haisbrough area on the coast of Norfolk, intending to steer thence via Cambridge to attack London from the north. At 6 p.m., within sight of the coast, Mathy, as senior commander, radioed orders designed to prevent a collision over the capital: "Attack course east to north-east, run off to the north-east. Immediately after attack report by radio, giving height, signature." Then, between 7:15 and 7:40, four of the ships, with *L 13* in the lead, crossed the coast together. Only *L 11* delayed, coming in at Bacton at 9:30. A few miles inland she came under fire of machine guns of the Eastern Mobile Section, and jettisoned her bombs on the villages of Horstead, Coltishall and Great Hautbois. Back in Nordholz, von Buttlar reported having flown up the Thames and dropping his bombs on "West Ham, the docks and Woolwich . . . on dropping the fourth bomb an especially heavy explosion was seen, and three big fires were started which a half hour later still glowed through the light cloud layer."

Though he was over England for the first time, Breithaupt in *L 15* set a good course for London. At first even parachute flares gave him no information, but after 9:10 p.m., the bright glow of the lights of London, reflected off the clouds ahead, led him straight to his goal. At Broxbourne a mobile 13-pounder tried to turn him back, but he replied with three explosive bombs which fell close enough to blow down the gunners. Breithaupt thought this

*L 12 dropping her trail-ropes for a landing at Friedrichshafen. Another photo appears on pages 116-117. (Luftschiffbau Zeppelin)*

*L 15 above the rooftops of London during the October 13, 1915 raid. (Illustrated London News)*

attack came from Tottenham, on the northern edge of the city. He therefore steered west to get the wind behind him. Previously Breithaupt had slipped two tanks of fuel; now he dropped all his ballast except "one breech forward," and got his ship up to 8,500 feet. At 10 p.m. he set his engine telegraphs on "flank speed" and bore down on the capital.

It was an impressive moment for the watchers below, unused as they were to war from the air. In New Palace Yard, adjoining the Houses of Parliament, His Majesty's Loyal Commons, who were debating late on an emergency taxation measure, gathered to watch the bold invader of England.

> For a few minutes the airship, crossing the Thames on a northeasterly course and passing almost directly over New Palace Yard, was then played upon by two searchlights, and in their radiance she looked a thing of silvery beauty sailing serenely through the night, indifferent to the big gun roaring at her from the Green Park, whose shells seemed to burst just below her.[8]

But from above the scene was no less sublime. Said Breithaupt;

> The picture we saw was indescribably beautiful – shrapnel bursting all around (though rather uncomfortably near us), our own bombs bursting, and the flashes from the anti-aircraft batteries below. On either hand the other airships, which, like us, were caught in the rays of the searchlights, were clearly recognizable. And over us the starlit sky![9]

[8] MacDonagh, p. 82.

[9] Joachim Breithaupt, "How We Bombed London," *Living Age*, January 1928.

*A rare photograph of an historic occasion – the start of the first raid on England. Taken by Leutnant zur See Hans von Schiller from the control car of L 11, it shows the attacking squadron over the North Sea. L 13 in the foreground (Mathy), then L 12 (Peterson), and the flagship L 10 (Hirsch) in the distance. This is one of the few photos ever taken of a World War I airship raid. (Luftschiffbau Zeppelin)*

*L 13 on July 25, 1915 being drawn out of Factory Shed II at Friedrichshafen, with Heinrich Mathy aboard. After relatively successful raids in 1915 and 1916, L 13 was decommissioned on December 11, 1917 and later dismantled. (Luftschiffbau Zeppelin)*

In spite of the gunfire, Breithaupt coolly withheld his missiles until he was able to strike at the heart of London. "I ordered bomb dropping to start at Charing Cross Station and continued to the Bank of England, with particularly good coverage over the newspaper district of Ludgate Hill." Despite the Naval Staff's preoccupation with the Admiralty, Breithaupt's first bombs fell a third of a mile to the east, in the theater district north of the Strand. The first exploded in Exeter Street, close to the Lyceum theater. The second burst in Wellington Street, shattered a gas main and set fire to the escaping gas. Here seventeen people were killed in the street, the greatest number of deaths caused by a single bomb in any raid up to that time. The third bomb fell in York Street, and the fourth barely missed the Strand theater. The fifth bomb landed on the pavement near the Waldorf Hotel; the sixth at the foot of Kingsway, and the seventh and eighth demolished the temporary headquarters of the Belgian Relief Fund in Aldwych. Two other theaters barely escaped from the last salvo. The audiences took alarm from the explosions, but the entertainers succeeded in preventing panic. More bombs rained down on the Inns of Court; an incendiary which burned out the robing room at Gray's Inn was later salvaged and mounted in the Benchers' law library.

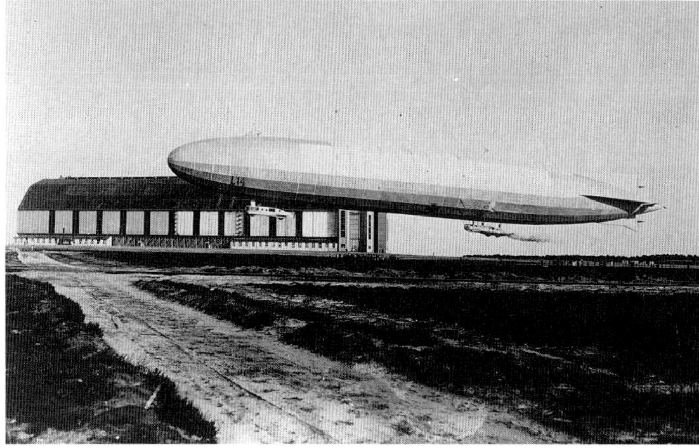

*Two views of L 14 at Nordholz. In the top left photo, the twin towers of the big home ship wireless station can be seen in the background. The top right photo shows the revolving shed in the background. (top left - Luftschiffbau Zeppelin, top right - Moch)*

*The German army Zeppelin LZ 74 on an early flight photographed from the roof of the Löwenthal shed. It was identical to the contemporary naval airships of the L 10 class. (Luftschiffbau Zeppelin)*

This ended the worst phase of the raid. Since Mathy's attack a month before, the Admiralty had obtained a mobile French 75 mm. anti-aircraft gun. Under Commander W. Rawlinson's direction it had been set up on the Honorable Artillery Company's grounds in Finsbury. Breithaupt was now within range, and Rawlinson let fly at the approaching Zeppelin. The shell exploded low, at only 7,200 feet, but it took Breithaupt by surprise. The gun crew reloaded, but just as Rawlinson prepared to fire again, *L 15* passed into the "dead circle" of the gun. The weapon could not elevate beyond 83 degrees, and Rawlinson had to watch helplessly as the Zeppelin, brilliantly illuminated, sailed straight overhead. As she made off to the east, Rawlinson got off a second round that burst close to the airship.

A further apparition had given Breithaupt cause for alarm – "over the City four airplanes were observed 500 to 1,000 meters [1,650 to 3,300 feet] below the ship; they were clearly recognizable in the searchlight illumination and by their exhaust flames." Five in all had taken off from the Royal Flying Corps fields at Joyce Green, Hainault Farm and Suttons Farm, to the east of London, armed, not with machine guns, but with small incendiary bombs to be dropped on the Zeppelins from above. Only one pilot saw *L 15*: climbing above the mist, he found her bathed in the dull radiance of the lights of London, but his plane had been seen by those on board and the airship climbed away from him. It was the first combat flight for the 18-year-old airman, who thirty-seven years later ended his career as Sir John Slessor, Marshal of the Royal Air Force and Chief of the Air Staff.[10]

Mathy in *L 13* had set himself the assignment, "firstly, to destroy the water works at Hampton and by this loss in weight to obtain the height necessary for an attack on London itself." At first he had little difficulty with his navigation, for a new moon in the west did not set until 8:30, while Cambridge and other towns up to the limits of the capital were easily recognized by their illumination. Near Hatfield, northwest of London, an anti-aircraft gun opened fire, and was answered with four 110-pound explosive bombs. At about 10:30 Mathy reached the Thames west of London at Staines, and correctly followed the river south and east to reach Hampton.

10 Sir John Slessor, *The Central Blue*, (New York: Frederick A. Praeger, 1957) P. 12.

Six miles below Staines the Thames bends sharply to the north, and is joined from the south by the River Wey. In the darkness after moonset, and nearly two miles up in the air, Mathy missed the bend and continued south along the smaller river. At 11:30 he was over the village of Shalford. Mathy dropped four parachute flares; only one floated in the air, the rest plunged earthward, but he decided "from its characteristic position" that this was Hampton. "In three crossings twelve 50 kg. explosive bombs were now dropped on the pumping and power stations; the hits were well placed." Minor damage was done to private houses.

Mathy then bore up north-east for London. Over Bromley, on the south-eastern edge of the capital, *L 14* was sighted close aboard; it is alleged that the Zeppelins barely escaped a collision,[11] and even that Mathy and Böcker quarreled over the responsibility,[12] but the stories are not borne out by either airship's war diary. At 12:45 under the impression that he was bombing the Victoria Docks, Mathy

[11] Jones, III, p. 131.

[12] *The Times*, September 21, 1920, p. 12.

*Two views of L 15. Above: In front of the construction shed at Löwenthal. (Kriegsmarinesammlung) Below: Landing at Nordholz. L 15 caused great damage to London on the October 13/14, 1915 raid. After a later raid on March 31-April 1, 1916, L 15 sank in the Thames estuary. The "Nora" and "Norbert" sheds are seen in the background. (Moch)*

*The Nordholz groundcrew taking charge of L 15 after her forced landing on October 14, 1915. Note the crumpled gondola strut and smashed window frames. After an effective raid on London, Breithaupt could not find the Nordholz base because of heavy fog. Lest the ship be blown out to sea, he released gas and landed on a railroad cutting after twenty-four hours of flight. (Luftschiffbau Zeppelin)*

*A rare photograph of the naval airship L 16 in her shed, with two officers posing in front of the control car. Note sandbags used to hold the ship down in the shed. (Luftschiffbau Zeppelin)*

dropped the remainder of his bombs, including a 660-pounder, in Woolwich Arsenal. Fortunately, they had little effect.

Böcker in *L 14* came inland past Norwich and Thetford in company with the other ships, and reported that, after passing these places and being fired on, he steered via Chelmsford to Woolwich. In fact, near Colchester *L 14* unaccountably slanted off to the south-east, crossed the lower Thames at the Isle of Sheppey, and flew south across Kent till 10:15 p.m. when she reached the sea near Hythe. Seemingly Böcker mistook the English Channel for the Thames, for at this time he reported "we crossed the Thames at Woolwich and attacked the dock facilities there as well as the arsenal with 9 explosive bombs and good results were observed." Six of these bombs were traced on an Army encampment overlooking the Channel, and fifteen soldiers were killed and eleven injured. Böcker then headed northwest, and actually succeeded in finding his way back to London. At 12:20 a.m. his ship appeared over the suburb of Croydon, where the rest of her cargo destroyed or damaged a number of private homes.

Peterson in *L 16* had suffered an unusual accident during the crossing of the North Sea. With the ship angled down by the bows, he had pulled the toggle of one of the forward "breeches" to bring her to an even keel, and most of the 220 pounds of water, falling on the control car roof, had poured down the ventilator of the radio transmitter. The operators spent the night tearing it down, drying and reassembling it, but short circuits persisted and Peterson could send no messages until next morning. Coming in with the other Zeppelins, Peterson passed Norwich and Cambridge, and saw *L 15* lit up over the capital. Thinking to approach while the defenses were distracted by Breithaupt's ship, Peterson reported dropping his bombs on big factories and railroad yards in Stratford, East Ham and West Ham. "Only a few searchlights and guns opened on *L 16* in contrast to the treatment of the other ship. Either they expected no attack from the north or their leadership failed." This was because Peterson's attack was made on the town of Hertford, nearly twenty miles north of London. Nine people were killed, and fifteen injured, by the 18 explosive and 30 incendiary bombs which Peterson sowed in a long line across the town and out into the fields beyond.

All the Zeppelins had trouble with fog during their homeward journeys. *L 13* strayed over the island of Vlieland and was fired on by Dutch guns. She landed at her base during the morning of the 14th, as did *L 11* and *L 16*. But *L 14* was kept in the air from 10:30 to 3:20, waiting for the fog to break

*L 16 at Nordholz. White bands around the nose identify the ships as a trainer – warning other ships. (Moch)*

and let her down at Nordholz. *L 15* did not even get back to her base. Steering by radio bearings, Breithaupt arrived over Nordholz at 10 a.m. with fuel for only two hours on board. At 11:40 he saw, thirty feet above the top of the fog, a captive balloon let up to mark the airship base. Repeatedly he descended into the fog, to within 360 feet by his altimeter, with no sign of the ground. Two of his engines were dead, the other two stopped at times because of water in the petrol. Towards noon Breithaupt knew he must land. He steered for the captive balloon, but lost sight of it as soon as the Zeppelin sank into the fog bank. At 250 feet, still unable to see the ground and unsure of where he was in relation to the big sheds and the gasometer, Breithaupt dropped his landing ropes, hoping the noise would be heard by the ground crew. Nobody found them, and *L 15* drifted north. At 12:08 p.m. the port engine, which had been running at half speed, stopped entirely; at 12:20 the last engine, the forward one, failed also. Rather than drift out to sea, Breithaupt valved gas forward to land at once. With no ballast left, the fore gondola crashed hard on the moorland near a railroad cutting. Most of the gondola struts broke, as well as ring and longitudinal girders up in the hull. Of the 1,379 gallons of petrol on board at take-off, only 36 gallons remained! Within an hour the ground troop arrived to walk the airship three miles back to Nordholz. Seven days later repairs were far enough advanced to enable *L 15* to transfer to Hage.

*On October 19, 1917, L 16, then a training ship (white ring around the nose) crashed into the Elbe in Altenbruch Reede after leaving Nordholz injuring all aboard. L 16 was eventually carried ashore on the north side of the Elbe. (Moch)*

*L 18 seen from underneath the fins and rudders, maneuvering to land at Hannover. (Moch)*

The October 13 raid was one of the deadliest of the war. The monetary damage was only a tenth of what Mathy had achieved on September 8, but in London alone 38 people were killed and 87 injured. Adding the casualties elsewhere, the total came to 71 killed and 128 injured, "a greater number, in proportion to the ships engaged and bombs dropped, than were inflicted by any other airship raid of the war."[13] Had the Zeppelins been able to continue such a record in frequent attacks, they might have exerted an influence on the outcome of the war. But this first squadron raid on London was also to be the last for nearly a year.

The airship commanders reported that the capital's defenses

were improving. Böcker, attacking London for the first time, was impressed:

> During the crossing of the city the ship was lit up bright as day by numerous searchlights (26 were counted), and was heavily fired on from all sides with explosive shells, whose bursts sometimes lay very near the ship. At the periphery of the city they were also firing incendiary rockets, some of which ascended very near to the ship.

Breithaupt long remembered his escape from the four airplanes, and Mathy reported that "compared with September 8-9, a considerable increase in the blackout and defenses was noticeable."

Winter weather brought a drastic reduction in air activity. The moon was new on November 7, but southeast gales and thick weather prevented even an attempted raid. There were several days in the last half of the month when the airships were out to cover mine sweepers working in the western portion of the German Bight. Peterson in *L 16* had a nerve-racking experience on November 22. Taking off from Hage at 7:20 a.m. to patrol off the Dutch Islands, he rose at once into dense, milky fog. A half-hour later he reeled in his antenna, cautiously felt his way down through the "soup", found the cloud base at 250 feet, and went on west at this altitude, getting his last navigational check from the island of Borkum. During the morning the after engine broke down. The starboard motor, disabled by a frozen wrist-pin, was torn down and repaired in flight by the mechanics working in the cramped after gondola. At noon, with the fog ever more dense, Peterson turned back. Flying at 130 feet to keep in sight of the water, Peterson came in over the German island of Baltrum on a course for

---

[13] Jones, III, p. 132.

his base. The Hage kite balloon was up, but heavy fog baffled him in four approaches to the field. The starboard engine again became useless when the propeller bracket broke up on the hull, and the forward motor failed from oiling up of the spark plugs at low speed. At 3:45 p.m., with only the port engine working, Peterson set his ship down without being able to see the ground, and found himself near the village of Hilgenriedersiel, three miles north of the Hage field. As always, Peterson brought off the landing without bending a strut. The villagers helped to hold *L 16* until the Hage ground troop arrived and walked her back to her shed at 6:45 p.m.

The only new airship delivered during the month promptly fell victim to an accident such as could so easily happen with hydrogen. *L 18* made her first flight at Löwenthal on November 3, and on the 6th was put in commission by Max Dietrich and started for the North Sea. Bad weather forced Dietrich to seek shelter in the Army shed at Hanover, and not until November 16 was he able to go on to Tondern, berthing in the big new "Toska" double shed.[14] Luckily the other side of the hangar was unoccupied. Early next morning, as the crew and maintenance group were filling a gas cell, there was an explosion in a gas line in a corner of the shed and *L 18* took fire. Fuel tanks blew up with loud reports, and the wreckage burned for an hour and a half. The charred corpse of one of Dietrich's machinist's mates was found near the remains of the fore gondola, and seven other people were injured. It was the first of three fires in the unlucky "Toska" hangar, in which five Zeppelins were destroyed.

December and early January were marked by a succession of southwest gales, fog, rain, sleet and snow. The moon was new on December 6 and January 4, but no raids were attempted. Scouting flights were few and far between. On December 13 the windward doors of *L 13*'s shed rolled open in a southwest storm, but Mathy's ship only suffered a damaged rudder which was repaired in two days. In the unheated hangars everything was clammy and beaded with moisture, and the airships suffered from the high humidity. The glued fabric strips on the outer covers, sealing over the laced fastenings of the big cotton panels, came unstuck and hung loose. High humidity of the gas meant that it lost some of its "lift," and the cells had to be emptied and refilled. The gold beaters' skin lining the gas cells, being animal tissue, grew mold and putrefied in the damp weather. Repeatedly the war diaries record, "take-off to dry out the ship."

The campaign against London had inflicted some painful injuries, though the results were far from what its sponsors had hoped. The rest of the island kingdom was now to taste the furor teutonicus, transported across the North Sea in the bellies of the monsters that old Count Zeppelin had created.

*The shortest life of any navy Zeppelin would be that of L 18. On its first flight, November 4, 1915, from Löwenthal it was ordered to the shed at Hannover because of bad weather. On November 16, L 18 flew to Tondern. On the following morning Kapitänleutnant Max Dietrich ordered all gas cells topped with hydrogen. There was an explosion and fire which killed one L 18 crewman, and six maintenance workers.*

14 Each shed at the naval airship base was designated by an individual code name. The first two letters of the shed name were the same as those of the base. Appendix C gives a complete list of all sheds at the naval airship bases, with dimensions, code names, etc.

L 21

# CHAPTER X

# FROM LONDON TO EDINBURGH

On January 8, 1916, Admiral von Pohl, dying of cancer, gave up command of the High Seas Fleet. His successor was *Vizeadmiral* Reinhard Scheer, commanding the III Battle Squadron. One of the Navy's leading "activists," Scheer's chief aim was to force England to her knees through unrestricted submarine warfare against merchant shipping. But it was over a year before he had his way, and thus 1916 at sea was marked by his aggressive handling of the Fleet. Scheer proposed to go much farther to sea than von Pohl had done, and particularly wished to execute operations against England, with battle cruisers bombarding coastal towns and the battle fleet in close support to fall upon enemy detachments pursuing the raiders. In all enterprises at sea, Scheer, commanding the weaker force, relied heavily on airships to protect the High Seas Fleet against surprise. He also intended to use them in intensified strategic bombing of England.

Between the Commander of the Naval Airship Division and the new Commander-in-Chief of the Fleet there developed in the next two years a respect and admiration which meant much to Strasser personally and to the arm which he represented. At their first meeting on January 18, a plan was drawn up for bombing the whole of England. Raids were to be made by as many airships as possible. Army Zeppelins were to participate, coordination being arranged between the Chief of the Naval Staff and the Chief of the General Staff. For the purpose of issuing simple attack orders, England would be divided into three areas:

> "England North" would mean Edinburgh and secondarily the Tyne.
> "England Middle" would mean Liverpool and secondarily the Humber.
> "England South" would mean London, secondarily Yarmouth, etc.

*OPPOSITE:*
*The naval Zeppelin L 21 in her shed at Nordholz. Note the fire ladder used for working on the outer cover of the hull. L 21 was shot down in flames on November 28, 1916 on the return leg of a mission to the British midlands. (Luftschiffbau Zeppelin)*

Strasser commented that an attack on Bristol would be difficult, while Southampton could be reached only from Belgian bases. The Naval Staff would be asked whether factories in undefended cities in the Midlands could be attacked en route to Liverpool; Strasser evidently received a prompt answer in the affirmative.

A few days later, on January 31, nine Zeppelins took off for England. Strasser was leading the raid aboard *L 11*, and his orders read, "Attack England middle or south, if at all possible Liverpool."

All of the ships reported low, thick fog over the North Sea, with deep rain clouds and snow off the English coast which heavily iced up the outer covers. They had to depend entirely on radio bearings to determine their position, and the "fixes" were unreliable. Many of the Zeppelins reached the coast at different places – usually to the south – from where they believed they made their landfalls. All of the raiders came inland, but none of them reached the west coast. Ground mist and low fog over England hampered their navigation, and it is not surprising that they were uncertain of their positions. Two airships claimed to have bombed Liverpool. The German commanders also thought that Sheffield was attacked three times, Manchester by two raiders simultaneously, and Nottingham, Goole, Immingham, and Yarmouth once each. Actually not a single bomb fell in any of these places. But there was no reason, as far as the British were concerned, why these cities should not have been attacked. The defenses in the Midlands were virtually non-existent, and the airships moved wherever they pleased. Their paths crossed and tangled, until the British ground observers could no longer keep track of their respective courses.

*L 13* and *L 21*, flying close together, were the first airships to come in over the coast near Mundesley in Norfolk at 5:50 p.m. A clear sunset suggested to Mathy that good weather might prevail to the west – a promise betrayed by the river mists which during the evening spread to cover much of the Midlands. At 9:15 he aimed seven explosive bombs at the glow of a blast furnace. These fell at Stoke-on-Trent and merely broke a few windows. Mathy then headed out of the mist-filled Trent valley, and tried to find his position with parachute flares. These lit up nothing but fog below, and *L 13* next was heard calling up the German direction-finding stations at Nordholz and Bruges. Plotting back from the intersection of the two bearings, Mathy was convinced that his first bombs had fallen near Manchester, and from the radio "fix" he set a course for the Humber. At 11:45 a momentary break in the clouds revealed "blast furnaces and other extensive installations" on which Mathy dropped his remaining bombs. He thought these fell in Goole, but actually he was over Scunthorpe, fifteen miles to the south-east. Three people were killed and 7 injured, and a steel works was slightly damaged.

Max Dietrich in *L 21* reported an attack on Liverpool. He soon outdistanced *L 13*, passing south of Nottingham and north of Derby, which he mistook for Manchester. He reported that railroad yards and factories were clearly visible, but he did not bomb them since he wanted to make a surprise attack on Liverpool. At 8:50 p.m. Dietrich thought he was over the west coast and:

> saw the lights of two cities which from dead reckoning and from their position were taken to be Liverpool and Birkenhead. Steered out to sea north of Liverpool, then attacked both cities on a southerly course. Docks, harbor works and factories of both cities were attacked with thirty-five so kg. [110 lb.] and twenty incendiary bombs. Explosion of all bombs and good results were clearly seen from on board.

Dietrich had overestimated a tail wind and actually was over the crowded residential suburbs of Birmingham, 75 miles south-south-east of Liverpool. The property damage was not great, but 33 people were killed and 20 injured.

At the time British ground observers thought that *L 11* had dropped the bombs on Scunthorpe, while Mathy was credited with an attack on Burton-on-Trent. Which ship made the attack on Burton is not clear, though possibly it was *L 15*, whose movements that night were traced with difficulty. Certainly it was not *L 11*, which carried all her bombs home with-her. Once again the crew had reason to believe that Strasser was a "Jonah." Be-

*Army Zeppelin LZ 97, a sister to the naval "Twenties", in a photograph that shows off the type quite well. Note the open bomb-traps amidship, and the small fish-shaped sub-cloud car hung ahead of the after gondola. (Luftschiffbau Zeppelin)*

fore reaching the coast, *L 11* was loaded with two tons of rain and ice, and, flying at a 10 degree angle, the ship could climb only to 6,700 feet. The rain and snow cleared over England, but mist and sometimes fog hampered von Buttlar. At 8:15 he sighted a large city which he identified, probably correctly, as Lincoln. South of Sheffield he found a big, brightly lit installation which appeared to be a prisoner of war camp. Towards 11 p.m. von Buttlar was sure he was over the west coast, but could see nothing because of heavy fog. After consultation with Strasser, *L 11*'s young commander decided to turn

AIRSHIP RAID, JANUARY 31–FEBRUARY 1, 1916

| *Ship* | *Flt. No.* | *Take-off* | *Landing* | *Time in Air* | *Distance (miles)* | *Av. speed (m.p.h.)* | *Max. alt. (feet)* | *Temp. (°F.)* | *Crew* | *Fuel (lb.) loaded/used* | *Oil (lb.) loaded/used* | *Ballast loaded (lb.)* | *Bombs (lb.)* | *Gas used (cubic feet)* |
|---|---|---|---|---|---|---|---|---|---|---|---|---|---|---|
| *L 11* | 57 | Nordholz 12.48 p.m. | Nordholz 10.50 a.m. | 22h. 02m. | 910 | 45·5 | 6,250 | 26·6 | 18 | 10,270/7,180 | 815/617 | 13,000 | 4,730 | 282,000 |
| *L 13* | 50 | Hage 12.45 p.m. | Hage 9.30 a.m. | 20h. 45m. | 875 | 41·4 | 9,150 | 19·4 | 16 | 9,250/7,050 | 925/440 | 12,820 | 4,850 | 390,000 |
| *L 14* | 36 | Nordholz 12.40 p.m. | Nordholz 1.06 p.m. | 24h. 26m. | 1,087 | 44·6 | 9,150 | 21·2 | 17 | 9,250/8,150 | 1,100/660 | 14,180 | 4,130 | 353,000 |
| *L 15* | 29 | Hage 1.00 p.m. | Hage 11.05 a.m. | 22h. 05m. | 1,071 | 51·6 | 8,700 | 14·9 | 17 | 9,610/7,740 | 837/573 | 12,430 | 4,750 | 512,000 |
| *L 16* | 26 | Hage 1.15 p.m. | Hage 9.00 a.m. | 19h. 45m. | 672 | 35·4 | 8,200 | 22·6 | 17 | 9,310/6,010 | 860/571 | 12,210 | 4,010 | 441,000 |
| *L 17* | 17 | Nordholz 12.17 p.m. | Nordholz 9.00 a.m. | 20h. 47m. | 805 | 38·8 | 8,540 | 18·5 | 18 | 10,570/7,490 | 880/231 | 13,650 | 4,430 | 314,00 |
| *L 19* | 14 | Tondern 12.15 p.m. | | | | | | | 16 | | | | | |
| *L 20* | 7 | Tondern 12.06 p.m. | Tondern 12.00 noon | 24h. 04m. | 817 | 34·1 | 8,060 | 20·3 | 18 | 12,520/9,100 | 1,308/604 | 13,580 | 5,600 | 392,000 |
| *L 21* | 7 | Nordholz 12.00 noon | Nordholz 11.45 a.m. | 23h. 32m. | 1,053 | 44·7 | 10,000 | 15·8 | 17 | 12,720/7,230 | 1,232/584 | 17,720 | 4,910 | 459,000 |

*Weather:* Calm. Fog in Trent valley, but mainly clear sky in Midland counties. Patches of mist and fog on East Coast.
*Bombs:* 379 (27,459 lb.).
*Casualties:* 70 killed, 113 injured.
*Monetary damage:* £53,832.

back. "It is pleasant to pay tribute to *Korvettenkapitän* Strasser for his high concept of his duty," writes the British air historian. "He had been over British soil for four hours or more and had sighted a number of possible targets, but as he recognized no objective of definite military importance he was content to take his bombs back as he had brought them."[1] Probably *L 11*'s "farthest west" was the high, sparsely inhabited Peak district between Manchester and Sheffield.

Böcker of *L 14* likewise thought he reached the west coast. Over the North Sea, he flew through light rain and snow which built up a heavy layer of ice on his ship. He correctly identified the cities of Nottingham and Derby, but was too eager to reach Liverpool to bomb these places. After passing Derby a thick wall of cloud rose up in the west, cutting off sight of the ground completely. About 11 p.m. Böcker thought he was over the west coast of England, but he saw nothing of Liverpool, although he searched up and down for an hour. At midnight he gave up. Böcker at no time had been farther west than Shrewsbury, but this was the westernmost point of the raid. On the way home he dropped 4,150 pounds of bombs on "big factories and blast furnaces" which he thought were in Nottingham, but which actually were in nearby Derby. Nine high-explosive bombs burst in the Midland Railway's maintenance shops, damaged the engine house and killed three men and injured two. Three bombs fell on the "Metallite" lamp works and did considerable damage, though no one was injured. The rest were ineffective, though a woman died of shock.

The other ships had more or less engine trouble, and most of them prudently cut short their journeys over England. *L 15* and later craft were fitted with the new Maybach 240 h.p. HSLu airship engine in place of the 210 h.p. C-X in use since early 1914. Lighter, more powerful and more efficient, the new power plant had been rushed into service before the "bugs" had been eliminated. For months, crankshafts fractured, connecting rods broke, and crank bearings and wrist-pins overheated, melted and "froze," until air-scoops were fitted to blow cool air from the slip-stream through the crank case.

Peterson had a bearing burn out in the fore engine of *L 16* before reaching the coast. The after engine was running roughly, and with only two reliable motors and a load of snow and ice, he gave up the attack on Liverpool and decided to bomb Great Yarmouth on the coast. At 8:20 p.m. he dropped his two tons of bombs from 7,000 feet on "such factories as could be made out in Great Yarmouth." As far as the British could ascertain, *L 16* came inland over the Wash at 7:10 p.m. and at 10:05 passed out to sea between Yarmouth and Lowestoft. The only bombs traced from her, two high-explosives, fell at Swaffham, 43 miles west of Yarmouth.

*L 17*'s mechanics spent the afternoon tearing down and reassembling the forward engine, after a piston ring had broken and "frozen" to the cylinder wall. Soon after the motor was set going at 6 p.m., a wrist-pin melted. The starboard engine failed repeatedly and *Kapitänleutnant* Herbert Ehrlich steered for the Humber. He believed he crossed the coast at 8 p.m. but could not determine his position due to thick cloud. A searchlight broke through the overcast to starboard; the glow of "blast furnaces" was seen nearby, and as *L 17* steered to attack, Ehrlich reported that small-caliber guns opened up on him. He made two runs over the "industrial area" and claimed the battery was silenced and all the lights extinguished by the end of the attack. Plotting back by dead reckoning, Ehrlich convinced himself that he had bombed Immingham. British records state that *L 17* drifted in over Sheringham in Norfolk at 7:40 p.m. and was picked up by the searchlight at the naval air station near Holt, whereupon she dropped her bombs in the surrounding fields.

During her approach to England, *L 20* had been weighted down by heavy rain and ice which prevented her from climbing over 6,500 feet, and the forward engine had been out of action most of the time while the starboard engine ran irregularly. *Kapitänleutnant* Franz Stabbert believed he came inland between the Humber and the Wash at 7:45. In hopes of orienting himself by provoking batteries into firing, he dropped 10 incendiary bombs with no results. At 8:45, according to Stabbert, *L 20*

---

[1] Jones, III, p. 140.

was faintly lit up by searchlights through the clouds and fired on; six explosive bombs silenced the battery. Fifteen minutes later Stabbert was sure that Sheffield was in sight, and because of his unreliable engines, he decided to attack this industrial city instead of continuing to Liverpool. Making six runs between 9:30 and 10:15, Stabbert reported dropping twenty-seven 110-pound explosive bombs on blast furnaces north and south of the city. He held on to three 220s, two 110s and ten incendiary bombs in case of being attacked while going out over the coast, and since his departure was peaceful, he carried these bombs home to Tondern. Stabbert had in fact made his entire flight more to the north than he realized. He missed the blacked-out city of Leicester on his way inland, and the "battery" was the town of Loughborough. Here 10 people were killed and 12 injured. *L 20*'s main attack was on Burton-on-Trent, the first of three made that night on the unfortunate town, which was well lighted. The total casualties here were 15 killed and 70 injured, and many houses and two breweries were wrecked or damaged.

Though two of *L 15*'s engines had been out of action for two hours during the crossing of the North Sea, Breithaupt reported having flown all the way to the west coast. At 7:45 p.m. he made out the lights of a big city which he thought was Sheffield, and aimed four 110-pound bombs at the station; the lights went out.

> At 9:30 p.m. the ship was over the west coast; a large city complex, divided in two parts by a broad sheet of water running north and south, joined by a lighted bridge, was recognized as Liverpool and Birkenhead. After dropping a parachute flare, the lights throughout the city mostly went out. From 2,500 meters [8,200 feet] 1,400 kg. [3,100 pounds] of explosive and 300 kg. [660 pounds] of incendiaries were dropped in four crossings of the city, mostly along the waterfront. All explosive bombs burst but fires were not seen to result. On the other hand, the incendiaries worked very well in my opinion; a great proportion seemed to have burst. A huge glow of fire was seen over the city from a great distance.

On the homeward voyage, *L 15*'s magnetic compass proved to be 90 degrees in error, and the rudder man had to steer by the stars. Radio bearings from Bruges proved very inaccurate, and Breithaupt reported, "If the sky had been overcast the failure of the only directional indicator would have been a very serious matter." British observations at the time are impossible to reconcile with the above account: *L 15* was believed responsible for dumping 40 bombs in the fen district north-east of Cambridge and then roaming off into Lincolnshire, but it is more likely that these came from *L 16* during her wanderings over Norfolk. It seems extremely probable that Breithaupt's main attack was the second made that night on Burton-on-Trent.

Last of the nine was Loewe's *L 19*, which remained over England for nine hours and was destined not to return. Just arrived in the North Sea with a new ship, Loewe apparently was determined to go all the way to Liverpool despite recent severe troubles with the HSLu engines. British records show that *L 19* came inland near Sheringham in Norfolk at 7.20 p.m. and at 10:45 made the third attack of the night on Burton-on-Trent. Loewe then headed south for the Birmingham suburbs which *L 21* had already bombed, but his missiles caused no casualties and did only minor damage. British observers then noted *L 19* wandering slowly eastward and not until 6:25 a.m. did she leave the country at Winterton. From *L 19*'s slow progress and varied headings, there can be no doubt that Loewe experienced engine trouble over the enemy's country.

At 3:53 a.m., *L 19* had been heard calling for bearings, and the stations at Bruges and Nordholz located her between King's Lynn and Norwich. At 5:37 Loewe sent his attack report: "At 12 midnight I was over the west coast. Orientation and attack there impossible due to thick fog; dropped incendiaries. 1,600 kg. [3,500 pounds] of bombs on return dropped on several big factories in Sheffield . . ." Nothing more was heard from *L 19* after a bearing at 6:41 a.m. located her near the Haisbrough Lightship, close to the English coast. Three flotillas of destroyers raised steam to search for *L 19*, but while they were leaving port, Nordholz at 4:05 p.m.

*L 19, commissioned by Kapitänleutnant Odo Loewe, experienced numerous problems after her commissioning on Noveber 22, 1915. L 19 did not return from her first raid on England on January 31, 1916, after it ran out of fuel and fell into the North Sea. The British trawler "King Stephen" refused to rescue the survivors and all sixteen of the crew perished. (Moch)*

again heard the airship's Telefunken signals: "Radio equipment at times out of order, three engines out of order. Approximate position Borkum Island. Wind is favorable." Bearings on this signal indicated that *L 19* was farther west than she had believed, 22 miles north of Ameland, and this information was sent to Loewe. The destroyers were recalled.

Nothing more was heard from *L 19*. At midnight the Fleet again sent out searches, but did not find the Zeppelin. All airships were ordered out to look for her, but fog and cross-winds kept them in their sheds. On the morning of February 2, the destroyers picked up one of *L 19*'s fuel tanks twelve miles north of Borkum; it still contained ten gallons of petrol.

On the same day the Fleet Command learned that *L 19* had appeared low over Ameland at 5 p.m. on the afternoon of February 1. Though the Dutch sentries had the impression that she had lost her way and was in difficulties, they opened fire and hit her repeatedly until she vanished in the mist. Undoubtedly *L 19* had been crippled by their gunfire and driven into the North Sea by the rising south wind.

On February 3 the Army radio station in Lille learned that an English trawler had sighted the wreck of a Zeppelin on the water 110 miles east of Flamborough Head. This could only be *L 19*. Detailed newspaper accounts came to hand during the next few days, and the Germans were horrified to learn that the trawler skipper, after speaking *L 19*, had sailed off and left the crew to their fate. By the time he reached port with his story, the airship had gone down. The *King Stephen*'s skipper pleaded that if he had rescued Loewe's crew, they might have overpowered his nine hands and taken the vessel to Germany. But it was not against the trawler's captain that the Germans directed their indignation. The Bishop of London publicly condoned his abandoning the "baby-killers" to drown in the cold North Sea, and for days the German press raged against the prelate, "who has acted less as an apostle of Christian charity than as a jingoistic hatemonger."[2]

Six months later, Loewe's last report arrived at Nordholz in a bottle that had been washed up on the Swedish coast:

> With 15 men on the top platform and backbone girder of the *L 19*, floating without gondolas in approximately 3 degrees east longitude, I am attempting to send a last report. Engine trouble three times repeated, a light head wind on the return journey delayed our return and, in the mist, carried us over Holland where I was received with heavy rifle fire; the ship became heavy and simultaneously three engines failed.
>
> February 2, 1916, towards 1 p.m., will apparently be our last hour.
>
> Loewe.

Although the Germans had lost one airship during this raid, the British defenses could claim no credit for her destruction. The ease with which the Zeppelins had wandered unopposed over the Midlands, twice and thrice bombing undefended towns, demonstrated the inadequacy of the existing defenses, and forced a shakeup that was long overdue. On February 16, 1916, responsibility for the defense of England against air attack reverted from the Admiralty to the War Office. The anti-aircraft batteries were augmented, and the former

2 *Frankfurter Zeitung*, February 9, 1916.

haphazard airplane defense establishment was replaced by an orderly array of squadrons whose sole duty was night-flying and fighting. The first of these had been formed in the Midlands on January 12, 1916, and during the year eleven more were organized in the Midlands, East Anglia, Sussex and Kent. No.39 Squadron, formed on April 15, 1916, to protect the London area, was to do more to end the Zeppelin menace than any other organization defending England. Standard equipment was the Royal Aircraft Factory's 90 h.p. B.E.2c, supposedly best suited for night-flying because it was inherently stable. Carrying only its pilot and fuel, it took nearly an hour to climb to its ceiling of about 13,000 feet. This barely sufficed to get within range of the 1916 model Zeppelins, and when the Germans increased the ceiling of their airships, the air defense system was rendered impotent. At first these airplanes carried small incendiary bombs to be dropped on the airships from above. When incendiary and explosive bullets were perfected in the summer of 1916, a Lewis machine gun firing the new ammunition became their sole armament.

The German Army airship service, not satisfied to limit its raids to the moonless half of the month, had made some trials with *LZ 77* near Cologne in November, 1915, and had concluded that the Zeppelins could not readily be seen from the ground even with a full moon. Pressure apparently was put on Strasser to accept these results. Suspecting that the haze over the big Rhineland industrial city had concealed the airship, he disagreed and, characteristically, preferred to obtain his own information. Two nights after the February full moon, under a clear, starry sky, Peterson flew *L 16* four times across the Hage base at 9,500 feet to 10,500 feet. Despite evasive maneuvers, the Zeppelin was clearly visible from the ground in the bright moonlight. An airplane of the Hage defense flight picked up the Zeppelin on climbing to 6,500 feet and thereafter had it continuously in sight, either as a dark silhouette against the moon, or as a light streak away from it; while the airplane itself could not be seen from the airship even though it fired signal flares. Peterson strongly advised against making raids during the full-moon period, particularly in view of the extreme danger of airplane attack. And within 24 hours, the deductions from the "Cologne Trials" were proven tragically in error. On the evening of February 20, the day before the German Army opened its great assault on Verdun, four Army airships were sent to bomb railroad junctions in the rear of the fortress. *LZ 77*, clearly visible to French gunners in the bright moonlight, took an incendiary shell amidships and crashed in flames at Revigny.

Exasperated with repeated failures of the new HSLu engines, Strasser had persuaded the Admi-

*Army airship LZ 77, seen here taking off at Friedrichshafen, was shot down in flames by French cannon with incendiary ammunition with all crew killed on February 21, 1916.*

ralty Aviation Department to order modifications of all these power plants which were in the hands of the Naval Airship Division. On March 4, 1916, *L 15*, *L 16* and *L 17* in the North Sea, and *L 20* and *L 21* temporarily at Seddin in the Baltic, were taken out of service, their engines were removed and shipped to the Maybach factory in Friedrichshafen, and their machinists' mates were sent along for advanced instruction in the care of their temperamental charges. Until the engines were returned at the end of the month, Strasser had to manage with only *L 11*, *L 13* and *L 14*, while the training ship *L 6* made "school scouting flights" to supplement the watch on the Bight by the older *L 7* and *L 9*.

Yet Strasser not only had ambitious plans for a series of intensive raids at the end of March, when all his ships should again be serviceable, but was looking even farther ahead to the delivery of the first "big six-engine ships," the 2,000,000 cubic foot giants which had been ordered from the Zeppelin Company in July, 1915. On February 11, 1916, he coolly proposed to Admiral Philipp that all these ships be turned over to the Navy, which especially required them because of their greater reliability with six engines, their bigger bomb load and 2,000-foot increase in ceiling. Philipp approved, pointing out that the Navy's airships had to travel farther than the Army's to reach their attack targets, while the air war against England fell mostly on the Navy. Admiral Dick at the Admiralty concurred, but feared the Navy would get nothing in the face of the Army's demands. But Strasser fought the matter through, even preparing a list of the dimensions of all the Army airship hangars in an effort to prove that only a few of them could accommodate the 650-foot "big six-engine ships." Ultimately the Navy got all but two of the new Zeppelins, as compensation for its losses in scouting cruisers at the Battle of Jutland.

Shortly after noon on March 5, three Zeppelins took off to "attack England north, chief target Firth of Forth." Unknown to the German weather service, whose westernmost observatory was at Bruges, a deep depression was fast approaching from Iceland. As the raiders passed Heligoland, the north-north-west wind was rapidly freshening, bringing snow-squalls which battered the airships and covered every exposed surface with a clinging layer of freezing slush. Towards 6 p.m. all the commanders gave up the attack on the Firth of Forth, which they considered they could not reach before 3 a.m., and bore away for the Midlands.

Steering to attack a munitions factory at Middlesbrough in Yorkshire, *Korvettenkapitän* Viktor Schütze in *L 11* was surprised when he made the coast at Tunstall, just north of Spurn Head. He had underestimated the strength of the north wind, which had carried him 70 miles south of his intended landfall. For two hours, plunging through one hail squall after another, Schütze fought to make his way north. Snow accumulated on the gondolas and top platform, ice built up on the cover though the temperature was only 3 degrees above zero F., and in the squalls St. Elmo's Fire blazed from the radio antenna, gondola struts and metal joints in the gangway. At 1 a.m., when the clouds rolled away, Schütze saw that *L 11* had been held to the spot by a north wind of 55 m.p.h. On the snow-covered countryside beneath, landmarks stood out as on a map. To the south, Hull, although well darkened, could be made out, with bombs exploding from another attacking Zeppelin. More snow-clouds then rolled over the target, but an hour later, after dropping fuel to get his ship up to 7,500 feet, Schütze was approaching Hull. The snow-covered houses, streets and docks contrasted sharply with the black water. For twenty minutes, *L 11* hovered over the town, holding herself against the gale with all engines running at flank speed, while the executive officer distributed 3,600 pounds of bombs. Schütze reported that great fires broke out, houses collapsed in a radiating circle around one bomb explosion, leaving a huge black hole on the mantle of snow, and through his binoculars he could see people running about in the glare of the flames. The forward engine stopped, and in the subzero temperature the oil congealed and the radiator water froze. On the way home *L 11* again passed through heavy snow and hail clouds with severe electrical phenomena. One squall carried her uncontrollably up 2,500 feet in two and a half minutes. She was flown down only to have the elevator jam in the up position, and despite sending men forward, she rose again to 10,500 feet before the elevator was repaired. At 5 a.m. the after motor failed, and the ship made the remaining 9-hour homeward flight on two engines.

Though *L 11* did much damage in Hull, it was less than it seemed from the air. The Zeppelin appeared to be hovering over the town at a low height (estimated at 3,000-4,000 feet) and a flash of light was seen through the hatches each time a bomb was released. The first missile, falling in the Humber opposite Earle's shipyard, caused a vessel on the stocks partly to collapse next day. Twenty more bombs destroyed houses, broke water mains, set fire to the Mariners' Almshouse, and to a shed on the docks. No guns or planes defended the town. The helpless population, in ugly mood, relieved its feelings by stoning a Royal Flying Corps vehicle in Hull, and a flying officer was mobbed in nearby Beverley.

*L 14* had made the earlier attack. Böcker had been steering for the Tyne, but likewise was carried south and made the coast north of Flamborough Head. He tried to work to the north to attack Newcastle and Shields, but gave up when he realized that the north wind was blowing at 54 m.p.h. "In the south the Humber showed up in the snowy landscape as a darker streak." At 1 a.m. Böcker began his attack with six bombs that fell in fields near Beverley. Seven explosives and thirteen incendiaries then followed as *L 14* crossed Hull at 9,500 feet. Most of the damage was suffered by houses near the docks. Like Schütze, Böcker had an exaggerated impression of the effect of his bombs. "The most striking result was the collapse of whole blocks of houses in a street running north and south, and these afterwards showed up against the snow as big black patches." The northerly gale drove *L 14* to leeward and prevented her from making a second run over Hull. Böcker reported intense St. Elmo's Fire in hail squalls. He submitted a special report of his "experiences," which included having two engines stop over Hull when water in the petrol (a constant problem in those days) froze at 4 degrees below zero F. and plugged the fuel lines.

Mathy found even more abominable weather, and nearly lost his ship. Half-way across the North Sea *L 13* lost her starboard engine when a crankshaft bearing burned out. From the Dogger Bank the Zeppelin was shrouded in snow squalls driven by a wind at sea level of 31 m.p.h. To compensate for the load of snow on the ship, Mathy dumped 1,300 pounds of fuel. At 8 p.m. he set his course for the Tyne instead of the Forth. For the next three hours the Zeppelin flew on blind in heavy snowclouds. "At 11 p.m. the lights of houses were seen through a hole in the clouds and heavy clouds were seen to the north." Mathy believed this was the coastal city of Sunderland, but like the others he had been driven far south, and came in at North Coates at the mouth of the Humber. An hour later "it became locally clear and fell almost calm. The region in sight for a short time was taken to be the inside of Solway Firth. To the north and east were thick cloud banks, so it was decided to attack the Humber, reckoning with a wind velocity of 10 meters per second from the north." Actually, as Mathy was to find later that night, the wind was blowing at double his estimate of 22 m.p.h. How little he was able to appreciate the strength of the gale is shown by the fact that he was then near Nottingham, a hundred and fifty miles south of his estimated position on the Scottish border.

Shortly after setting a course for the Humber the port engine briefly failed, and Mathy was forced to jettison fifteen of his explosive bombs and all of his thirty incendiaries to save his ship. On to the south-east drove *L 13*, making 53 m.p.h. over the ground. Then, at 2:10 a.m.:

> it became completely clear. *L 13* was over a river mouth which, from the shore contours, was not the Humber, but the Thames. The ship was brilliantly illuminated and very heavily fired on by numerous warships. In the brief interval between sighting and recognizing the region the ship had traveled from the north to the south shore. During the attempt to work to windward for an attack, it was realized that a north wind of about 20 meters per second [44 m.p.h.] was blowing, so that *L 13* could not advance and at 3:30 a.m., after three attempts, the attack here had to be given up.

The rest of the journey was a nightmare. Mathy passed close enough to Dover to identify it, but did not turn aside to attack. He feared he could not recover the distance he would have to go to leeward, and was also concerned about early-morning encounters with the Royal Naval Air Service. At 4 a.m. a radio directional "fix" placed *L 13* twenty miles north-east of Calais.[3] Considering the tempest and the permanent loss of one engine, Mathy decided to run before the wind to Namur. Still battling squalls, *L 13* crossed the Belgian coast at Ostend at 5:15 a.m., and went on under the cloud base at 300 feet. Presently the port engine packed up for good with a broken crankshaft. On two motors *L 13* made it to Namur at 8:50 a.m.

What happened next must have made Strasser wonder if the older Maybach C-X engines were any more reliable than the much-abused HSLus. After fueling, gassing up and possibly obtaining a little rest, Mathy and his men, still with two motors dead, took off at 1:50 p.m. for Hage. Two hours later a crank-bearing failed, putting the after engine out of action, and with the forward motor only, *L 13* crawled back to Namur. Substitute power plants were shipped by rail from Hage. On March 10, in a nine-hour flight, Mathy made it back to his base although the starboard engine failed at the take-off with a broken oil pump.

The moon would be new on April 2, and with his newer ships once more combat-worthy, Strasser planned and executed a series of attacks unparalleled throughout the war for persistence and determination. For nearly a week the Zeppelins took off every day to bomb England, covering the country from Edinburgh in the north to London in the south. The unprecedented scale of the great battle in progress at Verdun had inspired the Navy to match the sacrifices of the German Army. Unfortunately the results did not equal the intensity of the effort, and the strengthened London defenses were responsible for a painful loss.

Towards noon on March 31, seven Zeppelins took off with orders to "attack in the south, main target London." Aware at last of the effectiveness of British radio intelligence, Strasser forbade sending the usual take-off messages "in order not to alert the enemy to their approach." Two of the Zeppelins turned back off the Dutch islands. One of them, *L 9*, had a fantastic, near-fatal accident off Vlieland at 6:30 p.m. A bracing wire of the forward engine gondola carried away at its lower end and streamed into the propeller. With the engine still running, the wire wound around the propeller shaft, pulling the gondola bodily upward against the hull. Before it shattered, the 17-foot propeller slashed into the gangway overhead, severing the girders of Ring 11, the longitudinal girders, the cat-walk, both armored cables supplying power to the radio, and the control wires for the elevators and water ballast sacks. A broken piece of the propeller was flung clear through Cell 11, making a large hole. Suddenly bow-heavy from the loss of gas, *L 9* nearly dived into the sea from her altitude of 4,300 feet, and was checked only by stopping all engines and dropping all ballast forward. Emergency steering controls were connected up in the rear gondola, men were sent aft to bring her to an even keel, and *L 9* limped home, landing at Hage at 8:55 p.m. Her extensive repairs lasted until April 10.

Mathy in *L 13* found a temperature of 37.5 degrees F. at 6,700 feet – too warm to reach a safe altitude over London with his heavy load of 5,300 pounds of bombs. He decided first to drop part of his cargo on the New Explosive Works at Stowmarket. At 9:45 he was over the town and dropped a flare, but failed to locate the factory. He did arouse a battery of anti-aircraft guns, to which he replied with bombs. Mathy actually was over the factory, but his bombs merely broke window glass. After a sweep to the west, he again returned to look for the Explosive Works, and was fired on once more. The gunners thought they scored a hit. This was confirmed on the following morning when a German Navy message blank was found nearby. On it was scribbled:

> Commander-in-Chief High Seas Fleet, 10 p.m. Have attacked and hit a battery at Stowmarket with 12 bombs. Am hit, have turned back, hope to land in Hage towards 4 a.m. *L 13*.[4]

---

3 Strasser complained bitterly that German overseas news service broadcasts from the Norddeich radio station greatly interfered with radio bearings on this night.

4 In *L 13*'s War Diary this message is logged as having been sent.

*Heinrich Mathy's old ship L 13 at Hage, and now a training ship, April 28, 1917. It was dismantled there beginning December 11, 1917. (Kriegsmarinesammlung)*

Cell 10 amidships had been pierced and half its contents had escaped before *L 13*'s crew realized what had happened. Cell 16 in the nose was also holed. Mathy at once gave up the attack on London. Dropping the rest of his bombs as he crossed the coast north of Lowestoft, he sped home at 69 m.p.h. Due to great efforts by her crew, "whose conduct," Mathy generously reported "deserves special recognition for their success in closing the shot-hole," *L 13* made it safely back to Hage at 3:30 a.m.

Flying at 7,200 feet, Breithaupt came in with Mathy and set a course for London by way of Ipswich and Chelmsford. In spite of dropping all ballast, he could not get his ship up to a safe attack altitude. At 10:30, *L 15* was north-east of London, flying dynamically at 8,500 feet. The capital was well darkened, but the Thames was clearly visible. Fifteen minutes later, guns and searchlights near Dartford opened up on the lone raider, and the first salvo made a direct hit amidships. Swerving north to avoid the defenses, Breithaupt released fifteen explosive bombs to lighten the ship.

The airplanes now took a hand. Second Lieutenant A. de B. Brandon had been pursuing *L 15* for the past hour, and just as the searchlights lost the airship, he succeeded in getting above her and dropped a box full of explosive darts. The machine-gunners on the Zeppelin's top platform replied with spirit. Brandon was not to be discouraged:

I continued and circled in front of the Zeppelin, and turned round to get in its rear, and on going past there was a tremendous amount of machine-gun firing going on. At this point I switched off my lights, and continued in my direction for 2 or 3 hundred yards, and then turned and got in a direct line with the Zeppelin. I was then about 500 feet above it; I closed the throttle and volplaned towards the Zeppelin; the nose of my machine was pointed about quarter way from the rear. I then got out an incendiary bomb, and in trying to get it into the tube I had to take my eyes off the Zeppelin, and on looking up again I was astonished to find that in a very few seconds I would have passed the Zeppelin, so I quickly placed the incendiary bomb in my lap, and let off No.2 and No.3 lots of darts. I did not hear any report from this. I concluded that the Zeppelin was, in reality, coming towards me, so I opened up the engine again and turned completely round, and followed a southerly course, continuing for some considerable time, as I thought the Zeppelin had got a good start. In the meantime I turned on my lights again and I was at 8,000 feet; I cruised around at 8,000 feet for some time and saw nothing, and then dropped to 6,000 feet and cruised around for some considerable time without also seeing any sign of the Zeppelin.[5]

5 Brandon's report in Imperial War Museum file, "Pilots' Reports Relating to Destruction of Zeppelins."

*The broken wreck of the L 15 sinking off Westgate on the morning of April 2, 1916. (Illustrated London News)*

Breithaupt was finally alone in the darkness with his badly injured craft. Cell 11 amidships was already entirely empty. Cell 12 forward and Cell 9 aft were badly damaged and leaking, Cell 16 in the bow was almost entirely empty, and the ship was very nose heavy. Breithaupt's only chance was to reach Belgium. Meanwhile he jettisoned the rest of his bombs, all but four hours' fuel (later most of this too was dumped), the heavy Maxim machine guns, motor covers and spare parts. The secret documents, bound up with wire inside the radio room stool, tumbled into the Thames. Yet *L 15* gradually fell. When he saw he could not reach Belgium, Breithaupt radioed, "need immediate assistance between River Thames and Ostend." Then the wireless set went out of the window. At 12:15 a.m., with the Zeppelin down to 500 feet, the overloaded hull framework buckled in two places, at Rings 7 and 11, and the ship plunged into the sea a mile from the Kentish Knock Lightship.

Presently six armed trawlers loomed up in the darkness. Voices shouted, "Go to hell!" and one opened fire, but ceased after a few rounds with the arrival of the destroyer *Vulture*. Her captain picked up the 17 survivors, but not before demanding that they strip naked and embark not more than three in a boat. Two petty officers slashed every gas cell before leaving her, but had no other means of completing *L 15*'s destruction. Other destroyers took the airship in tow, but the hull framework gradually broke up and next morning *L 15* sank off Westgate. *Vulture* landed her prisoners at Chatham They were placed in individual cells at the naval barracks, and Breithaupt still remembers receiving the British Press in a state of nature. After a protest, he received his water-soaked uniform, and after further protests, his decorations and buttons which had been appropriated as souvenirs. There followed a series of interrogations by Major Trench, R.M., the head of the German section in Admiral Hall's Naval Intelligence Division. Having been imprisoned in Germany for two and a half years on a charge of espionage, Trench combined a fluent command of the language with a thorough dislike of everyone who spoke it. On April 6 the officers were sent to Donnington Hall. *L 15*'s executive officer, repatriated after a year and a half on condition that he would not participate in combat operations, spent the rest of the war on Strasser's staff.

*Kapitänleutnant Joachim Breithaupt in an English prison camp shortly after his capture in the L 15.*

Breithaupt did not return to the Fatherland until after the Armistice.

Both *L 14*, with Strasser on board, and *L 16* claimed to have reached London, but Böcker's main attack was on Thameshaven, twenty-two miles down-river from the capital, while Peterson's "London-Hornsea" bombs fell north of Brentwood. Martin Dietrich in *L 22*, delayed by strong head winds and engine trouble, steered for the Humber and claimed to have found Grimsby. His bombs landed a few miles away, and one, striking a chapel at Cleethorpes, killed twenty-nine soldiers of the Manchester Regiment and wounded fifty-three.

Daily for the next five days, Strasser sent out his Zeppelins against England, with varying success. On the night of April 2, *L 14* was the first to reach the Scottish capital. Despite his knowledge of the area from peace-time visits in the merchant service, Böcker was unable to find the Forth Bridge or Rosyth Dockyard, and dropped his 4,200 pounds of bombs on Leith and Edinburgh. In Leith, Messrs. Innes and Grieve's whisky warehouse was burned with its contents to the tune Of £44,000, and in Edinburgh many houses were struck and three hotels and Princes Street Station were damaged. But on April 4, the four ships sent out were recalled because of strong north-west winds. Fog over Nordholz obliged *L 22* to land at Düren in the Rhineland, and *L 14*, diverted to Hanover, was forced by thunderstorms there to fly 190 miles farther to Dresden.

On the night of April 6 the weather broke with an easterly gale, and the raiding airships were laid up for maintenance and engine overhaul. Never again did the Zeppelins attack England so persistently. The crews looked back on this week as a highwater mark in their flying careers. A year later the executive officer of *L 17* mourned for "the great days of 1916, when we took off to raid three times in five days, when we came home one day at 8 in the morning and at 2 took off again for England."[6] Eighty-four of the enemy population were killed and 227 injured, and £126,095 worth of damage was done – a third of this being attributable to the burning of the whisky warehouse in Leith. Yet the Naval Staff, on the basis of agents' reports, held the most exaggerated beliefs concerning the destruction wrought by these attacks, and on April 11, 1916, reported to the Kaiser concerning the March 31-April 1 raid:

> At Grimsby, in addition to the post office and several other houses, a battleship in the roadstead was heavily damaged by a bomb, and had to be beached. At Kensington an airplane hangar was wrecked, near Tower Bridge a transport ship damaged, in Great Tower Street a factory wrecked, and north of the Tower a bomb fell in George Street only 100 meters away from two anti-aircraft guns. It was reported that a big fire had broken out at West India Docks, and that at Tilbury Docks a munitions boat exploded (400 killed). Specially serious explosions occurred at the Surrey Commercial Docks and at a factory, close to the Lower Road, at which shells were filled with explosives. A railroad train already loaded with these shells was stated to be completely wrecked.

Not a word of this was true, but the fact that it was believed, not only by the deluded populace, but also by the Supreme War Lord and his responsible advisers, underlines the role of wishful thinking in determining national policy. More blood and treasure would be squandered before the German Navy abandoned its dreams of using the Zeppelins to blast and burn England into submission.

---

6 *Oberleutnant zur See* Dietsch, "Ein Luftschiffleben," *Zwei deutsche Luftschiffhäfen des Weltkrieges*, Ahlhorn u. Wildeshausen, ed. Dr. Fritz Strahlmann (Oldenburg: Oldenburger Verlagshaus Lindenallee, 1926), p. 85.

# CHAPTER XI

# THE BATTLE OF JUTLAND

During the spring of 1916 the airships were increasingly reserved for purely naval operations as the High Seas Fleet's activity worked up to the crescendo of the Battle of Jutland. The U-boats were also attached to the Fleet, as the Kaiser on March 6 had decided against unrestricted warfare against merchant shipping. From April 13 to 19, Scheer, warned by his Intelligence of an impending British attack on Tondern, had the High Seas Fleet standing by at "heightened readiness."

*L 22*, one of four ships out scouting on April 17, suffered very serious damage while being brought into the "Toska" shed at Tondern. Turning back early because of a rising south wind, Martin Dietrich landed at 11:40 a.m. "From 2 to 5 p.m. attempted to bring the ship in, but failed due to heavy gusts. As the wind dropped towards evening, attempted to bring her into the shed towards 11:30 p.m., wind 3 1/2-5 meters per second (8-11 miles per hour) at this time. As the ship was brought in, the port trolley broke, the ship struck with the port side of the bow against the shed door and was heavily damaged." The bow was smashed for 160 feet back from the nose. A work gang from Friedrichshafen came to Tondern to build on a new bow, and did not complete their task until May 24. Dietrich had been extraordinarily lucky. Eight months later, in a similar accident in the same hangar, *L 24* caught fire and destroyed her shed-mate, *L 17*. Still living in Hamburg, Dietrich recalls, "during three years of flying airships at the Front, I had every possible kind of experience except death."

On Easter Sunday, April 24, a rebellion broke out in Ireland. The German government endeavored to support the revolt by sending thousands of captured Russian rifles, and dispatched the renegade Irish leader, Sir Roger Casement, to Tralee Bay in a submarine. As a diversion, Scheer planned to bombard the seaport of Lowestoft. Late in the morning of the 24th the German battle cruisers, constituting

*OPPOSITE:*
*Kapitänleutnant Martin Dietrich.*

*Kapitänleutnant Martin Dietrich.*

the bombardment force, sailed from the Jade, followed by the dreadnought squadrons. From Tondern came *L 7* to escort the battle cruisers out of the German Bight. At 3:48 p.m. the flagship *Seydlitz* struck a mine. At first her people believed she had been torpedoed, but *Kapitänleutnant* Karl Hempel, flying low overhead, saw no torpedo track and was sure he could have seen a submarine, if present, in the clear water. *Seydlitz* remained afloat and Hempel escorted her back towards Wilhelmshaven. At 7:48 p.m., being low on fuel, *L 7* headed for Hage, where she landed ten minutes after midnight.

Independently of the Fleet operation, Strasser, flying in *L 21*, led eight Zeppelins on the afternoon of the 24th to "attack England south, London if at all possible." As they approached the Norfolk coast, the airships found a strong south-south-west wind blowing, and soon gave up the attack on London. They had little success in searching for worth-while objectives in East Anglia, for the whole region was hidden by mist and deep rain clouds. Anti-aircraft guns were everywhere and opened fire at every opportunity. Shell splinters struck the forward gondola of *L 13*, but did no damage. Many of the ships carried their bombs home with them. Wishful thinking resulted in three claimed attacks on Norwich and one on Cambridge; in fact, five houses were wrecked at Newmarket, and the only fatal casualty occurred when one of the raiders unloaded 45 bombs on the village of Dilham and a woman died of fright.

At 3:30 a.m., as the last Zeppelin went out to sea off the Norfolk coast, the four remaining German battle cruisers were still 65 miles east of Lowestoft. Ahead of them was a screen of light cruisers and destroyers, while the entire High Seas Fleet was in support 70 miles to the rear. Strasser had been previously ordered to send up the older airships to scout with the Fleet. At 9:55 p.m. the evening before, *L 9* had left Hage and by dawn of the 25th was in her station between the battle cruisers and the High Seas Fleet. At 12:15 a.m. the school ship *L 6*, with a crew in advanced training, left Nordholz to cover the northern flank of the German advance, but she was carried far north by the south-south-west wind and lost touch with the fleet. *L 7*, which had landed at Hage at 12:10 a.m., had been hastily fuelled, gassed and ballasted, and at 3:30 a.m. took off to overtake the Fleet. One can imagine the fatigued state of her crew, who had been in the air since 11:40 a.m. the previous day.

Shortly after 5 a.m. *Lützow, Derfflinger, Moltke* and *von der Tann* appeared off Lowestoft and shelled the town for six minutes. Going on north, they threw a few rounds into Great Yarmouth, and then turned for home. During the bombardment they were shadowed by Commodore Tyrwhitt, who had come up from Harwich with three light cruisers, two flotilla leaders and 16 destroyers. At 5:10 a.m. *L 9* sighted this force, and at 5:35 reported it as "8 enemy ships and destroyers running north at high speed."

A few minutes later *L 9*, which was flying at only 2,600 feet, was jumped by two enemy aircraft "from a great altitude." *Hauptmann* August Stelling logged them as seaplanes, but they were B.E.2c airplanes whose pilots, Flight Commander Nicholl and Flight Lieutenant Hards, had taken off nearly an hour before from Great Yarmouth after sighting the Zeppelin out at sea. Taken by surprise, Stelling

*L 22 at Nordholz. Note the "bluff cannon" on top platform that was intended to scare off enemy aircraft. (Kameradschaft)*

was unable to use his superior climbing ability to escape, and ran before the wind, while his executive officer clambered up to the top platform to warn the control car via speaking tube to change course whenever the British planes made bombing runs. In the face of machine-gun fire from the platform, both planes pressed home their attack and managed to get over the Zeppelin and drop bombs, which missed due to her evasive maneuvers. So close did they come that in later years Nicholl declared he would be able to recognize the German officer who, from the platform, coolly scrutinized him and his plane through binoculars. Had the Britishers carried machine-guns with incendiary ammunition, *L 9* would surely have been destroyed.

In the early afternoon of May 2, eight airships departed from Hage, Nordholz and Tondern to attack "England north, chief target Rosyth, Forth Bridge, English fleet." At first, with a following wind, the airships sped along at 50 knots. Later, as they climbed to higher altitudes for the attack on the Forth, they met freshening south winds. Further reports from Bruges indicated the approach of a new low-pressure area from over England. Except for *L 14* and *L 20*, all the raiders bore away for the Midlands.

The attack there miscarried, due to a curious accident. *L 23*, the first ship inland, dropped an incendiary bomb on Danby High Moor, and set fire to the heather. Some twenty-five minutes behind her came *L 16*. By this time the moor was well ablaze, and Peterson, attracted by the illumination, dumped most of his cargo on the blazing heath. He reported seeing the Stockton area all lit up, and as he headed to attack, another ship bombed the city. Peterson, following, reported "well-placed hits on buildings at the site of the fire, as well as clearly recognizable railroad tracks and embankments." *L 17*, after an attack on Skinningrove, dropped the

*L 22 in the "Toska" hangar, Tondern. While walking the ship out, a violent gust broke the port forward tackle and the door smashed the nose of the ship. Remarkably there was no fire. Note the top machine gun platform which is rarely seen. A Zeppelin Company crew built a new bow for the L 22 in seven days. (Moch)*

rest of her bombs on "a coastal city to the east, apparently Saltburn." At this time she was above Danby High Moor. *L 13* may also have added some bombs to the burning heath. If the reader finds it hard to understand why three airships should have wasted their bombs on a heath fire, it should be understood that all the East Coast towns were darkened, and heavy snow-clouds and driving wind made navigation and observation very difficult on this night.

Of the Zeppelins which held on for Scotland, *L 14* ran into heavy rain squalls mixed with snow, and icing up rapidly, stalled and fell from 9,000 to 6,000 feet. As the snow ceased, Böcker aimed five bombs at "two big warships underneath" and optimistically assumed they had been sunk. At 1:15 a.m. Böcker plotted his position over Edinburgh by dead reckoning, but was frustrated by more snow clouds. He finally went home without dropping any more bombs. In fact, he had been over the wrong estuary, the Firth of Tay, north of the Forth, and his bombs had fallen in a field near Arbroath.

Stabbert on *L 20* had kept more to the north, as he had intended to steer for the Firth of Forth Bridge by way of Dundee. At 7 p.m. he had dropped a water-flare and had taken bearings, and at that time had found the wind still blowing from the east. Comparing a radio bearing received at 10:21 p.m. with another two hours earlier seemed to show that meanwhile a brisk northwest wind had sprung up. After 10:45, however, the Zeppelin was flying over a solid layer of cloud, and Stabbert could not estimate his position or drift from the surface below. At 11:20 p.m. *L 20* plunged into heavy rain and snow squalls, and the outer cover began to ice up fast. Stabbert had to drop ballast and finally slipped fuel tanks. At midnight the Zeppelin was groping blindly through dense fog. Stabbert continued on to the west, believing that his progress was being retarded by a north-west wind. He was now completely dependent on his radio for a knowledge of his position, but when it was most needed, Stabbert found that the weak signals emanating from the ice-coated antenna would not reach Germany. At 1 a.m. the snow-clouds rolled away, and Stabbert was dismayed to find that a south-east wind had carried him to Loch Ness, far up in the Scottish Highlands. He at once turned about, hoping to reach the coast before dawn. On the way he saw lights, which he believed indicated a mine pit-head, and he dropped seventeen bombs. Stabbert was far north of the limit of the blacked-out area, and the occupants of Craig Castle naturally did not anticipate a Zeppelin raid in the barren Highlands. Windows and roof were damaged by bombs exploding within 40 feet of the building.

*L 20 stationed at Tondern. During a raid on May 3, 1916, radio bearings were weak, the C.O. did not know he was over the Scottish Highlands. Later crossing the North Sea and running short on fuel, L 20 crash-landed in Norway (see photo opposite below). Six of the crew were repatriated, and ten were interned. (Moch)*

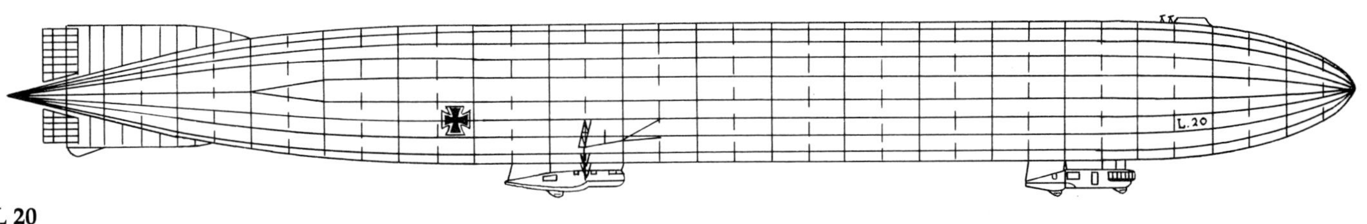


**L 20**

| | | | |
|---|---|---|---|
| Gas capacity | 1,264,400 ft.$^3$ | Engines | 4 Maybach HSLu, of 240 h.p. |
| Length | 585.5 ft. | Propellers | 4 Lorenzen |
| Diameter | 61.35 ft. | Weight empty | 52,500 lbs. |
| Useful lift | 39,250 lbs. | Maximum speed | 62 mph |
| Gas cells | 18 | Ceiling | 11,500 ft. |
| Crew | 18 | Full speed endurance | 3000 miles |

At 4 a.m. *L 20* reached the coast, not at the Firth of Firth, as Stabbert fondly believed, but at Peterhead, 100 miles to the north. At 6 a.m. he regained radio contact with Nordholz, obtained bearings, and found he was in the latitude of the Orkney Islands. Stabbert urgently requested assistance and more bearings, but was told to "wait." At seven he met the steamer *Holland*, descended to 60 feet to shout an inquiry concerning his position, and learned he was in 58 degrees north, 3 degrees east. As Stabbert pricked out the spot on his North Sea chart, the full hopelessness of his position came home to him. No matter how he figured or economized, he could not reach Germany with the fuel on board. At 7:49 he radioed, "require immediate assistance as I cannot reach my base," and was advised that cruisers and destroyers would steam to his aid off Denmark. An hour later, as he found the south-south-east wind freshening to 40 miles per hour, there came further disillusionment: he would now require ten hours to reach the northern tip of Denmark, but only five hours' fuel remained on board, while the surface craft could not reach Hanstholm until 7 p.m. He was further influenced to steer for Norway because his warrant machinist advised that the two side engines would not run much longer.

At 11 a.m. *L 20* was over the Norwegian coast south of Stavanger, with two hours' fuel on board. The secret documents had been weighted and

*L 20 crash landing, Norway, May 3, 1916. Three L 20 crewmen: (left to right) Ob.Masch. Maat Schknecht; Ob.F.T. Maat Hans Peters, radio man; and Ob.hzr. Noll, engine mechanic. All three were interned. (Moch)*

dropped in deep water, and the radio set smashed. In the fierce down-drafts spilling off the mountains the Zeppelin was almost uncontrollable, and Stabbert did not dare land on the beach. With two non-swimmers in the control car, the ship over 2 tons heavy, and the crew prepared to open the manoeuvreing valves and climb out of the windows when she struck, Stabbert brought his ship down on a fjord. *L 20* landed hard, struts of the forward engine gondola shattered, and as it dangled by a few wires, the machinist's mate leaped through the communicating door to the control car. A sea anchor was put out, but failed to hold the ship's head to the wind, and as she drifted towards a 150-foot cliff, eight men, including the commander and executive officer, leaped into the water. With the elevator man, Wilhelm Tinchon, left alone in charge of the control car, the ship rose and drifted over a tongue of land. The after gondola was torn off on a pinnacle, and Tinchon and four other men jumped or were spilled out on Norwegian soil. *L 20*, with her back broken, drifted off with three men still in the gangway. These slashed the gas cells and finally the wreck fell in the sea. Because they had been rescued by civilian fishing vessels, six of the crew, including the executive officer, were promptly repatriated as "shipwrecked mariners." Stabbert and the others were interned. Seven months later, after several attempts, Stabbert escaped and reached Germany.

The fate of some other airships remained for a time in doubt. Towering thunderstorms and lashing squalls of rain and hail blocked their homeward path over the North Sea. St. Elmo's Fire burned from all metal points, snow piled up on the outer covers, and ice, falling from the hull, was hurled by the propellers into the gas bags. In *L 17*, which, due to a broken winch, was unable to wind in her antenna in a hail squall, long sparks crackled from the antenna to the hull, lightning jumped from the control car to the top platform, and static electricity flickered on the fur collars of the lookouts. *L 23*, with her side engines running at only two-thirds power, fell towards the sea under a load of drenching rain and was saved only by dropping the last

*Above left: Norwegian soldiers inspecting the remains of L 20s after gondola, which was torn off before her final landing in the Hafs Fjord in Norway. Above right: Sight-seers viewing the broken hull of the L 20. (both - Illustrated London News)*

two "breeches" of water, machine guns, ammunition, and empty ballast sacks and fuel tanks. In *L 11*, Cell 6, over the after gondola, was riddled by ice particles thrown into it by the side propellers, and ran 70% empty. The stern-heavy ship was trimmed by shifting bombs and crewmen to the mooring point in the nose, and dismantling the after engine and carrying the parts to the crew room in the control car. In *L 14*, Cell 6 ran 90% empty, and Cell 7, 40% empty despite attempts to patch them. *L 21*, with Cell 7 leaking and a heavy load of snow, radioed for help, but was saved when the snow stopped and later melted in the morning sun. She was 2 tons heavy at landing and spent ten days repairing the resulting damage.

These experiences made Strasser aware for the first time of the dangers of "icing," in that particles of ice falling from the hull might be thrown into the gas bags. Subsequently, "ice shields" were fitted inside the outer cover above the propellers, but these, being made only of heavy canvas backed by light girders or wires, were themselves frequently riddled.

Strasser assured Scheer that "as a result of the extensive destruction of factories, etc., this attack must be considered as fully successful, despite the loss of *L 20*." British figures show that 9 were killed, 30 injured, and that £12,030 worth of damage was done in exchange for the loss of an airship that cost about £72,916.

While the airships were coming home from England on the morning of May 3, the seaplane carriers *Engadine* and *Vindex*, escorted by light cruisers and destroyers of the Grand Fleet, sailed to attack the airship base at Tondern. The purpose of the operation was to decoy the German High Seas Fleet out of Wilhelmshaven and under the guns of the Grand Fleet. At dawn on May 4 the carriers were off Sylt. With their usual bad luck, eight of the Sopwith "Baby" seaplanes failed to get off the water. The ninth flew into the radio antenna Or a destroyer and was lost with its pilot, and the tenth turned back soon after take-off with engine trouble. The eleventh and last seaplane was spotted coming on over Tostlund at a great altitude, and at Tondern the anti-aircraft crews stood to their guns and the local defence pilots took off. They did not find the enemy; the British seaplane had turned back, dropped one bomb on Danish soil, and returned to the carrier.

Meanwhile, the German Fleet had been alarmed. At 8:50 a.m., *L 7* left Tondern to scout towards Horns Reef, and at 8:35 a.m., *L 9* took off from Hage. Stelling cruised north from Terschelling towards Horns Reef, but sighted nothing and turned back during the morning.

At 9:58 a.m. *Kapitänleutnant* Hempel, in *L 7*, radioed that he was 16 miles off Sylt and proceeding towards Horns Reef. At 10:39, *L 7* obtained a bearing which placed her 20 miles south-south-west of the Horns Reef Lightship, but transmitted no further messages. Strasser considered that her radio was out of order and that she would return to Tondern about 2 p.m. When she did not appear, Strasser reported her as overdue to the Fleet Command. Seaplanes found no sign of the missing Zeppelin.

*L 14*, repaired after her recent adventures over England, took off from Nordholz at 4:20 p.m. to join in the hunt. At 7:23 p.m. she reported from the Horns Reef Lightship, "Nothing seen, very misty, visibility three miles, moderate east wind, course north-north-west." At 8 p.m. she started back for her base. Fifty-five minutes later *L 14* came within an ace of crashing into the sea: the elevators, put down to parry an updraft, jammed in this position, and only by instantly stopping all engines, dropping two "breeches" of water ballast forward, and sending men aft, was the Zeppelin checked in her dive a bare 250 feet above the water. The upper control cable of the starboard elevator had broken, and the lower one had jumped off its sheave and jammed. Men were sent out on the fins, the two horizontal control surfaces were disconnected, the starboard elevator was lashed in neutral position, and with only the port one functioning, *L 14* limped off to Tondern, where she made an emergency landing at 5:20 a.m. the next morning.

Weeks later the Germans learned what had happened to *L 7*. At 11:30 a.m. she had come in sight of H.M.S. *Galatea* and *Phaeton*, covering the seaplane carriers. The light cruisers opened fire and chased the airship for half an hour, but *L 7*, though at a low altitude, contrived to keep at a safe distance.

*L 7 probably at Tondern in the "Toni" shed. L 7 was shot down while scouting off shore over Horns Reef by the British cruisers "Galatea" and "Phaeton." Casualties were eleven dead, and seven survivors. Below: L 7 at Nordholz.*

*Above: L-7 as she landed afire on the sea. Right: The last of the L 7. Both photos were taken by the English submarine E. 31. ( both - Illustrated London News)*

The warships had already turned back when they saw the Zeppelin stand on her nose and plunge blazing into the sea. One of the last shells had got home in a fuel tank and started a fire that quickly enveloped the whole airship. The cruisers dared not close the spot because of the danger from U-boats, but a British submarine, E. 31, surfaced nearby and rescued seven survivors. Though the British hoped to be reported off Horns Reef, *L 7* did not send a contact report before her destruction. Thus the High Seas Fleet did not sortie until late in the evening, long after the British had started back for their bases.

During the rest of May the weather was unfavorable for airship operations, with prolonged spells of south-west winds. After May 23, Admiral Scheer ordered the airships to be held for a fleet operation against Sunderland. The bombardment of the English coastal town was intended to draw out portions of the British fleet which the Germans might smash up in detail, and after May 23 a force of 15 U-boats was stationed off Cromarty, Rosyth and Scapa.

Scheer had two alternate plans for the operation, the second to deal with the possibility that airship scouting could not be carried out:

> For the advance to the north-west [i.e. Sunderland] extensive airship reconnaissance was indispensable, since this would lead us into a sea area in which we must not allow ourselves to be brought to action against our will . . . For the operation to the north, for which the Jutland coast to the east offered a certain protection against enemy surprise, and further considering the great distance from the enemy's bases, this danger was less. Airship reconnaissance here was indeed desirable, but not absolutely necessary . . . Unfortunately, the weather was unfavorable for the scheme. The Fleet waited in vain from May 23 to May 30 for a day suitable for air reconnaissance.
>
> Since on May 30 a change in the weather did not seem likely, I decided, because the submarines could no longer be left in their attack positions, to give up the operation to the north-west and to carry out the operation to the north without airship scouting if the occasion required it.

Thus, it should be emphasized, the Naval Airship Division, by its inability to cover the High Seas Fleet in the western part of the North Sea, determined in a negative way the place as well as the time of the Battle of Jutland. Scheer's further orders to his battle cruisers to "carry on cruiser warfare before and inside the Skagerrak and beyond to the Norwegian coast" have, as Corbett remarks, "a pleasant old-world flavor of the days before directional wireless."[1] The British Admiralty knew that something was afoot, and before midnight on May 30 the Grand Fleet and the Battle Cruiser Fleet were

1 Corbett, III, p. 323.

*L 24 of the "p" class falsely reported part of the British Grand Fleet the day after the Battle of Jutland. (Moch)*

at sea. Scheer did not sail until the early morning of May 31.

Continuously changing his plans in accordance with the weather, Strasser on the evening of May 30 had issued orders for five Zeppelins to take off between 3 and 9 a.m. next day to cover the Fleet in its advance up the Jutland coast. Reading Strasser's operational order, it is apparent that Scheer had made a clean break with von Pohl's doctrine of confining the airships to close tactical missions. At last they were to be flung boldly out into the distant reaches of the North Sea for the strategic reconnaissance for which they were so pre-eminently suited by virtue of their great range, endurance, mobility, and powerful radio equipment. From the southern tip of Norway in an irregular semicircle extending to a point half-way between the West Frisian island of Texel and Cromer on the Norfolk coast, five Zeppelins were to patrol between assigned stations. The most distant was 325 sea miles from Nordholz, and in the south, one position was only 55 miles from the English coast.

*Landing L 24 at Tondern. The ground crew pulls her down by the car rail. Note the porcelain insulator for the radio wire. Kapitänleutnant Robert Koch is in the window.*

Yet on the morning of May 31 the weather was once again too uncertain for the Zeppelins to leave their hangars, and not until early afternoon did they get into the air and start for their distant patrol sectors. Since *L 11* and *L 17* could not leave their fixed sheds due to cross-winds, *L 21* and *L 23* in the revolving hangar in Nordholz took their places ("great military usefulness of the revolving shed!!!" wrote Strasser). Soon after taking off they found misty weather and a low cloud ceiling at 1,000 feet. At 3:30 p.m. the airships still were not far from the German coast.

This was the hour at which the German battle cruisers collided with their British opposite numbers off the Danish coast, and the Battle of Jutland was on. All through the afternoon they hammered at each other, and the British lost the *Indefatigable* and *Queen Mary*. The German and British battle fleets met briefly at dusk, and for a time it seemed that Scheer might be cut off from his base and brought to action next morning. During the night, however, he smashed his way through the British destroyer flotillas across his path, and by the early morning of June 1 his battered ships had a clear passage to Wilhelmshaven.

Of the fighting on May 31 the airships saw nothing. *L 14* and *L 23*, nearest to the battle, were handicapped by poor visibility. *Kapitänleutnant* Otto von Schubert in *L 23*, while still over the German Bight, logged at 3 p.m., "visibility one-half mile, wind 3-4 doms (13 1/2-18 miles per hour), overcast, top of clouds 750 meters (2500 feet)." At 5 p.m., receiving radio reports of the action, he steered to cover the German battle cruisers from the north and east, but did not find them. *L 14* also found nothing in very misty weather with visibility of three miles, though she and *L 23* were in sight of each other above the clouds at 6:10 p.m. *L 21*, to the west of the battle, remained over the Dogger Bank as her commander knew that *L 9*, scouting the next sector to the west, had had to turn back at 4:28 p.m. when her starboard propeller sheared off. *L 16* remained on her station off the Dutch coast.

At 10:06 p.m. Scheer radioed to Strasser, "early reconnaissance at Horns Reef urgently needed." As Frost observes, "that was an exceedingly dangerous message to send, because if the British could decipher it, his intentions would be revealed."[2] Admiral Hall's radio intelligence section did in fact intercept and decipher this message, but it was not forwarded to the British Commander-in-Chief because "the officer who received the air reconnaissance signal from Room 40 had had very little experience of German operational signals and German naval procedure, and was not aware of the significance of this signal."[3] And lastly, Strasser, to whom it was addressed, never received it, "apparently due to English jamming."

None the less, while the first group of Zeppelins was returning to Nordholz and Hage during the night of May 31-June 1, *L 11*, *L 13*, *L 17*, *L 22* and *L 24* were taking off with orders to proceed to the same patrol stations assigned on the previous day. Visibility was slightly better, and the two airships proceeding north saw some of the confused night fighting going on far below. *Kapitänleutnant* Robert Koch in *L 24*, flying under the cloud base so that he could rise into the overcast if surprised by enemy warships, noted gunfire to the north-east at 1:06 a.m. when at the Horns Reef lightship. He steered for it, but when it ceased he went on towards the Norwegian coast. Martin Dietrich in *L 22* still remembers the gunfire and searchlights marking the desperate night action between the British destroyers and the German dreadnoughts, and the gigantic flash of fire on the port bow at 3:10 a.m. – the exact moment at which the old battleship Pommern was struck by a British torpedo and vanished with all hands in a violent explosion.

*L 24*, going on north, soon began sending in a stream of enemy contact reports. At 2:38 a.m., 50 miles west of Bovbjerg:

> at dawn the ship was attacked by numerous torpedo-boats and U-boats. Own altitude 1,500 meters (5,000 feet). The boats were difficult to make out, but could be spotted by the muzzle flame and were estimated to include a destroyer flotilla and a half-dozen U-boats. The ship steered a zig-zag course over the boats and dropped salvoes of 3 or 5 bombs at boats particularly close together.

At 4 a.m., well after dawn:

> 20 miles off Hanstholm (near the northern tip of Denmark) and at 2,200 meters (7,200 feet), a squadron of ships was sighted in the Jammer Bay, consisting of twelve big vessels and many cruisers. Attempted on a southerly course to ascertain their type, but could only determine that the squadron was steaming at high speed

2 Holloway, H. Frost, *The Battle of Jutland* (Annapolis: U.S. Naval Institute, 1936), p. 419.

3 Admiral Sir William James, *The Code Breakers of Room 40* (New York: St. Martin's Press, 1956), p. 119.

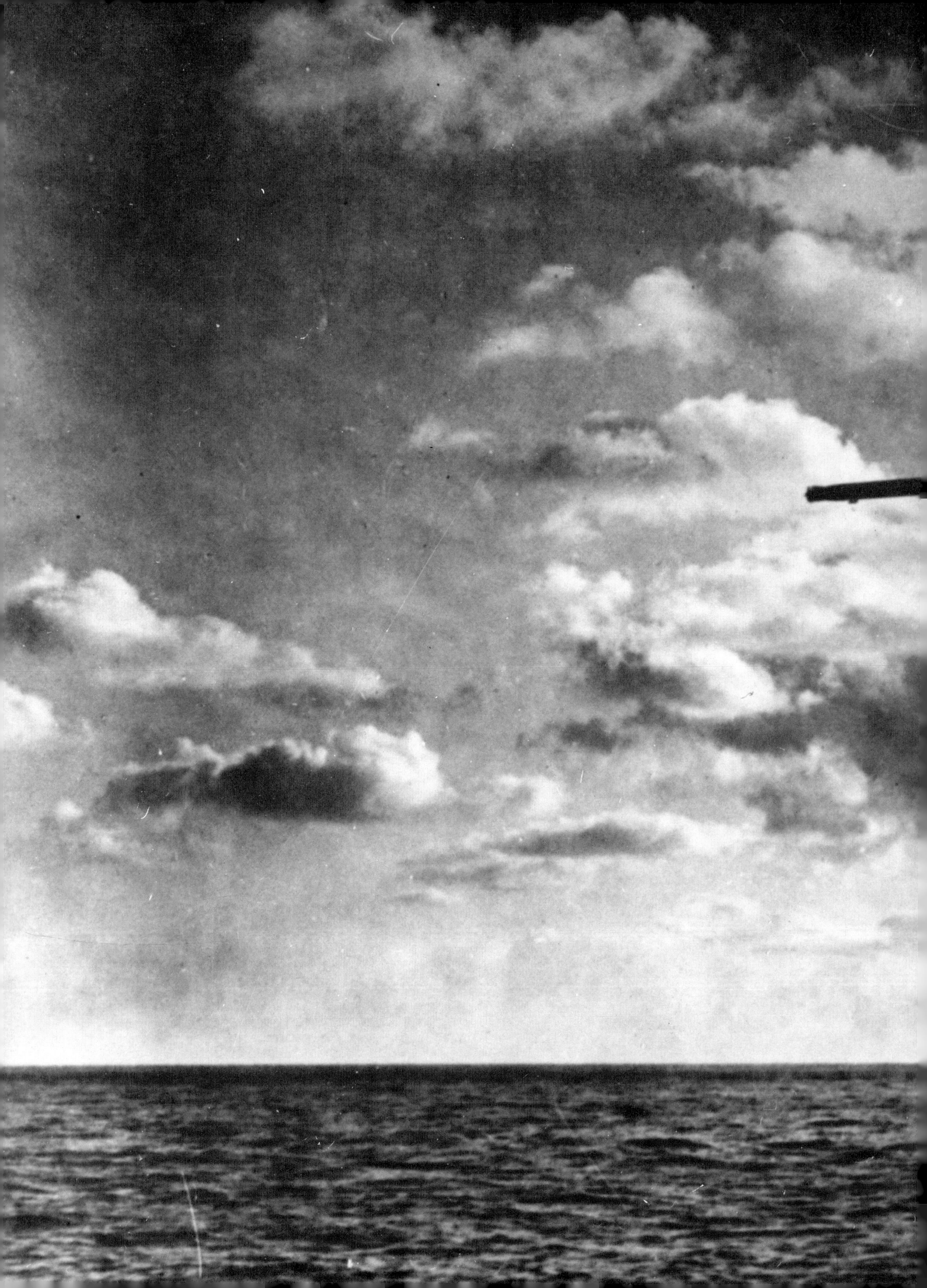

*PREVIOUS: L 11 on a scouting mission over the North Sea. A German destroyer is in the foreground. (Luftschiffbau Zeppelin)*

> on a southerly course, while at the first encounter it was steaming in line of bearing with cruisers out ahead. Two cruisers pursued the airship, therefore steered on a north-west course into clouds and on a west and northeast course repeated the attempt. Break-up of the clouds and hazy atmosphere made it impossible to get as close as necessary to the enemy main body without being chased and shot at again by the enemy small craft.

Scheer concluded that Admiral Jellicoe had divided his battle fleet and that one portion had been seen by Koch in Jammer Bay. Yet the forces reported by *L 24* simply did not exist. Corbett suggests that the ships in Jammer Bay might have been a convoy; "it was certainly no part of the British forces."[4]

Scheer paid more attention to reports from Viktor Schütze in *L 11*, who soon before dawn fell in with the bulk of the British Grand Fleet. Schütze, identifying the ships he contacted, stubbornly keeping in touch and developing the situation, was the only airship commander who succeeded in his scouting mission during the Jutland battle. At 4 a.m., forty miles due north of Terschelling, he saw smoke clouds. Ten minutes later:

> A strong enemy force of 12 large battleships with numerous lighter warships could be made out steering north-north-east at high speed. *L 11* attached herself to keep in contact, sending out radio reports, simultaneously making circles to the east. While doing this, the ship encountered in 043 β (east of the first unit) towards 4:40 a.m. a second squadron of six large English battleships with lighter warships, which on being sighted were turning by divisions to the west, apparently to join the first unit. Since this group was nearer to our own forces than the first, *L 11* remained in contact with it, but sighted in 029 β at 4:50 a group of three English battle cruisers with about four lighter warships coming down from the north-east, working in between *L 11* and the enemy main body. Visibility was so bad that it was very difficult to keep in contact, while the enemy could easily see the airship at 1,100 to 1,900 meters (3,600 to 6,200 feet) against the rising sun. At 4:15, after encountering the first battleship squadron, the enemy opened fire with all ships and weapons, with anti-aircraft and other guns of all calibers; the main turrets fired broadsides. These were well aimed for deflection and well grouped, and the line of ships could be made out from the muzzle flashes when the ships themselves were invisible. All ships coming into sight energetically fired, so that at times *L 11* was under fire from 21 large and small warships. Although the fire was without results, the passage of the big shells and the bursting of shrapnel nearby caused such heavy vibrations in the framework that it seemed advisable to increase the distance. The gunfire lasted till 5:20 a.m. At this time the battle cruisers, pushing up from south-west to within close range of *L 11*, forced her off to the north-east to escape their heavy fire. At the same time the visibility deteriorated markedly, and the enemy was lost from view.

The appearance of *L 11* caused at first excitement, and then profound disappointment, in the Grand Fleet. Somewhat scattered during the night, and ignorant of the fact that the Germans had broken through their rear and had reached the safety of the swept channel at Horns Reef, the British, well to the west, were hoping to find the enemy at dawn and fight him to a finish. Beatty's six battle cruisers, somewhat ahead of the battle fleet, had turned back to rejoin and it was these which Schütze encountered on a north-north-east course at 4:10 a.m. H.M.S. *Indomitable* fired a 12-inch armor-piercing shell from her fore turret, and the four ships of the 3rd Light Cruiser Squadron took up the tale. The shooting was heard farther east in the battle fleet, which turned towards the sound of the guns in

[4] Corbett, III, p. 416. Some historians have questioned whether the "destroyers and U-boats" which *L 24* reported bombing off Bovbjerg might have been the German II Flotilla of ten large destroyers, which had been detached during the night to proceed to Kiel via Skagen and the Little Belt. But the War Diary of the flotilla, as well as those of individual boats, have been examined, and fail to mention any such attack. Nor does a perusal of contemporary Danish newspapers (for which I am grateful to Hans Kofoed of Charlottenlund, Denmark) support a suggestion that *L 24* bombed Danish fishing boats.

hopes that Beatty had found the Germans; these were the vessels which Schütze found turning west by divisions at 4:40 a.m. Their disappointment was great when they realized that they undoubtedly had been reported to Scheer, who would now be able to give them a wide berth. The last group of "three English battle cruisers" was the four dreadnoughts of the 6th Division, which had become separated from the Fleet through torpedo damage to the division flagship H.M.S. *Marl-borough. Marlborough*'s 13.5-inch guns were "unloaded through the muzzle" at Schütze's craft, and she fired several rounds from her two 3-inch anti-aircraft guns. Other battleships took potshots at the target in the eastern sky, notably H.M.S. *Neptune.*

Convinced that much of the British fleet was in Jammer Bay, Scheer thought the warships reported by *L 11* were "reinforcements from the Channel." Schütze had looked carefully for signs of battle damage, "but since masts, funnels and bulwarks seemed intact, and they manoeuvred at high speed, they apparently had not been engaged on May 31." At 5:07 a.m. Scheer ordered all his ships to "run in by squadrons," recording in his War Diary, "I decided not to bring to action the enemy forces reported by *L 11*, since an action in the present circumstances and with insufficient air reconnaissance promised no success." At 7:26 a.m. he radioed to Strasser, "airship reconnaissance no longer necessary."

After the battle Scheer testified to his continuing faith in airship scouting: "This tactic provides the utmost possible security against surprise through the unexpected appearance of superior enemy forces . . . *therefore airship scouting is fundamental for more extended operations.*" Unlike some of the airship apologists of the 1920s, he did not claim that the Zeppelins had "saved the High Seas Fleet at the Battle of Jutland."[5] In truth, the airships did not distinguish themselves in this historic engagement. They saw nothing of the battle itself, and the good work done next morning by Schütze in *L 11* was balanced by the incomprehensible errors of Koch in *L 24*. But Scheer had not expected the Zeppelins to play a role in the action – the operation was specifically planned to overcome the difficulties resulting from their being unavailable – and only at the last moment were they flung into the air in hopes that they could be of assistance. Above all, the weather was against them. In the days before radar, when fog and haze obscured the surface, the most extensive reconnaissance revealed nothing. The airships alone were not rendered ineffective. The surface scouting forces of both fleets groped for each other in the mist, and many of the encounters which, taken together, go under the name of the Battle of Jutland, were chance clashes in low visibility, unheralded and fought without preparation.

---

5 German and American airship advocates refer repeatedly to a British memorandum dated Sept. 20, 1917, originally prepared at the Admiralty by supporters of the British rigid airship program, which asserted, "It is no small achievement for their Zeppelins to have saved the High Seas Fleet at the Battle of Jutland; to have saved their cruiser squadron on the Yarmouth raid (on April 25, 1916), and to have been instrumental in sinking the *Nottingham* and *Falmouth* (in the 'Sunderland Operation' of August 19, 1916, q.v.)". The public first heard of this document when Admiral William A. Moffett, the Chief of the U.S. Navy's Bureau of Aeronautics, read from it at a congressional hearing on airship policy on January 28, 1926. All these claims were false, but Moffett was acting in good faith, as accurate information concerning the war records of the Zeppelins was then hard to come by.

# CHAPTER XII

# SUPER ZEPPELINS VERSUS ANTI-AIRSHIP AMMUNITION

On May 30, 1916, after repeated postponements, there arrived at the "Front" the first of the "big 6-engine ships," *L 30*. She had made her first flight at Friedrichshafen on May 28. Two days later, *Oberleutnant zur See* von Buttlar put her in commission, and with old Count Zeppelin as a passenger, flew her to Nordholz. An embarrassing mishap marred her arrival: for the occasion, Strasser, his staff and the airship officers at Nordholz constituted themselves a "landing commission," and went out on the field. As *L 30* slowed her engines, her dashing young commander found that his ship was improperly "weighed off" and falling fast. Down went five "breeches" of water ballast – squarely on the heads of the landing commission! A few minutes later Strasser, soaked to the skin, greeted von Buttlar with the wry remark, "You came in like a watering cart!"

The genesis of the *L 30* type went back to March, 1915, when the Admiralty requested the Zeppelin and Schütte-Lanz firms to prepare designs for the largest vessels that could be accommodated in the standard hangars then in existence at the North Sea bases, which measured 604 feet long, 112 feet wide and 92 feet high. The airship builders responded with a design for a craft of 1,589,000 cubic feet with five engines. The Admiralty was dissatisfied with this solution, particularly as the height of the proposed craft – 87 feet – indicated that they would be difficult to handle in and out of the sheds. The Admiralty also wanted more engines for safety. On July 22, 1915, Admiral Dick, in charge of the Aviation Department, wrote to the Naval Staff:

> The two companies are therefore ordered to prepare a new project for a 6-engine ship without regard to shed measurements and are to prepare to build ships of this type. In order to house these ships, which will be about 200 meters [650 feet] long, since

*OPPOSITE:*
*Inside the hull of the L 30, looking forward, after application of the outer cover, but before the gas cells were in place. This photograph describes better than words the structural complexity of even a wartime airship. It shows the thirteen main longitudinal girders and the twelve "reefing girders", the cross-braced rings (indicated by king-posts) and intermediate rings, and the keel and catwalk at the bottom. Two water-ballast "breeches" are hung on either side of the keel in the foreground. (Luftschiffbau Zeppelin)*

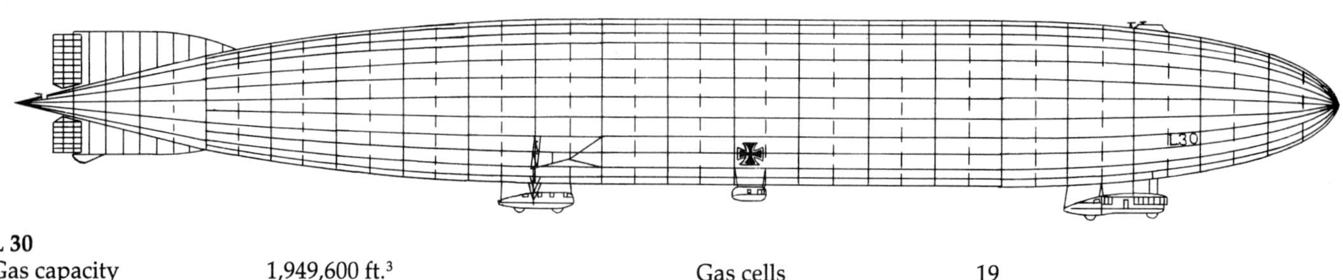


**L 30**

| | | | |
|---|---|---|---|
| Gas capacity | 1,949,600 ft.$^3$ | Gas cells | 19 |
| Length | 649.4 ft. | Crew | 22 |
| Diameter | 78.4 ft. | Engines | 6 Maybach HSLu, of 240 h.p. |
| Useful lift | 61,600 lbs. | Propellers | 6 Lorenzen |
| Fixed weights | 79,600 | Maximum speed | 62.2 mph |
| Fuel | 1585 Gal. | Ceiling | 12,500 ft. |
| Oil | 211 Gal. | Full speed endurance | 4600 miles |
| Bombs | 9250 lbs. | | |

> they will be completed before the new sheds now under construction, the double sheds which are now under construction in Tondern and Seddin are to be lengthened as quickly as possible to 240 meters [790 feet] . . . Without this measure the development of large airships will be delayed for several months. Construction of an intermediate type is not advisable, because burdening the works with two different types in rapid succession will merely retard delivery of ships and impair their best performance.

In one leap the gas volume increased to 1,949,600 cubic feet, marking the greatest advance in airship construction made throughout the war. The ships of this design were repeated, with modifications, for the rest of the war. Furthermore, they played an indispensable role in the airship programs of other countries. When *L 33*, the fourth "big 6-engine ship," made a forced landing in England on the night of September 23-24, 1916, her design was copied in R 33 and R 34, the first successful British rigid airships. The later *L 49* served as the basis for the construction of the U.S. Navy's first rigid, *Shenandoah*.[1]

1 Partly because the Schütte-Lanz firm dealt primarily with the Army, which preferred smaller craft, and partly because their building shed at Mannheim-Rheinau again had to be enlarged, their first two million cubic foot ship, *SL 20*, was not completed until September 10, 1917.

*The first of the "Super-Zeppelins": Naval airship L 30 coming in to land at Friedrichshafen. (Luftschiffbau Zeppelin)*

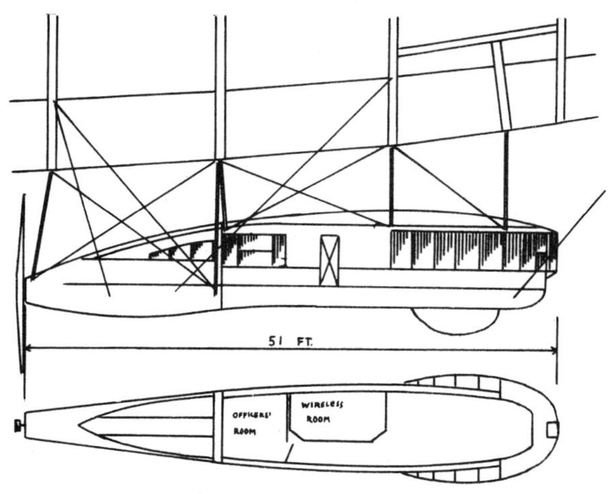


CONTROL CAR AND FORWARD ENGINE CAR

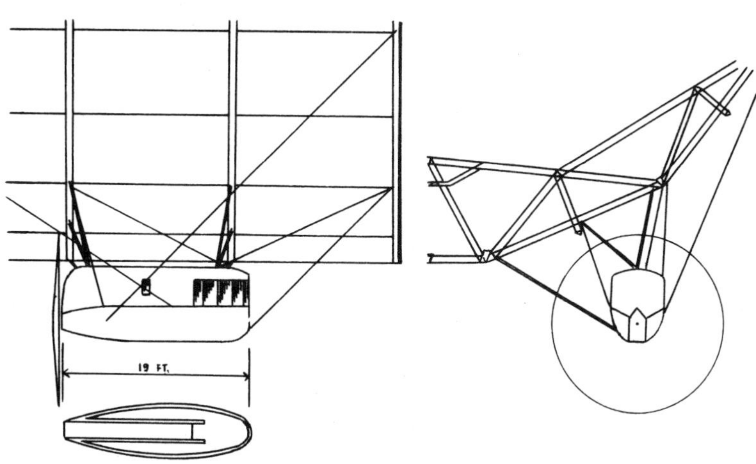


MIDSHIPS POWER CAR

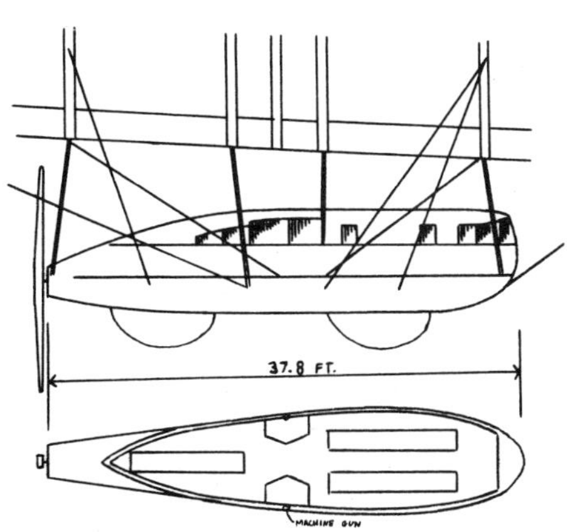


AFTER POWER CAR

**L 30 Class Detail**

(after Dürr)

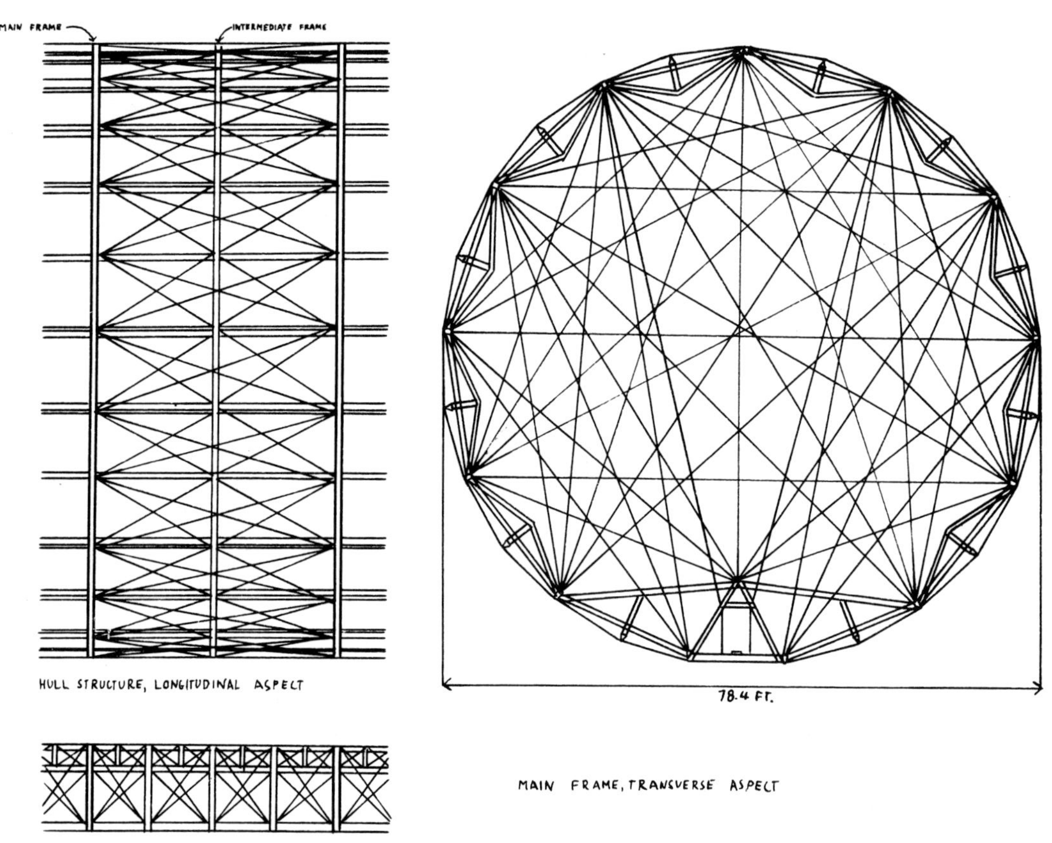


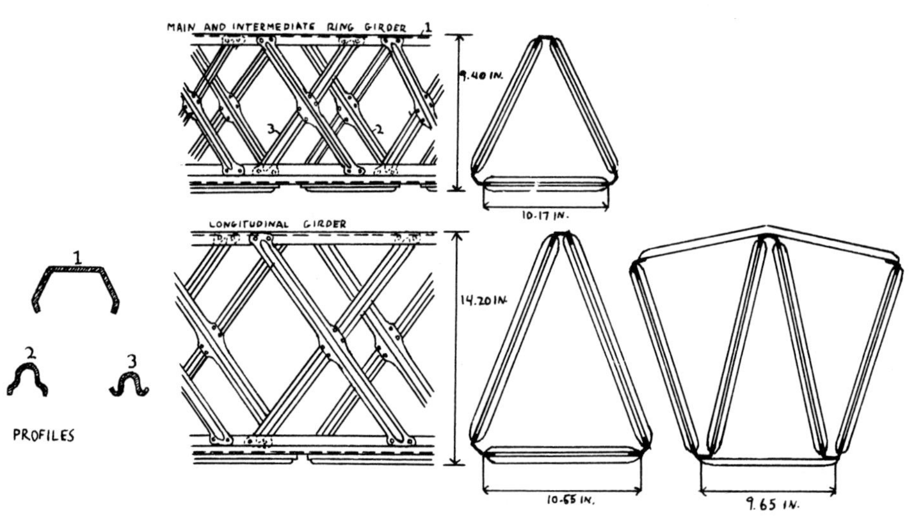


**L 30 Class Detail**

(after Dürr)

*L 30 over Strasser's headquarters and radio station in Ahlhorn. (Nonhoff-Strumann)*

The dimensions of *L 30* herself are impressive even in this day and age. She measured 649 feet 7 inches overall, 78 feet 5 inches in diameter, and stood go feet 10 inches high on her gondola bumpers. Six of the Maybach HSLu motors were fitted, the added engines being carried in two small gondolas slung on either side of the hull amidships. Maximum trial speed of *L 30* was 62 m.p.h. Though the maximum static ceiling was 17,400 feet, in raids over England she flew at about 13,000 feet. Out of a total lift of 141,200 pounds, a maximum of 61,600 pounds – 43-6 per cent – was available for useful load, a figure improved on in later ships. In two bomb rooms forward and aft of amidships, *L 30* could carry nearly 5 tons of bombs. At one time a total of ten machine guns were fitted – two in the control car, two in the after engine car, one in each of the side gondolas, one in the rear gun pit abaft the rudders, and no less than three on the top platform near the bows. The hull, with only a short parallel portion amidships, was much better streamlined than in earlier craft. Only in the rear engine gondola did *L 30* fail to show improvement over her predecessors, for two of the after engines still drove propellers on clumsy side brackets. These had been retained because of the simple reversing gear which had been incorporated with the side propeller drive since the earliest days of the Zeppelin airships. Though the need to make the midships gondola propellers reversible had been recognized, the development of a new gear drive, according to a Zeppelin Company engineer, required more time than the design and production of a new engine.

The sheer bulk of the "big 6-engine ships" made them even harder to handle on the ground, and confined them to their hangars on an increasing proportion of days because of winds across the shed axis. But the German Navy was committed to using large masses of men to handle the giant gas-

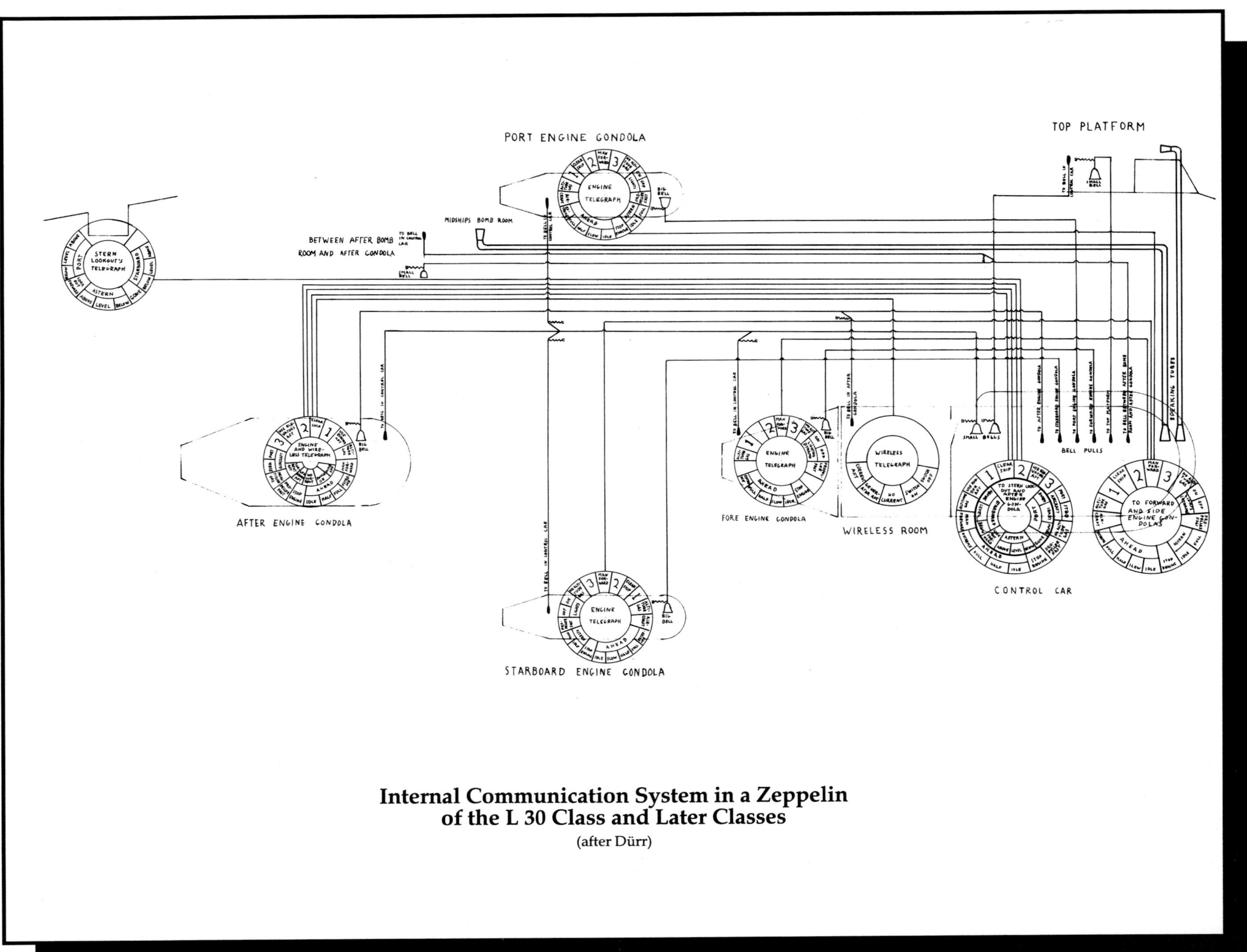


**Internal Communication System in a Zeppelin of the L 30 Class and Later Classes**
(after Dürr)

*L 30 being walked out of the "Aladin" shed at Ahlhorn. (Kameradschaft)*

bags in and out of their sheds, and mooring masts and other mechanical aids had to await the unhurried era of experimentation in the 1920s. All things considered, however, *L 30* deserved the attention with which she was received at Nordholz. Her capabilities were thoroughly investigated by Strasser and his staff, and she made five test flights, including altitude and endurance trials, before undertaking her first scouting mission on July 5.

The British, whose spies found little trouble in reaching Friedrichshafen from nearby Switzerland, promptly christened the new type the "super-Zeppelin." Actually *L 30* posed no new problems for the British defenses. She could carry more bombs, and was a trifle faster, but she still flew at approximately the same altitude as the earlier ships, and navigated in the same manner. Indeed, the British at this time were rushing a development that promised to put the quietus on the Zeppelin as a raiding weapon.

The British military authorities were well aware that the Zeppelins were inflated with hydrogen, one of the most inflammable gases known. But early in the war they convinced themselves that their enemies had eliminated the fire hazard by leading the exhaust gases from the engines into the hull.[2] For the time being the development of incendiary ammunition was abandoned, and it was thought that the only way to bring down a Zeppelin was to shoot her full of holes and destroy her buoyancy.

That the Royal Flying Corps eventually was able to arm its planes with effective anti-airship ammunition was due entirely to the perseverance of a few individuals. As early as August, 1914, a Mr. John Pomeroy had submitted an explosive bullet to the British War Office, but meeting with no encouragement, he returned to his home in Australia. Not until December, 1915, was his invention taken up by the Ministry of Munitions. At the same time, officialdom took an interest in a phosphorous incendiary bullet invented by Mr. J.F. Buckingham of Coventry, and in an explosive bullet developed by Commander F.A. Brock, R.N. Tests showed that

2 Not until 1917 did the Germans experiment with a double-walled gas cell in which a layer of inert nitrogen surrounded the inflammable hydrogen. The Zeppelin Company's investigations in this direction progressed to the use of live incendiary ammunition on a test cell, but the "weight penalty" of the double envelope, together with the reduction in lifting gas volume, led to the project being abandoned.

*L 30, the first of the 55,000 cubic meter Zeppelins, was built to carry up to 9,250 pounds of bombs. Many other countries used the L 30 as a model for their own airship development. (Luftschiffbau Zeppelin)*

the explosive bullet was required to blow holes in the outer cover and in the gas cells of the German airships, and the phosphorous ammunition would then ignite the escaping hydrogen. In the spring of 1916 over a million rounds of Brock, Pomeroy and Buckingham ammunition were ordered for the 303 caliber Lewis machine gun, and were used from the middle of the summer by the home defense squadrons. Great was the grief that this ammunition brought to the German airship services, and one of their number expressed the feeling of all when he labeled it "the invention of the devil." He added, "Had we caught the man who invented that bullet during the war we should gladly have burned him on the great flying ground at Ahlhorn in a stream of blazing hydrogen."[3]

But the Germans, with their newest and finest raiding airships coming forward, were not easily to be dissuaded from continuing the campaign against England.

3 (Heinrich Bahn), "In a German Airship Over England," *Journal of the Royal United Service Institution*, February, 1926, p. 107.

# CHAPTER XIII

# THE SUNDERLAND OPERATION

By the middle of August the German High Seas Fleet had repaired most of the damage of the Jutland battle, and Scheer was planning a new operation against the English coast. A bombardment of Sunderland was again intended to draw the British Grand Fleet across a series of submarine traps. Nine U-boats sailed on August 16 to take station in two lines off Blyth in Northumberland and Flamborough Head in Yorkshire, where they could ambush the Grand Fleet as it proceeded south. As in the planning before Jutland, Strasser's Zeppelins were to play a vital role in searching for the British fleet and in covering their own forces. "For the undertaking extensive airship reconnaissance is a prerequisite," wrote Scheer in his operational order. The concept was boldly strategic, and from the point of view of airship history makes the Sunderland operation the most interesting event of World War I at sea.

Since the entire plan depended on airship scouting, once more Strasser's evaluation of the weather would set the whole vast enterprise in motion. On the morning of August 16, Strasser had to report that the weather next day would not permit airship scouting. During the next two days, Zeppelins were sent out specifically on weather-reporting missions. On the 17th, Strasser advised Scheer, "weather unfavorable, but apparently better tomorrow." On the 18th he concluded, "weather situation good, persistent north-west wind," and at 9 p.m. on the evening of August 18 the High Seas Fleet put to sea.

Strasser had distributed an operational plan to his commanders which they were not to discuss even with the officers of the ground troop, as he believed espionage at the bases was responsible for British advance knowledge of airship flights. Between 1:30 and 4:40 a.m. on the morning of the 19th, eight Zeppelins took off to proceed to their stations in the North Sea. *L 30*, *L 32* (with Strasser on board), *L 24* and *L 22* were to patrol from Peterhead, north of Aberdeen, to Lindesnes, on the Norwegian coast, to give warning of the southerly

*Broadside view of L 31. Note the lightweight lifeboat under the hull abaft the control car. (Frau Mathy)*

advance of the Grand Fleet from Scapa Flow. *L 31* was assigned to watch the Firth of Forth, *L 11* was to reconnoiter off the Tyne, *L 21* was to cruise off the Humber, and *L 13* was to patrol from the "Hoofden"[1] to the south-west corner of the Swarte Bank, in the center of the southern part of the North Sea, to warn of British forces coming up from the Channel. Orders had been written for *L 14*, *L 16*, *L 17* and *L 23* to take off about midnight of August 19 and to patrol during the 20th.

1 "The Hoofden" was the German name for the waters off the Dutch coast.

The four northern airships were on station during the afternoon of the 19th with nothing to report. At 2:05 p.m. *L 30* sighted the Scottish coast at Aberdeen, and from 2:45 to 6:45 p.m., when she received the general recall, she cruised east and west on her patrol line. *L 32*, her neighbor to the east, covered her sector from 11:10 a.m. till 2 p.m.,

*L 31 being walked into the "Normann" shed at Nordholz on some date between July 17, 1916 when she arrived from Friedrichshafen, and August 7 when she was tranferred to Ahlhorn. In the left foreground is Peter Strasser, Leader of Airships. Not more than six months later a clear copy of this photograph appeared as the frontispiece of the British Admiralty Confidential Report, "German Rigid Airships, February 1917", C.B. 1265. (Frau Mathy)*

when she started back on receiving a message that strong British forces were to the south. At 12.30 another Zeppelin was sighted to the north-east; this was *L 24*, which patrolled on station from 1 to 6 p.m. At 7:25 her control car personnel suffered a bad fright when an over-charged storage battery burst into flames; it was promptly doused with a hand fire extinguisher and dropped overboard. *L 22*, patrolling westward from the Lister lighthouse on the Norwegian coast below Stavanger between 11 a.m. and 6:50 p.m., sighted many merchant ships in the Skagerrak as well as *L 24* and *L 32* at the eastern end of their patrol lines. None of these four Zeppelins saw anything of the British fleet.

Two remarkable assumptions stand out on every page of Admiral Scheer's War Diary: Firstly, it was inconceivable that the enemy could possibly have advance knowledge of his movements. Secondly, he was certain that the protective circle of airships would guarantee him against surprise by the superior Grand Fleet. Actually, as early as 11:30 a.m. on August 18, the British had guessed from German radio traffic that the High Seas Fleet was preparing to sail. Jellicoe departed from Scapa Flow with the Grand Fleet during the afternoon of the 18th, and thus passed the northern patrol line nearly a day before the Zeppelins were in position. At 9:30 that evening Beatty with the battle cruisers left Rosyth for a rendezvous with Jellicoe. At 11:30 p.m. the Harwich Force of light cruisers and destroyers also sailed to join him.

At 6 a.m. on the morning of the 19th the British Grand Fleet and the battle cruisers met 100 miles east-north-east of the Firth of Forth, and the combined force of 33 dreadnoughts proceeded south. The Harwich Force was still far down in the North Sea. *Kapitänleutnant der Reserve* Eduard Prölss, covering this sector in *L 13*, was hampered by increasing cloud. At 7:30 a.m., flying at 1,000 feet, he encountered Tyrrwhitt's vessels. Approaching on an

*L 31 being walked into the "Normann" shed. This photograph was taken from beneath its shedmate L 30 whose tail can be seen in the top foreground. Hans von Schiller was Wachoffizier of L 31. (Luftschiffbau Zeppelin)*

opposite course, he met heavy anti-aircraft fire and had to climb into the clouds to escape. Prölss reported to Scheer, "7:30 a.m. in 055 α 6 (70 sea miles east of Lowestoft), two enemy destroyer flotillas, cruiser squadron following them, making high speed to south-west. Being heavily fired on. *L 13.*" The Harwich Force was only temporarily steering south-west, but this caused Scheer to comment, "not related to us, as they were running towards the Channel. The enemy still seems to have no knowledge of our approach." At 9:40 a.m. Prölss again sighted one of Tyrwhitt's ships and radioed, "enemy light cruiser with three funnels, high speed on course east-south-east." "Apparent patrol forces for the Belgian and Dutch coast," was Scheer's comment.

At this time the four northern airships were still proceeding to their patrol line. *L 11*, passing within searchlight signaling distance, was ordered by Admiral Hipper in *Moltke* at 9 a.m. to "cover ahead of II Scouting Group." Though the air was clear in the vicinity of the Fleet, *L 11* also found visibility deteriorating towards the English coast, with heavy clouds forming down to 650 feet. *L 31*, to the north of the High Seas Fleet, steered around several thunderstorms. *L 21*, to the south, had good visibility despite scattered clouds.

At 6:56 a.m. the U-boat traps scored their first success when U 52 torpedoed the light cruiser *Nottingham* in the battle cruiser screen. At 8 a.m. Jellicoe, fearing further losses through submarine attacks, reversed course to the north. Half an hour later the battle cruisers turned after the battle fleet, and were sighted during this maneuver by U 53. At 9:10 she reported three large warships, four light cruisers and several destroyers on a northerly course 80 miles east of Farne Island. This report, decoded in Scheer's flagship at 10:40, was his first information of enemy units to the north.

Mathy in *L 31* was approaching U 53's position. It was a typical North Sea day, with a low, solid cloud ceiling at 650 feet. Occasional rain squalls limited visibility to less than a mile. By flying below the clouds to carry out his mission, Mathy risked being seen and shot down by enemy vessels before they could be sighted from the airship.

At 9:45 a.m. Mathy came upon the light cruiser screen on the eastern wing of the battle cruiser fleet. Anti-aircraft fire forced him up into the overcast, and he went away over the clouds on a northerly course, reporting "two light cruisers, two destroyers 028 α 5 (go miles east of Farne Island) on a northerly course, quickly lost to sight in rain." Descending again, and flying at 650 feet in ragged clouds, Mathy found farther to the north "the *Gros*[2] reported by U 53." Quickly coming under fire at a range of 5,000 to 6,000 yards, Mathy again climbed into the clouds and at 10:50 radioed to Scheer, "008 α 5 enemy *Gros* course north-east quickly lost to sight in rain." Once again deceived by a temporary course change, and firm in his conviction that the Grand Fleet – of which Mathy had seen a portion – could not be inside the airship cordon, Scheer noted, "should this be an isolated unit, it would be the best possible proof that the enemy does not suspect we are at sea. If it is a portion of a force seeking to join other units, we will have to await further reports from our airships. From their course and distance, they are not concerned with us." At 11:40 a.m., with somewhat better visibility, Mathy descended again, saw some ships to the north-east, but on approaching closer, found they were fishing vessels. He concluded that the British had turned south, and in fact, their official history states that they did so as early as 10 a.m.

Scheer received no further reports from his Zeppelins during the morning, but all the British commanders had the uneasy feeling that they were being shadowed and watched. Jellicoe relates:

> From 8:28 onwards (British time) Zeppelins were frequently in sight from both the Battle Fleet and the Battle Cruiser Fleet, and were fired at, but they kept at too long a range for the fire to be effective. The *Galatea* sighted the first at 8:28 a.m., and the second was seen by the Battle Fleet at 9:55 a.m.; at 10 a.m. Commodore Tyrwhitt, who was at sea with the Harwich Force, reported himself in position Lat. 52.5C N., Long. 3.38 E., and also being followed by a Zeppelin. He stated later that his force was

[2] This is an untranslatable word, meaning roughly "main body" or "central force." It should not be taken to mean that Mathy knew he had seen the Grand Fleet, nor was it so interpreted by Scheer.

*Flight crew and maintenance group of L 31 (Schiffpflegegruppe) who worked on the ship between flights, and which provided crew members as needed. Heinrich Mathy is on the far right in the foremost window of the control car. This photo was copied from a print found on one of the dead L 31 crewmen after the ship was shot down on October 2, 1916 over Potters Bar, England by British aircraft. All nineteen crewmen perished. Zeppelin flight crews were not drilled to empty their pockets as in World War II. (Moch)*

> shadowed by airships during the whole period of daylight on the 19th. Reports were also received from the patrol trawler *Ramexo* that she had two Zeppelins in sight in Lat. 57 N., Long. 1 E. It was evident that a very large force of airships was out. A total of at least 10 was identified by our directional wireless stations and they appeared to stretch right across the North Sea.[3]

The Zeppelin with the Harwich Force was *L 13*, while *L 31* was the only airship near the Grand Fleet during the morning. *Ramexo*'s two Zeppelins were *L 30* and *L 32*, patrolling off Peterhead.

After steaming north for two hours, Jellicoe had once again changed direction. Had he kept to his previous course the two fleets would have met by one o'clock. Scheer did not learn of Jellicoe's return to a southerly course. Undisturbed by the news of warships to the north and south both steaming away from him, Scheer concluded, "there is no necessity for altering the plan," and he kept on for Sunderland.

Soon after midday *L 13* regained contact with the Harwich Force:

> Again following a northerly course, at 12:30 p.m. a large group of enemy warships was sighted to the south. They opened heavy fire on *L 13*, which, after ascertaining their number, climbed to 2,000 meters (6,500 feet) and went off westward to leeward of them, keeping close behind them and trying through holes in the clouds to make out their type.
>
> Unfortunately at this time thunderstorm

[3] Admiral Viscount Jellicoe of Scapa, *The Grand Fleet, 1914-16* (London: Cassell & Co., Ltd., 1919), p. 439.

formations increased and after going around a thunderstorm the enemy could not be found in spite of going down to 300 meters (1,000 feet) under the cloud ceiling. Advancing to the north was without result, and therefore turned back.

With the initial contact, Prölss radioed to Scheer, "12:30, 155 ε 5 (sixty miles north-east of Cromer), strong enemy forces on a northerly course, about 30 units. Being heavily fired on." At 1 p.m. Prölss sent off the fateful results of his attempt to identify the half-dozen light cruisers and two destroyer flotillas of the Harwich Force: "1 p.m., 141 ε 5. Reported forces consist of 16 destroyers, light cruisers, battle cruisers (*Grosse Kreuzer*) and battleships (*Linienschiffe*)." A half hour later he signaled, "Reported enemy force proceeding in 144 ε 5 on a north-west course, keeping contact."

This series of messages produced an electric atmosphere on the flag bridge of S.M.S. *Friedrich der Grosse*. Ignorant of the menace of the Grand Fleet barely over the northern horizon, Scheer had been pressing doggedly on with the intention of bombarding Sunderland at dusk. The first report caused him at 1:15 p.m. to call in the Scouting Forces and turn south-east "so that in case heavy units are present, the very favorable opportunity will not be missed." With the next message, "my doubts as to whether it was correct to discontinue the advance after the first reports from *L 13* have been resolved by the latest reports that battleships are present." At 1:48 p.m. Scheer radioed, "report class of ships." But the deluded *L 13* could only reply at 2:30, "class of ships cannot be made out due to heavy clouds. Contact lost in circumventing thunder clouds." Nor did the High Seas Fleet meet the enemy. At 3:35 Scheer concluded that the British vessels had turned out of reach to the east. Sunderland was now too far distant, and he abandoned the operation and steered for Wilhelmshaven. He never had a chance of bringing to action the Harwich Force, whose fast light cruisers and destroyers could easily have outrun the ponderous German dreadnoughts. But Scheer's fruitless chase to the south had drawn him away from the overwhelming might of the Grand Fleet. By leading the German Fleet away from a battle in which it would have fought at a disadvantage and might have been worsted, Prölss's erroneous reports had an effect on the whole course of the naval war.

How had the fiasco occurred? The blame must be divided between Prölss, who submitted an erroneous report, and Scheer, who evaluated it incorrectly. As for Prölss, his difficulties in identifying, at a distance and through holes in heavy cloud, ships which were shooting at him is apparent from his narrative. Recognition of ship types at a distance under favorable conditions may be difficult for an experienced line officer. And it may be pertinent to add that Prölss, a reserve officer since 1889, was not, like the majority of his colleagues, a seafaring man by profession, but in peacetime was the Chief of the Fire Department of the City of Magdeburg. As for Scheer, it had always been his primary objective to cut off and annihilate a portion of the British fleet, and wishful thinking played a part in his decisions. At first he had believed that, "these could be the destroyer flotillas seen this morning by *L 13*," but later he had no trouble convincing himself that a force of battleships was coming up from the Thames. Admiral Hipper thought that the capital ships to the south were "Beatty's squadron or the Thames force."

At 3:03 p.m. Scheer received a message from U 53, 80 miles off Sunderland, "2:15 in 163 δ 5 enemy *Gros* steering south." Half an hour later *L 11* sighted four light cruisers coming out from under a cloud. At 4:03 p.m. U 53 reported a force of ten battleships. Scheer again failed to realize that the Grand Fleet had been found. He debated whether to attack these vessels or not, but was dissuaded by the shortage of fuel in his destroyers, and the hazards of a night encounter with British torpedo craft. He kept on for home.

At 2:30 p.m., when *L 31* picked up and decoded U 53's first message, she was 45 miles off the entrance to the Firth of Forth with nothing in sight but scattered patrol craft. Realizing that the German scouting groups were south-east of the High Seas Fleet, and that the British squadron off Sunderland was approaching the German rear, Mathy rang up "flank speed" to overtake the enemy to the south of him. At 3:25 heavy smoke clouds were seen ahead, and at 4:45, Mathy sighted

*Naval airship L 32 in flight over Oldenburg. This photograph was taken by von Schiller from L 30 while both ships were in flight to Bremen on September 22, 1916. This information was found in L 32's war diary which was found in the charred remains of L 32 after it was shot down in flames on September 24, 1916 over Great Burstead, England by British aircraft. All twenty-two crewmen perished.*

the British battle cruisers and radioed to Scheer, "in 127 δ 5 enemy heavy units, course south-west to south." (The square given, 25 miles east of Scarborough, was 50 miles too far to the west, as Mathy discovered later when he met Hipper's flagship, S.M.S. *Moltke*, and exchanged positions by searchlight.) At five o'clock Beatty's six battle cruisers reversed course, and at 5:10, *L 31*, which was still following, radioed "enemy steering north, enemy making high speed." "These reports," wrote Scheer, "prove that a further advance to the west would be useless, as the enemy is already close under the coast and steering north." Twenty minutes later Mathy broke off contact, as the airships had received general orders to return.

As the northern Zeppelins headed home, the British trawler *Ramexo* was rewarded for her day-long vigil. *L 30*, cruising in scattered cloud at 2,000 feet, was taken completely by surprise when the little fishing vessel opened fire, and the trawler's crew thought they scored two hits and started a fire in the airship's fore gondola. Von Buttlar, who had mistaken *Ramexo* for a harmless fisherman, had to drop half his bombs and most of his ballast to escape, and the first shells burst so close that the smoke blew into the control car windows.

During the Grand Fleet's homeward voyage, U 66 torpedoed the light cruiser *Falmouth*, and other U-boats attacked without success. The last act was a meeting between the German High Seas Fleet and the Harwich Force, which had been vainly sought earlier in the day. At 6:40 p.m. *L 11*, which was covering the southern flank of the Fleet, reported five light cruisers and 19 destroyers steering south-west at high speed. At 7:30 *L 21* also sighted the Harwich Force. "The possibility is not excluded," wrote Scheer, "that they were the forces with which *L 13* had lost contact . . . The heavy ships reported by *L 13* to the south had apparently retreated, perhaps because our superior battle force had been reported to them." For some hours during the evening the High Seas Fleet saw the British torpedo craft accompanying them on the southern horizon, apparently awaiting darkness to launch a night assault on the German dreadnoughts. But after 8 p.m., *L 11* and *L 21*, to their surprise, saw the British turn southwest and disappear at high speed under low-lying clouds.

The reader knows that this was the first occasion – and, as it happened, the last – in which the German naval airships carried out a strategic reconnaissance plan in connection with a major fleet operation. Lack of training, lack of experience, lack of doctrine, all played a part in the errors and failures of the Zeppelins on August 19. It would be unfair to expect Scheer and Strasser to have anticipated the systematic search plans flown by powerful, fast aircraft with carefully trained crews which played such a decisive role in World War II's fleet actions. It is very doubtful if the 13 Zeppelins in the North Sea could have provided the continuous searches for several days which would have been necessary to keep Scheer properly informed of the British fleet's whereabouts. As usual in the early days of aviation, too much was expected from too small a force.

# CHAPTER XIV

# "A CERTAIN MEANS OF VICTORIOUSLY ENDING THE WAR"

The autumn months of 1916 brought a final, all-out assault by the Naval Airship Division on the British capital. Denying the effectiveness of the improved defenses, Strasser ordered his ships to attack again and again. His best and bravest crews were literally consumed in the fire, and the newest and most marvelous products of Friedrichshafen were reduced to tangled piles of junk smoldering in the fields around London. Yet Strasser, with his heart and soul mystically identified with the gigantic gas-bags, refused to accept the verdict of trial by battle, and clung to his illusions with unrealistic optimism.

The reason for this desperate, suicidal effort is easily inferred. The Jutland battle had proved that the High Seas Fleet, though able to inflict shattering losses, was incapable of breaking the stranglehold of the British blockade. Scheer's most deadly weapon – the U-boat – still lay useless in his hands. On land, Germans and French for months had been locked in a bloody death-grapple before Verdun, and since July 1 the British Army, despite appalling casualties, had been hammering the German defenders of the Somme. In the east, the jerry-built Austrian military machine had collapsed in the face of the Brusilov offensive, and Rumania was about to take her ill-starred gamble on the side of Germany's enemies. It was time for the Zeppelins to win or perish in the Fatherland's bitter struggle for survival.

On August 10, 1916, Strasser wrote to Scheer:

> The performance of the big airships has reinforced my conviction that England can be overcome by means of airships, inasmuch as the country will be deprived of the means of existence through increasingly extensive destruction of cities, factory complexes, dockyards, harbor works with war and merchant ships lying therein, railroads, etc.

While von Pohl's establishment of 18 airships might suffice for Fleet scouting, Strasser demanded for the air war against England 22 airships in the North Sea. This would require four additional flight crews. Strasser concluded:

> I am well aware of the generally prevailing personnel problems, but I believe that the personnel must be made available, if necessary through reduction in other areas, since the airships offer a certain means of victoriously ending the war.

On the margin of this letter Scheer noted somewhat skeptically, "We will have to wait and see." Yet he gave Strasser his full support.

Already, with the new-moon period at the end of July, the Navy's Zeppelins had made a new series of attacks. Though the airships ranged from Dover to Berwick, in the first three raids they only injured one boy and did £1,192 damage. Confused by ground mists, the Zeppelins scattered so many bombs in open country that the British seriously believed they were trying to set the growing crops on fire with incendiary bombs. Mathy, claiming two attacks on London, actually had flown both times along the Kentish coast, dropping his bombs in the sea when he came under fire from Ramsgate, Deal and Dover. Realizing the deficiencies of his navigation, he wrote:

> The raids of July 31-August 1, August 2-3, and today's show that it is dangerous to fly for long periods at night and over solid cloud ceilings, because winds that cannot be estimated and which are often very strong can produce significant and even serious drift errors unless wireless bearings are used freely.

Only in the last raid of the series, on the night of August 8-9, did *L 24* cause appreciable damage in Hull, where ten people were killed and eleven injured. Yet Strasser – who had participated in one raid aboard *L 31* – claimed "extraordinarily successful results" in a report to Scheer.

The reorganized British defenses scored no successes, but there were omens of what was to come. The Admiralty ordered the small seaplane carrier *Vindex*, carrying two Bristol Scout airplanes on a short flight deck forward, to go to sea on nights when Zeppelins were expected. On the evening of August 2, *Vindex* intercepted four of the raiders off Lowestoft, and one of her pilots, armed only with bombs, made a determined but ineffective attack on *L 17*. On the night of August 8 the trawler *Itonian*, armed with a single 6-pounder, broke up a raid on the Northumberland coast and forced *L 17* and *L 23* to jettison their bombs in the sea.

On August 6, Strasser wrote to Scheer that he wished to make a "big effort" during the next raiding period from August 20 to September 6. To augment the twelve raiding airships in the North Sea, he proposed that *SL 8* and *SL 9* be transferred from the Baltic. Scheer and Prince Henry, commanding in the Baltic, gave their consent, and the two Schütte-Lanz ships came west on August 18, filling the last berths at Nordholz.

The first raiding opportunity came on August 24, when thirteen airships took off to "attack England south." Strasser was aboard L 32. The British had early warning of the raid from German radio signals, and during the afternoon the Harwich light cruisers (*Conquest*, *Carysfort* and *Canterbury*), with a number of destroyers, sailed to look for Zeppelins. *Vindex* remained in harbor.

At least six of the airships reported being fired on at sea. *L 14* claimed to have encountered as early as 3:28 p.m. a line of destroyers pushed eastward to catch the Zeppelins in daylight, and had diffi-

*SL 9 was lost on March 30, 1917. Her C.O. took off from Seerappen to return to Seddin against orders. It was struck by lightning off Pillau, and crashed in flames killing all twenty-two crewmen. (Moch)*

*All of the Zeppelins had a forward platform on top of the ship, and carried three machine guns. Most Zeppelins had a tail platform to drive off planes from the rear as shown here on the army ship LZ 90.*

culty outrunning them against a stiff headwind. *SL 8* as late as 11 p.m. was fired on by two ships, apparently light cruisers, which used no searchlights since the night was so bright and clear. *Conquest* reported herself in action at 7:24 p.m. and again at 9:24 p.m. when, after she had fired several rounds of 3-inch, her target dropped half a dozen bombs and made off hastily to the north-east. This was *L 13* which, flying at 8,000 feet, took a shell that passed clear through Cell 8 amidships and exploded above the airship's back, the splinters damaging Cell 9. Prölss sent a call for help and dropped all his bombs and some fuel, as the ship was heavily loaded with rain. But even though Cell 8 quickly ran empty, he was helped along by a strong tail wind, and at 12:45 a.m. when he landed at Hage, Cell 9 was still half full. As *L 13* quickly dived from her flight altitude, the gas temperature rose from 41 to 64 degrees F. due to adiabatic heating, and Prölss was able to land his ship practically "weighed off" and undamaged.

All the raiders encountered strong south-west to north-west winds at sea, and on this account, and because they could not attack the English coast before moonrise at 2 a.m., five ships turned back, dropping some of their bombs, they claimed, on outpost craft. *L 23*, heavily loaded with rain, had to dump all her bombs and 1,300 pounds of fuel, and even so landed hard and was under repair for

*Army Zeppelin LZ 97. (Luftschiffbau Zeppelin)*

*Sub-cloud car of LZ 90 which fell in East Anglia during the raid of September 2/3, 1916. In fact, LZ 90 dropped the car, and later the winch, to lighten the ship. (It is said that crew members enjoyed sub-cloud car duty as it was a chance for them to smoke).*

three days. The remainder likewise had many difficulties, and had little to show for their efforts. *SL 8*'s after engine broke down and she did not reach the coast. *SL 9*, flying at 9,000 feet through the tops of heavy clouds, aimed her bombs at "lights like those of a city," but she was not traced over England. Back in Nordholz, numerous breaks were found in the wooden hull girders, and *SL 9* was out of service until September 5, the end of the raiding period.

*Oberleutnant zur See* Kurt Frankenberg, Böcker's former executive officer now in command of *L 21*, believed he had bombed Harwich from 12,000 feet in the face of heavy anti-aircraft fire, but his missiles fell about five miles south of the naval base. Short of fuel which he had sacrificed to reach a high altitude over Harwich, Frankenberg had to take the shortest route home over Holland. He had expected the sun to warm the hydrogen after daylight and increase the ship's lift, but she encountered heavy rain at high altitude. Thoroughly soaked, *L 21* made a heavy landing and was out of service for six days while damage to hull and gondolas was repaired.

Mathy in *L 31*, and Peterson in *L 32*, avoided the enemy's surface ships, and much of the wind, by proceeding south via Düsseldorf to Aachen, and then west via Brussels to the Channel. During the afternoon *L 31* was delayed when a starboard midships gondola stay parted, and mechanics had to climb out on the gondola roof to rig a jury lashing. *L 32*'s mechanics changed a leaky exhaust muffler in the air. Above Belgium, Mathy flew at low altitude, in order to be hidden in the clouds from highflying airplanes. At 9 p.m. he went out to sea over Ostend.

Peterson, who had flown higher, was held back by strong head winds and did not leave the Belgian coast until 11:10 p.m. Making slow progress over the ground, *L 32* reached the English side of the Channel near Folkestone towards 2 a.m. It was now too late to raid London, so Peterson dropped his bombs on "numerous ships and naval vessels lying off Dover. A square hit on one ship caused a devastating explosion. Here likewise the airship was heavily fired on from land and sea, particularly with incendiary shells." These bombs fell harmlessly offshore, but made a grand spectacle for watchers along the coast, throwing up fountains of water and spray. *L 32* then turned out to sea, pursued by a plane from Dover. The pilot got off a drum-full of ammunition from below, but lost the Zeppelin in the clouds as he was reloading the gun; he was not seen from the airship. At 5:30 a.m. Peterson descended through the clouds to fix his position and found himself over the north-west corner of Vlieland. As she steered east outside territorial waters, *L 32* was heavily fired on by Dutch guns, but landed undamaged at Nordholz at 8:30 a.m. Mathy followed the Thames straight up to London. For the first time in almost a year the inner defenses were tested, and apparently they were caught napping. The searchlights were much hampered by clouds and mist, which Mathy cleverly utilized as cover during his attack. At 1:30 a.m. he began bombing the south-eastern districts (his report says, "All bombs struck blocks of houses in south-western London and the western part of the City"), and was not found by the searchlights until five minutes later, when 120 rounds were fired at the Zeppelin as she was retreating into a cloud bank.

Though the damage caused by this swift assault – £130,000 – was exceeded only by that in Mathy's record raid of September 8-9, 1915, it is the worst documented of any of the Zeppelin attacks on London. It seems difficult to account for the damage toll, for aside from a hit on a power station in Deptford, it appears that private homes were the chief sufferers from Mathy's 36 explosive and 8 incendiary bombs. The casualties were few: nine killed and forty wounded.

Mathy briefly dismissed an accident which concluded *L 31*'s homeward flight via Belgium and the Rhineland:

> The return was again made across Belgium; at 3:30 a.m. on the 25th the ship was again over Ostend. The landing followed at 8:50 a.m.; here the ship fell very hard, because she had become heavy due to an extraordinary load of rain, and no more emergency ballast was at hand. The radiator water of the three engines not needed for the landing was dropped beforehand also. The ship needs a new after gondola, otherwise she has sustained no significant damage.

Actually workmen had to be sent up from Friedrichshafen to make extensive repairs, and *L 31* was not again airworthy until September 21, when she made a test flight.

Freshening easterly winds caused an attempted raid on August 29 to be recalled. Then, four days later on September 2, Strasser sent out twelve airships – every one in the North Sea except the damaged *L 31* and *SL 9* – to "attack England south, chief target London." For the only time in the war, Army airships bombed the same target simultaneously, as *LZ 90*, *LZ 97*, *LZ 98* and the new *SL 11*, completed on August 2, 1916, took off from Rhineland bases. Sixteen airships in all – it was the greatest raid of the war, and at the same time destined to be a turning-point in the history of the Zeppelin as a combat weapon.

The weather was not entirely favorable, as the wind "upstairs" was blowing strongly from the south-west and west south-west. Near the coast the airships met rain and snow at higher altitudes, and several of them "iced up" alarmingly. Two of the raiders apparently did not reach England. Though *L 17*'s commander claimed to have bombed Norwich, and to have suffered damage from anti-aircraft fire, the British raid map shows her turning back thirty miles off the Norfolk coast. The Army Zeppelin *LZ 97* also reversed course about twenty miles off the Naze because of heavy rain squalls.

Of the remaining three military airships, *LZ 98*, commanded by *Oberleutnant zur See der Reserve* Ernst Lehmann – Dr. Eckener's co-worker in the years between the wars – was the first to approach the capital. Proceeding via Belgium, she crossed the Channel coast near Dungeness just after midnight, and wound northwards until reaching the Thames at Gravesend. Here Lehmann came under heavy fire from the guns at Tilbury and Dartford, and dropped all his bombs in the belief he was over the London Docks. *LZ 98* then rose to 13,800 feet and made off to the north-east at 60 m.p.h. A Royal Flying Corps pilot of No. 39 Squadron, Second Lieutenant William Leefe Robinson, saw the Zeppelin, but he sacrificed speed to keep his altitude, and Lehmann escaped into the clouds before the airplane could attack.

*LZ 90* came inland at Frinton, south of the Naze, at 11:05 p.m. At 11:20 she stopped her engines and lowered a sub-cloud car, which ran away and fell near Manningtree with about 5,000 feet of cable. The Zeppelin later dropped the winch, on which were found marks suggesting that the crew had tried to stop it from unreeling by jamming an iron bar into the gears. The airship went on to Haverhill, where she dropped six bombs, and at 1:45 a.m. went out to sea north of Yarmouth. Reports differ as to whether anyone was in the sub-cloud car, but the contemporary narrative of G.H.Q. Home Forces states: "There is no reason to suppose that an observer was in the car, which undoubtedly fell by accident."[1]

By an improbable coincidence, *Hauptmann* Wilhelm Schramm of *SL 11* was flying through the night to bomb his birthplace – London, according to German records. He came in over the River Crouch at 10:40 and made a wide sweep in order to approach the capital from the north. At 1:10 a.m. he was over St. Albans, and ten minutes later dropped his first bombs on London Colney. As *SL*

[1] Great Britain, Air Ministry. *Air Raids, 1916*. VII, Sept. 2-3, 1916. Compiled by the Intelligence Section, G.H.Q. Home Forces. Subsequently repaired, the sub-cloud car was hung in the Imperial War Museum, Lambeth. Built by the ship's Crew of sheet duralumin, it measured 14 feet long and 4 feet deep, with four fins at the rear and small celluloid windows at the front. Inside was a mattress for the observer to lie on, and a telephone connecting him with the airship above. According to the inscription attached, "a captured member of the crew of another ship stated that there was considerable competition for the post of observer in this car, owing to the fact that smoking was permitted in it."

AIRSHIP RAID, SEPTEMBER 2–3, 1916

| *Ship* | *Flt. No.* | *Take-off* | | *Landing* | | *Time in Air* | *Distance (miles)* | *Av. speed (m.p.h.)* | *Max. alt. (feet)* | *Temp. (°F.)* | *Crew* | *Fuel (lb.) loaded/used* | *Oil (lb.) loaded/used* | *Ballast loaded (lb.)* | *Bombs (lb.)* | *Gas used (cubic feet)* |
|---|---|---|---|---|---|---|---|---|---|---|---|---|---|---|---|---|
| *L 11* | 104 | Hage | 2.25 p.m. | Hage | 8.55 a.m. | 18h. 20m. | 846 | 46·1 | 9,850 | 33·8 | 15 | 7,190/6,680 | 550/344 | 10,100 | 3,640 | 335,500 |
| *L 13* | 117 | Hage | 2.30 p.m. | Hage | 8.30 a.m. | 18h. 0m. | 814 | 44·1 | 8,850 | 30·2 | 16 | 7,880/6,240 | 752/353 | 10,800 | 2,890 | 212,000 |
| *L 14* | 84 | Hage | 2.47 p.m. | Hage | 10.33 a.m. | 19h. 46m. | 835 | 42·3 | 9,500 | 32·9 | 16 | 8,080/6,620 | 729/440 | 10,340 | 3,105 | 354,000 |
| *L 16* | 84 | Hage | 3 p.m. | Hage | 9.34 a.m. | 18h. 34m. | 729 | 39·2 | 9,500 | 29·3 | 16 | 8,100/7,500 | 496/254 | 9,600 | 3,765 | 252,500 |
| *L 17* | 64 | Tondern | 1 p.m. | Tondern | 7.50 a.m. | 18h. 51m. | 763 | 40·4 | 9,700 | 30·2 | 16 | 9,370/7,060 | 926/419 | 9,050 | 2,980 | 270,000 |
| *L 21* | 52 | Nordholz | 2 p.m. | Nordholz | 4.52 p.m. | 26h. 48m. | 884 | 32·8 | 10,700 | 26·6 | 17 | 9,890/8,200 | 924/357 | 12,240 | 3,365 | 424,000 |
| *L 22* | 39 | Tondern | 12.25 p.m. | Tondern | 11.40 a.m. | 23h. 15m. | 948 | 40·7 | 10,500 | 26·6 | 15 | 8,830/6,460 | 728/335 | 13,900 | 3,890* | 405,000 |
| *L 23* | 32 | Nordholz | 2.16 p.m. | Nordholz | 8.05 a.m. | 17h. 50m. | 805 | 45·0 | 9,850 | 30·2 | 17 | 9,850/6,830 | 945/440 | 12,580 | 3,265 | 389,000 |
| *L 24* | 27 | Tondern | 12.45 p.m. | Tondern | 8.25 a.m. | 19h. 40m. | 909 | 46·6 | 11,500 | 24·8 | 16 | 8,320/5,630 | 631/254 | 14,800 | 4,850 | 390,000 |
| *L 30* | 31 | Ahlhorn | 1.16 p.m. | Ahlhorn | 8.13 a.m. | 18h. 57m. | 1,032 | 54·1 | 11,500 | 26·6 | 20 | 12,320/9,770 | 1,580/620 | 26,350 | 5,630 | 884,000 |
| *L 32* | 10 | Nordholz | 4.30 p.m. | Nordholz | 10.40 a.m. | 20h. 0m. | 1,058 | 52·8 | 12,500 | 23·0 | 21 | 12,790/11,470 | 1,233/702 | 26,450 | 5,650 | 884,000 |
| *SL 8* | 33 | Nordholz | 2 p.m. | Nordholz | 10.10 a.m. | 20h. 14m. | 779 | 38·9 | 10,800 | 34·7 | 19 | 8,340/6,930 | 440/357 | 15,650 | 4,850 | 350,000 |
| *LZ 90* | | Mannheim | | Mannheim | | | | | | | | | | | | |
| *LZ 97* | | Darmstadt | | Darmstadt | | | | | | | | | | | | |
| *LZ 98* | | Wildeshausen | 1 p.m. | Ahlhorn | 11 a.m. | 22h. 0m. | | | 8,600 | | | | | | | |
| *SL 11* | | Spich | | | | | | | 12,000 | | 16 | | | | 6,310 | |

*Weather:* Light W. wind. Good deal of cloud and some mist in the London area and in Norfolk.
*Bombs:* 463 (34,420 lb.), includes 60 (4,559 lb.) on London.
*Casualties:* 4 killed, 12 injured (none in London).
*Monetary damage:* £21,072.

* Includes armament.

11 proceeded southward, her commander distributed his missiles, a few at a time, on the northern suburbs – North Mimms, Littleheath, Northaw, Gordon Hill, Clayhill, Cockfosters and Hadley Wood. At Wood Green the raider was picked up by the searchlights at Finsbury Park and Victoria Park. The guns now came into action:

> From Tottenham, southwards, while the bombs were being dropped, the airship was under heavy fire from the greater part of the antiaircraft defenses of north and central London, even including those of Regent's Park, Paddington, and the Green Park, from which she was too far distant for the fire to reach her, though no doubt they contributed to the great volume of fire from London which compelled her to change course at Finsbury Park.[2]

Now heading north, *SL 11* dumped six bombs along the Enfield Highway, and twelve more on Forty Hill and Turkey Street. Now the airplanes took a hand in the game. Six pilots were in the air, and three of them were attracted by the commotion. Leefe Robinson was first on the scene:

> Remembering my last failure I sacrificed height (I was still 12,900 feet) for speed and made nose down in the direction of the Zeppelin. I saw shells bursting and night tracer shells flying around it. When I drew closer I noticed that the anti-aircraft aim was too high or too low; also a good many some 800 feet behind – a few tracers went right over. I could hear the bursts when about 3,000 feet from the Zeppelin. I flew along about 800 feet below it from bow to stern and distributed one drum along it (alternate New Brock and Pomeroy). It seemed to have no effect; I therefore moved to one side and gave it another drum distributed along its

2 Great Britain, Air Ministry. *Air Raids, 1916*. VII, Sept. 2-3, 1916.

*SL 11 near completion in the Leipzig double shed. Note the fabric "Crow's Foot" spreading the stress of the long landing ropes for pulling the ship down. SL 11 was shot down in flames near London on September 3, 1916.*

> side –without apparent effect. I then got behind it (by this time I was very close – 500 feet or less below) and concentrated one drum on one part (underneath rear). I was then at a height of 11,500 feet when attacking Zeppelin. I had hardly finished the drum before I saw the part fired at glow. When the third drum was fired there were no searchlights on the Zeppelin and no antiaircraft was firing. I quickly got out of the way of the falling blazing Zeppelin and being very excited fired off a few red Very's lights and dropped a parachute flare.[3]

As the flaming *SL 11* slowly descended to earth, shedding a brilliant light over miles of countryside, the naval airships were still making their approaches across Norfolk, Suffolk and Cambridgeshire. Official reports could not convey the horror and consternation that the German crews must have experienced as they saw the awful portent hanging in the sky. That some of them should have betrayed irresolution is hardly surprising, for even the bravest instinctively dreaded fire in the air.

*L 16*, which was nearest to London, had crossed the Norfolk coast near Sheringham at 10:40 p.m. Because of a heavy load of rain she dropped three explosive bombs on "a locomotive southwest of Norwich." These fell at Kimberley Station, on the Great Eastern Railway, ten miles west-south-west of Norwich. The searchlights of the capital were visible from more than 50 miles away, and *L 16*'s commander, *Kapitänleutnant* Erich Sommerfeldt, counted over 40. At 2 o'clock he began his attack, as he thought, on the north-west part of London,

3 Leefe Robinson's report in Imperial War Museum file, "Pilots' Reports Relating to Destruction of Zeppelins."

and reported that his bombs extinguished the searchlights and started fires. Sommerfeldt had been attracted to the village of Essendon, fifteen miles north of London, by the two searchlights mounted there. No guns were near and the village was badly damaged. Fifteen minutes later, *SL 11* burst into flames before the horrified gaze of *L 16*'s crew:

> During bomb dropping a large number of searchlights, more than a dozen, had seized an airship traveling from south to north, which was being fired on from all sides with shrapnel and incendiary ammunition. It had already passed the center of the city when it caught fire at the stern, burned with an enormous flame and fell. The fire lit up bright as day the *L 16*, which was only 1,000 to 2,000 meters [3,300 to 6,600 feet] to the north.

One of the pilots chasing *SL 11* saw *L 16* lit up by the glare of her consort's destruction, but the illumination gave out before he could come within range. At full speed, Sommerfeldt headed northeast for the coast, desperately aware that he had nearly been burned down in the same way as the ill-fated Army ship.

Peterson, in *L 32*, was at Tring, about twenty miles to the north-west, when the Schütte-Lanz ship was destroyed. He had crossed the coast at Cromer

*SL 13 in the Leipzig double shed. SL 13 never saw combat, and in the end burned, along with SL 18, in this shed on February 8, 1917. The Leipzig hangar was not rebuilt.*

*SL 13 at Wildeshausen, November 18, 1916. Note the lookout on top of the ship, and hoods over the gas shafts. Also note the large finger patch over the nose, and that the control car, and the fore engine car are separate. (Pochhammer)*

at 10:03 p.m. His ship had iced up severely in snow-squalls and had become so tail-heavy that Peterson dropped eight 110-pound bombs to trim her. At 11:27, and again at 11:35, he stopped to check his position by radio bearings. Just before midnight he dropped a fuel tank. At 12:24 a.m. Peterson checked his position again over Newmarket. On the port bow appeared the searchlights of London, thirty or more, and Peterson tried to work to the west-south-west of the capital to get to windward. Towards 2 a.m. other airships were in sight, several over London. At 2:20 a.m.:

denly burst into flames. The blazing mass radiated a red-yellow light, and illuminated the area over a wide radius and fell slowly. The resulting fire on the ground continued until out of sight. . . . Making a sweep to the south-west, *L 32* towards 3 a.m. ran up from the suburb of Kensington towards the City and from there off to the north-east. In this manner the bombs were well placed. Two fires were still to be seen from previous attacks. In spite of mist and scattered cloud the gunfire was again heavy. The number of searchlights has further increased.

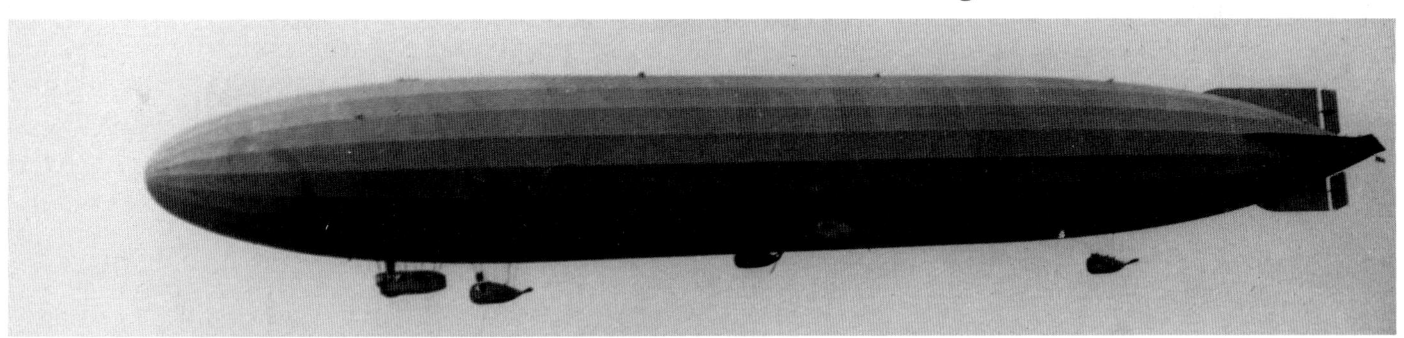

*SL 13 landing at Hannover on her delivery flight to Wittmundhaven. She was a sister ship to SL 8. (Blasweiler)*

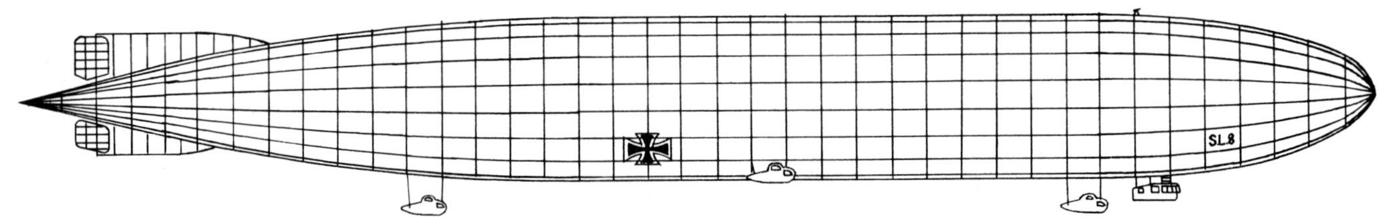


**SL 8**

| | | | |
|---|---|---|---|
| Gas capacity | 1,370,000 ft.$^3$ | Crew | 18 |
| Length | 571 ft. | Engines | 4 Maybach HSLu, of 240 h.p. |
| Diameter | 65 ft. | Maximum speed | 57.1 mph |
| Useful lift | 44,100 lbs. | Ceiling | 11,500 ft. |
| Gas cells | 19 | | |

Actually, from Tring *L 32* proceeded east and dumped her bombs on Ware. She then steered north-east and crossed the coast near Lowestoft at 4:15 a.m. Over the sea she was twice heard starting and stopping her engines as she obtained radio bearings.

*L 21* was at Hitchin, about thirty miles from London, when the Army ship fell. Her commander correctly deduced the cause of "the burning of *SL 11*, which from my own observation as well as testimony of the crew, was destroyed by the attack of two clearly visible airplanes, of which one fired a red, and the second a white or pale green light." At 3:15, feeling he could not reach London in the face of a freshening south wind, Frankenberg turned back to look for Norwich. He reported he could not find the city, which was completely darkened, but two incendiary and one explosive bomb aroused the defenses, four extremely powerful searchlights were uncovered and guns opened fire, and he at once dropped all his bombs. Sandringham, not Norwich, lay below, and the British, unaware that the Zeppelin commanders were forbidden to attack royal residences, were sure that Frankenberg had deliberately attempted to bomb the palace. His missiles did no damage, nor was the Zeppelin injured, though the Sandringham gun claimed a hit with the second of 12 rounds.

*L 21* was much delayed in returning to Nordholz. At 6:20 a.m., about two hours after leaving the coast, her starboard engine failed with a cracked cylinder. At eight o'clock the port engine also broke down with a defective magneto, putting the radio generator out of action so that Frankenberg could not send word of his plight. With two engines dead, *L 21* drifted north-east. At 11 a.m. the forward engine failed for a time. Because the gas was warmed by the sun's heat, *L 21*, in spite of being flown at a 15-degree down angle, rose to 10,700 feet and was checked there only by the use of the maneuvering valves. She would not answer the rudder due to the nose-down angle, and could not be brought back to her course till the forward engine was restarted. At 1:30 p.m. Borkum appeared on the starboard bow, and two hours later *L 21* was over her home field. The hydrogen was expanded by "superheat," and after dropping machine-gun ammunition, Frankenberg landed his ship "weighed off" and undamaged.

*Hauptmann* Manger reported that he had dropped six bombs on Boston at 10:45 p.m., then had steered south and at 2:15 a.m. had dropped 16 explosive and 20 incendiary bombs on northern London. Actually *L 14* had come inland near Wells-next-the-Sea at 9:50 and had steered erratically south to Thaxted, about 35 miles north-north-east of the capital, whence:

> the fall of the Army airship was observed by the crew. Shortly beforehand a green rocket had shot up from the ground through the overcast, which threw out a bright light. Then the ship itself was seen hanging in the air giving out a brilliant light and gradually sinking into the clouds. At the same time two Very signals, green and red, resembling plane recognition signals, were fired from above the ship. Therefore it is suspected the ship was destroyed by a bomb from a plane.

The British actually traced the bulk of *L 14*'s bombs on Haughley as she made off to the coast *after SL*

*11*'s destruction, and she went out to sea over Bacton at 4:05 a.m.

*Kapitänleutnant* Guido Wolff in *SL 8*, flying above clouds reaching up to 8,200 feet, did not see the coastline as he came inland over Holkham in Norfolk at 11:05, but at midnight it cleared and London was visible ahead. A heavy load of snow and rain dried quickly, but a strong head wind retarded her progress, and at 1:50 a.m., over Huntingdon, *SL 8* reversed course. She was thus on her way home when her crew saw their sister ship burning over London. Wolff thought he dropped his bombs on Norwich and Winterton, but could not see the results because of a ground mist. These missiles were scattered over northern Norfolk, and at 3:20 a.m. *SL 8* left the coast near her original landfall.

Schütze in *L 11* had passed through numerous rain and hail squalls out at sea which prevented him from reaching a safe attack altitude. At 1:45 p.m. the outer cover had burst between Rings 8 and 9 in a long tear from the top girder to No.1 longitudinal, and the engines ran at half speed for an hour until repairs were completed. At 10:18 p m. Schütze made his landfall at Yarmouth. Passing down the coast at 7,200 feet, he at first was uncertain of his position. He correctly identified Harwich, and standing offshore until 2:30 a.m., when a ground mist moved in, he aimed all his bombs at the naval base. They missed and caused no damage. Back at Hage, several small holes were found burned in the outer cover alongside the top girder at Ring 3, apparently from an incendiary shell which had burst short. Schütze saw other airships attacking London from 50 miles away, and in his War Diary recorded, "2:15, enormous flame over London, slowly sinking below cloud horizon, gradually diminishing. Burning airship."

Von Buttlar in *L 30* claimed an attack on London. Steering straight up the Thames, he asserted, he turned to windward and crossed the City from the south, dropping his first bomb at 11:10 p.m. Von Buttlar claimed his missiles were well placed and many fires and the collapse of houses resulted. Besides being fired on, von Buttlar reported that two planes pursued his ship for ten minutes. In fact, his bombs fell a good 90 miles from London. "*L 30* exhibited her now familiar tendency of just crossing the coast and then returning home,"[4] in the words of a contemporary British report. She was over land only a short time near Lowestoft, and dropped her bombs on the village of Bungay to the west of the fishing port.

Koch, in *L 24*, ran into heavy rain squalls which turned to snow at 8,500 feet. With a heavy load of snow, he was able to maintain an altitude of 10,000 feet only by flying his ship at an angle of 12 degrees, with a loss of speed. Fighting the south wind, Koch believed he got as far as Cambridge before giving up the attack on London and running before the wind to look for Norwich. At 12:40 he thought he saw the Norwich searchlight and aimed two explosive bombs at it, but further searchlights were not turned on as Koch hoped. Next the lights of Yarmouth opened up. In two runs, he reported, he silenced a battery and made hits on the air station, the railroad station and gas works. Koch had, however, come only a few miles inland. The "Norwich" bombs fell at Mundesley when a gun on a cliff overlooking the sea opened up on the airship. The "Yarmouth" bombs were aimed at lights burning on the Bacton night-landing ground north of Yarmouth. A plane in the air saw *L 24*'s missiles exploding south-east of the field, but could not find the attacker.

*Kapitänleutnant* Wilhelm Ganzel in *L 23* likewise abandoned the raid on London due to a heavy load of rain and hail, and likewise reported an attack on Norwich. In fact, he was farther to the west, over the Wash, where his bombs, falling on Boston, caused most of the meager casualty toll of the raid.

The two remaining Zeppelins made attacks on the English Midlands. *L 13* was carried so far north while waiting for darkness that Prölss decided to raid Nottingham. The weather was clear inland and he claimed to have found the city without difficulty. Nottingham, Prölss reported, was poorly blacked out, a row of factories was brightly lit up, and at 1 a.m. *L 13* began dropping her bombs. Several fires broke out and a factory exploded. "The streets of the town were clearly lit up for a time by the light of the big fire that followed, the ship herself at an

---

4 *Air Raids, 1916*, VII.

*Fore machine gun platform of L 22. The hatch over the climbing tunnel is to the left. Two Maxim 8mm machine guns with quilting to prevent cooling water freeze up. Note the two parachutes in the foreground. These were clipped to the crewman's harness, where the parachute was then drawn out as the crewman left the Zeppelin. There is no evidence that these were ever used. (Moch)*

altitude of 2,700 meters 19,000 feet] was lit up bright as day, and continued so until she had made 15 miles away from the scene of the fire." This attack was made in fact on East Retford, twenty-seven miles north-north-east of Nottingham. The town was well blacked out, but railroad lights attracted Prölss' attention. One of his explosive bombs went through a gasholder, and an incendiary falling nearby set fire to the escaping gas; ultimately all three containers in the nest were destroyed. This was the greatest single item of damage in the entire raid.

*L 22*'s forward engine went out of action with a broken crankshaft during the approach, causing Martin Dietrich to abandon the attack on London and to steer for Nottingham. After 10 p.m. he flew through very heavy snow squalls, and with a temperature of 25 degrees F. a mantle of ice built up on the airship. Only occasionally could Dietrich glimpse the surface through holes in the clouds. In this situation the radio bearings disagreed: Nordholz and Borkum placed *L 22* off the Wash, List off the Humber. Dietrich believed he came inland north of Spurn Point. Seven explosive and twenty incendiary bombs were sent down when he glimpsed "the lights of big factories in Halton on the south bank of the Humber," and he saw a heavy explosion and the glow of a big fire. At 1:20 a.m., after leaving the coast, the lookout on the top platform reported an airplane coming out of the clouds astern. As it flew over the Zeppelin, the ice-coated machine guns fired a few rounds and jammed, and Dietrich dived his ship into a cloud bank. The British, who had tracked *L 22* with difficulty as she circled over the Humber area, traced some bombs from her at Humberston, fifteen miles north-east of Halton.

So ended the greatest bombing effort that the German airship services made throughout the war. The sixteen ships participating had been carrying a total of 32 tons of bombs. The British traced 17

*Two famous training ships of the Naval Airship Service. L 11 (left) and L 6 together on the landing ground at Fuhlsbüttel. (Luftschiffbau Zeppelin)*

tons, of which 4,559 pounds landed within the boundaries of the Metropolitan Police District of London. Four British citizens had been killed, and twelve injured, and the damage totaled £21,072. Against this, the Germans had lost a trained airship crew of 16 men, together with *SL 11* which had cost the German taxpayers about £93,750.

September 3, 1916, was a Sunday, and the news of *SL 11*'s destruction was in every London home. The raider had fallen at Cuffley, and soon the lanes and byways leading to what was then a quiet farming hamlet were choked with excursionists in automobiles, in carts, on bicycles and on foot. What they saw in the hilltop beet field behind the Plough Inn was at that time both impressive and unique. A great tangle of steel bracing wire spread across the grass and tripped up Flying Corps personnel searching for more significant remains. The four Maybach engines lay in different parts of the field, more or less smashed and deeply imbedded in the ground. In the crankcase of one was found a shell-hole, plugged with cotton waste, proving that the airship had been hit before Leefe Robinson gave her the *coup de grâce*. The control car, which had fallen free, lay completely smashed but untouched by fire. Working parties were gathering damaged machine guns, ammunition boxes whose sides had been riddled by the explosion Or their contents, and the tinny remains of burst fuel tanks. Of the wooden girder framework, artfully joined with the cunning of the cabinet maker, only charred fragments survived. In one corner a green tarpaulin covered the blackened and mutilated bodies of the crew.

At first it was generally believed that *SL 11* had been set on fire by the guns alone. But presently there appeared an official announcement that Leefe Robinson had been awarded the Victoria Cross for destroying the airship. In his covering report, Lieut.-Colonel F.V. Holt, commanding the Home Defence Wing, stated that "it is very important that the successful method of attack remain secret, and instructions have been issued that the public are to be told that the attack was made with incendiary bombs from above."[5] But the country learned

*L 6 in the revolving shed at Nordholz on February 13, 1915. This damage was caused when the ship fell into a pine forest after a scouting flight. With the barometer falling, von Buttlar did not know that L 6 was too low. (Moch)*

enough to make Leefe Robinson the hero of the hour.

The spectacular downfall of *SL 11* within full view of London's millions had a heartening effect on the British populace. Too long had they patiently acquiesced in a policy of passive resistance that made little effort to stop the raiders, and merely sought to confuse them after they reached England. The people now believed that the Zeppelins would have to pay for any further intrusions over British soil. The authorities were also confident that this event marked the beginning of the end. Royal Flying Corps pilots would become more skilled in night-flying, while there was nothing the Germans could to armor their great inflammable gas-bags against the deadly flaming bullets.

The German Army airship service never again attempted to raid England, and was disbanded within a year. The Navy, however, was not ready to admit defeat. "The Navy was soon consoled of the loss of a military airship. The two services had little in common."[6]

At Fuhlsbüttel on the afternoon of September 16, the training airships *L 6* and *L 9* were destroyed in an inflation accident which emphasized the treacherous properties of hydrogen. Cells 9, 10, 11 and 12 of *L 6* had been connected up for inflation and the gas turned on. After ten minutes, there was

5 Letter, Lieut.Col. F.V. Holt to G.H.Q. Home Forces, September 3, 1916, in Imperial War Museum file, "Pilots' Reports Relating to Destruction of Zeppelins."

6 *The Times*, September 21, 1920, p. 12.

an explosion amidships, flames climbed rapidly up the sides of *L 6*, and promptly spread to *L 9*. Everyone in the hangar escaped, though one *L 6* crew member was blown out of a cabin window and injured a leg. The fire burned for nearly two hours. Though four-fifths of the shed roof was blown off, the towers and doors at the ends remained intact. Strasser suspected that rust particles in the high-pressure hydrogen storage flasks had been carried through the filling lines, building up a static electric charge which had sparked the fire; but the cause of the Fuhlsbüttel disaster was never proved.

Strasser still had faith in his airships, and was still confident of victory. In the first raid of the next new-moon period, on September 23, 1916, little concession was made to the enemy's proved ability to burn the Zeppelins out of the night sky. "Attack in the south," read his orders, "if possible with cloud cover, London. Middle permitted if wind veers to the right." Eight older airships, approaching via the North Sea, found a fresh south-west wind and no cloud cover, and raided the Midlands. Four of the new "thirties," led by Mathy as senior officer, flew south by way of Belgium in order to keep to windward of the capital.

Of the Midlands group, *L 17* proceeded farthest inland. *Kapitänleutnant* Hermann Kraushaar had set a course for Sheffield, and at 12:45 a.m. saw the lit-up factories of what he thought was his objective. Fire-belching chimneys in the northeast part of the town indicated blast furnaces, and heading into a 30 m.p.h. south-west wind, Kraushaar dropped his bombs deliberately. At 1:10, from north of Lincoln, Kraushaar saw, far in the distance, an evil omen: "Flaming airship falling to the south, the form was characteristic, it was followed in its nose first fall till it disappeared in the low ground mist." *L 17*'s attack was actually made on Nottingham. One of her first bombs cut the telephone wire between the lights and guns at Sneinton, and they had to act independently. Mist in the Trent Valley hampered the defenders, and Kraushaar met little opposition over the city. His eight explosive and eleven incendiary bombs killed three people and injured seventeen; the Midland Railway's freight station was badly wrecked, and the Great Central Station and tracks slightly damaged.

The other Zeppelins failed to reach the Midland cities. *L 21*, though flying at a 7-degree angle, was unable to climb higher than 8,000 feet. Her 36 bombs fell harmlessly near Suffolk villages. *L 22* again had trouble with radio bearings, which gave her a choice of locations – the Wash, the Humber, or Flamborough Head. Dietrich believed he made an attack on Grimsby; some bombs from his ship fell south-east of the town. At 1:20 a.m. the commander of *L 23*, *Kapitänleutnant* Ganzel, recorded in his War Diary, "Bright glow of fire towards Thames mouth, saw airship falling in flames." He was then near Lincoln, and had witnessed this latest disaster from nearly 150 miles away.

Of the four "super-Zeppelins," *L 30* claimed to have been the first to reach London. Von Buttlar reported having flown up the south bank of the Thames, and at 10:35 p.m., ninety minutes before any other Zeppelin reached the capital, he stated that he began dropping his bombs over eastern London. Because of the clearness of the night he did not go farther west against what he described as stiff opposition. He reported releasing his last eight explosives at Gravesend on the return journey. Yet British records show positively that no bombs fell either in London or in southern England at this time. The British raid map shows *L 30* slowly moving along the Norfolk coast from Cromer to Wells-next-the-Sea between 8:55 and 10:05 p.m., scattering her bombs in the water. Yet *L 30* could not have come so far north when at 8:17 p.m. she was over Blankenberghe on the Belgian coast, 125 miles to the south. The author believes that the airship off Cromer was *L 14*, which according to her War Diary was fired on in this area by outpost vessels and coastal batteries, and aimed 8 bombs at the ships. Yet where had *L 30* been between 8:17 p.m., when she left the Belgian coast, and 3:30 a.m. when she raised the Terschelling Bank Lightship on her way home?

Böcker in *L 33*, commissioned only three weeks before, was actually the first to reach London. Approaching the North Foreland from the Belgian coast, Böcker proceeded up the Thames Estuary. Some destroyers in the Edinburgh Deep opened fire on *L 33* at 10:12 p.m., but she held to her course and at 10:40 p.m. crossed the coast near the River

## AIRSHIP RAID, SEPTEMBER 23–24, 1916

| Ship | Flt. No. | Take-off | | Landing | | Time in Air | Distance (miles) | Av. speed (m.p.h.) | Max. alt. (feet) | Temp. (°F.) | Crew | Fuel (lb.) loaded/used | Oil (lb.) loaded/used | Ballast loaded (lb.) | Bombs (lb.) | Gas used (cubic feet) |
|---|---|---|---|---|---|---|---|---|---|---|---|---|---|---|---|---|
| *L 13* | 128 | Hage | 2.23 p.m. | Hage | 8.08 a.m. | 18h. 23m. | 741 | 41·4 | 9,500 | 35·6 | 16 | 9,750/7,600 | 894/476 | 10,580 | 2,910 | 214,500 |
| *L 14* | 91 | Hage | 2.36 p.m. | Hage | 6.58 a.m. | 16h. 22m. | 795 | 48·5 | 9,850 | 32·5 | 15 | 8,380/5,510 | 772/338 | 9,560 | 3,460 | 335,500 |
| *L 16* | 92 | Hage | 2.50 p.m. | Hage | 1.52 a.m. | 11h. 02m. | | | | | | | | | | |
| *L 17* | 67 | Tondern | 1.10 p.m. | Tondern | 10.25 a.m. | 21h. 14m. | 1,092 | 51·4 | 10,650 | 30·2 | 16 | 9,360/7,720 | 772/331 | 10,400 | 3,330 | 346,000 |
| *L 21* | 57 | Nordholz | 1.00 p.m. | Nordholz | 7.20 a.m. | 18h. 20m. | 935 | 51·0 | 9,500 | 35·6 | 17 | 9,880/5,890 | 868/364 | 11,900 | 4,410 | 382,000 |
| *L 22* | 43 | Tondern | 1.25 p.m. | Tondern | 7.15 a.m. | 18h. 05m. | 767 | 42·5 | 10,150 | 32·0 | 15 | 8,820/5,450 | 706/276 | 15,720 | 3,810 | 424,000 |
| *L 23* | 34 | Nordholz | 1.10 p.m. | Nordholz | 7.10 a.m. | 18h. 00m. | 902 | 50·1 | 10,500 | 32·0 | 16 | 9,330/6,910 | 915/386 | 13,920 | 4,440 | 424,000 |
| *L 24* | 33 | Tondern | 2.50 p.m. | Tondern | 10.35 a.m. | 7h. 45m. | | | | | | | | | | |
| *L 30* | 38 | Ahlhorn | 1.40 p.m. | Ahlhorn | 7.35 a.m. | 17h. 53m. | 966 | 53·6 | 11,000 | 33·8 | 20 | 13,730/10,190 | 1,370/443 | 27,000 | 5,860 | 883,000 |
| *L 31* | 15 | Ahlhorn | 1.35 p.m. | Ahlhorn | 8.45 a.m. | 18h. 50m. | 998 | 52·4 | 13,100 | 23·0 | 20 | 12,790/10,580 | 1,320/748 | 23,100 | 9,250 | 641,000 |
| *L 32* | 13 | Ahlhorn | 2.10 p.m. | | | | | | | | 22 | | | | | |
| *L 33* | 10 | Nordholz | 1.24 p.m. | | | | | | | 32·0 | 21 | | | | | |

*Weather:* Light S. and S.E. wind. Mist in the valleys of the Trent and the Lea.
*Bombs:* 371 (32,790 lb.), includes 101 (10,276) on London.
*Casualties:* 40 killed (37 in London), 130 injured (114 in London).
*Monetary Damage:* £135,068 (£64,662 in London).

## *L 31* DECK LOG IN RAID OF SEPTEMBER 23–24, 1916

| Cent. European time | Altitude (feet) | Temperature (°F.) Air | Gas | Pressure height (feet) | Release of ballast (lb.) | Wind Direction | Str. | Course | Distance (miles) | Speed (m.p.h.) | Position | Weather | Engines | Remarks |
|---|---|---|---|---|---|---|---|---|---|---|---|---|---|---|
| 1.35 | 165 | 58·1 | 60·8 | | | S.S.E. | 3–4 | | | | Takeoff | Overcast | | |
| 5.05 | | | | | 8,830 | | | 224° | 174 | | Cologne | | All | |
| 6.00 | | | | | | | | As | 53 | | Aachen | | | |
| 6.25 | | | | | | | | directed | 18·6 | | Visé | | | |
| 7.12 | | | | | | | | | 46·6 | | Louvain | | | |
| 7.25 | | | | | | | | | 16·8 | | Mechelen | | | |
| 7.50 | | | | | | | | | 24·8 | | Antwerp | | | |
| 8.45 | | | | | | | | | 52·1 | | Bruges | | | |
| 9.00 | 8,200 | 41·0 | 37·4 | 8,200 | 12,120 | W.S.W. | 4–6 | | 13·0 | | Ostend | | | |
| 9.20 | | | | | 1,320 | | | 333° | 12·7 | 52·4 | 059 β | | | 11.45: 1,279 lb. bombs dropped |
| 11.45 | | | | | Fuel | W.S.W. | 7–8 | 260° | 85·2 | | Dungeness | | | 1.20: 511 lb. bombs dropped |
| 1.17 | 12,500 | 24·8 | 28·4 | 12,500 | | | | 320° | 60·8 | | London | | | 1.31–1.46: 7,460 lb. bombs dropped |
| 1.50 | 13,100 | 21·2 | 26·6 | 13,100 | | | | As directed for attack on London | 34·5 | | London | | | |
| 2.50 | | | | | | | | 55° | 85·5 | | Yarmouth | | | |
| 5.10 | | | | | | | | 90° | 111·8 | | 112 δ | | | |
| 5.23 | | | | | | | | 60° | 58·2 | | 023 ϵ | | | |
| 6.45 | | | | | | | | 100° | 69·1 | | Borkum | | | |
| 8.45 | | 44·6 | 51·8 | | 11,985 | S.W. | 3 | 145° | 86·0 | | Landing Ahlhorn | Overcast | | |

## BALLAST SHEET

15TH FLIGHT OF THE AIRSHIP "L 31"

0 10 20 30 40 50 60 70 80 90 100 110 120 130 140 150 160 170 178

I II III IV V VI VII VIII IX X XI XII XIII XIV XV XVI XVII XVIII XIX

| Item | Distribution | Total |
|---|---|---|
| FUEL | 440, 440, 880, 880, 1320, 1760, 1760, 1760, 1760, 880, 880 | 12,760 |
| OIL | 660, 440, 220 | 1320 |
| BALLAST | 2200, 2200, 660, 530, 660, 2200, 2200, 350, 2200, 1320, 2200, 1760, 2200, 176, 2200 | 25,056 |
| CREW | 7, 3, 10 | 20 |
| ARMAMENT | 40 BOMBS 128 LB. EA.; 4 BOMBS 660 LB. EA.; 60 INCENDIARY BOMBS; MACHINE GUNS 981 LB. | 10,230 |
| SPARES | | 1320 |

| | LB. | | LB. |
|---|---|---|---|
| FUEL | 12,760 | PASSENGERS | |
| OIL | 1320 | PROVISIONS | |
| BALLAST | 23,056 | ARMAMENT<br>AMMUNITION<br>BOMBS | 10,230 |
| 20 CREW | 3520 | | |
| SPARES & STORES | 1320 | | |
| FREE LIFT | 1100 | | |
| SERVICE LOAD | 43,076 | USEFUL LOAD | 10,230 |

ADDITIONAL LOAD __________ LB.
(DEW, RAIN, SNOW)

USEFUL LIFT WITH 100% FILLING 53,306 LB.

| AIR: | | GAS: | |
|---|---|---|---|
| T. = | 57.2°F. | T. = | 60.0°F. |
| BAR. = | 30.16 IN. | SP. GR. = | 0.1000 |
| REL. H. = | 80% | | |

ADDITIONAL FILLING __________ CU. FT.

AHLHORN, SEPT. 24, 1916.

WEIGHED OFF BY
FRIEMEL
OBLT. Z. S.

THE COMMANDER
MATHY
KAPITÄNLEUTNANT

Crouch. Böcker then steered directly for London – "a determined attempt on the part of the airship to pass over the guns and searchlights without finesse"[7] – but the speed of his approach took the defenders by surprise. At 11:35 he dropped a parachute flare over South Brentwood, and another, twenty minutes later, over South Chadwell Heath. The second flare surprised the local searchlight crew, which was not cleared for action, nor could they find the Zeppelin behind the dazzling white glare of the burning magnesium. A few minutes later, says Böcker, "between 12:00 and 12:40, starting at Tower Bridge, two bombs of 300 kg., eight of 100 kg., thirty-two of 50 kg. and twenty incendiar-

7 Great Britain, Air Ministry. *Air Raids, 1916*, VIII, 23 September-2 October, 1916. Compiled by the Intelligence Section, G.H.Q., Home Forces.

*L 31 returning to Nordholz after the disastrous night of September 23/24, 1916. Large ground crew leads the ship towards the "Norman" shed. (Moch)*

*L 32 (commanded by Werner Peterson) over Oldenburg on September 22, 1916. This photo was said to be of her last flight, this is however, untrue. L 32 was destroyed over Billeracy two days later. This photograph is printed from a plate exposed in the control car of L 30 (commanded by von Buttlar) by her first officer, Leutnant zur See Hans von Schiller. (von Schiller)*

ies were dropped over the big warehouses along the Thames and over the City. Several enormous fires and the collapse of whole groups of houses were observed." These missiles fell in Bromley-by-Bow, on Bow itself, and on Stratford. Some of the incendiaries set fire to an oil depot and a lumber yard, "causing two of the most dangerous fires with which the Metropolitan Brigade had to cope throughout the entire period of the raids."[8] For a time these fires threatened to get out of hand, but were finally brought under control after several hundred empty oil barrels and some 43,000 cubic feet of lumber had gone up in flames. Only 26 of *L 33*'s explosive bombs were traced, leading the authorities to believe she must have dumped the rest in the mouth of the Thames. But one of the explosives demolished a whole row of tenements, killing six people and injuring twelve. Another destroyed a popular public house, the Black Swan, and killed four more people.

Böcker had done well to get his ship up to 13,000 feet on a relatively warm night – the temperature was just at the freezing-point – but the searchlights and batteries here were stronger than in any other sector. *L 33* could not long escape from the artillery barrage. Over Bromley a shell exploded inside Cell 14, abaft the forward engine gondola, severing the axial cable, fracturing the main ring and destroying the cell, while four adjacent gas-bags were torn by splinters. Shell fragments also riddled many of the after cells. Böcker turned towards the sea, his ship losing hydrogen with fatal rapidity. In the glare of the Kelvedon searchlight *L 33* was seen to release a "smoke screen" (actually the spray of her last water ballast), but still she fell at the rate of 800 feet per minute. Up in the hull the crew worked frantically to patch the torn gas cells. Once the sailmaker was overcome by escaping hydrogen, but

8 Frank Morison (Albert H. Ross), *War on Great Cities*, (London: Faber & Faber, 1937), p. 102.

*L 33 landing at Nordholz, September 1916. On September 24, 1916 during her first raid on England, she was forced to land through loss of gas after a raid on London near Little Wigborough. L 33's design was copied by British Admiralty draftsmen, and was reproduced as the post-war airships R 33 and R 34. (Moch)*

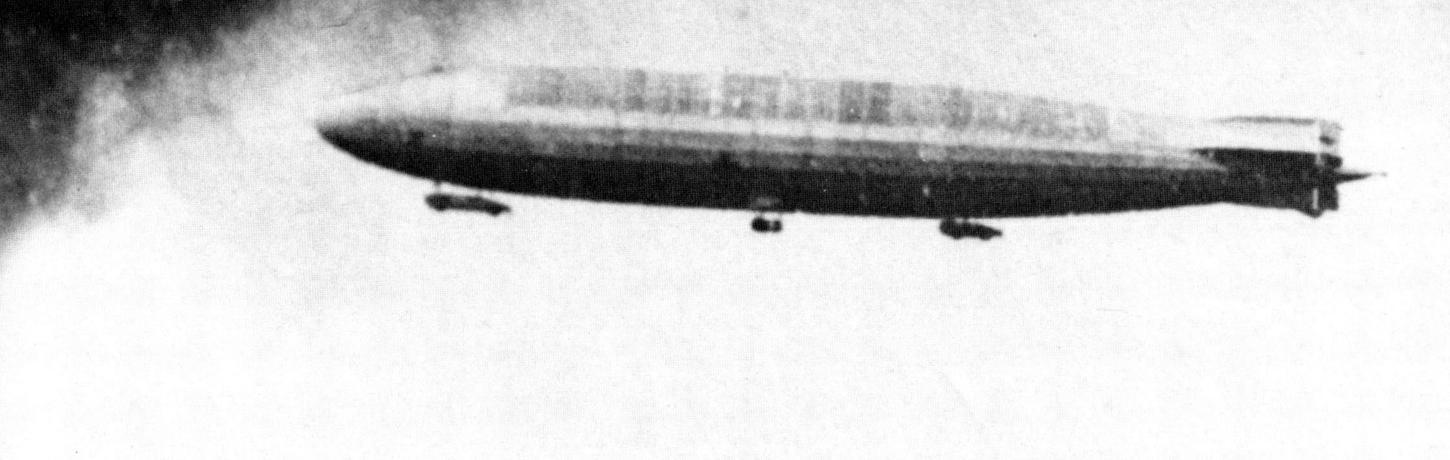

*PREVIOUS: The German naval airship L 33 on her one and only scouting flight, photographed from a vessel of the High Seas Fleet. (Kriegsmarinesammlung)*

he and his mates continued to work with cellon pots and brushes. Nor was the Zeppelin yet free from the defenses. Over Chelmsford an airplane attacked for twenty minutes, but failed to set her afire, though machine-gun bullets pierced several of the airship's fuel tanks The pilot was the same Lieutenant A. de B. Brandon who had unsuccessfully attacked *L 15* six months before. He reported:

> At 12:12 I saw a Zeppelin in the searchlights some distance away and made for it. Very shortly after this it escaped from the searchlights and I lost it, but I continued on and picked it up again. I went on climbing and managed with some difficulty to keep it in view, as there were no searchlights on it and my automatic pump had failed, and I had to work the cocking handle of the Lewis gun. After putting on a drum of ammunition I came up behind the Zeppelin and on raising the gun jerked it out of the mounting, the gun and the yoke falling across the nacelle. I managed to replace the gun but in the meantime had passed under and past the Zeppelin. I turned and passed along it again, but from the bow, but we passed each other too quickly for me to take aim. On turning I came up from behind and fixed a drum of ammunition. The Brock ammunition seemed to be bursting all along it but the Zeppelin did not catch fire. I was using Brock, Pomeroy and sparklet. I turned again and put on a fresh drum and came up from behind and fired again. The gun jammed after about nine rounds. I now decided to get above the Zepp and went on climbing but there was a large bank of grey cloud all

*Various views of L 33 after coming down near Little Wigborough.*

*Overview of L 33 after coming down near Little Wigborough, Essex. The stern is nearest to the camera.*

> around the horizon and it was impossible to see the Zeppelin against it, after I had got level with the Zeppelin. I first saw the Zeppelin at 12:13 and lost it at 12:33.[9]

Böcker struggled on, hoping to ditch his ship in the sea and sink her, but at Little Wigborough, in the marshes back of Mersea Island, 133 stalled and fell in a field about sixty feet from a farmer's cottage. After setting the wreckage alight with signal flares, Böcker set off with his men, hoping to reach the coast and seize a boat to escape across the North Sea. They were soon captured. While the crew members were questioned for fourteen days in London, Böcker was interrogated by Major Trench, who, he alleged, threatened him with a civil trial for murder. After Böcker refused to give information, Trench showed him plans of the latest Zeppelins, produced a list of their secret radio call signals, and claimed to have spent a day in Friedrichshafen since the start of the war. Early in 1918 Böcker was exchanged with the usual stipulation that he should not serve in combat. In June, 1918, he was once more in the air, and furthermore in command of his old *L 14*, now a school ship. As Director of Airship Training he finished the war in Nordholz.

*L 31* and *L 32* came down-Channel in company and at 10:45 p.m. made their landfall at Dungeness. Here, instead of coming inland, *L 32* circled for over an hour. Her last radio message had been sent three hours before and the cruiser *Stettin*, which heard her call letters, reported that the signal was too weak to read, but one may assume that Peterson had engine trouble. Mathy pressed straight on for the capital. With a load of nearly five tons of bombs, and an air temperature of 40 degrees F., *L 31*, was unable to reach a safe altitude for an attack on London. To lighten her, Mathy aimed ten 128-pound bombs at the Dungeness Lighthouse, but scored no hits At 11:30 he crossed Tunbridge Wells, and shortly afterwards picked up the London-Eastbourne railroad line. Following this north, Mathy from time to time checked his position by dropping parachute flares. At 12:10 a.m. he came in over Croydon at an altitude of 12,500 feet. Here the last flare proved of unexpected assistance. Floating between the ship and the ground, it so blinded the anti-aircraft gunners that they were unable to find *L 31*.

Mathy in the meantime was rapidly dropping his bombs in a line through Brixton and Streatham, where many of the thickly clustered houses were damaged or demolished. Others blew in the fronts of grocery stores, furniture shops, tailor shops, and many other establishments. One explosive bomb gutted a tram car on top of Streatham Hill. Altogether the casualties in these suburbs amounted to thirteen dead and thirty-three injured.

At 12:15, *L 33* was seen to the east, with two large fires in her wake. To the smoke from these fires, rather than the effect of the flares, Mathy attributed his immunity from the searchlights.

Crossing the heart of the capital from south to north, Mathy dropped ten more bombs on Lea Bridge Road and Leyton, and above a blanket of mist in the Lea Valley got away unscathed. How he missed the City, the goal of every London raid,

[9] Brandon's report in Imperial War Museum file, "Pilots' Reports Relating to Destruction of Zeppelins."

is a mystery. His War Diary particularly mentions having dropped ten 128-pound and two 660-pound bombs on it. Though Mathy insisted that he saw the Thames clearly in the light of his parachute flares, he actually was not so far north when these explosives fell. Visibility may have been none too good from his altitude of 13,000 feet. He stated in his report, "single bombs were released over Clapham, the bulk of them over Chelsea-Pimlico, in the City, and in Islington," indicating his belief that his two groups of bombs fell over the heart of the capital, and were much more closely spaced than was the case.

At 1:10 a.m.:

> The attack of a ship on the Woolwich area was observed. The ship was also very heavily fired on and, after dropping her bombs, appeared to have reached safety when additional searchlights opened up ahead of her and, after a brief, very intense bombardment, her destruction followed. The ship fell in flames at 1:15 a.m.

Under the circumstances, it is surprising to find the British defense authorities secretly perturbed by Mathy's bold crossing of the capital – the first time this had happened – and by the novel way in which he had confounded the defenses. Knowing with whom they were dealing, the British expected Mathy to try the same scheme again, probably followed by a fleet of airships employing the same tactics.

The flaming victim that night was *L 32*. At midnight Peterson began his approach to the capital, but deviated considerably to the east. At 12:50 he aimed seven bombs at the Crockenhill searchlight, south-east of London. At 1 a.m., when he reached the Thames, he was 12 miles east of the city. North of the river *L 32* came into clear air, and the lights seized her at once. Immediately the guns opened fire, and although the Zeppelin's height was estimated at 13,000 feet,[10] the Tunnel Farm gun claimed two hits. Peterson dumped the rest of his bombs – 23 explosive and 21 incendiary – and turned east to escape the fire. But already the airplanes were upon him. Second Lieutenant Frederick Sowrey reported:

> At 12:45 a.m. I noticed an enemy airship in an easterly direction. I at once made in this direction and maneuvered into a position underneath. The airship was well lighted by searchlights but there was not a sign of any gunfire. I could distinctly see the propellers revolving and the airship was maneuvering to avoid the searchlight beams. I fired at it. The first two drums of ammunition had apparently no effect, but the third one caused the envelope to catch on fire in several places; in the center and front. All firing was traversing fire along the envelope. The drums were loaded with a mixture of Brock, Pomeroy and Tracer ammunition. I watched the burning airship strike the ground and then proceeded to find my flares. I landed at Suttons Farm at 1:40 a.m., 24th instant. My machine was

*Oberleutnant zur See Werner Peterson commander of L 32, was killed when the ship went down on September 24, 1916. He was known as a superb ship handler. The mystery remains as to why he was carrying not only the L 32 logbook, but also the new German Navy secret signals book when the ship went down.*

10 L 32's bomb-sight, found subsequently in the wreckage of the control car, was in fact set for an altitude of 4,000 meters (13,100 feet).

*British soldiers guarding the wreck of the L 32. The tail cone and one of the rudders appear in the foreground, together with an oak tree onto which the airship fell, and which was completely stripped.*

*A British officer picking his way through the tangled remains of the hull of L 32. (Illustrated London News)*

B.E.2c 4112. After seeing the Zeppelin had caught on fire, I fired a red Very's light.[11]

The wreckage fell at Snail's Hall Farm, South Green, near Billericay, and burned on the ground for 45 minutes. All on board were killed. A propeller with gear-case was picked up three miles from the scene, and two of the huge elevating planes and rudders were found in a wood half a mile away. Officers of the Naval Intelligence Division, who stood by at all times to rush to the scene of a Zeppelin crash and to search the wreckage and bodies of the crew for intelligence material, were early on the scene and discovered a burned but usable copy of the latest secret signal book of the German Navy – a priceless item which they had sought in vain since it had last been changed just after Jutland.

The loss of *L 32* brought home to the other airship crews the deadly turn in the war over England. They were brave men and had often faced death without flinching, but the memory of their burn-

11 Sowrey's report in Imperial War Museum file, "Pilots' Reports Relating to Destruction of Zeppelins."

*The remains of L 32's port engine gondola lying upside down.*

ing sister-ship, haunting their dreams by night and their thoughts by day, was too great a strain on their over-wrought nerves. They discussed, not their chances of survival, but what they could do when the inevitable catastrophe should overtake them. Even here they could only echo the opinion of one of Peterson's men, who on the night before his own end had prophesied, "Death will come so quickly that there will be no time for deliberation or even for instinctive action."[12]

For the German Naval Airship Division this raid was a turning-point in the air war against England. The destruction of an Army Schütte-Lanz craft could be ignored. The loss of *L 32* and *L 33*, the Imperial Navy's newest Zeppelins, together with Peterson and Böcker – two men whose ability and experience made them irreplaceable – signaled the end of Strasser's dream of conquest. Never again would his men approach England with such high confidence, nor would his giant war machines strike such terror into the hearts of the enemy.

12 Pitt Klein, *Achtung! Bomben Fallen!* (Leipzig: Verlag von K.F. Koehler, 1934), p.135.

# CHAPTER XV

# "CAUTION IS ORDERED"

Strasser's reaction to the double catastrophe over London is shown by his orders for the next raid, on September 25, in which nine Zeppelins took part. The older ships were directed to "attack England middle and industrial area," and only the two "thirties" were authorized to "attack in the south, main target London, with the limitation that caution is ordered in case of clear weather." For the Naval Airship Division, proud of the distinction of having led in the assault on England, this was a bitter pill.

With the older ships heading for the Midlands via the North Sea, and *L 30* and *L 31* making for London via the Rhineland and Belgium, the attack fell into two parts. Three of the Midlands raiders turned back. Ganzel in *L 23* made three approaches to the Norfolk coast, and thrice reversed course, alleging that the forward engine had failed each time. He in fact was suffering already from a severe war neurosis, and two months later was transferred from *L 23* to the light cruiser *Kolberg*.

Martin Dietrich in *L 22* was heading for Sheffield from the start. Having had trouble recently with radio bearings, he flew west-southwest from Tondern to take his departure from the Terschelling Bank Lightship, but could not find it in thick weather. None the less, he made an accurate landfall at Mablethorpe on the Yorkshire coast at 10:40 p.m. At 12:15 a.m. lights were seen on the starboard bow, which Dietrich took to be those of Lincoln. Since heavy clouds and snow squalls were building up in the west, he turned aside and bombed this target of opportunity. Writing up his report next day, Dietrich, considering the southeast wind on his return, was inclined to believe he had attacked Sheffield rather than Lincoln. He was right: his bombs had fallen among the Sheffield armaments factories, and only by extraordinary luck did they escape severe damage. One incendiary started a small fire at the engine shops of the shipbuilding firm of John Brown & Co., but the rest of the bomb damage was suffered by nearby houses. Twenty-eight people were killed and nineteen injured.

The other airships were frustrated by the black-out and by the increased anti-aircraft defenses in their attempts to bomb the Midlands industrial cities. Making a flight of 970 miles, *L 21* claimed to have bombed Derby, but her main attack was on Bolton, 60 miles to the north-west in Lancashire. *L 14* claimed an attack on Leeds, but had been held away from the city by the gun at Collingham, ten miles to the north-east. Only three bombs were traced from *L 16* during a journey of nearly two hours over Yorkshire.

*L 30*, flying the southern route via Aachen, Liege, Antwerp and Ghent, left the Belgian coast at Blankenberghe at 8:20 p.m. and steered for the North Foreland. Finding a completely clear, starry night, with no cloud cover, von Buttlar abandoned the attack on London, and reported bombing Ramsgate and Margate. "Especially heavy explosions and several fires were seen." Yet no bombs fell in or near the two Kentish towns on this night. Once again the British raid map shows *L 30* reaching the coast far to the north near Cromer at 8:15, but since this time coincides with her departure from Blankenberghe, this report certainly refers to one of the northern airships – possibly *L 13*, which dropped some bombs in the sea before turning back for Hage.

Mathy again flew down the Channel to Dungeness, but found no "London weather." With hardly a cloud in the sky, and both the English and French coasts clearly visible, Mathy saw that it would be suicide to attack the capital. Instead, *L 31* would bomb the naval base at Portsmouth, where, as Mathy told his crew, "nobody has ever been, and it is sure to be very interesting!"[1]

At 10:15 p.m. Mathy was off Beachy Head. Shortly after 11, when over Selsey Bill, the last promontory east of Portsmouth, he descended to 4,000 feet and dropped a parachute flare to verify his position. A few minutes later he reached the east coast of the Isle of Wight and turned north on a compass heading for Portsmouth.

At 11:50, *L 31* came in from the sea at an altitude of 11,000 feet. Searchlights were uncovered at once, and the dockyard antiaircraft guns opened fire. The Zeppelin was beyond their range, however, and the unpracticed gun crews had several misfires. Mathy began an intense two-minute attack, but found that "observation of hits was very difficult, since the searchlights were blinding in the clear air." He reported that "by means of four parachute flares thrown out towards the end of the attack, it was ascertained that all bombs had fallen in the city and on the dockyard." Yet his daring *tour de force* was in vain, for his heavy load of 8,125 pounds of bombs was never traced by the British, and must have fallen in the sea. Mathy then steered east over land, pursued by an airplane from Calshot. At 12:40 a.m. he stopped his engines to obtain radio bearings, and at 1:15 left the coast at St. Leonard's. At 2:30 a.m., three bombs were heard exploding in the sea off Dover, presumably from *L 31* as she started her homeward journey across Belgium.

The British defense authorities, knowing from their deciphering service that Mathy had been the attacker, were much puzzled by his failure to bomb the dockyard. They concluded either that *L 31* had intended a reconnaissance and had dumped her bombs to regain altitude after her descent over Selsey Bill, or that the electrical bomb release gear had failed at the crucial moment. Curiously enough, they dismissed the true reason – "confusion from being blinded by lights and shell-fire" – as "most improbable," an unconscious tribute to Mathy's determination and ability.[2]

For several days the weather was too bad to permit raids, and the airship crews, left to themselves, brooded on the events of the past week. Mathy's men in particular were showing unmistakable signs of what later would be diagnosed as "combat fatigue":

> Even in the mess the old cheerfulness is gone. We discuss our heavy losses, particularly, of course, the most recent ones. Our nerves are on edge, and even the most energetic and determined cannot shake off the gloomy atmosphere.
>
> It is only a question of time before we join the rest. Everyone admits that they feel it. Our

1 Pitt Klein, p. 137.

2 *Air Raids*, 1916. VIII.

nerves are ruined by mistreatment. If anyone should say that he was not haunted by visions of burning airships, then he would be a braggart. But nobody makes this assertion; everyone has the courage to confess his dreams and thoughts.

The commander acts no differently than of old, but it is only natural that his appearance should become more serious and his features be more sharply and deeply graven in his face.

"We will be next, Pitt !" growls our first elevator man, Chief Quartermaster's Mate Peters.

"You're mad !" I defend myself. "We have already made a hundred and twenty successful war flights; we serve under the most outstanding commander. I trust our lucky star!"

He looks earnestly at me.

"Pitt, you know that I'm no coward; out in eastern Asia we made many hair-raising voyages through typhoons. But I dream constantly of falling Zeppelins. There is something in me that I can't describe. It's as if I saw a strange darkness before me, into which I must go."[3]

Yet *L 31* was ready on the afternoon of October 1, when eleven Zeppelins set out to raid England. They encountered gusty south-west to west-north-west winds over the German Bight, with squalls and deep clouds. Over England a nearly solid cloud ceiling hampered their navigation, while at higher altitudes the wind, veering into the north-west, picked up speed and brought rain, snow and hail.

[3] Pitt Klein, p. 144.

*Mathy and the crew of L 31 (another photo of this crew, along with maintenance personnel, appears on page 183). The crew wear their decorations, among them are the Iron Cross 1st, and 2nd Class. Mathy is at the extreme left, his Wachoffizier, Oberleutnant zur See Friemel is at Mathy's left. Of the twenty-three crewmen in this photograph, four were left behind on the last mission. (Moch)*

Almost all of the airships were carried south of their dead reckoning position. Three of them were obliged to return without having attacked, while *L 30*, though she reported bombing "extensive installations on the south side of the Humber," was not seen over England.

Blinded by a vile mixture of snow-clouds and mist, five Zeppelins wandered over Lincolnshire and Norfolk, attempting to find the big cities by radio bearings alone, and dropping bombs at intervals in hopes of arousing the defenses. Several craft iced up severely. For a full ten hours, Frankenberg in *L 21* saw neither land nor sea, and had no check on his position. He tried to find Manchester or Sheffield, but glimpsed only a few distant searchlights. Once the clouds parted, and with theatrical clarity, Frankenberg saw, seventy miles away, a Zeppelin held by the searchlights over London and dropping bombs. Visibility was again obscured, and then once more the strange craft was seen burning high in the sky. Soon afterwards *L 21* flew into a damp mist which froze on the outer cover. The Zeppelin iced up rapidly, and soon, although she was driven at an angle of 10 degrees, she became too heavy to be held in the air. Frankenberg had to drop his bombs one by one as ballast. Nor could he radio for bearings. The antenna was coated with ice three inches thick, and was useless.

*Kapitänleutnant* Koch had intended to steer for Manchester, but could not determine his position due to the solid cloud below. A star sight taken at dusk showed that *L 24* had been carried much farther south than radio bearings indicated, and her commander therefore decided to attack London. During the approach he saw another airship take fire high in the sky and smash to earth, "in my estimation in the region north-east of the docks." He held to his course and an hour later "the whole bomb load was dropped with good effect on the districts of Stoke Newington and Hackney." Actually Koch had been attracted by flares on the night-flying field at Hitchin, thirty miles north of London. His bombs killed a soldier on guard, but did no damage. *L 24* went out to sea south of Lowestoft at 3:35 a.m. A few hours later the tail-shaft of the forward propeller broke. Due to a heavy load of rain and shortage of ballast, Koch could not stop his ship and send a man out on the gondola roof to secure it, and after forty-five minutes the windmilling propeller pulled out and spun earthward.

The raider which had fallen in flames over London was *L 31*. Heinrich Mathy, courageous and aggressive to the end, did not know the meaning of the word "caution," and was determined to carry out his orders to "attack London if possible according to weather conditions." At 9 p.m. he made his landfall near Lowestoft, and for seventy miles followed a compass course of 245 degrees until reaching the line of the Great Eastern Railway at Chelmsford. At this point he slowed his engines to check his position by radio bearings. Had he followed the railroad line straight into London, Mathy probably would once again have got away, for the defending airplanes were still on the ground. But the searchlights were converging on him, and at 10:45 p.m. *L 31* was seen to sheer off to the north.

Hoping to surprise the defenders at another point, Mathy was circling the north-east fringe of the capital. At 11:20 p.m. he again checked his position by radio bearings. At 12:10 a.m. he was over Hertford. Apparently hoping to pass unheard and unopposed over the northern gun defenses, Mathy now throttled his engines and drifted with the wind south and east towards Ware. But at 12:30, when he opened up his engines, he found himself under a heavy fire from batteries ahead. Four defense pilots saw the disturbance and banked their machines to head for the enemy. Mathy undoubtedly saw them closing in, for *L 31* turned sharply west, salvoed all her bombs, and began to climb.

Second Lieutenant W.J. Tempest, who had taken off from North Weald Bassett at 11 p.m., was about fifteen miles away, but immediately headed straight across London for the Zeppelin, although the sky in his path was strewn with exploding antiaircraft shells. While still five miles away his fuel pump failed, but he succeeded in keeping up the pressure by hand.

> "As I drew up to the Zeppelin, to my relief I found that I was quite free from A.A. fire, for the nearest shells were bursting quite three miles away. The Zeppelin was now nearly

*Set on fire at 13,000 feet, L 31 fell at Potters Bar. A cordon of British soldiers guards the wreckage.*

15,000[4] feet high and mounting rapidly. I therefore decided to dive at her, for though I held a slight advantage in speed, she was climbing like a rocket and leaving me standing. I accordingly gave a tremendous pump at my petrol tank, and dived straight at her, firing a burst straight into her as I came. I let her have another burst as I passed under her and then banking my machine over, sat under her tail, and flying along underneath her, pumped lead into her for all I was worth. I could see tracer bullets flying from her in all directions, but I was too close under her for her to concentrate on me. As I was firing, I noticed her begin to go red inside like an enormous Chinese lantern and then a flame shot out of the front part of her and I realized she was on fire. She then shot up about 200 feet, paused, and came roaring down straight on to me before I had time to get out of the way. I nose-dived for all I was worth, with the Zepp tearing after me, and expected every minute to be engulfed in the flames. I put my machine into a spin and just managed to corkscrew out of the way as she shot past me, roaring like a furnace."[5]

The wreckage of *L 31* came to earth in a field outside Potters Bar. The forward half of the hull crashed on to a huge oak, from which several branches were stripped, and piled up around it to a height of twenty feet in a shapeless tangle of duralumin girders. The after half was strewn over the field several hundred feet away. The fire, fed by the airship's fuel supply, flared and smoldered for several hours, despite a weeping drizzle that set in before dawn.

Lying on his back half-imbedded in the soil in one corner of the field, the astonished villagers found an officer who had leaped from the blazing ship long before she reached the ground. By the light of the two piles of wreckage they saw that he

4 This is an exaggeration. In his official report, Tempest gives *L 31*'s altitude as 12,700 feet, while her bomb-sight was found set for only 3,500 meters (11,500 feet).

5 Tempest letter, "Ackworth Grange, September 15, 1920," in Imperial War Museum file, "Pilots' Reports Relating to Destruction of Zeppelins."

*Army airship LZ 86. The navy had little use for the army ships as their lift was limited. (Kameradschaft)*

still breathed, but he almost immediately expired. Royal Flying Corps officers later found from his identity disc that he was their most redoubtable foe – "*Kaptlt*. Mathy. *L 31*."

His death made a profound impression on the men of his service. One petty officer wrote:

> There was only one airship commander with whom I ever flew that I would have trusted to find his way over England without making a bad mistake. That was Heinrich Mathy. . . . It was the airplane firing the incendiary bullet that brought about his downfall and with him the life and soul of our airship service went out too.[6]

For the remaining twenty-two months of his life, Peter Strasser never forgot his most successful airship captain. To Mathy's young widow he sent a letter of condolence with the stiff, stereotyped phrases behind which this hard and determined man concealed from his associates a sensitive personality:

> In the circle of his comrades his memory will endure as a naval officer such as His Majesty the Kaiser required, daring, of tireless energy, his attention continually directed towards the destruction of the enemy, without consideration for his own person, and at the same time a cheerful, helpful and true comrade and friend, high in the estimation of his superiors, his equals and his subordinates.[7]

There followed an interlude in which, during the next full moon period, the airships once more participated in a Fleet operation. Scheer had planned to repeat the Sunderland operation, but on October 6 he was ordered to resume trade war with the U-boats under prize rules, and his future plans for the Fleet had to omit the submarines. Thus, the operation on October 19 proceeded no further than

6 (Heinrich Bahn,) p. 108.

7 Letter, Peter Strasser to Hertha Mathy, Nordholz, October, 3, 1916.

*Army LZ 98 entering a shed at the advanced base at Namur in Belgium. Under the command of Ernst Lehmann, LZ 98 made several raids on England in the spring and summer of 1916. (Author)*

*On September 4, 1917 Admiral Scheer visited Ahlhorn to confer the Pour le Mérite on Fregettenkapitän Peter Strasser. Subsequently, Scheer flew in L 35 commanded by Kapitänleutnant Ehrlich. (Kameradschaft)*

the eastern edge of the Dogger Bank, and there was no contact between the opposing fleets. At 1:30 p.m. *L 14* encountered a portion of the Harwich Force, but Scheer by then was already on his way home. The British, in fact, had no advance information of Scheer's sortie, and the Grand Fleet was in harbor.

The eight Zeppelins patrolling in a great arc ahead of the High Seas Fleet suffered a variety of mechanical breakdowns, which could have had serious consequences if the British had been at sea in strength. *L 21* had to leave her station at 10:15 a.m. when she lost her port propeller. *L 24* extended her patrol line accordingly, but at 2:02 p.m. she had to head for home when the after propeller shaft bearings seized. *L 17* took her place, but at 6:05 p.m. three of her engines failed all together; twenty minutes later, two were partially and one fully repaired. *L 23*'s port elevator jammed at 10:20 a.m., but she stayed in position. At 1:30, when it was repaired with a jury rig, she was ordered to return. *L 13*, which was only forty-five miles off Lowestoft when she received the general recall, was searching for Norderney Lighthouse at 12:20 a.m. next morning when both side engines failed completely, and the after motor began giving trouble due to a plugged fuel line. With the radio generator out of action she could send no distress messages, but she limped into Hage at 5 a.m.

On November 17 four airships were out scouting, including the new *L 36*, which flew to the mouth of the Skagerrak. Thereafter, storms and gales prevailed for days, and no long flights were possible. The officers at Nordholz had nearly given up hope of an improvement in the weather when they sat down to dinner at noon on November 27. It was a festive occasion, for Max Dietrich, the commander of *L 34*, was celebrating his 46th birthday. Suddenly Strasser's adjutant burst in with unexpected news: "Gentlemen, attack orders: the industrial areas of middle England, splendid prospects, the first ship must be in the air by 1 p.m. at the latest!"[8] The officers dropped their napkins and rushed from the table. Only Kurt Frankenberg of *L 21* paused to shout back, "Leave the birthday decorations, we'll celebrate tomorrow !" But his executive officer, young Hans-Werner Salzbrunn, soberly confided to his friend, Richard Frey of *L 22*, "I know we won't come back from this flight!"

Over the eastern North Sea the airships found weak south-west to north-west winds, and flew through great masses of vapor. *L 35* passed within half a mile of a water spout. *L 36*, charging out of a cloud bank close aboard, flew over *L 22* with only 600 feet to spare. Later in the evening the clouds disappeared and left the sea gleaming black and hard under a multitude of stars. Viktor Schütze, commanding *L 36*, complained that "there was no real darkness, such as one expects on a moonless winter night." From the north-west to the north-

8 *Korvettenkapitän* Heinrich Hollender, "Marineluftschiffe," *Die deutschen Luftstreitkräfte im Weltkrieg*, ed. Georg Paul Neumann (Berlin: E.S. Mittler u. Sohn, 1920), p. 395.

*These two photos show L 34 at Nordholz. Under the command of Max Dietrich, this ship was shot down in flames on November 27, 1916 off Hatlepool, England, with twenty crewmen perishing. (both - Luftschiffbau Zeppelin)*

east the sky glowed as over a big city. For hours before reaching the English coast, several ships were silhouetted against the sky glow to the north, and *L 36*'s disgusted skipper claimed he could still read his pocket watch in the control car. At 11:30 p.m. the glow in the north began sending flickering rays of soft light towards the zenith. After half an hour the aurora borealis vanished, but it was still "very bright like a bright moonlit night," with visibility of 20 miles towards the land. At higher altitudes the head wind increased, and the airships made slow progress.

*L 30* had suffered a burned-out crank-bearing in the starboard after engine ten minutes after take-off, and when the starboard midships engine failed at 8:10 p.m., von Buttlar turned back. The other ships split into two groups. *L 34*, *L 35*, which intended to attack Newcastle, and *L 36* heading for Edinburgh kept together on a course for the Durham coast, followed by *L 24* which planned to bomb a benzol plant at Stockton-on-Tees. The older Zeppelins held more to the south for Flamborough Head.

Dietrich, leading the northern group, crossed the coast at Black Halls Rocks, north of Hartlepool, at 12:30 a.m. At Hutton Henry *L 34* was picked up by a searchlight, and her commander aimed thirteen explosive bombs in reply. Dietrich evidently did not care to venture farther inland against alert defenses on such a clear night, for he turned back and on his way out to sea began dropping his bombs on West Hartlepool. Sixteen explosives fell here, killing four people and injuring eleven. Dietrich had made the mistake of flying no higher than 9,500 feet, and now found an airplane rapidly overhauling him. The pilot, Second Lieutenant Ian V. Pyott, had taken off from No.36 Squadron's field at Seaton Carew at 11:22 p.m.:

> I had been in the air for approximately an hour when I sighted a Zeppelin between Sunderland and Hartlepool in the beam of a searchlight (Castle Eden) coming south and towards me. At this moment I was at 9,800 and the Zepp seemed a few hundred feet below me. I flew towards the Zepp and flew at right angles to and underneath him amidships, firing as I went under. I then turned sharply east, the Zepp turning east also. We then flew on a parallel course for about 5 miles, firing 71 rounds at the Zepp. I estimated his ground speed to be approximately 70 m.p.h. I was aiming at his port quarter and noticed first a small patch become incandescent where I had seen tracers entering his envelope. I first took it for a machine-gun firing at me from the Zepp, but this patch rapidly spread and the next thing was that the whole Zepp was in flames. I landed at 12 midnight (British Time), engine and machine O.K. The Zeppelin, which fell into the sea at the mouth of the Tees, was still burning when I landed.[9]

Next day only a patch of scummy oil marked where Dietrich's birthday had ended in death for him and all his crew.

*L 35* was over Seaham Harbor, only eight miles away, when *L 34* fell. *Kapitänleutnant* Ehrlich had had trouble with the automatic valves of the midships gas cells. Moisture in the hydrogen, pouring out as *L 35* climbed to her attack altitude, had condensed and frozen on the valve seats to the thickness of a finger. The valves were supposed to be checked and cleaned by the sailmaker patrolling in the keel, but he could not keep ahead of the problem, the thin metal valve covers were deformed by the seating springs forcing them down on the uneven accumulation of ice around the edges, and thus, even after they were cleared of ice, they were no longer gas-tight. To prevent further loss of gas, Ehrlich had to fly below pressure height at 8,200 to 9,200 feet, and had to steer clear of the defenses. Ehrlich watched *L 34* steer inland ahead of him between Hartlepool and the Tees:

> *L 34* crossed the coast without being lit up, but then was caught by a searchlight and temporarily evaded it. After a while, after the ship had gone inland, the searchlight lit up and caught the ship at once. The ship must have been clearly visible from below. Soon afterwards 14 searchlights lit up in succession, forming a

9 Pyott's report in Imperial War Museum file, "Pilots' Reports Relating to Destruction of Zeppelins."

> semi-circle with its opening towards the land, between the Tees and Hartlepool. All held the ship fast and she steered westward brightly illuminated. Weak anti-aircraft fire and single guns opened up. After 5 to 7 minutes a rocket or flare went off, about level with the ship, whereupon the gunfire ceased. After 3 to 5 minutes the ship became a brightly glowing ball of fire, held her altitude a moment and then tipped to the vertical, burning over her whole length, and fell. Behind the ship and apparently separate from her there was a great red ball of burning gas streaming out of the ship. The ship fell not far from the coast, near the Tees (on land) and the fire went out almost at once. When a green star was fired in the air, all the searchlights went out. Reliable lookouts on the stern platform saw two planes, at first with the naked eye, then with glasses, which seemed to be going in for a landing.

*L 35* gave up the raid and turned out to sea at once. As the British official history says, "It was well for her she did, for had she persisted any farther, it is unlikely she could have evaded encounters with other airplane pilots who were patrolling in the vicinity.[10]

*L 24* was about fifteen miles out at sea when *L 34* fell. Her starboard engine was dead, and her commander, *Oberleutnant zur See* Kurt Friemel (Mathy's former executive officer) "gave up my plan of going inland on such a clear night with three engines, and steered along the coast to Scarborough." Friemel reported dropping his bombs here at 1:45 a.m., but they were not traced by the British.

Schütze was already steering up the coast for the Firth of Forth when the burning *L 34* lit up the southern heavens in her fall. At 1 a.m. he flew into an inversion, with the temperature rising from 3 degrees above zero F. at 8,500 feet to 14 above, persisting at this figure up to 10,500 feet, which was the highest he could drive his ship at a s-degree angle. This did not seem adequate for an attack on Edinburgh on such a clear night, and at 2 a.m. *L 36* turned west, to go inland and attack Blyth, Newcastle or Sunderland from the land side. A few minutes later the starboard midships engine failed.

---

10 Jones, III, p. 240.

*Naval airship L 35. (Luftschiffbau Zeppelin)*

The ship, now showing herself markedly stern-heavy, put up her nose to a 13-degree angle and despite hard-down elevators, rose out of control to 12,500 feet until she was checked by throttling the engines. To trim his ship, Schütze dropped 2,850 pounds of bombs and 880 pounds of fuel aft. Understandably, he now did not wish to attack. On the way home *L 36* had more engine trouble, had to drop more fuel and bombs as ballast, and at one time only two motors were running.

The older ships, coming inland farther south, were unable to ascend much above 8,000 feet, and repeatedly found themselves under fire from alert anti-aircraft batteries. None of their bombing attacks was effective. Making his first raid on England, *L 22*'s commander, *Kapitänleutnant* Heinrich Hollender, witnessed the fall of Dietrich's ship seventy miles away:

> "While returning to the coast I saw *L 34* caught by three searchlights near Scarborough and Whitby, and heavily fired on. Suddenly the batteries ceased firing and the searchlights went out. At the same time, at 12:45, *L 34* took fire with a bright yellow flame. The ship at first stayed on an even keel, then tipped up vertically and we saw the red-hot framework falling. *L 34* was flying at 3,600 to 3,700 meters [11,800 to 12,200 feet] and the fall lasted at least 8 minutes."

Shortly afterwards, while leaving the coast north of Flamborough Head, *L 22* came under intense anti-aircraft fire and was badly hit. Shell fragments made about 150 holes in the gas cells, and as Cells 5 and 12 emptied fast, the Zeppelin became heavy. All unneeded fuel and spare parts were jettisoned and the ship was held in the air at a nose-up angle of 6 degrees. As soon as he left England behind, Hollender brought his craft down to 2,000 feet to compress the gas into the less-damaged upper portions of the cells. The ship's electrical system was out of order, and some time passed before a distress signal could be composed with the aid of a flashlight. Dawn found *L 22* still in the air, and the rising sun warmed and expanded the gas. To land in Nordholz was out of the question, but at 8 a.m. *L 22* was over Hage. After dropping the last two tanks of fuel, parachutes, empty ballast sacks, and everything else detachable, the ship was still over three tons heavy, but the after gondola fell on a post supporting the fence around the field, which absorbed most of the impact. The post was driven completely into the earth, the rear gondola struts and side propeller shafts were bent and some girders were broken in the hull, but the damage was repaired in six days.

Nor did *L 21* return to Nordholz. Frankenberg had crossed the coast near Atwick at 10:20 p.m., but met such heavy fire from the defenses that he turned out to sea, to come in further to the north. Near the coast, *L 21* changed direction several times, apparently to avoid patrolling airplanes, but once inland she headed straight for Leeds. The gun at Brierlands, about ten miles east of Leeds, apparently held her away from the city, and Frankenberg headed south. *L 21* then passed between the blacked-out cities of Manchester and Sheffield without seeing them. At Chesterton the glare from some ironstone-burning hearths attracted 16 explosive and 7 incendiary bombs, which merely broke window glass. Some colliery waste-heaps also drew a few incendiaries. From radio bearings obtained at this time, Strasser believed *L 21* had attacked Manchester.

From here, Frankenberg steered an easterly course across the southern Midlands. Despite a fol-

*Oberleutnant zur See Frankenberg of the L 21 (at left), with fellow officers in front of the Kasino at Nordholz. Left to right: Frankenberg, Wendt (Strasser's adjutant), von Buttlar, and Gresser. (Luftschiffbau Zeppelin)*

*SL 12 was the first ship built at Zeesen near Berlin, and was stationed at Ahlhorn. On December 28, 1916, returning from an aborted mission, upon approach to the home field, she was slammed against the gasometer by a gale and was damaged beyond repair. (Moch)*

lowing wind, his progress was slow, averaging only 35 m.p.h. due to engine trouble. North of Peterborough *L 21* encountered two airplanes, but Frankenberg handled his ship so skillfully that they could not come near her. At East Dereham, another pilot was attracted by a light she was showing, but his engine failed just as he was about to attack. Shortly afterwards Frankenberg radioed that he was near Norwich, with a side engine out of order.

The naval air station at Great Yarmouth had been warned of the Zeppelin's approach, and three planes were in the air hunting for her. She was already out at sea when their pilots saw her against the early dawn. One after another they attacked, and the last assailant, watching her take fire at the stern, saw the German machine-gunner on the top platform run straight over the nose of the ship just before she exploded. *L 21* fell into the sea about ten miles east of Lowestoft. Surface craft found a broken propeller blade floating in a great pool of petrol and oil, but there was not a single survivor. Though Flight Sub-Lieutenant Pulling received credit for her destruction, Flight Lieutenant Egbert Cadbury's four drums of ammunition undoubtedly set her alight, for he alone was firing at the stern where she first began to burn and the other two pilots got off only three rounds between them.

Strasser, forced to realize that *L 21* and *L 34* had almost certainly been destroyed by planes outside London, was obliged to admit that the British had got the better of his beloved airships. On *L 22*'s report he noted, "Machine guns are no defense for the airship against airplanes, which are also superior in speed.[11] The only protection is for the ships to use cloud cover, therefore I shall have to issue the same order in all raids as previously issued for London, 'attack only with cloud cover.'" Experiments with camouflage paint in *L 11* at Nordholz would be accelerated, and if the results were successful, all "Front" airships would be similarly treated. Strasser also suggested that a searchlight on the top platform might assist in finding attacking planes, and for a short time this was carried.

Another month passed before there was an opportunity to send the Zeppelins against England. Six took off on the afternoon of December 28, 1916, with orders to "attack southern England, if at all possible, London. Attack only with cloud cover, otherwise turn back." Soon after leaving the German coast, their commanders found the south-west wind increasing, and they were not surprised when Strasser recalled them. *SL 12*, a ship of the small, obsolete Schütte-Lanz "e" type, commissioned only on November 15, 1916 was making her ninth flight in naval service, and it was to be her last. As her commander, *Kapitänleutnant* Waldemar Kölle, attempted to land at Ahlhorn, the ship was driven against the gasometer, laying the bow open. The

[11] Yet during the next two weeks *L 22*, *L 23* and *L 24* were laid up in succession while machine-gun platforms were being built in the tail.

nose was so badly crumpled that Kölle dared not drive the ship against the freshening wind, and he had no choice but to land outside the field. During the night the rising storm completed *SL 12*'s destruction, and next morning all that remained was a rumpled heap of fabric, from which splintered girders projected like pins from a pin-cushion.

On that same unlucky December 28, disaster overtook two of the Tondern ships. Soon after 6 a.m., *L 16* and *L 24* had taken off from Hage and Tondern to patrol the western and northern edges of the German Bight to protect their minesweepers. *L 24*, coming home ahead of the rising wind, had landed at 4:20 p.m., but as she was being walked into the "Toska" shed, the after tackle snapped and she broke her back across the shed entrance. *L 24* instantly blazed up, and the fire spread to *L 17* on the north side of the hangar. Both ships were a total loss.

Thus the year 1916, the year in which the German naval airships made their greatest effort, ended on a note of defeat. In 1915, 47 airships had sortied against England, and 27 had crossed the British coast. In 1916, 187 had taken off to raid England, and 111 had completed the journey across the North Sea. Yet in 1915, the damage done had amounted to £815,865, while the much larger bombing force over England in the year 1916 had achieved a damage toll of only £594,523, while the casualty toll had only slightly increased. Only one naval Zeppelin had been lost in the 1915 raids on English targets, while in 1916 the expanded defenses had accounted for a total of 6. Within a few weeks the Chief of the General Staff would propose the disbanding of the Army airship service. The big bombing plane was on the horizon – the famous Gotha had been flight tested in the autumn of 1916, and thirty of them were to be ready to attack London by the 1st of February, 1917. What lay in the future for the Naval Airship Division?

# CHAPTER XVI

# THE COMING OF THE "HEIGHT CLIMBERS"

The last series of attacks had proved that the naval airships could not expect to bomb England as in the past without suffering heavy losses. The Fleet Command in fact debated whether continuance of the raids was justified by the results. At a conference with Admiral Scheer, Strasser pleaded for his airships with all his usual passion and eloquence, and convinced his superior that:

> it was not on the direct material damage that the value of the airship attacks depended, but rather on the general result of the German onslaught upon England's insularity, otherwise undisturbed by war. The disturbance of transportation, the dread of the airships prevailing in wide strata of society, and above all the occupation of very considerable material and military personnel were considered outstanding reasons for continuing the attacks.[1]

Long afterwards the British official historian showed the correctness of this argument when he wrote:

> The reader cannot fail to have been struck by the comparative ineffectiveness of the attacks, but it would be misleading to lay stress on the direct results. . . . Had the Zeppelins been built and maintained solely for the raids, it must be admitted that, from a purely military standpoint, they would more than have justified the money and ingenuity that went to their building. The threat of their raiding potentialities compelled us to set up at home a formidable organization which diverted men, guns and airplanes from more important theatres of war. By the end of 1916 there were specifically retained in Great Britain for home anti-aircraft defense 17,341 officers and men. There were twelve Royal Flying

*OPPOSITE:*
*Inside the L 43's after gondola, looking forward between the 240 horsepower Maybach engines carried in the car. Engine telegraphs are seen hanging from the roof. (Luftschiffbau Zeppelin)*

---

1 Gladisch, VI, p. 290.

> Corps squadrons, comprising approximately 200 officers, 2,000 men, and 110 airplanes. The anti-aircraft guns and searchlights were served by 12,000 officers and men who would have found a ready place, with continuous work, in France or other war theatres.[2]

The Zeppelin raids, it might be said, were continued for their nuisance value. Though Strasser continued to believe that his ships could damage London, and even ordered it as a specific target, it was bombed only once more by an airship, and then by accident. For inflicting actual damage on the enemy capital the Germans turned to bombing planes, such as the twin-engine Gotha, and ultimately the "Giants" such as the 4-engine R. VI, built by the Zeppelin Works at Staaken, with a wing span of 138 feet 5 1/2 inches and a loaded weight of 25,318 pounds. But even from Belgian bases, these craft could not reach the Midlands and the north of England, and thither the naval Zeppelins continued to be sent, to harass if not destroy.

Obviously the Naval Airship Division could not afford to go on losing one or two ships in every raid. War-conscious schoolteachers in England put the question simply when they assigned as arithmetic problems: "If Germany has twenty Zeppelins, and makes two raids every month, losing two airships in each raid, how long will it be before there are no more Zeppelins?" The answer, five months, was about what Strasser could expect if intensive bombing were resumed on the old basis. The performance of the airships must be improved.

The first serious suggestion came from the Aviation Department of the Admiralty, and involved an increase in speed without raising the ceiling. This proposal was built around a new design for a highly streamlined engine gondola with two Maybach HSLus geared to a single propeller. This was a far more efficient power unit than the clumsy 3-engine after gondola of the "thirties" with two propellers on brackets on the hull driven by long shafting. The Zeppelin Company prepared two general arrangements utilizing the new twin-engine gondola. Design No. 157 was for a seven-engine ship of 2,090,000 cubic feet, 682 feet long – a "thirty" hull with one gas cell added. Still bigger was the 8-engine design No. 160 of 2,239,000 cubic feet, 716 feet long with still another gas cell. The 13,000-foot ceiling with full war load would actually be slightly less than in the "thirties." A speed of 65 1/2 m.p.h. was calculated for the 7-engine craft, and 67 1/2 for the 8-engine ship, though judging from experience with a later 7-engine Zeppelin, the No. 160 design would more likely have attained at least 75 m.p.h. But delays in development of the twin-engine drive prevented a prompt commencement of these designs, while Strasser soon afterwards decided on the opposite solution – high ceiling at the expense of speed.

Strasser wrote to the Admiralty on January 17, 1917, to recommend that the 2,000,000 cubic foot ships be lightened to enable them to climb to the unprecedented ceiling of 16,500 feet with war load. Just a few days before he had received a communication from one of *L 33*'s machinist's mates, Adolf Schultz, who, under a prisoner exchange scheme, had been sent from England to Switzerland, and had forwarded his recommendations, the product of bitter personal experience through the naval attaché in Bern. Perhaps these recommendations were responsible for shocking Strasser out of his complacency about the efficiency of the "big 6-engine ships."

> Churwalden, Dec. 31, 1916
>
> In order to be able to continue the very effective air attacks, without suffering such severe losses as in the recent past, the ships must be able to go to at least 6,000 meters [20,000 feet], where they will be able to escape airplane attack. In interrogations, English officers have spoken very contemptuously of the *L 30* type on account of the size of the target, the visibility and the loud noise of its engines.
>
> To reach an altitude of 6,000 meters will naturally require a great decrease in weight.... The engines are very much improved over formerly and since the speed of the ship is not so important in view of the inaccuracy of the enemy artillery, two motors could be removed, specifically the 2 side engines from the after

---

[2] Jones, III, p. 243.

> gondola. . . . For controlling the ship it would be immaterial whether the commander's position is in the forward or after car, so it could be moved to the after car in place of the 2 superfluous engines, and many long control cables could be dispensed with and transmission of orders greatly simplified. The forward gondola would be merely a small engine car. . . . Thorough tests would enable many articles to be dispensed with which the first ships did not have, in spite of which they made successful attacks on England. . . . In order to keep the ship in the air in case of dire emergency, all four gondolas should be arranged to be droppable, so that one could keep going with the two midline, the two side gondolas, or with a midships and two side gondolas.

Strasser adopted none of these suggestions, though his marginal comments show that he considered having the side gondolas detachable. In his letter to the Admiralty he stated that if the useful lift of the present "thirties" could be increased by 7,300 pounds, they could reach 16,500 feet easily. About half of this could be saved by substituting the streamlined 2-engine gondola with the single propeller for the ungainly 3-engine after car. Much of the remainder could be saved by making the hull frame lighter: "In order to reach great heights and to be able to attack, one should not try to be careful and should work to a low margin of safety."

These proposals took the Admiralty by surprise, and a conference was called for January 27. Admiral Starke, the head of the Dockyard Bureau (which included the Aviation Department) was chairman, and was accompanied by his airship expert, the brilliant *Marine-Schiffbaumeister* Engberding. Strasser represented the "Front," and Drs. Dürr and Dörr represented the Zeppelin Company. Starke in his opening remarks acknowledged that the present ships, with a ceiling of 13,000 feet, would suffer heavy losses if they continued raiding, and a ceiling of 16,500 feet was necessary, while 20,000 feet was desirable. Engberding questioned the removal of one engine from the attack ships – would not high speed be desirable for fighting storms ? And were the engines as reliable as the "Front" claimed? (Events only a few months in the future would prove that his forebodings were well warranted.) Perhaps there should be one type of ship for raiding at high altitude, and a more powerful one for scouting. Strasser argued that the small number of airships should be usable for both purposes. "High altitude is the best defense against airplanes, and a greatly increased attack altitude is so necessary for further airship offensive operations against England that all resulting disadvantages, including a reduction in speed, must be accepted." Engberding returned to the attack with a list of equipment that could be dispensed with. "The point of view that every gram of weight must be taken out must be strictly adhered to. Previously the 'Front' has always had its way by saying, 'it weighs only a few kilograms.' But many small weights add up to a large total!" Dr. Dürr, speaking for the Zeppelin Company, agreed that removing the sixth engine with its fuel lines and accessories would lighten the ship by 3,860 pounds. He had to tell his audience that there had been a delay in providing the forgings for the gears in the new streamlined 2-engine gondola. The first would be tried in *L 44*, then due to be delivered on March 20. All other new ships would have the old 3-engine gondola. Dr. Dürr pointed out that the hull frame had been lightened in each vessel of the *L 30* class by using progressively thinner duralumin sheet in the girder members, which could not be made of lighter material as it could not then be worked. Strasser demanded more weight saving in the framework: "A single ring fracture is no calamity." Engberding retorted that whenever some hull girder broke, the "Front" would complain that the whole ship was too weak. The conference closed with the appointment of a commission, including Dr. Dürr, Dr. Dörr, several naval architects and the commander of the ship, which would embody in a new craft building at Friedrichshafen the improvements agreed on. The chief innovations were:

> (1) Substitution of the 2-engine gondola with one direct-drive propeller for the 3-engine rear gondola with one rear and two side propellers. (2) Reduction of fuel tankage to a 30-hour instead of a 36-hour supply. (3) Removal of all

*Martin Dietrich's L 42, the first "Height Climber" to reach 19,700 feet. Shown here, L 42 is in for an overhaul – the outer cover is removed, and gas cells lift the ship just off the ground. (Moch)*

machine guns, of the forward and after gun platforms, and the gun mounts in the gondolas. (4) Reduction of bomb releases by half, leaving eight for 660-pound bombs, sixteen for 220-pound bombs, and 60 for incendiaries. (5) Lightened design of hull girders. (6) Design of a new, smaller control car. (7) Complete elimination of crew's quarters and comforts.

On his return to Nordholz, Strasser ordered the immediate application of the conference's recommendations to the four newest airships. The after engine in the rear gondola, and the port-side bomb releases were removed. The weight reduction ranged from 4,070 pounds in *L 35* to 4,890 pounds in *L 39*. On February 2 and 3 the ships made short altitude trial flights. *L 35*, with a useful load of 15,600 pounds still on board, reached 16,100 feet. With somewhat lighter loads, *L 36* reached 16,400 feet, *L 39* stopped her engines at 16,400 feet and continued rising statically to 17,700 feet, and *L 40* went to 17,100 feet. At high altitudes the temperature was 18 to 22 degrees below zero F. Ballast water partly froze despite the addition of glycerin; Strasser proposed carrying some sand ballast in 110-pound bags instead. The short stay at high altitude uncovered no other defects. The engines ran well, a few of the men experienced slight dizziness and mild palpitations, but a few whiffs of compressed oxygen relieved these symptoms. Strasser thus felt that his machines and men would have no difficulty resisting the effects of anoxia and cold. Longer flights at high altitude would prove to be another matter.

On February 28, Martin Dietrich commissioned in Friedrichshafen *L 42*, the first ship built to the recommendations of the January conference, and flew her to Nordholz. The hull was practically identical with that of the "thirties." While the gondolas were the same as in earlier ships, the stern engine

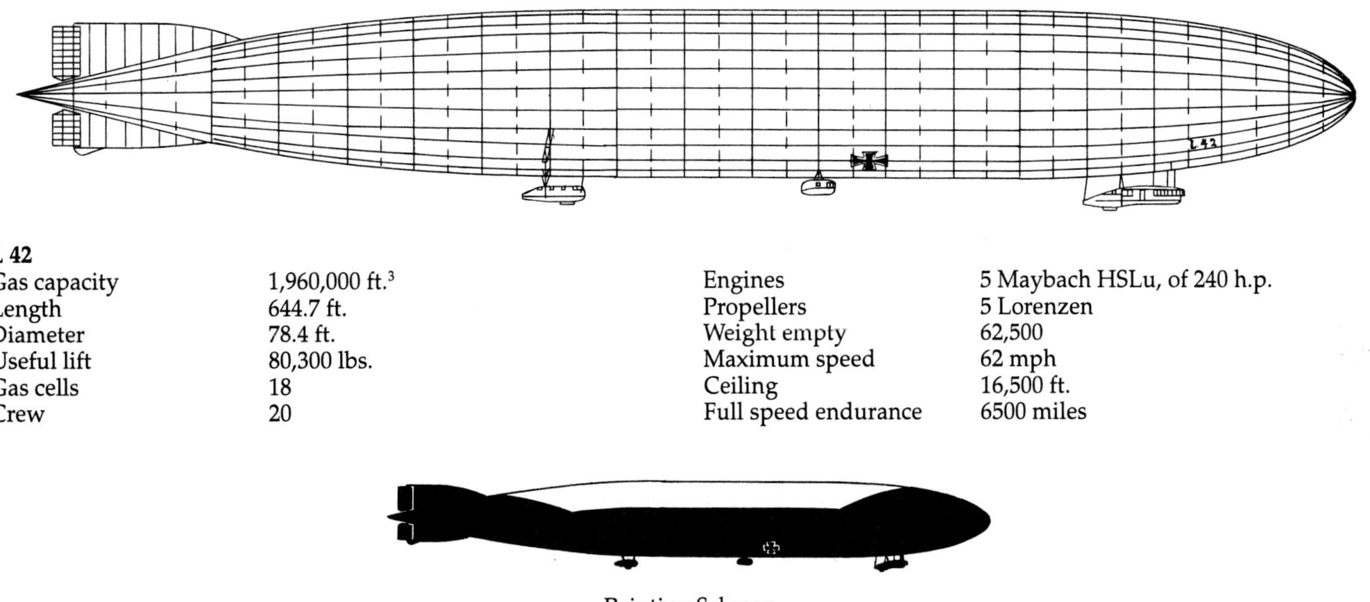

**L 42**

| | | | |
|---|---|---|---|
| Gas capacity | 1,960,000 ft.$^3$ | Engines | 5 Maybach HSLu, of 240 h.p. |
| Length | 644.7 ft. | Propellers | 5 Lorenzen |
| Diameter | 78.4 ft. | Weight empty | 62,500 |
| Useful lift | 80,300 lbs. | Maximum speed | 62 mph |
| Gas cells | 18 | Ceiling | 16,500 ft. |
| Crew | 20 | Full speed endurance | 6500 miles |

Painting Scheme

in the rear car was omitted. The port-side bomb releases and bomb bay doors were not installed, machine-gun mounts and gun platforms were suppressed, and to hamper the English searchlights, the underside of the hull, gondolas and fins were painted black. The useful lift of 80,300 pounds was an unprecedented 56 per cent of the total lift. On March 10, *L 42*, with Strasser as a passenger, made the altitude test flight which henceforth was part of the "working up" routine of every new airship. Three hours after taking off from Nordholz, and after dropping 23 tons of water ballast and glycerin anti-freeze, Dietrich had his ship flying at 19,700 feet. Slightly over 16,000 pounds of useful load was still on board, including 4,400 pounds of water which Dietrich had retained to represent bombs; if he had dropped this, Dietrich believed he could have attained 21,000 feet. Compressed oxygen was carried and some of the crew required it above 16,000 feet. Strasser went through the ship at her ceiling, and Dietrich still remembers him clambering painfully down the control car ladder, and, panting for breath in the rarefied air, explaining, "One-has-to-talk-slowly-up-here!"

Higher into the sub-stratosphere went the ships produced later in the year. *L 44*, completed in Löwenthal on April 1, 1917, not only had a lightened hull frame, but also was the first with the streamlined twin-engine after gondola with one propeller. During the summer and autumn the new gondola was fitted to all surviving Zeppelins in place of the old after engine car with the outrigger propellers, entailing a three- to four-week lay-up. *L 46* introduced streamlined amidships power cars, and a small, light control car in *L 48* made her 2,430 pounds lighter than *L 46*. On August 21, 1917, there was commissioned *L 53* which, with a major change in hull structure, had her nine largest frames spaced fifteen instead of ten meters apart. Her useful lift was 89,523 pounds – 62.7 per cent of the total – and she reached 20,700 feet on her first raid. The *L 53* class – too lightly built to withstand full-speed maneuvers at low altitude – remained the standard type in the North Sea until nearly a year later.

Other refinements improved the efficiency of the "height climbers," as the new Zeppelins were labeled by the British. To reduce skin friction, the entire outer cover was tightly doped, instead of being left porous on top to permit the escape of valved hydrogen – a step which led to some unusual accidents, as no provision had been made for equalizing air pressure within the huge hull. Gas-cell weight was reduced by using only two layers of gold beaters' skin instead of three, and in 1918 the gas cells were made still lighter through the use of silk fabric instead of cotton. While all machine guns and mountings were removed in Strasser's first determination to force the Zeppelins as high as possible, this decision was rescinded late in April, 1917. Top platforms were built in *L 43* and *L 44*, and two machine guns were carried in the control car on scouting flights, though they were left at home on raids. Still later, as airplane attacks occurred over the North Sea, Strasser promoted the development of the Becker 20 mm. machine cannon, designed to outrange the British 303 caliber machine guns. But the cannon were not mounted until the summer of 1918.

Strasser indisputably achieved one of his major aims: the "height climbers," raiding at altitudes of 16,000 to 20,000 feet, at one stroke rendered obsolete the entire British defense system. The slow B.E.2c, B.E.12 and F.E.2b aircraft, which formed the equipment of all the home defense squadrons through 1917, were hopelessly outclassed with their ceilings of 11,000 to 13,000 feet. A small number of high-performance single-seat fighters might have restored the balance, but the Western Front in France received priority. Only at the end of the war were Avros and Bristol Fighters, with ceilings of 18,000 and 20,000 feet, being issued to squadrons in the Midlands and the north. As for the guns, they caused no further losses to the black-painted raiders crossing England four miles up in the air.

But the high-altitude performance of the new Zeppelins brought new difficulties which other air forces did not begin to comprehend until the period between the wars. Though Strasser did his best

*BELOW: Naval airship L 43, a sister ship of the first "Height Climber" L 42, on a trial flight at Friedrichshafen in March 1917. Note the black color of the underside, intended to conceal the ship from enemy searchlights. (Luftschiffbau Zeppelin)*

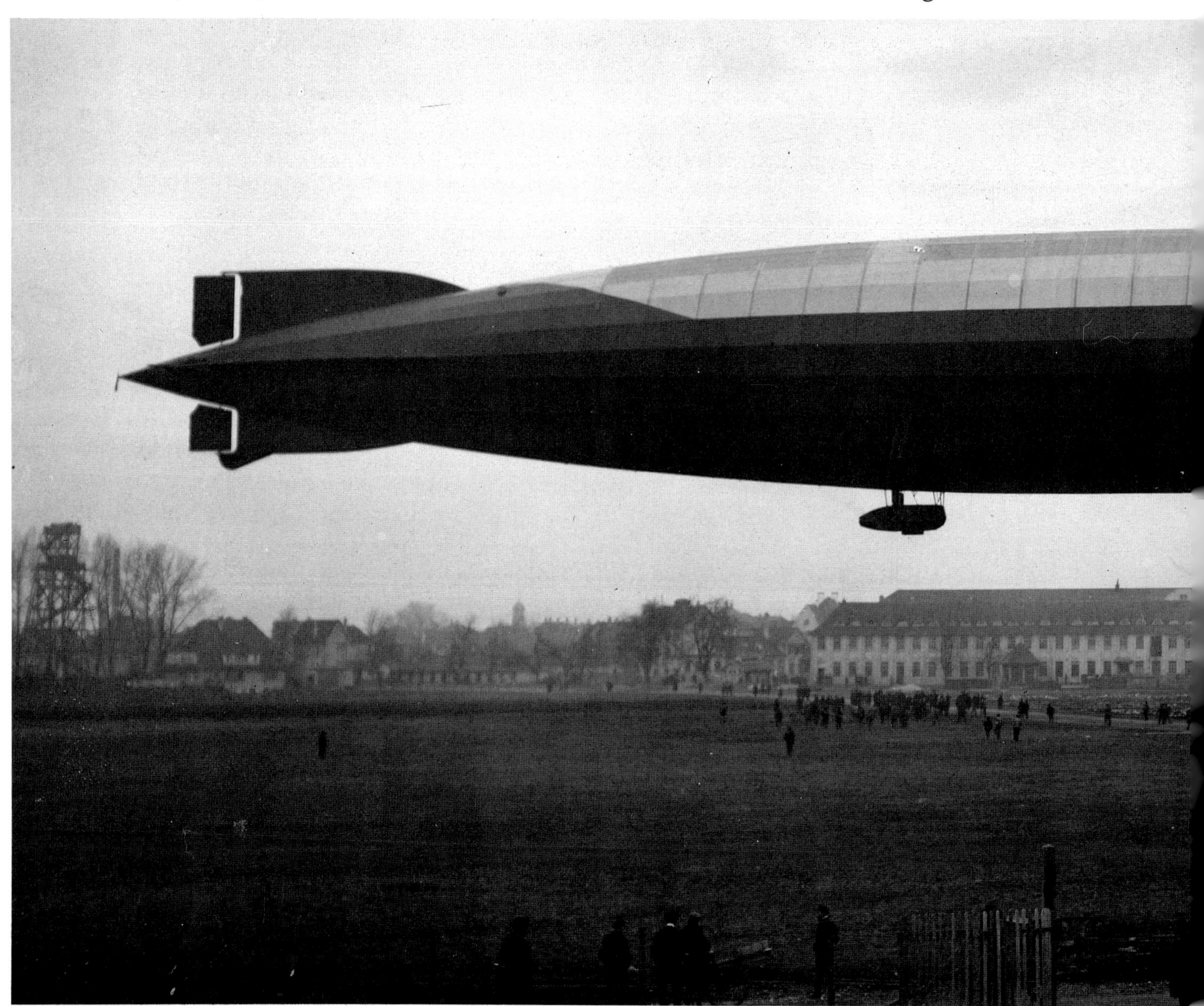

in the time left to him, his ships and men again and again found themselves helpless in the eerie new world of the sub-stratosphere.

The ground-bound weather experts of the Hamburg Observatory, handicapped by the fact that their westernmost station was only 235 miles away at Bruges,[3] found themselves unable to predict conditions in the upper air. On at least two occasions in the last years of the war, the airships were placed in great peril by winds of gale force above 15,000 feet which they did not even suspect until they had ascended to their attack altitudes.

3 Though German U-boats were frequently cruising in the Atlantic west of the British Isles, no attempt was made to use them as weather reporting stations.

Navigation also became more difficult. Inevitably, all clouds except the high cirrus lay below, rather than above, the airships. At great heights the features of the landscape were even more remote and indistinct than usual. At night, with a solid cloud ceiling beneath him and upper air currents hurrying him whither he knew not, the airship commander had little chance to find his position without external aid. Though they were now entirely dependent on radio bearings, the raiders were still using the system whereby the Zeppelins themselves had to send out signals on which the shore stations took bearings, with the added disadvantage that the British could in the same way determine the airship's position. With eight or ten ships in the air at one time, all asking for bearings every

*Above: Naval airship L 43 dropping her trail-ropes for a landing at Friedrichshafen. (Luftschiffbau Zeppelin) Below: L 43 at Ahlhorn during its first flight on March 15, 1917. It was shot down by British aircraft on June 14, 1917 with all twenty-four crewmen perishing. (Nonhoff-Strumann)*

hour or oftener, the pandemonium in the ether – the "Battle of the Wireless," as the radio operators called it – sometimes beggared description.

The new developments also found the medical department of the German Navy unprepared. Though its reputation stood high in wound surgery, shipboard sanitation, and the care of tropical diseases, it had failed to anticipate the development of aviation medicine. For flight personnel there was a strict intake physical examination, but no psychological tests, and no routine checks were made thereafter on their health.[4] Navy doctors had realized the need for oxygen at high altitudes, but no experimental studies had been done on the effects of low oxygen tension on human physiology.

While the human body can compensate for some decrease in oxygen tension, above 12,000 feet begin the symptoms of "altitude sickness," as described from experience by the ground troop medical officer at Ahlhorn:

> It was interesting for me to observe the crews from the medical aspect during high altitude flights [5-6,000 meters – 16,400-19,700 feet] and extended altitude flights up to 8 hours at 6,000 meters. Above 4,000 meters [13,100 feet] begin the well-known altitude symptoms, which manifest themselves as ringing in the ears, dizziness and headaches. At greater heights began a marked acceleration of respiration and cardiac activity. Pulse rates of 120 to 150 per minute were by no means uncommon. These serious developments could be controlled only by continuously breathing oxygen from cylinders. It was naturally difficult to provide the crews with any kind of nourishment on the long high-altitude flights. The only thing that could be agreeable at low temperatures was chocolate. The best thing was to eat as little as pos-

[4] On the night of August 7, 1917, *L 49*'s elevator man, suffering from undetected heart disease, dropped dead in the control car during a high-altitude trial.

*The experimental naval airship L 25 on the Wildpark field, near Potsdam. (Luftschiffbau Zeppelin)*

sible, or not at all. It can be appreciated that long high-altitude flights under these conditions were very exhausting for the crews, particularly the raids on England, which made the greatest demands.[5]

Initially, compressed oxygen was issued in individual bottles, so that each man could "suck air" as he felt the need. For long it was considered a sign of weakness to do so, and only gradually did the individual commanders, who were ahead of the medical department in comprehending the need, order the use of oxygen by all personnel above 16,000 feet. There were frequent complaints that "the 'air' tasted so strongly of oil or other impurities that the stomach often rebelled, and continued to do so for 30 or 50 hours afterwards."[6] At best, the oxygen left the user with cracked lips and a "morning-after" head on the next day. Later the bottles of compressed oxygen were replaced by thick-walled "bombs" containing liquid air. "The effect of liquid air was quite different. One did not feel either hungry or thirsty after it, but extraordinarily alert, and far from experiencing any feeling of fatigue one felt one could knock down a brick wall."[7]

The bitter, penetrating cold at high altitudes caused frostbite, and stiffened joints so that even simple movements were clumsily executed. No artificial heating was ever installed in the naval airships, and very little could be done about the cold,

5 Marine-Stabsarzt der Reserve Dr. Nonhoff, "Bericht über mein Kommando als Trupparzt des III. M.L.T. in Ahlhorn," Strahlmann, p. 92.

6 Dietsch, Strahlmann, p. 79.

7 Freiherr Treusch von Buttlar-Brandenfels, *Zeppelins over England*, trans. Huntley Patterson (New York: Harcourt, Brace & Co., 1932), p. 189.

*LZ 107 experimentally camouflaged. (Luftschiffbau Zeppelin)*

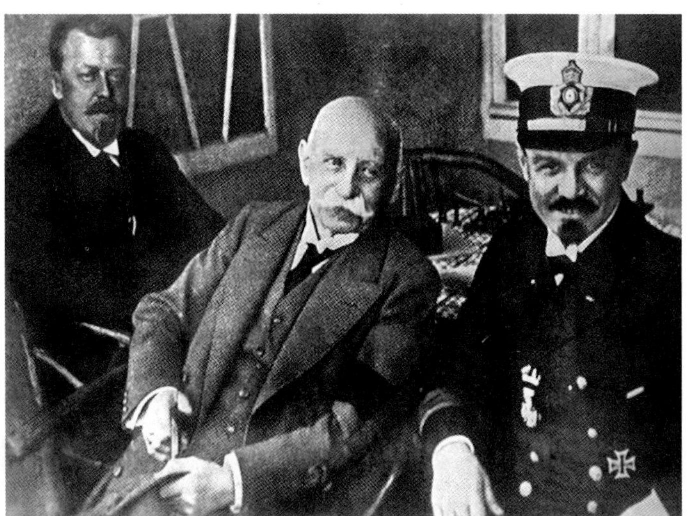

*Count Zeppelin with Dr. Eckener (left) and Korvettenkapitän Peter Strasser, on the occasion of the Count's last visit to Nordholz in late 1916. The Count died on March 8, 1917. (Luftschiffbau Zeppelin)*

except to bundle on more clothing. Ordinary naval uniforms, jackets and caps, which offered no protection against frostbitten noses and ears, were replaced by fur-lined flying suits and helmets, but many men in addition wore layers of newspapers under their clothes. Removal of the crew's hammocks from the gangway was no hardship, as "one would have frozen no matter how many blankets he tried to sleep under."

The engines, as well as the mechanics, suffered from oxygen deficiency at high altitudes. At each stroke of the pistons they took in the same volume of air, but it was so lacking in oxygen that the proportion of fuel had to be reduced. The engines thus could lose as much as half their power, and ships capable of reaching 62 m.p.h. at sea level were reduced to 45 m.p.h. at 20,000 feet. In August, 1916, the Maybach Company, with the help of the Daimler-Benz firm, had undertaken the development of an over-dimensioned "altitude motor" which would draw in an abnormal amount of air at each piston-stroke, and thus ensure a normal supply of oxygen at high altitude. An engine testing station was erected atop a 6,500-foot peak in the picturesque Bavarian Alps. Until November, 1917, however, the "height climbers" had to make do with the old HSLu power plant.

Once more filled with confidence in his weapon, Strasser on February 22 wrote to the Navy Minister that he wanted a total of 30 airships – 24 for the North Sea and 6 in the Baltic. For any two-day Fleet operation he would need 18 Zeppelins to form a tight scouting ring, with 6 in reserve in case any of the scouts were disabled, and to carry out routine reconnaissance. On ordinary days, two or three ships would be in the air to protect the German Bight and to cover the minesweepers. Strasser also wanted a large number of the new raiders, able to reach 16,500 feet, for continuing attacks on London. At this time he had only 6 such craft, but expected to have 14 more by July 20, 1917.

All these changes in the Naval Airship Division were proceeding against the background of dramatic alterations in the conduct of the war at sea. Hindenburg and Ludendorff, coming to the Army High Command on August 29, 1916, had broken the deadlock over unrestricted submarine warfare by throwing their weight behind Scheer and von Holtzendorff, its leading Navy advocates. The Kaiser's reluctant decision to release the U-boats on February 1, 1917, in a ruthless all-out assault on England's shipping – a desperate gamble that the chief enemy could be strangled and the war won in six months – determined the character of the entire German and Allied effort at sea till the Armistice. The small submarine arm moved into the limelight, while the other German naval forces, including the proud dreadnoughts which meant so much to the Supreme War Lord, were the handmaidens and supporters of the undersea corsairs. "Our Fleet became the hilt of the weapon whose sharp blade was the U-boat,"[8] wrote Scheer. The Zeppelins played their part. Sixteen days after the start of the unrestricted submarine campaign, Strasser sent his airships out in daylight across the North Sea to observe and report on merchant traffic in the newly proclaimed blockade area (*Sperrgebiet*) around the British Isles. These long flights, beyond the Dogger Bank towards the Humber, the Tyne, the Firth of Forth and the Moray Firth, were made at intervals during 1917 and 1918.

The immediate British answer to the submarine campaign was to intensify minelaying in the German Bight, in order to prevent the U-boats from

[8] Scheer, p. 256.

*This ship is possibly L 36 over Northern Germany. (Moch)*

leaving their bases. As the months passed, row after row of British explosive "eggs" extended ever farther outward into the North Sea. Instead of trying to sweep them all, the augmented German mine-clearing force merely tried to keep open certain channels leading to the open sea. "Route White" led north along the Danish coast, "Route Yellow" westward towards the Dogger Bank, "Route Black" hugged the three-mile limit off the Dutch islands. Along these *viae dolorosae* the submarines put to sea, preceded by minesweepers, escorted by destroyers, and only airship patrolling could provide security for the light forces involved. A Fleet Command order of July 18, 1917, laid down the exact squares between which three airships should patrol from dawn to sunset each day to protect the minesweepers, while a fourth should fly over the area of minesweeping operations. Detailed orders were issued, such as those to *L 42* on May 4, 1917:

> Minesweeper cover "middle" on line 055 β to 165 α 7. If possible observe whether there is an outer mine barrier west of the barrier reported by *L 43* (037 ε and 038 ε). Return according to the work of the minesweeper units. Land approximately at dusk. *L 23* has the north, *L 43* the west. Take-off 5 a.m. Report at 4 a.m.
>
> Leader of Airships.

*Wreck of L 36 on the ice of the river Aller on February 7, 1917. Kapitänleutnant R. Franz Georg Eichler had fought all day to keep his ship in the air, but she came down after exhausting her ballast, fuel, and gas. (both - Moch)*

Four days after her altitude test flight, the lightened *L 36* was lost in an operational accident that epitomizes many of the difficulties of flying the big rigids. Late in the evening of February 6 she took off from Nordholz on a scouting mission. During the night she became increasingly stern-heavy, while Cell 7, over the rear gondola, appeared to be losing gas. Strasser later concluded that this cell had lost most of its hydrogen, but had filled with air from a hole in the bottom, thus continuing to appear go per cent full. Out of trim and with a nose-up angle at times reaching 17 degrees, *L 36* had to drop much ballast aft, pump fuel forward, and have 5 bombs carried from the after bomb room to the mooring point in the nose. After dawn next morning, *Kapitänleutnant der Reserve* Franz Georg Eichler found he had to descend through a layer of fog which Nordholz reported reaching down to within 65 feet of the ground. With the ship 6,000 pounds "light," and a nose-down angle of 5 degrees, *L 36* entered the top of the fog at 1,600 feet. At 800 feet by the altimeter the temperature suddenly rose from 12 to 25 degrees F. The ship became very nose-heavy and began to drop fast with a down angle of 12 to 15 degrees, and Eichler had the engine telegraphs set to "full speed" to increase the air pressure on the elevators, which were hard up. Suddenly, at a height of only 200 to 300 feet (the altimeter was reading 520 feet) *L 36* broke out of the bottom of the cloud and her crew saw below the ice covered estuary of the Weser. The engines were immediately stopped and all "breeches" and ballast sacks forward were released, but a few seconds later the control car smashed hard on the ice. One man was spilled out of the shattered gondola, later making his way to shore on foot. The ship rebounded to 3,300 feet, but since the shattered control car threatened to tear off, and the ladder to the keel had been smashed, Eichler valved gas and landed again on the ice. The control car crew scrambled up into the ship, the emergency rudder and elevator controls in the after gondola were manned, and *L 36* once more ascended and continued east-south-east in bright sunlight above the fog. Soon after the second take-off the wrecked control car wrenched free and fell into the sea. The fog continued, the Nordholz captive balloon could not be found, and with no charts and no radio, Eichler was lost when at 1 p.m. unidentified mountains loomed above the clouds. With the loss of the gondola, and the gas superheated by 27 degrees F., the crippled airship was at least 5,500 pounds light. By valving gas – the controls had disappeared with the forward gondola, and men distributed through the gangway pulled the individual maneuvering valve wires on order – Eichler got his ship down under the clouds and at a height of 600 to 750 feet flew until he found the railroad between Verden and Celle, some go miles south-south-east of Nordholz. Suddenly the ship became stern-heavy. The last ballast aft was dropped, but she descended fast, the rear gondola dragged through treetops and tore down high-tension lines, and at 1:50 p.m. *L 36* crashed – permanently – on the ice of the River Aller. There was no more ballast or fuel. The wind drove the wreck across the ice to the river bank, and at 3 p.m. the hull broke in two.

Strasser's endorsement on the findings of the Court of Inquiry was critical, but took account of Eichler's difficulties:

> (1) Due to the progressive heaviness and stern-heaviness of the ship, the cause of which could not be clearly determined during the night, the ship's command was confronted with a very difficult technical problem. The error of setting the engines at "full speed" at a critical moment, although it was recognized and immediately countermanded, led to the loss of the control car.
>
> (2) The valving of gas during the afternoon, which cannot be absolutely condemned as incorrect, since the alternative, the valving of gas by ascending above pressure height, could have produced a critical situation, led to the stranding and loss of the airship.
>
> (3) Even though two errors of judgment have been proved against the commander, he should be absolved of blame. In airship operations slight mistakes can easily lead to serious consequences.
>
> Lest a fear of responsibility should be engendered, one should not construe every mistake as a court-martial offence.

> Considering that the commander did not abandon his badly damaged ship for one moment, but on the contrary, courageously strove to bring his ship home, and in consideration of his previously blameless airship record as well as his war service, I have no hesitation in entrusting him with the command of another airship.[9]

The first long daylight scouting flights into the U-boat blockade area were made on February 16. The orders for *L 30* read:

> Strip in submarine blockade area. 2 a.m. report if take-off will take place. 3 a.m. take-off. Course according to own judgment with respect to weather. Leave blockade area by 5 p.m. at latest. Usual radio reports from turning-points. *L 37* has same mission.
>
> Leader of Airships.

Both Zeppelins made a sweep far to the north, nearly to the latitude of Scapa Flow, then proceeded down the middle of the North Sea to the approximate level of Newcastle, and thence home. *L 37* sighted a four-funneled destroyer which, at 12 miles' range, opened fire on the airship. Finding Nordholz fogged in, *L 37* had to go inland to Ahlhorn. *L 30*'s patrol was uneventful.

Not until March 16 did the first raid on England with the new "height climbers" take place. Strasser's orders read:

> England south, London. With north wind return over Belgium. Participants: *L 35, L 39, L 40, L 41, L 42*. Leader of Airships aboard *L 42*. Direction from Nordholz by Commander of the Naval Airship Division.[10] Take-off about 1.30 p.m.
>
> Leader of Airships.

The bomb loads, of 3,500 to 4,000 pounds, were of course lighter than in the previous year. The weather conditions were quite unusual. A high pressure area over southern England and northern France extended into Germany, but to the north-west a violent depression was approaching from Iceland. Of this the airship commanders had no warning, for not only was Bruges unable to detect the approaching storm, but its observations, radioed to the Zeppelins at 4 p.m., extended only to 3,300 feet. Climbing to their attack altitude after sundown, the airships found a solid cloud ceiling below at 10,000 feet, which broke up as they neared the British coast. As the depression bore down on them, the north-north-west wind freshened – to a fierce 45 m.p.h. at 12,500 feet. The ships could not ascertain their position by reference to the ground. And on this night the British jammed the airship wireless wavelength almost continuously from 8:30 p.m. to 2 a.m., so that only fragments of messages got through. The Bruges radio bearing station failed at the height of the raid from 10 p.m. to 1:30 a.m., and the bearings from Nordholz, Borkum and List met at such an acute angle over England as to be nearly useless. All the raiders were carried south of their dead-reckoning positions.

*Kapitänleutnant* Robert Koch, in *L 39*, made the coast near Margate at 11:20 p.m. and moved south-west across Kent, going out to sea again at St. Leonards. His six bombs on land damaged two houses, and more were heard exploding out at sea as he proceeded south over the Channel. At 3:55 a.m., *L 39* reached the French coast west of Dieppe, and then drove with the gale south-south-east almost to Paris. Here Koch must have realized that he was letting himself be carried dangerously far from home, for he headed up into the wind and struggled northeast for an hour, past Chaumont and Beauvais. Before he could reach safety on the German side of the lines, the Zeppelin must have suffered an engine failure, for at 6 a.m. she faltered in her course and once more drifted south-east. At 6:40 a.m. she appeared in the half-light of dawn over Compiegne. For fifteen minutes the Zeppelin drifted aimlessly over the town while French anti-aircraft guns fired over a hundred shells in her direction. At last one of them got home and set her

---

[9] Report of Board of Inquiry on 1055 of *L 36*, "Bosse bei Rehben an der Aller, 9. Februar 1917," courtesy of F. Moch.

[10] With Strasser's promotion to "Leader of Airships" on November 23, 1916, *Korvettenkapitän* Viktor Schütze had given up command of *L 36* to become the Commander of the Naval Airship Division.

*L 39 departing the "Albrecht" shed at Ahlhorn. This photo is said to be of its first flight. L 39 was shot down in flames by anti-aircraft fire at Compiegne, France on March 17, 1917. (Moch)*

on fire, and *L 39* plunged earthward, smearing a greasy trail of smoke down the morning sky. Half-way to earth an explosion blasted the skeleton in two and spewed her hapless crew overboard. The twin balls of wreckage crashed to earth on opposite sides of a garden wall on the outskirts of town. The Germans learned next day of *L 39*'s destruction through a radio broadcast from the Eiffel Tower.

The other ships were also driven over France by the gale. *Kapitänleutnant* Ehrlich in *L 35*, and *Kapitänleutnant* Sommerfeldt in *L 40*, both claimed to have bombed London. Sommerfeldt reported seeing the blue lights of a plane above the city, and it may have been true, for 16 Royal Flying Corps machines were in the air that night. British observers actually saw *L 35*, *L 40* and *L 41* following Koch's ill-fated ship across the eastern corner of Kent, and their bombs fell in open country and caused no casualties. As they passed out to sea over the Channel, the Zeppelins' troubles were only beginning.

*L 35* made the French coast at Calais, and crossed the trenches north of Ypres. Steering for Ahlhorn, Ehrlich was surprised to find at 6 a.m. next morning that he was a hundred miles south of his base, between Münster and Hamm. At 9:37 a.m. came a directive from *Korvettenkapitän* Viktor Schütze in Nordholz, "drop in wind in north not to be expected. Try to reach Friedrichshafen or Mannheim." With only enough fuel to last till 1 p.m., Ehrlich steered for Hanover, but the violent north-west wind carried him still farther south,

AIRSHIP RAID, MARCH 16–17, 1917

| *Ship* | *Flt. No.* | *Take off* | | *Landing* | | *Time in Air* | *Distance (miles)* | *Av. speed (m.p.h.)* | *Max. alt. (feet)* | *Temp. (°F.)* | *Crew* | *Fuel (lb.) loaded/used* | *Oil (lb.) loaded/used* | *Ballast loaded (lb.)* | *Bombs (lb.)* | *Gas used (cubic feet)* |
|---|---|---|---|---|---|---|---|---|---|---|---|---|---|---|---|---|
| *L 35* | 36 | Ahlhorn | 1.00 p.m. | Dresden | 1.30 p.m. | 24h. 45m. | 1,050 | 42·6 | 18,400 | +5·0 | 17 | 11,200/10,770 | 937/772 | 53,950 | 3,245 | 1,088,000 |
| *L 39* | 24 | Ahlhorn | 1.18 p.m. | | | | | | | | 17 | | | | | |
| *L 40* | 16 | Ahlhorn | 12.30 p.m. | Ahlhorn | 2.27 p.m. | 25h. 57m. | 878 | 33·7 | 19,000 | −4·0 | 17 | 10,880/9,920 | 816/440 | 50,700 | 3,540 | 935,000 |
| *L 41* | 9 | Ahlhorn | 1.00 p.m. | Ahlhorn | 3.53 p.m. | 26h. 53m. | 969 | 36·1 | 17,000 | +3·6 | 17 | 11,000/10,120 | 1,018/756 | 47,100 water 4,740 sand | 4,060 | 918,000 |
| *L 42* | 6 | Nordholz | 1.30 p.m. | Jüterbog | 4.05 p.m. | 26h. 35m. | | | | | | | | | | |

*Weather:* Strong S.W. wind. Heavily overcast.
*Bombs:* 79 (9,620 lb.).
*Casualties:* Nil.
*Monetary Damage:* £163.

nearly to Kassel. At the same time, at 10:43 a.m., another message was received from Nordholz, "according to morning weather map, storm conditions over north and central Germany. South-west winds in south Germany." With two of her engines stopped to save fuel, *L 35* drove on for Dresden, making 50 m.p.h. with the storm on her tail On the ground there at last at 1:30 p.m., the ship rolled and thrashed "like a mad elephant" in a wind of 40 m.p.h. As her nose was entering the hangar door, a gust picked up the tail and smashed it down again, breaking the ship's back abaft the rear gondola. Not until June 14 were repairs complete and *L 35* back in Ahlhorn.

*L 40* traversed the Channel to the French coast at Wissant. At 4:20 a.m., with a rising moon, she passed high over the Western Front, and at 9 a.m. found her bearings over Euskirchen near Bonn, in the Rhineland. With the radio insulation burned

*The wreck of L 39 burning on the outskirts of Compiegne, France on the morning of March 17, 1917. (L'Illustration)*

out, Sommerfeldt had been unable to ask for bearings since midnight. He received Schütze's directive, but "since it seemed impossible to reach a south German base on account of shortage of fuel, kept on course for Ahlhorn." *L 40* arrived over the Ahlhorn field with only the forward engine working, and as she sank into the hands of the ground crew, the last motor failed for lack of fuel. Only 133 gallons remained of the 1,480 on board when *L 40* had left Ahlhorn 26 hours earlier.

*L 41* crossed the Channel to Boulogne, and entered German territory at 4 a.m. via the trenches near Cambrai. Due to lack of fuel, her commander, *Hauptmann* Manger, also steered for Ahlhorn. At 2 p.m. he was over his base, but could not land as *L 40* was ahead of him, and *L 41* drifted off into the fog with only two engines working. She landed at 3:53 p.m. after a flight of nearly 27 hours.

Strasser brought his usual bad luck to *L 42*, which did not reach England. Dietrich intended to cross the coast near Orfordness in Suffolk, and thence proceed to London. Recognizing a freshening north-west wind, he pointed up more to the north, for Lowestoft. Radio bearings failed completely, the forward engine broke down, and Dietrich found he had been carried south to within sight of Ostend Lighthouse. Here he steered due north, but with only four engines working, the ship was driven stern first southward. At 12:47 a.m. Dietrich started back towards Nordholz. After prolonged search in fog, and with petrol low, he ran east and at 4:05 p.m. landed in Jüterbog with only 1 hour's fuel on board.

There had been no casualties in England, and the 79 bombs traced on land had produced damage of only £163. There was considerable dissatisfaction in G.H.Q. Home Forces over the fact that none of the Zeppelins had been destroyed over England, or even intercepted; but the defenders had been outclassed by the increased ceiling of the new airships. *L 35*'s maximum altitude was 18,400 feet, *L 40* touched 19,000 feet, and *L 41* reached 17,100 feet. Despite his own experience in *L 42*, Strasser appears to have been pleased with the performance of his men and ships in this raid, particularly with the alleged bombing of London by *L 35* and *L 40*.

Next month, *Kapitänleutnant* Ludwig Bockholt created a sensation with the capture of a merchant vessel by an airship, the only instance of its kind during the war. On the afternoon of April 23, 1917, his *L 23* was off Hanstholm on the Danish coast when at 3:06 p.m. she sighted:

> Norwegian bark *Royal* on a westerly course, crew leave her in the boats on approach of airship. Ascertained ship is unarmed and abandoned. Deck cargo of wood. Therefore water landing close to the boats, one of which comes alongside without being asked. Bark bound for West Hartlepool. As prize crew, Warrant Quartermaster and two petty officers put on board with orders to steer for Horns Reef.

*Royal*'s papers showed that she was carrying pit-props – a contraband lading. By radio, Bockholt advised that his prize would be at Horns Reef at 8 a.m. next day, and she was in fact met by German destroyers and escorted into the Elbe. The capture of *Royal* – actually a schooner of only 688 tons – hardly affected the trade war against England, but Bockholt's flamboyant gesture appealed particularly to the men, and tales of the exploit were told from Tondern to Hage. To Strasser, however, it almost certainly appeared as a foolhardy stunt – the Zeppelin could so easily have been damaged in the water landing in the open sea, or even set on fire by a concealed rifleman using incendiary ammunition. He made sure that the performance was not repeated.

On May 1 the weather was favorable for long-distance scouting, and about 1 a.m., *L 43* and *L 45* took off, the former to observe shipping in the U-boat blockade area off the British coast south of the 56th parallel, which passed through the Firth of Forth, and the latter to scout north of this dividing line. *L 45* went to within 50 miles of Aberdeen, and landed at 8:15 p.m. with nothing to report. *L 43*, after sighting the wreckage of a Norwegian sailing vessel near the Dogger Bank South Lightship, went on north-west to a point within 140 miles of the Firth of Forth. Here, at 10 a.m., *Kapitänleutnant* Kraushaar turned south-south-west, and at noon was only 48 miles off Blyth. He had sent radio messages with each change of course, but there was no British reaction. An hour later, "since no vessels had been seen as yet, decided to advance into the coastal area off the Humber and Wash to observe coastal traffic." At 3 p.m. Kraushaar checked his position from the Outer Dowsing Shoal whistle buoy, only thirty miles east of Saltfleet on the Lincolnshire coast, and found that his dead reckoning was correct while radio bearings placed him 30 to 40 miles too far to the north. From here *L 43* steered for home via the Dogger Bank South Lightship, and landed at Ahlhorn at 9:27 p.m. after a flight of 20 hours and 27 minutes.

May 4 started in routine fashion with *L 23* providing cover for the minesweepers to the north, *L 42* in the middle and *L 43* to the west. Kraushaar in *L 43*, finding good visibility off Terschelling, decided to extend his patrol westward to the edge of the U-boat blockade area. This resulted in his encountering light forces of the Grand Fleet well out on the Dogger Bank. *L 43* was only 3,300 feet high when at 12:15 p.m. she saw light cruisers maneuvering at high speed near a sailing ship. Kraushaar radioed a contact report, and while climbing to 13,000 feet, watched other cruisers join up. "Chance to drop bombs at 2:15. Salvo of three 50 kg. [110 pound] bombs dropped. Light cruiser runs into line of bombs, third bomb not seen to burst on water, instead sudden smoke and fires spring up forward and continue till out of sight." As the vessels made off to the north-west, Kraushaar released his remaining bombs, but could only report near-misses. "During entire attack constant firing from all ships. . . . At times enemy fires with elevation of at least 80 degrees. Because of the extraordinarily skillful

*L 40 on the Ahlhorn landing ground, with the frames of Sheds V and VI in the background. (Luftschiffbau Zeppelin)*

maneuvering of the enemy, who steers a constant, unpredictable zigzag and circling course to the northwest, it was very difficult to maneuver for aimed bombing as own speed was reduced by a head wind." With all his bombs expended, and *L 42* coming in sight in response to his signals, Kraushaar turned back at 3:20 p.m. Dietrich, counting 60 warships in two groups, lost sight of the British when clouds moved in underneath. In one of the very few occasions throughout the war when a Zeppelin succeeded in attacking surface warships, Kraushaar was credited by the British with a "series of determined bombing attacks," but "the airship's bombs just failed to score hits, although splinters from them fell in several of the destroyers and in the *Dublin*."[11]

On May 23, three days after the new moon, Strasser sent out six Zeppelins to "attack south, London."

Kraushaar, in *L 43*, was the only commander to claim an attack on the British capital. Bruges had forecast strong south to south-west winds, and bearings on the Dutch coast and on the Terschelling Bank Lightship showed a speed of advance against the wind of only 30 knots, too low to reach London before dawn. At 7:05 p.m. an exhaust valve of the forward engine burned out, but Kraushaar had the cylinder cut out and the engine continued to run at 1,200 revolutions until the landing. From 7:45 p.m. to 12:15 a.m., *L 43* flew below 10,000 feet, and advanced more rapidly. At 2 a.m., reported Kraushaar, the lights of Sheerness were seen on the starboard bow. With favorable cloud cover and temperature conditions – it was 10 below zero F. later at 20,700 feet – he decided to go on to London.

> Since the upper cloud ceiling had dissolved over the city and only a thick layer of haze remained at low altitude, the course of the Thames and position of the docks could be readily made out from the lighted quays. Considering the hour and wind direction, an advance to the heart of the city was given up. Flew over Greenwich and held off far enough to the east [sic] so that the dock areas on both sides of the Thames and the Isle of Dogs could be crossed with a following wind. 3:15 to 3:30: These installations were attacked from 6,000-6,300 meters [19,700-20,700 feet] with all bombs –1,850 kg. [4,100 pounds] – on a north-east course. Due to the extraordinary speed with which we ran off – calculated at 70 knots, actually 90 knots – could

[11] Jones, IV, p. 16.

> only make out the bursts through the mist among the dock lights, but no details were observed.

Actually *L 43* had been set to the north, and had made the Suffolk coast between Felixstowe and Orfordness at 2:20 a.m. With the wind behind her, she drove north-north-west across Norfolk till she again reached the sea at Wells. The "London" bombs, of which thirty-eight were counted, were scattered between East Wrentham and Great Ryburgh. One man was killed and cottages damaged. Radio bearings on the way home showed that *L 43* had been carried far to the north, but by descending to 1,600 feet, she made more progress, crabbing across a south-south-west wind estimated at 49 to 54 m.p.h. To add to Kraushaar's worries, Nordholz broadcast, "To all airships. Airship base at Wittmund, thunderstorm. Airship bases Nordholz, Tondern, thunderstorms approaching. Ahlhorn clear." At 2:37 p.m., after a flight of nearly 23 hours, *L 43* slipped in between two thunder squalls to land at Ahlhorn.

*L 44*, with Strasser on board, was fortunate to get home. According to British records she was only briefly over England, coming in at Lowestoft at 2:23 a.m. and going out a few minutes later near Great Yarmouth. No bombs were traced from her. *Kapitänleutnant* Stabbert reported:

> 12:45 a.m. crossed coast at Harwich. Broken cloud ceiling. Several searchlights sought in vain to reach ship. Weak anti-aircraft fire. No planes observed. 2 engines failed over Harwich. Planned to attack London with three engines, as weather and cloud conditions unusually favorable. 3rd engine failed after passing Harwich. Ship dropped rapidly with 2 motors. Attack on London given up, turned back, all

*L 41 as she appeared on her arrival at Ahlhorn, before she was reconstructed and given an under coating of black paint. Two radiators over the after gondola show that one engine has been removed for higher altitude. Note arches for Sheds V and VI in the background. (Nonhoff-Strumann)*

*L 44 at Ahlhorn ("Alix"), was the first ship to carry a streamlined rear car with two engines and one propeller (see below). L 44 was shot down in flames in Lorraine during the "Silent Raid" on October 20, 1917. (Moch)*

*A direct-drive after power gondola of the type fitted to the L 44 and all later ships. The propeller was attached at the after (left-hand) end of the car. Note the two engines inside, placed to port and starboard of the center line, the ladder leading into the ship, and the retractable radiators with their flexible feed pipes. The light gondola frame was eventually covered with heavy fabric. (Luftschiffbau Zeppelin)*

> bombs dropped at 1:40 a.m. over Harwich when ship fell again. No unusual results seen due to overcast. Immediately after attack last 2 engines failed one after the other. Ship continued to descend and after slipping 6 fuel tanks, dropping water, radiator water, spare parts and most of ship's equipment, she was held at 3,900 meters [12,800 feet]. Attack altitude was 5,700 meters [18,700 feet]. Ship drifted as a free balloon for 3/4 hour from Harwich to Lowestoft. One engine was then set going. Then, due to serious mistrimming (20 degrees) and lack of trimming material, ship went up to 6,400 meters [21,000 feet]. Till 10 a.m. flew with only one motor. After 10, flying at times with 2-3 motors, two of them at half speed. Radio receiver working, sender not working. Return most of way with one engine full speed and one at half speed.

*L 44* came home in this condition, not because of engine trouble, but because all spare radiator water had been dumped overboard. There was much anxiety over her plight, particularly as Strasser was on board, and at 11:28 a.m., *L 23* took off from Tondern with orders from *Korvettenkapitän* Schütze: "*L 44* last bearing in 005 δ 7 [120 miles east of Flamborough Head] at 9:40 a.m., has radio trouble, appears to have engine trouble, apparently drifting north. *L 23* to go to 007 δ 7. . . . Purpose is to seek *L 44*, to serve as radio repeater, report on condition, in case of need to rescue personnel or to lead own surface forces to her. On making contact stand by while 2nd ship will cover to west." At 2:06 p.m., *L 23* sighted her crippled sister 30 miles to the west. At 5:10 p.m. Stabbert's ship limped past Heligoland, and at 6 p.m. landed at Nordholz.

"Almost simultaneous failure of all engines is neither attributable to material or personnel failure, but to an unfortunate coincidence," Stabbert insisted. No official document could mention the superstition that Strasser aboard a raiding airship was a "Jonah." The unprecedented plight of *L 44*, falling with dead engines over the enemy's country, had provoked Strasser to an outburst of rage, which Stabbert answered – so say former airshipmen – with, "Commander, don't shout so loud! The English will hear you down there!"

*L 42* came nearest to London on this night. Dietrich after 11 p.m. flew through hail squalls, and St. Elmo's Fire glowed inside and outside the ship. Still later, solid cloud underneath hid the ground. When Dietrich dropped some bombs in hopes of arousing the defenses, twenty searchlights opened up. These were taken to be at Sheerness. Bearings on burning incendiaries showed that *L 42* was making no progress against the wind at 18,700 feet. Abandoning the attack on London, Dietrich dropped all his bombs here, but heavy clouds hid the results. Actually crossing the coast south of the Naze, Dietrich had come inland as far as Braintree, then had turned off to the north and had traversed Norfolk at 56 m.p.h. with the wind, to go out to sea near Sheringham. The "Sheerness" bombs, distributed between Mildenhall and East Dereham, did no damage.

On the homeward flight *L 42* found a wall of black thunderclouds reaching up to 23,000 feet barring her way. Dietrich had no choice but to fly through them. With antenna wound in, and pressure height of 19,400 feet, *L 42* plunged into the black squall clouds at 16,400 feet. Hail drummed on the taut outer cover, and at 4:45 a.m. a blinding flash of lightning struck the ship. The metal structure was so heavily charged that a machinist's mate, sitting on a stool in the port midships engine car, got a severe shock when he touched the duralumin gondola wall. There was a strong smell of ozone in the rear gondola, and its personnel believed that the electrical charge left the ship along the port propeller bracket. Ten minutes later the Zeppelin was staggered by a second lightning bolt. This time the top lookout saw it strike near him and course along the ship's back, while people in the rear gondola saw the flash shooting out of the tail. The sailmaker patrolling the keel was astonished to see the lightning glaring through the translucent gas cells and outer cover. Fifteen minutes later there was a weaker lightning stroke which was seen from the control car to hit forward. A meticulous check of the ship at Nordholz revealed six holes in the cotton outer cover at the bow, the largest the size of the palm of the hand. Underneath, two bracing wires in contact had burned through, and a pea-sized hole had been punched in a duralumin girder member. Traces of fire were found on the port after propeller.

For Richard Wolff's new *L 47* the raid was also her altitude trial, as the weather had prevented her from making one since her commissioning on May 3. Wolff believed that he cruised for over two hours above England, flying at 18,400 feet with the stars above and solid cloud beneath, but the British did not trace *L 47* over land. *L 40* and *L 45* both crossed East Anglia with the wind, and both claimed to have bombed Norwich, but only three bombs from them were traced on land.

British records show that one man was killed, none injured, and £599 damage done in this raid. On the Naval Staff's report the Kaiser noted: "In spite of this success, I am of the opinion that the day of the airship is past for attacks on London. They should be used as scouts for the High Seas Fleet, and for strategic reconnaissance, not for bombing raids on London."[12] The Chief of the Naval Staff replied that large numbers of troops, guns and airplanes would be released for the Western Front if the airships should cease their attacks, and the Kaiser was persuaded to allow them to continue "when the circumstances seem favorable."

This raid demonstrated that the effects of altitude on men and machines could no longer be ignored. "At 16,000 feet and over, when a man climbed the ladder from the control car to the keel, walked aft to the 'head,' returned and climbed down the ladder into the control car again, he was so exhausted that he was useless for the rest of the raid," one former Zeppelin commander told the author. (The "head" was aft at Ring 35, and the round trip involved walking more than 800 feet.) Strasser, with his personal experience aboard *L 44* fresh in his mind, called for special reports from all the commanders who took part in the raid.

Much attention was devoted to "altitude sickness." The commanders agreed that flying for four hours or more above 16,000 feet led to severe headache which lasted for hours afterwards, abdominal discomfort, nausea, and sometimes vomiting. "The crew cannot perform as well at the new high altitudes," wrote Stabbert of men who had raided England in the previous year with von Schubert and Ganzel. At the start of *L 44*'s six-hour flight at high altitude, the sailmaker and a mechanic in the rear gondola were so fatigued that they had to be put in hammocks. The others, laboring to re-trim their derelict ship, "became rather exhausted and inefficient" carrying 66-pound cans of petrol forward, pumping fuel by hand and moving back and forth in the gangway with an up angle of 20 degrees. After looking into the rear gondola, Stabbert himself found that it took him 15 minutes, dragging himself from handhold to handhold, to struggle the 295 feet uphill to the forward gondola. Descending the ladder to the control car, Stabbert felt exhausted and was "absolutely gasping for air." In his opinion, the ship's safety was endangered by the crew's slowness in carrying weights forward to trim her. Remarking that the symptoms of altitude sickness began at 18,000 feet, Stabbert suggested that all heavy work (particularly hand-pumping petrol from the tanks along the keel to the gravity tanks over the engine cars) should be done before reaching this altitude. His crew made little use of oxygen, but henceforth Stabbert was determined to have them take it over 16,500 feet by orders relayed via engine telegraph, whether they felt the need or not. "To use oxygen when one begins feeling exhausted is too late."

In *L 42*, flying at 18,700 feet at a temperature of 4 below zero F., the starboard engine in the rear gondola had to be stopped due to a broken oil line. Efforts to drain the radiator failed because the warrant machinist and two of his men could not get out on the gondola roof, and the radiator froze solid. Nor could the men do the work needed to repair the motor. "They have always done their duty before," wrote Dietrich, who attributed their inefficiency to lack of oxygen.

The cold and high altitude had bizarre and even dangerous effects on material. Stabbert remarked on the rapid loss by evaporation of radiator water at high altitude, naively observing "whether due to addition of alcohol or the dry air at great heights is unknown."[13] Henceforth *L 44* would carry 660 pounds of reserve radiator water in sacks near the

12 Gladisch, VI, p. 290.

13 Strasser's endorsement provided the correct explanation in terms of reduced atmospheric pressure and lowered boiling point.

*Naval airship L 45 at Staaken. Note the rectangular rudders, an invariable feature of all of the Staaken-built Zeppelins. (Luftschiffbau Zeppelin)*

individual engine cars, and all radiators would be filled just before going up to attack altitude. A "reserve water central supply" had been set up in each ship before this raid, but Strasser determined to abolish it, even though it saved weight, as the men were too fatigued by having to walk from their individual gondolas to fetch water.

In *L 44*, different coefficients of expansion of duralumin and steel caused the engine telegraph wires and rudder and elevator control cables to slack off markedly in the cold at high altitudes, though they "took up" again at lower levels.[14] For the same reason, celluloid windows "set up" taut at the factory split at high altitude. In *L 45*, ice one millimeter thick covered the face of the compass after a long flight above 13,000 feet.

One raid in each "attack period" was now the rule. The moon would next be new on June 19, and on June 16, Strasser sent his ships to "attack in south, London." The shortest night of the year was only five days away. Two years earlier the capable and perceptive Klaus Hirsch had warned his chief against attacking England in the short midsummer nights, and by now the danger to the Zeppelins was tenfold greater. Why Strasser sent the airships out when they would find only three to four hours of semi-darkness over London is incomprehensible.

[14] It can be shown that the rudder and elevator control cables, "set up" at 50 degrees F., could slack off more than 4 inches at -25 degrees F., enough to permit them to jump off their sheaves.

Martin Dietrich, who flew in this raid, cannot explain it. But he recalls that his chief would never admit the existence of an effective British defense against the Zeppelins, and did not want to hear his officers report having sighted airplanes over England. "Sometimes he would argue with them and suggest they were overly nervous and imagining things." Possibly Strasser's deputy, Viktor Schütze, had been pressing to make this attack. If so, he paid the penalty in the disaster which followed.

Schütze, leading the squadron in *L 48*, was accompanying his old crew, now commanded by *Kapitänleutnant der Reserve* Eichler, on their first raid in their new ship. As the black-hued monster was walked out of the "Normann" hanger in Nordholz, the station band struck up "The Admiral of the Air." Half-way through the tune the cover of the bass drum split from top to bottom. Only then did the superstitious seamen remember that they were embarking on their thirteenth raid.

Two ships assigned to the operation, *L 46* and *L 47*, could not leave their sheds in Ahlhorn, apparently due to cross winds. *L 44* and *L 45* experienced repeated engine failures; the former limped home across Holland with only the port midships engine working. Only *L 42* and *L 48* reached England.

At 8:30 p.m. Martin Dietrich saw the English coast at Southwold 40 miles away, but did not steer for it as it was still too light, and thunderstorms loomed over the land. At 11:31 p.m. there came an

*Naval airship L 46 dropping ballast for a landing south of the hangars at Friedrichshafen. The Maybach engine factory is in the center background. Note the anti-aircraft machine-gun tower at the left background. (Luftschiffbau Zeppelin)*

optimistic message from Schütze in *L 48*: "To all airships. Weather good for London. Attack and departure course between east and north." Dietrich planned to come inland between Dover and Dungeness on a course for London, but at midnight, when he thought the lights of Dover were in sight, he found the south-south-east wind had freshened to 22 to 27 m.p.h. With thunderstorms and vivid lightning to the west, Dietrich resolved to drop some of his bombs on Dover and go on to London later if possible. Not until 2 a.m. was he able to reach a good attack position to windward. As he dropped his first bomb, fourteen searchlights opened up, guns commenced firing, and a plane was seen under the ship, but only two or three searchlights found *L 42* and could not hold her due to her black camouflage. "With the bursting of a 300 kg. [660 pound] bomb a gigantic explosion took place, which caused further explosions at intervals of ten minutes, until the whole district, apparently a munitions store, was completely in flames. The fire could still be seen an hour later on the way home." By now it was too late to raid London, and *L 42* kept on going east-north-east at 19,400 feet.

Dietrich reported having bombed Dover and Deal, but his actual target was Ramsgate. His third bomb, as he guessed from three miles in the air, exploded a naval ammunition depot near the Clock Tower and wrecked the naval base. Three civilians were killed and fourteen civilians and two servicemen injured, mostly by the ammunition explosion, while the damage totaled £28,159. Though Dietrich did not know it, three aircraft tried to attack him on the way home. A seaplane off Lowestoft was at 11,000 feet when she met the airship, but had no chance as *L 42* was flying at 14,800 feet. A few minutes later Flight Lieutenant Cadbury in a Sopwith "Pup" from Great Yarmouth gave chase, but found he could not gain on her. A Yarmouth H.12 flying boat also pursued *L 42* for 95 minutes to within 10 miles north of Ameland without being able to overhaul her. At 9:10 a.m. *L 42* landed at Nordholz after a nineteen-hour flight. For fourteen of those hours she had been above 13,000 feet, and for eleven hours over 16,500 feet, but her crew had fully met all the demands on them.

*L 48* was first seen about 40 miles north-east of Harwich at 11:34 p.m., but the starboard engine failed and the forward engine gave trouble that could not be rectified until 2 a.m. The liquid magnetic compass froze, and it was only with difficulty that Eichler could get his bearings. It was now much too late to reach London, so Eichler decided to bomb Harwich and head for home as rapidly as possible before dawn. *L 48* came inland south of Orfordness at 3:10 a.m. and bore down on Harwich

L 48

*L 48 At Friedrichshafen, ready to take off on a trial flight from the field south of the hangars. (Luftschiffbau Zeppelin)*

from the north. Her crew thought they salvoed their bombs into the naval base from 18,400 feet in the face of heavy gunfire, but they fell harmlessly in open fields about 5 miles to the north. It was an exceptionally clear night, and the Zeppelin could easily be seen moving across the starlit sky. Following her attack, *L 48* dropped down to 13,000 feet, and at 3:23 a.m. called up the stations in the German Bight to ask for bearings.

Meanwhile several airplane pilots had taken off from nearby flying fields, and one of them, Lieutenant L.P. Watkins of No.37 Squadron, presently found *L 48* steering north inside the coast. But for the frozen compass, she would have been well on her way home, instead of finding herself at low altitude over the enemy's country with the early dawn lighting the eastern sky. Watkins reported:

> I climbed to 8,000 feet over the aerodrome, then struck off in the direction of Harwich still climbing when at 11,000 feet over Harwich I saw the A.A. guns firing and several searchlights pointing towards the same spot. A minute later I observed the Zeppelin about 2,000 feet above me. After climbing about 500 feet I fired one drum into its tail, but it took no effect. I then climbed to 12,000 feet and fired another drum into its tail without any effect. I then decided to wait until I was at close range before firing another drum; I then climbed steadily until I reached 13,200 feet and was then about 500 feet under the Zeppelin. I fired three short bursts of about 7 rounds and then the remainder of the drum. The Zeppelin burst into flames at the tail, the fire running along both sides; the whole Zeppelin caught fire and fell burning.[15]

Dietrich was seventy miles away when he witnessed *L 48*'s destruction, and never forgot it:

> At 3:35, two points abaft the port beam, a red ball of fire suddenly appeared, which quickly grew bigger and in falling, showed the shape of a Zeppelin airship. The burning ship was at the same altitude as *L 42*, therefore 4,000-4,500 meters [13,000-14,800 feet]. Some 500 meters [1,600 feet] higher a plane was clearly visible, which twice fired a bright white light.

The wreck of *L 48* fell burning into a field at Holly Tree Farm, near Theberton. Already the early midsummer dawn was breaking, and the flames of her destruction showed pale against the cold radiance of the eastern sky. *Korvettenkapitän* Schütze, *Kapitänleutnant* Eichler, and 12 of the men either jumped out or were burned to death.[16]

*PREVIOUS: L 48 starting her motors after taking off for a trial flight at Friedrichshafen in May 1917 (another photo above). Smoke is caused by backfiring of the port engine. On her first raid to England on June 17, 1917, she was shot down in flames. Of the seventeen man crew, three survived and were later interrogated. Found on board, and contrary to orders, were secret code word lists, and ciphers. This is the best photograph in existence of one of the finest looking classes of Zeppelins ever built. (Luftschiffbau Zeppelin)*

15 Watkins' report in Imperial War Museum file, "Pilots' Reports Relating to Destruction of Zeppelins."

16 As with L 32, the destruction of *L 48* involved a breach of security. On June 22, 1917, Admiral Scheer was obliged to write to the Chief of the Naval Staff that *L 48*, at the time of her loss, had on board contrary to orders the general cipher table for the naval signal book and three code word lists and since it had been reported in the press that the Zeppelin had fallen on land, Scheer had to request that all of them be changed.

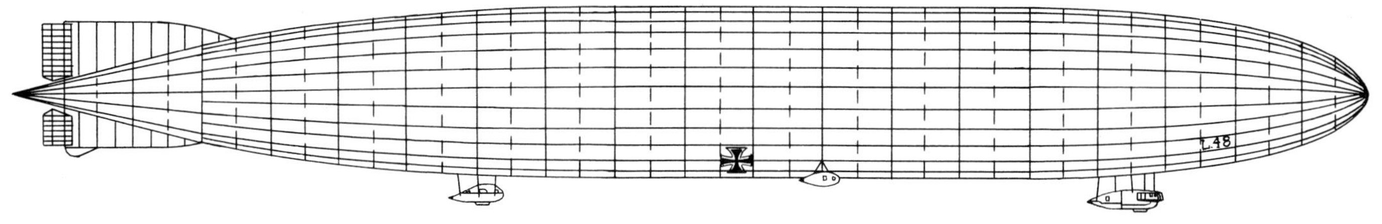


**L 48**

| | | | |
|---|---|---|---|
| Gas capacity | 1,970,800 ft.³ | Engines | 5 Maybach HSLu, of 240 h.p. |
| Length | 644.7 ft. | Propellers | 4 Jaray L.Z. |
| Diameter | 78.4 ft. | Weight empty | 56,900 |
| Useful lift | 85,800 lbs. | Maximum speed | 66 mph |
| Gas cells | 18 | Ceiling | 20,000 ft. |
| Crew | 20 | Full speed endurance | 7600 miles |

Three members of the crew of *L 48* survived the destruction of their ship. This case is unique in the eight-year history of the Naval Airship Division, for never before or afterwards did any of Strasser's men ride down to earth with two million cubic feet of blazing hydrogen and live to tell the tale. The fact that the bow structure survived intact, instead of the entire framework piling up in a shapeless tangle of crushed wreckage, suggests that *L 48* fell rather slowly. Badly injured, Machinist's Mate Wilhelm Uecker died on Armistice Day, 1918. The executive officer, *Leutnant zur See* Otto Mieth, survived with two broken legs, and Machinist's Mate Heinrich Ellerkamm, in charge of the starboard midships gondola, miraculously escaped with only superficial burns.

Ellerkamm, still at the age of 66 enjoying the blond hair, the clear blue eyes and the fair skin of youth, was not adverse to remembering his incredible experience when the author visited him in 1957. "My hour has not yet come," was his solemn remark as he recalled that not once, but twice, had his life been miraculously saved. An airship man from October, 1914, and a regular crew member under *Kapitänleutnant* Loewe in *L 19*, he had agreed before her last flight to give his place to a friend in the maintenance group who wished to earn the customary Iron Cross for making a raid. Told of the frozen compass having caused *L 48* to leave Harwich on a northerly instead of an easterly course, he remarked, "I still think it was that radio message telling us to go down to 3,400 meters. Just before they got us the machinist climbed down into my gondola on his rounds and told us that we had been advised by radio of a tail wind blowing at 3,400 meters [11,000 feet]. The English must have intercepted it." Continuing, he related:

> I thought we were over the sea on our way home. It was time to check the fuel supply for my motor – I had pumped petrol up to the gravity tanks above the gondola some hours before – and I told my helper to take over. There was a faint light of dawn in the east, and as I climbed the ladder, suspended in space half-way between the gondola and the hull, I heard a machine gun firing. There below us, dim in the light of dawn, was the English flyer. I stepped on to the lateral gangway inside the hull; we were below pressure height, and I could look aft. There was another burst of gunfire, and I could actually see flaming phosphorus bullets tearing through the after cells. I watched with a horrified fascination. This I knew must be the end!
>
> Any one of those bullets could set our hydrogen on fire. There was an explosion – not loud, but a dull "woof!" as when you light a gas stove. A burst of flame. Then another explosion. One gas cell after another was catching fire over my head. My first thought was not to be crushed under the wreckage in case we were over land, so I climbed farther up among the girders. Flames were dancing everywhere, and the heat was overpowering. My fur coat

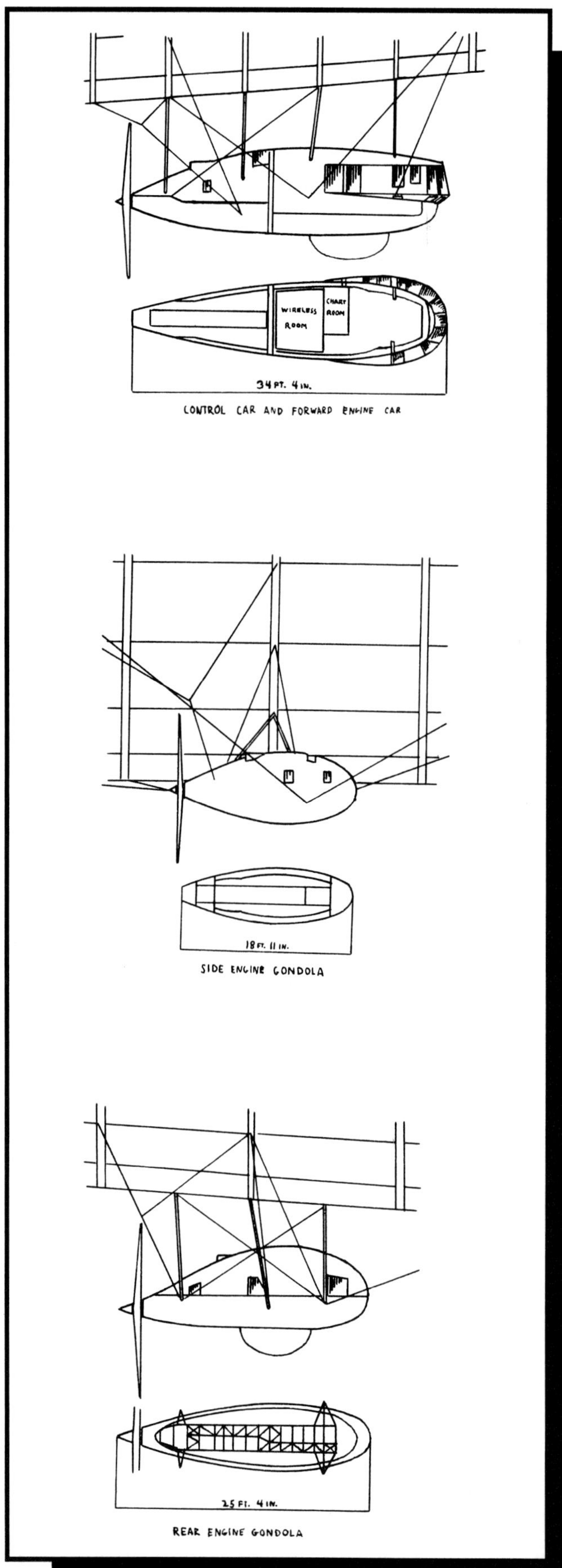


collar caught fire; I tried to beat it out with my hands. The weight of the big 2-engine gondola aft was dragging down the stern, the ship tipped vertically and down we plunged, a monstrous roaring banner of flame reaching hundreds of meters above my head, and the wind whistling through the bared framework. I noticed the draft was driving the flames away from me. But it was only a temporary respite. I thought of jumping, and remembered *Korvettenkapitän* Schütze, when he was our commander, saying, "Better to smash against the earth and perish at once than to burn to death trapped in blazing wreckage on the ground." No, it isn't true that we carried poison, or pistols to shoot ourselves when the ship caught fire. Hand guns were forbidden.

I was still arguing with myself when a light appeared below –whether on land or sea I could not tell. Suddenly there was a terrible, continuous roaring smashing of metal as the stern struck the ground and the hull structure collapsed beneath me. I found myself on the ground with the breath half knocked out of me, the framework crashing down on top of me, fuel and oil tanks bursting on impact and their burning contents flowing towards me through the shattered wreckage. I was trapped in a tangle of red-hot girders, the heat roasting me alive through my heavy flying coat. If I had lost consciousness I would have burned to death. But I could still think and move, and with all my strength I forced some girders apart – I never felt the pain of my burned hands until later – and burst out of my prison. I fell full length on cool, wet grass. In front of me, frightened horses were galloping away across the field, their tails in the air. I heard the roar of an engine, and saw a British plane circling low over the wreckage, the pilot waving to me. Already it was almost full daylight.

The fire was roaring at my back. Staggering to my feet, I turned back to the wreck. *Korvettenkapitän* Schütze had jumped, as he always said he would; he was dead, his legs buried up to the knees in the ground. English civilians helped me to drag *Leutnant zur See* Mieth, still alive, out of the wreckage of the radio cabin in the control car. One of them took me to his home, where I collapsed unconscious. Later I asked to be taken to see Mieth, but it was forbidden.

I can't explain how I survived. All I can say is that my gondola was 100 meters from the tail cone, and the tail structure broke the force of my fall, while the bow remained intact and did not collapse on me entirely.

The loss of *L 48*, with his valued subordinate, Viktor Schütze, was the most demoralizing blow that Strasser had yet sustained. That the newest of the "height climbers," with an experienced and tested crew – the flagship of an officer whose boldness and skill had been repeatedly proved – should have been destroyed by the British was shocking and inconceivable. Dietrich had sent word of *L 48*'s loss by radio, and Strasser was out on the field to meet him. Climbing aboard *L 42* as soon as she touched the ground, Strasser demanded details. "The English have no real defense against our airships!" he insisted. "But it *was* a plane!" retorted Dietrich. "I saw it myself!" One of the senior commanders, Dietrich had to be believed, and Strasser left the control car of *L 42* a dejected and temporarily beaten man.

"He stayed in his quarters the rest of the day, and was very depressed," continues Dietrich. "Then, after a day or two, he invited us commanders to a *Bowle*, which was very unusual – ordinarily we would give the party and invite him. I had been thinking about the last raid, and to try to cheer him up, I said, 'Commander, things aren't so bad, we can still get away from the planes. I know we can climb higher. We'll just have to use oxygen.' Next day he had recovered his good spirits, and said to me, 'I was very pleased that you, as senior commander, took the attitude that you did last night.'"

On June 23, Strasser wrote to Scheer:

The airship attacks on England constitute a burden on our main opponent not to be underestimated.

How disturbing these attacks are for the English is shown by the tremendous expense they go to prevent these attacks, and by the jubilation demonstrated when an airship is destroyed.

The deliberate minimizing of the effects of the attacks by the English press in my opinion is designed, in conjunction with our losses, to cause us to be doubtful of their success.

If the English should succeed in convincing us that the airship attacks had little value and thereby cause us to give them up, they would be rid of a severe problem and would be laughing at us in triumph behind our backs.

L48

# CHAPTER XVII

# BRITISH FLYING BOATS TAKE THE WAR INTO THE GERMAN BIGHT

Meanwhile the British Navy, annoyed by the Germans' ability to protect their minesweepers and submarines through their superiority in airships, and by their ability to observe the British Fleet whenever it entered the German Bight in fair weather, were preparing a two-pronged surprise assault on the Zeppelins in their own waters. Although the airships were now flying as high as possible over England to avoid airplane attack, they were still carrying out their reconnaissance's at comfortable altitudes, sometimes descending as low as 200 feet to spot mines. The Germans well knew that the British had no seaplanes able to fly to the German Bight and back, and had learned to feel contempt for the improvised seaplane carriers which had vainly brought float-planes into the Bight to attack them in previous years. To overcome this fault, the Grand Fleet in the first half of 1917 was taking Sopwith "Pup" land plane fighters to sea in converted cross-Channel steamers with short flying-off decks forward, but these vessels – *Manxman*, *Pegasus* and *Nairana* – sighted no Zeppelins and had no successes. In March, 1917, the Grand Fleet aircraft committee recommended that the fast "large light cruiser" *Furious* be fitted with a flying-off deck forward for airplanes. She re-entered service modified in this way in July, 1917, with five "Pups" which were not intended to land back on board, but to "ditch" in the sea. One vessel in each light cruiser squadron was also fitted to carry a "Pup" on a platform over the forward guns, and *Yarmouth*, the first so equipped, was eventually to achieve a brilliant success.

More prompt results were obtained with a new model of the more conventional flying-boat operating from shore bases. The American Curtiss Company led in the development of these craft, and in April and May of 1917 the first four "boats" of an improved Curtiss design, known as the "Large America" or H.12, were delivered to the Royal Naval Air Service stations at Great Yarmouth and Felixstowe. With two 275 h.p. Rolls-Royce Eagle I engines giving them a speed of 85

*OPPOSITE:*
*L 48 on a trial flight at Friedrichshafen. (Luftschiffbau Zeppelin)*

*Wittmundhafen in East Frisia. Built originally for the Army airship service, it was later turned over the German Navy on April 17, 1917. In the foreground are the "Wünsch", and "Wille" sheds. Since there were no gas works nearby (as in Nordholz), gas had to be brought in by special railroad tank cars. (Moch)*

m.p.h., a crew of four, and fuel for six or eight hours, the British Navy at last had in the H.12 a weapon which could carry the offensive to the enemy's waters.

Even more vital now was the role of the radio intelligence service in Whitehall. The Zeppelins had given up the self-betraying practice of signaling their take-offs on raids, but on scouting flights they not only continued the take-off announcement, but sent a message with each change of course, requests for bearings, and radio reports of sighting of ships or local weather. *L 22*, routinely covering the dangerously exposed western sector off Terschelling, sent no fewer than 9 radio signals during a patrol of 13 1/2 hours on April 7 – each one enabling the enemy to fix her position. The possibility of "fingering" the Zeppelins for the flying-boat hunters was not lost on the British Admiralty, and on April 26, 1917, a coded position chart was issued to the air stations, with instructions for its use. The first Zeppelin heard was labeled "Annie," the second "Betty," the third "Clara," etc.

On the morning of May 14, after a week of bad weather and no scouting flights, Strasser sent out *L 23* for defensive patrolling to the north, and *L 22* to the west from the big 2-hangar ex-Army base at Wittmundhaven in East Frisia. British listeners heard *L 22*'s take-off message, and knowing that she was probably heading for her routine patrol north and south off Terschelling, the Admiralty ordered the Great Yarmouth air station to send off a flying-boat to intercept her. At 4:30 a.m. the H.12 No.8666, with Flight Lieutenant Galpin, Flight Sub-Lieutenant Leckie and two petty officers, took off on a course for the Terschelling Bank Lightship. The "boat" was carrying three Lewis machine guns with explosive and incendiary ammunition, four 100-pound bombs, radio equipment, and 265 gallons of fuel, 40 of it in cans. When 80 miles from her base, the "boat" stopped sending radio messages in order to avoid discovery. At 5:48 a.m., in Galpin's words:

> We sighted a Zeppelin dead ahead about 10-15 miles away end on. We were then cruising at 60 knots, at 5,000 feet, and 2 minutes later passed the Terschelling L.V. on our port hand. We increased speed to 65 knots and height to 6,000

*Right: Aerial view of revolving double shed at Nordholz. It was 597 feet long, 114 feet wide, and 98 feet high and could rotate once in an hour. Pointed ends are additions added later by Busen to accomodate larger ships of the L 30 class (650+ feet). (Moch)*

feet. We dropped three of the bombs to lighten ship at 5.0 a.m. [British time] and Flight Sub-Lieutenant Leckie took over the wheel again. C.P.O. Whatling went aft to the rear gun and I went forward to the 2 Lewis guns mounted parallel in the bow. The Zeppelin turned north and then north-east exposing her broadside, and I concluded she was coming south-west when we first saw her, and had now reached the limit of her patrol. We were then about 2 miles astern of her so increased speed to 75 knots, descending to 5,000 feet. She seemed as yet unaware of us, probably owing to our background of dark fog and cloud; but when we came within half a

*Nordholz hydrogen gas plant. Low pressure gas store at lower left and near road. High pressure store with 150 cylinders buried under flat areas to the right. (Moch)*

mile of her she put her nose up and seemed to increase speed. We dived at her at 90 knots coming slightly astern at 3,800 feet, where we leveled out to 75 knots. In this position we overhauled her on the starboard quarter about 20 feet below the level of the gondolas. I opened fire with both guns at 50 yards' range and observed incendiary bullets entering the envelope on the starboard quarter slightly below the middle. After a few rounds the port gun jammed, but the starboard gun fired nearly a complete tray before jamming also. We were then 100 feet from her and turned hard-a-starboard while I tried to clear the starboard gun. As we began to turn I thought I saw a slight glow inside the envelope and 15 seconds later when she came in sight on our other side she was hanging tail down at an angle of 45 degrees with the lower half of her envelope thoroughly alight. Five or six seconds later the whole ship was a glowing mass and she fell vertically by the tail. C.P.O. Whatling, observing from the other hatch, saw the number *L 22* painted under the nose before it was consumed. We also saw two of the crew jump out, one from the after gun position on the top of the tail fin and one from the after gondola. They had no parachutes. When the airship had fallen to about 1,000 feet four large columns of water went up below in quick succession either from bombs or engines becoming detached from the framework. After 45 seconds from first ignition the envelope was burned off and the bare skeleton plunged into the sea, leaving a mass of black ash on the surface from which a column of brown smoke about 1,500 feet high sprang up and stood.[1]

Not only did the flying-boat succeed in destroying *L 22* on this first flight into the Bight; she managed also to conceal her presence, and the Germans had no warning that their airships might again be attacked by this formidable weapon.

While returning from the raid of May 23-24, 1917, Sommerfeldt in *L 40* became the first Zeppelin commander to see one of the new British flying-boats and live to tell the tale. Once again it was the H.12 No.8666 which, piloted by Flight Lieutenant Galpin, had left Yarmouth at 4:15 a.m. Flying to Terschelling, she proceeded east for about 15 minutes more without sighting anything. Galpin decided to return, and flew at 1,200 feet because of the poor visibility. At 6:38 a.m. a Zeppelin suddenly appeared out of the clouds at 1,600 feet. In Galpin's words:

On seeing us he dropped two white flares; we did not answer this signal, but put on full speed, dropped our bombs and climbed up at him. He then turned quickly through 16 points and started to climb hard. When he reached 3,000 feet we had gained on him and were actually 300 yards astern. He threw out a smoke screen, under cover of which he gained the main bank of clouds; it was not feasible for us to attempt to follow him there. As he disappeared I fired half a tray of Brock, Pomeroy and tracer into him, but was unable to observe the effect.[2]

Sommerfeldt's report of the encounter was inaccurate, and did not give the urgent warning of this new danger which his colleagues so badly needed. Apparently he assumed it was a short-range seaplane brought to the spot by a carrier:

During the return the ship was attacked in 005 ε 7 [ten miles north of Vlieland] by a seaplane which took off from the water, did not answer recognition signals, and dropped 2 bombs, apparently to lighten the load, and pursued the ship. The plane was fired on with one machine gun from 1,200 meters [4,000 feet]. The fight was ended by *L 40* entering a cloud. Enemy light warships were not seen in the vicinity. . . . Although the ship was at all times 100 meters [330 feet] higher than the plane, and at a distance to one side, the pilot succeeded in making three hits [12 bullet holes] on the ship. At the up angle at which she was flying, every bullet – coming up from below – pierced sev-

1 Galpin's report in Imperial War Museum file, "Pilots' Reports Relating to Destruction of Zeppelins."

2 C.F. Snowden Gamble, *The Story of a North Sea Air Station* (London: Oxford University Press, 1928), p. 242.

> eral cells. The distance from the plane was estimated at 1,200 meters [4,000 feet]. 75 rounds were fired at it from the ship. Results not seen.

On June 5, flying the westerly patrol off Terschelling, *L 40* was again attacked close in to the island by No.8666 with Galpin and Leckie in charge. The Zeppelin was first seen:

> cruising at 2,000 feet about 6 miles to the north-east of us. We came down to 4,000 feet, but lost sight of her in the mist, and when next seen at 8:10 a.m. [British time] she was east-by-north and level with us at 4,000 feet. She then fired one white light which we answered with one white Very light. We pursued her until 8:45 a.m., during which she climbed to 10,500 feet and were immediately under her. At 8:25 a.m. we opened fire at 600 yards with the two guns forward and two amidships, and continued firing at intervals until 8:45 a.m. Ten trays of Brock, Pomeroy and Buckingham ammunition were fired, the closest range attained being 1,000 feet.[3]

Over-generous Fate had granted Sommerfeldt a second opportunity to warn his chief and comrades-in-arms of this menace to the patrolling Zeppelins. And a second time he misidentified the aircraft type and permitted himself to believe that it was a harmless seaplane carrier operation:

> 9:30 a.m. in 044 ε, 20 hectometers distance [12 1/2 miles], plane sighted, did not answer recognition signals, steered for ship. Ship at 1,800 meters [6,000 feet], plane at 2,000 meters [6,600 feet]. Ran off on an east course to draw plane over seaplane station Borkum and climbed. . . . Plane approached close and opened fire with tracer ammunition. Ship ran off on zigzag course and took every opportunity to reply. Salvoes repeatedly covered target as could be ascertained from exploding tracer. Plane is a biplane resembling Nieuport type, carries 2 black circles on planes as recognition mark. 9:48 a.m. in 081 ε, plane at 3,200 meters [10,500 feet] under ship at 5,300 meters [17,400 feet]. Three bombs of 10 kg. [22 pounds] dropped. Plane turns off and steers for Terschelling.

Five hours later, "despite extraordinary visibility of about 40 sea miles, no enemy vessels can be found which could have brought the plane."

June 14, a fateful day, was one of full activity for the Naval Airship Division. About midnight of the 13th, in response to orders issued earlier in the evening, two of the latest Zeppelins, *L 46* and *L 48*, took off to scout in the U-boat blockade area. Strasser's orders for the former read:

> Operation in blockade area. With north winds towards Firth of Forth, observe especially traffic in Dogger Bank area and western portion of line Lindesnes-St. Abbs Head, Farne Island. Particularly observe whether traffic heavy or light, single steamers or convoys. With southerly winds cover blockade area from Hoofden to 54 degrees as northern boundary. *L 48* proceeding in direction Christiansand-Firth of Forth, in case of south winds north of 55th parallel. Take-off 10 p.m., report 9 p.m. Patrolling: *L 23*, *L 42*, *L 43*.
>
> Leader of Airships.

The last three took off about 2 a.m. to cover minesweepers working on "Route Yellow" where it had been fouled by British mines 40 miles north of Terschelling. *L 43* had the exposed western sector north of Terschelling. At 6:36 a.m. she radioed that she was at the Terschelling Bank Lightship and starting her patrol.

British radio direction finders had already located two airships over the German Bight, and as "Annie" (the first one heard) appeared to be heading west, the H.12 No.8677 took off from Felixstowe at 5:15 a.m. to meet her. Flight Sub-Lieutenants Hobbs and Dickey were in charge, and described their flight in a joint report:

> In accordance with your orders we proceeded at 5:15 a.m. B.S.T. and at 7:30 a.m., after making good course 72 magnetic, we sighted

[3] C.F. Snowden Gamble, *The Story of a North Sea Air Station*, p. 245.

Dutch coast at Vlieland. We carried on various courses which brought us at 7:58 a.m. off Amieland [sic] where we altered course for Felixstowe. At 8:40 a.m. we were again off Vlieland at 500 feet when we sighted a Zeppelin 5 miles on our starboard bow at about 1,500 feet steering due north. Its approximate position was 53 degrees 20 minutes North, 4 degrees 40 minutes East. We at once proceeded to attack at full speed, climbing to 2,000 feet. Flight Sub-Lieutenant Hobbs was piloting machine, Sub-Lieut. Dickey manned the bow gun, WIT Operator H.M. Davies A.M. II F. 20254 manned midship gun and A.M. I (E) A.W. Goody F. 12237 manned the stern guns. As we approached the Zeppelin we dived for her tail at about 100 knots. Her number *L 43* was observed on the tail and bow, also Maltese Cross in black circle. Midship gun opened fire with tracer ammunition and when about 100 ft. above Sub-Lieut. Dickey opened fire (Brock and Pomeroy ammunition), as the machine passed diagonally over the tail from starboard to port. After two bursts the Zeppelin burst into flames. Cutting off engines we turned sharply to starboard and passed over her again; she was by this time completely enveloped in flames and falling very fast. Three men were observed to fall out of her on her way down. Flames and black smoke were observed for some time after wreckage reached the water. We then set course for Felixstowe arriving at 11:15 a.m.[4]

So ended the three-month career of *L 43* and all her crew. The Secretary of the British Admiralty gave away nothing in his brief public announcement on the same day:

> Zeppelin *L 43* was destroyed this morning by our Naval Forces in the North Sea.
>
> Soon after being attacked she burst into flames fore and aft, broke in two, and fell into the sea.
>
> No survivors were seen.[5]

All that the Germans knew was that *L 43* had failed to acknowledge the weather map radioed from Nordholz at 10:14 a.m., but reports from *L 46* left little doubt as to the cause of her destruction. At 3:05 a.m. *Kapitänleutnant* Hollender had arrived at the Dogger Bank South Lightship. The wind was from the south-south-east, and in accordance with his orders, Hollender decided to cover the southern part of the submarine blockade area, instead of proceeding on his west-north-west course towards the Firth of Forth. At 8:18 a.m. *L 46* was within sight of the Hook of Holland, and steered north to scout towards the Humber. Meanwhile the indefatigable team of Galpin and Leckie had left Great Yarmouth at 8:05 a.m. in H.12 No.8660 "to search the area 25 miles east of Southwold for hostile-aircraft indicated by enemy WIT signals."[6] At 9:08 a.m. the "boat" reached the Noord Hinder Lightship and turned north. Seven minutes later *L 46* was sighted about 15 miles to the east, steering west at an altitude estimated at 10,500 feet. In Galpin's words:

> Leckie turned 8660 to meet her, climbing hard. She saw us 10 minutes later, threw out her water ballast and went up to 15,000 feet, at the same time turning north-north-east and making off. By 8:45 a.m. [British time] we had reached a height of 12,500 feet immediately under the Zeppelin, and fired four trays of Brock, Pomeroy and Buckingham into her. I observed the bursts of tracer going well on to the target, but the incendiary must have burnt out by the time it reached her; it is quite possible she was hit by explosive bullets, but no immediate results took place; four tracers were seen to be fired at us. At 9:15 a.m., after we had maneuvered without effect for another half an hour endeavoring to get up to her, as she showed no signs of coming down, I decided to break off the fight without wasting further fuel and ammunition.[7]

Hollender reported on this action:

> 9:45 in 157 ε 5 [45 miles north-east of Yarmouth], ship flying at 4,000 meters [13,000

4 Hobbs and Dickey joint report in Imperial war Museum file, "Pilots' Reports Relating to Destruction of Zeppelins."

5 The Times (London), June 15, 1917.

6 Gamble, p. 246.

7 Ibid.

> feet], pressure height 4,500 meters [14,750 feet]. English seaplane, bi-plane with two occupants and I machine gun forward seen coming up from astern. The plane came out of a cloud bank at about 2,500 meters [8,200 feet] and approached the ship very fast. I at once dropped all water except three "breeches" and in seven minutes climbed to 5,700 meters [18,700 feet] and ran off before the wind. As the plane was at about 3,000 meters [10,000 feet] his speed fell very markedly. He got up to about 3,500 meters [11,500 feet], 4,000 [13,000 feet] at the very most. Attempts to drive him off failed as the machine guns could not be depressed enough. Several attempts to get to one side of him were prevented by the plane keeping constantly right under the ship. The action went on from 157 ε 5 to 012 γ 7 and lasted an hour. Then the plane turned away and disappeared over the clouds. In climbing, the ship became sluggish and very stern heavy. Since I had only three "breeches" and feared cooling of the gas with evening, decided to turn back.

Thus the unsuccessful plane attack forced *L 46* to leave her patrol area at least six hours before Strasser recalled the other ships at 4:37 p.m. Understandably, Strasser believed *L 43* had been shot down by the same plane that had attacked *L 46*. Henceforth he ordered special precautions and minimum altitudes for the patrolling airships off Terschelling, as for *L 45* on June 30:

> Maximum alertness for enemy planes, therefore flight altitude 4,000 meters [13,000 feet]. Sharpest watch possible by lookouts. In case of meeting them, climb immediately with all possible speed, keep in touch with Borkum seaplane station by radio, report plane encounters, giving squared position, and end of action.

For the crews, this meant that each scouting flight became as strenuous as a raid on England. From the greater height it was also much more difficult to reconnoiter, for "only in theory does the range and quality of vision increase with altitude. In practice, cloud and mist layers intervene between the airship and the earth, even in the clearest weather, and particularly over the North Sea, so that uninterrupted observation is difficult."[8] At 13,000 feet it was impossible to detect or disturb submerged British submarines. The mine flights also had to be given up, as the airships could not possibly see the English "eggs" beneath the surface from two and a half miles in the air. Not only, then, did the British long-range flying boats jeopardize the airships themselves; they greatly restricted their value for their primary function of fleet scouting.

Before dawn on July 26, three airships took off to make patrols over the German Bight – *L 45* to the north, *L 44* in the middle, and *L 46* to the west. Their radio signals were heard by the British, and at 8:22 a.m. Galpin and Leckie left Great Yarmouth in the H.12 No.8666 to look for them. After reaching Texel they headed east, hugging the islands to be "between the sun and any Zeppelin," until, in Galpin's words:

> At 9:10 a.m. [British time] we sighted a Zeppelin, which later proved to be the *L 46*, about 15 miles north of us and proceeding northwards. We gave chase and got up to her about 9:35 a.m. We were both at about the same height, 10,000 feet, and the Zeppelin had turned westward, so that we were approaching her on her port beam. *L 46* appeared to be unaware of our presence, probably owing to the sun behind us, until we came within a mile of her. She then suddenly threw out ballast, at the same time putting her nose up to an angle of 15 to 20 degrees, and her helm hard over. She did not stop climbing until she reached 12,000 feet when she turned north-east and made off home. In this position we fired four trays of Brock, Pomeroy and Buckingham at her from 11,500 feet, which was our maximum attainable height, but without apparent effect. She dropped two bombs at us when we were immediately below her, and also fired a machine gun. Bullet holes were made in the top plane of the center section, on either side of the gravity petrol tank and just missing the hull.

8 Helmut Beelitz, *Der Werdegang und Wandel der Luftschiffverwendung im Seekrieg* (Düsseldorf: Verlag G.H. Nolte, 1936), p. 46.

At 10:00 a.m. we observed another Zeppelin about 10 miles north of us at about 8,000 feet, and so broke off the useless attack on *L 46*. We were within 3 miles of this Zeppelin when she also put her nose up, threw out ballast, and went up to 15,000 feet, turning eastward. I conclude she received a signal by WIT from *L 46*. At 10:23 we abandoned the chase as both Zeppelins were beyond our reach; when last seen they were both going eastward at 15,000 feet. We returned to Southwold at 1:54 p.m. and Yarmouth at 2:2 p.m.[9]

*Kapitänleutnant* Hollender's account of the fight shows that for some moments *L 46* was in great danger, but after releasing her ballast the flying-boat never had a chance to catch up with her. At 10:45 a.m. *L 46* was in:

position 009 ε [35 miles north of Vlieland], course south by west. At 3,000 meters [10,000 feet] on port bow enemy plane approaching on west course at same altitude as ship, seen at about 4,000 meters [13,000 feet] distance. Turned hard starboard at once and climbed. Due failure of 2 sacks forward to empty, markedly nose-heavy and did not at first ascend over 3,500 meters [11,500 feet]. Plane comes up from astern at same altitude. Sacks emptied from gangway, and all "breeches" forward. Plane 1,000 meters [3,300 feet] behind ship shooting steadily with tracer or incendiary ammunition, climb above him and open machine-gun fire, without regard to fact we are blowing off gas, as I consider ship's destruction certain. For same reason did not restrict sending of radio messages. Ship rose at rate of 15 meters per second [2,960 feet per minute]. Action continued with generally easterly course, steering to evade plane, to 029 ε [25 miles north of Terschelling]. Intention was to draw plane towards Borkum. After reaching 4,500 meters [14,700 feet], maneuvered to attack him and fired at plane steadily with two machine guns. At 5,500 meters [18,000 feet], with plane about 1,500 meters [5,000 feet] lower, he turned off north-west and attacked *L 44*. Length of action 23 minutes. Fired about 700 rounds.

*L 44*, the second ship, had in fact been warned by *L 46*'s message, sent during the attack, "020 ε in action with enemy planes. Course east." Receiving this at 11:08, *L 44*, which was flying at 10,200 feet, "climbed at once to 5,600 meters [18,400 feet]. At the same time the plane was seen to starboard on a course for *L 44* at about the same altitude – 3,500 meters [11,500 feet]. Turned to north-east course before the wind." At 11:30 "the plane, which had approached to within about 2,000 meters [6,500 feet] suddenly disappeared." In response to radio messages from the two Zeppelins, two squadrons of seaplane fighters left Borkum at 11:41 and 11:56, and at 12:09 land-based fighters took off from Wilhelmshaven. From 12:30 to 1:45 p.m., four fighters were flying escort underneath *L 44*, but by this time the British flying-boat was well on her way home.

At 3:50 a.m. on the morning of August 21, *L 23* took off from Tondern to make a routine patrol. At 5:40 a.m. her commander, *Oberleutnant zur See* Bernhard Dinter, reported sighting four Aurora class light cruisers and fifteen destroyers, thirty miles west of Bovbjerg. The larger vessels were the 3rd Light Cruiser Squadron of the Grand Fleet, making one of its periodic sweeps off the Jutland coast. Unknown to Dinter, H.M.S. *Yarmouth* was carrying a Sopwith "Pup" on a platform over her forward guns. As the Zeppelin followed the warships to sea, Flight Sub-Lieutenant B.A. Smart was ordered to take off and attack her. He reported:

At about 6:40 a.m. when in position 54 degrees 47 minutes N., 7 degrees 55 minutes E. I received orders to proceed to attack Zeppelin. I immediately left on Sopwith Pup No.6430. Bearing of Zeppelin being S.S.W. distance 10 to 15 miles. I had just previously had distinguishing marks on machine partially obscured with grey paint to avoid being recognized until very near Zepp.

I climbed steadily at 55 knots until 9,000 feet, keeping enemy in sight except when occasionally obscured by clouds. Then proceeded in slightly downward course as Zeppelin was far below me, air speed then 100 knots.

Finally when within firing distance Zeppelin was some 1,500 feet below me, my own

[9] Gamble, p. 254.

*L 23 based at Tondern and here at Nordholz. L 23 was shot down by a Sopwith "Pup" on August 21, 1917 off Lyngvig, Denmark. All eighteen crewmen perished. (Moch)*

height being 7,000 feet. I then got directly astern so that machine guns in gondolas were out of action owing to envelope obscuring same, and then dived at roughly an angle of 45 degrees getting up a speed of 130 knots. One man and machine gun was observed on top of envelope, but I zigzagged slightly until quite near, and as far as I know nothing hit any part of plane.

When within 150 to 200 yards fired burst of 10 to 15 shots, but they went rather high so nose-dived, flattened out and fired continuously until within 20 yards of stern when flames broke out and I made a sharp dive and swerve to avoid ramming Zeppelin. Having recovered myself I looked back to observe effect.

After end of Zeppelin was a mass of flames and dropped immediately. A part was adrift from forward end, which I later discovered to be a man descending by parachute. Framework crumbled up and flames quickly spread forward until by the time wreck finally hit sea only a very small portion of forward end was intact. This continued burning emitting a high column of dense black smoke until nothing but a few specks remained. My height was then 3,000 feet.[10]

Smart found his way back to the squadron and "ditched" ahead of a destroyer, which promptly rescued him and salvaged the plane's engine and machine gun. No messages were sent by *L 23* after 7 a.m. A large number of planes were sent out to look for her, and in the evening one of them found a patch of oil and petrol a thousand feet square on the water 25 miles south-west of Bovbjerg. Alighting on the sea, the plane crew picked up some small wooden parts and the blade of an airship propeller, charred at the hub end, but nothing else was seen. The Germans did not learn of the manner of *L 23*'s loss, and believed she had been shot down by gunfire from the surface vessels.

On the morning of September 5, *L 41*, *L 44* and *L 46* left Ahlhorn to cover the minesweepers working on "Route Yellow" forty miles north of

10 Smart's report in Imperial War Museum file, "Pilots' Reports Relating to Destruction of Zeppelins."

*"Height Climbers" L 41 and L 44 arriving at Ahlhorn on the morning of August 22, 1917 after a mission to England. (Luftschiffbau Zeppelin)*

Terschelling. They saw nothing of enemy surface vessels, but encountered a new danger in the air. During the summer the H.12 flying-boats, whose service ceiling was given as 10,800 feet, had found that the Zeppelins were flying too high over the North Sea to be attacked. Recently, however, the Aircraft Manufacturing Company had produced a two-seat day bomber, the D.H.4, with 200 h.p. R.A.F. 3a engine, of exceptional range and performance. Two of them received at Great Yarmouth during August were designated for anti-Zeppelin work. These planes had extra fuel tanks giving them an endurance of 14 hours, mounted five machine guns and could climb to 17,500 feet. In case the land plane should be forced down at sea, a flying-boat would be sent out in company. The "boat" pilot would also do the navigating.

On the morning of September 5 the Admiralty wired to Great Yarmouth that two Zeppelins had been heard off Terschelling. Flight Lieutenant Gilligan and Observer Lieutenant Trewin took off in one of the D.H.4s to look for them, while Flight Lieutenant Leckie followed in the H.12 flying-boat No.8666, carrying Squadron Leader Nicholl, the commander of the station, and two petty officers. At 2 p.m. the flying-boat sighted *L 44* and *L 46* about 30 miles from Terschelling; the two Zeppelins appeared to be about 9,000 feet high, the same altitude as the flying-boat. The D.H.4 experienced engine trouble and was unable to reach her ceiling. Both planes fired at *L 44* but could not get close enough to endanger her. *Kapitänleutnant* Stabbert, her commander, reported:

> 2:15 p.m. in 163 γ 7 [58 miles north-northwest of Terschelling], 2 biplanes in sight under ship. Ship at 4,500 meters [14,800 feet]. After making recognition signals, one plane fired 2 red stars apparently in answer to the signals. Both planes turned towards ship and climbed.

*Two views of the Staaken-built LZ 113. The Army received two of the 55,000 cbm. Zeppelins from the Navy of which LZ 113 was one. (both - Luftschiffbau Zeppelin)*

Soon afterwards recognized a cockade on the planes. Went to 5,500 meters [18,000 feet] and turned east, dropping ten fused 50-kg. [110-pound] bombs as ballast. The one plane with cockade was a big flying-boat, such as seen previously, the other which had fired the star signals was a small seaplane [sic], with no recognition marks on the planes, almost white in color, with only broad red stripes on the vertical tail surfaces. Latter was eventually recognized as enemy and both fired at with machine guns. The planes made four or five runs, coming up to one side from astern, climbing to within 1,000 meters [3,300 feet] under the ship and firing, apparently with weapons of larger caliber than our machine guns, then diving away. Several black bursts were seen behind the ship at the same altitude. While the seaplane was under the ship and being fired at with machine guns, it suddenly heeled over to starboard and dived nearly vertically for several hundred meters, leading to the belief it had been hit, and then went off to the west without attacking again. The second attacked once again and then also turned off west. During the action 850 rounds of machine-gun ammunition were fired.

*L 46 taking off at Ahlhorn for a night altitude training flight on the evening of August 11, 1917. (Luftschiffbau Zeppelin)*

*L 35, an experimental ship at Jüterbog where it tested the new Mb IVa altitude engine. It also carried the Albatross D III, and a torpedo glider (see below). (Moch)*

The D.H.4 was not hit by *L 44*, but by German light cruisers which made excellent practice, considering the range. A shell splinter went through the radiator of the land plane, and another damaged the "boat's" hull. Gilligan and Trewin presently had to land on the sea, as their engine had overheated and "seized" from lack of water. Leckie immediately abandoned the attack on the two Zeppelins, and went down to rescue his sinking comrades. Both were hauled safely aboard, but "old 8666" refused to take off from the rough sea. Leckie taxied towards England until his fuel ran out on the evening of the 5th, and the flying-boat then drifted until it was picked up on the afternoon of September 8. The occupants were then in the last stages of exhaustion.

*L 46*, taking in a warning message from *L 44*, had turned before the wind and climbed to 16,500 feet, and was in no danger. Stabbert was criticized by Admiral Hipper for leading the planes over the minesweepers; the enemy should not have been allowed to see them at work. Strasser replied that the visibility was 60 miles and the planes could see as far as "Route Yellow" in any case, while the Zeppelin had tried to draw the British planes towards Borkum so that they could be attacked by the seaplane fighters there, in accordance with standard operating procedure.

*L 35 with an Albatross D III (left), and a torpedo carrying glider hung for flight testing. (Moch)*

*Above and left: The Albatross D III dropped from L 35 on February 23, 1918.*

This was the last attack on a Zeppelin in the German Bight for eight months. There would be no further successes until nearly a year later, when a land-plane fighter would be taken to the German coast aboard a lighter. The "height climbers'" ascending powers kept them beyond the reach of all other aircraft.

Officers of the Aviation Department of the German Admiralty in Berlin envisaged another type of defense – a fighter plane hung under the airship which might be released in the event of an attack. A standard German Navy Albatros D III fighter was delivered to the Airship Experimental Command in Jüterbog, and hung up under *L 35*, which had been withdrawn from the "Front" on September 25, 1917, to make test flights with the new Maybach "altitude motors." On January 25, 1918, *L 35* carried the Albatros aloft, but it was not dropped. Next day the plane was released at 4,600 feet, and after diving about 150 feet, it picked up speed and flew away. On February 23, 1918, a conference was held at the Admiralty to discuss this experiment. Strasser, apparently learning of it for the first time, stated that if a special seaplane fighter could be developed, equipped with both wheels and floats and able to operate at the 13,000-foot altitude at which his ships were now making scouting flights, he might be interested. A senior seaplane pilot replied that it would be impossible to build a seaplane with such high-altitude performance. Strasser ended the discussion by stating that his airships no longer had to fear enemy planes off Terschelling, due to their improved performance, and Admiral Starke ordered the project to be discontinued.

# CHAPTER XVIII

# THE BALTIC AIRSHIPS & OPERATION "ALBION"

Rare indeed were the moments of glory for the small force of airships which, from bases in the eastern Baltic, kept watch on the inert Russian Navy. It was in this theatre that the German Naval Airship Division suffered its first wartime loss. On Christmas Day, 1914, *PL 19* had flown from Kiel to Königsberg, in the eastern Baltic, where she was to occupy the Army shed for three weeks. Her commander's orders show the most fantastic expectations of what this small pressure airship, with a useful lift of only 7,300 pounds, could accomplish. She was to raid the Russian naval base at Libau, 125 miles to the north, bombing if possible the foundry and rolling mills, the Nobel oil refinery and storage tanks, the submarine base and submarine docks, the Navy Yard barracks and machine shops, and the railroad and railroad bridge over the river on the main line to Vilna and Riga! In addition, *PL 19* was to search for mine-fields off Libau and Memel and make shorter scouting flights. Two raid attempts were defeated by the weather; then, on January 25, at 3:20 a.m., *Oberleutnant* Meier got his ship off the ground and disappeared in the darkness in the direction of Libau. There were seven men on board, ten hours' fuel and seven 110-pound bombs.

*PL 19* first flew north over the Baltic, being forced lower and lower by the cloud ceiling until she was only 650 feet above the water. At 8 a.m. her commander decided to go over land, rose into the overcast to be hidden from the ground, and flew the rest of the way in the clouds. Apparently the German airship men had never experienced icing conditions, for *PL 19*'s civilian "volunteer airship pilot," Dr. Rötzell, noted with astonishment that hoar frost an eighth of an inch thick accumulated over the fabric envelope, adding more than 500 pounds to the load. Ice formed on the starboard propeller (Rötzell naively thought it was congealed oil from the gear-casing) and large chunks were hurled off the whirling blades into the gas-bag overhead. Rötzell could not believe the heavy fabric could be pierced, but

*OPPOSITE:*
*Interior view of LZ 113, the Army ship at Sedden. Size of the men shows scale of the interior structure of Zeppelins. Gas cells have been removed. Gas shaft goes from keel to top of the ship. (Moch)*

*Naval airship SL 4 at Seddin. It was destroyed when shed doors opened, and the ship was blown out onto the field. (Grosz)*

saw it gradually riddled, one hole being as large as a man's hand. Also, after prolonged valving of damp gas, ice had formed on the seat of an automatic valve and even more of the vital hydrogen had leaked away. Towards 8:45 a.m. the crew recognized through a hole in the clouds a lake south of Libau. Bringing their ship down to 1,500 feet, they flew on under the clouds, and aimed their first bomb at a factory. It failed to explode, and as they dropped the rest, *PL 19* rose into the clouds and her crew could not see the results. A Russian account states that the first bomb fell on a pile of iron in a factory yard, and the rest caused no damage or casualties. *PL 19*, clearly visible in broad daylight at a low altitude, came under heavy rifle fire and the Russians claimed to have hit her. But as they headed out to sea "with joy, satisfaction and pride on every countenance," the Germans found the ship undamaged.

Their jubilation was short-lived. Suddenly there was a crash overhead, the starboard propeller jammed and the engine stopped. The gear-case had

*Seddin bei Stolp airship base covered the western Baltic. Double shed "Selinde" on left, and single shed "Selim." (Moch)*

*Wainoden airship base in Courland (Kurland). Deep cold caused problems with airships, and few missions were flown against the Russians. "Walther" shed on left, "Walhalla" shed on right. (Moch)*

fractured and the gears no longer meshed. The ship, half a ton heavy, descended swiftly. By dropping ballast and flying at a 20-degree up angle, she was held at 1,000 feet, but then the port engine failed – fuel would not flow uphill. The loss of all power was fatal. The blowers which maintained pressure in the ballonet were silent, the envelope buckled amidships, and at 9:40 a.m., *PL 19* fell into the Baltic seven miles offshore. At first the crew hoped they might be rescued by a German vessel, but the sea was deserted. When, towards noon, two Russian minesweepers appeared and fired on the derelict with machine guns, there was nothing to do but surrender and be taken on board. The prisoners last saw their ship, under fire from the Russian vessels, blazing fiercely on the water.[1]

Following the loss of *PL 19* there were no airships in the Baltic until *L 5* came east on July 14, 1915, to participate in the German assault on Riga. Before this occurred, she was lost in a rash daylight raid on Dunamünde. The Schütte-Lanz *SL 4* took her place and made several flights in connection with the German Fleet's attempt to force the entrance to Riga Gulf in mid-August, but after this failed, the Baltic airships settled down to a dull routine of uneventful patrol flights. It was to this secondary theatre that Strasser sent most of the despised Schütte-Lanz craft.

Admiral Prince Henry, the Kaiser's brother and commander-in-chief in the Baltic, was an air enthusiast and continually pressed for a raid on the Russian capital, St. Petersburg. Strasser, reluctant to divert any effort from the war in the North Sea, was consistently opposed to this, and it was a fact that the small airships of 1915 were quite incapable of making so long a flight. Beginning in August, 1916, the Kaiser began urging a raid on St. Petersburg in the hope that it might hasten the collapse of the tottering Russian war machine. Strasser was able to delay the Imperial command until winter, when the long nights would protect the airships from the Russian defenses. On November 29, 1916, "Operation Iron Cross" commenced with a telegram from Prince Henry to the Naval Staff, asking for a large airship for the raiding period starting December 15. Just before midnight on December 17, *L 35* and *L 38* left Ahlhorn heading east, and after a layover at Seddin, were housed on December 20 in the sheds "Walther" and "Walhalla" at Wainoden in Courland, in former Russian territory. From here it was only 400 miles to St. Petersburg.

On December 26 there were short flights to dry out the ships. On the 28th the weather seemed to improve – not enough to warrant a raid on the Russian capital, but sufficient to order "attack Reval, if weather permits, also Helsingfors and targets on Oesel, Dagö and western Esthonia." In the early dusk the two Zeppelins took off, carrying 24 hours' fuel and over three tons of bombs.

At 5 p.m. *L 35* was over Libau, intending to go on to Windau and thence to the Finnish Gulf. At 6:30 p.m. Ehrlich began climbing through a 3,000-foot layer of cloud to an altitude of 8,200 feet. The ship iced up heavily, and a thick layer of frozen snow on the horizontal stabilizers made her stern-heavy. At 7 p.m. *L 35* was flying on top of the overcast beneath a clear, starry sky. It was bitterly cold, and from radio bearings, the north-west wind was estimated to be blowing at 45 m.p.h. The port after engine failed when an oil line broke, and the Zeppelin advanced only slowly against the head wind. In the after and port midships engines the oil congealed in the feed-lines, and the mechanics had to

---

1 At least one man of *PL 19*'s crew, Ernst Lehmann, the survivor of the *L 1* disaster, got home to Germany during the war. Escaping from a prisoner-of-war camp in Siberia, he traveled by foot 500 miles to Manchuria, took ship from Shanghai to San Francisco, crossed neutral America and started the last lap on a steamer for Sweden – only to be seized by the British blockade. After further detention in a prisoner-of-war camp in England he was exchanged, and spent the last nine months of the war on ground duty with the Naval Airship Division.

dig the semi-solid lubricant out of the tanks and feed it to the engines by hand. To starboard a number of lights came in sight – probably Baltic Port – but at 1 a.m. Ehrlich abandoned the attack here as it would be dawn before he could reach the place against the wind. Steering south-west along the coast at 1,300 feet, Ehrlich was buffeted by heavy snow squalls and found the wind had veered into the south-south-east and was blowing at 45 m.p.h. The starboard outrigger propeller shaft broke at 4:16 a.m., and at times *L 35* made no progress over the ground. In desperation, Ehrlich descended to 500 feet in hopes of finding less head wind, and started up the port after engine without regard to damage to its bearings. At 9:10 a.m. on December 29, after a flight of nearly 17 hours, *L 35* landed at Wainoden.

*L 38* climbed through one layer of clouds between 1,300 and 3,300 feet, went on through another cloud layer from 5,000 to 9,200 feet, and came out under a clear black sky. Here, at 10,200 feet, the temperature was a numbing 8 degrees below zero F. The crew progressively wadded themselves in every piece of clothing they could lay their hands on. Even the compass began to freeze, and the rudder man had to turn on all its lights and pile coats on it to keep it warm. The oil lines of all engines were clogged with congealed lubricant, and in the darkness the machinists had to drag the go-pound oil tanks along the catwalk and down ice-coated ladders into the engine gondolas. The engines now received too much oil and the spark plugs fouled and had to be changed. At 9 p.m. *Kapitänleutnant* Martin Dietrich steered more to the north, intending to bomb installations on Oesel. To the north an aurora borealis simulated searchlights turned upward. Bearings received at 1:22 a.m. indicated that *L 38* was near the port of Arendsberg on Oesel, but the place could not be seen through heavy cloud. At 2:21 a.m. Dietrich abandoned the raid and steered south-south-west. The starboard midships engine failed with damage to the reduction gears. Dietrich also determined that the wind had come ahead, from the south-west. Till dawn he hovered over the clouds at 9,000 feet. At 4:45 a.m. the starboard after engine went out of action – the radiator had frozen while the sooted plugs were being changed. At 7 a.m. Dietrich descended to 1,000 feet and steered for the coast through driving snow. Immediately a layer of ice accumulated on the outer cover. Fragments breaking off fell into the after propellers, which hurled them into the gas cells, and the loss of hydrogen made the ship stern-heavy. The ice was driving everywhere – on the upper platform the look out dared not show his face above the canvas dodger, so heavy was the barrage. A big piece splintered the after propeller, and the engine had to be throttled to half speed. Suddenly the ship fell. Only by dropping most of the bombs and 880 pounds of fuel was she checked, and not before the tail skid and lower rudder had dragged in the freezing Baltic. Weighted down aft by snow on the horizontal stabilizers, *L 38* was badly out of trim, flying at an up angle of 15 degrees though the elevators were hard down, and steering erratically. Frequently the engines had to be stopped lest she rise uncontrollably into the clouds. To restore the trim, crew members were sent forward to the mooring

*L 38 down in the snow on December 29, 1916 at Seemuppen, Russia. The ship was later dismantled. (both - Moch)*

point, spare parts and the 1,200 pounds of bombs still on board were dragged forward along the catwalk, and fuel was redistributed by hand pumping. The ship became manageable once more, and at 8:50 a.m. staggered to the coast near Libau. At 10 a.m. *L 38* was struggling south in thick snow, and her crew could hardly see the ground. Suddenly, as the up angle increased to 20 degrees, the ship stalled and fell. The antenna was torn off, and only by dumping all reserve fuel, incendiary bombs, spare parts and machine guns was she caught at 700 feet. Lest *L 38* drift out to sea, where her crew would surely have perished, Dietrich decided to land at once. Since the ship was at least 6,600 pounds heavy, the gondolas surely would have been torn off in a landing in open fields. When an evergreen forest came in sight the engines were stopped, the trees caught the weight of the falling ship, and *L 38* came to rest with fir-trees peeking into the hull. While two petty officers went to fetch help, the rest of the crew tried to moor their ship. The wind was too strong: within ten minutes the hull had broken amidships, and gradually it collapsed in the snow, one ring breaking after another.

*L 38*'s forced landing had been made at Seemuppen, former Russian territory now in German hands. For her commander, the "Russian adventure" was summed up in a facetious post-card, addressed to "Herr *Kapitänleutnant* Dagobert Dietrich" by his fellow officers in Ahlhorn, with the verse:

*Above all the treetops is peace.*
*On all the peaks one feels*
*Hardly a breath of air!*

Strasser on January 8 wrote to the Naval Staff to state that not only did he not wish to send a ship east to replace *L 38*, but he wanted *L 35* returned. The Naval Staff agreed, ordered Prince Henry to release Ehrlich's craft, and offered the usual hollow consolation – that two more big Zeppelins might be sent east for the next attack period. On January 23, 1917, *L 35* made the return flight to the North Sea. Almost everyone was happy except the Kaiser, who complained, "When they spent the whole summer waiting for good weather for long-distance flights, they can hardly look for better conditions in January with its short days and the rain and snow we are having this winter." No further attempts were made by the naval airships to bomb St. Petersburg.

The late spring of 1917 brought reinforcements for *SL 8* – the only airship then in service in the Baltic. The obsolescent *L 30* and *L 37* came east from the North Sea, followed by four Army craft, two of which, *LZ 113* and *LZ 120*, were the military service's only 2,000,000 cubic foot "big 6-engine ships." It was a different kind of war from that in the North Sea, and the chief enemy was boredom. The Russian Air Force, demoralized by the March revolution, was entirely inert, and the Zeppelins patrolled at low altitude. *Oberleutnant zur See der Reserve* Lehmann, commanding the Army's *LZ 120*, wrote:

> Our work was by no means gratifying in spite of being very strenuous at times. The job was to determine daily the presence or absence of enemy naval forces in the Baltic, to keep a close check on the Russo-English submarine stations in the Gulf of Finland, patrol the sea for mines and observe the movements of merchant vessels along the Swedish coast. The routine was for us to be out 24 hours on a patrol and then rest for a similar period. We made a great number of flights that summer of 1917, mostly in wonderful weather which lent an atmosphere not unlike that of our peace-time operations. . . . By and large we had time to study the manifold beauties of the Baltic shores – blue skies, little white clouds, blue sea, and all this enveloped in the mellow haze peculiar to that part of North Europe. . . .
>
> We learned to feel very much at home aboard ship and since we could then afford to carry some extra weight in the control car, which was exceptionally roomy, we made that and the crew's quarters comfortable by adding wicker chairs, pictures, table cloths and invariably fresh flowers on the table.[2]

During the long summer a constantly recurring theme in the conversation of *LZ 120*'s officers was the optimum length of patrol flights:

2 Lehmann and Mingos, p. 233.

> It was the consensus of opinion that it would be better, from a military viewpoint, to maintain a ship on patrol for much longer periods of time – for example, 100 hours or more. We also concluded that the length of a flight might be limited solely by the petrol capacity of the ship. I say that was the consensus of opinion. It was universal among the members of our crew, but the other officers largely disagreed, for two reasons. They thought the motors would require overhauling before the completion of such a long trip and further, that the men could not stand the exertion and strain for such extended periods.[3]

The impending dissolution of the Army airship service on August 1 may have inspired Lehmann to test the proposition as a grand finale. Loading the Zeppelin with 2,650 pounds of bombs, 7,700 pounds of water ballast, 6,600 pounds of machine guns, ammunition, equipment and provisions, and deducting 5,500 pounds for the weight of the 29 men on board, Lehmann found enough useful lift remaining for 2,400 pounds of oil and 37,300 pounds of petrol – some of which was carried in the 42 regular tanks, the rest in 37 tanks temporarily hung up in the gangway and draining through rubber hoses into the permanent fuel system. This amount of petrol would last for 56 hours at cruising speed on all engines, or more than 100 hours at reduced speed. Considerable attention was paid to meals and living quarters, but the results still left something to be desired:

> The food supply from time to time gave rise to indigestion (thick pea soup and bad quality bread) but no other diet could be supplied with the provisions on board. A double-walled heating kettle of about 13 gallon capacity had been produced, which was connected to the radiator water line of one of the engines. By this means a hot noon meal could be prepared, and coffee heated at other times. . . . 160 gallons of drinking water was available in two water tanks, and proved sufficient. 1,100 pounds of water was withdrawn from ballast sacks for washing.
>
> No provision was made for accommodating the crew members off watch, other than distributing hammocks through the keel according to trimming requirements. Construction of sleeping quarters for the officers forward, and two crews' bunk rooms forward and aft, with light flooring and canvas partitions, would be desirable in the future, as well as a washroom and a second "head." Furthermore, a mess and dining-room for personnel off watch could be arranged amid-ships.[4]

At 10:40 p.m. on the night of July 26, *LZ 120* took off from Seerappen to begin her long flight. It almost ended disastrously at the start, for as she climbed out of the hollow enclosing the "Seraphine" shed, *LZ 120* rose into an inversion. As the air became warmer, the lift became less, and the Zeppelin flew past, rather than over, the houses on top of the hill. Once in the air the ship was put in order and the crew divided into watches, and those off duty climbed into the 20 hammocks along the gangway. Part of the experiment was to determine if the crew could tolerate the strain of prolonged flying by being divided into watches. Officers and men of the seaman branch stood alternate watches of 6 hours' duration. By running most of the time on three engines, the machinists could be divided into three watches on duty 8 hours at a time.

Dodging thunderstorms kept the duty section busy on the first night, but the remainder of the flight was uneventful. Depending on the weather, the ship at first cruised in the western Baltic, and later in its eastern and northern portions. Twice the starboard after engine ran so roughly that connecting bolts at the upper end of the outrigger drive-shaft were sheared through. Each time the Zeppelin free-ballooned while the outer cover was unlaced, and men climbed out on the propeller bracket to replace the bolts. Every morning the officers had a "shower bath" from a bucket of water slung overhead at the mooring point in the bow, and crewmen off watch sun-bathed on the top and rear platforms.

3 Lehmann and Mingos, p. 235.

4 Ernst Lehmann, "Report of 100 hour flight of *LZ 120* from July 26-31, 1917," courtesy F. Moch.

*L 37 was the first Zeppelin built at Staaken, and served exclusively in the Baltic. It was broken up at Seddin in 1920, and the parts were sent to Japan. (Moch)*

*SL 8 at Seddin, commanded by Guido Wolf. After Operation "Albion", SL 8 was dismantled at Seddin in the "Selim" shed. (Moch)*

*Kapitänleutnant Guido Wolf's last command was the 2,000,000 cubic ft. SL 20. It was flown to Ahlhorn on December 11, 1917, and was later destroyed in the Ahlhorn explosion of January 5, 1918. (Luftschiffbau Schütte-Lanz)*

*Interior of SL 20 looking forward. Barrel structure at the bottom of gas shafts, collected overflow of hydrogen and conveyed it to hoods on the back of the airship. (Luftschiffbau Schütte-Lanz)*

*Interior of SL 21 at Zeesen showing inside of the framework before outer cover is applied. Dismantled at Zeesen in Febvruary, 1918. (Luftschiffbau Schütte-Lanz)*

The weather map on the evening of July 30 indicated an approaching storm, and at 8:20 p.m. Lehmann set a course for Seerappen, running on all six engines. *LZ 120* landed at 3:40 a.m. on July 31. She had been in the air for 101 hours, and fuel for three engines for 14 hours more still remained in the tanks. This endurance record stood for two years, until the R 34 bettered it with a time of 108 hours in the first crossing of the Atlantic from east to west. This was the last great flight of the Army airships. During the month of August the military service was dissolved, and most of its craft were dismantled. The two "big 6-engine ships," *LZ 113* and *LZ 120*, were turned over to the Navy and commissioned with Navy crews.

September and October, 1917, saw the climax and the end of the Baltic detachment of the Naval Airship Division. The German Army, advancing against Russian forces demoralized by the March revolution, had at last captured Riga, and on September 9 proposed to the Naval Staff that the Fleet cooperate in an amphibious assault (Operation "Albion") on the islands of Dagö, Oesel and Moon. The main landing would be in Tagga Bay on the north-west side of Oesel, avoiding the heavy batteries at Zerel on the Sworbe Peninsula at the south end of the island. While the British Grand Fleet remained idle, most of the High Seas Fleet – its ten newest dreadnoughts, the battle cruiser Moltke, six light cruisers and 47 destroyers – went east to provide the gunfire support force. During the pre-assault phase of "Albion" the Baltic airships were to make diversionary raids on ports on the eastern side of the Gulf of Riga, and if possible would bomb the heavy batteries on the Sworbe Peninsula. During the landing they were to patrol and cover the assault shipping, and make raids as ordered. *L 30, L 37, LZ 113, LZ 120* and *SL 8* were available, together with the first of the 2,000,000 cubic foot Schütte-Lanz ships, *SL 20,* which had been completed in Mannheim on September 11, 1917.

The increased activity of the six airships in the Baltic abruptly exposed the operational Achilles' Heel of the Naval Airship Division – the supply of hydrogen gas. The crux of the problem was the enormous expenditure of gas by the 2,000,000 cubic foot ships in high altitude operations. Strasser and his technical advisers insisted on refilling the airships to 100 per cent fullness after each flight, and on keeping the gas at a slight positive pressure by daily servicing, in order to maintain the purity of the gas. Should the cells be only partly full, they would "rise" and a partial vacuum would exist on the under surface which would accelerate the inward diffusion of air. This would not only decrease the purity and lift of the hydrogen, but would increase the danger of fire and explosion.

Yet, as Strasser noted at this time, to refill one of the standard Zeppelins to 100 per cent fullness after even a routine scouting flight required 1,060,000 cubic feet of gas – somewhat more than half her capacity. After one raid on England in September, 1917, the six Ahlhorn ships required a total of slightly less than 6,000,000 cubic feet of hydrogen to replace what they had blown off during their ascent to high altitudes.

The gas plants at the various bases – really miniature industrial works producing hydrogen by passing steam over heated iron – had been planned and built in 1914-15, when such enormous requirements had been undreamed of. In 1917 the two largest gas works, at Ahlhorn and Nordholz, produced 1,060,000 cubic feet of hydrogen daily. At both bases, 1,060,000 cubic feet could be stored at atmospheric pressure in a conventional aboveground gas holder, and buried in the earth, protected from tem-

*Jüterbog airship base, south of Berlin. At left is the single "Albrecht" shed, at right is the double "Baer" shed. (Kameradschaft)*

*Seerappen near Königsburg. The double shed was completed in September 1916. This base covered the eastern Baltic. (Moch)*

perature changes and air attacks, were numerous large steel flasks holding 4,400,000 cubic feet of hydrogen at 100 atmospheres' pressure. A further bottleneck was the capacity of the compressor which filled the high-pressure store. At Ahlhorn it could handle 425,000 cubic feet of gas per day, and thus it would take about ten days to refill all the high-pressure flasks. Considering that the Zeppelins did not make high altitude flights every day, these amounts barely sufficed for four big "Front" ships and two small school ships at Nordholz. With six big ships at Ahlhorn it was not enough. In the autumn of 1917, it was planned to expand production at Ahlhorn to 2,120,000 cubic feet of gas per day, and the underground storage would be increased to 7,760,000 cubic feet. Compressor capacity would rise to 1,270,000 cubic feet per day, but none of this was achieved until 1918. To meet the chronic Ahlhorn deficit, hydrogen was imported from the Zeppelin plant at Staaken in forty railroad tank cars whose high-pressure cylinders held a total of 2,120,000 cubic feet of gas at 100 atmospheres' pressure.

The other bases were even less capable of meeting their own needs. Tondern, with two 2,000,000 cubic foot ships, had a gas plant turning out 350,000 cubic feet of hydrogen daily, a low pressure gas holder containing 1,060,000 cubic foot, and a high pressure store of 880,000 cubic feet. Here, ten gas wagons were in constant use, but there is a suggestion that even with outside help, operational demands were not completely met. Wittmundhaven, with underground storage but no gas works, was dependent on the still-operating gas plant at the decommissioned Hage base. The Hage daily output of 700,000 cubic feet was transported to Wittmund in 50 railroad cars carrying 2,675,000 cubic feet – enough to maintain two ships, but to service three, more gas wagons would be needed – and they could not be procured. In the Baltic,

*L 37 in the Baltic, probably at Seddin for an overhaul. Structure of the hull is uncovered. Note the reinforced keel over the control car. (Moch)*

Seerappen and Wainoden received their hydrogen in 75 gas wagons from the plant at Seddin which turned out 700,000 cubic feet per day.

Demand and supply were balanced most precariously – a balance that could be upset by any trivial cause – and such a cause occurred on June 7, 1917, when an explosion put the Seddin gas plant out of commission. The effects were at first limited to the Baltic theatre. Because the 75 tank cars had to be sent to the interior to pick up gas, the Seerappen and Wainoden airships had to proceed to Seddin to be filled up. Very little flying was done in the Baltic during August, and *L 30* was put out of service in Seerappen from August 4 to 27 because of the gas shortage.

The increased demands of the "Albion" operation immediately exposed the weakness of the improvised gas-supply organization. On September 14 Strasser received from Admiral Prince Henry in the Baltic the complaint that there was no gas at Wainoden or Seerappen, and the Seddin gas plant had not been restored to full production. No scouting flights could be made, and the airships could make only one raid, after which they would have to lie empty and idle. The Baltic Command begged that all available railroad gas wagons be rushed east to meet the emergency. Strasser's covering letter to the Admiralty barely concealed his annoyance. He reminded his superiors that twice in 1916 he had requested a high-pressure gas plant at Seddin, but had been refused. Again, in July, 1917, he had asked if the Baltic gas problem would be dealt with, but nothing had happened. Now, he implied, the Admiralty could take the consequences of its indifference. The North Sea had its own gas problems. There were only 201 of the railroad tank cars, each carrying 70,000 cubic feet of hydrogen, in the naval service. One hundred of these were indispensable to North Sea operations, nor could the North Sea gas plants spare any of their output. Staaken could provide little more as it was already supplying Ahlhorn and filling newly built ships. The Army, Strasser suggested, might be persuaded to release its 40 high-pressure hydrogen tank cars, and the gas plant at the Army's Schneidemühl base might help. Meanwhile, Strasser would order that the North Sea airships be kept go per cent instead of 100 per cent full, but any further economies in this direction would result in the gas rapidly becoming contaminated with air.

The Baltic Command was of course not satisfied to have its complaints so summarily dismissed, and on September 23 the Chief of the Naval Staff advised Admiral Scheer, Prince Henry and Strasser that "by Imperial Command" every effort would be made to supply the gas required for the airships in the "Albion" operation, and 40 more gas wagons would be sent east. Strasser sourly informed Scheer next day that he could continue scouting flights with three airships daily under these circumstances, but if more ships were required on any one day, it might be impossible to carry out the missions ordered. Despite all these efforts, the Baltic Command telegraphed on September 29 that 40 gas wagons, received from the North Sea, had been sent back after being emptied, and there was only enough hydrogen in Seerappen and Wainoden for one filling of the ships there. Strasser, replying on October 8, stated that an additional 40 gas wagons would be made available for the Baltic theatre, which would then have a total of 155, and the output of the works at Staaken, Nordholz and Ahlhorn would be sent east even if scouting flights and raids in the North Sea had to be sharply curtailed.

*Control car inside SL 15. Engine annunciators on right, rudder wheel on bow of car, elevator wheel to the left. Pulls overhead are for dropping water ballast, or to release hydrogen if ship is too light. (Schütte-Lanz Archives)*

The Baltic airships accomplished less than had been hoped for in the "Albion" operation, being hampered particularly by bad weather and south-west winds that kept them in their sheds for days at a time. Their achievements in raids are impossible to evaluate in the absence of Russian data. Actually, a small bombing offensive started before the decision to invade the Baltic islands, when all four of the Zeppelins were sent out early in September to attack railroad junctions at Walk and Wolmar east of Riga Gulf. Bad weather then forced a suspension of operations until the night of September 24, when *LZ 113* and *LZ 120* attacked the batteries at Sworbe and Zerel on the south end of Oesel. Both commanders claimed direct hits on the batteries; *LZ 120*'s commander, *Kapitänleutnant* Johann von Lossnitzer, reporting that the 12-inch guns at Zerel were bracketed by a stick of bombs. On October 1, *L 30*, *L 37* and *LZ 120* went to the eastern side of the Riga Basin to attack the small ports of Salismünde and Sophienruhe "to direct Russian attention from our operational objectives." These places were poorly defended and *L 30* bombed from only 4,100 feet.

On October 9, 23,000 German troops had embarked in nineteen transports at Libau, and on October 11, escorted by the warships, they sailed for Tagga Bay on Oesel. Three airships had taken off early that morning to cover the advance of the invasion fleet – *L 30* to the north-east to watch over the Riga Basin; *LZ 113* to fly north to the mouth of the Finnish Gulf and bomb the Sworbe batteries on her way home; and *SL 20*, on her first "war flight," to accompany the Fleet. They encountered thick, deep clouds and thunderstorms, with freshening south-west winds, and at 11.30 a.m. were ordered to turn back. At 3 p.m. *LZ 113* passed the invasion fleet and reported by searchlight to the flagship *Moltke*: "Nothing seen before the Finnish Gulf."

The bad weather prevailed until October 14, and thus the airships were unable to cover the landing on Oesel on October 12. Mines damaged two of the German dreadnoughts, but the Russians put up little resistance and their surface vessels did not interfere. On October 14 the German battleships bombarded the Zerel batteries, and on October 17, Oesel Island was secured. The other garrisons promptly surrendered, and by October 19, Dagö Island was in German hands and the amphibious operation was over.

With a break in the weather on October 15, three Zeppelins set out to bomb Pernau at the north-east corner of the Gulf of Riga, the last naval base left to the Russians in the Riga Basin. All three commanders reported the target well defended by antiaircraft guns, but claimed to have placed their bombs in the center of town with the aid of captured Russian General Staff maps. On October 16, *L 37* bombed Pernau again and returned to Seerappen with the port midships gondola burned out by a serious fire in the air. *SL 20* did not reach the target, and after trouble with three of her five engines, made it back to Seddin after a flight of 31 hours.

Though the German Navy in the spring of 1918 participated in the occupation of Finland, the Baltic airship detachment was disbanded after Operation "Albion." Between November 13 and 26 the obsolete *SL 8* was broken up at Seddin. *LZ 113* and *L 37* were deflated and hung up in the "Selinde" shed at Seddin, and *L 30* and *LZ 120* were similarly preserved in the "Seraphine" hangar at Seerappen. *SL 20*, being considered possibly suitable for service in the North Sea, went to Ahlhorn on December 11.

All the airship commanders wrote special reports on Operation "Albion." They all complained of the uncertainty of scouting and raiding to leeward of their bases in prevailing south-west winds, and of the impossibility of obtaining radio bearings after the Oesel landing due to excessive radio traffic. Admiral Schmidt, commanding the naval task force, felt the airships could not have done more, considering the advanced season. *Kapitänleutnant* von Lossnitzer of *LZ 120* concluded his report with an impassioned defense of the airship, notwithstanding its poor showing in the German Navy's only amphibious operation:

> The incomparable advantage which we may anticipate in a naval battle from this peculiarly German weapon of naval reconnaissance requires that its absence be taken into account if we are obliged to operate in unfavorable

*SL 20, the first 2,000,000 cubic ft. Zeppelin, probably at Sedden. It flew to Ahlhorn on December 11, 1917, and was destroyed in the January 5, 1918 explosion. Shown here are the control car, and the port midship gondola. (Moch)*

weather. Neither now, nor in the foreseeable future, will our Fleet be able to do without airships, not only because of our limited number of cruisers, but also because in the Zeppelin airship we have a scouting weapon that the enemy dreads, since he has nothing equivalent to oppose to it. It is our responsibility to develop this weapon to its utmost.

Von Lossnitzer had penned an appreciation of the airship in a manner after Strasser's own heart. His next assignment was as Strasser's adjutant, and nine months later, placed in command of the newest and finest naval airship, von Lossnitzer perished with his chief in the last raid on England. Perhaps this memorandum of December 12, 1917, started him on the road to the fatal rendezvous with a British plane off the coast of Norfolk on August 5, 1918.

# CHAPTER XIX

# THE SILENT RAID

After three years of war the Army General Staff succeeded in clipping the wings of the Naval Airship Division. *General* Ludendorff, taking seriously the empty boasts of American politicians that myriads of war planes from beyond the seas would darken the skies of Europe in 1918, was busy during the summer of 1917 with his "Amerika-Programm" of greatly expanded aircraft production. Germany's limited supplies of raw material should, he felt, be channeled into airplane construction. Up to this time the Navy had been receiving an average of two new Zeppelins every month. Now, on July 27, Ludendorff made the drastic proposal in a letter to the Chief of the Naval Staff that the Navy's airship building program should be halted completely to conserve aluminium and rubber. Scheer's instant reaction shows the value he placed on the airship and his faith in it as a scouting weapon: writing to the Naval Staff on August 9, he flatly insisted that planes could not take the place of airships, and 18 at least would still be needed for scouting even if the raids were stopped. Nor would the Army, he submitted, really wish to have the airship raids discontinued. While bombing planes could threaten south England, only the Navy's airships could reach the central and northern portions. Should the attacks there cease, industrial production, particularly shipbuilding, would increase, while the considerable defense organization would be disbanded and sent to fight in France. The Naval Staff's reply to Ludendorff, based on this argument, went on to state that the Navy would require an establishment of 25 airships, with one new Zeppelin per month, if raids on northern and central England were to continue. Should the raids be abandoned, "1/2 ship per month" would still have to be delivered to replace losses. Ludendorff's reply, on August 11, acknowledged the need to continue raids on central and northern England, but asked that replacements be limited to 1/2 ship per month.

*Coming home to Ahlhorn after a six ship raid on August 21-22, 1917. Top ship may be L 35, then L 41, then L 44. (Moch)*

The Naval Staff carried its fight to the Kaiser, who decided in favor of Ludendorff in an Imperial Order dated August 17, 1917. Germany's rubber and aluminium would be conserved to build up the Army's strength in aircraft. The Fleet henceforth would generally use its airships for scouting only. The High Seas Fleet would be limited to 18 airships, with replacements of 1/2 ship per month, and the Navy total would be 25 ships and 27 crews. "These numbers are not to be exceeded in any circumstances."

These limitations, which of course had major repercussions on operations and tactics, appear to be unknown to all German and British air historians, and are only briefly mentioned by Scheer.[1] If the British naval forces operating in the German Bight in the last year of the war complained that the Zeppelins were unduly shy and circumspect, this was not only well justified by the presence of British planes, but was due to a knowledge that combat losses could not be replaced. Similarly, the few raids of 1918 were made on exceptionally dark, cloudy nights when the Zeppelins could be sure of getting home, but at the same time could do little damage.

On August 21, Strasser sent eight Zeppelins out to raid England, flying himself in *L 46*. Remarkably, only one of them – *L 41* – was credited by the British with reaching England; bombs from her fell east of Hull, destroying a chapel and injuring one man. Yet several other raiders turned in circumstantial reports of journeys inland, claiming attacks on Grimsby, Lincoln and Louth. Years later the Brit-

1 Scheer, p. 210.

*Strasser with his commanders outside the Kasino at Ahlhorn, on September 4, 1917, with his Pour le Mérite invested by Admiral von Scheer. Left to right: Manger, L 41; von Freudenreich, L 47; Schwonder, L 50; Prölss, L 53; Bockholt, L 57; Strasser; Gayer, L 49; Stabbert, L 44; Ehrlich, L 35; Martin Dietrich, L 42; Hollender, L 46; Dose, L 51; Friemel, L 52. (Kameradschaft)*

ish air historian found a sheaf of messages, labeled, "Hot Air," which reported a Zeppelin passing over Pontefract on this night and going on into Lancashire, while Doncaster heard bombs exploding in the distance. He admits, "It is not impossible that the *L 46* and one or two other ships came over land, but if they did, what happened to their bombs? Could they all have found a resting place on moorland wastes remote from habitation?[2] This confusion and uncertainty illustrate the difficulties which plagued the Observer Corps during 1917, when the ground posts were depleted by the demand for men to supply the armies in France, and the airships flew at great altitudes where they were difficult to trace.

The official history sums up:

> The raid was ineffective, but it had one very disturbing feature, and that was the height at which the attack near Hull was made. At 20,000 feet the Zeppelins had nothing to fear from the night-flying airplanes with which the defense squadrons were equipped, none of which could get near this "ceiling." Nor did the airships' commanders need to concern themselves over much with the searchlights or gun defenses.[3]

There was another side of the picture, however, for the airships and their crews again had trouble on account of the cold, thin air at high altitudes. In a technical memorandum prepared after the raid, six ships reported that the liquid in the magnetic compasses, although containing 44 per cent alcohol, first turned a thick, muddy brown and then froze at temperatures of zero to 6 below zero F. In *L 44* the fluid in the air thermometers separated, the gas thermometers did not function, and the rudder cables grew slack and jumped off their sheaves in the cold of high altitudes. The crew of *L 46*, which was making her first raid, had a great deal of trouble with the compressed oxygen equipment. The gas was contaminated with glycerin, so that most of the men preferred to do without it. As a result the steersmen collapsed several times, the machinists were frequently incapacitated, and the warrant quartermaster became "completely apathetic." On the other hand, *Kapitänleutnant* Hollender, who had taken a great deal of oxygen in order to be alert for any emergency, became violently ill from the effects of the glycerin. For the young executive officer, Richard Frey, the scene in the control car over England still aroused poignant memories forty years later. "Hollender was 'out on his feet' and I had to lead him into the radio room and make him sit down. Strasser's judgment may have been impaired by altitude sickness – he hadn't taken any oxygen – and I can still see him raging at Hollender, 'What's wrong with you? Why are you standing there with your hands in your pockets?' When he could not arouse him, Strasser ordered me to take command, and I had to remove the binoculars from around Hollender's neck. Later, when Hollender regained partial consciousness, he was angry at me for taking over the ship." Not until *L 46* was on the landing ground at Ahlhorn did her commander awaken.

As Frey points out, this raid indicated the danger of high-altitude flying without reliable artificial oxygen supplies. "We were lucky that everybody in the control car was not rendered unconscious. With nobody in charge of the ship the results could hardly be imagined. Had this happened over England, it would have meant the certain loss of the ship." Immediately after this raid, however, the compressed oxygen equipment was replaced by liquid air.

2 Jones, V, p. 56.

3 Jones V, p. 56.

*L 50 rises from outside the "Alrun" shed at Ahlhorn. Note the large amount of water being released. (Luftschiffbau Zeppelin)*

Strasser ordered nine ships to raid England on September 12, but stormy weather forced them to stay on the ground. There they remained, while day after day the routine patrols were canceled, until September 24, when Strasser took advantage of a lull between two low-pressure areas to send the Zeppelins against England. The order read "attack middle or north." Again the raid was ineffective, with only £2,210 worth of damage. Ehrlich, flying the oldest ship, *L 35*, made the deepest penetration inland. He stated that at 1 a.m. he came inland near Mablethorpe, intending to attack Sheffield. At 3:55 a.m., when *L 35* had reached the industrial area south of Doncaster, the head wind had increased and Ehrlich had to abandon the attack on Sheffield. To the south appeared "blast furnaces and railroad yards," whose lights were not turned off until just before the attack. "From the lack of any defense activity as well as failure to darken the extensive industrial area it would appear that the attack came as a surprise. Furthermore it would seem that the sound of the ships cannot be perceived at great altitudes." The lights actually were those of the Parkgate Steel Works and the Silverwood Colliery, north of Rotherham, which did not receive the air-raid warning until *L 35* was actually bearing down

*Detail of L 50's streamlined control car. (Moch)*

*Three views of L 52 at Wittmundhaven. L 52 survived the war, but was destroyed by airship crews on June 23, 1919. In the photo below, the Imperial Cown can be seen in the center of the Iron Cross on the front of the ship.*

on them. The lights were extinguished just in time to save the works from a severe bombing, and the best Ehrlich could do was to drop his missiles in a long line where he thought the lights had been. They missed their targets and merely broke windows and blew down a wall.

On the morning of October 19, 1917, commanders in Nordholz, Tondern, Ahlhorn and Wittmundhaven received orders by telephone:

Attack middle England. Industrial region of Sheffield, Manchester, Liverpool, etc. . . . Take-off Nordholz, Tondern, Ahlhorn 12 noon, Wittmundhaven 1 p.m. Participants *L 42, L 51, L 53, L 45, L 54, L 41, L 44, L 46, L 47, L 50, L 55, L 49, L 52*. Ostend measurements at 4, 7, 10 p.m., 3 a.m Ostend night measurements cannot be counted on. Wind measurements as required from the German Bight. Weather map will not be wirelessed. Pay careful attention to wireless discipline. In case of thunderstorms, do not try to fly above them. If impossible to go around them, go through at low altitude under pressure height.

Leader of Airships, Ahlhorn.

Dies irae! All the shortcomings of the "height climbers," all the unsolved problems of operation at high altitudes, were about to recoil on the heads of Strasser and his men. They had no way of knowing that a deep depression over Iceland was fast bearing down on the British Isles, bringing north to north-east winds of gale force. During the morning Strasser got in touch by telephone with the outlying bases, and the last words *L 45*'s commander heard from his beloved chief were, "The weather conditions are good, Kölle; go right into the interior, and good luck!"[4]

Thus, bravely enough, started the last great airship raid of the war. *L 42* and *L 51* were held in the "Normann" shed at Nordholz by a cross wind, but by 1:54 p.m. the eleven others were in the air. They were heading for an appalling disaster: four of that proud company would never see the Fatherland again.

Conditions over the eastern North Sea were not unusual. *L 41* found a flat calm at 9,000 feet over Norderney, but later had to detour around several thunderstorms. The other ships reported light south-west winds over the German Bight. At 5 p.m., because the air temperature at 11,500 feet was only 15 degrees F., *L 52* dropped the last of her water ballast without anti-freeze, and went on west at 13,000 feet. From Ahlhorn came an optimistic forecast:

5:51 p.m. Especially favorable weather situation for central England. Winds German Bight west to south-west. To westward, moderate west to north-west currents up to high altitude.

Leader of Airships.

Already several craft had risen to 16,000 feet, and were finding conditions far different from Strasser's confident prediction. Here the wind had veered towards the north, and was rapidly freshening. Of these conditions the Zeppelin commanders had received no warning, for the gale raged only in the upper air and no observations had been made above 10,000 feet.

[4] Waldemar Kölle, "Marineluftschiffe im Kriege, in Sturm und Not," *Deutsche Rundschau*, January 1926, p. 49.

AIRSHIP RAID, OCTOBER 19–20, 1917

| *Ship* | *Flt. No.* | *Take off* | *Landing* | *Time in Air* | *Distance (miles)* | *Av. speed (m.p.h.)* | *Max. alt. (feet)* | *Temp. (°F.)* | *Crew* | *Fuel (lb.) loaded/used* | *Oil (lb.) loaded/used* | *Ballast loaded (lb.)* | *Bombs (lb.)* | *Gas used (cubic feet)* |
|---|---|---|---|---|---|---|---|---|---|---|---|---|---|---|
| *L 41* | 31 | Ahlhorn 12.29 p.m. | Ahlhorn 3.08 p.m. | 26h. 39m. | 1,022 | 38·7 | 18,400 | – 7·6 | 18 | 10,750/10,300 | 662/406 | 44,100 | 3,850 | 955,000 |
| *L 44* | 26 | Ahlhorn 1 p.m. | | | | | | | | | | | | |
| *L 45* | 26 | Tondern 12.20 p.m. | | | | | | | 17 | | | | | |
| *L 46* | 31 | Ahlhorn 1.20 p.m. | Ahlhorn 1 p.m. | 23h. 37m. | 865 | 36·6 | 19,300 | – 17·5 | 18 | 10,580/8,210 | 883/375 | 52,500 | 3,970 | 1,130,000 |
| *L 47* | 33 | Ahlhorn 12.15 p.m. | Ahlhorn 12.40 p.m. | 24h. 25m. | 1,136 | 46·3 | 15,750 | – 0·5 | 19 | 10,180/9,460 | 610/580 | 51,400 | 4,010 | 884,000 |
| *L 49* | 16 | Wittmund 1.54 p.m. | | | | | | | 19 | 10,630/ | 655/ | 56,000 | 4,410 | |
| *L 50* | 19 | Ahlhorn 1.27 p.m. | | | | | | | 20 | 11,000/ | 1,100/ | 48,100 | 5,230 | |
| *L 52* | 13 | Wittmund 1.35 p.m. | Ahlhorn 3.40 p.m. | 26h. 6m. | 1,198 | 46·5 | 19,700 | – 27·5 | 19 | 10,280/9,440 | 896/574 | 56,900 | 4,450 | 918,000 |
| *L 53* | 13 | Nordholz 12.15 p.m. | Nordholz 3.45 p.m. | 27h. 25m. | 1,058 | 38·7 | 21,350 | – 14·8 | 20 | 10,030/8,930 | 1,016/485 | 54,100 | 6,620 | 1,003,000 |
| *L 54* | 12 | Tondern 12.50 p.m. | Tondern 9.40 a.m. | 20h. 50m. | 862 | 41·0 | 21,350 | + 12·2 | 16 | 8,800/7,280 | 915/429 | 58,700 | 6,410 | |
| *L 55* | 12 | Ahlhorn 12.36 p.m. | Tiefenort 6.15 p.m. | 28h. 40m. | 1,178 | 41·0 | 24,000 | – 24·8 | 19 | 10,580/10,580 | 883/883 | 52,250 | 6,620 | 1,978,000 |

*Weather:* Light N.W. winds at low altitudes. At higher altitudes, strong N.W. winds increasing to gale force. Very cloudy sky.
*Bombs:* 275 (30,621 lb.), includes 20 (2,454 lb.) on London.
*Casualties:* 36 killed (33 in London), 55 injured (50 in London).
*Monetary Damage:* £54,346 (£48,205 in London).

*Kapitänleutnant* von Buttlar, recognizing the increasing strength of the north wind, abandoned the idea of attacking Sheffield or Manchester. Coming inland south of the Humber, he claimed that at 9:50 p.m. he dropped his bombs on Derby and Nottingham from 21,300 feet. *L 54* started her return early, and at 3:35 a.m., according to her report, was in sight of The Helder. At 7 a.m. bearings showed that she was far north of her course. Von Buttlar concluded that he had been set north by a strong south-south-west wind over the German Bight, and with fuel for only 4 to 5 hours on board, he asked for destroyers to stand by. But at 9:40 a.m. he brought his ship into Tondern with 205 gallons of petrol still in her tanks.

The British records are entirely at variance with *L 54*'s report. At 8:55 p.m. she was seen to make the Norfolk coast near Happisburgh, but instead of coming overland, von Buttlar's ship coasted down the shoreline nearly to Harwich, where she turned inland. The "Derby and Nottingham" bombs fell in open country, between Ipswich and Colchester, doing no damage, and *L 54* then went out to sea near Clacton. Proceeding north along the coast, *L 54* nearly fell victim to a B.E.2c from Great Yarmouth. The plane was at 9,000 feet, and *L 54* was only 5,000 feet high, but the plane was unable to overhaul her even though it pursued the airship twenty miles to sea. Flying at low altitude, von Buttlar was not affected by the gale in the upper air, and was the only commander to bring his ship home via the usual North Sea route.

Hollender in *L 46* had hoped to reach the industrial Midlands via the Humber, but after 7 p.m. found the wind veering and blowing harder. Steering north-north-west by compass, *L 46*, flying at 19,400 feet, was slowly forced southward past the Wash by a north wind of 45 to 50 m.p.h. At 11:20 p.m. she was carried inland stern-first over the Norfolk coast. Expecting the wind to veer further towards the east, Hollender decided not to go into the interior, and put up his helm to attack Norwich on his way back to the sea. He claimed to have dropped his 4,900 pounds of bombs on the city at 11:30 p.m. Actually *L 46* passed ten miles east of Norwich, making 75 m.p.h. over the ground, and her twenty bombs fell harmlessly near Happisburgh on the coast. From the control car of *L 46*, nearly four miles in the air, Hollender could see the guns flickering at Harwich, along the Thames, and even on the Western Front in Flanders. Steering north-northeast by compass, the airship hardly advanced over the ground, and was carried away south-east towards the mouth of the Scheldt. "Considering the strong wind, which was now blowing from the north-north-east, and the complete breakdown of wireless bearings, continued the return over Holland, which was made at 3,500 meters [11,500 feet] above largely solid cloud without the defenses being aroused." Descending through the clouds at 5 a.m., *L 46* was greeted by inaccurate German antiaircraft fire and round herself over the Ruhr industrial area. At 10 a.m., *L 46* was over Ahlhorn, and at 1 p.m. came down through the fog to a safe landing.

*L 47* likewise made her way home across Dutch territory. *Kapitänleutnant* Michael von Freudenreich had intended to cross the coast at Scarborough in order to be to windward of his target, but was sent south by the wind and believed he came inland south of Flamborough Head at 8:30 p.m. Fighting his way west at 14,800 feet, von Freudenreich thought he had the lights of Leeds in sight at 9 p.m., but *L 47* was blown south in spite of steering a northerly course at times. The compass failed. Rapidly the ship drove southward, past Sheffield, as her commander thought, without being able to attack. At 10 p.m., *L 47* crossed a city which von Freudenreich believed was Nottingham, and here he dropped 3,000 pounds of bombs. So fast was he going that there was no time to release one 660-pound and three 110-pound bombs. Steering by a small chart table compass and the stars, *L 47* made for the coast on a north-east course, but was carried south-east over the ground. Just before leaving the country at 11:40 p.m., the rest of the bombs were dropped on a "blast furnace installation, possibly near Ipswich." Actually *L 47* came inland even farther south than her commander believed, at Sutton, north of the Wash, and never came within sight of Leeds, Sheffield or Nottingham. The "Nottingham" bombs went down while she was circling over Rutlandshire, and the last group in fact exploded west of Ipswich, but did no damage.

At 12:41 a.m. radio bearings showed that *L 47* was over Ostend, and descending to 3,300 feet she was below the gale and made good progress to the north-east. At 3:50 a.m. both the after engines failed from lack of fuel, and the forward engine also with a broken radiator pipe. The ship drifted over Dutch territory at The Helder, and was briefly under rifle fire at an altitude of only 2,600 feet. The after engines were quickly set going and *L 47* made her way home along the Frisian Islands. She landed at Ahlhorn at 12:40 p.m. with only 98 gallons of fuel left on board.

Other ships penetrated farther inland, and made their way home across France. Even though she was only 9,500 feet high over the North Sea, *L 41* after 6:30 p.m. had to point up 10 degrees, then 15 degrees to windward to make good her course over the ground. *Hauptmann* Manger was correct in reporting that he came inland past Spurn Point at 7:45 p.m. Flying at 16,400 feet, Manger made for Manchester. With the ship's head pointing north-west, and later, north-north-west, to make good a westerly course over the ground, *L 41* instead was carried southwest. At 10 p.m., when he thought he was over Sheffield, Manger was circling near Derby, 37 miles to the south. Here he "considered whether in view of a further increase in the wind I should give up Manchester and attack Sheffield. I decided, however, to go on." Driving farther with the wind, Manger at 11:45 p.m. believed he had reached Manchester at last, but he was in fact on the outskirts of Birmingham, where his bombs did some damage to the Austin Motor Works at Longbridge. Manger evidently referred to this plant when he reported that "hits were observed in a brightly lit-up, big new factory and in an iron foundry with blast furnaces."

If Manger previously had not realized the violence of the northerly gale, he now had an opportunity to measure its effects:

> While running off, it was ascertained that the ship made very little headway on a 60-degree course, and was still being carried south. At go degrees she made no speed at all. The wind had therefore freshened to 9-10 doms [40 to 45 m.p.h.]. Direction north to north-north-east. The return on an easterly ground course was thus impossible. It was only possible to go forward with a simultaneous set to the south. I next steered on a north-east compass course. The ship did not make speed enough, combined with the drift, to get away from the coast before dawn. I then had her headed east-north-east, and finally east.

*L 41* left England north of Dover. Above the Channel, Manger descended to 8,500 feet, but climbed back to 16,400 feet when he thought warships fired at him. Once more he had no success in trying to advance on a north-east course, and on a northerly course drove stern-first over the ground. In the grip of the gale, *L 41* was carried south-east across northern France, and at 5:50 a.m. crossed the Western Front near La Bassee. Fearing air attack, Manger requested the Flanders naval command to send out a plane which escorted *L 41* beyond Brussels. Once past the Front, Manger brought his ship down to 3,300 feet, turned north at Aachen, and at 3:08 p.m. made a hard landing at Ahlhorn, damaging the forward gondola. Only 60 gallons of petrol remained of the 1,465 which *L 41* had carried when she took off 26 hours and 39 minutes before.

*Kapitänleutnant* der Reserve Prölss in *L 53* claimed to have attacked Birmingham, but was so uncertain of his course that he did not submit a track chart with his report. He believed he came inland at 8 p.m. just north of the Wash. A bearing at 8:30 p.m. indicated that *L 53* was near Cambridge, showing that the wind must be freshening from the north. Prölss claimed to have compensated for his drift, and at 9:30 to have reached a big city which he believed was Birmingham, on which he dropped 4,400 pounds of bombs. At 11:30 "another big city was in sight, the remaining 1,000 kg. [2,200 pounds] of bombs were dropped; extraordinarily strong anti-aircraft fire, 25-30 searchlights seen through the clouds, but could not pierce them; ship had driven over London and making little progress east." Prölss reported leaving the country at Dover on a course for Ostend. Instead, heavy gunfire to port showed that he was on the wrong side of the Western Front. Using cloud cover, *L 53* crossed the Front and at 10:10 a.m. was over Celle by radio bearings.

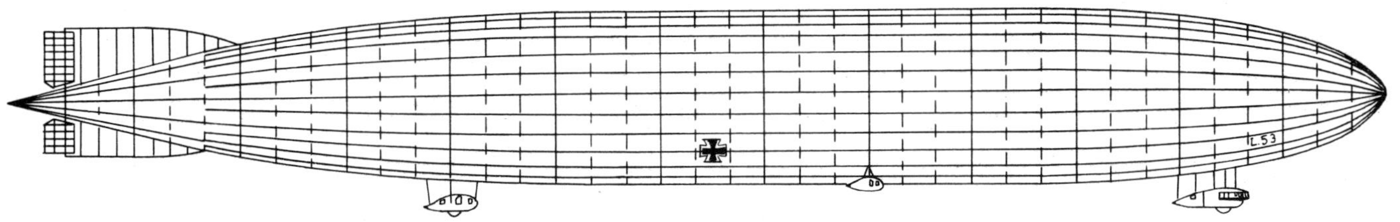

**L 53**

| | | | |
|---|---|---|---|
| Gas capacity | 1,977,900 ft.$^3$ | Engines | 5 Maybach HSLu, of 240 h.p. |
| Length | 644.7 ft. | Propellers | 4 Jaray L.Z. |
| Diameter | 78.4 ft. | Weight empty | 37,500 |
| Useful lift | 88,200 lbs. | Maximum speed | 67 mph |
| Gas cells | 14 | Ceiling | 21,000 ft. |
| Crew | 20 | Full speed endurance | 8400 miles |

*In place of the three engine gondola and propellers on brackets on the hull, was a streamlined gondola aft, with two engines turning on a single propeller. This detail is from L 53. (Luftschiffbau Zeppelin)*

At 3:45 p.m. she made a safe landing at Nordholz.

From comparing British records with *L 53*'s War Diary, the author has concluded that Admiral Hall's organization confused *L 53* with *L 44*. For example, "*L 53*" is shown passing Arras in the British sector of the Western Front at 11:30 p.m., at which time Prölss believed he was over London. No bombs, however, fell in France during this raid. I believe it was *L 53*, not *L 44*, which came inland over the Wash at 8:30 p.m., and which at 10 p.m. was near Bedford. Here an engineering works and a military school were showing lights which attracted a string of 110-pound bombs. This ship then swung south-east and at 10:40 p.m. dropped ten bombs, including a 660-pounder, near Leighton Buzzard. No damage resulted and she then passed east of London. At 12:30 a.m. she went out to sea near Dover.

Other ships, more or less crippled and unable to battle the north-east gale, followed *L 53* in her long slant across France to Lorraine. *L 52* was competently handled by *Oberleutnant zur See* Friemel, who was more sure of his navigation than Prölss. He came inland at Theddlethorpe, south of the Wash, at 8:30 p.m., exactly where he stated in his report. Over the land Friemel found a layer of mist which hampered orientation. Heading north-west

*Naval airship L 53 at Friedrichshafen. (Luftschiffbau Zeppelin)*

*OPPOSITE: Inside a Zeppelin of the L 53 class, looking aft. Note spacing of the main braced frames, with two intermediate frames intervening. Attachment of the cantilever tail fins shows well at the stern. Fuel tanks and water ballast sacks appear in the gangway in the foreground. (Luftschiffbau Zeppelin)*

and flying at 16,400 feet, he held on for Sheffield, but found no cities or industrial targets. *L 52* hardly advanced, and the north wind grew even fiercer. Shortly after 10 p.m., when he believed he was south of Sheffield, Friemel turned east, to bomb Norwich or south-east coast towns. At this time, without knowing it, he was very near Northampton. At 11:05 p.m. he saw many searchlights to starboard, steered for them, and as he dropped all his bombs, Friemel realized he was over the eastern defenses of London. The 26 bombs traced by the British fell at Hertford and Waltham Marshes, but did little damage. As *L 52* passed east of London she was chased by a Royal Flying Corps pilot, but he could not get his B.E.2e to her estimated altitude of 15,000-16,000 feet. Friemel steered northeast after his attack, intending to go home over Belgium, but although he descended to 13,000 feet over the Channel, he could not reach the Belgian coast. At 1 a.m., as Friemel records, he was off Boulogne, and at 6:30 a.m., just before dawn revealed *L 52* to the gunners below, Friemel crossed the trenches near St. Die, south-east of Verdun. He descended to 3,300 feet and at 8 a.m. fixed his position precisely over Worms. Being short of fuel, *L 52* landed at Ahlhorn at 3:40 p.m. instead of going on to Wittmundhaven.

*Kapitänleutnant* Hans Kurt Flemming in *L 55* believed he came inland south of Flamborough Head, and at 9:25 p.m. thought he dropped 4,400 pounds of bombs from 19,000 feet on Mappleton and Hull. At 10:50 p.m. he dropped his remaining 2,200 pounds of bombs from 20,700 feet on a large city which he believed was Sheffield, but from later bearings decided was Birmingham. With a northerly course and wide-open engines, *L 55* drove down on the London defenses. Flemming described a heavy barrage from the London batteries, and saw two night-flying fields north of the city. At 1:25 a.m., according to her report, *L 55* skirted London to the west, descending to 10,000-11,500 feet protected by a ground mist. From here, reported Flemming, he proceeded via Dover to the Hook of Holland.

*L 55* actually came inland with *L 47* and *L 52* south of the Humber at 8:30 p.m. Following a winding course, she dropped the "Mappleton and Hull" bombs at Holme, south of Peterborough, and then drove very rapidly on London. But the sixteen explosives she scattered between Hitchin and Hatfield were those which Flemming thought he had dropped on Birmingham. *L 55* did in fact pass west of London, but by 11:20 p.m. she was leaving England at Hastings.

*L 55 taking off from Nordholz. During the "Silent Raid" on October 19, 1917, L 55, after taking off from Ahlhorn, she attempted to out-climb enemy aircraft, and eventually reached 24,000 feet – the altitude record at the time. L 55 did not make it back to Ahlhorn, and in fact was blown over Thuringia where it crash landed, and was later dismantled. (Moch)*

*L 55 control car. Note the hatch in the keel forward. (Moch)*

At 3:20 a.m. the forward engine failed permanently and both after engines went out of action with burned-out exhaust valves. Since the latter drove the radio generator, the main transmitter was silent and the battery-powered emergency set could not reach Germany. Fearful that the ship might fall in enemy territory, Flemming had the attack order, the radio signals, and the attack charts of Newcastle, Hull, Sheffield, Liverpool and Manchester torn in small pieces and thrown overboard. At 4 a.m., *L 55* was fired at through holes in the clouds. Flemming believed he was at Dover, but in fact the ship had drifted over France and about this time was crossing the Western Front between St. Quentin and Reims. At dawn Flemming climbed again to 19,700 feet. At 6 a.m. an airship was seen at a great distance on the starboard bow. For half an hour the port midships engine was out of action, and then the starboard midships engine had to be stopped temporarily. At 8:40 a.m., seeing two planes to the north at low altitude, Flemming turned south-east and "climbed to 7,300 meters [24,000 feet] to make the ship heavy at the same time." Thus casually does he record the greatest altitude reached by an airship in history! At 10:45 a.m. Flemming believed he passed Maastricht on the Meuse, and at 11:30 a.m. was over a large town which he assumed was Aachen. Here he threw down a message for Strasser, "Over Aachen, request orders. *L 55*." Shortly afterwards the emergency radio picked up, "Head for Ahlhorn. Leader of Airships." In fact, *L 55* was over Darmstadt, 125 miles east-south-east of Aachen, and she must previously have passed Mainz instead of Maastricht. Ignorant of the gross error in his position – which Strasser's reply did nothing to correct – Flemming steered north-north-east by compass above the overcast, expecting to be over Ahlhorn in a few hours. At 2:40 p.m. he brought his ship down through thick cloud, expecting to find Hamm below. Instead, between heavy rain squalls, *L 55*'s commander glimpsed a rolling, wooded landscape. At 1,650 feet the big antenna was torn off in a wood. On a small railroad station the officers read the name "Immelborn," and from a railroad guide they found they were over Thuringia, 200 miles south-south-east of their base. "Since the ship at times had an angle of 45 degrees, only enough fuel for two hours, and darkness was approaching, landing was planned." At 6:15 p.m., *L 55* fell hard in a forest clearing near Tiefenort on

*The wreck of L 55 in Tiefenort, Thuringia. L 55 commander Kapitänleutnant Hans Kurt Flemming survived this crash, but was later killed on May 6, 1937 when the "Hindenburg" went down in Lakehurst, New Jersey. (Moch)*

*L 44 at Ahlhorn with the "Alix" shed in the background. During the "Silent Raid" L 44 was hit by French 75mm cannon and brought down in flames. (Kameradschaft)*

*L 54 landing at Nordholz with the "Nora" and "Norbert" sheds in the distance. (Kameradschaft)*

the River Werra. The forward and after gondolas were smashed, with heavy damage to the hull framework above them, the port midships and forward propellers were shattered, and Cell 9 amidships was found to have run empty. The ship could not be saved, and by October 31, Flemming and his crew had completed dismantling the wreck.

They were fortunate, for many of their comrades did not return. For *L 44* there are no German reports. Though Stabbert had escaped with his life from the disaster to *L 20* a year and a half before, he was not to be so lucky a second time. The "*L 53*" of the British records is, I believe, his *L 44*, which must already have been in trouble as she reached the Norfolk coast east of the Wash at 7:45 p.m. With little change in course, this ship drove aimlessly southward towards the mouth of the Thames. At 9:40 p.m. the first bombs traced from her descended near Herne Bay, damaging an inn. At 9:52 p.m. this ship is shown reaching the Channel between Dover and the North Foreland. Certain it is that it was indeed *L 44* which the dawn discovered in Lorraine, some forty miles on the wrong side of the trenches. Considering Stabbert's slow progress from the Wash, where he had made his landfall nearly twelve hours earlier, it is certain that he must have experienced repeated engine breakdowns. None the less, he made a bold attempt to get back to Germany. Close to the Front, French 75 mm. anti-aircraft guns opened fire on the Zeppelin, which rose quickly from 12,000 to 19,000 feet. At 7:45 a.m. an incendiary shell pierced the hull, and *L 44* caught fire and

*The only photograph showing L 49 in flight. L 49 was forced down in France during the "Silent Raid." The Allies made complete drawings which were later developed into the U.S.S. "Shenandoah", and the British R 36. (Moch)*

*Two views of the damage to L 49 after its delivery flight to Löwenthal on July 15, 1917, from an implosion after descending from 12,000 feet. It was fitted with a new bow at Wildeshausen, and was made airworthy on July 13, 1917. (both - Moch)*

fell nose-first in flames. With Gallic realism, French photographers recorded the scattered corpses and shattered machinery at St. Clement: the first streamlined twin-engine gondola, which, with its occupants, had torn loose and fallen free, crushed into the ground; the staring, sightless eyes of *L 44*'s dead executive officer, young Armin Rothe, still recognizable to his friends; the smoking heap of duralumin girders dominating the scene, smashed beyond recognition except for the tail cone, from which hung a filthy rag – all that remained of the war ensign of the Imperial German Navy.

*L 49* and *L 50*, hopelessly lost and depending on *L 44* to lead the way, were following close behind and witnessed her destruction. *L 49*'s forward engine had failed before she reached England, and further, while *Kapitänleutnant* Hans-Karl Gayer waited out at sea for complete darkness, the north wind carried him to leeward. As a result, he came inland, not at Scarborough as he thought, but at Holkham in Norfolk, nearly a hundred miles to the south. In a brief report which Gayer smuggled out of prison nearly a year later, he claimed to have bombed two batteries, two flying fields, and a railroad station with good success. No locations were given. *L 49* dropped forty-two bombs as she crossed Norfolk, most of them falling west of Norwich, but they only killed cattle and damaged farm buildings. Two more engines failed, almost certainly due to altitude sickness affecting the personnel. At 10:20 p.m. *L 49* left the land at the Naze, at 10:48 she drifted down on the North Foreland, and, circling down the Kentish coast, she headed out over the Channel from Folkestone (described by Gayer as "a lighted seaport") at midnight. At 12:40 a.m. she reached France at Cape Gris Nez, but her crew believed they were passing over the Dutch coast. Heading north-north-east and then east-north-east, *L 49*, with only two engines working and her radio useless, still drove south-east. At dawn Stabbert's ship was seen ahead, and Gayer steered to follow her. The sudden blaze of fire as *L 44* was destroyed was a demoralizing blow for *L 49*'s crew, but, unable to conceive how far he had been carried by the wind, Gayer believed that *L 44* had been shot down by Dutch anti-aircraft guns. He turned back to the west. A few minutes later, as he descended to 6,500 feet in an attempt to orient himself by sight of the ground, he was jumped by five airplanes bearing French cockades. This was disillusionment unexpected and complete. The planes, Nieuports of Escadrille N.152 (the "Crocodiles") carried only tracer and ball ammunition, and did not succeed in setting *L 49* on fire, but they completed Gayer's discomfiture. He himself states he "could not go east," and he made no attempt to outclimb them. Gayer finally brought his ship down in the woods on the slopes of the River Apance, near Bourbonne-les-Bains. The 19 exhausted Germans stumbled out of the gondolas and Gayer endeavored to set the ship afire. His Very pistol misfired, the igniter in the fore gondola refused to function, and while he was still working on it, an ancient Frenchman who had been hunting nearby rushed up and disarmed

*L 49 after being forced down in France by French Nieuports. Note the supports for midship engine cars. The bow is to the left. (Scamerhorn)*

the Germans. The Zeppelin had to be dismantled by her captors, but not before her design had been copied and distributed to all the Allied powers. The plans of America's first rigid airship, the *Shenandoah*, were largely based on those of *L 49*.

The citizens of Bourbonne-les-Bains must have been sufficiently surprised to have *L 49* on their hands, without having another Zeppelin fall in their midst a few hours later. Yet such was the fate of *Kapitänleutnant* Roderich Schwonder's *L 50*. One of her engines failed over the North Sea, and another over England, due to neglect by the height-sick crew, while the radio was rendered useless. In a rather garbled report which a medical officer com-

*Two views of L 49 after its force-landing in France.*

mitted to memory and forwarded to Strasser on his release from a French prison, Schwonder said he believed he had bombed Grimsby and Hull from 16,400 feet. Since the defenses were extraordinarily strong, he later decided he had been over London. In fact, *L 50* had crossed the Norfolk coast at Cley-next-the-Sea at 8:45 p.m., and went out to sea again north of Harwich at 9:50 p.m. With the wind blowing 40 m.p.h. at her altitude, *L 50* too was carried away south-east over France, with her commander having no idea of her position. She crossed the trenches into German-held territory near Valenciennes, but made no effort to better her course, and drifted back to the French side of the lines east of Reims. From here *L 50* actually flew west till reaching Provins at 3:50 a.m., and then wandered south-east into Lorraine. At 6 a.m. Schwonder saw the ground through a hole in the clouds, and believed he was over Holland. *L 44*, flying nearby, was fired on with phosphorus ammunition and crashed in flames. Schwonder at once reversed course, and for nearly two hours flew west in broad daylight at 6,500 feet as far as Tonnerre, some 125 miles from the Front. Still with no idea of what country lay beneath, Schwonder descended to 800 feet. "The shape of the railroad cars showed it was not Germany." Through binoculars, he saw on a house the sign "Cafe du Centre," and knew he was over France. Towards noon, *L 50* wandered back east to Bourbonne-les-Bains, and Schwonder saw *L 49* on the ground apparently undamaged, with French planes about to take off. Up he went to 6,500 feet, but found that with three engines he could not make headway against the wind towards Germany. Then, states his report, Schwonder decided to destroy *L 50* by diving her vertically into the ground from 6,500 feet to crumple up her bows "like an accordion." It is a fact that *L 50* was flown at high speed into the ground at Dammartin, but her descent was more nearly horizontal. The control car was torn off and several men leaped from the side gondolas. Schwonder was knocked unconscious by a blow from the engine telegraphs, and as he awakened he saw the hull of the ship, her nose crushed in, drifting along several hundred feet in the air. The crew were running after it, trying without success to set it afire with Very pistols. Suddenly the floating wreck tilted up to 45 degrees, and disappeared. A muster showed that sixteen of the crew were safe, but four had been carried off with the ship. Two machinists in the rear gondola were probably dead or injured, for the car had been crushed against a tree. The fuel mate in the gangway, and the relief rudder man, standing watch on the top platform, were probably disabled by altitude sickness, else they would have valved gas to save themselves. For the rest of the day the black-painted derelict drove south with the wind, swinging playfully on her tail at 23,000 feet and mocking the French aviators who reeled and buzzed futilely at the top of their ceiling 3,000 feet below. At 6:30 p.m. *L 50* drifted out to sea near Frejus, and was still dipping and swaying in the thin upper air when last seen by some seaplane pilots who pursued her until nightfall. Presumably she and her luckless passengers went down in the Mediterranean. Strasser charitably noted in his endorsement that the medical man lacked technical knowledge, and it would be unfair to Schwonder to criticize his decisions and actions from the doctor's verbal report.

Lastly, Kölle's *L 45* made a remarkable journey "from Denmark to the Riviera by way of London and Paris in twenty hours,"[5] according to a member of her crew who must have been a travel agent at heart. Kölle had been aware of the northerly wind from 4:20 p.m., when a bearing had shown the ship being set to the south, and *L 45* came in most northerly of the raiding Zeppelins. Kölle was aiming for Sheffield, but once in the clutches of the upper gale, *L 45* whirled southward with the other ships. Says he:

> We were now flying over a layer of broken clouds. In quick succession we saw short flashes, we saw the play of searchlights, and then – once more darkness and calm. Precise orientation from the ground was impossible. Also no fixed points could be discerned. We should have to have our position ascertained, and secure bearings. The executive officer came out of the wireless cabin. Bearings could not be

---

5 Jones, V, p. 97.

obtained; all the ships were calling. Well! the visibility seemed to be obscured everywhere. Then we should have to wait with our calls until wireless silence again prevailed. We would have to find Sheffield eventually. The course had been carefully checked, and the thin clouds over the great city would certainly be lit up by the bright industrial works.[6]

This is the account of the seaman and officer entirely concerned with directing himself, his ship and his crew to doing the greatest possible damage to the enemy. The rudder man, a cog in the machine, saw the weakness of the instrument under Kölle's hand far more clearly than did his commander:

> We should, so I believe, have crossed the Lincoln coast; but from an argument we had with the officers our navigating warrant officer, Hashagen, expressed grave doubts as to the landfall. I felt sure we were a long way south of that. Kölle, however, though looking anxious would not give way. I looked at my comrades in the car to see if I could read their thoughts, but only cold and anxiety was there. The wind must have freshened from the north, for even then, like the lightning, some searchlights cut the air; all I could see by their warm beams was the leeway that we were making. Kölle swore and jumped at the ballast control cords. The ship rose rapidly. "5,800," read Hashagen off the altimeter; the height and the cold made him look ghastly in the pale searchlight beam as he leaned on the glass panels. I shall never forget his face. I felt, too, that I would get little sympathy from him if I dropped out, for the height and anxiety were telling on him already. Guns opened on us, too, but that did not trouble us. For nearly two hours we struggled to keep our westward course, but the wind blew ever stronger and I could tell that our navigation was getting more and more uncertain. We dropped a few bombs at some faint lights, but providence alone knows where they went. I scarcely believe that Lieutenant Schütz, our second-in-command, troubled to set the bomb sight.[7]

These bombs fell in Northampton, where twenty-three were traced from *L 45* at 10:50 p.m. A woman and two children were killed, but little damage was done. Kölle later believed that this attack had been made on Oxford. *L 45* then drove straight down on London. The rudder man continues:

> At about 11:30 we began to see lights below and as the lights continued so it suddenly dawned upon us that it could only be the city of London that we were crossing in the air. Even Kölle looked amazed at the dim lights as Schütz suddenly shouted, "London!" It was then that we first realized the fury of the savage tempest that had been driving us out of our course. But Kölle clearly had but one thought – that was higher. So he released more ballast and the bombs – first two sighting shots and then the rest . . . Fortunately for us we were unseen; not a searchlight was unmasked; not a shot was fired; not an airplane was seen. If the gale had driven us out of our course, it had also defeated the flying defenses of the city! It was misty or so it seemed, for we were above a thin veil of cloud. The Thames we just dimly saw from the outline of the lights; two great railway stations I thought I saw, but the speed of the ship running almost before the gale was such that we could not distinguish much. We were half frozen, too, and the excitement was great. It was all over in a flash. The last big bomb was gone and we were once more over the darkness and rushing onwards.[8]

Most of Kölle's bombs fell to the north-west of London, but three 660-pounders exploded in the Administrative County and accounted for most of the casualties of the raid. Peculiar conditions in the upper air muffled the sound of *L 45*'s engines and also deadened the crash of her sighting shots on the outskirts of the capital. Consequently people were moving about when Kölle's first 660-pounder descended near Piccadilly Circus. It blew in the glass fronts of many fashionable stores and tore a hole in the road 5 feet deep and 100 feet across. Seven people were killed, and eighteen injured.

6 Kölle, p. 49.

7 (Heinrich Bahn,) p. 110.

8 Ibid.

Kölle's next bomb fell across the river. In Camberwell the second 660-pounder struck a party wall between two houses and utterly destroyed them, at the cost of 12 lives. The last of the "big ones" demolished four houses in Hither Green, while twenty-six neighboring villas were damaged by blast. Fourteen people were killed and nine injured.

Having reoriented himself by the lights of the capital, Kölle got his ship's head around and painfully worked his way eastward. No doubt he would have got back to Germany across France or Belgium, had he not met Second Lieutenant T.B. Pritchard in a B.E.2e over the Medway. Pritchard was at 13,000 feet and opened fire on *L 45*, which he estimated to be 2,000 feet higher. The Zeppelin rose quickly and turned south to run before the gale. Nor did she get back again to her easterly course, for troubles were crowding on her fast:

> It was then that our misfortunes began. Hahndorf reported to Kölle that the engine of the port wing car was scarcely working – he thought owing to the sooting of the plugs. The plugs were cleaned by the engineers but alas! their hands were so cold and they themselves so clumsy with lassitude and fatigue owing to the height that, by the time the plugs were cleaned and replaced, the engine had ceased to function – the cooling water had frozen, the radiator had split and there was no means in our power to get the engine into action again. From this moment our journey became one long story of misery and pain. The cold grew intense and we all began to feel dejected at the consciousness that our real attack on England must have failed. The jubilation at having flown over the enemy's capital gave way to anxiety. At the helm of the ship we began to feel that the gale was driving us away, still further out of our course. We were so high that the earth was scarcely visible. Clouds were obviously being driven beneath us until we could not distinguish the sea. It was somewhat after midnight that Hahndorf came in to report to the commander that the sailmaker could scarcely go on with his duties; his feet were frostbitten and the poor fellow was now lying in his hammock unable to do more. The petrol rating was complaining of weariness and sickness, leaning up against his tanks. Two engineers were suffering from height; one of these had been relieved by the man from the port wing car. Even Schütz, usually so cheerful, looked pale and anxious. So we went on in gloomy silence.[9]

During the night the condition of the crew became worse. The navigating warrant officer was too sick to attend to his work, and the ship drove steadily south, past Amiens, Compiegne and Auxerre. Just before dawn the forward engine stalled for lack of fuel, and the radiator froze. The fuel mate, down with altitude sickness, had not noticed the loss of two tanks of petrol through a leak in the feed line. Dawn silhouetted two German airships against the eastern sky. At first the crew thought they were over Germany, but anti-aircraft fire from below undeceived them. *L 45* crossed Lyons in broad daylight, but the French guns could not reach her. Over the mountainous country to the south, Kölle brought the ship lower and for an hour made good progress towards Switzerland. Then a third engine failed – this time in the after car, where the men had been refilling a radiator that had been boiling away rapidly in the rare atmosphere at high altitude. The cap had not been tightly secured, the water had shaken out, and the engine had become red hot and seized up before the mistake was noticed.

With only two engines working, *L 45* drifted incontinently southward. The warrant engineer came in and reported that the fuel would last only an hour more. At 11 a.m. *L 45* crossed Sisteron, and Kölle circled to land. The shallow bed of the River Bueche offered a good spot, but on the first approach an eddy drove the ship against a rock and tore off the port midships gondola. The ship rose and drifted down the valley to an island in the middle of the river, where she stranded again. Kölle lined up the men and fired a signal ball into the top of the hull. A puff of smoke, a roar of flame, and *L 45*'s duralumin bones were quickly bared of their fabric integument. The crew waded the stream and surrendered to some French soldiers guarding

---

9 (Heinrich Bahn), p. 110.

*The bare bones of L 45 in the bed of the river Bueche, near Sisteron. Faint arrow at upper right marks the lost port wing gondola. (L'Illustration)*

German agricultural prisoners. Later in the day *L 45*'s crew had the double humiliation of seeing the derelict *L 50* drift overhead on her way to the Mediterranean.

There followed a whole series of Intelligence interrogations. Kölle gives a fascinating picture of his interview with Major Trench, the head of the German Department in Admiral Hall's Naval Intelligence Division:

> Claiming the right to refuse to answer, I withheld all information. The Major then assured me that he had no intention of using force, and tried in vain to trick me into conversation. Through statements of his own opinions he tried to provoke my reactions in order to draw conclusions from them. Method employed covert accusations, assertions that bomb-dropping was contrary to the Geneva Convention, to which England strictly adhered, because they were dropped at random and, in violation of our orders, on undefended places. Finally, he described all my raid flights with times and targets listed with astounding accuracy, together with a correct description of my last flight, which he called my best. His transparent aim of getting me to relax failed completely. Similar procedure in interrogating Schütz, expressing opinions about personnel of the operations section and organization. Showed astonishingly detailed knowledge of even the most recently joined personnel of the Naval Airship Division. With warrant officers and petty officers, attempts to impress them by bragging of his extensive information. This information accurate in the most minute detail, causing petty officers to declare it made their heads swim. The major knew where and when the crew had been assembled; what changes in personnel had later occurred; what ships they had flown in; how long they had been at each base; that *L 45* had

*Kapitänleutnant Herrmann Kraushaar in his office in the "Alix" shed where his L 43 lay. L 43 was shot down in flames by a British flying boat on June 14, 1917. Kraushaar's body came ashore near the big stone church at Hage. He was buried in the Hage graveyard. (Moch)*

lain on the south side of the shed, the *L 54* on the north; who of the crew had remained behind on the last flight; when I had lost the *SL 12*; that the crew had 14 days' leave in January, during which the commander had been married; when Dinter had been detached and sent to the *L 23*; when various individuals had been sent on machine-gun courses and which men of the other crews they had met there; what stations individuals manned in the ship. The major knew all the commanders by name; all the school commanders with opinions as to which were the best pilots; the change of command between Buttlar and Bockholt, and the destruction of the *L 57*. Here he suggested that the ship had been lengthened, and for what purpose. Surprise questions as to why Buttlar had lost out as commander of the *L 57*; the general opinion of Bockholt; whether the Leader of Airships was very ambitious; whether Kraushaar was considered reliable; whether it was known that his wife was an Englishwoman; whether after the current losses further raids on England were likely; the physical effects of high altitude; what altitudes we could attain, and our fuel consumption; the flight performance of the new ships; whether the Schütte-Lanz ships gave satisfaction.[10]

10 Kölle special report to Strasser, November 1, 1917. Copy provided by F. Moch.

But Kölle had the last laugh on the major. By April 25, 1918, the above report, carried by a repatriated German prisoner in the heel of his shoe, was on Strasser's desk in Nordholz. It is said that after an investigation, three men were tried and shot in Tondern, Kölle's home base, and two in Nordholz.

It was most unfortunate that Strasser, contrary to his usual custom, was directing the raid from his headquarters at Ahlhorn. After recognizing from radio bearings that the airships were in trouble, he further hesitated to overload the special airship wavelength with warning messages. Had he been aboard one of the Zeppelins, as he had been in the two previous attacks, Strasser would have recognized early the development of the north-east gale in the upper air, and would have ordered the squadron back before reaching England. Certain experienced commanders, such as von Buttlar, Hollender, Manger and Friemel, could diagnose the unusual conditions and take appropriate measures. Others, such as Gayer and Schwonder, could only have been saved by direct orders.

In his report to Scheer, Strasser wrote as if this had been just another raid instead of a catastrophe. He put most of the blame on the weather service, for failing to obtain high altitude wind measurements from Ostend. Only a few weeks earlier, he had emphasized that such measurements could be of decisive importance for the airship raids on England. Strasser pointed out that towards midnight, just when the situation of the raiders became dangerous, traffic on the special airship wavelength became garbled, increasing the difficulty in obtaining bearings. He briefly referred to the significance of engine breakdowns, the loss of engine power at high altitudes, and the occurrence of altitude sickness among the personnel. Some commanders had hesitated too long: "With wind velocities such as prevailed at high altitudes on the night of October 19-20, lost quarter and half hours played a decisive role." Some of the ships, by pointing up too far to windward, failed to make enough progress to the east to clear the English coast by dawn. They should have held a more easterly heading, accepting the fact that they would have been carried to leeward, and if heavily fired on by anti-aircraft batteries, should have run with the wind. On the other hand, "those ships which got to the south of the 52 parallel (running through the mouth of the Thames) were in a critical situation."

In England, the attack is still remembered as the "Silent Raid," not only because the guns were muzzled lest they guide the Zeppelins to London, but also because the airships' engines were unheard at great altitude. The disastrous outcome was again hailed as the "beginning of the end" of the Zeppelin, but there were some dissenting voices. Rawlinson, formerly commanding the air defense of London, wrote:

> Of all the raids of which I have had experience, this was by far the most dangerous and at the same time unquestionably the most difficult to meet. . . . The most outstanding feature of the raid was that conclusive proof was afforded that, on that occasion at any rate, the defense was powerless to offer any effective resistance to the attack, which successfully achieved its main object. That is to say, the enemy were able to place their fleet in a commanding position over London, in spite of every effort on the part of the defense to prevent their doing so.[11]

The British official air historian presents a more balanced view, but admits that their escape from severe damage was largely fortuitous:

> There were no casualties or damage inflicted by the bombing other than what have already been noted, but although the Germans had little to show for their appreciable losses, it should be realized that things might have gone very differently. The defense system did not have much to do with the disastrous ending of the night's attack. The searchlights and guns were of small use, and not one of the seventy-three pilots who went up in England was equipped with an airplane capable of reaching the "ceiling" heights of the Zeppelins. Had it not been for the unusual meteorological conditions there seems no reason why the airships should not have bombed at their will and escaped. It is true that there could have been little discrimination of targets, and it is true, also, that the height-sickness, from which most of the crews suffered, impaired efficiency. The fact remains, however, that had the Zeppelins come and gone without let or hindrance, as they well might, the airship menace would, once again, have become a very live one.[12]

11 A. Rawlinson, *The Defence of London, 1915-18* (London: Andrew Melrose Ltd., 1923), pp. 216-222.

12 Jones, V., p. 101.

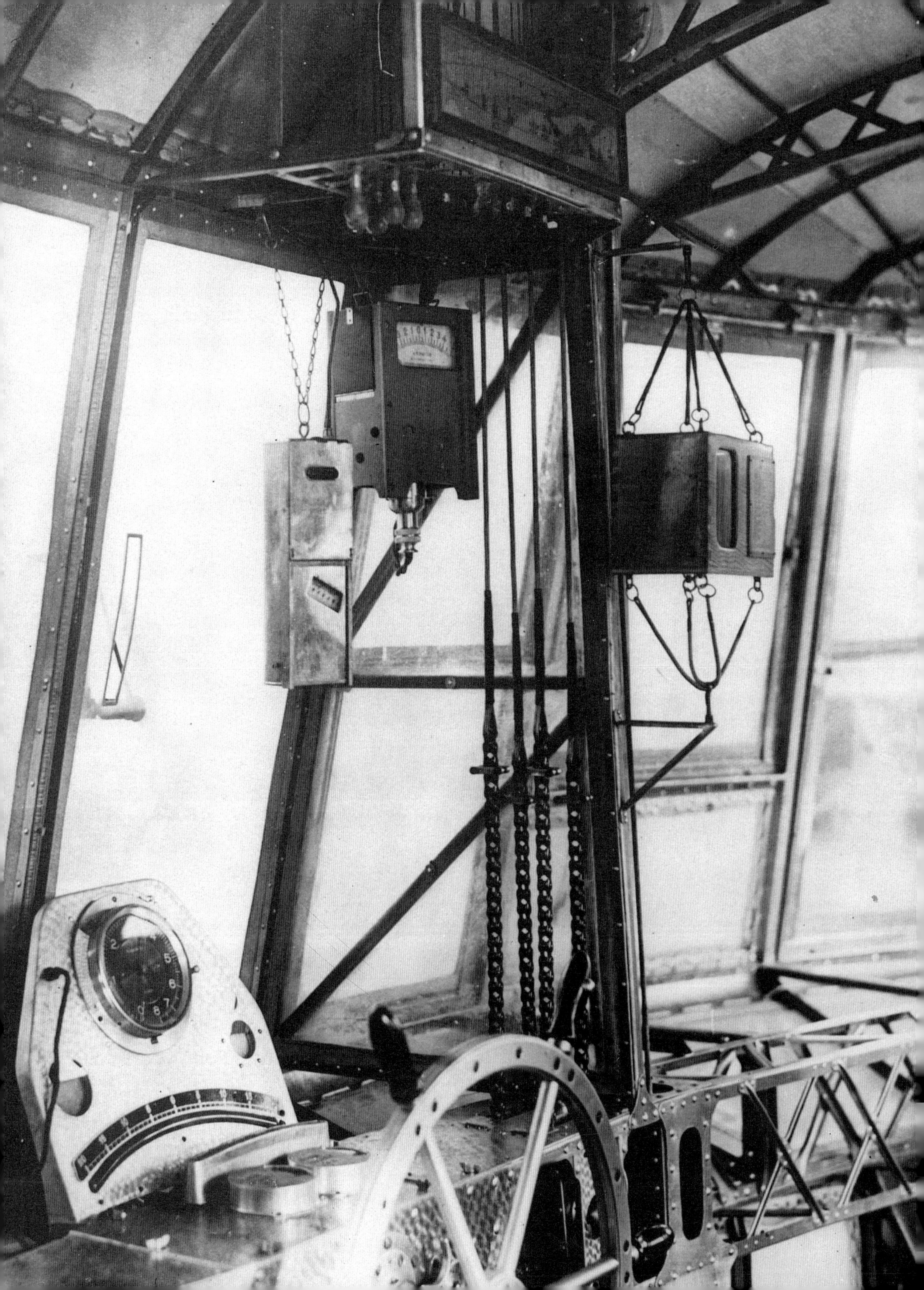

# CHAPTER XX

# THE AFRICAN ADVENTURE

The scene now shifts from the shores of the North Sea to the steaming jungles of German East Africa, where General Paul von Lettow-Vorbeck, with a handful of white troops and some native *askaris*, was still holding out against the British. Cut off from the Fatherland by the blockade, he lacked for everything. Dr. Zupitza, the former chief medical officer of the German West Africa garrison, had given much thought to the plight of the German colonial troops, and in May, 1917, suggested to the Colonial Office that a Zeppelin be sent to von Lettow-Vorbeck with medical supplies. At the Admiralty the project was approved by the Navy Minister, Admiral von Capelle, and his subordinate in charge of aviation, Admiral Starke. The idea of succoring their compatriots in East Africa had a romantic appeal, and a successful flight would raise the prestige of the German Navy. The 101-hour endurance cruise of *LZ 120* in July stimulated a joint study by the Admiralty, the Protectorate troops, the Leader of Airships and the Zeppelin Company.

The southernmost airship base in territory held by the Central Powers was at Jamboli in Bulgaria. The airline distance from there to Mahenge, in the heart of von Lettow-Vorbeck's territory, was 3,600 miles. A ship intended to cover this distance should have a still-air range of 4,350 miles, and traveling with four engines at a speed of 40 m.p.h., she would be in the air for 108 hours, or 4 1/2 days. With a cargo of sixteen tons – eleven tons of small arms ammunition and only three tons of medical supplies – a ship of 2,365,000 cubic foot capacity would be required.

The Colonial Office, emphasizing the desirability of having at least one colony in German hands at the peace conference, endorsed the project. Strasser also concurred: "Completion of the operation will not only provide immediate assistance for the brave Protectorate troops, but will be an event which will once more enthuse the German people and arouse admiration throughout the world."

OPPOSITE:
*The elevator man's post on the port side of the control car of L 59. Shown are the elevator wheel, inclinometer, altimeter and above, pulls for gas valves and water-ballast controls. (Luftschiffbau Zeppelin)*

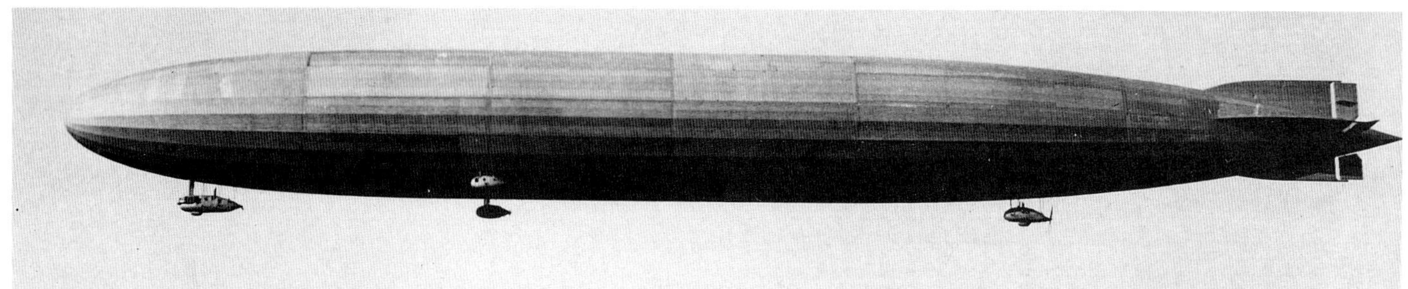

*Two views of the L 57 at Friedrichshafen. Its first flight was September 26, 1917. Photos of the L 57 are sometimes confused with the L 59, however the two can be differentiated by the square-cut Staaken rudders on L 59. L 57 was destroyed by high winds at Jüterbog on October 8, 1917, and burned with all of its valuable cargo. (Luftschiffbau Zeppelin)*

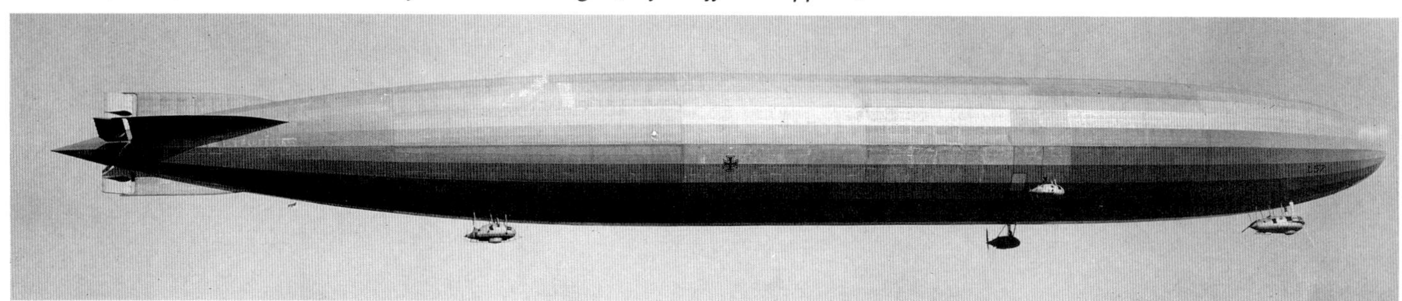

Even before reporting the plan officially to the Naval Staff, or seeking the consent of the Kaiser, the Admiralty ordered a special ship built and designated her commander. To save time, *L 57*, a series ship of the *L 53* class building at Friedrichshafen, was ordered to be lengthened by two 15-meter gas cells. Since the Zeppelin would not be able to return to Germany, one of the less-experienced officers, *Kapitänleutnant* Ludwig Bockholt, was chosen to command her.

Not until September 19 was the plan, code-named "China Matter," forwarded to the Chief of the Naval Staff, Admiral von Holtzendorff. The Kaiser's consent was necessary, and if it could be obtained by September 27, wrote von Capelle, the flight could be male in the new-moon period from October 12 to 20. A conference at the Admiralty on September 25 was mostly concerned with the Army and its possible attempts to influence the Kaiser against the project. "The Admiralty and the Colonial Office both fear that because of Colonel Thomsen's dislike of airships, the matter will be left undecided." In fact, the formidable Thomsen, Chief of the Army's Field Aviation, was in a mellow mood on October 4, when the scheme was presented to the Kaiser. Thomsen promised to support the plan unconditionally and would himself report the results to *General* Ludendorff. The Imperial consent was readily given, and on October 6 the Naval Staff notified the Governor of East Africa by radio that the airship would arrive some time after the middle of the month.

Meanwhile, on September 26, *L 57* had made her first flight. 743 feet long and with 2,418,700 cubic feet of hydrogen, she was the biggest airship built up to that time and had nearly the capacity of the transatlantic *Los Angeles* of 1924. Bockholt found her underpowered and difficult to handle. On long-distance flights she could fly up to 5,500 pounds heavy at an angle of 6 degrees with four engines making full power, with a marked loss of speed and almost complete loss of rudder control. "From my experience," wrote Bockholt, "the type should not be flown continuously at more than 3 degrees."

After two trial flights, *L 57* came to Jüterbog, and by noon of October 7, 1917, had completed loading the special cargo, including 85 cases of precious medical supplies. Because of fuel shortage the big Zeppelin had made no full-speed trials, so Bockholt chose the evening of the 7th to bring *L 57* out of the shed for this purpose. A low-pressure area was approaching rapidly and there was a stiff south-west wind at higher altitudes, but it had been calm at 4 p.m. and Bockholt convinced himself that he could make a 2-hour flight in the vicinity of the base, and house his ship again before the storm broke. At 5:10 p.m. he ordered *L 57* walked out. With the stern barely out of the hangar, a gust struck

*Wreck of L 57 after damage and fire at Jüterbog on October 8, 1917. (Moch)*

broadside, the inexperienced ground crew cast off the after trolley tackles, and the airship had to be run out as fast as possible lest she break her back across the shed door in swinging to the wind. In unseemly haste *L 57* took off, her commander hoping that the wind would drop while in the air. Instead, radio messages advised that it was blowing harder and the barometer falling fast. Bockholt decided to land and wait until the wind backed parallel to the shed axis. Once on the field, he called for 300 Army troops to reinforce the 400-man ground crew. For the moment there was no hope of bringing *L 57* into the shed in a stiff cross wind. Bockholt then resolved to take off again, ride out the storm in the air, and if necessary, go east to the Army shed at Kovno or all the way to Jamboli. But he delayed for food and foul-weather clothing to be loaded aboard, and this proved fatal. The storm was blowing up ever more fiercely, and at 11:50 p.m. a squall picked up the ship, slammed her hard on the ground, and broke most of the struts of the control car. The rudder and elevator controls, the ballast wires and engine telegraphs were useless, and there was no hope of taking off again. At 12:40 a.m. the wind dropped and Bockholt tried to bring the damaged *L 57* into the hangar. Just in front of the shed door, the ship floated up to 60 feet, and the eddies on the lee side sucked her into the entrance, crushing the nose. Dragging the landing party with her, she blew across the field. To keep her from driving away in the storm, Bockholt valved gas and had men with rifles shoot holes in the tops of the cells. Suddenly the rear gondola collapsed, the 743-foot hull pivoted on the starboard midships gondola, swinging broadside to the wind, and the bow and stern sections broke, cocking up into the air. Away went the derelict, across the field and into the fence. Sparks flickered across the surface of the gas cells, and there was a burst of flame. At 2 a.m. there was a great explosion of hydrogen, and the fire, fed by petrol and ammunition, burned until dawn. The valuable special cargo was a total loss.

The Admiralty sponsors of the enterprise met less than 48 hours later, and resolved to continue the project, ordering that *L 59*, then building at Staaken, be lengthened in the same manner as *L 57*. Bockholt accepted the blame for having ordered the last flight of *L 57* in disregard of the weather situation. Though Strasser did not want him court-martialled, he did wish to replace him with *Kapitänleutnant* Ehrlich, already assigned to command *L 59*. The Admiralty and the Naval Staff defended Bockholt, and Strasser was overruled. But Bockholt's errors of judgment delayed the enterprise by a month-long enough to render the whole undertaking futile.

On October 25, sixteen days after her reconstruction was ordered, *L 59* was completed and made her first flight. Hastily she was loaded with 15 tons of cargo.[1] On October 30, Bockholt received "by command of the All Highest" his orders to proceed to Jamboli, and thence to East Africa. After landing there, he and his crew were to join the ground forces. To avoid enemy air fields, he was to proceed to the African coast via the Aegean, or alternatively, over the Turkish mountains to Kos. On approaching the East African protectorate he would endeavor to make radio contact with the troop

---

[1] *L 59*'s cargo was itemized as follows (J. Goebel u. Walter Förster, *Afrika zu Unseren Füssen* (Leipzig: Verlag von K.F. Koehler, 1925), p. 50):

In pounds
311,000 rounds of ammunition: 16,950
230 machine-gun belts with 57,500 cartridges in the belts: 3,955
54 machine-gun ammunition boxes with 13,500 cartridges: 972
30 machine guns: 1,125
4 infantry rifles (for the crew in case of forced landing): 530
9 spare machine-gun barrels: 377
61 sacks of bandages and medicines: 5,790
3 sacks of sewing materials: 265
Mail: 55
Binoculars: 62
Spare rifle-bolts: 110
Bush knives and sheaths: 168
Spare radio parts: 73

Total: 30,332

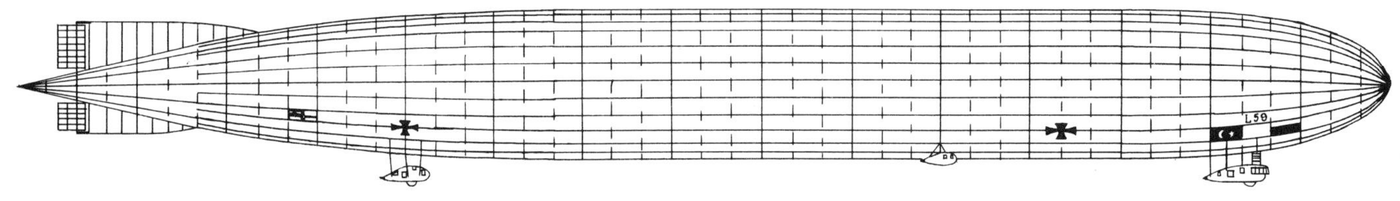


**L 59**

| | | | |
|---|---|---|---|
| Gas capacity | 2,419,400 ft.³ | Ceiling | 26,900 ft. |
| Length | 743.1 ft. | Full speed endurance | 10,000 miles |
| Diameter | 78.4 ft. | | |
| Useful lift | 115,000 lbs. | **On the Africa Flight** | |
| Gas cells | 16 | Cargo | 30,332 lbs. |
| Crew | 22 | Fuel | 48,000 lbs. |
| Engines | 5 Maybach HSLu, of 240 h.p. | Oil | 3365 lbs. |
| Propellers | 4 Jaray L.Z. | Ballast | 20,200 lbs. |
| Maximum speed | 64 mph | Crew and supplies | 5975 lbs. |

headquarters, supposed to be southeast of Mahenge, and otherwise was to land north-east of Liwale.

With these sketchy directions, Bockholt on the morning of November 3, 1917, departed from Staaken for Jamboli. *L 59* spent the night in the air, and early next morning ascended to 5,200 feet to clear the Balkan mountains. At noon on November 4 she dropped her landing lines on the Jamboli field, completing in 28 hours a journey which in those days took the Balkan Express three days to perform.

Bockholt made two abortive attempts to fly to Africa. On November 13, rising into an inversion, he had to drop so much ballast to avoid hitting the hangar that there was no possibility of going on. Three days later he was half-way across Asia Minor, following the railroad from Panderma to Smyrna, when he encountered a thunderstorm. The 15,400 pounds of water aboard was not enough, a ton of cargo was jettisoned also, and being unable to continue without ballast, Bockholt turned back. After a bumpy flight home, *L 59* landed at Jamboli after 32 hours in the air. Bockholt blamed both fail-

*L 59 being walked out of her shed at Staaken. (Luftschiffbau Zeppelin)*

*L 59 at Jamboli being walked out. Note the Navy flag painted on stern to port. (Moch)*

*L 59 from an unusual angle showing the forward car. Note man on roof. (Moch)*

ures on insufficient ballast, and undoubtedly he was right, considering the difficulties of flying the clumsy and low-powered *L 59* dynamically.

For the men in East Africa, the sands were running out, and every day counted. Since early July the German forces had been under heavy attack, gradually falling back. The final debacle occurred at the end of November, when the Germans in the interior surrendered, while the bulk of the forces led by von Lettow personally were defeated and captured north of the Ruvuma River. The doughty general, with a few hundred followers, made his way across the river to Mozambique, and on November 25 and 26 captured from the Portuguese[2] supplies more than equal to those carried by *L 59*. Von Lettow-Vorbeck himself doubted that *L 59* could have found him at this time, and believed that the flight would have had to be made a month earlier to fulfill its purpose. This was the exact measure of the delay caused by the loss of *L 57*. Furthermore, enemy intelligence, despite most stringent secrecy, was fully aware of *L 59*'s mission. British forces in East Africa had been advised that a Zeppelin might arrive about November 20, and planes were standing by to attack her.

As early as October 15, after the decision to continue the operation with *L 59*, the Naval Staff had noted, "the actual execution of the operation will

2 Germany had declared war against Portugal on March 6, 1916.

naturally depend on information coming in from the 'China Area,' where a certain deterioration of the situation seems to have taken place according to recent information." British reports of the capture of the Makonde Highlands, in the final drive against von Lettow-Vorbeck, reached the German Colonial Office on November 19. In forwarding these to the Naval Staff, the Colonial Office commented that reports such as these had often been found exaggerated. German resistance appeared to be fairly stiff, and the British had not yet overrun the Makonde Highlands. "Thus no real change has occurred in the military situation."

Meanwhile in Jamboli on November 20, the weather service reported a polar air mass coming down from the north. The forecast was generally favorable. Bockholt would have clear weather and tail winds at least to the African coast, though he might expect vertical convection currents, cumulus clouds, and even thunderstorms over the warm Mediterranean. This time there would be enough ballast – 20,200 pounds, together with 47,800 pounds of petrol, the cargo amounting to 35,800 pounds, and Dr. Zupitza, on board as liaison officer, and the crew of 21.

On the morning of November 21 the Bulgarian ground party walked *L 59* out on to the landing ground. It was cloudy, the temperature was exactly freezing, with a north wind, Force 2. At 8:30 a.m. came the cry, "Up ship!" and *L 59* was off on her long journey. During the morning, aided by the tail wind, *L 59* made good time southward. At 9:45 she crossed Adrianople in European Turkey, and then steered for the Sea of Marmora. On its southern shore, at Panderma, she reached Asia Minor and made for Smyrna along the railroad. After sunset *L 59* passed east of Smyrna, followed the railroad south by moonlight, and at 7:40 p.m. left the Turkish coast on a course for Lipsos Strait. By 10:15 p.m., *L 59* was off the eastern tip of Crete, and found black clouds in her path. Thunder roared, and flashes of lightning close aboard lit up faces in the gondolas brighter than day. Soon came the familiar report from the top lookout, "The ship is burning!" It was St. Elmo's Fire, an old story to Bockholt and his crew. Presently *L 59* was out in clear air, with the cloud banks astern, the stars shining overhead, and a faint glow to the south indicating the North African coastline. But for several hours in the storm the antenna had been wound in, and Bockholt had been cut off from the outside world.

The November 21 take-off had been too late. All day on the 20th the Colonial Office in Berlin had been studying enemy claims of victory over von Lettow-Vorbeck. On the morning of the 21st came further news of British advances in the Makonde Highlands, and three and a half hours after Bockholt's take-off, the Colonial Office advised the Naval Staff that it could no longer be responsible for the operation. Von Holtzendorff notified the Kaiser at once that the flight was being abandoned, and Jamboli was directed to recall the airship. In a few hours came the reply, "*L 59* can no longer be reached from here, request she be recalled through Nauen." Repeatedly the powerful overseas radio station at Nauen, near Berlin, called up the airship on the night November 21, but in vain. During the thunderstorm south Crete she could not receive messages.

So Bockholt went on in ignorance of the recall, and at 5:15 a.m. reached the continent of Africa at Ras Bulair, near Mersa Matruh. Below stretched the grey, monotonous wastes of the Libyan Desert, so appalling in their emptiness that *L 59*'s crew felt they had been transported to the surface of the moon. The sun blazed down from a cloudless sky, heating the gas, and quantities blew off through the automatic valves. Thoroughly dried out and very light from consumption of fuel, *L 59*, to prevent further loss of gas, flew during the day nose down with an excess load of 1,650 pounds aft to counteract her extreme nose-heaviness in this attitude. Heat bumps rising from the baking sands, more violent than any Bockholt's crew had ever experienced, tossed the ship about. Some of them, veteran seamen of many years' service, were ashamed to find themselves airsick.

Shortly after noon the crew turned out to stare at the green palms of Farafrah Oasis. Then more desert. Some of the men were complaining of headache, from gazing too long at the bright reflections off the sand. Soon after 3 p.m., *L 59* crossed Dakhla Oasis. Bockholt's success in hitting these pin-points in the trackless desert demonstrated the accuracy

IMPORTANT FLIGHTS OF *L 59*

| *Des-cription* | *Flight No.* | *Take-off* | *Landing* | *Time in air* | *Dis-tance (miles)* | *Av. speed (m.p.h.)* | *Max. alt. (feet)* | *Temp. (°F.)* | *Crew* | *Fuel (lb.) loaded/used* | *Oil (lb.) loaded/used* | *Ballast loaded (lb.)* | *Cargo/ Bombs (lb.)* | *Gas used (cubic feet)* |
|---|---|---|---|---|---|---|---|---|---|---|---|---|---|---|
| Trans-fer flight | 2 | Staaken Nov. 3, 1917 7.00 a.m. | Jamboli Nov. 4, 1917 12.30 p.m. | 28h. 30m. | 1,188 | 41·6 | 5,250 | | | | | | | |
| 1st Africa att'pt | 3 | Jamboli Nov. 13, 1917 | Jamboli Nov. 13, 1917 | 2h. 0m. | | | | | | | | | | |
| 2nd Africa att'pt | 4 | Jamboli Nov. 16, 1917 8.08 a.m. | Jamboli Nov. 17, 1917 4.08 p.m. | 32h. 0m. | 892 | 27·5 | 7,200 | | | | | 15,400 | Cargo 30,200 | |
| Africa flight | 5 | Jamboli Nov. 21, 1917 8.30 a.m. | Jamboli Nov. 25, 1917 7.40 a.m. | 95h. 5m. | 4,199·4 | 44·2 | 9,850 | | 22 | 47,800/25,050 | 3,360/ 1,107 | 20,200 | Cargo 35,800 | 930,000 |
| Trans-fer flight | 14 | F'hafen Feb. 20, 1918 9.00 a.m. | Jamboli Feb. 21, 1918 8.25 a.m. | 23h. 25m. | | | | | | | | | | |
| Naples raid att'pt | 15 | Jamboli Mar. 3, 1918 6.25 a.m. | Jamboli Mar. 4, 1918 6.07 p.m. | 17h. 42m. | | | | | | | | | | |
| Naples raid | 16 | Jamboli Mar. 10, 1918 6.30 a.m. | Jamboli Mar. 11, 1918 7.42 p.m. | 37h. 12m. | 1,608 | 43·2 | 15,750 | −4·0 | 23 | 21,150/12,300 | 1,790/794 | 48,300 | Bombs 14,100 | 1,148,000 |
| Nile Delta raid | 17 | Jamboli Mar. 20, 1918 3.53 a.m. | Jamboli Mar. 22, 1918 7.16 a.m. | 51h. 23m. | 2,391 | 48·5 | 16,400 | | | | | | Bombs 14,100 | |
| Malta raid att'pt | 18 | Jamboli Apl. 7, 1918 | | | | | | | 22 | | | | | |

of his navigation, which, over sea and land, both day and night, was celestial as far as possible. The ship's shadow, being of known length, also yielded both ground speed and drift, by sunlight or moonlight, with the help of a simple table.

At 4:20 p.m. the reduction gear housing of the forward engine cracked. Emergency repairs were made, but the motor was not used again. Since it drove the radio generator, *L 59* could no longer send messages, though she could still receive them. The other four engines lasted till the end of the flight. For rest and maintenance, each engine was shut down one or two hours in every eight.

The character of the country was gradually changing from formless sand to rugged, towering rock. A cloud of rose-colored flamingoes passed just before sunset, indicating that the Nile was not far away. At 9:45 p.m., just after dark, *L 59* reached the great river at Wadi Halfa, and continued south at a distance from its course.

Bockholt, expecting the ship to be heavy during the night because of the loss of gas during the heat of the day, had dropped 4,400 pounds of ballast and believed he could carry the rest of the load dynamically, flying 4 degrees nose up with four engines. The problem was further complicated by *L 59* entering the zone of the north-east monsoon. The air in the Nile Valley was humid and oppressive, the temperature at flight altitude was 68 degrees F. at 10:30 p.m., and rose to 77 degrees at 3 a.m. Super-cooling of 9 degrees F. contracted the gas and further diminished the lift. Bockholt was expecting trouble, and at 3 a.m. it came. Her laboring engines no longer able to hold her up dynamically in the warm air, *L 59* stalled and dropped from 3,100 to 1,300 feet, losing the big antenna and almost crashing into a mountain-peak. The engines were stopped and the ship relieved of 6,200 pounds of ballast and ammunition. Then at last she rose. "To fly steadily at 4 degrees heavy at night can easily be catastrophic with sudden temperature changes in the Sudan, as at Jebel Ain," wrote Bockholt later, "particularly if engines fail from overheating with warm outside temperatures. . . . Ship should have 3,000 kg. (6,600 pounds) or 4 per cent of her lift for each night to take care of cooling effect."

Meanwhile the recall had finally been taken in from Nauen. At 12:45 a.m. on November 23, *L 59*'s War Diary records, "Break off operation, return.

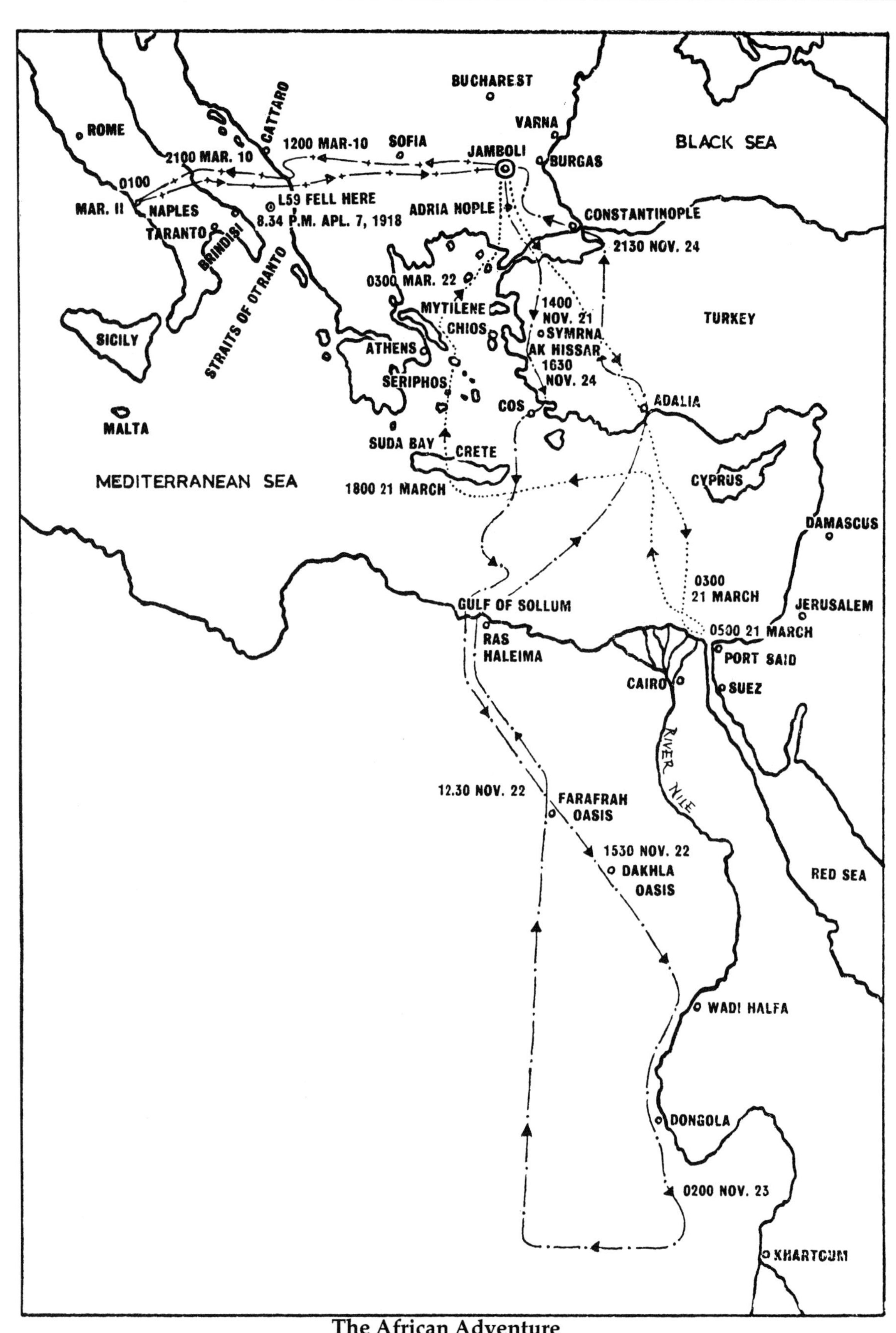

The African Adventure

*L 59 "down under" at Jamboli. Note the ground crew handling frame ahead of the after car. L 59 was unable to find the German troops in the jungles of German East Africa. It then returned to Jamboli and hence home where it was then reconstructed as a bomber. L 59 blew up over the Straits of Otranto on a mission to bomb Malta. All twenty-three crewmen perished. (Luftschiffbau Zeppelin)*

Enemy has seized greater part of Makonde Highlands, already holds Kitangari, Portuguese are attacking remainder of Protectorate forces from south." One of the many legends of the Naval Airship Division is that the British robbed Bockholt of success by sending a false recall message in captured German code. At 2:30 a.m. *L 59* reversed course, being then about 125 miles due west of Khartoum.

The return to Jamboli was an anticlimax, and Bockholt admits that "the realization of being on the verge of fulfilling the mission after overcoming all difficulties made it very difficult to turn back, and affected morale." Despite ancient and indigestible self-heating canned food and a thirst-provoking diet of preserved ham, preserved sausage, bread and butter; despite the hammocks slung too low above the noisily flapping outer cover along the keel; despite a temperature of 82 degrees in the keel over the desert by day, and of 14 above zero F. at night above the mountains of Asia Minor – the crew's morale had been sustained by the imminent success of their mission. There was now a reaction to nervous tension, to say the least. Some of the men became feverish, very fatigued and suffered from insomnia, though they still stood their watches of 4 hours on and 4 hours off.

At 3:30 a.m. on November 24, *L 59* left the African continent at Sollum. Once again there were thunderstorms over the Mediterranean. These were left behind at dawn, and the Zeppelin continued at 10,000 feet on a north-east course for the Gulf of Adalia on the south coast of Turkey. At 2 p.m., *L 59* reached Cape Chelonia on the western edge of the Gulf.

The night flight over Asia Minor brought a repetition of the near-catastrophe in the Sudan, and for the same reason – insufficient ballast released to compensate for evening cooling. Shortly after dark, *L 59* was flying "heavy" 1,300 feet above the mountains north of Ushak, nose up at an angle of 5 to 6 degrees with four engines running at full power to carry the load dynamically. Suddenly the gusty mountain wind caused her to drop precipitately, and 6,600 pounds of ballast had to be discharged at once. At 4:30 a.m. the ship was over Jamboli, but not until 7:40 a.m. on November 25 did she settle into the hands of the holding crew. The twenty-two adventurers climbed stiffly down. They were cold, they were tired, some were feverish, and all of them staggered as if they were still in the heaving gondolas of the airship. But despite the failure of their mission, there was pride in what they had achieved. They had been in the air for 95 hours – nearly four days – and had covered 4,200 miles through the greatest extremes of climate ever experienced by an airship. The 22,750 pounds of fuel remaining on board could have driven the ship for 64 hours more.

Nobody had expected *L 59* to return, and now there was the question of what to do with her. Strasser, the Naval Staff, Bockholt himself, and ultimately the Kaiser, were all involved in a debate that went on for weeks. Both Strasser and the Naval Staff were opposed to another African flight; the British had been warned by *L 59*'s appearance near Khartoum, and in the present situation in East Africa, the Zeppelin would probably fall into the hands of the enemy. The Kaiser himself is said to have sponsored a plan for *L 59* to fly 2,300 miles to Yemen in Arabia with arms and gold for the beleaguered Turkish Army of Enver Pasha. The Naval Staff on November 29 proposed that she make some mine-search flights off Constantinople, the approaches to which had been blocked by the Russians. Strasser objected to both operations: the distance to Yemen was too great and he was not certain that *L 59* could return. In the tropical heat, with a limited amount of landing ballast, she might fall hard and be damaged beyond repair. As for mine-flights from Jamboli, Strasser rightly insisted that the base could not handle and service so large a ship for frequent missions: the gas supply was inadequate, there were few trained men in the ground troop, the ship was too big for safe handling in and out of the shed and would inevitably be damaged, and repairs would be difficult and prolonged. Strasser proposed that *L 59* should return to the North Sea to be rebuilt with 7 engines, and remain as a high-speed scouting ship. On November 30 the Naval Staff decided to bring her home pending a decision as to her future use.

Bockholt himself seems to have been responsible for the plan finally adopted – that *L 59*, after reconstruction as a bomb carrier, should return to Jamboli to make long-distance raids of several days' duration in the Mediterranean. His letter of December 4 by-passed the Leader of Airships and went direct to the Naval Staff, adding to Strasser's dislike of his subordinate. Among possible targets, wrote Bockholt, were Valona, Brindisi, Naples and Malta to the west; Tripoli to the south-west; Alexandria, Cairo, Port Said, Suez and Assuan to the south, and a large British ammunition dump at Baghdad to the south-east. Bockholt expected important military results from attacking these places, as (1) the enemy would be forced to erect defenses at each place, taking the equipment from the Western Front, (2) enemy trade would be disturbed, particularly in the harbors of Port Said and Alexandria, (3) it would produce a great political effect on the North African natives, particularly in Cairo and Assuan, (4) it would be a morale stimulant for the Naval Airship Division to attack such distant places beyond the range of any other aircraft from European bases.

Not until December 17 did Strasser receive a copy of this letter, and his comments to the Chief of the Naval Staff two days later found fault with the proposed operation at every point. Bockholt, he argued, had been carried away by his own enthusiasm resulting from the African flight, but "the East African flight was aeronautically a great risk, which could be taken only because of the great importance of the mission. The return of the ship must be attributed to extraordinary circumstances, first of which should be mentioned that the ship found a south wind at altitudes of 2,000 meters (6,500 feet) and over." On long flights, comparatively little ballast could be carried, hence high attack altitudes would be unattainable, yet much ballast would have to be expended because of the expansion and contraction of the gas with high day and low night temperatures. Few raids could be made with only one airship – "experience shows that a ship is as often out of service as ready to fly." Lastly, returning to a favorite theme, *L 59* and 400 men would be tied up in a secondary theatre where prospects of success would be slight. "England would be very pleased to have this airship kept away from her. . . . Airship operations have never been worth while and never will be worth while except in the North Sea in scouting for the Fleet and in raids on England. . . . The airship is and remains a weapon of opportunity which, when suitable opportunities are seized, can render extraordinary service. But as soon as one concludes from such performance that regular results of the same nature can be obtained, one is badly disappointed, which can only damage the prospects of a really useful weapon." Bockholt, he concluded, was "a fine airship commander and skillful officer," but "has not had enough experience of the capabilities of airships."

The Kaiser himself decided on January 5, 1918, against Strasser and in favor of Bockholt. But the outcome proved Strasser right. After her return to Jamboli on February 21, 1918, *L 59* made only one raid in the space of six and a half weeks. After one abortive attempt, she attacked Naples on the night of March 10. Flying across the Adriatic from Scutari to Manfredonia, Bockholt attacked from 12,000 feet and claimed to have placed his 14,000 pounds of bombs on the naval base, the gas works, and the Bagnoli steel plant. *L 59*'s total time in the air on this flight was 37 hours and 12 minutes. At the end of a telegram to the Naval Staff protesting about the bad food issued to his crew, Bockholt facetiously added, "If I ever get married I won't go to Naples on my honeymoon." He did not live to do either.

On March 20, Bockholt left Jamboli to attack Port Said, but at 4:40 a.m. on the morning of March 21, fighting a stiff headwind, he had to abandon his attack when he was only 3 miles east of the town due to the approaching dawn. There would be no second chance to bomb Port Said. An attempt that evening to attack the British naval base at Suda Bay in Crete was thwarted when a cloud sheet moved in beneath the airship and cut off all sight of the ground. Most of her bombs were still on board when she landed at Jamboli after a flight of 52 hours and 23 minutes.

*L 59* was out of service for 5 days for a major engine overhaul, and then, on April 7, 1918, she took off from Jamboli for the last time. Bockholt planned to attack the British naval base at Malta, and proceeded across the Balkans to the Straits of Otranto.

That evening a submarine of the German Mediterranean Flotilla, U.B. 53 under *Oberleutnant zur See* Sprenger, was heading south from Cattaro for the Otranto barrage when an airship was seen coming up in her wake. Sprenger, who knew nothing of *L 59*'s mission, at first took her for an Italian craft, but presently felt such doubts that he ordered the guns secured. He and his crew watched in silence as the airship flew by, less than 700 feet high and so close that they could distinguish her gondolas. Ninety minutes later, at 9:30 p.m., Sprenger observed:

> Bearing about 200 degrees, distance from U.B. 53 estimated at 25-30 miles, two points of fire seen in the air, apparently shrapnel bursts. Shortly thereafter a gigantic flame, which lit the entire horizon bright as day for a short time and then slowly fell to the water, where it continued to burn over the horizon for 20 minutes longer. When the fire started several heavy explosions were heard. From all appearances ship was shot at and fell burning. Later appearance of searchlights in direction where she fell made it appear that a search was being made. On passing the approximate spot three hours later nothing was visible. Position about 41 degrees 2 minutes N., 18 degrees 53 minutes E.

Such is the testimony of the only witnesses to *L 59*'s destruction. An oil slick, with some pieces of wood floating in it, and ultimately one of the airship's droppable fuel tanks, were found off Durazzo. When the Italians made no claim to have destroyed her, the Germans concluded that *L 59* had fallen victim to an accident. Since her crew had complained of frequent leaks in the fuel lines, the best German opinion is that the hydrogen was ignited by a petrol fire.

On April 22 the Naval Staff proposed replacing *L 59*, but Strasser successfully objected, pointing out that he had only 11 airships in the North Sea and none could be spared. The Chief of the Naval Staff advised that in view of the enemy's obvious intention of attacking Palestine in the autumn, a Zeppelin might then be sent to Jamboli to raid Port Said and Alexandria, but nothing ever came of this plan.

Bockholt and his crew have been dead for many years, but their pioneering intercontinental journey should not be forgotten. Between the wars *Graf Zeppelin* and *Hindenburg* made many such flights, but it was the experiences of the men of *L 59* that first demonstrated the feasibility of the post-war global airship services.

# CHAPTER XXI

# "ALTITUDE MOTORS" & THE AHLHORN DISASTER

One of the reasons for the loss of five out of eleven Zeppelins in the "Silent Raid" was lack of engine power at high altitudes. The 1917 "height climbers," with cleverly streamlined hulls, light enough to be able to reach 20,000 feet with war loads, were still fitted with a 1915 power plant designed for 1914 conditions – the 240 h.p. Maybach HSLu. At high altitudes this engine lost as much as half its power, due to the diminished oxygen content of the atmosphere, and the speed of the Zeppelins fell from 62 to 45 m.p.h. It was not enough to drive them against the raging gales of the upper air.

This problem had been foreseen, but only now was the answer ready, in the Maybach MB IVa "altitude motor." With oversize cylinders, and compression ratio increased to 6.08 to 1, it could not be run at full throttle until reaching 5,900 feet, and up to this altitude it produced a constant 245 h.p. At 19,700 feet it still delivered 142 h.p., and a later model with aluminium pistons and a compression ratio of 6.7 to 1 produced 162 h.p. at this altitude.

The first of the improved power plants was installed in *L 58*, which arrived in Ahlhorn on November 3, 1917. If Strasser was still depressed by the outcome of the "Silent Raid," *L 58*'s speed trials revived his customary optimism. The new ship not only made 67 m.p.h. at sea level, but at 19,700 feet could still achieve 60 m.p.h. On November 6, Strasser wrote to Scheer urgently requesting that all new ships should have the MB IVa's. "High winds at high altitudes make it nearly impossible for ships with the old motors to carry out missions," he insisted. Apparently the new power plants were being hand-made in small quantities,[1] for Strasser concerned himself with the distribution of the next ten production models which would be completed on December 15, 1917. so impressed was he that he demanded that these ten engines be installed in the forthcoming *L 60* and *L 61*, even if this

[1] Only 110 Maybach MB IVa's were built for airships, though many more were used in German high-altitude reconnaissance airplanes in the last year of the war.

*OPPOSITE:*
*The Ahlhorn explosion. Aerial photograph showing the south sheds, III and IV.*

*L 47 at Ahlhorn, burned in Shed I on January 5, 1918. (Moch)*

meant delaying their completion. On November 26, Admiral Starke at the Admiralty directed that all new construction should have the "altitude motors," and furthermore, the older ships in service with the HSLu were re-engined during early 1918 with the MB IVa.

The failure of the radio direction-finding organization had been in part responsible for the heavy losses in the "Silent Raid," and during the winter of 1917-18 it was drastically modified. Two new sending stations were erected at Tondern and at Cleve, 250 miles to the south-south-west in the Rhineland. These transmitted directional signals on a regular schedule, fifteen minutes before and fifteen minutes after the hour, and an airship could determine her bearing from each station with her own radio receiver and the long trailing antenna, using no special equipment except a stop-watch and great circle charts.[2] No longer could the British track the Zeppelins by their requests for bearings, nor would the "airship special wavelength" be overloaded with their calls. And the new system could still be used by a ship whose transmitter was out of order, as so frequently happened with the numerous engine failures during the "Silent Raid."

On November 17, a day of thick, foggy weather – possibly chosen because it was known that such conditions would prevent airship reconnaissance – the British sent a force into the German Bight for what proved to be the last action of the war between capital ships. In the early morning the battle cruiser *Repulse*, with the 15-inch-gunned *Courageous* and *Glorious* and smaller warships, fell upon the German minesweepers and their covering forces. Four German light cruisers interposed themselves between the heavy British ships and their own

2 The transmitting stations had 16 pairs of antennas pointing towards the 32 points of the compass, and a rotating contact, revolving through 360 degrees once every 32 seconds, transmitted signals in succession from each set of directional wires. The stop-watch aboard the ship had a compass rose on its face, and its hands likewise revolved once every 32 seconds. Punching the stop-watch when a special tone indicated transmission of the signal from the "north" wire of the ground station, the airship's radio operator stopped it when the minimum signal was heard, and the stop-watch hand then indicated the bearing of the station from the ship. Five different readings were taken and averaged.

*L 51 being walked out into the revolving shed at Nordholz. L 51 was destroyed during the Ahlhorn disaster when gasoline flowing on the "Aladin" shed floor ignited near the rear gondola. (Moch)*

small craft, and during the running fight to the east gave better than they received. Presently the British found themselves trading shots with the dreadnoughts Kaiser and Kaiserin – for the Germans for some time had been sending battleships out to support the minesweepers – and when the battle cruisers *Hindenburg* and *Moltke* came up, the British broke off the action.

Routine airship flights for this day had been canceled, but Strasser, on receiving news of the battle, sent up two airships to "scout north-west of Heligoland, seek contact with enemy forces, *L 47* more northerly, *L 41* more westerly." Not surprisingly, both found scouting impossible due to a deep, solid overcast and turned back in the late afternoon without seeing the enemy.

Henceforth battleships were always at sea in support of the German minesweepers, which now operated as far as 180 sea miles north, and 140 sea miles west of the High Seas Fleet base in the Jade. But, as proof of Admiral Scheer's faith in the airship, when the Zeppelins were able to fly patrols, the surface support was reduced by half.

Strasser had lost none of his determination to destroy England and on December 12 dispatched five Zeppelins to "attack middle industrial area, Sheffield, Manchester, Liverpool or north: Tees, Tyne, Firth of Forth, etc." The break in the weather proved illusory, the ships finding north-west winds that freshened to a gale before they left the German Bight. Even the peerless *L 58*, with her new "altitude motors" and Strasser on board, was unable to make headway. At 4:03 p.m. her commander ascertained that the wind at 13,000 feet was blowing from the west-north-west at 45 m.p.h. Towards evening all ships reported the wind veering more to the north, and *L 56* at 7:34 p.m. dramatically messaged, "Stationary near Borkum for 2 hours, turned back since advance impossible." At 8:30 Strasser ordered the airships to return to base.

From December 18 to the 22nd, daily patrols were made over the German Bight, and then, to the end of the year, there were a succession of storms that kept the airships in their sheds. The New Year came in with a gale, and on Saturday, January 5, 1918, the weather was still bad. That morning the commanders of the five ships in Ahlhorn saw to the daily gassing of their craft to 100 per cent fullness, and *Kapitänleutnant* Walter Dose of *L 51*, which lay on the south-west side of Shed I, ordered his men to clean out the floors of the engine gondolas. The crew of *L 47*, which occupied the other side of the shed, found little to do, for their craft had not been in the air since December 22. *Korvettenkapitän* Arnold Schütze of *L 58* met his executive officer, quartermaster and machinist in Shed II to discuss preparations for the next raiding period. The crew and maintenance group had roll-call and were dismissed before noon. Not much was happening in Shed III, where *L 46* had lain idle since December 21. Only in Shed IV, which housed *SL 20*, was there any activity. The big Schütte-Lanz had suffered several breaks in Ring 4 in the stern in a trial flight on December 27, and a gang of workmen from the factory were still repairing the damage.

It was an overcast, sunless winter day. At noon Schütze trudged a quarter mile through the slushy snow to the officers' mess on the edge of the field, where he ate with Strasser and his brother officers. It was a simple meal, and the conversation centered on the war. After dinner, Schütze returned to his quarters for a nap, and at about 5 o'clock went out for a walk. Happening to see Strasser in the operations office, he dropped in to discuss a few problems. The two men spoke briefly, and paused to look out of the windows at the hangars, whose angular outlines were gradually softening in the early winter dusk.

Suddenly, from Shed I, a broad orange flame shot up into the darkening sky. Schütze did not have time to say, "What is that?" before his own shed, 200 feet beyond, took fire. A few seconds later came the blast of two mighty explosions. Without a word the two officers dashed through the door and out on to the field. All hell let loose as Sheds III and IV, half a mile from the first pair, flew into the air with earth-shaking detonations. Within a minute the four hangars and five ships of the mighty Ahlhorn base had been reduced to flaming, tangled junk.

"Air raid!" was the thought that flashed through the minds of the airshipmen and officers tumbling out of their barracks. But as the explosions died

*PREVIOUS: An unusual view from the top of the "Alrun" shed at Ahlhorn, showing the "Front" ships L 47 (left) and L 46. Hydrogen filling hoses are on the floor 115 feet below. Both ships were lost in the Ahlhorn disaster. (Moch)*

away with no answering echo from aircraft engines, they hastened to fling a cordon about the field to catch possible saboteurs. Their next move was to bring what aid they could to the men known to have been in the sheds.

Before his headquarters stood Strasser, looking with black sorrow and anguish on the wreckage of his years of work. He roused himself as *Oberleutnant zur See* Heinrich Bassenge of the ground troop came up to report that the teletype was out of order, the emergency telephone current would last only an hour, the radio receiver would take some minutes to repair, and the transmitter could not be used for lack of current. "Thanks," he answered dryly. "Get me a telephone connection at once with the Fleet Command in Wilhelmshaven. Also request medical assistance from Oldenburg as soon as possible, and reserve hospital space for many wounded. Then go at once to the sheds and report on conditions there!"[3]

Bassenge rode off on his bicycle. At Shed II he had to dismount, for one of the giant doors had fallen flat across the road. Of the hangar structure only the framework remained. The explosion had blown off the roof like paper, and strewn the sidewall material over the landscape. Inside, the petrol tanks of *L 58* were keeping up a hot fire, while the chill wind whistled eerily through the gaunt steel structure.

Shed I, the first to take fire, had not been so badly damaged. The side walls and doors were intact, though the roof was gone. Bassenge met the

3 *Oberleutnant zur See* Heinrich Bassenge, "Die Zerstürung des Luftschiffhafens Ahlhorn," Strahlmann, p. 222.

*January 5, 1918, the Ahlhorn explosion. Shown are sheds I and II in the background, and sheds III and IV in the foreground. Repair work was done on sheds I and II only. (Moch)*

*Various views of the Ahlhorn disaster, January 5, 1918. (all - Moch)*

executive officer of *L 47* and received the first information as to how the fire started: "Over *L 51*'s rear gondola the hull suddenly started to burn. In a moment the whole ship was alight and set fire to *L 47* lying beside her."[4] Fortunately there were no dead here. Returning to Shed II, Bassenge learned that the ship's sentry was missing. The guard outside could only say, "I saw the glow of fire within, and as I opened the door quickly I saw the ship rolling to and fro, and then she suddenly exploded!"[5]

Bassenge rode on half a mile to Sheds III and IV. Three hundred feet from his goal he had to abandon his bicycle. The explosion here had been far more violent, and of Shed III only the massive north-west door remained standing. Stone slabs and steel beams were piled up round about and scattered far down the road. The crew of *L 46* were working feverishly amid the burning wreckage, looking for the ship's sentry and missing members of the maintenance group. Momentarily they had to draw back as several fuel tanks blew up. Nearby their commander lay on a door, his leg broken by a falling beam.

Of Shed IV, there remained only four acres of twisted and collapsed steel girders. The wooden-built Schütte-Lanz had been almost entirely consumed, and with her had gone four of the six civilian workmen engaged in repairing her. The survivors, who were in the top of the shed when *SL 20* caught fire, escaped with severe burns.

How had the fire started? All the stories clearly showed that it began in the vicinity of the after gondola of *L 51*, and since the explosion there was not severe, most of the people in Shed I appeared at the Court of Inquiry. Both men working at the time in *L 51*'s rear gondola told their stories, but without shedding much light on what had happened. Seaman Lamotte related:

4 Ibid, p. 223.

5 Ibid., p. 224.

*Ahlhorn sheds V and VI being erected. Shed at right is the "Alma" shed which was completed on April 17, 1918. The "Alarich" shed at left was completed on July 18, 1918.*

We had been ordered to clean out *L 51*'s gondolas. We had several days for this work. On Saturday at 1:30 p.m. we started work again and turned on both our cable lamps. The cable led from the shed wall over the floor and through the gondola window facing the wall. The lights burned properly without any trouble. Towards the end we were cleaning up the stains left by leaks from the radiators. We don't use petrol in our work. We didn't smoke either, or use fire. From the way my stomach felt and from the darkness it must have been about 5 o'clock, when I heard an explosion in the shed. It was a noise like a motor backfiring. Since the noise seemed to be coming from the shed, I went to the gondola window looking towards *L 47* and looked into the shed, without leaning out of the window. I saw the glow of fire in the shed, without being able to say where the glow came from. Anyhow I can't say for sure that the glow came from under *L 51*'s gondola. Right away, after calling to my comrade that "It's high time we got out of this gondola!" I jumped out of the gondola window. Here I burned my head and both hands. I had to jump through the fire coming up from below. At this time both cable lamps were burning without disturbance. For a moment I was knocked out, but leaped up again and ran under *L 47* to the side door. There was no fire near *L 47*. But I saw, as I looked back a moment to discover if the fire under *L 51* could be put out, that the middle of the gondola was burning, particularly from below. My lamp cable led out of the forward window on the port side, Bleikamp's led through the other window on the port side of the gondola, about the middle of the gondola. As I left the shed door several small pieces of the roof fell on my head. When I was about ten meters away from the shed the explosion came.

All the testimony indicated that the conflagration began underneath, not inside, the after gondola of *L 51*, and that probably it started as a petrol fire. As an accident, it was difficult to explain, though the Court theorized:

> There is one possibility: that an asbestos slab or piece of iron in the roof of Shed I might have come loose and fallen through the ship, striking and destroying one of the fuel tanks in the gangway just ahead of the after gondola. Although the roof of Shed I was in good condition, this assumption is reasonable since the shed during the winter had been through heavy storms, which might have damaged it. This assumption explains the dull explosion before the start of the fire. The piece falling through the ship could have broken bracing wires, which would certainly have struck sparks. These sparks would have set fire to the outpouring fuel and would have started the fire.

It is difficult to understand how the fire spread so rapidly to the other ships, and particularly why they exploded with such violence. The situation was incredible to Strasser, who had always held that such a catastrophe would be limited to the one or two ships in the shed in which the fire started. Now, he admitted pessimistically in his report to Scheer, "I cannot suggest any way to prevent such occurrences in the future." He was certainly right in theorizing that the burning *L 51* would generate heat and expand the hydrogen in *L 47*, causing its discharge through the automatic valves, and an explosion would follow. In Shed II, he conjectured, the blast wave would first compress and then expand the cells of *L 58*, tearing them in many places. Numerous pieces of the roof might fall through the ship, an explosive mixture would form, and could be ignited by falling embers from Shed I. The blast would increase in violence in each succeeding shed; progressively greater cell damage would increase the accumulation of explosive hydrogen in the hangars, and therefore the final detonation in Shed IV was the most destructive of all.

Like many airship accidents, the Ahlhorn catastrophe is difficult to explain in spite of the large number of competent witnesses. Although no infernal machine was found in the wreckage of Shed I, the suspicion of sabotage still lurks in the minds of former airshipmen with whom the author has discussed the Ahlhorn disaster. They point out that the fire started in the only shed containing two ships, and at the commencement of an attack period. They refer to the widespread disaffection among the ground troop, many of whom in the last year of the war had embraced the defeatist propaganda of the Independent Social Democrats. They speak of the former petty officer who in 1928 "confessed" he had set the fire for a hundred thousand pounds of "Judas money", but the officers at least dismiss this man as a drunkard and a liar. Some believe that the two men in the after gondola started the conflagration by using petrol as a cleaning agent, contrary to stringent orders, instead of non-inflammable "Benzinoform."

*Kapitänleutnant* Dose, commander of *L 51*, admitted to the author almost 40 years later:

> The matter is still a puzzle to me, and I cannot feel completely certain about it. Perhaps the light cable leading into the gondola was defective – there was a desperate shortage of rubber in Germany at that time. Personally, I have been inclined to believe that the men in the after gondola were wearing shoes with nails against orders, which struck sparks and ignited the petrol fumes always present in the car. I am convinced that the shed roof was too strongly built for pieces to fall through the ship, and even so, this could hardly have started a fire. I wish to state emphatically that it could not have been sabotage. I had absolute confidence both in my flight crew and maintenance group, and they all went with me to *L 65*, including the two men who were in the after gondola when the fire started.

The disaster cost the Naval Airship Division 10 dead, 30 badly injured, and 104 slightly injured. In addition, 4 civilian workmen were killed while repairing *SL 20*. Among the seriously injured was *Kapitänleutnant* Hollender, commanding *L 46*,

*L 58 at Ahlhorn. It was the first Zeppelin to use the Maybach MbIVa engine (see drawing below). (Moch)*

whose leg was broken. He spent months in hospital, and never flew again. Strasser is said never to have recovered from this blow, though in a private letter he wrote: "It was terrible to see the proud Ahlhorn base collapse in wreckage before my eyes in the space of a minute. But we can overcome it. We have sheds and ships to fill the gap, and the determination is there to triumph over all difficulties with head held high."[6]

[6] Letter, Peter Strasser to Hertha Mathy, Nordholz, January 19, 1918.

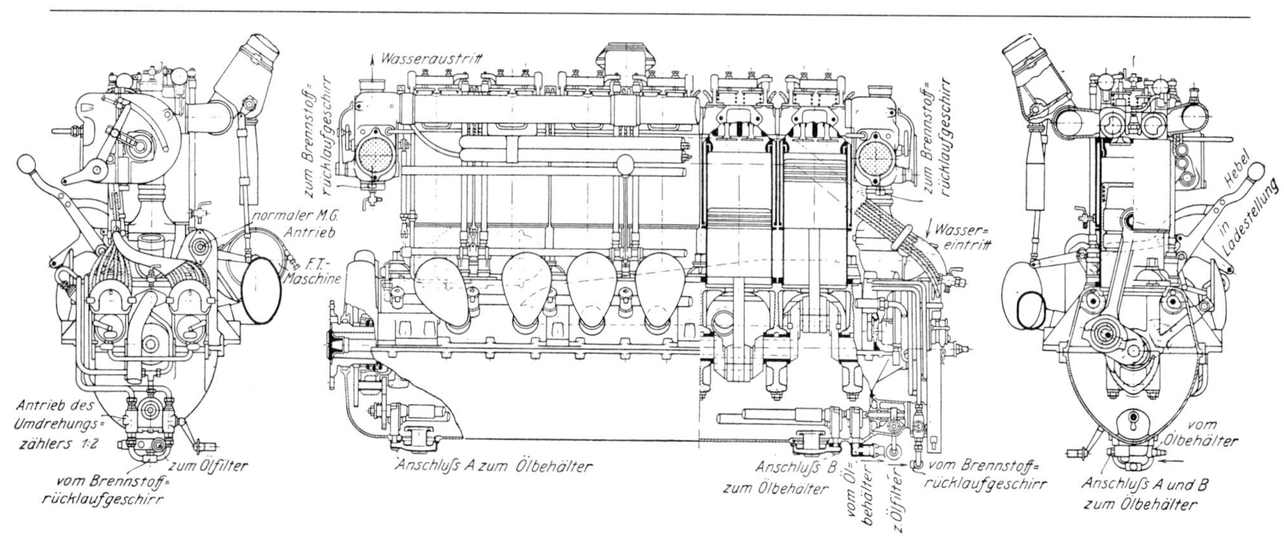


Abb. 141 bis 143. MBIVa-Motor von 245 PS Leistung

# CHAPTER XXII

# THE FIRST SUCCESSFUL CARRIER STRIKE IN HISTORY

The first scouting flight in the month of January, 1918, was on the 29th, and next month there was only one "war flight," an abortive attempt by *L 53* on February 20 to reconnoiter the Skagerrak and Kattegat. On the afternoon of March 12, five of the newest Zeppelins set out for England – including *L 63*, delivered to Nordholz only two days before – with Strasser in the lead in *L 62*. The target was the Midlands industrial region. It was clear over the German Bight, but as they neared England, the airships found a solid overcast forming below their altitude of 16,000 to 18,000 feet. Inability to determine their position visually, together with errors in the radio bearings, led the commanders to believe they were farther west than they were. Though *L 61* claimed to have attacked "a heavily fortified place on the Humber," none of her bombs were traced on land. *L 62* claimed an attack on Leeds, but her bombs fell in fields 35 miles to the east; *L 63* thought she attacked Leeds and Bradford, while 6 of her explosive bombs damaged houses in Hull. *L 54* claimed an attack on Grimsby. Von Buttlar's report states that the ship came under heavy fire, the machinists in the port gondola were shaken up by a shell exploding close aboard, and immediately afterwards Cell 9 amidships was found to be emptying fast. All ballast was dropped, followed by three tanks of fuel. On the way home the warrant machinist, making his rounds of the engine cars, found the two machinists' mates in the starboard gondola unconscious from carbon monoxide poisoning. They were quickly revived with liquid air. *L 54*'s bombs had actually fallen among trawlers in the North Sea, some of which had fired at her with their small anti-aircraft guns. But a later technical report makes it appear that the holes in Cell 9, including 17 along the backbone girder, were caused by ice particles thrown by the propellers of the midships gondolas, rather than by gunfire.

*L 53*, attracted by searchlights which her commander thought to indicate Hull, dropped all her bombs, but the ship was not traced

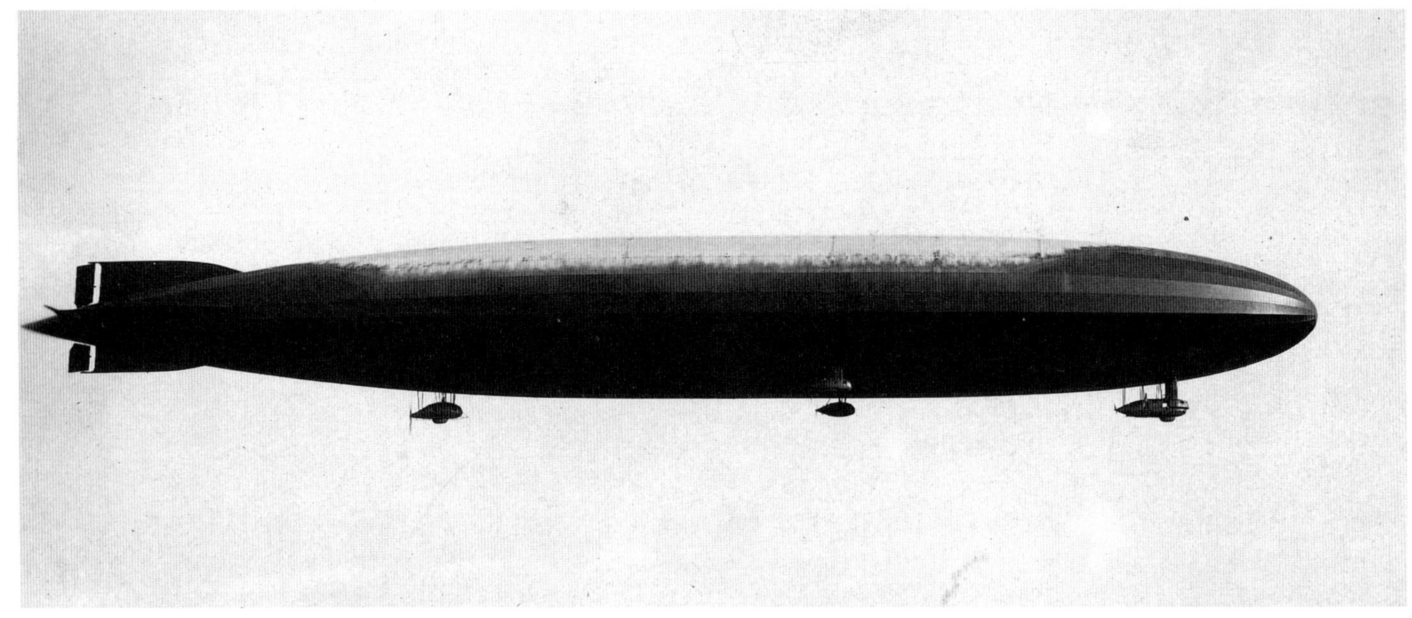

*The Naval airship L 61. (Luftschiffbau Zeppelin) The two photos below show L 61 at Wittmundhafen in spring of 1919 in a movie sequence. L 61 was flown by Hans von Schiller during the filming. The 'L 61' in the bottom right photo was later scratched in, as there were no markings on the airship during filming. (both below - Moch)*

over England. With a west-south-west to south-west wind of 36 to 40 m.p.h. at her altitude of 18,400 feet, *L 53* made a fast flight home with her engines running at full speed. At 5 a.m. she was over Nordholz, and "weighed off" 220 pounds light, she came in towards the revolving shed for what Prölss expected would be an easy landing. The telegraph for the forward engine was set for "slow ahead," those of the two after engines were on "stop," and the two midships engines were idling in reverse, ready to check the ship's headway. Unexpectedly the Zeppelin drove fast across the landing ground, even though the forward engine was stopped and the two midships ones were run full astern. The landing ropes tore out of the hands of the ground crew and *L 53* charged straight towards the revolving shed. Prölss quickly dropped three "breeches" – 1,650 pounds of water – forward, speeded up the forward engine and pulled the nose up sharply with the elevators. So steep was the up angle that the after gondola struck the ground, but *L 53* cleared the hangar. Prölss' second landing attempt, with all engine telegraphs set on "half speed," likewise failed when the light wind veered through 180 degrees. The forward engine broke down during the approach, the port motor failed when the clutch overheated, and it was noticed that the two after engines had stopped. With only the starboard motor running, *L 53* floated past the revolving shed and managed to put down outside the "Normann" hangar. Here, for the first time, it was remarked that the after propeller was shattered and the gondola crew was not answering signals. Looking inside, their shipmates beheld a ghastly sight. All four of the men lay sprawled in grotesque positions, and the engine throttles were still set on "full speed."

Two revived after they had been dragged into the fresh air, but the others were pronounced dead of carbon monoxide poisoning. The gas had seeped out of a 2-inch crack in the exhaust pipe of the foremost of the two engines in the gondola. From the story of the two survivors, it appeared that all had been unconscious throughout the 6-hour flight from the English coast. The untended engines had continued to run at full speed, spoiling the first landing attempt, until they had been shut off by the governors after the propeller had splintered on the ground. The warrant machinist, who was responsible for making rounds and checking all the engine gondolas, had himself been overcome, and none of the frozen, half-stupefied men in the other cars had investigated when he failed to appear.

The attack was ineffective, with only one man killed and damage limited to £3,474. The weather was largely responsible: low clouds and mist had hidden all landmarks from the high-flying airships, and the radio bearings, though the Germans did not know it, were worse than useless. At the same time, however, the weather prevented the British from putting up any effective opposition. The searchlights could not pierce the clouds, and only ten airplanes got off the ground. The conditions well illustrate the dilemma facing the airship raiders in the last year of the war; they could attack on clear nights, when targets on the ground were visible and relatively easy to locate, with the prospect of losing a ship or two to the defenses; or they could choose dark, cloudy nights, when the Zeppelins could be sure of getting home, but at the same time could do little damage. Because of the recent heavy losses, and the restricted building program, Strasser had to choose the latter alternative.

For the first time in a year and a half, a second attack was made in the same raiding period. Three Zeppelins took off on the afternoon of March 13 to raid the industrial Midlands, but at 7:13 p.m. Strasser recalled them because the wind was veering easterly. *L 52* and *L 56*, which had been coasting along the Frisian islands, turned back for Wittmundhaven.

*L 42*, which had found good weather well out at sea, was off the Northumberland coast when Strasser's order was received. She did not acknowledge the recall, although Strasser at 8:40 p.m. sent a direct hint, "To *L 42*. Revolving shed. Leader of Airships." Dietrich humorously confesses today that he disobeyed orders. "We had seen two convoys, and were maneuvering to attack the second one, when the recall came in. We thought we could bomb them before starting back to Nordholz, but then the English coast came in sight. It was too much! It had been half a year since we had had a chance to raid England, and now, with the island in plain sight, we were being ordered to go home without attacking. 'We'll keep going,' I said to my executive officer. But I knew it had to be a success. If I failed, I would have to quit the service."

For 40 minutes Dietrich stood off the coast, waiting for complete darkness. All the seaside cities were brightly lit, and Dietrich believed the enemy was not expecting a raid. The British official history admits, "We had followed the movements

*L 42 at the time of the Hartlepool raid. Considerably modified and improved since going into service on February 28, 1917, she has both after engines now driving a propeller at the rear of the car, midship gondolas raised and fitted with reversing gear, and wears the straight-sided German aircraft cross introduced in the spring of 1918. (Kriegsmarinesammlung)*

of the three airships across the North Sea with some difficulty, and because of uncertainty no warning had been given to the north-east coast towns."[1] At 10:05 p.m. *L 42* swooped in from the north on Hartlepool at 16,400 feet. Twenty-one bombs exploded in West Hartlepool and destroyed or damaged many buildings for a monetary loss of £14,280, while eight people were killed and twenty-nine injured. In ten minutes *L 42* was on her way out to sea, climbing to 17,700 feet after dropping her cargo.

The predicted north-east wind "blew into the ship's nose" all the way home, and it was 10:25 a.m. before *L 42* landed at Nordholz. "Strasser was a stickler for the regulations," continues Dietrich, "and I wondered what kind of trouble I'd be in. When I saw he was not out on the field according to his usual custom, I prepared for the worst. Von Lossnitzer, his adjutant, warned me, 'The old man is furious with you for disobeying orders. You're in for at least three days' confinement to quarters.' 'It was worth it to be able to make an attack on England,' I replied, and went off to get some much-needed sleep. In the afternoon when I gave Strasser my verbal report, he was very cool at first, and said hardly anything, but presently he smiled and remarked, 'In honor of your successful attack, I name you "Count of Hartlepool."' Of course, he couldn't report to higher authority that I had disobeyed orders. The raid was described as 'additional to a scouting mission.' Later I saw a copy of my report, on which the Kaiser himself had written, 'Very gratifying!'"

Five Zeppelins were ordered to attack England on April 4, but bad weather forced a cancellation. Then, on April 12, came an apparent opportunity: while *L 52* and *L 53* encountered thick fog on routine scouting flights that day, five of the newest Zeppelins set out to raid the Midlands industrial area. A last-minute telegram from Strasser added, "If weather permits, 'south' also. London only by my express orders."

The attacking Zeppelins were each carrying 6,600 pounds of bombs, including four of 660 pounds. Over the North Sea they found thick, solid cloud with numerous rain squalls. Towards evening it cleared in the upper air, but clouds beneath still concealed the surface. Once again the Zeppelins had to rely on radio bearings. At first there was a light west-north-west wind, but later, at 20,000 feet, an east-north-east wind was found.

Three airships penetrated only a short distance inland. Navigating by radio bearings, *L 60*, *L 63* and *L 64* claimed attacks on Leeds, Grimsby and Hull, but they missed these cities. The latter two had repeated engine failures and *L 64*, making a heavy landing without ballast at Nordholz, was badly damaged and not again air-worthy until April 29.

The bold flights inland of the other two ships gave the country a scare. *Hauptmann* Manger, in *L 62*, was over land for 6 hours and made a determined effort to bomb the Midland industrial centers. He believed that he had crossed the coast at Mablethorpe at 10 p.m., but he was considerably farther south than the bearings indicated, coming inland over Norfolk. At 10:35 p.m. Manger reported aiming three bombs at a lighted night-flying field near Lincoln, and at 11:05, recognizing Nottingham "from its ring of searchlights," he dropped half his bombs. The night-flying field was at Tydd St. Mary, 42 miles south-south-east of Lincoln; the "Nottingham" bombs were not traced. Manger's real goal was Birmingham. Between 11:45 and midnight he reported dropping the rest of his load on the big industrial city. He stated that the craters of the 660-pound bombs could be seen as black holes in the lit-up streets and there was heavy gunfire, but the "gas shells" did not ascend to *L 62*'s altitude of 18,700 feet. The first of Manger's bombs actually descended as he was passing south of Coventry, 15 miles east-south-east of Birmingham. *L 62* then continued on towards Birmingham, dropping bombs in open country, and the last, two 660-pounders, fell on Hallgreen and Shirley when she again came under anti-aircraft fire. The British official historian states: "The *L 62*, which had come within striking distance of Coventry and Birmingham, and of the congested industrial area in between, had dropped 2 1/2 tons of bombs with no effect, and we were, it must be admitted, fortunate to escape so lightly."[2]

A few minutes later, *L 62* encountered Lieutenant C.H. Noble-Campbell of No.38 Squadron, flying an F.E.2b. For half an hour the Englishman

[1] Jones, V, p. 123.

[2] Jones, V, p. 126.

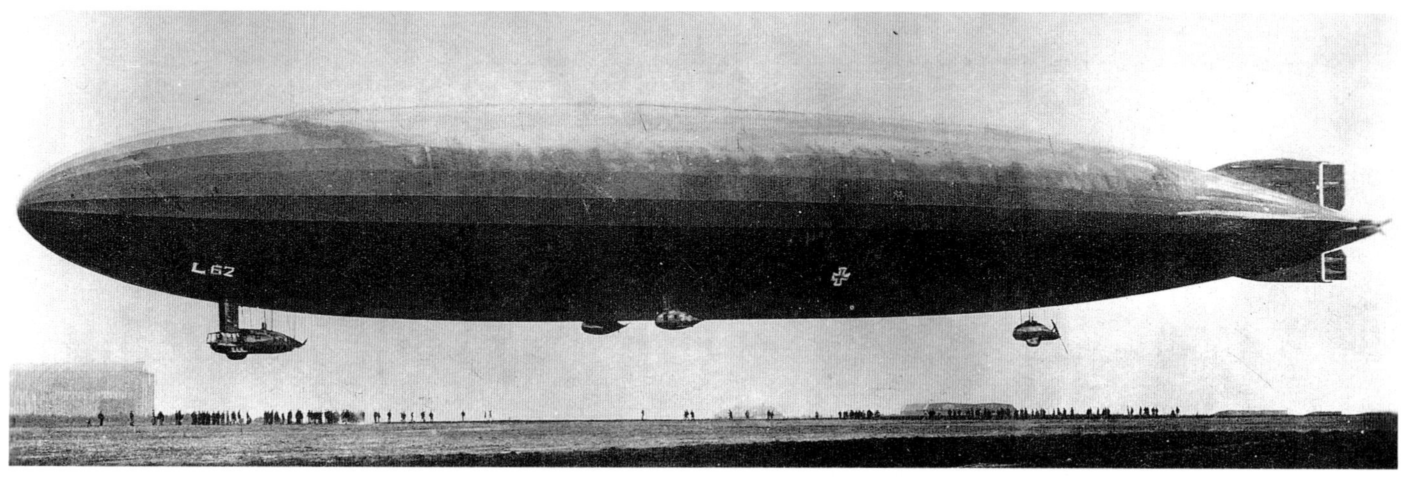


*A clumsily retouched, but undoubtedly authentic photograph of L 62 at Nordholz. (Luftschiffbau Zeppelin)*

chased the Zeppelin, and finally got close enough to open fire. The mechanics in the airship's gondolas replied with spirit, and by luck or skill wounded the pilot in the head and forced him to land his damaged craft at Coventry. On no other occasion throughout the war was an attacking plane worsted in combat with a Zeppelin.

Yet Manger makes no reference to this victory in his War Diary. On his way east he descended to 11,000 feet because of the head wind, and passing Norwich, *L 62* was fired on, he says, with incendiary shells, shrapnel and "air torpedoes" that ascended to 16,500 feet. Over the sea *L 6*, went down to 4,600 feet. Cell 9 was found to have lost a large amount of gas from a hole near the backbone girder, presumably from a shell fragment.

It was *L 61* which on this night caused even more anxiety to the British defenders, and which, through a series of incredible mischances, failed by a hair's breadth to win a glittering success which Strasser's men had sought in vain for over three years. Liverpool – the great West Coast port which two Zeppelins had claimed to have attacked in January, 1916 – had never been reached, though it was high on the German priority list. On this night, six months before the Armistice, it escaped the full treatment with three tons of bombs by a margin of only a few minutes' flying time. *L 61*'s veteran commander, Herbert Ehrlich, died in December, 1921, without knowing how narrowly he had missed the most prized target in middle England.

Ehrlich was heading for Sheffield. Between 9:30 and 9:50 p.m. he reported having been fired on by outpost ships, but British observers saw him then coming inland at Withernsea, Yorks, and the incendiary shells undoubtedly came from the coastal batteries. He was at 16,400 feet and there was a solid overcast beneath. Ehrlich reported that a radio bear-

*Naval airship L 63 at Ahlhorn. (Luftschiffbau Zeppelin)*

## AIRSHIP RAID, APRIL 12–13, 1918

| Ship | Flt. No. | Take-off | | Landing | | Time in air | Distance (miles) | Av. speed (m.p.h.) | Max. alt. (feet) | Temp. (°F.) | Crew | Fuel (lb.) loaded/used | Oil (lb.) loaded/used | Ballast loaded (lb.) | Bombs (lb.) | Gas used (cubic feet) |
|---|---|---|---|---|---|---|---|---|---|---|---|---|---|---|---|---|
| *L 60* | 6 | Tondern | 2.02 p.m. | Tondern | 10.00 a.m. | 19h. 58m. | 976 | 48·8 | 21,350 | −20 | 19 | 12,090/9,510 | 750/353 | 55,600 | 6,900 | 1,060,000 |
| *L 61* | 13 | Wittmund | 3.07 p.m. | Wittmund | 12 noon | 20h. 57m. | 930 | 44·2 | 22,300 | −22 | 19 | 10,300/9,150 | 1,055/496 | 53,900 | 6,600 | 1,320,000 |
| *L 62* | 17 | Nordholz | 1.57 p.m. | Nordholz | 12.30 p.m. | 22h. 33m. | 1,165 | 51·7 | 21,650 | −26 | 20 | 10,580/7,720 | 660/298 | 49,200 | 6,460 | 1,095,000 |
| *L 63* | 11 | Nordholz | 2.19 p.m. | Nordholz | 11.10 a.m. | 20h. 49m. | 716 | 34·7 | 20,000 | −24 | 19 | 10,580/5,700 | 663/196 | 57,400 | 6,870 | 1,060,000 |
| *L 64* | 7 | Nordholz | 2.00 p.m. | Nordholz | 4.23 p.m. | 26h. 23m. | 855 | 32·4 | 21,000 | −22 | 20 | 11,300/10,200 | 772/210 | 59,400 | 6,510 | 1,223,000 |

*Weather:* Very light N.N.E. wind. Sky overcast.
*Bombs:* 141 (21,527 lb.).
*Casualties:* 7 killed, 20 injured.
*Monetary damage:* £11,673.

## *L 61* DECK LOG IN RAID OF APRIL 12–13, 1918

| Cent. European time | Altitude (feet) | Temperature (°F.) Air | Gas | Pressure height (feet) | Release of ballast (lb.) * | Wind Direction | Str. | Course | Distance (miles) | Speed (m.p.h.) | Position | Weather | Engines | Remarks |
|---|---|---|---|---|---|---|---|---|---|---|---|---|---|---|
| 3.07 | 33 | 51·8 | 57·2 | 650 | 145, 146 } 993 | W. | 1·5 | 294° | | | Takeoff | Overcast | All idle | |
| 3.40 | 3,300 | 52·7 | 57·2 | 3,300 | 69, 71, 129, 131 } 9,270 | W.S.W. | 3·5 | 272° | 13·7 | 24·8 | Norderney | Misty, 1,470 ft. cloud ceiling | All full<br>Port stern stopped | 3.39 a ship in sight (Borkum) |
| 7.07 | 4,900 | 33·8 | 44·6 | 4,900 | 1 "breech" for'd, 1 aft | W.N.W. | 5·5 | 263° | 80·8 | 23·4 | 040 δ | ,, | Port stern full<br>Fore motor idle | 4.40 rain increasing<br>6.40 fine rain |
| 7.31 | 6,500 | 32·0 | 42·8 | 6,500 | 1 "breech" for'd, 1 aft | W.N.W. | 5·5 | | | | | ,, | Fore motor full<br>5.40 p.m. idle | Bruges 5°, Nordholz 272°, List 243° |
| 7.57 | 9,850 | 21·2 | 32·0 | 9,850 | 85, 86, 113, 114 } 9,270 | W.N.W. | 5·5 | | | | | 9,000 ft. cloud ceiling | 6.65 p.m. full | |
| 8.34 | 9,850 | 15·8 | 19·4 | 9,850 | 66, 68, 130, 132 } 9,270 | N.W. by W. | 3·5 | 258° | 41 | 28·2 | 086 ϵ 7 | ,, | | List 252°, Nordholz 270°, Borkum 270°, Bruges 340° |
| 10.00 | 16,400 | −0·4 | +3·2 | 16,400 | 70, 72, 83, 84 } 9,270 | S.E. | 2·0 | 274° | 49 | 34·2 | Market Rasen | ,, | | Heavily fired on by outpost ships 9.35–9.50<br>List 256°, Nordholz 267°, Bruges 314° |
| 11.35 | 18,400 | −7·6 | −5·8 | 18,400 | 78, 100 } 4,850 | S.E. | 2·0 | 258° | 31·0 | 19·6 | Sheffield | ,, | | 11.17 first bomb fell<br>11.35 last bomb fell |
| 11.47 | 20,000 | −13·0 | −14·8 | 20,000 | 145, 146 } 1,100 | S.E. | 2·0 | | | | | ,, | All flank | 12.50–2.30 prolonged heavy bombardment |
| 1.28 | 22,300 | −22·0 | −15·6 | 22,300 | 126, 128 } 4,560 | E.S.E. | 5 | 140° | 40·4 | 21·4 | Spurn Point | ,, | | List 255°, Nordholz 266°, Bruges 322° |
| 3.28 | 13,500 | +3·2 | +6·8 | 20,800 | | E.S.E. | 5 | 82° | 42·9 | 21·4 | 056 ϵ 5 | ,, | Stbd. aft stopped | List 264°, Borkum 275°, Bruges 334° |
| 5.16 | 6,900 | 24·8 | 14·0 | 20,400 | | S.S.E. | 5 | 99° | 52·8 | 29·3 | 059 δ 7 | ,, | | List252°,Nordholz268°,Borkum271°,Bruges5° |
| 6.30 | 18,400 | −9·4 | −7·6 | 21,700 | | E.S.E. | 4 | | | | | ,, | Fore<br>Port mid'ps<br>Stbd. Mid'ps } Stopped | 5.45 070 δ 7 an enemy plane in sight to stbd. |
| 7.25 | 9,850 | 15·8 | 3·2 | 21,100 | | N. by W | 6 | Various | 37·3 | 17·7 | 020 ϵ 7 | ,, | Fore<br>Stbd. mid'ps<br>Port mid'ps } Full | Nordholz 213°, List 240°, Bruges 25° |
| 8.34 | 3,000 | 48·2 | 68·0 | 17,150 | | Same | 6·5 | 43° | 31·0 | 26·3 | | Ceiling altitude | | 4 engines stopped. Nordholz 248°, List 220° |
| 10.37 | 650 | 55·4 | 66·2 | 17,250 | | N.N.E. | 6 | 115° | 28 | 20·6 | 113 ϵ 7 | 2,600 ft. | All half | Borkum 26°, Nordholz 276° |
| 11.25 | 330 | 59·0 | 62·6 | 17,360 | 1 "breech" for'd, 1 aft | W.S.W. | 3 | Various | 11·2 | 35·0 | Carolinensiel | Under cloud ceiling, 330ft., rain | All idle<br>Stbd. midships reverse | Over Wittmund |
| 12.04 | 33 | 42·8 | 55·4 | 17,750 | 1 "breech" for'd, 1 aft | W. | 0·5 | Various | | 17·2 | Landing | Overcast | All stopped | |

* Figures in this column indicate ring from which ballast was dropped.

ing at 10 p.m. showed *L 61* about 15 miles southwest of Grimsby, on a direct course for Sheffield. This in fact was close to her true position at that time. "The British give away the position of defended localities through the use of searchlights, and it is possible to find good attack targets despite poor orientation," Ehrlich noted. But at 10:30 p.m., pushed along by an easterly wind whose strength he had underestimated, he passed four miles south of Sheffield, which was blacked out, without seeing it. On sped *L 61*, headed straight for Liverpool, sixty miles distant. But at Runcorn, barely ten miles from the teeming warehouses of the great seaport, she turned north, and between 11:15 and 11:35 p.m. dropped all her bombs on a well-lit city which Ehrlich thought was Sheffield, but which was actually Wigan. The town had received no air-raid warning, and the blast furnaces

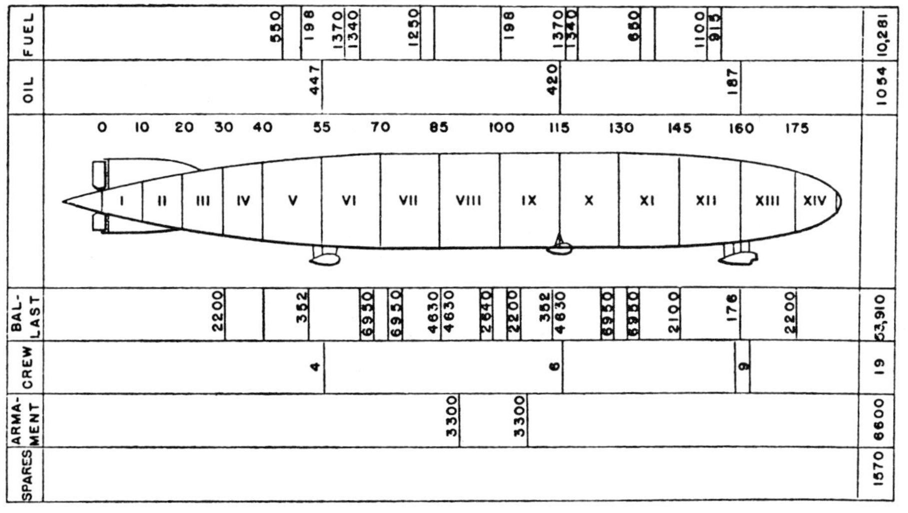

BALLAST SHEET

13TH FLIGHT OF THE AIRSHIP "L 61"

| | LB. | | LB. |
|---|---|---|---|
| FUEL | 10,281 | PASSENGERS | |
| OIL | 1054 | PROVISIONS | |
| BALLAST | 53,910 | ARMAMENT | 6600 |
| 19 CREW | 3350 | AMMUNITION | |
| SPARES & | 1570 | GUNS | |
| STORES | 110 | LIGHT BOMBS | 31 |
| SERVICE LOAD | 70,275 | USEFUL LOAD | 6631 |

ADDITIONAL LOAD (FREE LIFT) 1100 LB. (DEW, RAIN, SNOW)

USEFUL LIFT WITH 98% FILLING 78,006 LB.

| AIR: | GAS: |
|---|---|
| T. = 50.9° F. | T. = 57.2° F. |
| BAR. = 29.88 IN. | SP. GR. = 0.0945 |
| REL. H. = 88% | |

ADDITIONAL FILLING______________CU. FT.



WITTMUNDHAVEN, APRIL 12, 1918.

REDUCED USEFUL LIFT 79,516 LB.

WEIGHED OFF BY DIETSCH OBLT. Z. S. & EXECUTIVE OFFICER

THE COMMANDER EHRLICH KAPITÄNLEUTNANT

NO. D 72 (LZ 106) LUFTSCHIFFBAU ZEPPELIN G.M.B.H. FRIEDRICHSHAFEN

*Von Buttlar (seated), wearing his Pour le Mérite, and Schiller in their quarters at Tondern. (Luftschiffbau Zeppelin)*

of the Wigan Coal and Iron Company were throwing a ruddy glow far out into the night. Eight bombs on the suburb of Ince injured a man and damaged several houses and a railroad line. Fifteen bombs on Wigan itself killed seven people injured twelve, and accounted for most of the £11,673 worth of damage done in this raid. The last bombs, four 660-pounders, fell in open fields near Aspull, but they damaged cottages by their blast and injured four people. *L 61* then headed east, and at 1:28 a.m. a radio bearing placed her just off Spurn Point. In fact she was then circling north of Hull and did not leave the country until 2:35 a.m.

At 4:30 a.m. an F.2a flying-boat had left Great Yarmouth "to search for a Zeppelin north-north-east 60 miles from Yarmouth."[3] At 5:45 a.m. the flying-boat and *L 61* sighted each other simultaneously at a distance of 10 miles. The airship was flying at 6,500 feet because of the head wind. "In the south a flying-boat in sight steering for the ship. Turned away to the north, the ship climbing very fast to 6,800 meters [22,300 feet]. The plane was lost to sight in the still-dark west." At 3:30 a.m. one of the after engines had failed with a damaged cylin-

[3] Gamble, p. 379.

*PREVIOUS: Naval airship L 63 about to go into commision at Friedrichshafen. The naval ensign has been hoisted at the stern, and only a few shores remain to be removed. The small traps along the bottom of the gangway cover the apertures for the hydrogen filling hoses. Note light weight lifeboat bottom-up on the floor in right foreground, and the fire ladders used to work on the hull. (Luftschiffbau Zeppelin)*

der, and at 8:25 a.m. three more motors failed with fuel line trouble, leaving only the port engine in the after gondola working. With a strong north-north-east wind, Ehrlich believed that the ship, flying above solid cloud, had drifted over Holland. After two hours the three engines were again running, and at noon *L 61* landed at Wittmundhaven with the ceiling at 300 feet and heavy rain.

The weather over England again had been thick and foggy. One of the twenty British pilots who took to the air on this "filthy night" later wrote: "I went through 4,000 feet of clouds, to emerge in a clear stratum between the cloud levels, went through the next lot to 8,000 feet, but found more clouds – enough to hide thousands of Zeppelins. The Germans *really are absolute experts* in foretelling the weather."[4]

The naval Zeppelins were ordered to stand by for a raid on April 13, but it was canceled because of the weather. Then, on April 23, the High Seas Fleet sailed for the last time on its boldest operation of the war, and the one that took it farthest from Germany. Scheer intended to attack the Scandinavian convoys running from Lerwick in the Shetlands to Bergen in Norway. Knowing that Grand Fleet dreadnoughts were escorting them, he realized that the battle cruisers, backed by the entire battle force, would be needed to ensure success. On the morning of April 24 the Battle Fleet was off Stavanger in Norway, and the five battle cruisers under Hipper were to the north off Haugesund. Of the convoy nothing was to be seen. Scheer had in fact chosen the wrong day, an error for which the Naval Airship Division was in part responsible, as the weather had permitted no long-distance scouting to the north. To add to Scheer's troubles, the battle cruiser *Moltke* suffered a major engineering casualty and had to be towed home. Scheer had enjoined strict radio silence, and the British had no knowledge of the operation until *Moltke* had signaled her difficulties off the Norwegian coast.

Late in the evening of April 23, Strasser had sent out *L 41*, *L 42* and *L 63* to escort the High Seas Fleet northward. Two hours later, at 1:30 a.m., he ordered them to return because of an increasing north-east wind.

During the winter and early spring, routine scouting flights had been few and far between. There was an improvement in May, and from the middle of the month, patrols were made almost daily. Usually only two airships scouted by day in the German Bight, one from the Terschelling Bank Lightship to the Dogger Bank South Lightship, and the other from the Dogger Bank South to the Dogger Bank North Lightship and thence east to Lyngvig on the Danish coast. In practice, the dangerous waters off Terschelling seem to have been left more and more to the seaplanes based on Borkum and Norderney. Longer airship reconnaissance flights were made by night in this last year of the war. Whenever possible, one Zeppelin flew north by night to within sight of Christiansand on the Norwegian side of the Skagerrak, while two other ships flew west to within 50 miles or so of the coast of England, usually on the north and south sides of the 54th parallel passing near Flamborough Head. The British made no effort to deal with these night reconnaissance's. The orders for these operations were rather detailed, as for *L 61* on May 16, 1918:

> Late and early reconnaissance to the west with intervening night advance into submarine blockade area. Take-off so that westerly patrol line [squares 146 δ to 152 γ 7] is reached in its northern portion about 10 p.m. After patrolling this line proceed into blockade area south of 55 degrees latitude according to your evaluation of the situation. At dawn be on the above line again, fly patrol here till 6 a.m., then run in. Take-off about 7 p.m. *L 53* will perform middle scouting and north of 55 degrees.
>
> Leader of Airships.

Only rarely were any vessels seen in these nocturnal excursions, and *Kapitänleutnant* Heinz Bödecker,

[4] Ibid., p. 378.

*L 56 at Wittmundhaven taking off from "temporary" shed "Wille." (Moch)*

commanding *L 61*, allowed himself to complain that:

> from 4,000 meters [13,000 feet] (ordered because of danger from planes) it is not possible to distinguish individual ship types accurately even on a bright moonlit night. (For example to differentiate between own and British light cruisers.) It is necessary to go down to within gunfire range to identify or to exchange signals with own vessels.

British minelaying operations in the German Bight were stepped up in the spring of 1918, with the 20th Flotilla, consisting of eleven destroyers, adding steadily to the minefields in the south, while a tremendous barrage was started across the northern

*L 56 in shed "Wille" at Wittmundhaven.*

*L 56. This photograph illustrates quite well the German technique of manhandling airships on the landing ground. (Luftschiffbau Zeppelin)*

outlet of the North Sea to bar the U-boats from the Atlantic. The Grand Fleet's light craft, accompanied after March, 1918, by the carrier *Furious*, with a new flying-on deck aft, covered the minefields in the northern and eastern portions of the Bight. The mines around Terschelling were watched over by flying-boats from Great Yarmouth, and the Harwich Force was charged with surveillance of the fields in the western Bight. To assist in this latter mission, the Harwich light cruisers towed to sea high-speed lighters each carrying a large flying-boat. On reaching German waters, the "boat," usually an F.2a, would be floated off and would rise from the surface of the sea. On the first such operation by the Harwich Force, on March 19, 1918, three flying-boats were taken into the Bight.

The first scouting flights of the month of May were by *L 61* and *L 64* on the 3rd. There were no more until May 10, when *L 56* took off at Wittmundhaven at 7:30 a.m. to scout to the west, and at 8:50, *L 62* departed from Nordholz to patrol to the north. *L 62* was seen to rise at once to 3,300 feet, and at 9:25 was heard signaling to the Commander-in-Chief of the Fleet, "Takeoff, course for Dogger Bank North Lightship." Forty minutes later, at 10:05 a.m., she flew over some German patrol craft about ten miles north-west of Heligoland at an altitude of only a thousand feet, and disappeared into a towering cumulus cloud. Almost immediately there was a heavy explosion, and the shattered remains of *L 62*, blasted in two, fell blazing into the sea. The trawler *Bergedorf* was directly under the cloud, and the wreckage plunged into the water a bare 100 feet from her, while fragments landed on her deck. Five bodies were recovered, but no survivors were found. Strasser was unable to determine the cause of *L 62*'s destruction. Since she was flying well under the "pressure height" she had established after taking off from Nordholz, there could be no question of an escape of hydrogen. Strasser believed that an electrical charge in the thundercloud had caused an explosion of either fuel or bombs. General opinion today among surviving naval airship men is that one of the bomb fuses – three-foot tubes inserted in the tail of the weapons after leaving the German coast – had been sabotaged to explode when the bomb was armed.

The radio station at the Admiralty in Whitehall heard the airships' signals off Heligoland, and after a message at 1:08 p.m. indicated that one of them was headed west, the naval air station at Killingholme was directed to intercept her. At 1:20 p.m. a twin-engine F.2a flying-boat was on its way, with Captains T.C. Pattison and A.H. Munday, Royal Air Force, a radio man and an engineer on board. At 4:30, when they were about 50 miles north-north-west of Borkum Reef Lightship, they saw a Zeppelin on the port beam, about a mile away. The "boat" was at 6,000 feet and the airship was estimated to be at 8,000 feet. The Zeppelin at once dropped bombs and ballast, and started to climb. The flying-boat pursued her, ascending to her ceiling, and firing both her forward and midships guns:

> We were now at a height of 11,000 feet and the Zeppelin's height was approximately 12,500 feet. I opened fire again and fired another 130 rounds of explosive and tracer bullets. I noticed the propeller of the Zeppelin's port engine almost stop and the craft suddenly steered hard to port. I concluded that the port engine had been hit by our gunfire as well as other parts of the craft, as the envelope and gondolas seemed a background for all the flashes of the explosive and tracer bullets. There was much more outpouring of ballast and articles and considerable smoke. I concluded that we had finished the Zeppelin and informed Captain Pattison that we had bagged it. But the craft again headed for Holstein in a crabwise fashion emitting much smoke.[5]

Research by the author in the German archives has proved that the airship they attacked was *L 56*. A report by her commander, *Kapitänleutnant* Walter Zaeschmar, shows that the Zeppelin was not damaged, despite Captain Munday's definite belief to the contrary. It also shows that the flying-boat crew had grossly underestimated the airship's altitude, and were well out of range all the time they were firing at her:

5 Munday's report in Imperial War Museum file, "Pilots' Reports Relating to Destruction of Zeppelins."

At 4:50 p.m. *L 56*, according to R.S.A. bearings at 4:15 p.m. plus dead reckoning, was in 081 δ [90 miles north-west of Terschelling] at 4,700 meters [15,400 feet] altitude and steering on a south course, when an enemy flying-boat was sighted to the west at 2,500 meters [8,200 feet]. Distance about 12,000 meters [7 1/2 miles].

The plane was put astern and ship climbed to an average altitude of 6,600 meters [21,700 feet]. The enemy at first approached fast and climbed rapidly, while ascending in circles. The altitude he attained was estimated at 5,000 meters [16,400 feet] judging from relative positions.

The distance was estimated at 3,000 meters [10,000 feet].

The enemy pursued the ship until 5:40 p.m. and then disappeared from sight. His speed decreased with altitude; for a considerable time – 30 minutes – he remained on the same bearing and could not gain on the ship. As far as could be made out, he was half-stalled at an angle of 10-15 degrees. Our speed estimated at 20 m/sec. [45 m.p.h.] with 4 degree up angle.

Whether the plane was firing could not be observed, as he had the sun behind him. As the plane gained altitude, the bombs and 3 tanks of fuel had to be dropped as ballast. With the signals of 5:05 and 5:35 p.m. wireless bearings were requested, so as to advise the seaplane station at Borkum of our position. The east course steered led with the north wind towards Borkum. The enemy followed as far as 034 ε [60 miles north of Terschelling].

The Killingholme flying-boat's attack did cause *L 56* to break off her patrol prematurely at 6:20 p.m. for lack of fuel and ballast, and she landed at Wittmundhaven at 8:15 p.m. British intelligence, confused by the accidental loss of *L 62* on the same date, incorrectly attributed her destruction to Pattison and Munday, an error perpetuated in the official air history.[6]

On the morning of May 18, *L 52*, patrolling after a night-time advance into the submarine blockade area, sighted for the first time the Harwich Force with the new seaplane lighters north-northeast of the Dogger Bank South Lightship. This was the fourth such operation with the lighters, and ended with the flying boats taking off from the water near the Horns Reef light buoy. Possibly the planes had already been flown off when Friemel first sighted the force at 4:15 a.m. He noted that three enemy light cruisers, steering north in line ahead, were each towing a broad-sterned barge, but was positive they were not carrying aircraft and suggested it might be a new minesweeping device. After half an hour the Harwich Force ran under a deep bank of thunderclouds where *L 52* could not follow.

Significant was the reaction of *Kapitänleutnant* Ehrlich's veteran crew when, on May 21, 1918, they turned over their *L 6* to *Kapitänleutnant* Bödecker and went to Jüterbog to take back their old *L 35* as an experimental ship. They were not sorry to be leaving the "Front." "The physical, technical, navigational and meteorological difficulties had risen immeasurably; visibility conditions and flying possibilities were becoming ever more circumscribed. The zenith of the airship's reign had been passed."[7]

Routine patrols in the German Bight, and night-time advances into the submarine blockade zone off the English coast, continued uneventfully through the month of June and into July. The British could expect no further successes against the high-flying Zeppelins from the heavy flying-boats, and *Furious* and shipborne fighters had not been able to catch them in the air. Instead, it was determined to destroy the airships in their sheds. Tondern was chosen for the first attempt, because, with its command of the northern approaches to the German Bight, its Zeppelins were particularly well placed to watch the Grand Fleet. Thus was set up a prophetic and historic operation – the first carrier strike in history against a land target, the first faltering exhibition of the weapon which, in the hands of the United States Navy twenty-five years later, was to play a major role in annihilating the maritime power of Japan.

Late in June, two specially trained flights of Sopwith "Camels" were embarked in the aircraft carrier *Furious* to make the raid. On June 29 the car-

6 See Jones, VI, p. 355.

7 Dietsch in Strahlmann, p. 87.

rier, with the 1st Light Cruiser Squadron and accompanying destroyers, was off the Danish coast, but the weather was unfavorable and the operation was abandoned. No Zeppelins were out scouting on this date. On July 17 the force departed from Rosyth on its second attempt. Next morning, at 3:30 a.m., the carrier was off Lyngvig Light, but thunderstorms caused the strike to be postponed for 24 hours. They also kept the patrolling Zeppelins in their sheds.

Early on the morning of July 19, *Furious* was off the Schleswig coast and sent away the two flights of 2F.1 "Camels," each carrying two 50-pound bombs. Of the seven pilots, only Captains W.F. Dickson and B.A. Smart returned, and because of the faulty design of the landing-on deck of *Furious* they were forced to ditch in the sea. Four others were forced by bad weather to land in Denmark, while a fifth fell in the sea and was drowned before reaching the coast. Dickson's report present a graphic picture of the first flight, which did most of the damage:

> I saw Captain Jackson at about 3,000 feet above me and a good distance to the east of the town, coming down in a dive, with Lieutenant Williams about half a mile astern of him, I climbed a little and joined with him and observed two very large sheds, larger by quite a considerable amount than the main shed at East Fortune Air Station, and also a smaller one. These were at least 5 miles to the north of the town and were standing up quite apart from anything else on flat ground. . . .
>
> There was absolutely no sign of life until Jackson began diving on the shed when a battery on the Tondern-Hoyer road opened fire, besides this no other battery opened fire during our dropping. Captain Jackson dived right onto the northernmost shed and dropped two bombs, one a direct hit in the middle and the other slightly to the side of the shed. I then dropped my one remaining bomb and Williams two more. Hits were observed. The shed then burst into flames and enormous conflagration took place rising to at least 1,000 feet and the whole of the shed being completely engulfed.
>
> After dropping, Jackson went straight on, Williams to the left, and I to the right. Two or more batteries then opened fire on us while we were returning but the shooting was not good. This is the last I saw of the other two.[8]

The early-morning attack took the Tondern base by surprise. At 4:32 a.m. a sentry at Scherrebeck, south-east of the field, phoned that three unidentified aircraft were approaching. Three minutes later the three "Camels" were diving on the sheds. The prime target was the big double "Toska" hangar to the north, housing *L 54* and *L 60*. The small "Tobias"' shed merely contained the base captive balloon, while the "Toni" shed was being dismantled. From 100 feet above the hangars the first flight dropped three bombs into the "Toska" shed, and *L 54* and *L 60* instantly took fire and burned with tremendous outpouring of thick black smoke. One bomb hit the "Tobias" hangar, and splinters damaged the captive balloon. The three planes then flew off west at a height of 70 feet and disappeared into a cloud bank. Ten minutes later the second flight (mistaken by the Germans for the first trio returning) swept in from the east and attacked the "Tobias" shed. Two bombs which went through the roof set fire to the captive balloon; four others fell nearby, one on a gas wagon with hydrogen flasks charged at 100 atmospheres' pressure, but none of them exploded, though the carriage was damaged. A plane in the second wave lost a wheel; otherwise the Germans did no damage to the low-flying Britishers.

Tondern was protected only by small arms in the hands of the ground troop. On March 6, 1918, its five Albatros D-III fighter aircraft had been withdrawn – a fact undoubtedly well known to British intelligence – and had not returned. One man of the ground troop was slightly wounded by a splinter; an *L 54* crewman was slightly injured, and another burned, while an *L 60* crewman was severely wounded in the abdomen by a penetrating bomb fragment. The two modern airships in the "Toska" shed were of course a total loss. Fortunately they had burned slowly instead of exploding, and the

8 Dickson's report in Imperial war Museum file, "Pilots' Reports Relating to Destruction of Zeppelins."

*The Tondern base. Small "Tobias" shed in foreground, with double shed in the background. L 54 is landing. (Kameradschaft)*

big hangar was hardly damaged except for bomb holes in the roof.

Until the Armistice the Naval Airship Division lived in constant fear of a similar attack on one of the other bases. The "Toska" shed was quickly repaired, but because of its exposed position, Tondern was maintained on a standby basis as an emergency landing ground only. At Nordholz, hundreds of acres of sandpine were burned over, lest they be set afire in a raid and destroy the base. Only Ahlhorn, far from the sea, was relatively safe. Yet Furious never came back. With the realization that planes still could not land on board because of turbulence around the funnel and superstructure amidships, she was deprived of her aircraft and relegated to the kite-balloon service.

The loss of *L 54* and *L 60* had to some extent been balanced by the development of a new type of Zeppelin. Strasser later claimed to have recommended as early as February 18, 1917, that a larger airship be built with both high speed and high ceiling, but his letter cannot be found in the files. Not until the "Silent Raid" had shown the need for such a design did the Admiralty, on December 10, 1917, propose to the Chief of the Naval Staff the construction of a "lengthened experimental ship with 7 pro-

*The "Toska" shed with the wrecks of L 54 and L 60 after the carrier raid of July 19, 1918. (both - Moch)*

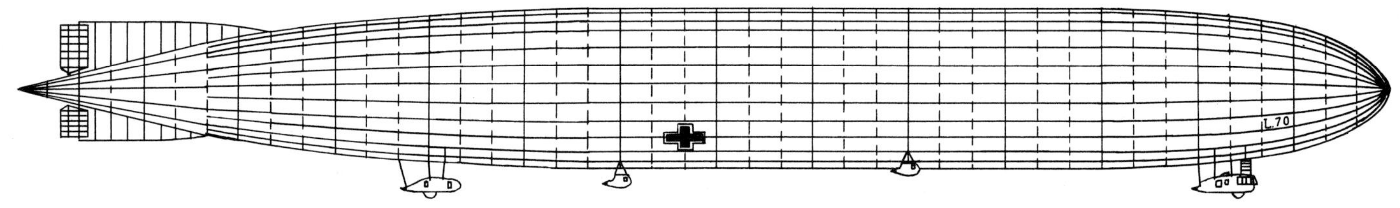


**L 70**

| | | | |
|---|---|---|---|
| Gas capacity | 2,196,900 ft.[3] | Engines | 7 Maybach Mb IVa, of 245 h.p. |
| Length | 693.9 ft. | Propellers | 6 Jaray L.Z. |
| Diameter | 78.4 ft. | Maximum speed | 81.5 mph |
| Useful lift | 98,000 lbs. | Ceiling | 21,000 ft. |
| Gas cells | 15 | Full speed endurance | 7460 miles |
| Crew | 25 | | |

pellers." No firm decision was taken, however, until April, 1918, when Admiral Starke ordered the construction of four lengthened craft of about 2,190,000 cubic foot capacity with a maximum speed estimated at 78 m.p.h., the first to be ready about June 1. Strasser on April 22 wrote to the Naval Staff that "the 4 new ships to be delivered, in order to be capable of reaching the great altitudes over the North Sea and England which are now required to carry out their missions, will at my insistence be high climbing 7-engine ships of great speed." *L 70*, the first of the type, made her maiden flight at Friedrichshafen on July 1, 1918. Fundamentally a "height climber" of the *L 53* class with an extra 15-meter gas cell amidships, she was 693 feet 11 inches long with a gas capacity of 2,196,900 cubic feet, and carried seven of the Maybach MB IVa "altitude motors." On her trials she reached 19,700 feet statically, and 23,000 feet dynamically, with an unspecified load. Her maximum trial speed was 81 m.p.h., making her the fastest airship built up to that time. Her useful lift was 98,000 pounds, and it was intended that she should carry 8,000 pounds of bombs in raids on England.

The command of this fabulous ship went, not to one of the veteran commanders, but to Strasser's recent adjutant, *Kapitänleutnant* von Lossnitzer. "A splendid fellow, incomparable in his determination, a rarely capable person and a good comrade, to whom Strasser was particularly attached."[9] But the fact remained that von Lossnitzer had made only eight "war flights" in *LZ 120* in the Baltic, and two reconnaissance's in the North Sea in the "school ship" *L 41* early in 1918. He brought his new com-

[9] Letter, Peter Wendt to Hertha Mathy, August 23, 1918.

*Naval airship L 70 on a trial flight at Friedrichshafen. (Luftschiffbau Zeppelin)*

*The port after engine car of L 70, attached to the hull, but before being covered with fabric. Note the 245 horsepower Maybach MB IVa engine, showing its exhuast side; note the ungeared Jaray LZ propeller; the water radiator in the nose of the gondola; the oil tank, and oil cooler on the outside of the gondola; the folding ladder leading to the hull; and the engine telegraph in the gondola roof. (Luftschiffbau Zeppelin)*

mand to Nordholz on July 8, but cross winds prevented housing her in the "Nordstern" shed, and *L 70* spent the night in the revolving hangar with 40 feet of her tail sticking out in the open. Next day she was flown to her proper berth.

Strasser had the greatest confidence in the new ship. Others were not so impressed. Admiral Starke recalled later that on July 28, 1918:

> I had a conversation with Captain Strasser in which he spoke of *L 70* as the final type. He tried to convince me that the danger of aircraft to this ship was not great. Here I could not agree with him. I told him I did not feel *L 70*'s performance was sufficient protection against attacking aircraft and on this account the Admiralty was ordering the experimental ship *L 100*. He then assured me that he could not use a ship that could not be housed in the revolving shed. He brought up every possible argument against building the experimental ship.

The new design – initiated by the Admiralty over Strasser's objections – was for a 6-engine craft of 2,648,250 cubic feet, 743 feet long and 82 feet 5 inches in diameter. Her anticipated dynamic ceiling of 27,150 feet was over 4,000 feet higher than that of *L 70*, though her speed was less. *L 100* was scheduled to complete at Friedrichshafen on November 1, 1918, but very little work was ever done on her.

*In the last months of the war, Strasser pressed to have his airships armed with the Oerlikon 20mm cannon as it could out-range the .303 machine gun. Shown here is an example in the control car of L 70 at Friedrichshafen. (Luftschiffbau Zeppelin)*

Thus, Strasser in the last summer of the war was still the same – believing passionately in his weapon, still underestimating his opponents, and determined to the point of obstinacy in pursuing what he conceived to be the good of the service. Not only was he feuding with the Admiralty over the unwanted *L 100*, but the Naval Staff had incurred his ire by trying to force on him another Schütte-Lanz craft. On June 5, 1918, the last of the wooden ships, *SL 22*, had made her first flight in Mannheim. Strasser, however, refused to accept her because of her low useful lift and combat ceiling. On July 22 the Naval Staff, no doubt mindful of the investment of more than a hundred thousand pounds of public money in the ship, wrote to Strasser begging him to accept *SL 22* at least for limited scouting and patrolling in the North Sea. In recent trials, the Naval Staff related, she had developed a useful lift of 82,993 pounds, and with a load of 11,706 pounds on board had risen to 19,000 feet statically and 20,450 feet dynamically.

Strasser tartly replied on July 30 that the reported useful lift of *SL 22* was about the same as that of *L 42*, which the Admiralty had recently permitted him to take out of "Front" service because of her inferior performance. Furthermore, he knew that *SL 22*'s "ceiling" figures had been attained in cool morning air, and she would not rise so high in the event of a midday airplane attack. She lacked the new "altitude motors" and her speed was inferior, and if the MB IVa's were installed, her lift would be even less. "The airship therefore is useless for Front service, that is, if it were used it would surely be destroyed if it encounters enemy aircraft."

The last official letter ever written by the Leader of Airships concludes with characteristically blunt and pungent phrases:

> If such experimental ships as *SL 22* and *PL 27* are built against the advice of the Front, there must be good ground for thinking that special interests are behind their development. However, I can never permit ships unsatisfactory for Front service to be forced on the Front just because they have visited a Front base.

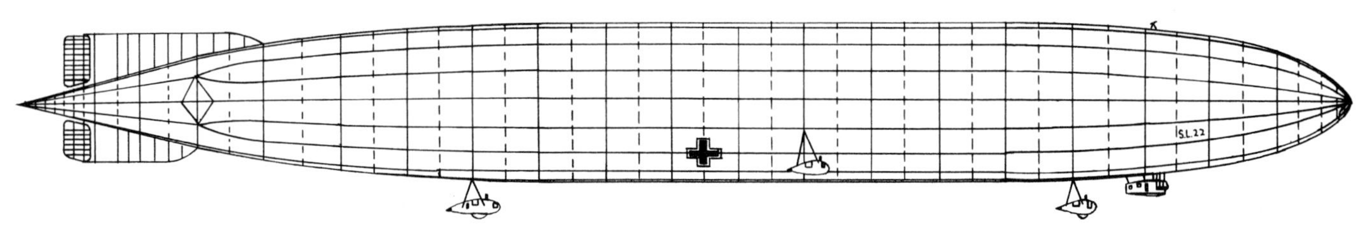


**SL 22**

| | | | |
|---|---|---|---|
| Gas capacity | 1,989,700 ft.[3] | Gas cells | 20 |
| Length | 651 ft. | Engines | 5 Maybach HSLu, of 240 h.p. |
| Diameter | 74 ft. | Maximum speed | 65 mph |
| Crew | 22 | Ceiling | 16,400 ft. |

*SL 22. Strasser refused her for combat missions as it was heavier than Zeppelins. SL 22 visited Wildeshausen, and ended the war at Jüterbog, where she was dismantled after the war. (Schütte) Below: SL 22 at Rheinau shed. (Bleston)*

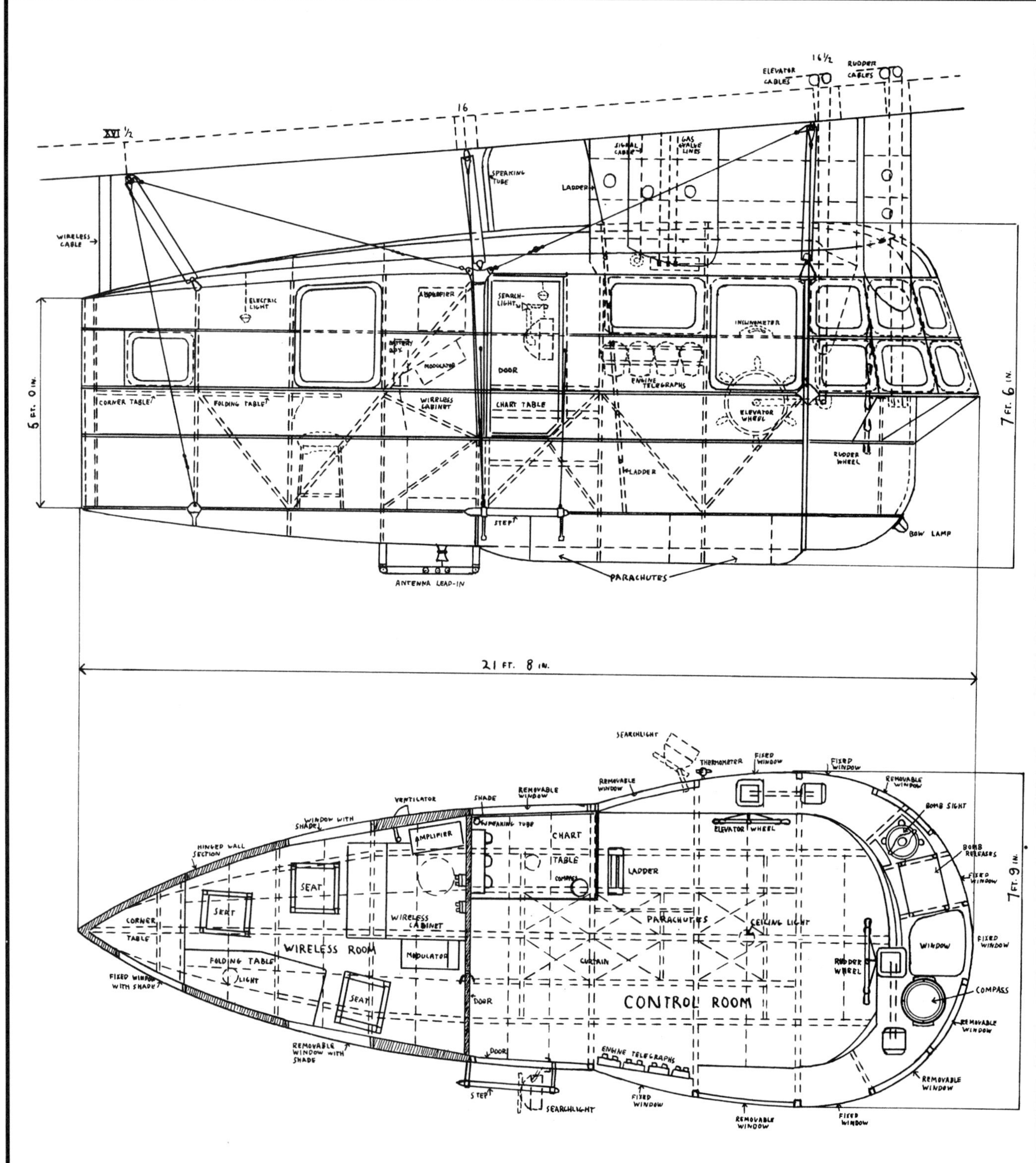


**Control Car of the SL 20 Class**

(after Schütte)

*Parseval PL 27 at Ahlhorn. (Luftschiffbau Zeppelin)*

*Götterdämmerung* awaits, but this remarkable man, secure in his faith in his sky giants, has no intimation of doom. To the end, Peter Strasser is utterly devoted to his ships and his men, and the men in turn will follow him literally to their deaths. A strange man, accustomed to making the most rigorous and incessant demands on himself, he has developed an appearance of sternness, not to say hardness, that appears almost inhuman. Nobody ever knew Peter Strasser completely. What lay beneath the uniform, the mask of duty, that he turned towards the outer world? A few who had the fortune to stand close to him glimpsed a sensitive, even poetic spirit. "The service was his whole life," recalls the widow of one of his commanders. "It was most unusual for an officer of his rank in the Imperial Navy to remain a bachelor. Undoubtedly he would have been warmer and more human if he had found the right woman to marry. I know that he felt very deeply the deaths of the men who served under him, but he had forced himself to repress his feelings completely."

# CHAPTER XXIII

# GÖTTERDÄMMERUNG

The last two weeks of the Naval Airship Division as a combat organization were filled with drama and tragedy. On the day after the Tondern attack, *L 52* and *L 64* had been out for daytime reconnaissance in the Bight, but after eight hours of battling heavy rain and snow squalls, Strasser ordered them to return. For eleven days the weather prevented further scouting flights. Then, on July 31, three ships were out to cover a demonstration by half the High Seas Fleet in support of the minesweepers. The airships' orders read:

> Protection of a force assembling at 4 a.m. in Karl 87, 4 minesweepers, 2 trawlers, 2 escort half flotillas, 2 torpedo boat flotillas, light cruiser *Königsberg* with Leader of Minesweepers, I Scouting Group, I or III Battle Squadron, *Graudenz* with Second Leader of Torpedo Boats and aircraft mother ship. Will steer via Karl 140 to about Karl 442, then back.[1]

The I Scouting Group comprised all five of the German battle cruisers, and the battle squadron would have included at least 5 dreadnoughts. *L 61* was to patrol the southern edge of the German Bight from the Terschelling Bank to the Dogger Bank South Lightship; *L 63* was to fly between the Dogger Bank South and Dogger Bank North Lightships; and *L 65* was to scout between the Dogger Bank North Lightship and Lyngvig. Taking off between 1:30 and 2 a.m., the airships encountered heavy, broken cloud over the North Sea. *L 65*, finding an overcast along her entire patrol line, flew north to within sight of the Norwegian coast at Egersund and reported visibility there of 80 miles. *L 63* was in sight of the surface vessels at 6:25 a.m., and at 1:25 p.m., some miles to the south of their course, saw a big, dark-painted submarine which did not answer recognition signals and

*OPPOSITE: Inside the hull of L 65, looking aft, shortly before her completion at Friedrichshafen. Outer cover has been applied but gas cells, which will fill this space completely, have not been installed. Note keel at bottom, and king post bracing of main frames spaced fifteen meters apart. (Luftschiffbau Zeppelin)*

1 The "Karl" designations refer to a new secret squared position chart of the North Sea which had been distributed on July 15, 1918.

*Nordholz in the summer of 1918. Huge double hangar in the foreground: "Nordstern" shed 853 feet long was completed in March 1918, "Nogat" shed not completed but was nearly finished by August. "Normann" shed in the distance, and at right, two single sheds for training ships. (Moch)*

dived as the Zeppelin approached. At 2:15 p.m., when it half-emerged, von Freudenreich aimed eleven 110-pound bombs at it; four burst around the boat and he claimed a direct hit on the conning tower. At 4 p.m., *L 61* saw a submarine a few miles to the southwest, probably the same one.

By coincidence, the Harwich Force put to sea the same day. Motor torpedo boats had been developed to attack German vessels in the Bight, and three previous expeditions had been attempted with these craft since June 30. On the morning of August I the Harwich Force, with six 40-foot "coastal motor boats" on davits in the light cruisers, was approaching the western edge of the German Bight. At 6:15 a.m. it was sighted and reported by a German seaplane 87 miles north-north-west of Terschelling.

Three Zeppelins had taken off between 1:50 and 2:27 a.m. on routine reconnaissance. *L 56*, on westerly patrol, was nearest to the scene, and at 6:25 a.m. sighted and reported the British cruiser squadron. Her commander, *Kapitänleutnant* Zaeschmar, was hampered by huge, puffy clouds floating close together above the water, and obscuring sight of the surface. At 8:05, *L 56* reported seeing several large warships with an anti-submarine screen some miles to the west. At 9:30 a.m. Zaeschmar logged a "large single-masted vessel surrounded by destroyers," which he believed was a "land-based aircraft mother ship," and because he expected she would fly off planes in pursuit, Zaeschmar turned off to the southeast to open the distance. His observation was evidently inspired by German intelligence descriptions of *Furious*, but the carrier in fact was not with the Harwich Force.

*L 70*, to the north, had picked up the seaplane's and *L 56*'s messages, and steered for the Dogger Bank South Lightship to find the enemy. At 8:50 a.m., flying at 15,700 feet, von Lossnitzer saw through a hole in the clouds a kite balloon at 2,300 feet, but could not see the vessel towing it. A few minutes later he saw destroyers to the west. Turning to starboard, *L 70* boldly advanced to attack in the face of heavy anti-aircraft fire whose shells exploded under the ship. At 9:08 a.m. von Lossnitzer believed he saw an enemy battle cruiser (none was present), screened by destroyers, turning to port under the clouds. He aimed ten 220-pound bombs at two of the destroyers on opposite courses, but the overcast covered them before the bombs exploded. At 9:36, *L 70* radioed, "In contact with one enemy battle cruiser, one destroyer flotilla at Dogger Bank South Lightship." Unable to find the British ships again beneath heavy clouds, von Lossnitzer returned to his patrol line, and at 2:26 p.m. broke off his reconnaissance due to poor visibility.

*L 70, Strasser's flagship in the last raid of the war, shown on the field at Nordholz just before taking off on the fatal raid over England on August 5, 1918. Valuable intelligence material was salvaged from her control car where she fell off the Norfolk coast. (Kameradschaft)*

The light cruisers had just put the motor boats in the water when *L 70* was seen approaching through a gap in the clouds. The attack surprised them, accustomed as they were to the Zeppelins' cautiously keeping their distance. Four large bombs fell close to the ships, but did no damage. "It seemed that the Zeppelin commanders were losing their sense of caution, and that it would be worth while, next time, to take a fighting airplane in company."[2] Commodore Tyrwhitt could not know that his experience had been exceptional, and that the attack had been made by an overbold newcomer, in a hurry to make his reputation in the North Sea. The idea of taking a fighter plane to sea with the Harwich Force was soon to bear bitter fruit for another Zeppelin commander.

Zaeschmar, who had prudently seen without being seen, undoubtedly was right in sounding a contrasting note of caution:

> On meeting enemy forces we have to expect the use of land-based aircraft; but since they are tied to their carrier, it is my opinion that the airship is not exposed to danger if it follows at a distance of 30 miles. The possibility of surprise is present, however, with cloud conditions like today; particularly when the airship, coming out of the German Bight, is silhouetted sharply against the sky, while she herself has very limited vision.

Next day, on August 2, *L 53* was patrolling on the north side of the Bight, and *L 64* to the west. The latter ship had several encounters with enemy

2 Jones, VI, p. 370.

*L 64 first flew on March 11, 1918 and is shown here at Ahlhorn. (Luftschiffbau Zeppelin)*

*Above: L 53 taking off from Friedrichshafen. Its first flight was August 12, 1918. Below: L 53 being walked stern first into the construction shed at Friedrichshafen. (both - Luftschiffbau Zeppelin)*

forces. Her commander, *Korvettenkapitän* Arnold Schütze, reported the first as follows:

> At 8:45 a.m. on a south-west course in Square Karl 430 (42 miles north-west of Terschelling) an enemy fighting squadron came in sight consisting of a particularly large biplane (Curtiss boat) and five almost equally large biplanes, approaching on a north-east course at 2,000 meters altitude [6,500 feet] under the ship. The planes climbed under the ship to 4,000 meters [13,000 feet] and fired heavily on her. Brown explosive bursts seen astern. The machine guns were not used as the ship was climbing hard and the distance was too great. Instead, all bombs were dropped on the squadron flying below the ship, so that all the planes immediately turned off on a south course and gave up the attack. The combat lasted from 8:45 to 9:20 a.m.

*L 64* during the action had climbed from 14,700 to 19,000 feet, and had little ballast left on board. Pushing on to the west, she found an enemy destroyer flotilla of 7 boats steaming into the Bight, and was heavily fired on. Because no bombs were left on board, Schütze turned away and lost the vessels under the clouds. He found them again at 2:45 p.m., and followed them for half an hour as they proceeded to the south-east. This appears to be the only occasion on which the British minelaying 20th Flotilla was discovered by the airships in its numerous forays into the German Bight.

The flying-boat attack off Terschelling resulted indirectly in severe damage to *L 64* in her landing at Ahlhorn at 8:30 p.m. The weather was squally and gusty, the ship was "exhausted" (*Ausgefahren*), with only half her buoyant gas and no ballast, and she was unusually heavy aft. The ground crew was unable to drag her towards her hangar, and as the ship rolled and pitched on the ground, Schütze felt obliged to order the heavy 2-engine after gondola cut off in order to get her into the "Alarich" shed. She was several weeks under repair, and did not make another flight until September 5, 1918.

*L 52* was patrolling on August 4, and on the morning of August 5, *L 61*, having exchanged a torn gas cell, took off from Wittmundhaven at 2:46 a.m. for routine scouting in the German Bight. The moon would be new next day, and the other "Front" ships were standing by for a raid. Late in the morning Strasser's order was issued:

> Attack on south or middle (London only at order of Leader of Airships). Bombs: Four of 300, eight of 100, twelve of 50 kg. For *L 70*, eight of 300, eight of 100, eight of 50 kg. Take-off for *L 56*, 3 p.m., the others at 2 p.m. Approach along 54th parallel as far as 4 degrees east. Participants: *L 53*, *L 56*, *L 63*, *L 65*, *L 70*. Blankenberghe wind measurements at 2, 5 p.m., 5 a.m. Wind measurements from German Bight as required. Afternoon weather map will be wirelessed, night map will not. Preserve careful wireless discipline. Airship special wavelength. Leader of Airships aboard *L 70*. Direction from Nordholz on Leader of Airships' instructions.
>
> Leader of Airships.

With the war already lost, Strasser still dreamed of bombing London!

For the last time, the huge gas-bags, their bellies full of bombs, lifted slowly from the fields along the North Sea coast and headed west for England. With von Lossnitzer in *L 70* was Peter Strasser, leading in person the first raid on England in four months. Strasser, the chief who did not believe that *L 70* could be attacked by British aircraft, and von Lossnitzer, inexperienced, rash, making his first raid on England under the eye of the man who had given him the finest airship in the world as a special favor. Neither man would be a restraining influence on the other. It was a bad combination.

Over the North Sea the airships, flying at 16,400 feet, found the familiar low cloud ceiling underneath. Fresh head winds had been expected at high altitudes, but in fact the westerly wind decreased as the Zeppelins climbed higher, and at 6:30 p.m., *L 53*, *L 65* and *L 70* together placed themselves within 60 sea miles of the English coast, still in broad daylight. Because of the high air temperature and low barometric pressure, *Kapitänleutnant* Dose in *L 65* had not been able to reach a safe attack altitude despite release of 43,000 pounds of ballast. After dropping 2,200 pounds of unfused bombs, his ship ascended to 17,700 feet. At 9 p.m. Strasser sent final orders to his commanders: "To all airships. Attack according to plan from Karl 727. Wind at 5,000 meters [16,400 feet] west-south-west 3 doms [13 1/2 m.p.h.]. Leader of Airships."

Strasser's former comrades-in-arms believe that this message – the last they ever received from their beloved chief – betrayed him to the enemy. Actually, *L 53*, *L 65* and *L 70* had been seen as early as 8:10 p.m. from the Leman Tail Lightship, thirty miles north-east of Happisburgh on the Norfolk coast. When first sighted, the Zeppelins were on parallel courses, but presently they deployed into "V" formation. Within forty minutes the news was traveling over the whole East Coast defense network. Thirty-five minutes later, the Great Yarmouth air station, nearest to the path of the attackers, had thirteen planes in the air. Ten of them steered to look for the enemy inland, but three aircraft flew out to sea to intercept the airships before they should reach the coast. In the lead was a D.H.4 two-seater with a Rolls-Royce 375 h.p. Eagle VIII engine – a magnificent combat aircraft for its day, with a speed at 15,500 feet of 122.5 m.p.h., and a service ceiling of 22,000 feet. The pilot was Major Egbert Cadbury, who had participated in the destruction of *L 21*, and his observer, Captain Robert Leckie, had piloted the flying-boat that had shot down *L 22*. Following Cadbury and Leckie were Captain C.S. Iron and Sergeant Wills, and Captain B.S. Jardine and Lieutenant E.R. Munday, in lower-powered D.H.9s. Forty minutes' climbing brought the three planes through the clouds, and up ahead the enemy was in sight. Says Iron:

> Darkness had closed in below us, but our quarry, silhouetted against the faint glow which lingered in the evening sky, remained clearly visible above us. By this time we had become aware of not one Zeppelin, but three. We had been climbing steadily out to sea, and as we worked our way round to make our point, two more raiders had come into view. There they were: three Zeppelins in line abreast, their noses pointing landward, waiting, apparently, for some prearranged zero hour to launch them upon their voyage of frightfulness.
>
> Surely the Zeppelin commanders had blundered. Strong currents in the upper air, possibly, had carried them a long way south of their intended rendezvous, so that instead of making their landfall with the secrecy planned they had unwittingly drifted down over a veritable hornets' nest. . .
>
> Curbing our impatience we continued to climb, with painful slowness, up through the thousand-foot gap which separated us from our target, when, suddenly, a startling metamorphosis took place before our astonished gaze. A small ball of fire had appeared at the after end of our Zeppelin; with amazing rapidity this grew into a blaze; a few seconds later we could see that the whole of the Zeppelin's tail was well alight.
>
> Fascinated by the spectacle of the burning ship we sat watching the progress of the fire. Very gradually our quarry began to sink by the tail, and we could see the flames spreading upwards and forwards towards the bow. A vertical draught, induced by the falling stern, was fanning the blaze along the whole length of the hull. A few seconds more and the airship's doom was sealed. She had become a roaring furnace from end to end.
>
> Her stern sank lower, and the blazing ship had assumed almost a perpendicular position before starting off on her plunge to earth. After swinging my machine off its course, to avoid falling debris, we sat enthralled at the appalling spectacle.
>
> At the beginning of her dive the now derelict airship broke in two, and her after-part came hurtling down beside us; several portions broke away and continued their headlong career with added velocity. The forepart of the ship fell more slowly, and as it passed us we could see the burning skeleton of the mangled framework glowing with a terrific heat.
>
> As the blazing mass fell through the upper cloud layers, six thousand feet below us, they threw back immense fans of light, making everything about us as bright as day. Slowly the

### AIRSHIP RAID, AUGUST 5–6, 1918

| Ship | Flt. No. | Take-off | Landing | Time in air | Distance (miles) | Av. speed (m.p.h.) | Max. alt. (feet) | Temp. (°F.) | Crew | Fuel (lb.) loaded/used | Oil (lb.) loaded/used | Ballast loaded (lb.) | Bombs (lb.) | Gas used (cubic feet) |
|---|---|---|---|---|---|---|---|---|---|---|---|---|---|---|
| *L 53* | 52 | Nordholz 1.55 p.m. | Nordholz 5.50 a.m. | 15h. 55m. | 852 | 54·0 | 19,350 | −0·4 | 16 | 9,700/6,400 | 937/207 | 42,800 | 6,450 | 779,000 |
| *L 56* | 33 | Witt'haven 3.1[illegible] p.m. | Witt'haven 6.15 a.m. | 15h. 3m. | | | 22,000 | −4·0 | 18 | 9,700/6,240 | 905/165 | 49,600 | 5,740 | 1,220,000 |
| *L 63* | 33 | Ahlhorn 1.47 p.m. | Ahlhorn 5.05 a.m. | 15h. 18m. | 899 | 58·7 | 20,650 | +1·4 | 18 | 10,100/5,980 | 565/249 | 53,800 | 6,610 | 991,000 |
| *L 65* | 17 | Nordholz 2.35 p.m. | Nordholz 6.55 a.m. | 16h. 20m. | 811 | 49·7 | 19,350 | +3·0 | 19 | 10,200/8,390 | 551/375 | 47,200 | 6,120 | 1,060,000 |
| *L 70* | 7 | Nordholz 2.13 p.m. | | | | | | | | | | | 7,950 | |

*Weather:* Light southerly wind. Sky overcast, intermittent rain.
*Bombs:* No bombs dropped on land.
*Casualties:* Nil.
*Monetary damage:* Nil.

reflected brilliance faded, until only a pin-point of light, far down in the cloud-mass, was left to indicate the course of the falling wreckage.[3]

Cadbury and Leckie had got home first on the leader of the raiding squadron, *L 70* herself. In his report, Cadbury says:

> At approximately 21:45 the Zeppelins, which were flying in "V" formation, altered course North. At 22:10 Zeppelin abeam 2,000 feet above us, at 17,000 feet. At 22:20 we had climbed to 16,400 feet, and I attacked Zeppelin head on, slightly to port so as to clear any obstruction that might be suspended from airship. My observer trained his gun on the bow of the airship and the fire was seen to concentrate on a spot under the Zeppelin 3/4 way aft.
>
> The Z.P.T.[4] was seen to blow a great hole in the fabric and a fire started which quickly ran along the entire length of the Zeppelin. The Zeppelin raised her bows as if in an effort to escape, then plunged seaward a blazing mass. The airship was completely consumed in about 3/4 of a minute. A large petrol tank was seen to become detached from the framework and fall blazing into a heavy layer of clouds at about 7,000 feet below.[5]

The wreckage of *L 70* landed quite close to the schooner Amethyst, near which some bombs had already exploded, and left a great pool of petrol that burned on the water for almost an hour. The mate of the schooner looked through his night glasses, but saw no survivors. For Peter Strasser, death had come as he would have wished it, while fighting at the head of his men in a last battle for a cause already lost.

Cadbury continues:

> On seeing the fate of their companion, the remaining two Zeppelins immediately altered course East and proceeded in that direction at high speed.
>
> At this moment, my engine cut out completely, owing, I presume, to a temporary block in the petrol system. I managed to get my engine going again, and closed second Zeppelin. I again attacked bow on and my observer opened fire, when within 500 feet of airship. Fire immediately broke out in the midships gondola. At this point my observer's gun jammed owing to a double feed, which in the darkness could not be cleared. The fire on the Zeppelin became extinguished. I maintained contact with Zeppelin for approximately five minutes while my observer attempted to clear jam, but without success. I was unable to use my front gun, as I had reached my ceiling.[6]

The second airship was *L 65*. Her commander, Walter Dose, recalled:

3 C.S, Iron, "The Last of the Zeppelins," *Blackwood's*, January 1936, p. 137.

4 The Pomeroy explosive bullet.

5 Cadbury's report in Imperial War Museum file, "Pilots' Reports Relating to Destruction of Zeppelins."

6 Cadbury's Report.

> I was only 3,000 meters from *L 70* when it happened. We had been feeling quite uneasy for some time. First, there was that long radio signal from Strasser, which was surely plotted by the English direction finding stations. Then, as the twilight deepened, we could see streams of flame shooting from her short exhaust stacks. Suddenly we saw a small light on the otherwise darkened ship which rapidly spread, and soon afterwards the whole ship was in flames. She started to fall with running engines, first slowly, then faster and faster, and broke to pieces shortly before entering the clouds below. Immediately afterwards the plane attacked us. Later, bullet holes – 340 in all – were found in the after gas cells. There was no fire of course. The mechanic in the port midships gondola lifted the black window-curtain without turning out the light, producing the illusion of a fire inside.

Turning north to evade this attack, Dose believed he was fired on by ground batteries, and replied with 3,750 pounds of bombs, partly to get his ship above 17,500 feet and to escape the plane. He believed these batteries were near King's Lynn, but could not see the effect of his bombs because of heavy clouds underneath. Actually, Dose had been deceived by radio bearings into believing he was farther west than he was, and his bombs fell far out at sea, 65 miles north-east of King's Lynn. *L 65* made for home at 19,400 feet. On the return journey, Cell 7, which had a hole the size of a fist, ran out 90 per cent empty, while Cells 4, 5 and 6 lost 10 to 15 per cent more gas than the others due to numerous bullet holes. At 11 p.m. the two after engines were set at half speed, to reduce the stresses on the fragile hull which threatened to break in two. Dose was lucky to be able to land his ship without damage at Nordholz at 6:55 a.m., and the repairs to the gas cells lasted until August 23. Since Cadbury and Leckie had got off only a few rounds against *L 65*, she must have been attacked by another plane – probably Jardine and Munday's D.H.9, which was lost at sea with her crew.

Prölss in *L 53* was also not far distant when the flagship was destroyed. "At 10:10 p.m. to port over Norfolk a ship was seen falling in flames and therefore, since I had to consider that with the brightness prevailing at this hour, a plane had shot down the ship, the idea of pushing farther into the interior was given up." Prölss had been planning to attack Nottingham or Sheffield, but, he says, after the loss of *L 70* he rose to 19,400 feet and dropped his bombs on the coastal town of Boston. He was aiming entirely by radio bearings, and they fell in the sea 65 miles to the east off Cromer.

*L 56* and *L 63* had approached the English coast together some 30 miles south of the others. Von Freudenreich in *L 63* intended to come inland south of the Humber, but could not get a 9:45 p.m. radio bearing as the stop-watch failed. A bearing at 10:15 showed he was off the mouth of the Humber. In actual fact, he had made the land just north of Yarmouth, had turned sharply north across the tracks of the other three ships, and had *L 65* and *L 70* on the port quarter about 5 miles distant. "At this moment *L 70* took fire with a large flame, stood up vertically and fell. An external cause was not apparent. Because it was not fully dark I expected it had been done by a plane and steered north to escape, climbing to 6,300 meters [20,700 feet]." Soon afterwards, he reported, he was heavily fired on by batteries on the north side of the Humber and on Spurn Point, and because of the overcast beneath, the accurate anti-aircraft fire up to great altitudes, and the fact that it was still light enough for airplane attack, he aimed his entire bomb load at these batteries. In fact, *L 63* was at least 40 miles east of her position by radio bearings, and these bombs must have fallen far out in the North Sea.

At 9:45, while still well out to sea, *Kapitänleutnant* Zaeschmar in *L 56* had seen the lights of Yarmouth ahead, and *L 53*, *L 65* and *L 70* at a great distance to the north against the light evening sky. At 10:15, "observed at distance of 60 to 70 miles a burning airship fall and continue burning on the ground." At 11:30 p.m., he reported, he came inland south of Lowestoft, saw lights through a hole in the clouds, and decided from radio bearings that this must be Norwich. Here, from 20,400 feet, he dropped all his bombs. The flight home was uneventful, but *L 56*'s landing at Wittmundhaven was delayed till 6:15 a.m. because of ground mist, and because the ship was heavy and her commander waited for sunrise to warm and expand the gas. In fact, *L 56*, after flying north up the Norfolk coast with *L 63*, had turned back and at 11:45 p.m. had dropped some bombs in the sea, then came over land near Lowestoft, crossed the town, and dropped another group of bombs offshore.

Strasser's conduct of the raid was deservedly criticized by the anonymous author of the Air Ministry's secret intelligence survey, *Enemy Aircraft North Sea and Baltic*. "Whether in view of the cloudy weather, or trading on the immunity enjoyed in previous raids, *Korv. Kap*. Strasser showed remarkable recklessness in allowing his fleet to approach the English coast at a slow speed, a comparatively early hour, and a comparatively low altitude."[7] This judgment must stand today. Leckie, now retired after reaching Air Marshal's rank and after serving as Chief of the Air Staff of the Royal Canadian Air Force, believes that Strasser deserved better luck with the weather: "Following an almost perfect day with sky unusually clear of clouds, a heavy bank of nimbus spread from the *West*, and *before* the attack, had covered the East coast and sea to the east to 10/10ths. I feel it is more probable that Strasser was assured by his Met. organization that he could count on clear weather in the Bight of Heligoland and vicinity of the Dutch islands (making for easy and accurate navigation) and a thick cloud cover during the last 100-150 miles to his objective. We know the cloud cover did arrive but probably about 2 hours late. Unquestionably, however, Strasser exercised poor judgment in persisting with his operation without waiting for the cover of clouds."

On receipt of the news of *L 70*'s destruction, the naval commander on the East Coast of England, Admiral Sir Edward Charlton, determined to salvage the wreck. It could be expected that *L 70* might yield classified documents – signal books, cipher keys and codes – which would greatly assist British naval intelligence. In addition, technical information to be derived from the Zeppelin remains would be of great value to British Admiralty designers striving to overtake the German lead in airships.

[7] Great Britain, Air Ministry, *Enemy Aircraft North Sea and Baltic*, Sept. 6, 1918, p. 5.

Two days after *L 70* was destroyed, H.M. Trawler, *Scomber*, out of Immingham, located and buoyed the graves of Strasser and his men. The wreck was down among the sand banks and shallows off the Lincolnshire coast, five miles north-west of the Blakeney Overfalls bell buoy, and submerged in eight fathoms of water.

From August 9 to September 22, 1918, the little ships wearing the White Ensign spent a total of 22 days over the wreck. *Scomber* was flagship of the operation, and the other trawlers participating were *Driver*, *Bullfrog*, *Peking*, *Topaz*, and *Star of Britain*. Working in pairs, the trawlers, dragging wires between them underneath the wreckage, succeeded in bringing most of the structure of the airship to the surface, and large amounts were carried ashore to be landed on the quay at Immingham. Here were piled heaps of duralumin girders, most if not all of the gondolas complete with engines, radiators and propellers, gas valves, and even fragments of gas cells and the fabric outer cover.

Intensive examination of the wreckage, and more particularly, of operating records found in her control car, soon gave the British a complete picture of the design features and capabilities of the new type of Zeppelin. A personal notebook found on von Lossnitzer's body gave valuable information on the Maybach "altitude motor," its actual power output at different altitudes, and its fuel and oil consumption. Probably from this source, correct figures were derived for length, diameter and gas volume. The formidable speed capabilities of the new ship – with a maximum of 77 1/2 m.p.h. at 7,550 feet – probably came from the notebook, though a bombsight found in the control car was graduated for a maximum speed of only 62, m.p.h. Probably also from von Lossnitzer's notebook the British obtained such details as the rate of climb dynamically at various nose-up inclinations, and the bomb loadings for the class of 2,200 pounds on North Sea patrols, 6,600 pounds for attacks on London, and a maximum of 10,580 pounds against other targets. The figure of 8,800 pounds of bombs carried on this raid evidently came from the ballast sheet and deck log which probably was the authority for the statement that "for a normal raid on England with 4,000 kg. of bombs, the airship was intended to rise statically to 18,400 feet, with an additional climb dynamically to 19,700 feet. After the discharge of the bombs at this height she would rise to 21,000 feet and would have enough fuel left for the return journey." The airship's rough War Diary was almost certainly recovered, to reveal that "it was apparently the intention of the commander of *L 70* to use all seven motors on the outward journey and only five on the return." Direct examination of the salvaged wreckage revealed such new details as the girder structure being "lighter even than in the Height-Climbing class, where drastic reductions of weight were made throughout the structure. The ballonets in the ship destroyed are made of very light mixed silk and cotton." From black-painted portions of salvaged fabric it was concluded that *L 70* was painted identically to earlier ships – black beneath, and clear-doped above.

The secret *Enemy Aircraft North Sea and Baltic* is silent on the salvage of codes and ciphers, but this is hardly surprising as such material would be placed under a higher classification. From a letter which Strasser's successor wrote on August 7, 1918, to the Chief of the Naval Staff, it is known that *L 70* had on board "various weather codes and Name List 1090 Vol.2, with Exchange Table (a cipher key) for 31 July to 15 August No.1373." He added, "one can assume complete destruction and that they are not in enemy hands." Unfortunately this was not the case. Mr. G. Edward Bray of Grimsby, at that time mate of the trawler *Topaz*, recalls the scene as *L 70*'s control car was recovered: "As soon as the gondola came out of the water, the officer jumped down and salvaged a dispatch case of papers which were rushed ashore by a naval pinnace."

What of the bodies of Strasser and the 21 members of the crew? As invariably happened, some had jumped, even though they wore no parachutes, while others who had ridden the wreckage down were trapped in the structure or gondolas. Sir Egbert Cadbury recalled very distinctly that he was told by Admiral Charlton that Strasser's body was recovered and a search revealed "all the German codes and also a complete history of all the other German airship raids." He added that "all the bodies were recovered intact, and that of Captain

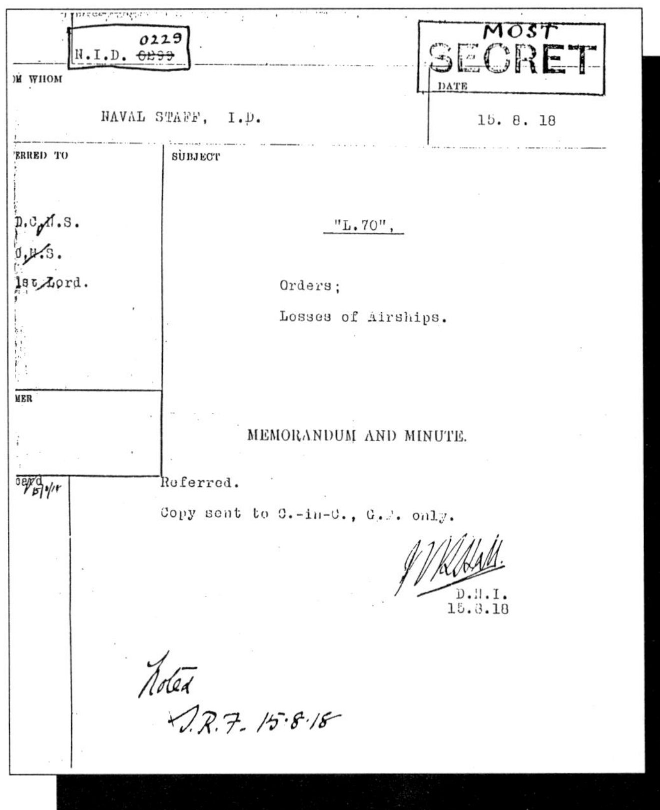

N.I.D. 0229 ~~0899~~

MOST SECRET

M WHOM: NAVAL STAFF, I.D.

DATE: 15. 8. 18

ERRED TO: D.C.N.S. / D.N.S. / 1st Lord.

SUBJECT: "L.70". Orders; Losses of Airships.

MEMORANDUM AND MINUTE.

Referred.

Copy sent to C.-in-C., G.F. only.

D.N.I.
15.8.18

Noted
J.R.F. 15.8.18

The three documents shown above, below and opposite are the documents found on Peter Strasser's body and translated by the British Admiralty. They are published here in their original English translation. (Public Records Office)

TRANSLATION OF ORDERS RECOVERED FROM "L.70".

ORDERS - Attack South or Midlands.

BOMBS - 8 : 300, 8 : 100, 8 : 50 kg.

ASCENT - 3.30 p.m.

Proceed first to 4°E. on the parallel of 54°N.

AIRSHIPS TAKING PART - L.53, L.56, L.63, L.65, L.70.

Blankenberghe measurements - 6 p.m., 10 p.m. and 3 a.m.

Wind measurements from the Bight of Heligoland as required.

Afternoon weather chart will be sent by wireless.

No evening weather chart.

Special care must be taken to observe wireless discipline.

Special wave-length for air-ships. Control (station) Nordholz.

Leader of Airships (F. d. L.) in "L.70".

Control; Nordholz I Adjutant in accordance with my directions.

AIR-SHIP LOSSES.

(Translation of a Document recovered from L.70)

enemy action ... with crew ...... L.7, L.19, L.21, L.22, L.23
L.31, L.32, L.34, L.39,
L.43, L.44, L.48, L.59

Total ... 13

without crew ... L.5, L.8, L.12, L.15, L.33
L.45, L.49, P.L.19, L.50

Total ... 9

the act of God .. with crew ...... L.10, L.62, S.L.6, S.L.9,

Total ... 4

without crew ... L.3, L.4, L.16, L.20,
L.36, L.38, L.40, L.55,
L.57, S.L.3, S.L.12,
S.L.14

Total .... 12

the ~~hangars~~ sheds ..................... L.6, L.9, L.17, L.18,
L.24, L.46, L.47, L.51,
L.58, S.L.4, S.L.20,

Total .... 11

49

ng up (in the sheds ~~?work suspended~~) ......... L.11, L.13, L.30, L.37,
L.Z.113, L.Z.120,
S.L.8, L.41.

st before the war ................ L.1, L.2.

Deutschland

ismantled ........................ Sachsen, Viktoria Luise.

existence ~~commission~~ ..................... [L.14, L.35, L.42] , L.52,
L.53+, L.54, L.56, L.60,
L.61, L.63, L.64, L.65, L.70+

t built .......................... L.26-29, L.66-69; S.L.21

overleaf) L.52* Friemel, L.53+ Prölss, L.54* Büttler, L.56 Zaeschmar ~~Hoeschler~~, L.60* Flemming, L.61 Bödecker, L.63 Freud~~enreich (?)~~, L.64 Schütze, L.65 Dose, L.70+ Lossnitzer; Ehrlich, Hausser; L.71 Dietrich.

Strasser was completely untouched and his death was due either to drowning or to the shock of the impact with the water – I am not sure which – but he showed no disfigurement or burns or injuries of any kind." Mr. Bray confirmed that the body of Strasser was recovered and buried at sea. Five bodies were found in the wreckage brought aboard H.M.T. *Topaz*, and after being searched for documents and papers, they were weighted with furnace bars from the fire room and returned to the sea. Along with a quantity of flotsam, six or seven dead Germans drifted up together on the Lincolnshire coast. The local people refused to permit their burial in the churchyard, and Mr. Henry Drinkall of Grimsby recalls that his drifter, the *Venus*, was dispatched under sealed orders to carry the bodies out to sea for burial.

Without their leader, Strasser's bereaved subordinates carried on with routine flights in the German Bight. For four days after the disaster off the Norfolk coast there were no reconnaissance's. Then, on August 10, *L 52* and *L 63* were out scouting. Next day, on August 11, *L 56* took off from Wittmundhaven at 2:13 a.m. to patrol to the north, and *L 53* left Nordholz at 2:40 a.m. to scout from Terschelling to the Dogger Bank South Lightship. And once more disaster struck.

Since May, 1918, several officers of the Royal Air Force had been experimenting with a lighter designed to take a high-performance fighter plane into the Zeppelins' side of the North Sea. It was intended that a destroyer should tow the lighter at high speed into the wind, and the 2F.1 "Camel" would then be able to get into the air with the short run that the lighter's deck provided. Lieut.-Colonel C.R. Samson was nearly killed in the first attempt to take off from the lighter on May 30. Lieutenant S.D. Culley then took over the equipment in improved form and on July 31 made a successful flight.

The decision to test the lighter under service conditions coincided with *L 70*'s bold attack on the Harwich Force on August 1. Thinking that a similar opportunity might offer itself again, Commodore Tyrwhitt took the lighter, with Culley and the "Camel" on board, on the next expedition into the German Bight. On the night of August 10, four light cruisers and thirteen destroyers left Harwich for the waters north of Terschelling. The chief purpose of the operation was to send off six motor torpedo boats to attack enemy vessels. The lighter was in the tow of the destroyer *Redoubt*.

At dawn on the 11th, Tyrwhitt's squadron hove-to off Terschelling and sent the motor boats on their way east to the German Bight. Three hours later a Zeppelin – *L 53* – appeared at a great altitude to the north-east. Commodore Tyrwhitt ordered his force to head out to sea and make smoke-screens, and Prölss, his curiosity aroused, followed after the cruisers and destroyers. At 8:58 a.m. Culley took off from the deck of the lighter. By 9:30 the "Camel" had climbed to 18,000 feet, but the Zeppelin was still a thousand feet higher. In the thin air of the heights, Culley's plane reeled and mushed as he tried for half an hour to coax it a few hundred feet farther. At 9:58 a.m. the "Camel" was only 300 feet below the Zeppelin, and they were headed straight

*Korvettenkapitän Eduard Prölss died when his L 53 was shot down in flames on August 11, 1918.*

for each other. Culley pulled back the stick and opened fire. One gun jammed after seven rounds, but the other Lewis on the upper wing spat out a complete double drum of incendiary and explosive ammunition. The Zeppelin made no effort to save herself, and as he looked back over his shoulder, Culley saw small bursts of flame along her black underside. A few moments later she was on fire forward and sinking by the head. The bow broke away and the Zeppelin plunged vertically. Bombs and gondolas tore free and fell faster than the framework, sending up tall columns of water as they struck the surface. One or two men jumped overboard. They had no parachutes. Long before reaching the water the wreckage had burned itself out, leaving a smudgy trail of brown smoke which, to Culley, assumed the shape of a huge question mark.

These two losses in six days marked the end of the German Naval Airship Division as a fighting service. The death of Strasser was the final blow. "After the loss of *L 70* with the Leader of Airships on board in August, 1918, there were no more airship raids on England, primarily *because the driving force behind them was gone.*"[8] Tributes and eulogies poured into Nordholz. Scheer, who believed whole-heartedly in Strasser and the airship, telegraphed:

> The airship, which was created by the inventive genius and stubborn perseverance of Count Zeppelin, was developed by Captain Peter Strasser, as Leader of Airships, with untiring zeal, and in spite of every obstacle, into a formidable weapon of attack. The spirit with which he succeeded in inspiring his particular arm on many an air raid he has crowned by his heroic death over England. As Count Zeppelin will live for ever in the grateful memory of the German people, so also will Captain Strasser, who led our airships to victory.[9]

More dispassionate estimates must recognize Peter Strasser as one of the outstanding subordinate commanders on either side in World War I. Perhaps too closely identified with his weapon to be suited for flag rank, he was ideally qualified to lead an elite service which lived dangerously even when not facing the enemy, and which took terrible risks every time it went into combat. Zealous for the cause, but careless of his own future, Strasser shared his men's dangers and never asked them to do what he would not dare himself. By his death in the last raid of the war he sealed a relationship with his men which they still recall with deep emotion as one of absolute loyalty, faith and trust. Yet bravery and patriotism do not sum up Peter Strasser. In a sense he was ahead of his time. In an era when bulldog courage and marlinspike seamanship were considered enough, Strasser was one of the first naval officers to combine a knowledge of war and of men with special technical skills which enabled

[8] Beelitz, p. 41.

[9] Hans von Schiller, "Acht Jahre Marineluftschiffahrt," *Luftfahrt*, July-August, 1922.

him to get the utmost out of a complex and novel weapon. Even his faults – which led to his death – were those of a strong character: overestimation of his own arm, disregard of the capabilities of his enemies, and devotion to friends and – favorites, some of whom proved unworthy of him.

Yet Strasser actually belongs to more than the German Navy, or even the German people. Although his work is little known outside the circle of his former associates, only Count Zeppelin and Dr. Eckener contributed more than he to the cause of the airship. The men who manned the Zeppelin Company's postwar commercial ships, including the world-girdling *Graf Zeppelin* and the luxurious *Hindenburg*, were members of the so-odd flight crews trained in the Naval Airship Division, and followed the principles of intensive theoretical knowledge and expert airmanship evolved by Strasser and Eckener in their five-year association. And not only the German ships, but also the American Navy's *Shenandoah*, *Akron*, *Macon*, and countless "blimps," owed much to the continuous technical improvements and the navigational and meteorological advances which Strasser fostered among his associates and subordinates. Among the pioneers of the air, Peter Strasser's place is secure.

# CHAPTER XXIV

# CONCLUSION

At Nordholz, it might have seemed as if nothing had changed. *Korvettenkapitän* Paul Werther, formerly heading the ground troop and the airship schools, stepped into Strasser's shoes and later was confirmed as the last Leader of Airships. With the help of the officers at Nordholz, Werther formulated detailed proposals for a new type of Zeppelin with improved high-altitude performance. They envisaged a ship with a ceiling of at least 26,000 feet, capable of carrying 6,600 pounds of bombs and ten hours' fuel, able to make at least 76 m.p.h. at her maximum altitude, and armed with fourteen 20 mm. machine cannon. But with Strasser dead, and Scheer, his patron, leaving Wilhelmshaven on August 11 to become Chief of the Naval Staff, the atmosphere had changed. On August 16, Admiral Hipper, the new Commander-in-Chief of the High Seas Fleet, led a conference at Nordholz that laid down a new policy for the Naval Airship Division. Recent experiences, particularly the destruction of *L 53* by a landplane fighter, had demonstrated that the airplane was once again superior to the airship. Therefore, stated Hipper, airship scouting would be ordered only in situations where the results would be of unusual value. Werther and his commanders had proposed that steps be taken to give the Zeppelins an operational ceiling of 26,000 feet. To this, Hipper replied by pointing out that clouds beneath the airships often prevented effective scouting from their present altitude of 20,000 feet. He concluded by assuring the airship officers that scouting activities would not be halted entirely. Hipper confirmed this policy in a letter of August 26. Seaplanes, he wrote, had been developed to the point where they could fly routine reconnaissance in the German Bight,[1] and this was no longer an airship mission. They would still be

[1] On February 19, 1918, the Zeppelin Werke Lindau had delivered to the seaplane station at Norderney the first all-metal "Giant" monoplane of the Dornier Rs III type with a wing span of 121.4 feet and four Maybach 245 hp. engines. With a take-off weight of 23,000 pounds, the endurance was 10 hours and the maximum speed 90 m.p.h. After a series of tests, three more were ordered, and had the war continued into 1919, these flying-boats would have assumed most of the missions of the naval airships.

*OPPOSITE:*
*Wreck of L 63 in "Nogat" shed on June 23, 1919 showing starboard gondola. (Moch)*

*L 71 on a trial flight at Friedrichshafen on July 28, 1918, before being enlarged and modified. Note large amount of water falling from the ship. (Luftschiffbau Zeppelin)*

required for long-distance scouting and to cover the outer reaches of the North Sea as far as the Skagerrak and the Norwegian coast. Germany's technical superiority in airships could not be surrendered without sacrificing military advantages. On the subject of future raids, Hipper was equivocal: "The right to engage in raids and combat must not be taken away from the airship . . . but possibilities of success must not conflict with executing the mission. With respect to attacks on England, it must be considered that tying down great amounts of defensive equipment and manpower provides significant relief for the Army." Meanwhile, continued efforts should be made to improve the performance of the airships.

*SL 22 was the last Schütte-Lanz flown, though it was not accepted by the Navy. It was dismantled at Jüterbog in June 1920. (Bleston)*

On September 7, 1918, there was a conference at the Admiralty to discuss proposals for improving the performance of present and future airships.[2] The conference decided on a three-part program.

The recently delivered *L 71*, a sister of *L 70*; *L 72*, scheduled to complete at Löwenthal on October 1, and subsequent Zeppelins of the same type, would be lengthened by one gas cell to a capacity of 2,418,700 cubic feet, and would have one engine removed. Rebuilt in this fashion, they would have a dynamic ceiling of 26,200 feet. Werther, Flemming and Dietrich, representing the "Front," wanted these ships to have 5 engines for the sake of increased ceiling, but agreed to accept 6 when the loss of speed was emphasized.

By adding two gas cells, *L 56*, *L 61*, *L 63*, *L 64* and *L 65* could be similarly reconstructed to the same gas volume by January or February, 1919.

After some debate, it was decided to order one large new ship of 3,813,480 cubic foot capacity, 780 feet 10 inches long and 96 feet 6 inches in diameter, to be delivered in June, 1919. This new *L 100* would be the largest craft that could be accommodated in the standard double sheds in the North Sea, and approximated to the later *Graf Zeppelin* in size. With ten Maybach "altitude motors," the new ship would attain 26,200 feet statically, where she could still reach 68.3 m.p.h., and 28,600 feet dynamically. Her calculated useful lift of 183,680 pounds would have been devoted largely to water ballast in order to reach extreme altitudes.

In fact, of the whole program laid down at the September 7 conference only the reconstruction of *L 71* was carried out. On October 3, Dietrich flew her to Friedrichshafen, where she was cut in two for the insertion of an additional 15-meter gas cell, while the heavy 2-engine rear gondola was replaced by a smaller single-engine car. On October 28, *L 71* returned to the North Sea, berthing in the "Alarich" shed in Ahlhorn. The same modifications were made in *L 72*, which was ready for trials at the outbreak of the German Revolution.

A more realistic view of the limitations of the Zeppelins, together with the shortage of raw materials, led to the cancellation of the other ships. A memorandum by *Korvettenkapitän* Werther, dated October 2, 1918, shows that if the war had continued into 1919, the size of the Naval Airship Division would have been sharply limited. After the delivery of *L 72*, Werther expected to operate with only seven "Front" ships, *L 56*, *L 61*, *L 63*, *L 64*, *L 65*, *L 71* and *L 72*. *L 42* and *L 52*, serving as school ships, would occupy the "Normann" shed in Nordholz, while *L 14* would be laid up in the small "Nora" shed.

Only the two big "Nordstern" and "Nogat" hangars would remain in "Front" service in Nordholz, and the revolving shed, which could not accommodate the 743-foot craft of the lengthened *L 71* type, would be dismantled. In Ahlhorn the rebuilt Shed I, and the giant new Sheds V and VI, would continue in service. Tondern and Jüterbog would be maintained as emergency landing fields, and all the other bases would be decommissioned or turned over to the Navy's aviation branch.

As a result of this decision, the Naval Staff canceled the big new *L 100* on October 6. On November 2 it was decided that *L 73* would be completed, and possibly *L 74*, but all later contracts were canceled.

Judging by its very limited activities in the last months of the war, the Naval Airship Division would have played only a minor role had the struggle continued into 1919. On August 12, the day after *L 53*'s destruction, *L 63* took off at Ahlhorn on a routine patrol. Six and a half hours later she was recalled, ending the last scouting flight for two months. There were occasional practice flights near the bases. Then, on October 12, 1918, came an order for a long-distance reconnaissance the next day. For *L 65* it read:

---

[2] The September 7 conference considered the following design proposals, given here with their estimated performance (*L 70* included for comparison from the same set of original tables):

| No. | Engine number | Static ceiling | Dynamic ceiling | Static ceiling without bombs | Speed at altitude 6,500 ft. | Speed at altitude 16,400 ft. | Static ceiling |
|---|---|---|---|---|---|---|---|
| L 70 type, 2,195,800 cu. ft., length 693 ft. 11 in., diam. 78 ft. 6 in., height 90 ft. 10 in.* | | | | | | | |
| 1 | 7 | 21,200 ft. | 24,500 ft. | 22,400 ft. | 78·4 m.p.h. | 74·3 m.p.h. | 70·7 m.p.h. |
| L 70 lengthened, 2,418,700 cu. ft., length 743 ft. 2 in., diam. and height same | | | | | | | |
| 2 | 7 | 22,450 ft. | 25,250 ft. | 23,600 ft. | 77 m.p.h. | 73 m.p.h. | 70·5 m.p.h |
| 3 | 6 | 23,650 ft.† | 26,200 ft. | 24,800 ft. | 74 m.p.h. | 70·3 m.p.h. | 64·5 m.p.h |
| 4 | 5 | 24,500 ft.† | 26,650 ft. | 25,700 ft. | 69·5 m.p.h. | 65·8 m.p.h. | 59 m.p.h. |
| L 100 type, 2,648,250 cu. ft., length 743 ft. 2 in., diam. 82 ft. 5 in., height 97 ft. 8 in. | | | | | | | |
| 7 | 6 | 24,800 ft. | 27,150 ft. | 25,850 ft. | 73·2 m.p.h. | 69·5 m.p.h. | 62·7 m.p.h. |
| Proposal 112a, 3,177,900 cu. ft., length 738 ft. 3 in., diam. 96 ft. 6 in., height 109 ft. 11 in. | | | | | | | |
| 9 | 7 | 25,800 ft. | 28,000 ft. | 26,750 ft. | 74·7 m.p.h. | 71 m.p.h. | 63·1 m.p.h. |
| Proposal 112c, 3,813,480 cu. ft., length 780 ft. 10 in., diam. 96 ft. 6 in., height 110 ft. 3 in. | | | | | | | |
| 11 | 9 | 26,700 ft. | 28,900 ft. | 27,500 ft. | 78·4 m.p.h. | 74·4 m.p.h. | 65·4 m.p.h. |
| 12 | 10 | 26,200 ft. | 28,600 ft. | 27,000 ft. | 81 m.p.h. | 76·7 m.p.h. | 68.3 m.p.h. |

* Height including gondola bumpers.

† Can save 1,760 pounds more and increase ceiling by 650 feet.

*L 63 on the floor, wrecked by loyal personnel June 23, 1919, in the Nordholz shed "Nugat." (Kameradschaft)*

*L 65, her back broken and ribs caved in, as she looked after her crew pulled away the supporting shores and slacked off suspension tackle at Nordholz, June 23, 1919. (Luftschiffbau Zeppelin)*

Take-off about 11 a.m. so that ship can search extended area from Dogger Bank North Lightship north of 56 degrees before dark, and also can cover friendly units which tonight are putting to sea along Route 750. Control by I Minesweeper Flotilla.

Return with onset of darkness. Carry out mission according to your estimate of capabili-

*"Alarich" shed VI at Ahlhorn with L 71 and L 64. On October 3, 1918, L 71 flew to Friedrichshafen for lengthening, and returned on October 28. The last flights of these two ships were to England in July 1920. (Martin Dietrich)*

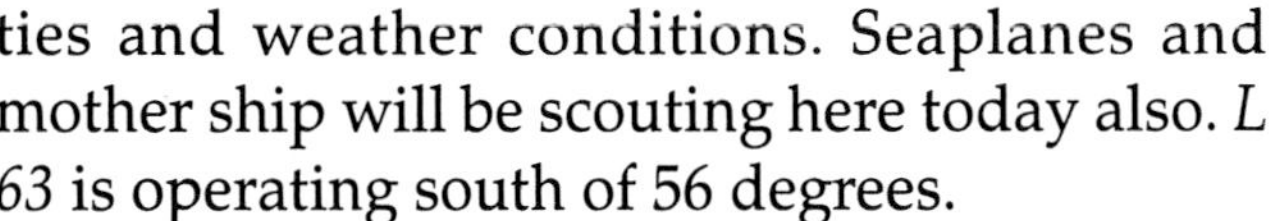

*Seddin at the end of the war with L 30 being dismantled, with LZ 120 intact in the background. LZ 120 was eventually surrendered to Italy. (Moch)*

*The remains of L 37, broken up by the Japanese at Seddin.*

> ties and weather conditions. Seaplanes and mother ship will be scouting here today also. *L 63* is operating south of 56 degrees.
>
> Leader of Airships.

Four battleships of the High Seas Fleet were to sortie that evening in support of their minesweepers. A solid overcast at sea prevented the Zeppelins from carrying out their orders. At 5:16 p.m., *L 63* turned back near the Dogger Bank North Lightship. *L 65* was off Lyngvig when she abandoned the mission. To *Kapitänleutnant* Gerhold Ratz, and to *Oberleutnant zur See* Werner Vermehren, had fallen the distinction of leading the last combat flights ever made by rigid airships.

With the Central Powers reeling towards disaster, Admiral Scheer at Imperial Headquarters or-

*LZ 120 awaiting surrender at Seddin.*

L63

L 42

*PREVIOUS: "Front ship" L 63 and training ship L 42, destroyed by their crews at Nordholz on June 23, 1919. (Luftschiffbau Zeppelin)*

dered a final fleet operation. Cruisers and destroyers, covered by the battle cruisers and battle fleet, were to raid shipping off the Flanders coast and in the Thames Estuary, and the Grand Fleet, hurrying to intercept, was to be brought to action off Terschelling. "Airship reconnaissance if practicable,"[3] read Admiral Hipper's operations order issued October 24. The consequence would probably have been a German disaster instead of the British defeat calculated to improve Armistice conditions. But the last battle never took place. The seamen of the High Seas Fleet, subverted by socialist politicians and persuaded that the officers intended to save their honor by perishing with their ships, broke out in mutiny on October 28. The revolt spread to Wilhemshaven and Kiel. For the Imperial Government it was the end, as Soldiers' and Sailors' Councils assumed power throughout the land.

With minor exceptions, the flight personnel of the Naval Airship Division remained loyal to the Kaiser till the end. But cases of disaffection and even outright insubordination had become increasingly frequent among the men of the ground troop. When the Fleet gave the signal, these immediately took control of the airship bases. There was no bloodshed, but the officers were arrested, and after a few days' detention, were sent home. On November 9, 1918, the airships were hung up in their sheds and deflated. Two days later the Armistice was signed. Paragraph XXVII read:

> All naval aircraft are to be concentrated and immobilized in German bases to be specified by the Allies and the United States of America.

With the revolutionary seamen in complete control, the airship bases, like the other facilities of the Imperial Navy, became scenes of chaos and looting. At all of them were large stocks of gasoline and oil, quantities of spare parts, new and used Maybach "altitude motors," parachutes, instruments – worth a fortune to unscrupulous speculators. "I remember how it all gradually disappeared," recalls a rating who was then in Nordholz. "The Sailors' Soviet didn't care. Most of them were in on it themselves. Those profiteers sold it all for millions of marks in Sweden."

Early in December an inter-Allied commission arrived in Germany to inspect naval vessels, seaplanes and airships at their bases, and to ensure that they had been disarmed in accordance with the Armistice terms. At the head of the airship party was Brigadier E.A.D. Masterman, one of England's leading airship pioneers. Between December 7 and 10 the Commission visited all the North Sea bases. At Friedrichshafen other officers examined *L 72*, and were told that frames hung up in Shed I were for *L 73*.

Winter dragged into spring, while at the airship bases the Soldiers' and Sailors' councils debated whether they should join the Republic of Oldenburg-East Frisia, the Republic of the Lower Elbe, or start a *putsch* of their own. And outside the limelight, regarding "the Bolsheviks" with scorn and hatred, were a small group of seamen still *Kaiserlich* in their hearts. The flight crews had remained loyal to the old regime, and with the revolution swirling around them, those who remained at the airship bases – the long-term professionals – began organizing a counterplot. The scuttling of the surrendered German warships by their crews at Scapa Flow on June 21, 1919, was the signal for them to act. On the morning of the 23rd, the conspirators at Nordholz and Wittmundhaven entered the echoing sheds unchallenged by the Sailors' Soviet, pulled away the shores under the empty hulls, slacked off the suspension tackles and let the giant structures crash down on the concrete floors with all their dead weight of 40 tons. With their framework crushed in and their backs broken, the Zeppelins were beyond repair. All the Nordholz ships – *L 14*, *L 41*, *L 42*, *L 63* and *L 65* – were thus demolished. At Wittmundhaven *L 52* and *L 56* were destroyed. At Ahlhorn the plot was betrayed to the Sailors' Soviet, and *L 64* and *L 71* remained intact.

The plotters, acting on their own initiative, had sworn a joint oath never to reveal the part any of them had played in the conspiracy, for fear of re-

3 From Admiral Hipper's operational order, given in Ludwig Freiwald, *Last Days of the German Fleet* (London: Constable & Co., Ltd., 1933), p. 114.

*L 72 on her first trial flight over Lake Constance, on July 9, 1920. Note the small single-engine power car fitted aft, and was in both ships of the reconstructed L 70 class. (Luftschiffbau Zeppelin)*

prisal from the revolutionary government. Thirty-eight years later the author met a former machinist's mate and flight crew member who had participated in the destruction at Nordholz, and who was willing to talk. "We weren't thinking about the Allies getting the ships," he related. "We didn't want them falling into the hands of those damned Communists in Berlin!"

This deed brought swift reprisal from the Inter-Allied Commission of Control. It immediately demanded the surrender of the remaining "Front" ships – *L 61*, *L 64*, and *L 71*. Also to be given up were the obsolete *L 30*, *L 37*, *LZ 113* and *LZ 120*, laid up in the Baltic one and a half years before. *L 72*, which had just been completed at Löwenthal at the time of the Armistice, was demanded, though the Germans argued that she was still the private property of the Zeppelin Company. Two small commercial Zeppelins were likewise seized – the *Bodensee* and *Nordstern*, which had been built for a revivified DELAG to operate between Friedrichshafen and Berlin. The Zeppelin works at Friedrichshafen were to be demolished. The Allies were clearly bent on exterminating the German airship industry, the French from motives of revanche, the British to secure for themselves a monopoly of world airship commerce.

Yet the desperate act of the counter-revolutionary seamen proved in the end to be the salvation of the Zeppelin enterprise. The United States had expected to share in the division of the craft destroyed in the North Sea bases, and still expected to be compensated for its loss. Negotiations were prolonged, the other Allies insisting that the United States could not own an airship larger than those destroyed. On December 16, 1921, the Conference of Ambassadors approved "the request of the United States Government to have constructed in Germany at Friedrichshafen a dirigible of approximately the *L 70* type (about 70,000 cubic meters)."[4] The result was *LZ 126*, later the U.S. Navy's long-lived *Los Angeles*. Her construction enabled the Zeppelin Company to survive, and by the time the ship was completed, in the autumn of 1924, the Allies were persuaded to lift their death sentence on the German airship industry.

In the summer and autumn of 1920 the last of the German Navy's airships were delivered to their new owners. So bitter was nationalistic feeling that the civilian crews risked injury as well as insult in carrying out the agreement. France, having first choice, received *L 72*, *LZ 113* and the commercial Zeppelin *Nordstern*. To Britain went *L 71* and *L 64*. To Italy were awarded *L 61*, *LZ 120* and *Bodensee*. Belgium received *L 30*, but had no place to house her and had her dismantled at Seerappen. *L 37* was allotted to Japan, but her new owners likewise broke her up and merely saved important parts. The wooden Schütte-Lanz *SL 22* was dismantled at Jüterbog and specimens of her structure were distributed to all the victorious powers. After demanding the ships, the Allies seized many of the sheds that had housed them. The big double hangar at Jüterbog was taken down and later re-erected

---

4 Letter of Ambassador Herrick to Secretary of State, December 16, 1921, in Frederick S. Hardesty (ed.), *Key to the Development of the Super-Airship: Luftfahrzeugbau Schütte-Lanz, Mannheim-Rheinau, Germany, 1909-1930* (New York 1930), p. 147.

*The German Navy Airship Combat Badge was made and distributed in 1920. Not all personnel received these because of the turmoil after the war. (Moch)*

at Kasumigaura, Japan, where in 1929 it housed the *Graf Zeppelin* on her world flight. Other sheds were demolished by German contractors.

Considering the amount of material that the Allied airship services had taken from their late enemy, their program should have met with more success. But as Beelitz remarks, "The seizure of twelve German airships did not result in revealing to the rest of the world the secret of the German success with airships."[5] For one thing, the Germans planned it that way, and sullenly refused all operating and technical information to their French and British opposite numbers. For another, after two years of neglect, the ships were in bad condition, particularly their gas cells. Lastly, the Zeppelins in use at the end of the war were highly efficient war-machines, designed expressly for bombing from great altitudes, and so lightly built that only highly trained crews could fly them safely. The Allies, lacking the extensive operating experience painfully built up by the Germans over twenty years, achieved very little with the surrendered "height climbers." Most, in fact, became "hangar queens" and were ignominiously scrapped before the end of 1921. An exception was *L 72*, renamed *Dixmude,* which, in the hands of the French Navy's Lieutenant de Vaisseau Jean du Plessis de Grenedan, made a number of flights in the latter part of 1923. After setting an endurance record of 118 hours and 41 minutes over the Sahara Desert, *Dixmude* was lost with fifty persons aboard in an explosion off Sciacca, Sicily, in the early morning of December 21, 1923. Her dark and violent end brought to a fitting conclusion the career of the last of the German naval airships.

What was the promise, and what was the performance, of the rigid airship as a weapon in World War I? "The bombs on England had little material effect," admits Martin Dietrich, who commanded five naval airships, with the detachment of a man looking back on the events of forty years ago. "But the moral effect was something else. It was important to remind the English that their island empire was no longer safe from attack – attack from the air." In other words, the Zeppelin airships are seen in the end as a psychological weapon, and their effect was most largely in the minds of those who possessed them and of those who were subjected to the threat of their attacks. Their real achievements as strategic bombers were mere pin-pricks compared to the devastation wrought by the *Luftwaffe* in the Battle of Britain, or by the Royal Air Force and U.S. Army Air Force in Germany. In fifty-one raids on England (a few by Army airships),[6] 5,806 bombs were traced, weighing a total of 196 tons in round figures. 557 people were killed and 1,358 injured. The total damage done by the airship raiders throughout the country amounted to £1,527,585, including £850,109 in the County of London. Only once could the Zeppelin airship have appeared as a real threat to the British war effort, when Mathy set fire to the heart of London on the night of September 8, 1915 (it is worth noting that Mathy alone, in two raids on the capital, caused £660,787 worth of the total damage). As previously pointed out, the most effective year was 1915, when the defenses had not been organized, and the big effort of 1916 yielded proportionately lower returns. In the last two years of the war, the airships were operating inefficiently at high altitudes, most of their "useful lift" being devoted to water ballast, and Strasser was frankly continuing the raids in this manner to tie down the defenses in the north of England.

The Germans grossly overestimated the psychological effect on the average Britisher, as when

5 Beelitz, p. 65.

6 Data following from Jones, Appendices, Appendix XLIV, p. 164

Admiral Behncke in the autumn of 1914 anticipated that the raids might "cause panic in the population which may possibly render it doubtful that the war can be continued." Yet the Zeppelin attacks, and the blackouts which resulted, brought with them a nameless terror, an imminent awareness of danger, which contributed to war-weariness among British civilians twenty-four years before the Battle of Britain:

> In London one of the strangest sights resulting from the raids was provided by the rush of people to the cover of the Underground railways. For many nights following the attack on the capital on the 23rd/24th of September 1916 many thousands of people flocked to the tube railways without waiting for any warning. Many of them began to take up their places about 5:30 p.m., prepared to camp out until the danger, real or imaginary, was over. They went in family parties and carried with them pillows, bedding, provisions, and household treasures.[7]

The number of guns, planes and men withheld from the Western Front for defense of Britain at the height of the Zeppelin menace has already been given. After 1916, the ineffectiveness of the "height climbers" in raids on the north permitted the British to reduce the gun and searchlight batteries there, while the inability of the defending airplanes to climb to the Zeppelins' altitude caused no official concern. Yet, had the Naval Staff discontinued the airship raids – something which Scheer and Strasser would have fought with their last breath – the north would have been spared a real though vague threat.

The popular German conviction that in the Zeppelin they possessed a magic weapon which would destroy their enemies' cities was a significant factor in maintaining home-front morale until the heavy losses in the autumn of 1916. Disillusionment thereafter was extreme and almost universal, and some airshipmen interviewed by the author forty years later were still smarting under the ingratitude of their countrymen. Students of psychology, contemplating the German *Kulturgeist* in action, have postulated a deep-seated national inferiority complex. For such insecurities the sight of the Zeppelin in the sky, the *Kolossal* symbol of Teutonic supremacy, must have been an unrivaled antidote – until its weaknesses could no longer be denied.

Yet bombing raids were not the primary mission of the German naval airships. Their chief task was defensive scouting for an inferior fleet, in which they compensated for a shortage of cruisers. In this role, despite the pre-war hostility of *Großadmiral* Tirpitz, they enjoyed the unlimited confidence of Admiral Scheer, the Naval Staff, the Admiralty, and until 1917, of the Kaiser himself. It may be surprising to find German naval officers over-rating an aerial weapon in its infancy, but they had to believe that the airships would enable them to meet the superior British Fleet on equal terms, and would keep them secure from a surprise seaborne invasion. This the lighter-than-air craft could do in good weather, and as Scheer states, "The Fleet had to make its actions dependent on those of the airships, or do without them."[8]

Not only did storms at sea keep the Zeppelins in their hangars, but many scouting flights were canceled because fog or low cloud hid the surface completely. Without mooring masts, the airships also were often trapped in their sheds by cross winds of 12 m.p.h. or more. The charge that the Zeppelin of 1914-18 was a fair weather weapon is borne out by the following statistics, showing the percentage of days on which reconnaissance flights were made in the North Sea:

| | | |
|---|---|---|
| 1914 | 35 days out of 148, | or 23.6% |
| 1915 | 124 days out of 365, | or 34.0% |
| 1916 | 89 days out of 366, | or 24.3% |
| 1917 | 96 days out of 365, | or 26.3% |
| 1918 | 55 days out of 315, | or 17.5% |

While weather was the largest factor, the declining percentages further reflect the emphasis on raiding in 1916, the difficulties of manhandling on the ground the bigger ships introduced in that year, and of course, all the increased problems of high altitude operations in 1917 and 1918. It must be recalled that airship scouting practically ceased in 1918 after Strasser's death, and the percentage of

[7] Jones, III, p. 246.

[8] Scheer, p. 211.

days on which scouting flights were made prior to that event was 23.5 per cent.

Yet the narrow North Sea was not the proper theatre for realizing the potentialities of the large rigid airship as a naval weapon. Unless fog or storms prevented the Zeppelins from landing, the usual North Sea scouting flight lasted no more than 20 hours. The 101-hour endurance cruise of *LZ 120*, and *L 59*'s 95-hour journey to Khartoum and return, showed what could have been done. Loaded to capacity with more than thirty tons of petrol, the 1917 and 1918 "height climbers," particularly the high-speed ships of the *L 70* class, would have had a range of 3,000 miles – enough to enable them, flying via the north of Scotland, to cruise for several days in the Atlantic. What could they not have done to aid the unrestricted U-boat war by seeking out Allied convoys and directing the submarines on to them? Instead, carrying three tons of bombs and 27 tons of water ballast, they were sent out in ineffective high-altitude raids against England. The charge that the German Navy failed to exploit the true capabilities of the rigid airship as a long-range scouting craft of great endurance is a fair one. It remained for Maitland and Scott, in R 34's crossing of the Atlantic in 1919, for du Plessis, with the 118-hour endurance cruise of *Dixmude* in 1923, and for Zachary Lansdowne in the 1924 voyage of *Shenandoah* from Lakehurst to Seattle and return, to demonstrate what the big rigid was best fitted to perform.

The indispensability of the airship as an aerial scout in the early days of aviation is generally conceded. With low-powered and unreliable motors, the airplane could not lift from the ground enough fuel to fly for extended periods. Using its engines only for forward motion, the airship, supported in the air by buoyant gas, could carry quantities of fuel and, cruising with engines throttled back, had an endurance of several days. But after 1916, when development of the airplane had surpassed the performance of the airship, only Scheer's and Strasser's faith in the Zeppelin kept them in service in the North Sea. Their vulnerability to weather conditions, their reliance on manpower for ground handling, their inability to navigate accurately, the refusal of their leaders to face the realities of aerial warfare after 1916 – above all, the hydrogen with which the Zeppelins were inflated – were the reasons that they accomplished less than had been expected by the German Navy and the German people.

The cost in money can only be guessed at, but must have been enormous, considering that during the conflict the German Navy purchased and placed in service 73 airships – 59 Zeppelins, of which 38 were of the largest size, 8 Schütte-Lanz ships, 3 Parseval non-rigids, the ex-Army M IV and 2 former passenger craft used as training ships. In addition, the Navy ordered and built after war's outbreak 14 small single hangars, and 15 sheds for large ships, most of which were double. A few figures can be presented. It is known that the contract price for *L 1* was £35,800 and for *L 3*, £42,500. An official memorandum of the Aviation Department of the Admiralty, dated February 20, 1915, indicates that for the 16 hangars built or building at that time for the service, £1,143,292 had been spent, including £345,521 laid out before the war for the revolving shed at Nordholz. For the eight Zeppelin airships put in service up to that date, £407,000 had been expended. The same memorandum shows that for *L 4* the Zeppelin Company was paid £43,600, and for *L 8*, £50,850. After the war the Inter-Allied Commission of Control set the original value of *L 14* at £68,100, of *L 41* at £140,000, while the later *L 42*, *L 52*, *L 56*, *L 63* and *L 65* were appraised at £163,200 apiece. The expansion of the Ahlhorn base, with construction of the 853-foot-long double hangars "Alma" and "Alarich," cost about £1,522,000.

The cost in personnel was proportionately greater than that of any branch of the German Navy, exceeding, according to some figures, the percentage of losses in the submarine service. Of the 50-odd flight crews trained during the war, about 40 per cent were killed – 40 officers, 34 warrant officers, 264 petty officers, and 51 ratings. A few of these died in industrial-type accidents at the bases – like *L 30*'s sailmaker, Johannes Heesen, who on August 14, 1916, was asphyxiated by hydrogen gas while working between the cells of the ship in the "Normann" hangar in Nordholz. But the majority were killed in combat or in flight operations. Seventeen airships were lost with all hands, and in every case, except that of *L 19*, the ship's destruction resulted from a hydrogen fire. In addition, *L 7* and *L 48* burned in the air with heavy loss of life. In the early years of the war, the airship crews were the finest procurable, and all were volunteers. Later, as the submarine service received priority, Strasser had to be content with older officers and men of lower quality, and at least one machinist's mate has told the author that he was ordered to airships against the wishes of his family. A notable feature of the personnel situation in the Naval Airship Division was the fine combat performance of reserve officers.

What remains for the airman and the historian forty years later? As strategic bombers, the hydrogen-filled rigid airships of 1914-18 failed, as in retrospect they were almost bound to do. Furthermore, their crews, thinking to destroy legitimate military targets such as harbor and railroad installations, munitions factories and government buildings, found themselves execrated as "Huns" and "baby-killers" because their bombs in fact caused civilian casualties. (Even today, the moral implications of indiscriminate bombing plague virtuous Americans as well as wicked Germans.) As Fleet scouting units the Zeppelins were undependable, and were further handicapped by a lack of planning and doctrine. Wishful thinking substituted for hardboiled analysis and interpretation of the results. But for two years of war the rigid airship was the premier long-range weapon of airborne destruction. That it was not equal to the demands made on it was not the fault of its personnel.

What the German flight crews suffered and endured in trying to do their duty still commands admiration. To fly combat missions in the slow, fragile, monster gas-bags, at the mercy of the elements and inflated with inflammable hydrogen, demanded the coldest kind of courage, particularly after the autumn of 1916 when almost every crew had seen their comrades burning in the sky over England. Only the most devoted and highly motivated could have carried on thereafter when the hardships of flying in the thin, freezing air four miles up were added to the other hazards. And it must be remembered that there was no limited tour of duty, no "fifty missions" for these men, who went on leave only when they were to take over a new ship.

Yet they left a heritage of technical skill and knowledge which, in the post-war years, was directly responsible for the fabulous success of the passenger-carrying *Graf Zeppelin*, almost all of whose personnel had previously served in the German Navy. This success would have been even more impressive had not the destruction of *Hindenburg* in a hydrogen fire, and the outbreak of World War II two years later, ended German airship development for ever.

As I concluded my work years ago, I was able to write of the airships and the airship men of the United States Navy who drew on the German Zeppelin heritage in operating large pressure airships in airborne early warning and antisubmarine warfare duties. Today these are gone, the last United States Navy airship squadron having been decommissioned on October 31, 1961. The three Goodyear Corporation advertising blimps, *Mayflower*, *Columbia*, and *America*, and the similar German advertising blimp D LEMO, are the only airships flying in the world at present. Nor do they adequately suggest the fascination and romance of the giant rigids. Ships of the air in the truest sense, majestic and mysterious as they moved almost silently across the sky, they had an unforgettable hold on the emotions of those who saw them, and of those who manned them. Some of this magical aura is conveyed, I hope, in this chronicle of the rigid airship in its great days of tragedy and glory.

# RIGID AIRSHIP TECHNOLOGY & TERMINOLOGY / GLOSSARY

Though the rigid airships used by the German Navy were built by two different firms, the Luftschiffbau Zeppelin G.m.b.H. of Friedrichshafen and the Luftschiffbau Schütte-Lanz G.m.b.H. of Mannheim-Rheinau, they eventually differed little from each other except in the material used for girders – duralumin in the former, and plywood in the latter. The rigid, streamlined hull was built up of a series of polygonal main rings, braced radially by hard-drawn steel wire running from a central fitting to the angles of the polygon, and tied together by longitudinal girders running from bow to stern of the ship. The two lowermost longitudinals formed the base of a triangular section keel, in which the heavy loads were concentrated, and which gave the crew access to the various parts of the ship. The main rings were spaced 8, 10 and eventually 15 meters apart, and between each set of main rings was a gas cell, made of fabric lined with gold beaters' skin to make it gas-tight. Larger ships had unbraced intermediate rings between the main ones, and light longitudinal girders between the heavy main ones, to support the outer cover. This was made of light cotton fabric, doped to render it taut and waterproof and to present a smooth outer surface to the air. Stabilizing fins and control surfaces were fitted at the stern, and the engines were slung below the hull in small enclosed cars or gondolas.

The rigid airship was essentially a powered balloon, which was supported in the air by a force equal to the weight of air it displaced, less the weight of the gas. It was German practice to assume that with standard atmospheric conditions (barometer 760 mm., relative humidity 60 per cent, and air and gas temperatures 0 degrees centigrade) a cubic meter of hydrogen of specific gravity 0.1 would lift a load of 1.16 kg., or 72 pounds per 1,000 cubic feet. On this basis one of the bigger wartime Zeppelins, such a *L 30* with a gas volume of 1,949,600 cubic feet, would have a gross lift of 141,200 pounds.

This would not represent the load that could be carried by the airship, as the fixed weights would have to be subtracted – the weight of the structure, the girders and wires of the frame, the gas cells, outer cover, gondolas, engines, and other structural features that could not be removed from the ship. In *L 30*, these totalled 79,600 pounds; the remainder, 61,600 pounds, was the useful lift, which could be used for carrying the useful load – crew, stores, water ballast, petrol, oil, armament and bombs.

But the lift under standard conditions would vary with changes in temperature, barometric pressure, and relative humidity. In addition, contamination of hydrogen by air diffusing into the gas cells obviously increased the weight of the gas and decreased the airship's lift. With higher air temperatures, or lower barometric pressures, the weight of the displaced air was less, and the lift of the airship was less. With low air temperature or high barometric pressure, the lift was greater. Therefore the Zeppelins could carry a greater load of bombs in winter than in summer. Humidity had a relatively slight effect, though a high air humidity somewhat decreased the lift. In addition, gas temperature relative to that of the air significantly affected the lift. When superheated (usually by the sun's rays), the gas was less dense than it would otherwise be, and the lift was increased; supercooling of the gas (usually late at night) had the opposite effect.

At take-off and fully loaded, the Zeppelin was "weighed off" and in equilibrium, or sometimes had a few hundred pounds "free lift." The gas cells were always 100 per cent full, or nearly so, at take-off. Burning petrol made the ship "lighter" and she would gradually ascend; since the barometric pressure decreased with increasing altitude, the hydrogen would expand, and at a certain relative pressure, spring-loaded automatic valves in the bottom of the gas cells would open and "blow off" gas until the pressure was equalized. In addition the commander could release water ballast to ascend, or if the ship was "heavy" due to loss of gas or a load of rain, snow or hail. If his craft was "light," possibly at the end of a flight after consumption of fuel, or with the gas superheated by the sun, he could release hydrogen from manually controlled valves in the top of some of the gas cells. Furthermore, a certain degree of heaviness or lightness could be compensated for by the dynamic lift derived from the thrust of the engines by flying the ship at an angle. Usually a "heavy" ship was held at altitude by positive dynamic lift developed when flown nose up, but sometimes gas might be conserved when "light" by flying nose-down to develop negative dynamic lift.

## Glossary of Airship Terms

**Adiabatic Heating**: When a gas is compressed, its temperature rises due to the work done on it. (The converse is true when the gas expands.) Occasionally an airship commander might take advantage of this physical fact. The text gives an example of a commander with a "heavy" ship warming the gas by a rapid descent from high altitude, and then making a quick landing "weighed off" before the warmed and expanded gas had time to cool.

**Airspeed Meter**: Pitot-tube actuated, it presented the speed through the air in meters per second. Corrections had to be made for decreased air density with increased altitude, and it did not of course give speed over the ground.

**Altimeter**: An aneroid instrument, actually a barometer measuring air pressure, graduated to give the altitude in meters. Changes in barometric pressure after take-off could produce false readings, though corrections might be obtained by radio. The altimeter of *SL 11*, in the author's possession, reads only to 2,500 meters [8,200 feet]; in later airships it read up to 8,000 meters [26,250 feet].

**Anti-freeze**: Alcohol was used throughout the war in airship engine cooling systems. Glycerin was used in water ballast sacks, until shortages required the use of calcium chloride, whose damaging corrosive effects on duralumin were not at first realized.

**Armament**: The 8 mm. Maxim machine gun was standard in naval airships throughout the war. Until 1917, two were carried in the control car, two in the after engine car, one in each wing engine gondola, two or three on the top platform and one on the tail platform. After 1917 only two were carried in the control car, and sometimes none. Beginning in the summer of 1918 it was intended to arm all airships with two 20 mm. Becker machine cannon in the control car, firing ball, tracer and explosive ammunition.

**Automatic Valves**: Spring-loaded valves in the bottom of each gas cell opened automatically whenever the internal pressure exceeded the external by 8 to 10 mm. of water, as when an airship with full gas cells ascended to a higher altitude, expanding the gas. The larger valves in the large cells had a diameter of 31 1/2 inches. Schütte-Lanz ships had exhaust trunks leading to the top of the ship to carry off hydrogen from the automatic valves; these were fitted in Zeppelins after *L 34*.

**Axial Cable**: A stranded wire cable running through the gas cells from bow to stern of the ship, and connecting the wire bracing of all the main rings at their centers, reducing the loads on the framework if there was an inequality of pressure between adjacent gas cells. A Schütte-Lanz patent, the axial cable (Zentralverspannung) was introduced in the Zeppelin *L 30*.

**Ballast**: To enable the airship to ascend to higher altitudes, or to compensate for gas loss or increased loads on the ship, droppable ballast was carried. Though Strasser briefly had sand carried in 110-pound sacks early in 1917, water was the usual form of ballast.

**Ballast sacks**: Most of the ballast was carried along the keel in rubberized cloth sacks holding 2,200 pounds of water. Fourteen such were fitted in *L 30*. Toggles in the control car were pulled by the elevator man to empty them as necessary, and the big sacks would drain completely in 60 seconds.

**Ballonet**: In pressure airships (q.v.), an air-filled compartment inside the main envelope which, being kept under pressure by a blower or other means, maintains a constant pressure in the large bag, regardless of changes in the volume of the gas.

**Bomb**: Explosive bombs carried in German naval airships were thick-walled, pear-shaped with a stabilizing ring at the tail, and came in 110, 128, 220 and 660 pound sizes. The incendiary bombs, made of thermite wrapped in tarred rope, weighed only about 25 pounds. Bombs were carried on racks on either side of the keel approximately amidships, and were released from a switchboard in the control car. The heaviest bomb load ever carried over England was by *L 31* on the night of September 23, 1916, and comprised four of 660 pounds, forty of 128 pounds, and 60 incendiaries, totalling 9,250 pounds.

**Bomb-sight**: A rather complicated instrument produced by Carl Zeiss of Jena, located in the control car to the right of the rudder man, and handled during the attack by the executive officer. Setting on the sight the ship's altitude as obtained from the altimeter, he then measured the speed over the ground by timing with a stop-watch the passage of an object between two cross-hairs supposedly measuring an interval of 300 meters on the ground. Compensating curves permitted the sight to be adjusted for the different ballistic properties of both 110- and 220-pound bombs. The sight was capable of considerable precision, but training in its use was sketchy and bombing practice was infrequent.

**"Breeches"**: To quickly lighten the ship at bow or stern, as in take-off or landing emergencies, water ballast was carried in small sacks near the nose and tail. *L 30* and later ships had four sacks holding 550 pounds each at each end of the ship. These, because their shape suggested half a pair of pants, were called "breeches," and unlike the large 2,200 pound sacks in the keel, the "breeches" emptied their entire contents instantly (often on the heads of the ground crew!) when the elevator man pulled their toggles in the control car.

**Ceiling**: The maximum altitude attainable by an aircraft under certain conditions. For the naval airships, the ceiling varied with the amount of useful load retained on board and prevailing temperature conditions and barometric pressure. Maximum altitudes attained in practice appear frequently in the text.

**"Cellon"**: German trade name for a widely used brand of aircraft dope (q.v.).

**Compass**: Weight considerations forbade carrying gyro compasses in naval airships. A liquid magnetic compass was carried in the control car within sight of the rudder man; despite addition of alcohol, the liquid frequently froze.

**Control Car**: The foremost car or gondola slung under the ship, fully enclosed and with good all-round visibility through glass and celluloid windows, except directly aft. Here were the flight stations of the commander, the executive officer, and the navigating warrant officer. The rudder man handled the rudder wheel in the bow of the car, with bomb sight and bomb release switches on his right. On the port side of the car was the elevator wheel, with ballast releases and maneuvering valve controls also in charge of the elevator man. A small chart table was on the starboard side of the car, with engine telegraphs overhead to transmit orders to the engine gondolas aft. In the rear of the control car was the sound-proofed radio cabin with transmitter and receiver.

**Cover**: Made of light cotton fabric. In earlier ships, applied in circular fashion around each section of the ship. Beginning with *L 44*, applied lengthwise in gores 65 to 130 feet long, laced to the girders, and the lacings covered with glued-on fabric strips. For camouflage purposes, the fabric came printed with tiny light blue dots or lines. At first it was clear-doped, later black dope was used on the underside of the ship. In *L 49*, the top outer cover weighed 110 grams per square meter undoped, and 140-158 grams per square meter doped; the bottom cover weighed 80-90 grams per square meter undoped, and 125 grams per square meter doped. The entire outer cover weighed 4,704 pounds.

**Crew**: The naval airships carried a standard complement as follows:
Commanding officer, usually a *Kapitänleutnant*.
Executive officer, usually an *Oberleutnant zur See*.
Navigator (*Steuermann*), a warrant officer, heading the seaman branch.
Engineer, a warrant officer, heading the engineering department. His flight station was in the after engine gondola.
Two petty officers, usually signalmen, to handle the elevator controls.
Two petty officers, usually boatswains' mates, to handle the rudder controls.
Two radio men, one a petty officer, one a striker.
One petty officer rated as sailmaker, in charge of gas cells and outer cover. His flight station was in the keel.
Two machinists' mates for each engine.

This number permitted the crew to be divided into two watches, but on "war flights" the steersmen off duty stood lookout watches on the top platform, and the machinists' mates off duty acted as lookouts in the engine gondolas. On raids, several men might be left behind to lighten the ship. Usually one rudder man, one radio man, and two or three of the machinists in the after gondola would remain behind.

**Cruciform**: A heavy cruciform-like structure in the stern of the ship which gave added strength to the rudder and elevator seatings.

**DELAG**: Abbreviation for *Deutsche Luftschiffahrt Aktien-Gesellschaft*, the commercial airship transportation company founded by Count Zeppelin in 1909. Its personnel played an important role in training Army and Navy flight crews before and during the war.

**Docking rails**: The only mechanical ground-handling aid used with the German naval airships. Running through the sheds and for 200 yards out into the field on each side, the rails carried so-called trolleys (q.u.) to which the ship was made fast fore and aft by tackles, so that she was prevented from moving sideways in a wind while entering or leaving her shed.

**"Dope"**: A solution of cellulose acetate in acetone, brushed on to the outer cover after it was in place, to tauten and waterproof it. Used clear or with black pigment on undersides after the spring of 1917.

**Drift**: The lateral motion of an aircraft over the ground, due to wind blowing at an angle to its course. To steer a true course over the ground, the wind strength and direction must be known.

**Duralumin**: Name applied to a family of alloys of aluminium with small and varying amounts of copper and traces of magnesium, manganese, iron and silicon. Its properties were first discovered by Wilm in 1909 and it was first manufactured in Düren, Germany. Being much stronger than the parent metal, duralumin was used for all Zeppelin girder-work beginning with *LZ 26* of 1914.

**Dynamic Lift**: The positive (or negative) force on an airship hull, derived from driving it at an angle with the power of its engines. With a large amount of engine power, flying a ship "dynamically" could readily compensate for considerable degrees of lightness or heaviness. At full power and at an angle of 8 degrees, *Los Angeles* developed a dynamic lift of over eight tons.

**Elevators**: Movable horizontal surfaces at the tail of the airship (though in very early Zeppelins they were fitted forward also); motion upward or downward inclined the ship's nose up or down, and caused her to ascend or descend.

**Engine cars**: Small streamlined enclosures attached by struts and wires to the hull of the airship, designed to accommodate an engine or engines, and personnel attending them, and to provide enough space to work on the engines in case of a breakdown.

**Fins**: Vertical or horizontal stabilizing surfaces at the tail of the airship, at the after ends of which were attached the movable control surfaces. Fins were flat, with extensive wire bracing, up until *L 65* which had thick cantilever-section fins and a minimum of external bracing.

**Fixed weight**: Total weight of structure and other permanent installations of an airship – in a Zeppelin, includes framework, bracing wire, gas cells, outer cover, gondolas, engines, fuel tanks and piping, ballast sacks, instruments, etc. In wartime Zeppelins, these might be as low as 37 1/2 per cent of the gross lift; safety requires a heavier structure in commercial airships, and the figure should then be nearer 45-50 per cent.

**"Free lift"**: At take-off, it was German practice to drop about 500 pounds of water ballast, to give an equivalent ascending force, or "free lift."

**Gangway**: *See keel.*

**Gas capacity**: The gas content of all cells filled 100 per cent full. Usually derived from calculation; "usable gas volume" sometimes given, and may represent actual measured amount of gas taken by the ship.

**Gas cells**: Filling the entire interior of the airship when 100 per cent full of gas, the cells were held in place by wire and cord netting, and made to be both light in weight and as gas-tight as possible. Initially, rubberized cotton fabric was used, with a weight of 240 grams per square meter. Gas loss was excessive, and there was a Feat improvement about 1911 when bags were first made of 6 layers of gold beaters' skin (q.u.). This material weighed about 150 grams per square meter. These cells were fragile and expensive. With *L 3* in 1914 was first used "skinned fabric" cells – two or three layers of gold beaters' skin glued to light cotton fabric. The weight of this was 145 grams per square meter. "Skinned fabric" cells were used throughout the war, and with silk substituted for cotton in 1918, the weight was reduced to 135 grams per square meter. The blockade caused a shortage of gold beaters' skin (principally imported from Argentina) and in the last two years of the war, inferior types of ordinary gut produced in Germany had to be substituted.

Analysis of gas-cell material from *L 49* showed the following breakdown of weights: Fabric (cotton) 60 grams per square meter. Thick outside coating of paraffin and soft wax, 9-15 grams per square meter. Two layers of gold beaters' skin inside, glued to each other and to the fabric, weighing together 42-45 grams per square meter. Total weight of gas-cell material, 147-162 grams per square meter. Total weight of all eighteen gas cells of *L 49*, 8,875.

**Girder**: Transverse rings, and longitudinal members, being required to resist compression and bending loads, were built up of light girders of triangular section. The Zeppelin Company employed rolled duralumin channels connected by stamped lattice pieces. A section of main longitudinal girder, 16.4 feet long, 14.17 inches high and 10.63 inches wide, weighed only 10.2 pounds but could support a compression load of 4,928 pounds. The Schütte-Lanz girders were built up of aspen plywood bonded with one of the earliest applications of casein glue, and waterproofed with paraffin and lacquered. A section of their wooden girder 8.6 feet long, 3.4 inches wide and 9.45 inches high, weighed 6.45 pounds but could support a compression load of 9,930 pounds.

**Gold beaters' skin**: Superb gas-tightness, together with light weight, was attained by lining the inside of the gas-bags with gold beaters' skin. This was the delicate outer membrane covering the caecum of cattle, each animal yielding only one skin measuring not more than 39 x 6 inches. For a single large gas cell, some 50,000 skins would be needed. The careful handling required in the slaughter houses, the quantity of skins required, and the skilled hand-work needed in assembling the skins at the gas-cell factory, caused the bags so made to be enormously expensive – in 1917 a single large gas-bag cost £2,000.

**Gondola**: Generic name for any car suspended below an airship, possibly derived from the fact that the early Zeppelin gondolas were not only shaped like open boats, but were intended to float on the water.

**Gondola bumpers**: One or two located under each center-line gondola, to cushion the shock of landing. These were rubberized air bags enclosed in a framework of canes and covered with strong canvas.

**Gravity tanks**: Fuel tanks permanently installed over each engine car and feeding the engines by gravity. Machinists' mates of the different cars were responsible for keeping them filled by handpumping petrol up from the slip tanks (q.v.) along the keel. In *L 30* there were eight gravity tanks each holding 148 gallons.

**Gross lift**: The total lift of the gas contained in an airship; equal to the total weight of air displaced minus the weight of the gas.

**Ground crew**: German naval airships were walked in and out of their sheds, and manhandled on the ground, by trained teams of enlisted men. Three or four hundred men would be required to handle one of the larger airships, and large numbers of men were stationed at each airship base for this purpose – 5,100 officers and men altogether at the seven airship bases operating in April, 1917.

**Hangar**: Large buildings at the airship bases, designed to contain one or two airships each, and with huge rolling doors at either end. The leeward door was always used for entry and exit except in very light winds. German practice required that the airships be housed in hangars when not in the air, and no mooring-out equipment was used.

**Helium**: The second lightest gas known, developed for airship use by the United States, which has a monopoly of its production from natural gas. Helium has the great advantage for airship use of being non-inflammable, but it has only 93 per cent of the lifting force of hydrogen. In rigid airships, the expense of helium required the installation of heavy condensers to recover water from the engine exhausts to compensate for the weight of fuel burned and to eliminate the need to valve the lifting gas as fuel was consumed.

**Hydrogen**: The lightest gas known, cheaply manufactured by a variety of methods. Produced for German naval airships at the airship bases in large plants utilizing the Messerschmitt process of passing steam over hot iron. Hydrogen is not only inflammable, but is also explosive when contaminated by as little as 6 per cent of air. The Germans were able to use hydrogen in their airships with relative safety by very strict attention to gas purity. Between flights the gas cells were kept inflated 100 per cent full and under slight positive pressure to minimize inward diffusion of air, and purity was checked almost daily; if the purity fell too low, the cell was emptied and filled with fresh hydrogen.

**Ice shields**: Fitted inside the outer cover of the airship above the propellers, to prevent them from throwing ice particles into the gas cells. Initially the ice shields were made of plywood, backed by light girder-work. Later, for the sake of lightness, these were replaced by heavy canvas, backed by wires. The canvas shields were frequently riddled.

**Inclinometer**: An instrument which informed the elevator man of the up or down angle of the airship.

**Keel**: A triangular-section corridor running from end to end of a rigid airship, composed of the two bottom longitudinals of the hull and an apex girder. At the bottom of the keel was the catwalk, about a foot wide. (Though there were no hand-rails, nobody was ever lost by stepping off it and through the outer cover!) Heavy loads, such as bombs, fuel tanks and water-ballast sacks, were hung from sturdy box-girders along the keel, and here were slung hammocks for the crew.

**Landing-ropes**: A long landing-rope 410 feet in length, and two shorter ones 249 feet in length, were stowed in the nose on hatches which could be opened by wires from the control car. When low over the field, these would be released and the bows of the airship would be hauled down by the ground crew. Other shorter ropes were attached along the keel.

**Lift equation**: The German Navy's standard formula for calculating the lift with changes in atmospheric conditions and gas purity was:

$$\text{Gross lift} = \text{Gas volume of ship} \times \frac{1.293 \times 273}{760}\left(1 - \text{specific gravity of Gas} \times \frac{\text{air temperature}}{\text{gas temperature}} - 0.38 \times \frac{\text{relative humidity} \times \text{water vapor pressure}}{\text{barometric pressure}}\right)\frac{\text{barometric pressure}}{\text{air temperature}}$$

It should be noted that:

Barometric pressure is expressed in millimeters of mercury. Temperature is on the absolute scale, whereon absolute zero is 0, and freezing temperature is +273 degrees.

Relative humidity as a percentage must be multiplied by a factor giving the water vapor pressure for the prevailing air temperature. Airship piloting handbooks included convenient tables for this factor. Longitudinals: The main longitudinal girders were the main lengthwise strength members of the airship. In *L 30* there were thirteen, twelve of them triangular, 14.17 inches deep and 10.63 inches wide, and the top longitudinal was a doubled girder of W-section. The intermediate longitudinals, of which there were twelve in *L 30*, were lighter, did not extend all the way to the tail, and were designed primarily to support the outer cover.

**Maneuvering values**: Fitted in the tops of certain gas cells, these enabled the commander to trim his ship by releasing gas from one end, or on occasion, to make the entire ship heavy. The valve pulls were handled by the elevator man. Because the maneuvering valves in the top of the ship were practically inaccessible and might stick open, standing orders in the German Naval Airship Division were to make the ship heavy by driving her over pressure height (q.u.), and discharging gas from the automatic valves. When the maneuvering valves were used to make the ship heavy, they were opened all together for a measured interval of time. In *L 70*, with cells 75 per cent full, opening the maneuvering valves for one minute would make her 1,100 pounds heavier.

**Maybach**: In 1909, Count Zeppelin had backed the construction in Friedrichshafen of an engine designed by Carl Maybach especially for airships. The engine was further developed and manufactured by the Maybach Motor Company, a Zeppelin subsidiary, and because of its superior reliability and fuel economy, was used by all German airships during World War I. The following table gives specifications of the 6-cylinder in-line Maybach engines used in 1914-18:

| Year | Type | H.P. | R.P.M. | Wt. (lb.) | Wt. lb. h.p. | Fuel consumption gm./h.p./hr. | Compression ratio | Total No. built |
|---|---|---|---|---|---|---|---|---|
| 1914 | C-X | 210 | 1,250 | 913 | 4.34 | 225 | 4.8/1 | 125 |
| 1915 | HSLu | 240 | 1,400 | 805 | 3.35 | 200 | 5.45/1 | 490 |
| 1917 | MBIVa | 245 | 1,400 | 882 | 3.59 | 200 | 6.08/1 | 110 (1917–1919) |
| 1919 | MBIVa | 245 | 1,400 | 860* | 3.51 | 200 | 6.7/1 | |

* Aluminum pistons replacing cast iron.

**Mooring mast**: Realizing that the Germans' inability to walk their Zeppelins in and out of their sheds in stiff cross winds imposed a severe operational handicap, Major G.H. Scott in the early post-war period devised the mooring mast, to which a rigid airship could be moored in the open, ready to take the air regardless of the wind direction. At the "high" mast developed by the British, the ship required constant attention because of changes of buoyancy, and for this and other reasons, the U.S. Navy later developed the "low" mast, to which the Aluminium pistons replacing cast iron airship was secured on the ground. The nose was held by the mast while the tail, resting on the ground, swung with the wind on a weighted car.

**Mooring point**: A reinforced fitting in the keel forward of the control car, to which the landing ropes (q.v.) were made fast.

**Non-rigid airship**: A small pressure airship (q.v.) consisting of a rubberized fabric gas-bag whose streamlined shape is maintained by gas pressure, and from which a single gondola is suspended.

**Oxyhydrogen**: A gaseous mixture of oxygen and hydrogen, or loosely, of air and hydrogen; always potentially explosive.

**Parachute flares**: A number of magnesium flares, attached to parachutes, were carried in the control car, and thrown out by hand to illuminate the ground at night, or to blind enemy gun and searchlight crews.

**Parachutes**: German naval airships carried individual parachutes for crew members for a short time early in 1917. These were of the "attached" type. No "live" parachute drop was ever made from a naval airship, in an emergency or otherwise, and because parachutes for 20 men weighed a total of 365 pounds, they were soon discarded because of their weight.

**Pressure airship**: Generic term including both the non-rigid and semi-rigid airship (q.v.), in both of which the shape is maintained by gas pressure. Contrasts with the rigid airship, which (though very rarely) may be described as a "pressureless airship."

**Pressure height**: The height at which decreasing atmospheric pressure permits the hydrogen to expand and build up a relative pressure inside the cells such that the automatic valves open and gas is "blown off." Following ascent to a pre-selected pressure height, the commander may ascend or descend at any altitude below this height without fear that gas will be released – an important consideration in flying through thunderstorms.

**Propellers**: German 2-bladed airship propellers were handsomely made examples of cabinet work, built up of laminations of West African and Honduras mahogany and American walnut, and often covered with walnut veneer. Usually they were geared down to about 540 r.p.m. from an engine speed of 1,400 r.p.m. Thus they could be made of large diameter, averaging about 17 feet. In *L 70* and *L 71*, the engines in the wing gondolas drove small, ungeared, high-speed propellers slightly over 10 feet in diameter.

**Rate of climb indicator**: An instrument which indicates to the elevator man the rate of ascent or descent in meters per second.

**Rigid airship**: An airship with a rigid frame which maintains its shape regardless of whether it is inflated with gas.

**Ring**: Main rings or frames were the chief transverse structural members of the rigid airship, and were polygons built of girders (13-sided in *L 30*). The ability of the main ring to withstand the forces exerted by the lifting gas and by the weight of the ship's structure and lading was a basic consideration in airship design. Main rings were heavily braced with both radial and chord wires. In *L 30*, where the main rings were 10 meters apart, an intermediate ring – unbraced – occurred between each pair of main rings; in *L 53* and later ships, with main rings spaced 15 meters apart, there were two intermediate rings. Beginning with *L 30*, main and intermediate rings were numbered with the distance in meters from the stern-post, which was Ring 0, and locations in the ship were referred to by the ring numbers.

**Rudder**: Movable vertical surfaces at the tail of the airship, whose motion steered the ship to port or starboard.

**Semi-rigid airship**: A pressure airship with a rigid keel running the length of the bag, either suspended beneath it or faired into its underside, for the attachment of engines and gondolas and the distribution of fuel, ballast and other loads. Permits construction of airships large than the non-rigid type.

**Shear wires**: Hard-drawn steel wires providing diagonal bracing in all rectangular panels formed by longitudinal girders and transverse rings, and taking the shear loads on the rigid hull.

**Shed**: *See hangar.*

**Slip-tanks**: Aluminium fuel tanks distributed along the keel. In *L 30* there were thirty-two of 64 gallon capacity, and any one of these could be dropped through the cover in an emergency if no other ballast was available.

**Stall**: In aircraft, a condition where an excessive nose-up attitude causes a loss of lift, and the aircraft falls out of control. It should be noted that while a "heavy" airship can stall downward like heavier-than-air craft, it can also "stall upward." When flying "light" and nose down, it may be inclined downward so far that the dynamic force on the top of the hull diminishes and the excess static lift of the "light" condition will cause it to rise out of control.

**Static lift**: The lift of an airship without forward motion, and due solely to the buoyancy of the gas. Contrasts with dynamic lift (q.v.).

**Streamlining**: The shaping of a body so as to cause the least possible disturbance in passing through the air, and hence causing a minimum of resistance, or "drag." Early in the war, much research on streamlining was done by Paul Jaray in the Zeppelin Company's wind tunnel at Friedrichshafen. Among Jaray's discoveries was that even at relatively low speeds, careful streamlining of all structural protuberances – fins, gondolas, struts and wires – was important for aerodynamic efficiency of airships.

**Supercooling**: A condition (usually obtaining at night) where the gas is cooler than the surrounding air; since the density of the gas is increased, its lifting power is less. As much as -9 degrees F. of supercooling has been recorded.

**Superheating**: A condition (usually due to sun's heat being trapped within the hull) where the gas is warmer than the surrounding air. Since the density of the gas is decreased, its lifting power is greater. During her flight to America, on July 4, 1919, R 34 experienced superheating of +66 degrees F.

**Thermometer**: In the control car was an air thermometer, and a remote-reading electrical thermometer giving (somewhat inaccurately) the temperature in one of the gas cells. The data provided by these instruments was essential to determining the lift of the airship, particularly with superheating or supercooling.

**Tail platform**: Abaft the rudders in the extreme tail was a small seat for a stern lookout, who manned a machine gun. It was suppressed at the end of 1916.

**Top platform**: Protected only by a low windscreen, and located on top of the ship above the control car, the top platform served as a lookout station and mounted up to 3 machine guns. It was reached by a vertical climbing shaft from the keel.

**Trim**: The attitude of an airship in the air in response to static forces. When weights and lifting forces are properly balanced so that the center of gravity is located directly under the center of lift, the airship is on an even keel and said to be "in trim." If this is not the case, she is "out of trim"; if the nose is inclined downward, "trimmed by the bow," if the tail is inclined downward, "trimmed by the stern."

**Trolley** (Laufkatze): A wheeled truck, pulled by hand and rolling on docking rails (q.v.). Trolleys served as points of attachment for tackles made fast to the airship fore and aft.

**Useful lift**: The amount of lift remaining after subtracting the fixed weights of the airship from the gross lift.

**Useful load**: The load that the airship can carry, equal in weight to the useful lift. Includes fuel, oil, water, ballast, crew, spare parts, armament and bombs.

**"Weighed off"**: The state of an airship whose lift and load have been adjusted so as to be equal, or whose excess of lift or load has become known by test. (Colloquially, if said to be "weighed off," an airship is in equilibrium, while she will otherwise be said to be "weighed off – pounds 'heavy'," or "weighed off – pounds 'light.'") Before leaving the hangar an airship, through release of ballast, was weighed off so precisely that one man at each end could lift her off the trestles. In flight, an experienced elevator man could tell a good deal about her static condition from the "feel" of the ship, but good practice demanded that before landing, the ship should be "weighed off" in the air. The engines were stopped, and ballast released if it were found that she sank, while gas was valved if she rose.

# BIBLIOGRAPHY


**OFFICIAL DOCUMENTS**

Germany. "Tambach Archives." This book is based largely on official German Navy records, now in the joint custody of the British Admiralty and U.S. Navy Department, and including War Diaries of all German naval airships and a quantity of correspondence relating to airships in the files of the German Admiralty, the Naval Staff, the High Seas Fleet Command, and other departments.

Great Britain. Air Ministry. Air Raid Reports. Compiled by the Intelligence Section, G.H.Q. Home Forces.
*Air Raids, 1915. Airship Raids,* August-September, 1915. (Compiled February, 1918.)
*Air Raids, 1916.* VII, 2-3 September, 1916.
*Air Raids, 1916.* VIII, 23 September-2 October, 1916.
Prepared during the war by Colonel H.H. de Watteville, these Intelligence reports show an astonishing familiarity with the Naval Airship Division, its ships and men, derived largely from radio intelligence. Only rarely do the courses of the Zeppelins over England require correction from post-war data.

*Enemy Aircraft North Sea and Baltic,* June-October 1918. Monthly Intelligence Summary.

Great Britain. Imperial War Museum. *Pilots' Reports Relating to Destruction of Zeppelins.*

Great Britain, Admiralty War Staff, Intelligence Division. C.B. 1265, *German Rigid Airships* (Confidential). London: Ordnance Survey, February, 1917. An extraordinarily accurate and detailed 118 page compilation, with 106 plates, of information on Zeppelins available to the Admiralty at this date. Partly from Intelligence sources, but more largely from a meticulous examination of the wreck of *L 33*, burned by her crew after forced landing at Little Wigborough, September 24, 1916. Author owns Copy No.1.

**BOOKS**

(a) ***German airships before World War I***

Berezowski, Alexander. *Handbuch der Luftpostkunde, Abschnitt "Zeppelin-Luftpost."* Neustadt (Orla): J.K.G. Wagnersche Buchdrückerei, 1930. A handbook for stamp collectors, but has a quantity of material on early DELAG passenger airship operations that is unobtainable elsewhere.

Eckener, Hugo. "Der lenkbare Ballon" in *Die Eroberung der Luft.* Stuttgart: Union Deutsche Verlagsgesellschaft, 1909. Detailed history of Zeppelin and other airship development, by Count Zeppelin's collaborator and successor.

Eckener, Hugo. *Graf Zeppelin.* Stuttgart: J.G. Cott'sche Buchhandlung Nachfolger, 1938. The author's favorite biography of Count Zeppelin.

Gruttel, Else. *Im Luftschif über Hamburg, Lübeck, Schleswig-Holstein.* Stuttgart: Verlag von Gustav Eyb, 1913. One of a series of guidebooks for DELAG passengers, with much detail concerning these early passenger Zeppelins and their operation.

Hacker, Georg. *Die Männer von Manzell.* Frankfurt a.M.: Societäts-Druckerei G.m.b.H., 1936. Entertaining – and accurate – reminiscences of a naval warrant officer who was rudder man in all Count Zeppelin's early airships, beginning with LZ 3.

Hildebrandt, Hans (ed.) *Zeppelin-Denkmal für das deutsche Volk.* Stuttgart: Germania-Verlag G.m.b.H., n.d. (1925). Ornate commemorative volume on Count Zeppelin, predictably presenting him as a German folk-hero. Article by Hans von Schiller on Naval Airship Division has numerous errors and omissions.

Kriegswissenschaftliche Abteilung der Luftwaffe. *Die deutschen Luftstreitkräfte von ihrer Entstehung bis zum Ende des Weltkrieges 1918. Die Militärluftfahrt bis zum Beginn des Weltkrieges 1914.* Berlin: E.S. Mittler u. Sohn, 1941. Official history. Several lengthy chapters on the airship in the pre-war German Navy are based on documents not now to be found in the Tambach Archives.

Luftschiffbau Zeppelin. *Das Werk Zeppelins, Eine Festgabe zu seinem 75. Geburtstag.* Stuttgart: Kommissionsverlag Julius Hoffmann, 1913. Artistically presented volume of anonymous articles by Zeppelin Company staff on development of Zeppelin's concepts to 1913, commemorating his 75th birthday.

Zeppelin, Dr.Ing. Graf. *Erfahrungen beim Bau von Luftschiffen.* Berlin: Verlag von Julius Springer, 1908. Count Zeppelin's personal views on airship design, presented as a lecture to the Union of German Engineers.

(b) ***German airships during World War I***

Beelitz, Helmut. *Der Werdegang und Wandel der Luftschiffverwendung im Seekrieg.* Dusseldorf: Verlag G.H. Nolte, 1936. A doctor's thesis by a former naval airship commander, largely abstracted from published sources and containing very little original material. Beelitz apparently received his degree from Heidelberg on the strength of his important position in the Nazi press bureau.

Buttlar-Brandenfels, Freiherr Treusch von. *Zeppelins over England,* trans. Huntley Patterson. New York: Harcourt, Brace & Co., 1932. The only pre-war officer of the German Naval Airship Division still flying at the Armistice, and the only airship commander awarded Germany's highest decoration, the *Ordre Pour le Merite*, von Buttlar, by his own account, enjoyed the war.

Colsman, Alfred. *Luftschiff Voraus!* Stuttgart and Berlin: Deutsche Verlags-Anstalt, 1933. Reminiscences of the business director of the Zeppelin Company, and the head policy-maker in 1919-21 until replaced by Dr. Eckener. Noteworthy for objective criticism of policies – and even personnel – of the Zeppelin Company in the early days.

Eckener, Hugo. *Im Zeppelin über Länder und Meere*. Flensburg: Verlagshaus Christian Wolff, 1949. The world-famous German airship expert's autobiography. Some comments on his five-year association with Strasser in World War I.

Gamble, C.F. Snowden. *The Story of a North Sea Air Station*. London: Oxford University Press, 1928. Ostensibly the story of the Royal Naval Air Service Station at Great Yarmouth, which took a leading part in anti-Zeppelin operations, it also tells with superb scholarship the whole story of naval air operations in the North Sea.

Goebel, J., and Forster, Walter. *Afrika zu unseren Füssen*. Leipzig: Verlag von K.F. Koehler, 1925. Well-written history of the Jamboli airship base by two officers who served there; much material on the Africa flight of *L 59*.

Goote, Thor (Langsdorff, Werner von). *Der F.d.L.* No publisher, n.d. (1938). Prizewinning fictional biography of Strasser with laudatory introduction by Air Minister Goering. Disappointing. described by Strasser's acquaintances as "a propaganda book."

Klein, Pitt. *Achtung! Bomben Fallen!* Leipzig: Verlag von K.F. Koehler, 1934. Popularly written recollections of Heinrich Mathy's crew, by one of the four men left behind on *L 3*'s last flight.

Kriegswissenschaftliche Abteilung der Luftwaffe. *Mobilmachung, Aufmarsch und ersten Einsatz der deutschen Luftstreitkräfte in August, 1914*. Berlin: E.S. Mittler u. Sohn, 1939. Official history. Mobilization and first combat employment of German air forces, including Naval Airship Division.

Lehmann, Ernst A., and Mingos, Howard. *The Zeppelins*. New York: J.H. Sears & Co., 1927. Composed of Lehmann's personal experiences as an airship commander, plus general airship history, often inaccurate.

Lehmann, Ernst A., and Adelt, Leonhard. *Auf Luftpatrouille und Weltfahrt*. Leipzig: Schmidt u. Günther, 1936. Expansion of above, with a nationalistic flavor and added material on operation of Graf Zeppelin and Hindenburg.

Marben, Rolf (ed.). *Zeppelin Adventures*, trans. Claud W. Sykes. London: John Hamilton, Ltd., 1931. Reminiscences by former personnel of the German Naval Airship Division.

Morison, Frank (Ross, Albert H.). *War on Great Cities*. London: Faber & Faber, 1937. Detailed record of events on the ground during the more important airship and aeroplane raids on London in World War I.

Morris, Joseph. *The German Air Raids on Great Britain*. London: Sampson, Low, Marston & Co., Ltd., n.d. Early history from British official records, superseded by The War in the Air.

Neumann, George Paul (ed.). *Die deutschen Luftstreitkräfte im Weltkrieg*. Berlin: E.S. Mittler u. Sohn, 1920. Encyclopedic account of organization, operations and materiel of German air forces in World War I. Technical airship article by Engberding. Summary articles by Steegmann and Stahl constitute the best history in print of the German Army Airship Service. Naval airship article by Hollender superficial, disappointing.

Neumann, George Paul (ed.). *In der Luft Unbesiegt*. Munich: J.F. Lehmanns Verlag, 1923. Reminiscences by wartime aviators. Articles by Lehmann, von Schiller and Breithaupt on naval airship operations.

"P.I.X." (Hallam, T.D.). *The Spider Web*. Edinburgh and London: William Blackwood & Sons, 1919. Personal reminiscences of a senior officer of the Royal Naval Air Service Station, Felixstowe. Includes anti-Zeppelin operations.

Raleigh, Sir Walter, and Jones, H.A. *The War in the Air*. 6 vols. Oxford: At the Clarendon Press, 1922-35. Official history. Vols. III and V, with detailed maps in separate case, give excellent and unbiased account of the Zeppelin raids and include German material.

Rawlinson, A. *The Defence of London, 1915-18*. London: Andrew Melrose Ltd., 1923. Personal reminiscences, valuable for his service in the autumn of 1915 as assistant to Admiral Sir Percy Scott, commander of the London defenses.

Saager, Dr. Adolf. *Zeppelin*. Stuttgart: Verlag Robert Lutz, 1915. Hysterical praise for Count Zeppelin as the savior of the Fatherland.

Scott, Admiral Sir Percy. *Fifty Years in the Royal Navy*. New York: George H. Doran Company, 1919. Reminiscences; one chapter on the author's organization of the London anti-aircraft defenses in the autumn of 1915.

Slessor, Sir John. *The Central Blue*. New York: Frederick A. Praeger, 1957. Opens with description of the author's anti-Zeppelin flights in 1915.

Strahlmann, Dr. Fritz (ed.). *Zwei deutsche Luftschffhäfen des Weltkrieges, Ahlhorn u. Wildeshausen*. Oldenburg: Oldenburger Verlagshaus Lindenallee, 1926. Numerous valuable articles by airship officers formerly serving at the Ahlhorn base.

Sueter, Rear-Admiral Sir Murray. *Airmen or Noahs*. London: Sir Isaac Pitman & Sons, Ltd., 1928. Some comments on anti-Zeppelin operations included in the author's story of his fight to give the Royal Navy an air arm.

Vissering, Harry. *Zeppelin, the Story of a Great Achievement*. Chicago: Privately printed, 1922. Persuasive propaganda by a whole hearted admirer who was also the Zeppelin's Company's agent in America. Excellent photographs from the *Luftschiffbau Zeppelin* collection.

### (c) *Technical Publications*

Bleston, Walter. Manuscript notebook. Extensive statistical tables on Schütte-Lanz airships, by one of the firm's chief engineers.

Bruce, J.M. *British Aeroplanes, 1914-18*. London: Putnam & Co., Ltd., 1957. The ultimate authority on design, construction and performance of aeroplanes used for anti-Zeppelin operations.

Burgess, Charles P. *Airship Design*. New York: The Ronald Press Co., 1927. Technological, mostly on rigid airships, by an American expert.

Durr, Ludwig. *25 Jahre Zeppelin-Luftschiffbau*. Berlin: V.D.I.-Verlag G.m.b.H., 1924. Much detailed technical information on development of Zeppelin airships, by chief designer of the Zeppelin Company. Many good drawings.

Eckener, Hugo. *Kurze Anleitungen und praktische Winke für die Führung von Zeppelin-Luftschifen*. Privately printed (1919). Flight manual for officers of the DELAG airship Bodensee, a condensation of the manual written by Dr. Eckener for the German Naval Airship Division about 1917.

Engberding, Dietrich. *Luftschiff und Luftschiffahrt in Vergangenheit, Gegenwart und Zukunft*. Berlin: V.D.I.-Verlag, 1926. Exhaustive description of airship technology, construction and operations, by the leading airship authority at the German Admiralty in World War I.

Hardesty, Frederick S. (ed.). *Key to the Development of the Super-Airship: Luftfahrzeugbau Schütte-Lanz, Mannheim-Rheinau, Germany, 1909-30*. New York: privately printed, 1930. Much valuable incidental information in a thick volume written to prove the legal claims of the Schütte-Lanz Company to have developed all technical features of the large rigid airships.

Keen, R. *Wireless Direction Finding*. London: Iliffe & Sons Ltd., 1938. Includes material on German direction finding equipment in World War I, with comments on its shortcomings and errors.

Kollmann, Franz. *Das Zeppelinluftschiff*. Berlin: Verlag von M. Krayn, 1924. Authoritative developmental history, based on Zeppelin Company records. Excellent photographs.

Lewitt, E.H. *The Rigid Airship*. London: Sir Isaac Pitman & Sons, Ltd., 1925. "A treatise on design and performance."

*Rangliste der Kaiserlich Deutschen Marine*. Berlin: E.S. Mittler u. Sohn, 1913 and other years. Official annual German Navy list of officers and their assignments.

Rasch, F., and Hormel, W. *Taschenbuch der Luftflotten*. Munich, J.F. Lehmanns Verlag, 1914 and other years. Annual, with photographs and data, especially detailed on German airships and aeroplanes.

Schütte, Professor Johann (ed.). *Der Luftschiffbau Schütte-Lanz, 1909-1925*. Munich and Berlin: Druck u. Verlag R. Oldenbourg, 1926. The talented, though difficult, chief designer of the Schütte-Lanz concern edits a series of articles by his subordinates and others on development and construction of its airships. Excellent illustrations.

*Technical Notes on Direction Finding Wireless Telegraphy*. London: H.M. Stationery Office, 1921. The state of the art of radio direction finding at the end of World War I.

Thetford, Owen. *British Naval Aircraft, 1912-58*. London: Putnam & Co., Ltd., 1958. Brief but authoritative histories of British naval aircraft types used against Zeppelins in the North Sea, with photographs and accurate 3-view drawings.

U.S. Navy, Bureau of Aeronautics. *Rigid Ship Manual*. Washington: Government Printing Office, 1927. Invaluable compilation of operating instructions for rigid airships, much of it translated from the German Navy's "Praktischen Anleitungen für die Fuhrung von Zeppelin-Luftschiffen."

### (d) *General History*

Churchill, Winston S. *The World Crisis*. 4 vols. New York: Scribner's, 1923-31. Considerable material in Vol.I on anti-Zeppelin operations initiated by the author as First Lord of the British Admiralty.

Corbett, Sir Julian S., and Newbolt, Henry. *History of the Great War – Naval Operations*. 5 vols. London: Longmans, Green & Co., 1921-31.

Freeman, Lewis R. *To Kiel in the "Hercules."* New York: Dodd, Mead & Co., 1919. Popular account of visit of the Naval Armistice Commission to Germany in December, 1918; visits to Tondern, Nordholz.

Frost, Holloway H. *The Battle of Jutland*. Annapolis: U.S. Naval Institute, 1936.

Groos, Otto, and Gladisch, Walter. *Der Krieg in der Nordsee*. 6 vols. Berlin: E.S. Mittler u. Sohn, 1920-27; 1936. Official History. Vols. I-V by Groos, Vol. VI by Gladisch. Disproportionate attention to naval Zeppelins, whose aggressiveness contrasted with inactivity of the High Seas Fleet. Based on official records, but with significant omissions. Only Vol.VI utilizes British material. This history never carried beyond May, 1917.

Hopman, Admiral. *Das Logbuch eines deutschen Seeoffziers*. Berlin: August Scherl G.m.b.H., 1924. Autobiography of one of the German Navy's ablest junior flag officers, covering period 1884-1914. A mine of information on the Imperial Navy, particularly on its higher command organs, in which Hopman served and which he evaluates objectively and at length.

James, Admiral Sir William. *The Code Breakers of Room 40*. New York: St. Martin's Press, 1956. The story of Admiral Hall's radio intelligence organization at the British Admiralty.

Jane, Fred T. (ed.). *Fighting Ships*. London: Sampson, Low, Marston & Co., 1914.

Jellicoe of Scapa, Admiral Viscount. *The Grand Fleet, 1914-16*. London: Cassell & Co., Ltd., 1919.

MacDonagh, Michael. *In London During the Great War*. London: Eyre & Spottiswoode, 1935. A reporter for the London Times, MacDonagh was greatly interested in the Zeppelin raids on the capital, and visited the wrecks of *L 31* and *L 32* for his paper.

Parkes, Oscar, and Prendergast, Maurice (eds.). *Jane's Fighting Ships*. London: Sampson, Low, Marston & Co., Ltd., 1919.

Scheer, Reinhard. *Germany's High Seas Fleet in the World War*. London: Cassell & Co., Ltd., 1920.

Tirpitz, Alfred von. *My Memoirs*. 2 vols. New York: Dodd, Mead & Co., 1919.

Wilson, H.W. *Battleships in Action*. 2 vols. London: Sampson, Low, Marston & Co., Ltd., n.d. (1926).

Wollard, Commander Claude L.A., R.N. *With the Harwich Naval Forces, 1914-18*. Antwerp: Geo. Kohler (Belgium) S.A., n.d. Personal reminiscences, partly remedying the undeserved neglect

**PERIODICALS**

(Bahn, Heinrich). "In a German Airship over England." *Journal of the Royal United Service Institution*, February, 1926. Personal experiences of the rudder man of *L 45* in the "Silent Raid."

Breithaupt, Joachim. "How We Bombed London." *Living Age*, January, 1928. *L 15* in the raid of October 13, 1915, by her commanding officer.

Iron, C.S. "The Last of the Zeppelins." *Blackwood's*, January 1936. Gripping eye-witness account of destruction of *L 70* on August 5, 1918, quoted in text.

Kölle, Waldemar. "Marineluftschiffe im Kriege, in Sturm und Not." *Deutsche Rundschau*, January, 1926. Well-written reminiscences by commander of *L 45*.

Koreuber, "Prall-Luftschiffe." *Illustrierte Flugwelt*, October 27, 1920. Authoritative information and tables on German Parseval and military airships.

Mieth, Otto. "Shot Down by the British." *Living Age*, April, 1926. Personal account by the surviving executive officer of *L 48*.

Müller-Breslau, Professor Dr. Ing. "Zur Geschichte des Zeppelin-Luftschiffes." *Verhandlungen zur Beforderung des Gewerbfleisses*, January 1914. Muller-Breslau's story of the design that Count Zeppelin presented to the 1894 commission, of which he was a member, and of his own role in developing the later "Zeppelin" design.

Outhwaite, Cedric. "The Sea and the Air." *Blackwood's*, November 1927. The operation that resulted in the destruction of *L 53* on August 11, 1918.

Robinson, Douglas H. "The Destruction and Salvage of Zeppelin *L 70*." *Cross and Cockade*, winter 1963.

Robinson, Douglas H. "The Airplane-Carrying Airship: The First Experiment." *American Aviation Historical Society Journal*, winter 1959.

Detailed account of the aeroplane-carrying experiment by *L 35* in January, 1918, from official records.

Roskill, Capt. S.W. "The Destruction of Zeppelin *L 53*." *U.S. Naval Institute Proceedings*, August, 1960, p. 71. Comprehensive account with information and photographs provided by Group Captain S.D. Culley, D.S.O., R.A.F.

Schiller, Hans von. "Airships in the World War." *Monthly Information Bulletin*, Office of Naval Intelligence. Washington: Government Printing Office, 1924. Prepared for the U.S. Navy from German Navy official records. Printed by von Schiller in condensed form in Marine-Rundschau, March, 1922.

Stahl. "Zeppelin-Luftschiffe" in *Illustrierte Flugwelt*, November 24, 1920, et seq. Authoritative information and tables on Zeppelin airships.

"The Strafing of *LZ 76*." *Blackwood's*, February, 1922. Detailed account of destruction of *L 53*, includes Culley's 6-sentence report.

## APPENDIX A

# SHIPS OF THE GERMAN NAVAL AIRSHIP DIVISION: STATISTICAL DATA

## (*a*) ZEPPELINS

| *Navy number* | *Builder's type* | *Volume (cubic feet)* | *Length ft.* | *in.* | *Diameter ft.* | *in.* | *Height ft.* | *in.* | *Gas cells (number)* | *Weight empty (pounds)* | *Useful lift (pounds)* | *Engines: number and type* | *Total horse-power* | *Pro-pellers (number)* | *Trial speed (m.p.h.)* | *Remarks* |
|---|---|---|---|---|---|---|---|---|---|---|---|---|---|---|---|---|
| *L 1* | h | 793,600 | 518 | 2 | 48 | 6 | 61 | 6 | 18 | 36,800 | 20,700 | 3M C-X | 495 | 4 | 47·4 | 8 metre ring spacing |
| *L 2* | i | 953,000 | 518 | 2 | 54 | 6 | 61 | 6 | 18 | 44,500 | 24,500 | 4M C-X | 660 | 4 | 47·0 | Internal keel, separate control car |
| *L 3* | m | 794,500 | 518 | 2 | 48 | 6 | 60 | 3 | 18 | 37,250 | 20,250 | 3M C-X | 630 | 4 | 47·4 | First "skinned fabric" gas cells |
| *L 4* | m | 794,500 | 518 | 2 | 48 | 6 | 60 | 3 | 18 | 37,400 | 20,100 | 3M C-X | 630 | 4 | 51·4 | First simple cruciform fins and rudders |
| *L 5* | m | 794,500 | 518 | 2 | 48 | 6 | 60 | 3 | 18 | 37,250 | 20,250 | 3M C-X | 630 | 4 | 52·1 | |
| *L 6* | m | 794,500 | 518 | 2 | 48 | 6 | 60 | 3 | 18 | 38,350 | 19,150 | 3M C-X | 630 | 4 | 52·0 | |
| *L 7* | m | 794,500 | 518 | 2 | 48 | 6 | 60 | 3 | 18 | 39,000 | 18,500 | 3M C-X | 630 | 4 | 52·0 | |
| *L 8* | m | 794,500 | 518 | 2 | 48 | 6 | 60 | 3 | 18 | 38,700 | 18,850 | 3M C-X | 630 | 4 | 52·0 | |
| *L 9* | o | 879,500 | 529 | 3 | 52 | 6 | | | 15 | 39,200 | 24,365 | 3M C-X | 630 | 3 | 52·8 | First with 10 metre ring spacing |
| *L 10* | p | 1,126,400 | 536 | 5 | 61 | 4 | 79 | 4 | 16 | 46,500 | 35,000 | 4M C-X | 840 | 4 | 57·7 | |
| *L 11* | p | 1,126,400 | 536 | 5 | 61 | 4 | 79 | 4 | 16 | 46,700 | 34,800 | 4M C-X | 840 | 4 | 57·0 | |
| *L 12* | p | 1,126,400 | 536 | 5 | 61 | 4 | 79 | 4 | 16 | 46,600 | 34,900 | 4M C-X | 840 | 4 | 59·5 | |
| *L 13* | p | 1,126,400 | 536 | 5 | 61 | 4 | 79 | 4 | 16 | 47,400 | 34,250 | 4M C-X | 840 | 4 | 59·7 | |
| *L 14* | p | 1,126,400 | 536 | 5 | 61 | 4 | 79 | 4 | 16 | 47,800 | 33,800 | 4M C-X | 840 | 4 | 59·2 | |
| *L 15* | p | 1,126,400 | 536 | 5 | 61 | 4 | 79 | 4 | 16 | 47,000 | 34,600 | 4M HSLu | 960 | 4 | 59·7 | First HSLu motors |
| *L 16* | p | 1,126,400 | 536 | 5 | 61 | 4 | 79 | 4 | 16 | 47,450 | 34,200 | 4M HSLu | 960 | 4 | 59·7 | |
| *L 17* | p | 1,126,400 | 536 | 5 | 61 | 4 | 79 | 4 | 16 | 48,500 | 33,100 | 4M HSLu | 960 | 4 | 58·1 | |
| *L 18* | p | 1,126,400 | 536 | 5 | 61 | 4 | 79 | 4 | 16 | 47,800 | 33,800 | 4M HSLu | 960 | 4 | 59·7 | |
| *L 19* | p | 1,126,400 | 536 | 5 | 61 | 4 | 79 | 4 | 16 | 47,900 | 33,700 | 4M HSLu | 960 | 4 | 60·4 | |

| *Navy number* | *Builder's type* | *Volume (cubic feet)* | *Length ft.* | *in.* | *Diameter ft.* | *in.* | *Height ft.* | *in.* | *Gas cells (number)* | *Weight empty (pounds)* | *Useful lift (pounds)* | *Engines: number and type* | *Total horse-power* | *Pro-pellers (number)* | *Trial speed (m.p.h.)* | *Remarks* |
|---|---|---|---|---|---|---|---|---|---|---|---|---|---|---|---|---|
| *L 20* | q | 1,264,100 | 585 | 5 | 61 | 4 | 79 | 4 | 18 | 52,500 | 39,250 | 4M HSLu | 960 | 4 | 55·7 | One 10 and one 5 metre gas cell added |
| *L 21* | q | 1,264,100 | 585 | 5 | 61 | 4 | 79 | 4 | 18 | 52,950 | 38,800 | 4M HSLu | 960 | 4 | 57·5 | |
| *L 22* | q | 1,264,100 | 585 | 5 | 61 | 4 | 79 | 4 | 18 | 53,200 | 38,600 | 4M HSLu | 960 | 4 | 59·0 | |
| *L 23* | q | 1,264,100 | 585 | 5 | 61 | 4 | 79 | 4 | 18 | 51,000 | 40,700 | 4M HSLu | 960 | 4 | 57·3 | |
| *L 24* | q | 1,264,100 | 585 | 5 | 61 | 4 | 79 | 4 | 18 | 51,400 | 40,300 | 4M HSLu | 960 | 4 | 57·3 | |
| *L 30* | r | 1,949,600 | 649 | 7 | 78 | 5 | 90 | 10 | 19 | 79,600 | 61,600 | 6M HSLu | 1,440 | 6 | 62·2 | |
| *L 31* | r | 1,949,600 | 649 | 7 | 78 | 5 | 90 | 10 | 19 | 78,800 | 62,500 | 6M HSLu | 1,440 | 6 | 63·8 | |
| *L 32* | r | 1,949,600 | 649 | 7 | 78 | 5 | 90 | 10 | 19 | 76,500 | 64,900 | 6M HSLu | 1,440 | 6 | 62·6 | |
| *L 33* | r | 1,949,600 | 644 | 8 | 78 | 5 | 90 | 10 | 19 | 75,300 | 66,100 | 6M HSLu | 1,440 | 6 | 64·2 | |
| *L 34* | r | 1,949,600 | 644 | 8 | 78 | 5 | 90 | 10 | 19 | 72,800 | 68,600 | 6M HSLu | 1,440 | 6 | 64·0 | First Zeppelin with gas shafts |
| *L 35* | r | 1,949,600 | 644 | 8 | 78 | 5 | 90 | 10 | 19 | 73,500 | 67,900 | 6M HSLu | 1,440 | 6 | 64·2 | Feb. 1, 1917, No. 1 engine removed. Mar. 17–June 13, 1917, streamlined rear gondola installed, midships gondolas raised and reversing gear installed. |
| *L 36* | r | 1,949,600 | 644 | 8 | 78 | 5 | 90 | 10 | 19 | 69,700 | 71,600 | 6M HSLu | 1,440 | 6 | 64·0 | Feb. 1, 1917, No. 1 engine removed. |
| *L 37* | r | 1,949,600 | 644 | 8 | 78 | 5 | 90 | 10 | 19 | 79,000 | 62,400 | 6M HSLu | 1,440 | 6 | 63·0 | |
| *L 38* | r | 1,949,600 | 644 | 8 | 78 | 5 | 90 | 10 | 19 | 69,750 | 71,550 | 6M HSLu | 1,440 | 6 | 64·2 | Midships gondolas located on ring 110 instead of ring 100. |
| *L 39* | r | 1,949,600 | 644 | 8 | 78 | 5 | 90 | 10 | 19 | 69,700 | 71,600 | 6M HSLu | 1,440 | 6 | 63·5 | Feb. 1, 1917, No. 1 engine removed |
| *L 40* | r | 1,949,600 | 644 | 8 | 78 | 5 | 90 | 10 | 19 | 69,700 | 71,600 | 6M HSLu | 1,440 | 6 | 62·4 | Feb. 1, 1917, No. 1 engine removed |
| *L 41* | r | 1,949,600 | 644 | 8 | 78 | 5 | 90 | 10 | 19 | 78,500 | 62,900 | 6M HSLu | 1,440 | 6 | 63·5 | Feb. 5, 1917, No. 1 engine removed. May 5–June 17, 1917, streamlined rear gondola installed, midships gondolas raised and reversing gear installed. |
| *L 42* | s | 1,959,700 | 644 | 8 | 78 | 5 | 90 | 10 | 18 | 62,500 | 78,900 | 5M HSLu | 1,200 | 5 | 62·0 | June 29–July 24, 1917, streamlined rear gondola installed, midships gondolas raised and reversing gear installed. |
| *L 43* | s | 1,959,700 | 644 | 8 | 78 | 5 | 90 | 10 | 18 | 61,900 | 80,300 | 5M HSLu | 1,200 | 5 | 62·0 | |

| *Navy number* | *Builder's type* | *Volume (cubic feet)* | *Length ft. in.* | *Diameter ft. in.* | *Height ft. in.* | *Gas cells (number)* | *Weight empty (pounds)* | *Useful lift (pounds)* | *Engines: number and type* | *Total horse-power* | *Pro-pellers (number)* | *Trial speed (m.p.h.)* | *Remarks* |
|---|---|---|---|---|---|---|---|---|---|---|---|---|---|
| *L 44* | t | 1,970,300 | 644 8 | 78 5 | 90 10 | 18 | 59,300 | 83,400 | 5M HSLu | 1,200 | 4 | 64·5 | First streamlined rear gondola. |
| *L 45* | r | 1,949,600 | 644 8 | 78 5 | 90 10 | 19 | 72,600 | 68,800 | 5M HSLu | 1,200 | 5 | 64·2 | Aug. 26–Sept. 20, 1917, streamlined rear gondola installed, midships gondolas raised and reversing gear installed. |
| *L 46* | t | 1,970,300 | 644 8 | 78 5 | 90 10 | 18 | 59,300 | 83,400 | 5M HSLu | 1,200 | 4 | 64·2 | First streamlined midships gondolas. |
| *L 47* | r | 1,949,600 | 644 8 | 78 5 | 90 10 | 19 | 70,700 | 70,600 | 5M HSLu | 1,200 | 5 | 63·4 | Sept. 26–Oct. 7, 1917, streamlined rear gondola installed, midships gondolas raised and reversing gear installed. |
| *L 48* | u | 1,970,300 | 644 8 | 78 5 | 92 4 | 18 | 56,900 | 85,800 | 5M HSLu | 1,200 | 4 | 66·9 | First streamlined control car. |
| *L 49* | u | 1,970,300 | 644 8 | 78 5 | 92 4 | 18 | 55,500 | 87,200 | 5M HSLu | 1,200 | 4 | 65·8 | |
| *L 50* | r | 1,949,600 | 644 8 | 78 5 | 92 4 | 19 (18?) | 70,600 | 70,800 | 5M HSLu | 1,200 | 4 | 62·6 | Streamlined gondolas as in *L 48*. |
| *L 51* | u | 1,970,300 | 644 8 | 78 5 | 92 4 | 18 | 55,700 | 87,000 | 5M HSLu | 1,200 | 4 | 66·1 | |
| *L 52* | u | 1,970,300 | 644 8 | 78 5 | 92 4 | 18 | 56,000 | 86,600 | 5M HSLu | 1,200 | 4 | 66·4 | April 26–May 15, 1918, MBIVa engines fitted. |
| *L 53* | v | 1,977,360 | 644 8 | 78 5 | 91 1 | 14 | 54,000 | 89,200 | 5M HSLu | 1,200 | 4 | 66·0 | 15 metre ring spacing. April 16–23, 1918, MBIVa engines fitted. |
| *L 54* | u | 1,970,300 | 644 8 | 78 5 | 92 4 | 18 | 55,600 | 87,100 | 5M HSLu | 1,200 | 4 | 66·6 | Mar. 15–31, 1918, MBIVa engines fitted. |
| *L 55* | v | 1,977,360 | 644 8 | 78 5 | 91 1 | 14 | 53,600 | 89,600 | 5M HSLu | 1,200 | 4 | 64·6 | |
| *L 56* | v | 1,977,360 | 644 8 | 78 5 | 91 1 | 14 | 58,200 | 85,100 | 5M HSLu | 1,200 | 4 | 66·0 | July 8-22, 1918, MBIVa engines fitted. |
| *L 57* | w | 2,418,700 | 743 0 | 78 5 | 91 1 | 16 | 60,600 | 114,700 | 5M HSLu | 1,200 | 4 | 64·0 | |
| *L 58* | v | 1,977,360 | 644 8 | 78 5 | 91 1 | 14 | 55,900 | 87,200 | 5M MBIVa | 1,225 | 4 | 66·5 | First "altitude motors". |
| *L 59* | w | 2,418,700 | 743 0 | 78 5 | 91 1 | 16 | 60,900 | 114,400 | 5M HSLu | 1,200 | 4 | 64·0 | Dec. 17, 1917–Feb. 14, 1918, rebuilt, gondolas re-located. |
| *L 60* | v | 1,977,360 | 644 8 | 78 5 | 91 1 | 14 | 58,100 | 85,200 | 5M MBIVa | 1,225 | 4 | 66·1 | Weights may be with HSLu engines. |
| *L 61* | v | 1,977,360 | 644 8 | 78 5 | 91 1 | 14 | 58,300 | 85,000 | 5M MBIVa | 1,225 | 4 | 68·9 | |
| *L 62* | v | 1,977,360 | 644 8 | 78 5 | 91 1 | 14 | 57,700 | 85,500 | 5M MBIVa | 1,225 | 4 | 66·8 | |
| *L 63* | v | 1,977,360 | 644 8 | 78 5 | 91 1 | 14 | 56,200 | 87,000 | 5M MBIVa | 1,225 | 4 | 71·6 | |

| *Navy number* | *Builder's type* | *Volume (cubic feet)* | *Length ft. in.* | *Diameter ft. in.* | *Height ft. in.* | *Gas cells (number)* | *Weight empty (pounds)* | *Useful lift (pounds)* | *Engines: number and type* | *Total horse-power* | *Pro-pellers (number)* | *Trial speed) (m.p.h.* | *Remarks* |
|---|---|---|---|---|---|---|---|---|---|---|---|---|---|
| *L 64* | v | 1,977,360 | 644 8 | 78 5 | 91 1 | 14 | 57,200 | 86,100 | 5M MBIVa | 1,225 | 4 | 66·0 | |
| *L 65* | v | 1,977,360 | 644 8 | 78 5 | 91 1 | 14 | 56,900 | 86,200 | 5M MBIVa | 1,225 | 4 | 71·6 | First cantilever section fins. |
| *L 70* | x | 2,195,800 | 693 11 | 78 5 | 91 1 | 15 | 62,300 | 97,100 | 7M MBIVa | 1,715 | 6 | 81 | |
| *L 71* | x | 2,195,800<br>2,418,700 | 693 11<br>743 2 | 78 5<br>78 5 | 91 1<br>91 1 | 15<br>16 | 61,100<br>62,900 | 98,500<br>112,700 | 7M MBIVa<br>6M MBIVa | 1,715<br>1,470 | 6<br>6 | 72·7 | Rear wing gondolas re-located from ring 85 to ring 100. Oct. 3–28, 1918, lengthened, small single engine gondola aft. |

## (*b*) SCHÜTTE-LANZ

| *Navy number* | *Builder's type* | *Volume (cubic feet)* | *Length ft. in.* | *Diameter ft. in.* | *Height ft. in.* | *Gas cells (number)* | *Weight empty (pounds)* | *Useful lift (pounds)* | *Engines: number and type* | *Total horse-power* | *Pro-pellers (number)* | *Trial speed (m.p.h.)* | *Remarks* |
|---|---|---|---|---|---|---|---|---|---|---|---|---|---|
| *SL 3* | c | 1,143,500 | 502 4 | 64 10 | 81 1 | 17 | 51,800 | 31,300 | 4M C-X | 840 | 4 | 52·6 | |
| *SL 4* | c | 1,146,500 | 502 4 | 64 10 | 80 6 | 17 | | | 4M C-X | 840 | 4 | 52·8 | Gondolas arranged differently from *SL 3* |
| *SL 6* | d | 1,240,300 | 534 5 | 64 10 | 80 6 | 18 | 55,600 | 34,750 | 4M C-X | 840 | 4 | 57·9 | |
| *SL 8* | e | 1,369,300 | 570 10 | 65 11 | 81 0 | 19 | 57,100 | 42,500 | 4M C-X | 840 | 4 | 56·1 | |
| *SL 9* | e | 1,369,300 | 570 10 | 65 11 | 81 0 | 19 | 56,400 | 43,200 | 4M HSLu | 960 | 4 | | |
| *SL 12* | e | 1,369,300 | 570 10 | 65 11 | 81 0 | 19 | | | 4M HSLu | 960 | 4 | | |
| *SL 14* | e | 1,369,300 | 570 10 | 65 11 | 81 0 | 19 | 54,100 | 47,800 | 4M HSLu | 960 | 4 | | |
| *SL 20* | f | 1,989,700 | 651 0 | 75 3 | 90 5 | 19 | 61,400 | 83,000 | 5M HSLu | 1,200 | 5 | 62·8 | |

## (*c*) PARSEVAL

| *Navy number* | *Builder's type* | *Volume (cubic feet)* | *Length ft. in.* | *Diameter ft. in.* | *Height ft. in.* | *Gas cells (number)* | *Weight empty (pounds)* | *Useful lift (pounds)* | *Engines: number and type* | *Total horse-power* | *Pro-pellers (number)* | *Trial speed (m.p.h.)* | *Remarks* |
|---|---|---|---|---|---|---|---|---|---|---|---|---|---|
| *PL 6* | | 317,800 | 246 0 | 49 4 | 72 5 | 2 Bal-lonets | 16,380 | 6,620 | 2 N.A.G. | 220 | 2 | 31·3 | 4-bladed cloth propellers. Engines by Neue Auto-mobil-A.G., Berlin. |
| *PL 19* | | 353,100 | 319 0 | 50 9 | 74 11 | 2 Bal-lonets | 18,290 | 7,280 | 2M C-X | 360 | 2 | 44·3 | 4-bladed wood propellers. |
| *PL 25* | | 497,870 | 369 0 | 54 2 | 80 1 | 2 Bal-lonets | 22,548 | 13,300 | 2M C-X | 420 | 2 | 45·2 | |

## (*d*) GROSS-BASENACH

| *Navy number* | *Builder's type* | *Volume (cubic feet)* | *Length ft. in.* | *Diameter ft. in.* | *Height ft. in.* | *Gas cells (number)* | *Weight empty (pounds)* | *Useful lift (pounds)* | *Engines: number and type* | *Total horse-power* | *Pro-pellers (number)* | *Trial speed (m.p.h.)* | *Remarks* |
|---|---|---|---|---|---|---|---|---|---|---|---|---|---|
| *M IV* | | 688,540 | 417 0 | 49 3 | | 1 Bal-lonet | 30,400 | 15,620 | 3M C-X | 510 | 3 | 45·4 | Engines enclosed in keel. |

## APPENDIX B

# SHIPS OF THE GERMAN NAVAL AIRSHIP DIVISION: HISTORICAL DATA

## (*a*) ZEPPELINS

| *Navy number* | *Builder's number* | *Built at* | *First flight* | *Commissioned* | *Commanding Officer* | *Executive Officer* | *Based at* | *Works flights* | *Scouting flights* | *Raids* | *Total Navy flights* | *Total flights* | *Remarks and end of service* |
|---|---|---|---|---|---|---|---|---|---|---|---|---|---|
| *L 1* | *LZ 14* | Friedrichshafen Ring Shed | Oct. 7, 1912 | Oct. 17, 1912 | From Oct. 17, 1912: Kptlt. Hanne | From Oct. 17, 1912: Oblt. z. S. v. Maltzahn | From Oct. 17, 1912: Johannisthal<br>From Apl. 21, 1913: Fuhlsbüttel<br>From May 29, 1913: Johannisthal<br>From Aug. 15, 1913: Fuhlsbüttel | | | | | 68 | Sept. 9, 1913: went down in sea off Heligoland in storm. 14 dead, 6 survivors. |
| *L 2* | *LZ 18* | Friedrichshafen Ring Shed | Sept. 6, 1913 | Not commissioned | Designated: Kptlt. Freyer | Designated: Oblt. z. S. Hirsch | From Sept. 20, 1913: Johannisthal | 5 | | | 5 | 10 | Oct. 17, 1913: Burned in air at Johannisthal. 28 dead, no survivors. |
| *L 3* | *LZ 24* | Friedrichshafen Ring Shed | May 11, 1914 | May 23, 1914 | From May 23, 1914: Kptlt. Fritz | From May 23, 1914: Oblt. z. S. v. Buttlar<br>From Sept. 1914: Lt. z. S. v. Lynckner | From May 23, 1914: Johannisthal<br>From June 1914: Fuhlsbüttel<br>From Sept. 25, 1914: Nordholz ("Nobel")<br>From Nov. 24, 1914: Fuhlsbüttel<br>From Dec. 5, 1914: Nordholz ("Nobel")<br>From Dec. 23, 1914: Fuhlsbüttel | | 27 | 1 | 74 (after Aug. 1, 1914) | 138 | Feb. 17, 1915: lost in forced landing on Fanö Island, Denmark. 16 interned. |
| *L 4* | *LZ 27* | Friedrichshafen Ring Shed | Aug. 28, 1914 | Sept. 1, 1914 | From Sept. 1, 1914: Kptlt. v. Platen | From Sept. 1, 1914: Oblt. z. S. Peterson<br>From Sept. 1914: Lt. z. S. Kruse | From Sept. 2, 1914: Fuhlsbüttel | 2? | 11 | 1 | 46? | 48 | Feb. 17, 1816: Lost in forced landing at Blaavands Huk, Denmark. 11 Interned, 4 missing. |
| *L 5* | *LZ 28* | Friedrichshafen Ring Shed | Sept. 22, 1914 | Sept. 24, 1914 | From Sept. 24, 1914: Kptlt. Hirsch<br>From April 14, 1915: Kptlt. d. R. Böcker<br>From July 1915: Kptlt. Ehrlich | From Sept. 24, 1914: Oblt. z. S. d. R. Wenke<br>From April 14, 1915: Lt. z. S. Frankenberg<br>From July 1915: Lt. z. S. Dietsch | From Sept. 25, 1914: Fuhlsbüttel<br>From Nov. 5, 1914: Nordholz ("Nobel")<br>From Feb. 20, 1915: Fuhlsbüttel<br>From May 6, 1915: Nordholz<br>From June 15, 1915: Fuhlsbüttel<br>From July 14, 1915: Seddin ("Selim") | 2? | 47 | 1 | 90? | 92 | Aug. 6, 1915: Forced landing at Plungiany, Russia, due gunfire damage over Dünamünde. Severely damaged and dismantled by Aug. 16, 1915: One man injured. |
| *L 6* | *LZ 31* | Friedrichshafen Ring Shed | Nov. 3, 1914 | Nov. 6, 1914 | From Nov. 6, 1914: Oblt. z. S. v. Buttlar<br>From May 3, 1915: Kptlt. Breithaupt<br>From Aug. 4, 1915: Kptlt. d. R. Blew | From Nov. 6, 1914: Fähnrich z. S. v. Schiller<br>From May 3, 1915: Oblt. z. S. Kühne | From Nov. 6, 1914: Fuhlsbüttel<br>From Nov. 24, 1914: Nordholz ("Nobel")<br>From Dec. 9, 1914: Fuhlsbüttel<br>From Dec. 23, 1914: Nordholz ("Nobel")<br>From April 10, 1915: Fuhlsbüttel<br>From May 4, 1915: Hage<br>From July 31, 1915: Dresden<br>From Sept. 21, 1915: Fuhlsbüttel | 2? | 33 | 1 | 89? | 91 | Sept. 16, 1916: Burned in Fuhlsbüttel shed in an inflation accident. One man of crew injured. |
| | | | | | | | | Aug. 4–Sept. 16, 1915: Elementary training ship | | | 165 | 165 | |
| | | | | | | | | Sept. 16, 1915–Sept. 8, 1916: Advanced training ship | 3 | | 156 | 156 | |
| | | | | | | | | Sept. 8–16, 1916: Elementary training ship | | | 7 | 7 | |
| | | | | | | | | Grand total: 2? | 36 | 1 | 417 | 419 | |
| *L 7* | *LZ 32* | Friedrichshafen Ring Shed | Nov. 20, 1914 | Nov. 24, 1914 | From Nov. 24, 1914: Oblt. z. S. Peterson<br>From June 1, 1915: Kptlt.d.R. Max Dietrich<br>From Sept. 5, 1915: Kptlt. Stabbert<br>From Nov. 12, 1915: Kptlt. v. Schubert<br>From Jan. 11, 1916: Kptlt. Sommerfeldt<br>From Apl. 18, 1916: Kptlt. Hempel | From Nov. 24, 1914: Lt.z.S. Brodrück<br>From June 1, 1915: Lt.d.r.d.M.A. v. Nathusius<br>From Sept. 5., 1915: Lt. z. S. Schirlitz<br>From Nov. 12, 1915: Lt. z. S. Rothe<br>From Jan. 11, 1915: Lt. z. S. d. R. Gebauer<br>From April 18, 1916: Oblt. z. S. d. R. Wenke | From Nov. 24, 1914: Leipzig<br>From Jan. 23, 1915: Nordholz ("Nora")<br>From Apl. 25, 1915: Tondern ("Toni") | | 78 | 1 | | 164 | May 4, 1916: Shot down in flames off Horns Reef by H.M. cruisers "Galetea" and "Phaeton." Finished off by H.M. submarine *E. 31.* Eleven dead, seven prisoners. |

| Navy number | Builder's number | Built at | First flight | Commissioned | Commanding Officer | Executive Officer | Based at | Works flights | Scouting flights | Raids | Total Navy flights | Total flights | Remarks and end of service |
|---|---|---|---|---|---|---|---|---|---|---|---|---|---|
| *L 8* | *LZ 33* | Friedrichshafen Ring Shed | Dec. 17, 1914 | Dec. 22, 1914 | From Dec. 22, 1914:<br>Kptlt. Konradin Maver<br>From Jan. 10, 1915:<br>Kptlt. Beelitz | From Dec. 22, 1914<br>Lt. z.S. Kühne | From Dec. 22, 1914:<br>Düsseldorf (City Shed)<br>From Feb. 27, 1915:<br>Gontrode (Army Shed) | | 0 | 0 | 17 | | Mar. 5, 1915: Lost in forced landing at Tirlemont after gunfire damage over Nieuport during attempted raid on England. |
| *L 9* | *LZ 36* | Friedrichshafen Ring Shed | Mar. 8, 1915 | Mar. 15, 1915 | From Mar.15,1915:<br>Kptlt. Mathy<br>From June 24, 1915:<br>Kptlt. Loewe<br>From Oct. 19,1915:<br>Kptlt. Martin Dietrich<br>From Dec.22,1915:<br>Kptlt. d. R. Prölss<br>From Mar.27,1916:<br>Hauptmann Stelling<br>From June 10,1916:<br>Kptlt. Kraushaar<br>From July 14,1916:<br>Kptlt. Ganzel<br>From Aug. 8, 1916:<br>Kptlt. Hollender<br>From Sept.8,1916:<br>Kptlt. Gayer | From Mar.15,1915:<br>Oblt. z. S. Friemel<br>From June 24, 1915:<br>Lt. z. S. Braunhof<br>From Oct. 19,1915:<br>Lt. z. S. Eisenbeck<br>From Dec. 22,1915:<br>Lt. z. S. Brand<br>From Mar. 27,1916:<br>Oblt. z. S. Schüz<br>From June 10,1916:<br>Lt. z. S. Zimmermann<br>From July 14,1916:<br>Lt. z. S. Frey<br>From Aug.8,1916:<br>Lt. z. S. Frey<br>From Sept.8,1916:<br>Lt. z. S. Loewisch | From Mar. 18, 1915:<br>Nordholz<br>From Apl. 10, 1915:<br>Hage ("Hanne") ("Hasso")<br>From July 2, 1916:<br>Tondern<br>From Aug. 3, 1916:<br>Seddin<br>From Sept. 7, 1916:<br>Fuhlsbüttel | 2 | 74 | 4 | 145 | 147 | Sept. 16, 1916: Burned in Fuhlsbüttel shed due to to inflation fire in *L 6*. No casualties to crew. |
| | | | | | | | | Sept. 8–16, 1916: Advanced training ship | | | 1 | 1 | |
| | | | | | | | | Grand total: 2 | 74 | 4 | 146 | 148 | |
| *L 10* | *LZ 40* | Friedrichshafen Factory Shed I | May 13, 1915 | May 17, 1915 | From May 17,1915:<br>Kptlt. Hirsch<br>From July25,1915:<br>Oblt. z. S. d. R. Wenke<br>From Aug.26,1915:<br>Kptlt. Hirsch | From May 17,1915:<br>Oblt. z. S. d. R. Wenke<br>From July 25,1915:<br>Oblt. d. R. Sticker<br>From Aug.26,1915:<br>Oblt. d. R. Sticker | From May 17, 1915:<br>Nordholz ("Nobel") | 2 | 8 | 5 | 26 | 28 | Sept. 3, 1915: Struck by lightning and fell in flames off Neuwerk Island. 19 dead, no survivors. |
| *L 11* | *LZ 41* | Löwenthal | June 7, 1915 | June 8, 1915 | From June 8,1915:<br>Oblt. z. S. v. Buttlar<br>From Feb.9,1916:<br>Korv. Kap. Viktor Schütze<br>From Sept.12,1916:<br>Kptlt. Hollender<br>From Sept.19,1916:<br>Kptlt. d. R. Blew | From June 8,1915:<br>Lt. z. S. v. Schiller<br>From Feb.9, 1916:<br>Lt. z. S. Mieth<br>From Sept.12,1916:<br>Lt. z. S. Frey | From June 9, 1915:<br>Nordholz<br>From June 23, 1915:<br>Hage<br>From June 28, 1915:<br>Nordholz ("Norbert")<br>From Aug. 17, 1916:<br>Hage<br>From Sept. 19,1916:<br>Nordholz<br>From Apl. 5, 1917:<br>Hage | 1 | 31 | 18 | 117 | 118 | Apl. 5, 1917: To Hage and decommissioned. Dismantled there beginning Nov. 24, 1917. |
| | | | | | | | | Sept. 19, 1916–Apl. 5, 1917: training ship | | | 276 | 276 | |
| | | | | | | | | Grand total: 1 | 31 | 18 | 393 | **394** | |

| Navy number | Builder's number | Built at | First flight | Commissioned | Commanding Officer | Executive Officer | Based at | Works flights | Scouting flights | Raids | Total Navy flights | Total flights | Remarks and end of service |
|---|---|---|---|---|---|---|---|---|---|---|---|---|---|
| *L 12* | *LZ 43* | Friedrichshafen Factory Shed I | June 21, 1915 | June 22, 1915 | From June 22,1915:<br>Oblt. z. S. Peterson | From June 22,1915:<br>Lt. z. S. Brodrück | From June 23,1915:<br>Nordholz<br>From June 28,1915:<br>Hage | 1 | 5 | 1 | 13 | 14 | Aug. 10, 1915: Towed into Ostend after gunfire damage over England, and burned while being dismantled. |
| *L 13* | *LZ 45* | Friedrichshafen Factory Shed I | July 23, 1915 | July 25, 1915 | From July 25,1915:<br>Kptlt. Mathy<br>From Apl.19, 1916:<br>Kptlt. d. R. Prölss<br>From Sept.13,1916:<br>Kptlt. d. R. Eichler<br>From Dec.6,1916:<br>Kptlt. Schwonder<br>From Feb.17,1917:<br>Oblt. z. S. Flemming | From July 25,1915:<br>Oblt. z. S. Friemel<br>From Apl.19,1916:<br>Lt. z. S. Brand<br>From Sept.13,1916:<br>Oblt. z. S. Westphal<br>From Feb.17,1917:<br>Lt. z. S. Kohlhauer | From July 26, 1915:<br>Hage ("Hannibal")<br>From Apl. 5, 1917:<br>Wittmundhaven ("Wille")<br>From Apl. 28, 1917:<br>Hage | 1 | 45 | 17 | 158 | 159 | Apl. 29–30, 1917: Decommissioned in Hage. Dismantled there beginning Dec. 11, 1917. |
| *L 14* | *LZ 46* | Löwenthal | Aug. 9, 1915 | Aug. 10, 1915 | From Aug.10,1915:<br>Kptlt. d. R. Böcker<br>From June10,1916:<br>Hauptmann Manger<br>From Dec.1,1916:<br>Kptlt. Dose<br>From Apl. 5, 1917:<br>Kptlt. d. R. Blew | From Aug.10,1915:<br>Oblt. z. S. Frankenberg<br>From June10,1916:<br>Lt. z. S. Gruner<br>From Dec.1,1916:<br>Lt. z. S. Trube | From Aug.12,1915:<br>Nordholz ("Nobel")<br>From July 8, 1916:<br>Hage<br>From Apl. 5, 1917:<br>Nordholz ("Nora") | 1 | 42 | 17 | 126 | 127 | Decommissioned Sept. 8, 1918. June 23, 1919: wrecked by airship crews in Nordholz, "Nora" shed. |
| | | | | | | | | Apl. 5, 1917–Sept. 8, 1918: Elementary training ship: | | | 399 | 399 | |
| | | | | | | | | Grand total: 1 | 42 | 17 | 525 | 526 | |
| *L 15* | *LZ 48* | Löwenthal | Sept. 9, 1915 | Sept. 12, 1915 | From Sept.12,1915:<br>Kptlt. Breithaupt | From Sept.12,1915:<br>Lt. z. S. Kühne | From Sept. 12, 1915:<br>Nordholz ("Nora")<br>From Oct. 21, 1915:<br>Hage | 1 | 8 | 3 | 35 | 36 | Apl. 1, 1916: Fell in sea at Knock Deep due gunfire damage over England, later sank. 1 dead, 17 prisoners. |
| *L 16* | *LZ 50* | Friedrichshafen Factory Shed I | Sept. 23, 1915 | Sept. 24, 1915 | From Sept.24,1915:<br>Oblt. z. s. Peterson<br>From May31,1916:<br>Kptlt. Sommerfeldt<br>From Nov.15,1961:<br>Kptlt. Gayer | From Sept.24,1915:<br>Lt. z. S. Brodrück<br>From May 31,1916:<br>Oblt.z.S.d.R.Gebauer<br>From Nov.15,1916:<br>Oblt. z. S. Dehn | From Sept. 25, 1915:<br>Hage ("Harald," "Hanne")<br>From Mar. 3, 1917:<br>Nordholz ("Norbert") | 1 | 38 | 16 | 131 | 132 | Oct. 19, 1917: Wrecked in landing at Nordholz. 5 injured. |
| | | | | | | | | Mar. 13–Oct. 19, 1917: Advanced training ship | 6 | | 103 | 103 | |
| | | | | | | | | Grand total: 1 | 44 | 16 | 234 | 235 | |

| Navy number | Builder's number | Built at | First flight | Commissioned | Commanding Officer | Executive Officer | Based at | Works flights | Scouting flights | Raids | Total Navy flights | Total flights | Remarks and end of service |
|---|---|---|---|---|---|---|---|---|---|---|---|---|---|
| *L 17* | *LZ 53* | Friedrichshafen Factory Shed I | Oct. 20, 1915 | Oct. 22, 1915 | From Oct.22,1915: Kptlt. Ehrlich<br>From Aug.10,1916: Kptlt. Kraushaar | From Oct.22,1915: Oblt. z. S. Dietsch<br>From Aug.10,1916: Lt. z. S. Zimmermann | From Oct.22,1915: Nordholz ("Nora")<br>From Aug.17,1916: Tondern ("Toska") | 1? | 27 | 11 | 72 | 73? | Dec. 28, 1916: Burned in "Toska" shed at Tondern due to destruction of *L 24*. |
| *L 18* | *LZ 52* | Löwenthal | Nov. 4, 1915 | Nov. 6, 1915 | FromNov.6,1915: Kptlt. d. R. Max Dietrich | From Nov.6,1915: Lt. d. R. d. M. A. v. Nathusius | From Nov.16,1915: Tondern ("Toska") | 2? | 0 | 0 | 2 | 4? | Nov. 17, 1915: Burned in inflation accident in "Toska" shed in Tondern. 1 dead, 7 injured. |
| *L 19* | *LZ 54* | Friedrichshafen Factory Shed I | Nov. 19, 1915 | Nov. 22, 1915 | FromNov.22, 1915: Kptlt. Loewe | FromNov.22,1915: Lt. z. S. Braunhof | From Nov.22,1915: Dresden<br>From Jan.29,1916: Tondern | ? | 0 | 1 | ? | 14 | Feb. 2, 1916: Lost in North Sea returning from raid on England. 16 dead, no survivors. |
| *L 20* | *LZ 59* | Friedrichshafen Factory Shed I | Dec. 21, 1915 | Dec. 22, 1915 | From Dec.22,1915: Kptlt. Stabbert | From Dec.22,1915: Lt. z. S. Schirlitz | From Jan.18,1916: Tondern<br>From Feb.21,1916: Seddin<br>From Apl. 6, 1916: Tondern | 2 | 6 | 3 | 17 | 19 | May 3, 1916: Forced landing in Norway after raid on England. 6 Repatriated, 10 interned. |
| *L 21* | *LZ 61* | Löwenthal | Jan. 10, 1916 | Jan. 19, 1916 | FromJan.19,1916: Kptlt. d. R. Max Dietrich<br>FromJune24,1916: Hauptmann Stelling<br>FromAug.15,1916: Oblt. z. S. Frankenberg | FromJan.19,1916: Lt. d. R. d. M. A. v. Nathusius<br>FromJune24,1916: Oblt. z. S. Schüz<br>FromAug.15,1916: Lt. z. S. Salzbrunn | From Jan.29,1916: Nordholz ("Norbert")<br>From Feb.21,1916: Seddin<br>From Apl. 5, 1916: Tondern ("Toska")<br>From Apl. 16, 1916: Nordholz ("Nobel") | 4 | 17 | 13 | 66 | 70 | Nov. 28, 1916: Shot down in flames off Lowestoft by British planes after raid on England. 17 dead, no survivors. |
| *L 22* | *LZ 64* | Löwenthal | Mar. 3, 1916 | Mar. 10, 1916 | FromMar.10,1916: Kptlt. Martin Dietrich<br>From Oct. 7, 1916: Kptlt. Hollender<br>FromFeb.14,1917: Kptlt. Hankow<br>FromFeb.22,1917: Oblt. z. S. Lehmann | FromMar.10,1916: Lt. z. S. Eisenbeck<br>From Oct. 7, 1916: Lt. z. s. Frey<br>FromFeb.14,1917: Lt. z. S. v. Knobelsdorff | From Mar.14,1916: Tondern<br>From Mar.15,1916: Nordholz<br>From Apl.16,1916: Tondern ("Toska")<br>From Sept.26,1916: Nordholz ("Nobel," ("Norbert")<br>From Mar. 3, 1917: Hage<br>From Apl. 5, 1917: Wittmundhaven ("Wille") | 3 | 30 | 11 | 78 | 81 | May 14, 1917: Shot down in flames off Texel by British flying boat. 21 dead, no survivors. |

| Navy number | Builder's number | Built at | First flight | Commissioned | Commanding Officer | Executive Officer | Based at | Works flights | Scouting flights | Raids | Total Navy flights | Total flights | Remarks and end of service |
|---|---|---|---|---|---|---|---|---|---|---|---|---|---|
| *L 23* | *LZ 66* | Potsdam | Apl. 8, 1916 | Apl. 16, 1916 | FromApl.16,1916: Kptlt. v. Schubert<br>FromAug.10,1916: Kptlt. Ganzel<br>FromDec.20,1916: Kptlt. Stabbert<br>FromJan.30,1917: Kptlt. Bockholt<br>FromJune14,1917: Oblt. z. S. Dinter | FromApl.16,1916: Oblt. z. S. Rothe<br>FromJan.30,1917: Lt. z. S. Maas<br>FromJune14,1917: Lt. z. S. d. R. Hamann | From Apl.21,1916: Tondern<br>From Apl.29,1916: Nordholz<br>From Nov.9,1916: Tondern ("Tobias") | 3 | 51 | 8 | 98 | 101 | Aug. 21, 1917: Shot down in flames off Lyngvig, Denmark, by British plane. 18 dead, no survivors. |
| *L 24* | *LZ 69* | Potsdam | May 20, 1916 | May 21, 1916 | From May 21,1916: Kptlt. Koch<br>From Oct.17,1916: Oblt. z. S. Friemel | From May 21,1916: Lt. z. S. v. Collani<br>From Oct.17,1916: Lt. z. S. d. R. Berger | From May 22, 1916: Tondern ("Toska") | 2 | 19 | 5 | 43 | 45 | Dec. 28, 1916: Burned at Tondern after breaking her back across entrance of "Toska" shed. |
| *L 30* | *LZ 62* | Friedrichshafen Factory Shed I | May 28, 1916 | May 30, 1916 | From May 30,1916: Oblt. z. S. v. Buttlar<br>From Jan.11,1917: Oblt. z. S. Friemel<br>From Apl.20,1917: Oblt. z. S. Bödecker<br>From Sept. 16, 1917: Lt. z. S. Vermehren<br>From Nov. 1, 1917: Oblt. z. S. Bödecker | From May 30,1916: Lt. z. S. v. Schiller<br>From Jan.11,1917: Lt. z. S. d. R. Berger<br>From Apl.20,1917: Lt. z. S. Vermehren<br>From Sept. 16, 1917: Lt. z. S. Schwabach | From May 30,1916 Nordholz ("Normann")<br>From Aug.21,1916: Ahlhorn ("Aladin")<br>From Apl. 5, 1917: Tondern ("Toska")<br>From May 2, 1917: Seerappen ("Seraphine") | 2 | 31 | 9 | 113 | 115 | Nov. 17, 1917: Decommissioned in Seerappen. Broken up 1920 and parts delivered to Belgium. |
| *L 31* | *LZ 72* | Löwenthal | July 12, 1916 | July 14, 1916: | FromJuly14,1916: Kptlt. Mathy | FromJuly14,1916: Oblt. z. S. Friemel<br>From Oct.1,1916: Lt. z. S. Werner | From July 18, 1916: Nordholz ("Normann")<br>From Aug.7,1916: Ahlhorn ("Albrecht") | 2 | 1 | 8 | 17 | 19 | Oct. 2, 1916: Shot down in flames at Potters Bar by British aircraft. 19 dead, no survivors. |
| *L 32* | *LZ 74* | Friedrichshafen Factory Shed II | Aug. 6, 1916 | Aug. 7, 1916 | From Aug.7,1916: Oblt. z. S. Peterson | From Aug. 7, 1916: Lt. z. S. Brodrück | From Aug. 8, 1916: Nordholz ("Normann")<br>From Sept. 19, 1916: Ahlhorn ("Alrun") | 2 | 1 | 3 | 11 | 13 | Sept. 24, 1916: Shot down in flames at Great Burstead by British aircraft. 22 dead, no survivors. |
| *L 33* | *LZ 76* | Friedrichshafen Factory Shed I | Aug. 30, 1916 | Sept. 2, 1916 | From Sept.2,1916: Kptlt. d. R. Böcker | From Sept.2,1916: Lt. z. S. Schirlitz | From Sept. 2, 1916: Nordholz ("Normann") | 2? | 0 | 1 | 8 | 10? | Sept. 24, 1916: Forced by gunfire damage to land at Little Wigborough. 22 prisoners. |

| Navy number | Builder's number | Built at | First flight | Commissioned | Commanding Officer | Executive Officer | Based at | Works flights | Scouting flights | Raids | Total Navy flights | Total flights | Remarks and end of service |
|---|---|---|---|---|---|---|---|---|---|---|---|---|---|
| *L 34* | *LZ 78* | Löwenthal | Sept.22,1916 | Sept.27,1916 | From Sept.27,1916: Kptlt. d. R. Max Dietrich | From Sept.27,1916: Lt.d. R. d. M. A. v. Nathusius | From Sept.27,1916: Nordholz ("Normann") | 3 | 3 | 2 | 8 | 11 | Nov. 27, 1916: Shot down in flames off Hartlepool by British aircraft. 20 dead, no survivors. |
| *L 35* | *LZ 80* | Friedrichshafen Factory Shed II | Oct. 12, 1916 | Oct. 18, 1916 | From Oct.18,1916: Kptlt. Ehrlich<br>From Sept.26,1917: Kptlt. Sommerfeldt Oblt.z.S.Vermehren<br>From June 7, 1918: Kptlt. Ehrlich | From Oct.18,1916: Lt. z. S. Dietsch<br>From Sept.26,1917: Oblt. z. S. Gebauer<br>From June 7,1918: Oblt. z. S. Dietsch | From Oct. 18, 1916: Ahlhorn ("Albrecht")<br>From Dec. 20, 1916: Wainoden<br>From Jan. 3, 1917: Seerappen ("Seraphine")<br>From Jan. 23, 1917: Ahlhorn ("Albrecht")<br>From Mar. 17, 1917: Dresden (Army Shed)<br>From June 14,1917: Ahlhorn ("Alix")<br>From Sept. 25, 1917: Jüterbog ("Baer") | 2 | 14 | 5 | 52 | 54 | Nov. 15, 1918: Broken up at Jüterbog. |
| | | | | | | | | Sept.26, 1917–Sept. 1918, Experimental ship | | | 34 | 34 | |
| | | | | | | | | Grand total: 2 | 14 | 5 | 86 | 88 | |
| *L 36* | *LZ 82* | Friedrichshafen Factory Shed I | Nov. 1, 1916 | Nov. 7, 1916 | From Nov.7,1916: Korv. Kap. Schütze<br>From Dec. 9, 1916: Kptlt. d. R. Eichler | From Nov.7,1916: Lt. z. S. Mieth | From Nov.10,1916: Nordholz ("Normann") | 3 | 3 | 1 | 17 | 20 | Feb. 7, 1917: Lost in forced landing at Rehben-an-der Aller after severe damage in crash on ice of Weser Estuary. |
| *L 37* | *LZ 75* | Staaken North Shed | Nov. 9, 1916 | Nov. 27, 1916 | From Nov.27,1916: Kptlt. d. R. Prölss<br>From May 1, 1917: Kptlt. Gärtner | From Nov.27,1916: Oblt. z. S. d. R. Brand<br>From May 1, 1917: Lt. z. S. Jahn | From Nov.27,1916: Ahlhorn ("Alrun")<br>From Dec. 18, 1916: Nordholz ("Normann")<br>From May 4, 1917: Tondern ("Toska")<br>From May 31,1917: Seddin ("Selinde")<br>From June 28, 1917: Wainoden ("Walhalla")<br>From Aug. 7, 1917: Seddin ("Selinde")<br>From Sept. 20, 1917: Seerappen ("Seraphine")<br>From Oct.19,1917: Seddin ("Selinde") | ? | 19 | 4 | 45 | ? | Nov. 24–Dec. 14, 1917: Decommissioned in Seddin. Broken up 1920 and parts delivered to Japan. |

| Navy number | Builder's number | Built at | First flight | Commissioned | Commanding Officer | Executive Officer | Based at | Works flights | Scouting flights | Raids | Total Navy flights | Total flights | Remarks and end of service |
|---|---|---|---|---|---|---|---|---|---|---|---|---|---|
| *L 38* | *LZ 84* | Löwenthal | Nov. 22, 1916 | Nov. 26, 1916 | From Nov.26,1916: Kptlt. Martin Dietrich | From Nov.26,1916: Lt. z. S. Eisenbeck | From Nov.27,1916: Ahlhorn ("Alrun")<br>From Dec.20,1916: Wainoden | 2? | 0 | 1 | 8 | 10? | Dec. 29, 1916: Forced landing at Seemuppen, Russia, and dismantled. |
| *L 39* | *LZ 86* | Friedrichshafen Factory Shed II | Dec. 13, 1916 | Dec. 18, 1916 | From Dec.18,1916: Kptlt. Koch | From Dec.18,1916: Lt. z. S. v. Collani | From Dec. 19,1916: Ahlhorn ("Alrun," later "Aladin") | 2 | 2 | 1 | 22 | 24 | Mar. 17, 1917: Shot down in flames by A.A. fire at Compiègne, France. 17 dead, no survivors. |
| *L 40* | *LZ 88* | Friedrichshafen Factory Shed I | Jan. 5, 1917 | Jan. 7, 1917 | From Jan.7,1917: Kptlt. Sommerfeldt | From Jan.7,1917: Lt. z. S. d. R. Gebauer | From Jan.7, 1917: Ahlhorn ("Alrun")<br>From May 1,1917: Wittmundhaven ("Wille") | 2 | 7 | 2 | 28 | 30 | June 17, 1917: Crashed at Nordholz, fell at Neuenwald and dismantled. |
| *L 41* | *LZ 79* | Staaken South Shed | Jan. 15, 1917 | Jan. 30, 1917 | From Jan.30,1917: Hauptmann Manger | From Jan. 30,1917 Oblt. z. S. d. R. Gruner | From Jan.30,1917: Ahlhorn ("Alrun")<br>From Dec.11,1917: Nordholz ("Normann") | 4 | 15 | 4 | 32 | 36 | May 29, 1918: Decommissioned. June 10, 1918: Hung up in "Norbert" shed. June 23, 1919, wrecked there by airship crews. |
| | | | | | | | | Dec. 11, 1917–May 29,1918: Advanced training ship | 2 | | 18 | 18 | |
| | | | | | | | | Grand total: 4 | 17 | 4 | 50 | 54 | |
| *L 42* | *LZ 91* | Friedrichshafen Factory Shed II | Feb. 21, 1917 | Feb. 28, 1917 | From Feb.28,1917: Kptlt. Martin Dietrich | From Feb.28,1917: Lt. z. S. Eisenbeck | From Feb.28,1917: Nordholz ("Normann," "Nobel")<br>From Apl. 17, 1918: Ahlhorn ("Alma")<br>From June 4, 1918: Nordholz ("Normann") | 2 | 21 | 6 | 51 | 53 | Nov. 9, 1918: Decommissioned. June 23, 1919: Wrecked by airship crews at Nordholz, "Nogat" shed. |
| | | | | | | | | June 6–Nov. 9, 1918: Advanced training ship | | | 12 | 12 | |
| | | | | | | | | Grand total: 2 | 21 | 6 | 63 | 65 | |
| *L 43* | *LZ 92* | Friedrichshafen Factory Shed I | Mar. 6, 1917 | Mar. 15, 1917 | From Mar.15,1917: Kptlt. Kraushaar | From Mar.15 1917: Lt. z. S. Zimmermann | From Mar. 15, 1917: Ahlhorn ("Alix," "Albrecht") | 3 | 6 | 1 | 11 | 14 | June 14, 1917: Shot down in flames off Vlieland by British aircraft. 24 dead, no survivors. |
| *L 44* | *LZ 93* | Löwenthal | Apl. 1, 1917 | Apl. 5, 1917 | From Apl. 5, 1917: Kptlt. Stabbert | From Apl. 5, 1917: Oblt. z. S. Rothe | From Apl. 5, 1917: Ahlhorn ("Alix")<br>From May 8, 1917: Nordholz<br>From May 24, 1917: Ahlhorn ("Alix") | 3 | 8 | 4 | 22 | 25 | Oct. 20, 1917: Shot down in flames by A.A. fire at St. Clement, France. 18 dead, n.s. |

| Navy number | Builder's number | Built at | First flight | Commissioned | Commanding Officer | Executive Officer | Based at | Works flights | Scouting flights | Raids | Total Navy flights | Total flights | Remarks and end of service |
|---|---|---|---|---|---|---|---|---|---|---|---|---|---|
| *L 45* | *LZ 85* | Staaken South Shed | Apl. 2, 1917 | Apl. 7, 1917 | From Apl. 7,1917: Kptlt. Kölle | From Apl. 7, 1917: Oblt. z. S. Dinter From May 1917: Oblt. z. S. Schüz | From Apl. 7, 1917: Ahlhorn ("Aladin") From June 5, 1917: Tondern ("Toska") | 2 | 13 | 3 | 24 | 27 | Oct. 20, 1917: Forced landing at Sisteron, France. 17 prisoners. |
| *L 46* | *LZ 94* | Friedrichshafen Factory Shed II | Apl. 24, 1917 | May, 1, 1917 | From May 1, 1917: Kptlt. Hollender | From May 1, 1917: Oblt. z. S. Frey | From May 1, 1917: Ahlhorn ("Alrun") | 5? | 19 | 3 | 31 | 36 | Jan. 5, 1918: Destroyed in Ahlhorn explosion. |
| *L 47* | *LZ 87* | Staaken North Shed | May 1, 1917 | May 3, 1917 | From May 3, 1917: Kptlt. d. R. Richard Wolff From June 29,1917: Kptlt. v. Freudenreich | From May 3, 1917: Lt. z. S. Fischer From Oct. 1917: Lt. z. S. Horstmann | From May 3, 1917: Ahlhorn ("Alrun") From Sept. 26, 1917: Wildeshausen ("Seibert") From Oct. 17, 1917: Ahlhorn ("Aladin") | 1 | 18 | 4 | 43 | 44 | Jan. 5, 1918: Destroyed in Ahlhorn explosion. |
| *L 48* | *LZ 95* | Friedrichshafen Factory Shed I | May 22, 1917 | May 23, 1917 | From May 23, 1917 Kptlt. d. R. Eichler | From May 23,1917: Lt. z. S. Mieth | From May 23, 1917: Nordholz ("Normann") | ? | 4 | 1 | 8 | ? | June 17, 1917: Shot down in flames by British aircraft at Theberton, Suffolk. 14 dead, 3 survivors. |
| *L 49* | *LZ 96* | Löwenthal | June 13, 1917 | June 15, 1917 | From June15,1917: Kptlt. Gayer | From June15,1917: Oblt. z. S. Dehn | From June 15, 1917: Ahlhorn ("Aladin') From June 16,1917: Wildeshausen ("Seibert") From July 12, 1917: Wittmundhaven ("Wünsch") | 2 | 2 | 1 | 13 | 15 | June 15, 1917: Severe damage on delivery flight. Oct. 20, 1917: Forced landing at Bourbonne - Les-Baines, France. 19 prisoners. |
| *L 50* | *LZ 89* | Staaken South Shed | June 9, 1917 | June 12, 1917 | FromJune12,1917: Kptlt. Schwonder | FromJune12,1917: Oblt. z. S. Westphal | From June 13, 1917: Ahlhorn ("Alrun") | 3 | 4 | 2 | 16 | 19 | Oct. 20, 1917: Lost fore gondola at Dammartin, France. Ship lost in Mediterranean. 4 missing, 16 prisoners. |
| *L 51* | *LZ 97* | Friedrichshafen Factory Shed II | July 6, 1917 | July 26, 1917 | FromJuly26,1917: Kptlt. Dose | From July26,1917: Lt. z. S. Trube | From July 26, 1917: Nordholz ("Normann," "Nobel") From Dec. 12, 1917: Ahlhorn ("Aladin") | 7? | 4 | 1 | 13 | 21 | Severe damage in altitude trial. Jan. 5, 1918: Destroyed in Ahlhorn explosion. |

| Navy number | Builder's number | Built at | First flight | Commissioned | Commanding Officer | Executive Officer | Based at | Works flights | Scouting flights | Raids | Total Navy flights | Total flights | Remarks and end of service |
|---|---|---|---|---|---|---|---|---|---|---|---|---|---|
| *L 52* | *LZ 98* | Staaken North Shed | July 14, 1917 | July 24, 1917 | FromJuly24,1917: Oblt. z. S. Friemel | FromJuly24,1917: Lt. z. S. d. R. Berger From Aug., 1918: Lt. z. S. Fritsche | From July 24, 1917: Wittmundhaven ("Wünsch") From Sept. 24, 1918: Nordholz ("Nobel") From Oct. 22, 1918: Wittmundhaven ("Wünsch") | ? | 20 | 1 | 40 | ? | Nov. 9, 1918: Decommissioned. June 23, 1919: Wrecked by airship crews at Wittmundhaven ("Wünsch"). |
| *L 53* | *LZ 100* | Friedrichshafen Factory Shed I | Aug. 18, 1917 | Aug. 21, 1917 | From Aug.21,1917: Kptlt. d. R. Prölss | From Aug.21,1917: Oblt. z. S. d. R. Brand From June 1918: Lt. z. S. v. Proeck | From Aug. 21, 1917: Nordholz ("Normann," "Nobel") | 6? | 19 | 4 | 45 | 51? | Aug. 11, 1918: Shot down in flames by British aircraft off Terschelling. 19 dead, no survivors. |
| *L 54* | *LZ 99* | Staaken South Shed | Aug. 13, 1917 | Aug. 20, 1917 | From Aug.20,1917: Kptlt. Bockholt FromSept.16,1917: Kptlt. v. Buttlar | From Aug.20,1917: Lt. z. S. Maas FromSept.16,1917: Oblt. z. S. v. Schiller | From Aug. 20, 1917: Wittmundhaven ("Wille") From Sept. 5, 1917: Tondern ("Toska") | ? | 15 | 2 | 43 | ? | July 19, 1918: stroyed at Tondern in "Toska" shed by carrier strike from H.M.S."Furious." |
| *L 55* | *LZ 101* | Löwenthal | Sept. 1, 1917 | Sept. 8, 1917 | From Sept.8, 1917: Kptlt. Flemming | From Sept. 8, 1917: Lt. z. S. Kohlhauer | From Sept. 8, 1917: Nordholz ("Nobel") From Oct. 6, 1917: Ahlhorn ("Albrecht") | ? | 1 | 2 | 6 | ? | Oct. 20, 1917: Lost in forced landing at Tiefenort, Germany, after raiding England. |
| *L 56* | *LZ 103* | Staaken North Shed | Sept. 24, 1917 | Sept. 28, 1917 | FromSept.28,1917: Hauptmann Stelling From Apl.1,1918: Kptlt. Zaeschmar | FromSept.28,1917: Lt. z. S. Upmeyer | From Sept. 28,1917: Wittmundhaven ("Wille") From Aug. 24, 1918: Nordholz ("Nobel") From Sept. 5, 1918: Wittmundhaven ("Wille") | ? | 18 | 1 | 35 | ? | Nov. 8, 1918: Decommissioned. June 23, 1919: Wrecked by airship crews at Wittmundhaven ("Wille"). |
| *L 57* | *LZ 102* | Friedrichshafen Factory Shed II | Sept. 26, 1917 | Sept. 26, 1917? | FromSept.26,1917: Kptlt. Bockholt | FromSept.26,1917: Lt. z. S. Maas | From ? Jüterbog ("Baer") | ? | 0 | 0 | ? | 4 | Oct. 8, 1917: Wrecked and burned in storm at Jüterbog. |
| *L 58* | *LZ 105* | Friedrichshafen Factory Shed I | Oct. 29, 1917 | Nov. 3, 1917 | From Nov.3,1917: Korv. Kap. Arnold Schütze | From Nov. 3, 1917: Lt. z. S. Liessmann | From Nov. 3, 1917: Ahlhorn ("Albrecht") | ? | 2 | 0 | 10 | ? | Jan. 5, 1918: Destroyed in Ahlhorn explosion. |

| Navy number | Builder's number | Built at | First flight | Commissioned | Commanding Officer | Executive Officer | Based at | Works flights | Scouting flights | Raids | Total Navy flights | Total flights | Remarks and end of service |
|---|---|---|---|---|---|---|---|---|---|---|---|---|---|
| *L 59* | *LZ 104* | Staaken South Shed | Oct. 25, 1917 | Nov. 3, 1917 | From Nov. 3,1917: Kptlt. Bockholt | From Nov.3,1917: Lt. z. S. Maas | From Nov. 4, 1917: Jamboli<br>From Dec. 12, 1917: Jüterbog ("Baer")<br>From Dec. 20, 1917: Friedrichshafen (Factory Shed II)<br>From Feb. 21, 1918: Jamboli | 4 | 1 | 1 | 17 | 21 | April 7, 1918: Burned in air over Straits of Otranto. 23 dead, no survivors. |
| *L 60* | *LZ 108* | Staaken North Shed | Dec. 18, 1917 | April 1, 1918 | From Apl. 1, 1918: Kptlt. Flemming | From Apl. 1, 1918: Lt. z. S. v. Kruse | From Apl. 1, 1918: Tondern ("Toska") | ? | 10 | 1 | 17 | ? | Commissioning delayed by wait for MB IVa engines. July 19, 1918: Destroyed at Tondern in "Toska" shed by carrier strike from H.M.S."Furious" |
| *L 61* | *LZ 106* | Friedrichshafen Factory Shed II | Dec. 12, 1917 | Dec. 19, 1917 | From Dec.19,1917: Kptlt. Ehrlich<br>From May21,1918: Kptlt. Bödecker | From Dec.19,1917: Oblt. z. S. Dietsch<br>From May21,1918: Lt. z. S. Schwabach | From Dec. 19, 1917: Wittmundhaven ("Wille")<br>From Sept. 5, 1918: Nordholz ("Nobel")<br>From Sept. 24, 1918: Wittmundhaven ("Wille") | 4 | 11 | 2 | 28 | 32 | Nov. 9, 1918. Decommissioned. Aug. 29, 1920: Surrendered to Italy at Ciampino. |
| *L 62* | *LZ 107* | Löwenthal | Jan. 19, 1918 | Jan. 21, 1918 | From Jan.21,1918: Hauptmann Manger | From Jan.21,1918: Lt. z. S. Gruner | From Jan. 29, 1918: Nordholz | 3 | 2 | 2 | 16 | 19 | May 10, 1918: Exploded in air near Heligoland. No survivors. |
| *L 63* | *LZ 110* | Friedrichshafen Factory Shed I | Mar. 4, 1918 | Mar. 9, 1918 | From Mar.9,1918: Kptlt. v. Freudenreich<br>From Aug.25,1918: Kptlt. Ratz | From Mar. 9,1918: Lt. z. S. Horstmann | From Mar. 10, 1918: Nordholz ("Nordstern")<br>From June 9, 1918: Ahlhorn ("Alma," "Alarich")<br>From Oct. 23, 1918: Nordholz ("Nogat") | 2? | 16 | 3 | 35 | 37? | Nov. 9, 1918: Decommissioned. June 23, 1919: Wrecked by airship crews at Nordholz ("Nogat"). |
| *L 64* | *LZ 109* | Staaken South Shed | Mar. 11, 1918 | Mar. 13, 1918 | From Mar.13,1918: Korv. Kap. Arnold Schütze<br>From Aug.25,1918: Oblt. z. S. Frey | From Mar.13,1918: Lt. z. S. Liessmann | From Mar. 13, 1918: Nordholz ("Nordstern")<br>From May 2, 1918: Ahlhorn ("Alma," "Alarich") | 2? | 15 | 1 | 24 | 26? | Nov. 9, 1918: Decommissioned. July 21, 1920: Surrendered to England at Pulham. |

| Navy number | Builder's number | Built at | First flight | Commissioned | Commanding Officer | Executive Officer | Based at | Works flights | Scouting flights | Raids | Total Navy flights | Total flights | Remarks and end of service |
|---|---|---|---|---|---|---|---|---|---|---|---|---|---|
| *L 65* | *LZ 111* | Löwenthal | Apl. 17, 1918 | May 3, 1918 | From May 3, 1918: Kptlt. Dose<br>From Aug.15,1918: Oblt. z. S. Vermehren | From May 3, 1918: Lt. z. S. Trube | From May 3, 1918: Nordholz ("Nordstern") | 5 | 11 | 1 | 23 | 28 | Nov. 9, 1918: Decommissioned. June 23, 1919: Wrecked by airship crews at Nordholz, "Nordstern" shed. |
| *L 70* | *LZ 112* | Friedrichshafen Factory Shed II | July 1, 1918 | July 8, 1918 | From July 8, 1918: Kptlt. v. Lossnitzer | From July 8,1918: Lt. z. S. Krüger | From July 9, 1918: Nordholz ("Nordstern") | 3? | 1 | 1 | 4 | 7? | Aug. 5, 1918: Shot down in flames by British aircraft off Norfolk coast. 22 dead n.s. |
| *L 71* | *LZ 113* | Friedrichshafen Factory Shed I | July 29, 1918 | Aug. 10, 1918 | From Aug.10,1918: Kptlt. Martin Dietrich | From Aug.10,1918: Lt. z. S. Eisenbeck | From Aug. 11, 1918: Nordholz<br>From Oct. 3, 1918: Friedrichshafen (Factory Shed II)<br>From Oct. 28, 1918: Ahlhorn ("Alarich") | 2? | 0 | 0 | 6 | 8? | Nov. 9, 1918: Decommissioned. July 1, 1920: Surrendered to England at Pulham. |

## (*b*) SCHÜTTE-LANZ

| Navy number | Builder's number | Built at | First flight | Commissioned | Commanding Officer | Executive Officer | Based at | Works flights | Scouting flights | Raids | Total Navy flights | Total flights | Remarks and end of service |
|---|---|---|---|---|---|---|---|---|---|---|---|---|---|
| *SL 3* | *C 1* | Mannheim-Rheinau | Feb. 4, 1915 | Feb. 5, 1915 | From Feb. 5, 1915: Kptlt. Boemack<br>From July15,1915: Oblt. z. S. Guido Wolff<br>From Oct.23,1915: Kptlt. Koch<br>From Feb.19,1916: Kptlt. v. Wachter | From Feb. 5, 1915: Oblt. z. S. Guido Wolff<br>From July15,1915: Lt. z. S. Kretschmann<br>From Oct.23,1915: Lt. z. S. v. Collani<br>From Feb.19,1916: Oblt. z. S. Dehn | From Feb. 5, 1915: Leipzig<br>From Feb. 20, 1915: Nordholz ("Hindenburg")<br>From Jan. 28, 1916: Seddin | 2 | 30 | 1 | 69 | 71 | May 1, 1916: Crashed on water between Gotland and Backofen. Crew rescued, ship destroyed. |
| *SL 4* | *C 2* | Mannheim-Sandhofen | April 25, 1915 | May 2, 1915 | From May 2, 1915: Kptlt. d. R. Richard Wolff | From May 2, 1915: Lt. z. S. Fischer | From May 2, 1915: Dresden<br>From June 16, 1915 Nordholz ("Nora")<br>From Aug. 11, 1915: Seddin ("Selim") | 2 | 21 | 2 | 30 | 32 | Dec. 11, 1915: Doors of "Selim" shed opened in gale, *SL 4* blown out on field and wrecked. Dismantled by Dec. 23, 1915. |
| *SL 6* | *d 1* | Leipzig | Sept. 19, 1915 | Oct. 9, 1915 | From Oct. 9, 1915: Kptlt. Boemack | From Oct. 9, 1915: Lt. z. S. d. R. Schaper | From Oct. 9, 1915: Seddin ("Selinde") | ? | 6 | 0 | 7 | ? | Nov. 18, 1915: Exploded in air 6km. north of Seddin. 20 dead, no survivors. |

| Navy number | Builder's number | Built at | First flight | Commissioned | Commanding Officer | Executive Officer | Based at | Works flights | Scout-ing flights | Raids | Total Navy flights | Total flights | Remarks and end of service |
|---|---|---|---|---|---|---|---|---|---|---|---|---|---|
| *SL 8* | *e 1* | Leipzig | Mar. 30, 1916 | Mar. 30, 1916 | From Mar.30,1916:<br>Kptlt. Guido Wolff<br>From May31,1917:<br>Kptlt. v. Wachter<br>From Oct.5, 1917:<br>Oblt. z. S. Ratz | From Mar.30,1916:<br>Lt. z. S. Kretschmann<br>From May31,1917:<br>Lt. z. S. Goldmann | From Mar. 30, 1916:<br>Dresden<br>From Apl. 20, 1916:<br>Seddin<br>From Aug. 18, 1916:<br>Nordholz<br>From Sept. 7, 1916:<br>Seddin<br>From Sept. 23, 1917:<br>Wainoden<br>From Oct. 4, 1916:<br>Seddin<br>From Jan. 16, 1917:<br>Wainoden<br>From Jan. 26, 1917:<br>Seddin<br>From June 10, 1917:<br>Wainoden<br>From June 28, 1917:<br>Seddin ("Selim") | 2 | 32 | 5 | 88 | 90 | Nov. 13–26, 1917: Dismantled in "Selim" shed, Seddin. |
| *SL 9* | *e 2* | Leipzig | May 24, 1916 | May 31, 1916 | From May 31,1916:<br>Kptlt. d. R. Richard Wolff<br>From Jan.26,1917:<br>Kptlt. Kölle<br>From Feb.28,1917:<br>Kptlt. Jöhnke | From May31,1916:<br>Lt. z. S. Fischer<br>From Jan.26,1917:<br>Oblt. z. S. Dinter<br>From Feb.28,1917:<br>Lt. z. S. d. R. Martin | From May 31, 1916:<br>Seddin<br>From July 24,1916:<br>Wainoden<br>From July 27, 1916:<br>Seddin<br>From Aug. 18, 1916:<br>Nordholz<br>From Sept. 7, 1916:<br>Seddin<br>From Oct. 21, 1916:<br>Wainoden<br>From Nov. 11, 1916:<br>Seddin<br>From Dec. 19, 1916:<br>Seerappen ("Seraphine")<br>From Dec. 20, 1916:<br>Seddin ("Selinde")<br>From Jan. 29, 1917:<br>Wainoden ("Walhalla")<br>From Jan. 31, 1917:<br>Seddin ("Selinde")<br>From Feb. 13, 1917:<br>Wainoden ("Walhalla")<br>From Feb. 28, 1917:<br>Seddin ("Selinde")<br>From Mar. 29, 1917:<br>Seerappen ("Seraphine") | 2 | 13 | 4 | 46 | 48 | Mar. 30, 1917: Burned in air in thunderstorm off Pillau while returning to Seddin. 23 dead, no survivors. |

| Navy number | Builder's number | Built at | First flight | Commissioned | Commanding Officer | Executive Officer | Based at | Works flights | Scout-ing flights | Raids | Total Navy flights | Total flights | Remarks and end of service |
|---|---|---|---|---|---|---|---|---|---|---|---|---|---|
| *SL 12* | *e 5* | Zeesen | Nov. 9, 1916 | Nov. 15, 1916 | From Nov.15,1916:<br>Kptlt. Kölle | From Nov. 15,1916<br>Oblt. z. S. Dinter | From Nov. 15, 1916:<br>Ahlhorn ("Alrun," "Aladin") | ? | 1 | 0 | 9 | ? | Dec. 28, 1916: Damaged in landing attempt at Ahlhorn, and wrecked in forced landing outside the base. |
| *SL 14* | *e 7* | Mannheim-Rheinau | Aug. 23, 1916 | Aug. 24, 1916 | From Aug.24,1916:<br>Kptlt. v. Wachter | From Aug.24,1916:<br>Oblt. z. S. Dehn<br>From Sept. 1916:<br>Lt. z. S. Lossow | From Aug. 24, 1916:<br>Seddin<br>From Sept. 4, 1916:<br>Wainoden<br>From Sept. 9, 1916:<br>Seerappen ("Seraphine")<br>From Nov. 17, 1916:<br>Wainoden<br>From Dec. 19, 1916:<br>Seerappen ("Seraphine")<br>From Mar. 22, 1917:<br>Wainoden | 2 | 2 | 1 | 18 | 20 | May 9, 1917: Badly damaged on field at Wainoden. Dismantled May 18–22, 1917. |
| *SL 20* | *f 1* | Mannheim-Rheinau | Sept. 10, 1917 | Sept. 11, 1917 | From Sept.11,1917:<br>Kptlt. Guido Wolff<br>From Nov.16,1917:<br>Oblt. z. S. Ratz | From Sept.11,1917:<br>Lt. z. S. Kretschmann | From Sept. 11, 1917<br>Seddin ("Selinde")<br>From Dec. 11, 1917<br>Ahlhorn ("Alix") | ? | 3 | 0 | 15 | ? | Jan. 5, 1918: Destroyed in Ahlhorn explosion, "Alix" shed. |

## (c) PARSEVAL

| Navy number | Builder's number | Built at | First flight | Commissioned | Commanding Officer | Executive Officer | Based at | Works flights | Scout-ing flights | Raids | Total Navy flights | Total flights | Remarks and end of service |
|---|---|---|---|---|---|---|---|---|---|---|---|---|---|
| *PL 6* | | Bitterfeld | June 30, 1910 | Aug. 9, 1914 | From Aug. 9, 1914:<br>Oblt. a. D. Meier | From Sept. 1914:<br>Lt. z. S. v. Lynckner | From Aug. 9, 1914:<br>Kiel | | 4 | 0 | 33 | | Requisitioned from Parseval Co. Dec. 27, 1914: Deflated in Kiel and stored. |
| *PL 19* | | Bitterfeld | Summer 1914 | Sept. 17, 1914 | From Sept.17,1914:<br>Hauptmann Stelling<br>From Jan.23,1915:<br>Oblt. Meier | From Sept.17,1914:<br>Ob. Steuerm. Schenck | From Sept. 17, 1914:<br>Kiel<br>From Dec. 25, 1914:<br>Königsberg | ? | 6 | 1 | 21 | ? | Built under British Admiralty contract. Jan. 25, 1915: Lost by accident in raid on Libau, 7 prisoners. |

| Navy number | Builder's number | Built at | First flight | Commissioned | Commanding Officer | Executive Officer | Based at | Works flights | Scouting flights | Raids | Total Navy flights | Total flights | Remarks and end of service |
|---|---|---|---|---|---|---|---|---|---|---|---|---|---|
| PL 25 | | Bitterfeld | Feb. 25, 1915 | Mar. 23, 1915 | From Mar.23,1915: Hauptmann Stelling From Aug. 8, 1915: Hauptmann Manger | From Mar.23,1915: Hauptmann Manger From Aug.8,1915: Oblt.z.S.Westphal | From Mar. 23, 1915: Tondern From Nov. 4, 1915: Fuhlsbüttel | 10 | 41 | 0 | 85 | 95 | Mar. 30, 1916: Flown to Biesdorf and decommissioned. |
| (d) GROSS-BASENACH | | | | | | | | | | | | | |
| M IV | | Tegel | Aug. 25, 1914 | Dec. 16, 1914 | From Dec.16,1914: Hauptmann v. Jena | From Dec.16,1914: Lt. z. S. Schüz | From Dec. 16, 1914: Biesdorf From Dec. 27, 1914: Kiel | ? | 27 | 0 | 83 | ? | July 13–Aug. 10, 1915: Deflated and overhauled. Nov. 3, 1915: Decommissioned and deflated in Kiel. |

## APPENDIX C
# GERMAN NAVAL AIRSHIP BASES

| *Shed names* | *"Clear inner dimensions" Length × width × height (feet)* | *Shed axis* | *Shed builder* | *Date completed* | *Remarks* |
|---|---|---|---|---|---|
| **NORDHOLZ**<br>H.Q. Naval Airship Division, Oct. 14, 1914–July 25, 1917: Jan. 10, 1918–Nov. 9, 1918. | *Ground troop:* Nov. 1914: 543<br>May 1915: 545<br>Mar. 1916: 692<br>Apl. 1917: 1,293 | *Gas Works ("Bamag") 1918:* | | | Production: 1,520,600 cu. ft. per day.<br>Compressor capacity: 720,624 cu. ft. per day.<br>Low-pressure gas holder: 1,060,000 cu. ft.<br>High-pressure store (150 cylinders): 5,280,000 cu. ft. |
| "Hertha," later "Nobel" | 597·1 × 114·8 × 114·8 × 98·4 | Revolving | | 1st half Aug. 20, 1914<br>2nd half Nov. 1914 | Revolving double shed, weight 4,000 tons. Lengthened to 656·2 ft. Dec. 1916–May 1917. Demolished 1921. Underground petrol store (Martini-Hünecke) 7,926 gallons. |
| "Nora" | 603·7 × 115·5 × 91·8 | S.W.-N.E. | Zeppelin Hallenbau | Jan. 1915 | Single shed. School ships after autumn 1916. Demolished 1921. |
| "Hindenburg," later "Norbert" | 603·7 × 115·5 × 91·8 | S.W.-N.E. | Zeppelin Hallenbau | Jan. 1915 | Single shed. School ships after autumn 1916. Demolished 1921. |
| "Normann" | 787·4 × 196·8 × 114·8 | W.N.W.-E.S.E. | | Apl. 26, 1916 | Double shed. Demolished 1921. Underground petrol store (Martini-Hünecke) 7,926 gallons. |
| "Nordstern" | 853·0 × 246·0 × 118·1 | N.N.E.-S.S.W. | | Mar. 1918 | Double Shed. Demolished 1921 } Underground petrol store (Martini-Hünecke) between sheds, 15,852 gallons. |
| "Nogat" | 853·0 × 246·0 × 118·1 | N.N.E.-S.S.W. | | August 1918 | Double Shed. Demolished 1921 |
| **AHLHORN**<br>H.Q. Naval Airship Division, July 25, 1917–Jan. 10, 1918. | *Ground troop:* Mar. 1916: 911<br>Apl. 1917: 1,299 | *Gas Works (Messerschmitt):* | | | Production: Autumn 1917, 1,056,000 cu. ft. per day. Autumn 1918, 2,534,400 cu. ft. per day.<br>Compressor capacity: Autumn 1917, 425,000 cu. ft. per day. Autumn 1918, 1,270,000 cu. ft. per day.<br>Low-pressure gas holder: 1,056,000 cu. ft. (882,750 cu. ft. usable).<br>High-pressure store: Autumn 1917 (120 cylinders) 4,400,000 cu. ft. Autumn 1918 (220 cylinders) 7,744,000 cu. ft.<br>Also 40 railroad tank cars from Staaken, 2,120,000 cu. ft. |
| I "Aladin" | 787·4 × 196·8 × 114·8 | N.N.E.-S.S.W. | Gute-Hoffnungs-Hütte | August 1916 | Double shed. Damaged in explosion Jan. 5, 1918. Rebuilding contracted for May 30, 1918, to complete Jan. 1919. Delivered to Italy, not erected. } Underground petrol store (Martini-Hünecke) 15,852 gallons between sheds I and II, to serve sheds I-IV. |
| II "Albrecht" | 787·4 × 196·8 × 114·8 | N.N.E.-S.S.W. | Gute-Hoffnungs-Hutte | August 1916 | Double shed. Heavily damaged in explosion Jan. 5, 1918. Rebuilding contracted for July 31 1918, cancelled Oct. 2, 1918. Demolished 1921. |
| III "Alrun" | 787·4 × 196·8 × 114·8 | E.S.E.-W.N.W. | Hein-Lehmann Co. | Sept. 11, 1916 | Double shed. Destroyed in explosion Jan. 5, 1918. |
| IV "Alix" | 787·4 × 196·8 × 114·8 | E.S.E.-W.N.W. | Zeppelin Hallenbau | Sept. 11, 1916 | Double shed. Destroyed in explosion Jan. 5, 1918 |
| V "Alma" | 853·0 × 246·0 × 118·1 | N.N.W.-S.S.E. | Gute-Hoffnungs-Hütte | Apl. 17, 1918 | Double shed. Delivered to Italy. Not erected. } Underground petrol store (Martini-Hünecke) 7,926 gallons between sheds. |
| VI "Alarich" | 853·0 × 246·0 × 118·1 | N.N.W.-S.S.E. | Gute-Hoffnungs-Hütte | July 18, 1918 | Double shed. Delivered to France (Marignane). Not erected. |
| **HAGE**<br>(Originally Norden)<br>Closed down Apl. 5, 1917 | *Ground troop:* Nov. 1914: 541<br>May 1915: 563<br>Mar. 1916: 468 | *Gas works ("Bamag") 1918:* | | | Production: 591,360 cu. ft. per day.<br>Low-pressure gas holder: 176,000 cu. ft.<br>High-pressure store (50 cylinders): 1,760,000 cu. ft. |
| I "Tirpitz," later "Hanne" | 603·7 × 111·5 × 91·8 | S.W.-N.E. | Arthur Müller Co. | Apl. 1915 | Single shed. Demolished 1921. |
| II "Luise," later "Hannibal" | 603·7 × 111·5 × 91·8 | S.W.-N.E. | Arthur Müller Co. | Apl. 1915 | Single shed. Demolished 1921. |
| III "Lücilin," later "Harald" | 603·7 × 111·5 × 91·8 | S.W.-N.E | Arthur Müller Co. | June 1915 | Single shed. Demolished 1921 |
| IV "Goeben," later "Hasso" | 603·7 × 111·5 × 91·8 | S.W.-N.E. | Arthur Müller Co. | June 1915 | Single shed. Demolished 1921. |
| **TONDERN**<br>Stand-by status after July 1918. | *Ground troop:* Nov. 1914: 307<br>May 1915: 537<br>Mar. 1916: 466<br>Apl. 1917: 504 | *Gas works (Pintsch):* | | | Production: 1917, 350,000 cu. ft. per day. 1918: 211,200 cu. ft. per day.<br>Low-pressure gas holder: 1,056,000 cu. ft.<br>High-pressure store: 1917 (25 cylinders) 888,000 cu. ft. 1918 (30 cylinders) 1,056,000 cu. ft.<br>Compressor capacity 1918: 425,000 cu. ft. per day.<br>Also 10 railroad tank cars, 529,650 cu. ft. |
| "Marine," later "Toni" | 603·7 × 111·5 × 91·8 | E.-W. | Arthur Müller Co. | Mar. 1915 | Single shed. Underground petrol store (Martini-Hünecke) 4,284 gallons. Demolished summer 1918. |
| "Joachim," later "Tobias" | 603·7 × 111·5 × 91·8 | E.-W. | Arthur Müller Co. | Spring 1915 | Single shed. Underground petrol store (Martini-Hünecke) 4,284 gallons. Demolished 1921. |
| "Toska" | 787·4 × 196·8 × 114·8 | E.-W. | Maschinenfabrik Augsburg-Nürnberg | Nov. 1915 | Double shed. Originally 590·5 ft., lengthened during construction. Underground petrol store (Martini-Hünecke), 7,926 gallons. Demolished 1921. |
| **WITTMUNDHAVEN**<br>Taken over from Army, April 5, 1917 | *Ground troop:* April 1917: 592 | *Gas:* | | | Delivered from Hage in 50 railroad tank cars (2,675,000 cu. ft.)<br>High-pressure store (16 cylinders): 564,960 cu. ft. |

| Shed names | "Clear inner dimensions" Length × width × height (feet) | Shed axis | Shed builder | Date completed | Remarks |
|---|---|---|---|---|---|
| I "Wille" | 787·4 × 196·8 × 114·8 | E.N.E.-W.S.W. | Zeppelin Hallenbau | Nov. 1916 | Double shed. Conventional design. Delivered to France (Maison Blanche), partly re-erected. |
| II "Wünsch" | 787·4 × 196·8 × 114·8 | N.E.-S.W. | Zeppelin Hallenbau | June 1917 | Double shed. Slanted sides. Delivered to France (Maison Blanche). Not erected. |

(I and II:) Underground petrol store(Martini-Hünecke) between sheds—3 cisterns of 4,284 gallons each.

## FUHLSBÜTTEL BEI HAMBURG

*Ground troop:* Nov. 1914: 293 / May 1915: 368 / Mar. 1916: 306 — *Gas:* Delivered in cylinders.

| Shed names | Dimensions | Shed axis | Shed builder | Date completed | Remarks |
|---|---|---|---|---|---|
| | 524·9 × 157·6 × 85·3 | W. by S.-E. by N. | H. C. E. Eggers and Co. G.M.B.H | June 1912 | Double shed. Built for *DELAG*. Used by navy from April, 1913. Heavy fire damage Sept. 16, 1916, and demolished. Navy cancelled contract Oct. 1, 1916. |

## KIEL

*Ground troop:* Nov. 1914: 255 / May 1915: 330 — *Gas:* Delivered in cylinders.

| Shed names | Dimensions | Shed axis | Shed builder | Date completed | Remarks |
|---|---|---|---|---|---|
| | 557·7 × 82·0 × 82·8 | E.-W. | | 1910 | Built for *Verein Für Motorluftschiffahrt in der Nordmark*. Navy use from Aug. 9, 1914. Navy cancelled contract Feb. 1, 1916. |

## WILDESHAUSEN

From Army June 1917

*Ground troop:* varied: June 1917: 130 / June 1918: 300 — *Gas:* delivered in cylinders.

| Shed names | Dimensions | Shed axis | Shed builder | Date completed | Remarks |
|---|---|---|---|---|---|
| "Seibert" | 787·4 × 131·2 × 114·8 | N.E.-S.W. | Maschinenfabrik Augsburg-Nürnberg | May 13, 1916 | Single shed. Used by navy only for reconstruction and repairs. Demolished 1921. |

## SEDDIN-JESERITZ

*Ground troop:* May 1915: 407 / Mar. 1916: 394 / Apl. 1917: 495

*Gas works ("Bamag"):* Production: 1917, 700,000 cu. ft. per day. 1918, 811,000 cu. ft. per day.
Compressor capacity: 383,720 cu. ft. per day.
Low-pressure gas holder: 1,056,000 cu. ft.
High-pressure store (25 cylinders) 880,000 cu. ft.
Stored also in 75 railroad tank cars (5,826,150 cu. ft.) and distributed to other bases.

| Shed names | Dimensions | Shed axis | Shed builder | Date completed | Remarks |
|---|---|---|---|---|---|
| "Bertha," later "Selim" | 603·7 × 114·8 × 91·8 | | | June 15, 1915 | Single shed. Retained for civil use. Used by Parseval-Naatz Co. to build PN 28, PN 29, 1929–30. Housed "Italia" 1928. |
| "Selinde" | 787·4 × 196·8 × 114·8 | | | Sept. 1915 | Double shed. Originally 590·5 ft., lengthened during construction. Demolished 1921. |

(Both sheds:) Underground petrol store(Martini-Hünecke) 10,568 gallons between sheds.

## WAINODEN COURLAND

*Ground troop:* April 1917: 463 — *Gas works (Silicon field works):* Production: 141,240 cu. ft. per day.

| Shed names | "Clear inner dimensions" Length × width × height (feet) | Shed axis | Shed builder | Date completed | Remarks |
|---|---|---|---|---|---|
| "Walther" | 787·4 × 137·8 × 114·8 | | | May 19, 1916 | Single shed. Temporary wooden structure. |
| "Walhalla" | 787·4 × 137·8 × 114·8 | | | Oct. 24, 1916 | Single shed. Temporary wooden structure. |

## SEERAPPEN

*Ground troop:* Mar. 1916: 311 / Apl. 1917: 457

*Gas works ("Bamag") completed 1918:* Production: 422,400 cu. ft. per day.
Low-pressure gas holder: 176,000 cu. ft.
High-pressure store (30 cylinders): 1,056,000 cu. ft.

| Shed names | Dimensions | Shed axis | Shed builder | Date completed | Remarks |
|---|---|---|---|---|---|
| "Seraphine" | 787·4 × 196·8 × 114·8 | | Zeppelin Hallenbau | Sept. 11, 1916 | Double shed. Delivered to Italy, not erected. Underground petrol store (Martini-Hünecke) 15,852 gallons at south-east corner of shed. |

## NAMUR (COGNELÉE)

*Ground troop:* Nov. 1914: 490 / May 1915: 443 / Jan. 1916: 220 — *Gas:* delivered in cylinders.

| Shed names | Dimensions | Shed axis | Shed builder | Date completed | Remarks |
|---|---|---|---|---|---|
| "Friedrich" | 590·5 × 91·8 × 98·4 | S.W.-N.E. | Ermus Co. | April 1915 | Single shed. Slanting sides. |
| "Baldur" | 590·5 × 104·9 × 98·4 | S.W.-N.E. | Ermus Co. | June 1915 | Single shed. Slanting sides. |
| "Eitel" | 590·5 × 104·9 × 98·4 | S.W.-N.E. | Ermus Co. | June 1915 | Single shed. Slanting sides. |

## DÜREN

*Ground troop:* Nov. 1914: 262 / May 1915: 318 / Mar. 1916: 241 — *Gas:* delivered in cylinders.

| Shed names | Dimensions | Shed axis | Shed builder | Date completed | Remarks |
|---|---|---|---|---|---|
| "Siegfried," later "Dietrich" | 590·5 × 91·8 × 98·4 | S.W.-N.E. | Ermus Co. | Jan. 1915? | Single Shed. Slanting sides. |

## JÜTERBOG (NIEDERGORSDORF)

*Gas works ("Bamag"):* Production: 633,600 cu. ft. per day.
Compressor capacity: 211,860 cu. ft. per day (but no high-pressure store).
Low-pressure gas holder: 176,000 cu. ft.

| Shed names | Dimensions | Shed axis | Shed builder | Date completed | Remarks |
|---|---|---|---|---|---|
| I | 603·7 × 114·8 × 91·8 | N.E.-S.W. | | | Single shed. Demolished 1921. |
| II "Baer" | 787·4 × 196·8 × 114·8 | E.-W. | | | Double Shed. Delivered to Japan and re-erected at Kasumigaura |

(I and II:) Underground petrol store (Martini-Hünecke) 4,284 gallons.

## JAMBOLI (BULGARIA)

Army Base. Navy use Sept. 1917–April 1918.

*Ground troop:* Nov. 1917: 400

*Gas works:* Production: 672,900 cu. ft. per day.
Low-pressure gas holder: 70,620 cu. ft.
High-pressure store in flasks: 416,650 cu. ft.

| Shed names | Dimensions | Shed axis | Shed builder | Date completed | Remarks |
|---|---|---|---|---|---|
| | 787·4 × 131·2 × 114·8 | N.E.-S.W. | | | Large single shed. |

## APPENDIX D
# PERSONNEL EXPANSION: NAVAL AIRSHIP DIVISION

| | *Nov. 26, 1914* | *May 31, 1915* | *Mar. 7, 1916* | *April 1, 1917* | *Aeroplane Defence Staffels—Mar. 25, 1916* |
|---|---|---|---|---|---|
| Flight crews | (25)412 | 380 | (24)533 | (33)760 | |
| Headquarters staff | 53 | 67 | 107 | 84 | |
| Nordholz | 543 | 545 | 692 | 1,293 | 62 |
| Ahlhorn | | | 911 | 1,299 | |
| Wittmundhaven | | | | 592 | |
| Tondern | 307 | 537 | 466 | 504 | 61 |
| Hage | 541 | 563 | 468 | | 60 |
| Fuhlsbüttel | 293 | 368 | 306 | | |
| Kiel | 255 | 330 | | | 51 |
| Düren | 262 | 318 | 241 | | |
| Düsseldorf | 262 | 325 | 394 | | |
| Namur | 490 | 443 | | | |
| Seddin | | 407 | 241 | 495 | 60 |
| Seerappen | | | 311 | 457 | |
| Wainoden | | | | 463 | 60 |
| Field Airship Company | 34 | | | | |
| "One Belgian Shed" | 288 | | | | |
| Spare flight crews | | | (2) 42 | (1) 18 | |
| Total | 3,740 | 4,283 | 4,747 | 5,965 | 354 |

# AIRSHIP BUILDING PLANTS

*Luftschiffbau Zeppelin:*
*Friedrichshafen:*
August 1914: 135 salaried, 840 workers
1917: 850 salaried, 6,400 workers (including Löwenthal).
*Staaken:*
1917: 700 salaried, 4,000 workers (many working on "Giant" aeroplanes).
*Maybach Motorenbau,* Friedrichshafen:
1917: 2,500–3,000
*Ballon-Hüllen-Gesellschaft,* Tempelhof: (Gas-cell manufacture)
1917: 2,000
*Luftschiffbau Schütte-Lanz:*
*Mannheim-Rheinau:*
August 1914: 5 salaried, 60 workers
May 1917: 279 salaried, 1,483 workers
*Zeesen:*
Dec. 1917: 181 salaried, 1,536 workers (only 324 for airships, 882 for aeroplanes).
*Luft-Fahrzeug-Gesellschaft* (Parseval Co.):
*Bitterfeld:*
1917: 103 salaried, 507 workers
*A. Riedinger Ballonfabrik A. G.,* Augsburg: (Gas cells for Schütte-Lanz ships):
1917: 800

## APPENDIX E

# SUMMARY OF GERMAN NAVAL AIRSHIP OPERATIONS

*1914:*

| | |
|---|---|
| Scouting flights—North Sea | 48 |
| Scouting days—North Sea | 35 out of 148 (23·6 per cent) |
| Scouting flights—Baltic | 10 |
| Losses | 0 |

*1915:*

| | |
|---|---|
| Scouting flights—North Sea | 297 |
| Scouting days—North Sea | 124 out of 365 (34·0 per cent) |
| Scouting flights—Baltic | 53 |
| Raid flights—North Sea | 47 (sorties), 27 (ships over England) |
| Damage in England | £815,866 |
| Raid flights—Baltic | 4 |
| Losses | 10 |

*1916:*

| | |
|---|---|
| Scouting flights—North Sea | 253 |
| Scouting days—North Sea | 89 out of 366 (24·3 per cent) |
| Scouting flights—Baltic | 30 (Navy)<br>29 (Army in Navy service) |
| Raid flights—North Sea | 187 (sorties), 111 (ships over England) |
| Damage in England | £594,523 |
| Raid flights—Baltic | 15 |
| Losses | 16 |

*1917:*

| | |
|---|---|
| Scouting flights—North Sea | 242 |
| Scouting days—North Sea | 96 out of 365 (26·3 per cent) |
| Scouting flights—Baltic | 42 (Navy)<br>56 (Army in Navy service) |
| Raid flights—North Sea | 54 (sorties), 28 (ships over England) |
| Damage in England | £87, 760 |
| Raid flights—Baltic | 27 |
| Losses | 16 |

*1918:*

| | |
|---|---|
| Scouting flights—North Sea | 131 |
| Scouting days—North Sea | 55 out of 315 (17·5 per cent) |
| Raid flights—North Sea | 18 (sorties), 11 (ships over England) |
| Damage in England | £29,427 |
| Losses | 11 |

*Totals:*

| | |
|---|---|
| Scouting flights—North Sea | 971 |
| Scouting days—North Sea | 399 out of 1,559 (25·6 per cent) |
| Scouting flights in Baltic | 135 (Navy)<br>85 (Army in Navy service) |
| Raid flights—North Sea | 306 (sorties), 177 (ships over England) |
| Damage in England | £1,527,544 |
| Raid flights—Baltic | 46 |
| Losses | 53 |

# INDEX